Painted Journeys

The Charles M. Russell Center Series on Art and Photography of the American West

B. Byron Price, *General Editor*

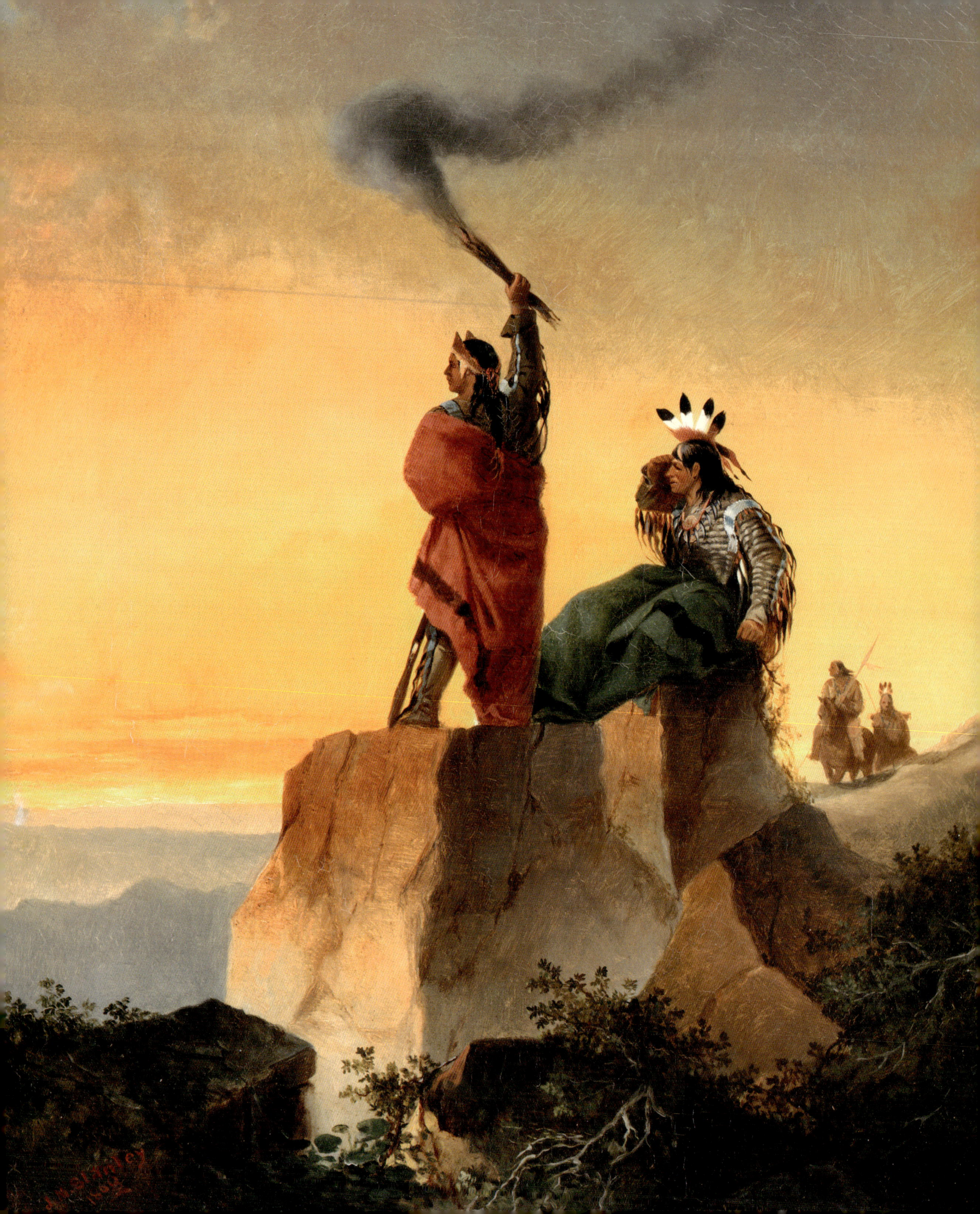

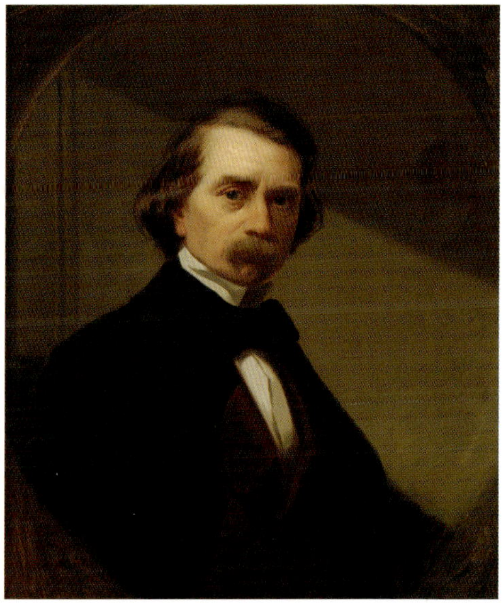

Painted Journeys

The Art of John Mix Stanley

Peter H. Hassrick and Mindy N. Besaw

with

Emily C. Burns, Scott Manning Stevens, Lisa Strong, Melissa Speidel, Jacquelyn Sparks, and Emily C. Wilson

Foreword by Bruce B. Eldredge

University of Oklahoma Press : Norman
In cooperation with the Buffalo Bill Center of the West, Cody, Wyoming

The following images appear uncaptioned on the pages noted:

Page ii: J. M. Stanley, *Indian Telegraph*, 1860 (cat. no. 169)

Page vi: J. M. Stanley, *Butte on the Del Norte* (detail), 1847 (cat. no. 032)

Page viii: J. M. Stanley, *Gambling for the Buck* (detail), 1867 (cat. no. 206)

J. M. Stanley, *Untitled, Teton Valley Scene* (detail), c. 1855 (cat. no. 132)

J. M. Stanley, *A Family Group* (detail), c. 1856 (cat. no. 145)

Page ix: J. M. Stanley, *The Last of Their Race* (detail), 1857 (cat. no. 159)

J. M. Stanley, *The Trial of Red Jacket* (detail), 1869 (cat. no. 213)

Page 130: J. M. Stanley, *Ko-rak-koo-kiss, a Towoccono Warrior* (detail), 1844 (cat. no. 017)

EXHIBITION VENUES AND DATES:

Buffalo Bill Center of the West, Cody, Wyoming, June 6 – August 29, 2015
Gilcrease Museum, Tulsa, Oklahoma, October 3, 2015 – January 3, 2016
Tacoma Art Museum, Tacoma, Washington, February 1 – April 29, 2016

Library of Congress Cataloging-in-Publication Data
Painted journeys : the art of John Mix Stanley / Peter H. Hassrick and Mindy N. Besaw ; with Emily C. Burns, Scott Manning Stevens, Lisa Strong, Melissa Speidel, Jacquelyn Sparks, and Emily C. Wilson ; Foreword by Bruce B. Eldredge.
pages cm — (The Charles M. Russell Center Series on Art and Photography of the American West ; volume 17)
Includes bibliographical references and index.
ISBN 978-0-8061-4829-8 (hardcover : alk. paper)
ISBN 978-0-8061-5155-7 (pbk.)
1. Stanley, John Mix, 1814–1872—Exhibitions. 2. Indians in art—Exhibitions. 3. West (U.S.)—In art—Exhibitions.
I. Hassrick, Peter H., author. II. Besaw, Mindy N., author.
ND237.S648A4 2015
759.13—dc23
2014039223

Copyediting by Melanie Mallon
Index by Debra A. Lindblom
Design by David Skolkin
Typesetting by Angela Taormina
Image prepress by University of Oklahoma Printing Services
Printed by TWP Sdn. Bhd., Malaysia

Painted Journeys: The Art of John Mix Stanley is Volume 17 in The Charles M. Russell Center Series on Art and Photography of the American West.

The paper in this book meets the guidelines for permanence and durability of the Committee on Production Guidelines for Book Longevity of the Council on Library Resources, Inc. ∞

1 2 3 4 5 6 7 8 9 10

This project, a thorough catalogue and scholarly assessment of John Mix Stanley's life work as well as a major traveling retrospective exhibition, would not have been possible without the generous support of many donors.

For this funding, the Buffalo Bill Center of the West is profoundly grateful.

These donors are listed below in alphabetical order:

Anson M. Beard, Jr.
Christie's
The Family of Helga and Erivan Haub
The Herndon Foundation
Mrs. J. Maxwell Moran
Ranney and Terri Moran
National Endowment for the Arts
Gerald Peters Family Foundation
Mr. William B. Ruger, Jr.
Mary A. H. Rumsey Foundation
John and Meredith Sullivan
Naoma Tate and the family of Hal Tate
TEX-OK Energy, in honor of Glenn E. Nielson's many contributions to the Cody community
Mr. and Mrs. William D. Weiss
Lisa and William M. Wirthlin, Jr.
Wyoming Arts Council

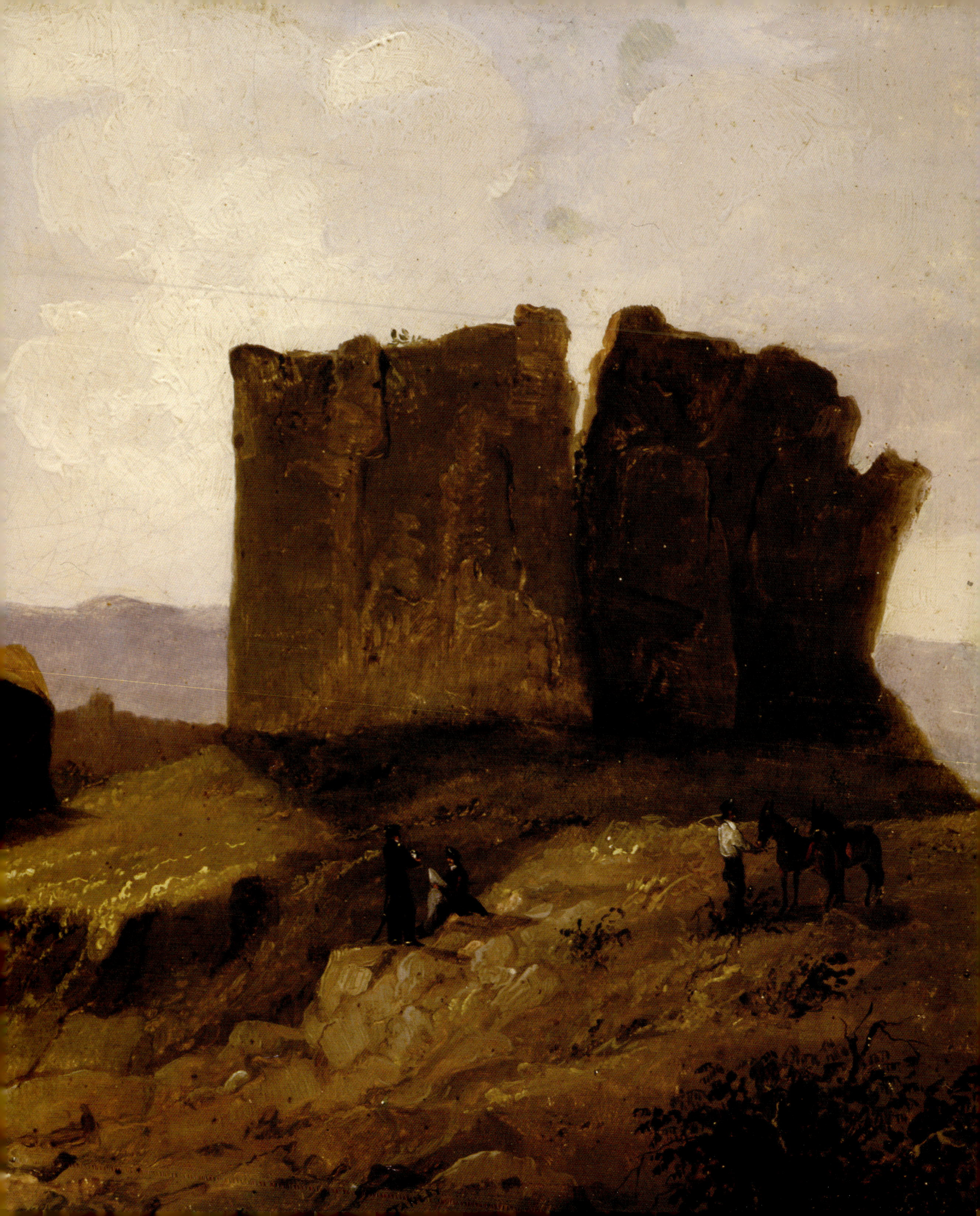

This book is dedicated to Julie Ann Schimmel,
whose remarkable devotion to American art scholarship has enlightened so many
and whose consummate study of John Mix Stanley's life and work
has made this volume possible.

Contents

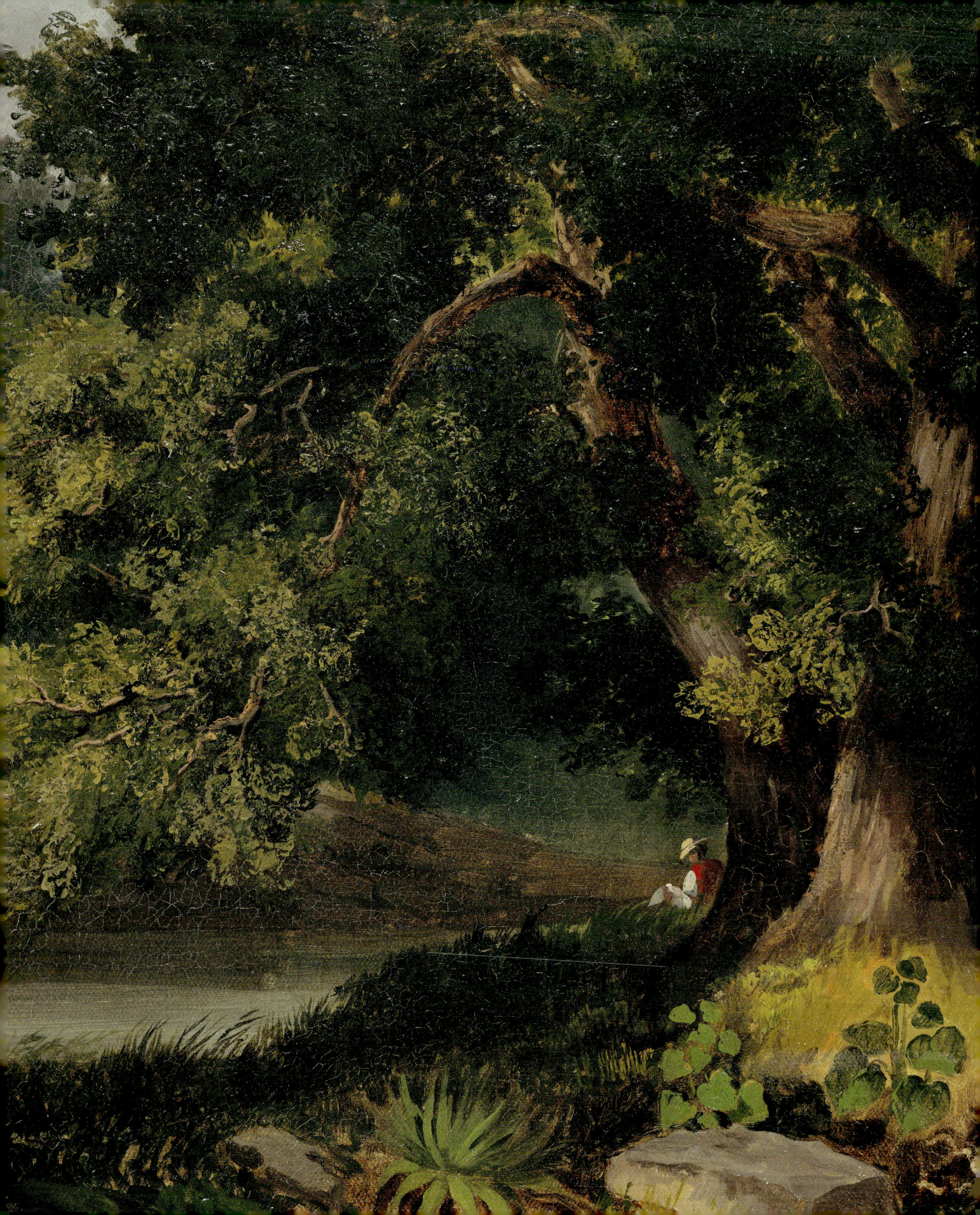

Foreword

Bruce B. Eldredge

Executive Director and Chief Executive Officer, Buffalo Bill Center of the West

Throughout its long history, the Buffalo Bill Center of the West has focused on American art and two special elements of that art: adventure and record. In organizing this major retrospective exhibition of the painter John Mix Stanley and marshaling the scholarship behind this accompanying catalogue on the artist and his times, we have delved deeply into those two worlds. No other American artist of the nineteenth century was such a well-traveled explorer, such an ardent adventurer, and such an inspiring recorder of frontier life and the western scene as was John Mix Stanley. The breadth of his travels, the scope of his artistic vision, and the caliber of his art are unequaled. It is therefore an honor and a remarkable accomplishment for this institution to have embarked on such an ambitious project of bringing the full range of Stanley's work to public attention for the first time.

This book features essays by noted American art scholars, including two from our own staff: Mindy N. Besaw, the former Margaret and Dick Scarlett Curator of Western American Art and Peter H. Hassrick, the museum's director emeritus and senior scholar. The outside authors of the volume—Emily C. Burns, Lisa Strong, and Scott Manning Stevens—have provided profound insights as well. In the course of the in-house research, over 225 Stanley works were uncovered. These are listed, illustrated, and discussed in a special section of the book compiled by Hassrick and devoted to a selected catalogue of known, extant works.

The exhibition, *Painted Journeys: The Art of John Mix Stanley,* co-curated by Hassrick and Besaw, comprises sixty works from all periods of the painter's career. Collectively, they reveal

OPPOSITE

J. M. Stanley, *Self-Portrait Sketching by a Stream*, c. 1854 (cat. no. 083)

the remarkable breadth and quality of Stanley's art, and elevate him to an ascendant position in American art through their quality and uniqueness. Through the exhibition, we have striven to revive the work of a leading but heretofore little-known American artist. The exhibition and catalogue, together, aim to define Stanley as a seminal painter of American Indians and to explore his role in shaping America's identity in the nineteenth century. They reveal how important he was in creating the western legacy in particular, a legacy that was inextricably intertwined with our national self-estimation at the time.

We are honored to be able to share this exhibition with two other important museums. It will travel, as Stanley did in the early 1840s, to Oklahoma, where it will grace the galleries of the Gilcrease Museum in Tulsa. Then, following the Gilcrease Museum's showing, the exhibition will move to the West Coast and find a temporary home at the Tacoma Art Museum in Washington, a state Stanley visited and painted in 1847–1848 and again in 1853. Both institutions are also major lenders to the exhibition. We trust that, with this traveling exhibition and well-researched and embellished catalogue, American audiences will be at last enlightened about Stanley's contribution to American cultural history and that he will find his long-deserved place in the canon of American art.

Acknowledgments

This volume and exhibition are the result of four years of research at the Buffalo Bill Center of the West. The project was originally slated as a stand-alone book based on research compiled since the 1970s by eminent John Mix Stanley scholar Julie Schimmel. Gerald Peters of Santa Fe, New Mexico, graciously provided access to the extensive Stanley archive for research. But, as the project developed under the aegis of Peter H. Hassrick, the center's director emeritus and senior scholar, and his assistant, Melissa Speidel, the museum, with the enthusiastic encouragement of the museum's senior staff, began to take interest as a sponsoring institution. Soon, *Painted Journeys: The Art of John Mix Stanley* took on the shape of a full-fledged, multi-venue, major retrospective exhibition and an expansive accompanying catalogue with multiple contributing authors.

It is with great pleasure, therefore, that the Buffalo Bill Center of the West offers thanks to Julie Schimmel, Gerald Peters, and Peter Hassrick for initiating such an undertaking. They are responsible for moving the project from conceptual to realizable form. Within the museum, special thanks go to the director, Bruce B. Eldredge, for helping to move the project forward and to Mindy N. Besaw, Margaret and Dick Scarlett Curator of Western American Art, for her enormous good work and welcome collaboration. The museum's development team indefatigably and efficaciously pursued funding for the project, securing major contributions from the National Endowment for the Arts, the Wyoming Arts Council, and many private donors, highlighted by the personal generosity of those who contributed $25,000 or more toward the effort: Naoma Tate and the family of Hal Tate; John and Meredith Sullivan; the Moran family, Betty, Ranney, and Terri; Lisa and William M. Wirthlin, Jr.; William B. Ruger, Jr.; the Herndon Foundation; the family of Helga and Erivan Haub; the Mary A. H. Rumsey Foundation; and a gift from TEX-OK ENERGY in honor of Glenn E. Nielson's many contributions to the Cody community.

We are exceptionally appreciative of the many lenders to the exhibition, all of whom have not only shared their treasures with us for an extended time but handled copious amounts of paperwork, assisted with research, and secured loan arrangements. Thanks go to many individuals and institutions, including Sarah Anschutz Hunt and Darlene Dueck, American Museum of Western Art–The Anschutz Collection, Denver; Andrew J. Walker, Margaret C. Conrads, John Frembling, and Jana Hill, Amon Carter Museum of American Art, Fort Worth, Texas; Richard West, Amy Scott, and Marilyn Van Winkle, Autry National Center of the West, Los Angeles; George Miles, Ingrid Lennon-Pressey, and Anne Marie Menta, Beinecke Rare Book and Manuscript Library, Yale University, New Haven, Connecticut; Walter J. Mayer, Buffalo and Erie Historical Society, Buffalo, New York; Fred Bollerer, Lisa Strong, and Sarah Cash, Corcoran Gallery of Art, Washington, D.C.; Rod Bigelow and Jeremy Munro, Crystal Bridges Museum of American Art, Bentonville, Arkansas; Michelle Jeske, Jim Kroll, and Coi E. Drummond-Gehrig, Denver Public Library, Colorado; Graham W. J. Beal and Kenneth Myers, Detroit Institute of Arts, Michigan; Alma Simmons, Detroit Public Library, Michigan; Marcee Craighill, Diplomatic Reception Rooms, U.S. Department of State, Washington, D.C.; John Vanausdall, James Nottage, and Christa Barleben, Eiteljorg Museum of American Indians and Western Art, Indianapolis; Randy Morger, Fort Benton Museums, Fort Benton, Montana; Rachel O'Neill, and Ray Werner, Galena–Jo Daviess County Historical Society and U. S. Grant Museum, Galena, Illinois; Duane King, Robert Pickering, Carole Klein, and Michelle Maxwell, Gilcrease Museum, Tulsa, Oklahoma; Elizabeth Mankin Kornhauser, Thayer Tolles, and Catherine MacKay, The Metropolitan Museum of Art, New York; Melanie Alexander, Kathy Doherty, and Virginia Cooper, Muscatine Art Center, Muscatine, Iowa; Jake Homiak and Daisy Njoku, National Anthropological Archives, Smithsonian Institution, Washington, D.C.; Nancy Anderson, National Gallery of Art, Washington, D.C.; Tim and Elaine Peterson, Boston; Brian Carter, Scott Rook, and Nicole Yasuhara, Oregon Historical Society, Portland; Jeffrey Quilter and Genevieve Fisher, Peabody Museum of Archaeology and Ethnology, Boston; James K. Ballinger and Jerry N. Smith, Phoenix Art Museum, Arizona; Kristin Swain, James Peck and Tim Decker, Rockwell Museum of Western Art, Corning, New York; Robert Rockwell, Corning, New York; Elizabeth Broun, Karen Lemmey, Emily Guth, and Richard Sorensen, Smithsonian American Art Museum, Washington, D.C.; Sarah Boehme and Alicia Benitez-Booker, Stark Museum of Art, Orange, Texas; Stephanie A. Stebich, Margaret Bullock, Laura Fry, and Ellen Ito, Tacoma Art Museum, Washington; Helen A. Cooper, Suzanne Greenawalt, Margaret Neil, and Suzanne Boorsch, Yale University Art Gallery, New Haven, Connecticut; and numerous private collectors from Wyoming, Texas, Utah, and Washington, D.C.

Countless individuals have assisted with the current research, helped with the loans, and provided counsel over the past several years. We are pleased to offer thanks to Eleanor D. Acheson, Washington, D.C.; Archives of American Art, Washington, D.C., and Amon Carter Museum branch, Fort Worth, Texas; Linda Ballinger, Phoenix, Arizona; Roger E. Belson, Henniker, New Hampshire; Kajette Solomon and Leslie Wong, Bridgeman Art Images, New York; Kerry Gaertner, Art Resource, New York; Tia Reber, Bishop Museum, Honolulu, Hawaii; Paige Kestenman, Christie's, New York; Rob Desongchamps, Anne Buening, and Lisa Delong,

Cincinnati Art Museum, Ohio; Scott L. Gampfer, Cincinnati Museum Center, Ohio; Aimie Westphal, Currier Museum of Art, Manchester, New Hampshire; Deedee Wigmore and Emily Lenz, D. Wigmore Fine Art, New York; Karen Brooks McWhorter, Denver Art Museum; Adam Lovell, Detroit Historical Society; Mark Bowden, Burton Historical Collection, Detroit Public Library; Ken Robinson and Jack Lepley, Fort Benton Museums; Peter B. Frantz, Essexville, Michigan, and his son Peter S. Frantz, Fairbanks; Jerry Peters and Ana Archuleta, Gerald Peters Gallery, Santa Fe, New Mexico; Haston C. Harris and Carlene Lebous, Nashville, Tennessee; Janis Davis, Harry S. Truman Library, Independence, Missouri; Swannee Bennett, Historic Arkansas Museum, Little Rock, Arkansas; Pauline Sugino, Honolulu Museum of Art; Elizabeth Le, Hunter Museum of American Art, Chattanooga, Tennessee; Ben Huseman, Arlington, Texas; Michael Juen, Iolani Palace, Honolulu; Doug Nelson, I. S. O. Art, Hamilton, Montana; Michael Frost, J. N. Bartfield Galleries, New York; John Howard, John Howard Fine Art, Missoula, Montana; Brook Masek, Joslyn Art Museum, Omaha, Nebraska; Martha Fleischman, Kennedy Galleries, New York; Jesse Talbot, New York Historical Society, New York; Craig Williams, New York State Museum, Albany; Jerry Bloomer, R. W. Norton Art Gallery, Shreveport, Louisiana; Thomas Nygard and Matt Cameron, Thomas Nygard Gallery, Bozeman, Montana; Claire Blechman, Peabody Essex Museum, Salem, Massachusetts; Jennifer Johns, Pennsylvania Academy of the Fine Arts, Philadelphia; Stacy Pomeroy Draper, Rensselaer County Historical Society, Troy, New York; Kelly-Ann Turkington, Royal British Columbia Museum, Victoria, Canada; Charlotte Mitchell, Sotheby's, New York; William H. Truettner, Washington, D.C.; Ashley Taylor, Tuscaloosa Museum of Art, Alabama; Kristen B. Schmidt, University of Arizona Museum of Art, Tempe; Laura F. Manaker, Merrill Lavine and Tracy Baetz, U.S. Department of the Interior, Washington, D.C.; the U.S. Department of Justice, Washington, D.C.; Merrill Lavine, U.S. Department of the Treasury, Washington, D.C.; Cheryl Gunselman and Trevor James Bond, Washington State University Libraries, Pullman; Vicki Catozza, Western Reserve Historical Society, Cleveland, Ohio; Clayton Lewis and Diana Sykes, William L. Clements Library, Ann Arbor, Michigan; and Gerold Wunderlich, Wunderlich and Company, New York.

At the Buffalo Bill Center of the West, this exhibition and publication have been adroitly overseen and implemented by the following: Emily Wilson, curatorial assistant; Jaclyn Rubino, research assistant; Emily Kassebaum, curatorial intern; the education team of Emily Buckles, Gretchen Henrich, Megan Smith, and George Miller; the development team of Lynn Pitet, Kelly Jensen, Gina Schneider, and Tom Roberson; Elizabeth Holmes and Patricia Lord, registrars; Gary Miller, collections manager; Desiree Pettet and Jessica McKibben, graphics; Beverly Perkins, conservation; Mary Robinson, Char Gdula, Karen Preis, and Mack Frost of the Harold McCracken Research Library; John Gallagher, Seth Johnson, and Lloyd Johnson of the museum's Information Technology Department, who have provided invaluable advice in working to convert database information into entries in the catalogue; and Lynn Rodgers, chief financial officer.

This volume would not have taken shape without the encouragement and ongoing effort of the University of Oklahoma Press. We offer special gratitude to the associate director and editor-in-chief of the press, Charles E. Rankin, for his energetic oversight of the project, and to the press's director, B. Byron Price, for recognizing the importance of this venture. To Price we owe additional thanks, because the Charles M. Russell Center for the Study of Art of the American West, which he directs, has provided a gracious subsidy for the book as well. In addition, Rowan Faye Steineker, editorial assistant, has been extremely helpful with many details concerning the publication.

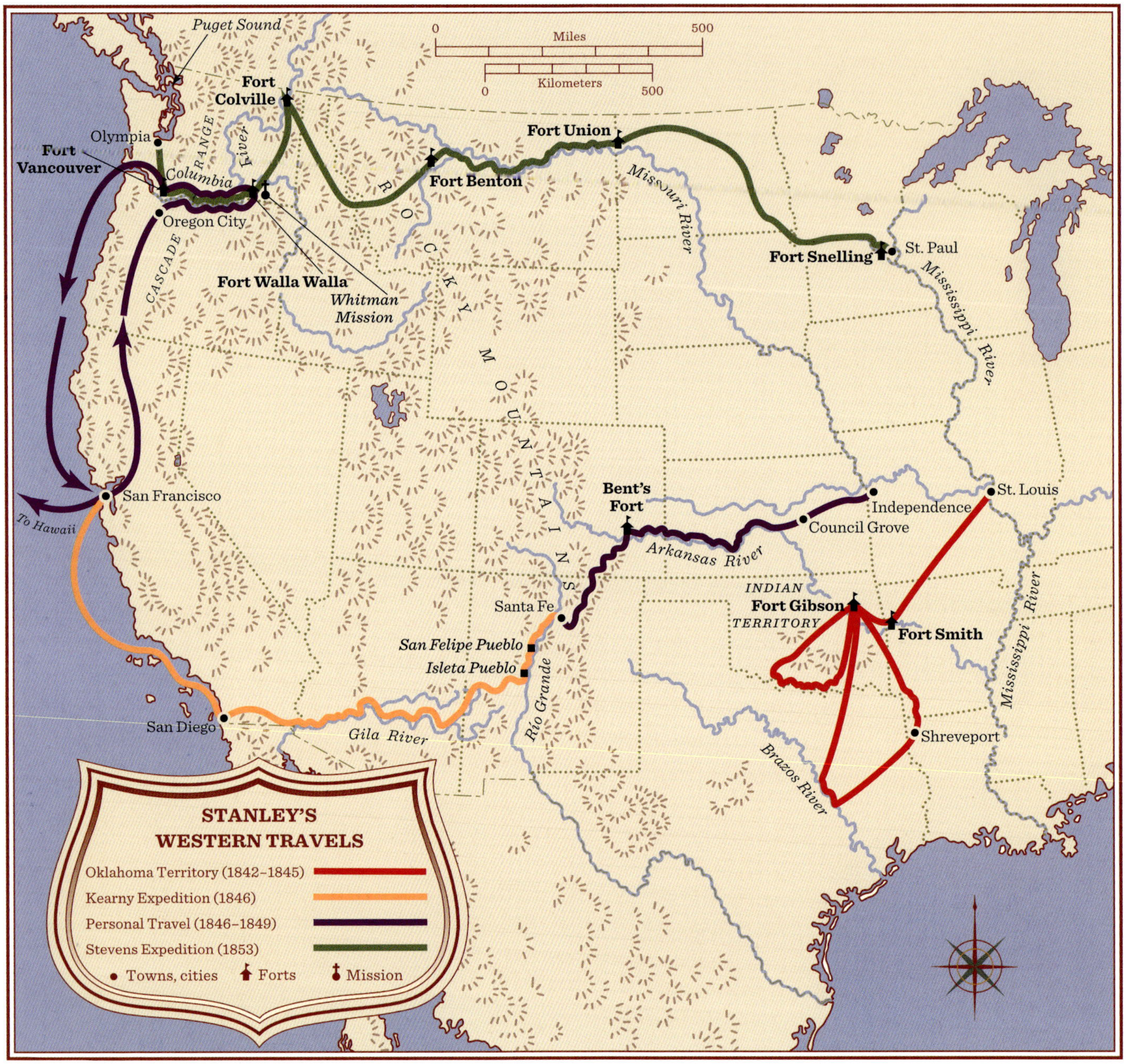

Map by Deborah Reade, www.DeborahReadeDesign.com.

Painted Journeys

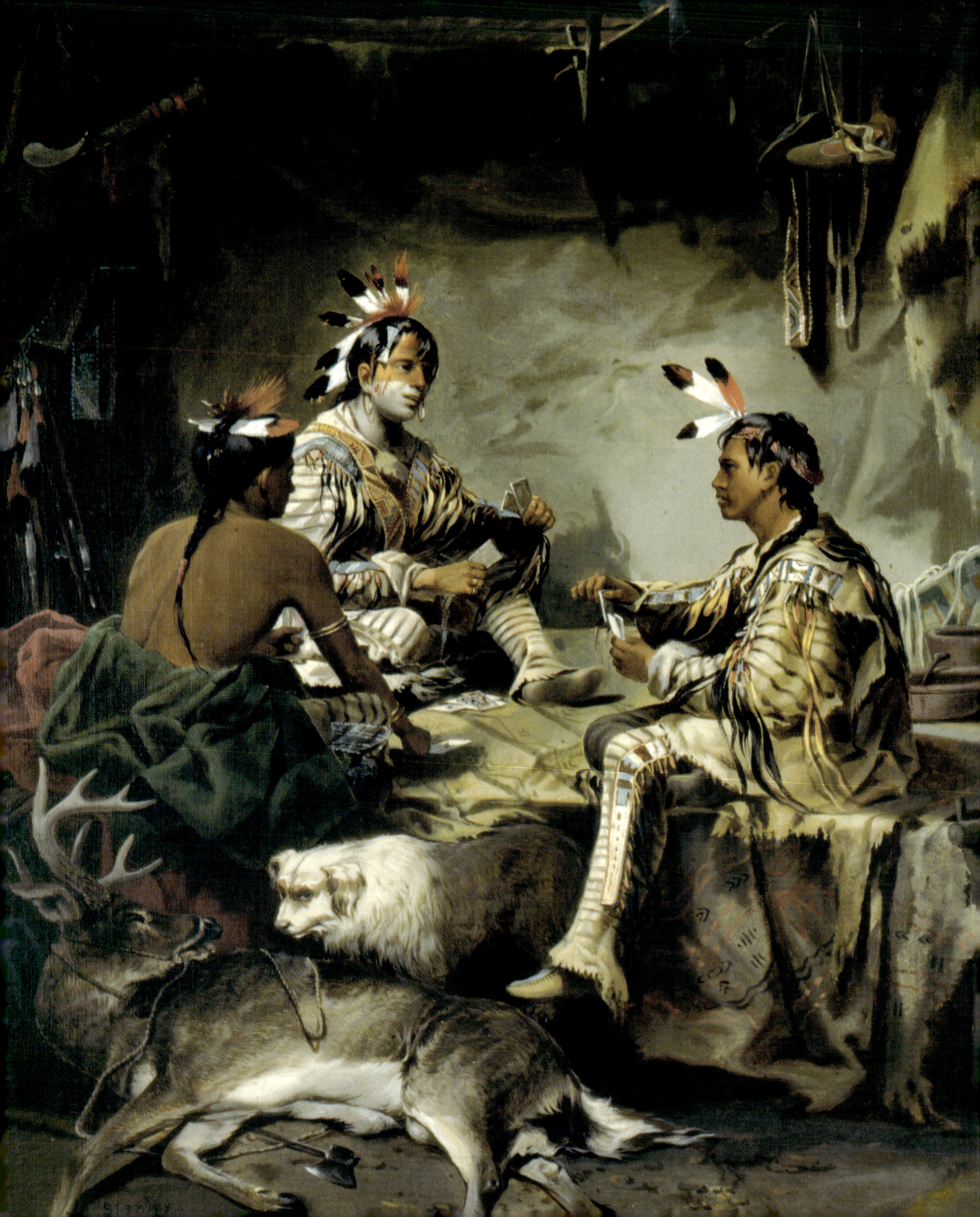

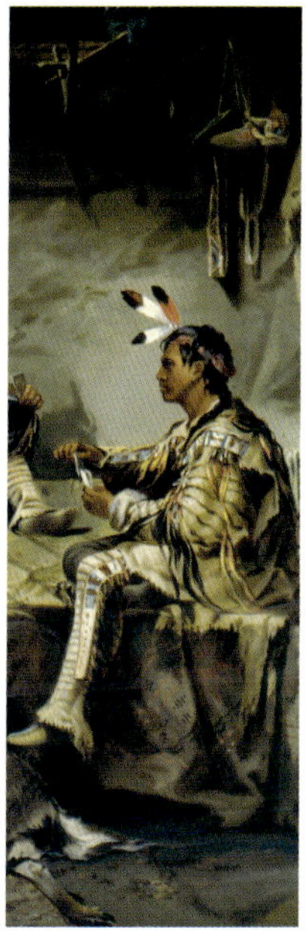

1

The Itinerant John Mix Stanley and the Circulating Spectacle of the West in Mid-Century America

Emily C. Burns

While traveling with the Pacific Railroad Survey in 1853, the artist-explorer John Mix Stanley (1814–1872) produced an evocative self-portrait in his sketchbook (fig. 1.1, cat. no. 073). A series of parallel dotted lines denote the structure of his tent, held up by a wooden frame. He sits on the ground, tucked in the right side of the composition, creating a shadow on the wall of the tent from the light source of a single candle on a stool beside him. Though the objects are modest, Stanley surrounds himself with the accoutrements of his travel: rock and plant specimens; small boxes; a large box with a folding lid, perhaps to hold his painting supplies or the daguerreotype equipment he carried on this journey; scattered papers; and even an American Indian smoking pipe. He does not depict himself in the act of sketching; rather, he contemplatively fiddles with an object from his travels. The small folding chair is labeled "Stanley," as though the artist associates himself with his peripatetic seat of art production.

In this self-representation, Stanley imagines himself as a solitary artist and explorer. He implies the itinerancy of traversing what his contemporaries described as a "comparatively unexplored region" of the western landscapes on the American continent.[1] Stanley's artistic career took him by government caravan and ship across and around the North American continent several times over more than a decade. He was one of a coterie of nomadic artists who sought patronage from documenting and imagining the geographic features, flora, fauna, and indigenous peoples of a volatile landscape as yet little explored by white settlers.[2] When his paintings were displayed in the midwestern and eastern United States, critics emphasized the

OPPOSITE

(detail) J. M. Stanley, *Gambling for the Buck*, 1867 (cat. no. 206)

FIG. 1.1.
John Mix Stanley,
My Prairie Home,
1853. Pencil on brown paper; 6⅞ × 10 in. (17.5 × 25.4 cm). Courtesy National Anthropological Archives, Smithsonian Institution, Washington, D.C.

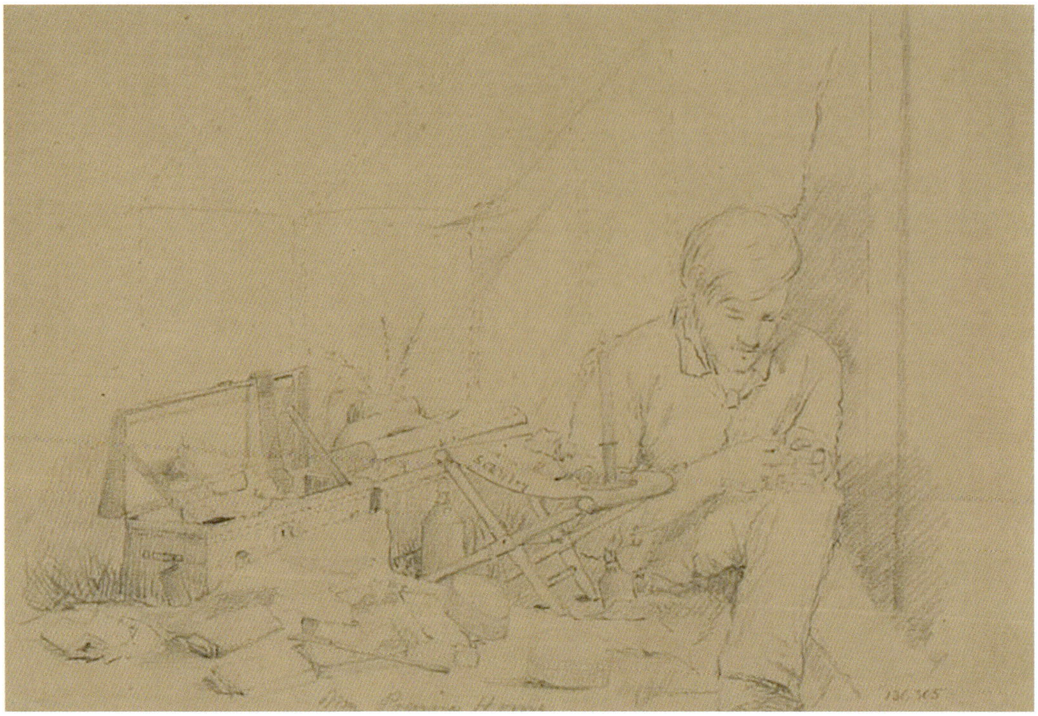

privation, adventure, and danger that the "pioneer" artist must have endured to obtain the material for the images.[3] Stanley activated this perception in his introverted self-portrait of the isolated artist on the prairie.

Scholarly research on Stanley has emphasized his role as a follower of George Catlin (1796–1872). An artist of a slightly earlier generation, Catlin conceived and produced a gallery of American Indian portraits in the 1830s, which he toured around the United States and in Europe and unsuccessfully attempted to sell to the U.S. government.[4] Stanley's travels were sponsored by U.S. government expeditions and sometimes self-funded through portraiture. As he journeyed and encountered members of different American Indian tribes, he created his own Indian gallery in the shadow of Catlin's project. He similarly toured his collection of paintings and American Indian artifacts, on view in urban locales even in the evenings by gas light.[5] Stanley offered his assembly of paintings to the U.S. government in the wake of Catlin's failed attempts to cajole a purchase. Some reviewers seemed convinced that galleries like Stanley's would "command an extravagant price, for a national or great public museum," but government support was not forthcoming.[6] Stanley had no better luck than Catlin in unloading his collection, despite press proclamations that Stanley's project was "superior," as historian Brian W. Dippie has charted. The government did borrow approximately 150 of Stanley's paintings, however, which were hung together in the Smithsonian Institution gallery (fig. 1.2) from 1852 to 1865, when most of the collection burned in a fire.[7] At the moment of their destruction, Stanley had been pursuing a more promising buyer for the collections in Michigan. In spite of this disastrous loss, the artist continued to produce new paintings and to search for new venues for display until the end of his life.

This retrospective exhibition seeks to catalogue a large but select number of Stanley's known surviving paintings and to consider his manifold contributions to art and spectacle in mid-nineteenth-century America. Although much of Stanley's artistic production has been destroyed, enough remains to enable scholars to consider critically the artist's engagement with the cultural conversations of this period. He left remarkably little writing, yet his production shows his deep engagement with both the realities and the mythologies of western settlement. A thorough analysis of Stanley's oeuvre shows that although Catlin's gallery was a central model for Stanley's project early in his career, the latter sought to differentiate himself from his predecessor. This thematic chapter offers a broad discussion of Stanley's artistic paths and his strategies for cultivating diverse audiences and venues for his work. Drawing from primary sources, such as newspaper reviews, and secondary sources, such as scholarly criticism on art and the American West, I interrogate the cultural, social, artistic, nationalist, and political climate in which Stanley's work was produced and viewed. The chapter is organized into five sections that offer a brief summary of Stanley's life and travel; discuss the role of modern spectacle in the circulation of Stanley's art; consider the critical responses to his North American Indian Gallery, as well as the ways in which he sought to differentiate his project from Catlin's; and present some concluding remarks about his legacy. Through a discussion of Stanley's artistic strategies, historians of art and cultural studies can gain a sense of the ways in which a mid-nineteenth-century artist cultivated audiences by seeking subjects that would capture popular attention and by constantly diversifying his markets around an unfixed western frontier.[8]

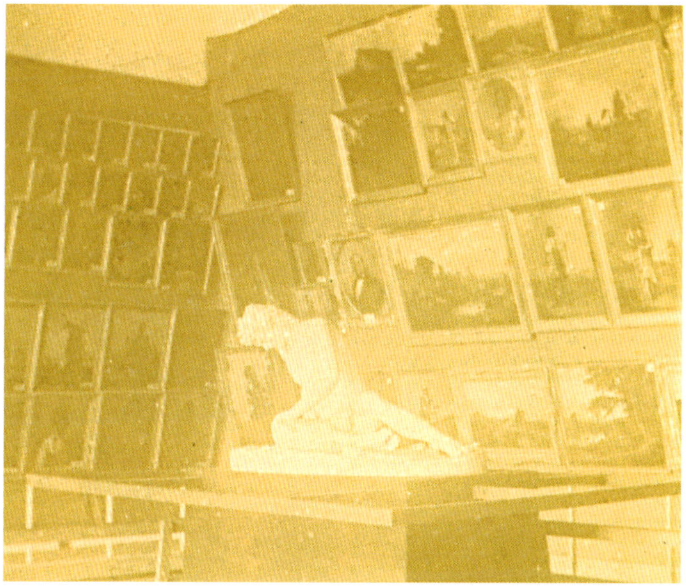

FIG. 1.2.
American Stereoscopic Co., Langenheim, Lloyd & Co., *A Corner in "Picture Gallery," Showing Part of the Stanley Collection before the Fire of January 24, 1865*, 1858. Albumen print mounted on cardboard; 3¼ × 6¾ in. (8.3 × 17.1 cm). Courtesy Smithsonian Institution Castle Collection, Washington, D.C. (SI.2004.020)

STANLEY'S PEREGRINATIONS

Stanley's travels as an explorer, documenter and arbiter of the landscapes and peoples of the West took him as far as present-day New Mexico, California, the Pacific Northwest, and even the kingdom of Hawaii.[9] He was born in 1814 in Canandaigua, New York, and was raised in Buffalo, where he may have worked as a sign painter in the early 1830s.[10] In 1834, he moved to Detroit, Michigan, where he studied portraiture and began to travel in the Midwest as an itinerant artist. He made his way to Troy, New York, by the early 1840s. Between 1842 and 1846, he traveled to present-day Oklahoma and Texas, and in 1845, he and a business partner, Caleb Sumner Dickerman (1819–1882), opened a North American Indian Gallery in Cincinnati, Ohio, which then toured to Louisville, Kentucky.[11] In 1846, he traversed the Santa Fe Trail and traveled with William H. Emory's military expedition during the Mexican-American War. Stanley spent the next two years in Oregon Territory, before traveling to Hawaii in the summer of 1848, where he remained for a little over a year.

Upon his return to Troy, New York, in 1850, he reopened the North American Indian Gallery with additional paintings and objects. The exhibition traveled from Albany to the Alhambra on Broadway in New York City, then on to New Haven and Hartford, Connecticut, before finally resting in Washington, D.C., in 1852. In the nation's capital, he met Alice Caroline English (1826–1891), who would become his wife in 1854. Stanley's time in Washington, D.C., was abbreviated, however, by his participation in another survey project; in 1853, he embarked on the northern railroad survey led by Isaac I. Stevens (1818–1862) to present-day Minnesota, North Dakota, Montana, Idaho, and Washington.[12] After Stanley's return to Washington, D.C., he worked on illustrations for government expedition volumes and continued to produce paintings based on his travels while petitioning the U.S. Congress to purchase his gallery of Indian portraits and artifacts. In 1864, Stanley and his family moved back to Detroit, where he remained for the rest of his life, except for a trip to Europe in 1868. He continued to make paintings, which he toured in single painting exhibitions, and explored reproduction opportunities in new techniques like chromolithography. He died of a heart attack on April 10, 1872.

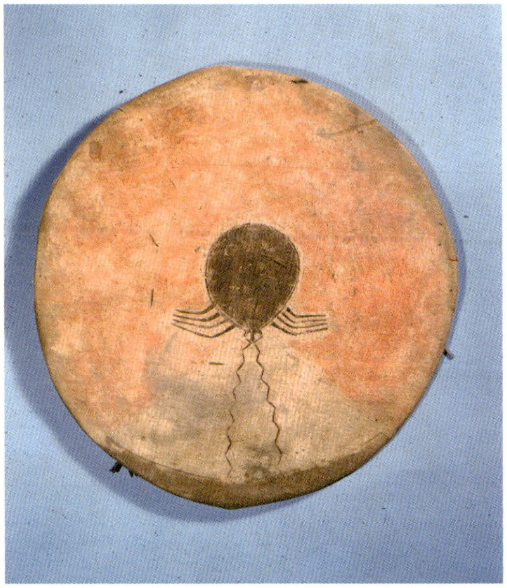

FIG. 1.3.
Pikuni Blackfeet (Piegan), *Buffalo Hide Shield and Skin Cover with Painted Decoration,* nineteenth century. Buffalo hide, skin. Courtesy National Museum of the American Indian, Smithsonian Institution, Washington, D.C.

Stanley's western travels largely occurred between 1842 and his marriage in 1854, but the impetus for these initial forays is not clear.[13] In his engagement with government survey projects, Stanley followed in the footsteps of the earlier survey artists from the time of the Lewis and Clark expedition in 1804, such as Titian Ramsay Peale (1799–1885).[14] These expeditions offered a model of survey representations and of collecting American Indian artifacts that mid-nineteenth-century excursions replicated.[15] Stanley likewise acquired many American Indian objects throughout his travels. His first collection of these objects was lost on a foundered ship in 1848, but he then began collecting anew. His second collection, today in the National Museum of the American Indian in Washington, D.C., included a shield (fig. 1.3), moccasins, clubs, saddles, clothing, lassoes, pipes, painted animal hides, jewelry, and arrows, mainly from the Blackfeet Nation, though the lost objects presumably came from the tribes Stanley encountered in his travels prior to 1848. The shield, donated among the other objects in 1929 to the Museum of the American Indian, was described as a "buffalo-hide shield with a deerskin cover on which is a painted decoration representing an insect."[16] In his North American Indian Gallery, the artifacts from his travels supplemented his displays of American Indian lands and peoples.[17] Artists who, like Stanley, traveled with expeditions occupied a middle ground between the expectations of documentation and the desire to show that the western territories were accessible.[18] American perceptions of the Midwest and Far West were also colored by the language of James Fenimore Cooper's Leatherstocking series, published in the 1820s and widely circulated. In producing paintings, Stanley moderated between these culturally determined expectations and his actual experiences in the West.

CIRCULATION AND SPECTACLE

Over his career, Stanley transitioned from making ethnographic portraits in the vein of Catlin to producing a wider array of paintings that subtly blended ethnography, history, genre, portraiture, and landscape. His experimentation with a variety of subjects and styles signaled his participation in a rising culture of modern spectacle. In the mid-century, artists were increasingly aware of the need to market their art to a mass audience, and thus artistic production, such as Stanley's, became intertwined with popular entertainment.[19] Echoing the artist's own peregrinations, Stanley's paintings circulated, primarily in the tours of the North American Indian Gallery. He made two panoramas that reflected on contemporary events, one in 1854 entitled *Stanley's Western Wilds*, and one in 1862 of the Civil War, with painter Alban Jasper Conant (1821–1915), entitled *Stanley and Conant's Polemorama! Or, Gigantic Illustrations of the War*.[20] Neither work survives, but the broadside for the latter suggests the drama, dynamism, and gore in his depiction of a Civil War battle. One reviewer argued for its didactic role for a mass audience, explaining, "A more vivid idea of the great struggle in which our country is engaged can be obtained in an evening than in months of reading."[21] The iconography and critical response highlights Stanley's engagement with visualizing the events of contemporary U.S. politics.

Stanley's representations also disseminated through media that brought his images into the home, such as government survey volumes.[22] Stanley anticipated this audience in his early portrait of Eleanora Ross (1830–1861) of 1844 (cat. no. 021), which depicts the sitter holding open a volume with a horizontal landscape engraving, inscribed by J. M. Stanley at lower left. The image is perfectly tilted so that the viewer can perceive this scene, as well as admire Stanley's portrait-painting techniques. Toward the end of his career, he became wrapped up in the popular rise of chromolithography in the 1860s, a medium that offered detailed color reproductions of some of his paintings.[23] Perhaps given the fire that destroyed many paintings at the Smithsonian, chromolithography enabled Stanley "to secure their preservation" in reproduction.[24] Print historian Peter C. Marzio suggests that Stanley made contacts during his 1868 trip to Europe to chromolithograph seven of his paintings.[25] Indeed, Germany's fascination with the American West would have meant that Stanley's images were as marketable overseas as in the United States.[26] Stanley also reproduced at least two paintings with the Detroit-based Calvert Lithographing, Engraving and Map Publishing Company when his German service was interrupted by the Franco-Prussian War in 1871.[27]

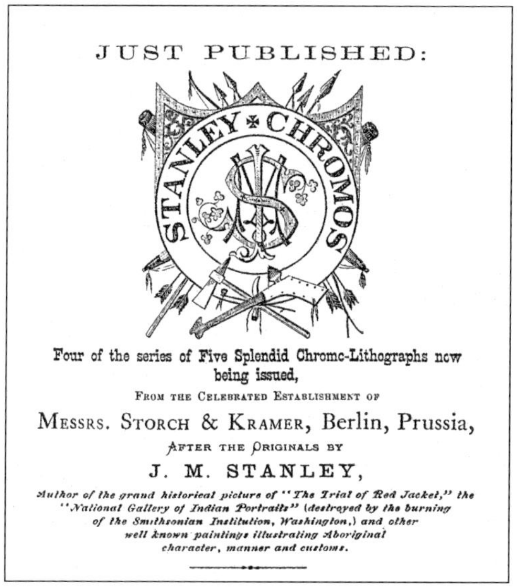

FIG. 1.4.
German advertisement for Stanley Chromos, c. 1870s. John Mix Stanley Papers, 1830–1973, Archives of American Art, microfilm copy, reel 687, Smithsonian Institution; courtesy Library of Congress, Washington, D.C.

Advertisements (fig. 1.4) from the Berlin-based chromolithography firm Storch and Kramer announced reproductions of Stanlcy's work with a bold heraldic insignia that included a tomahawk, arrows, and a cannon. The company sold chromolithographs of *Uncas, the Young Chief* (fig. 1.5), drawn from Cooper's *The Last of the Mohicans; The Deer-Slayers* (fig 1.1, cat. no. 209)*; The Indian Telegraph* (cat. no. 208); and *Gambling for the Buck* (cat. no. 206).[28] These images reveal Stanley's transformation of his ethnographic studies into genre scenes that constructed legible narratives accessible to wide audiences. Perhaps with an eye to the market, Stanley produced a second version of *Young Chief Uncas* (*Young Chief,* fig. 1.6, cat. no. 211) to be used in the production of the chromolithograph (as compared to cat. no. 210). The later version more clearly silhouetted the boy against the landscape setting because the figure and rock are higher in the compositional space, giving a greater sense of the figure sitting on a precipice. The colors are more varied, and the dark storm clouds from the original painting are calmed to a bluer sky. Stanley's adaptation of his painting for reproduction reveals his attention to public reception. A comparison between the chromolithograph of *Uncas, the Young Chief* (fig. 1.5) and the painting (fig 1.6, cat. no. 211) reveals the close replication enabled by reproductive technology, though the color in the painting is not quite as saturated as in the print. Still, the U.S. press celebrated Stanley's chromolithographs as difficult to distinguish from the original paintings.[29] The chromolithograph also boasts the printer's name in large letters at the lower center and Stanley's name at lower right. These chromolithographs, "to be found scattered all over the country" by the time of Stanley's death in 1872, extended the audience for his images.[30] Stanley began to develop a large

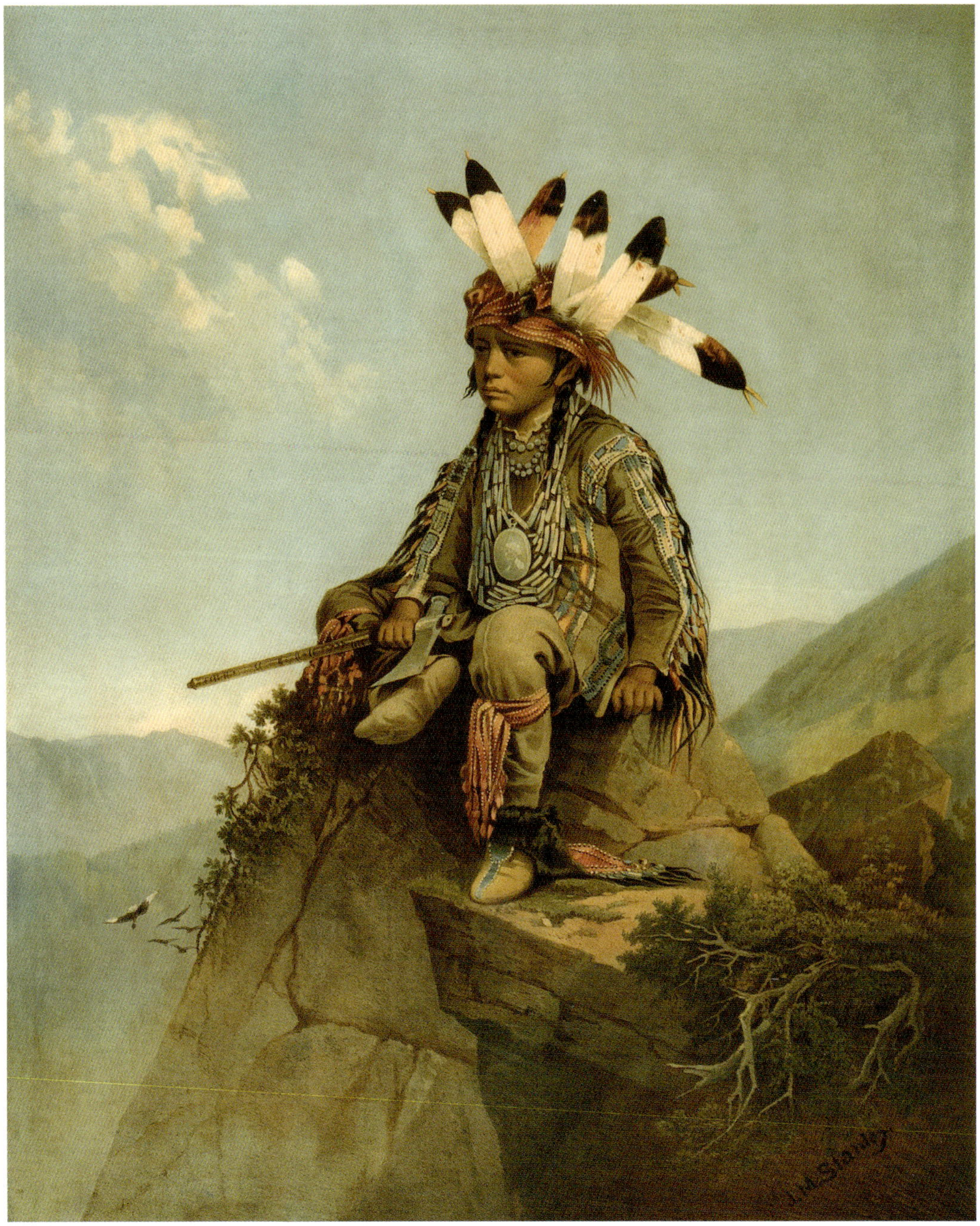

FIG. 1.5.
John Mix Stanley, *Uncas, the Young Chief*, 1869.
Chromolithograph; 19.94 × 15.5 in. (50.6 × 39.4 cm).
Courtesy Amon Carter Museum of American Art, Fort Worth, Texas (2007.10)

album of chromolithograph representations to combine with narrative texts about his subjects, though this project remained in progress at the time of his death.[31]

Stanley also made daguerreotypes during his travels, although, as photograph historian Martha A. Sandweiss has observed, he treated these objects as ethnographic tools and did not

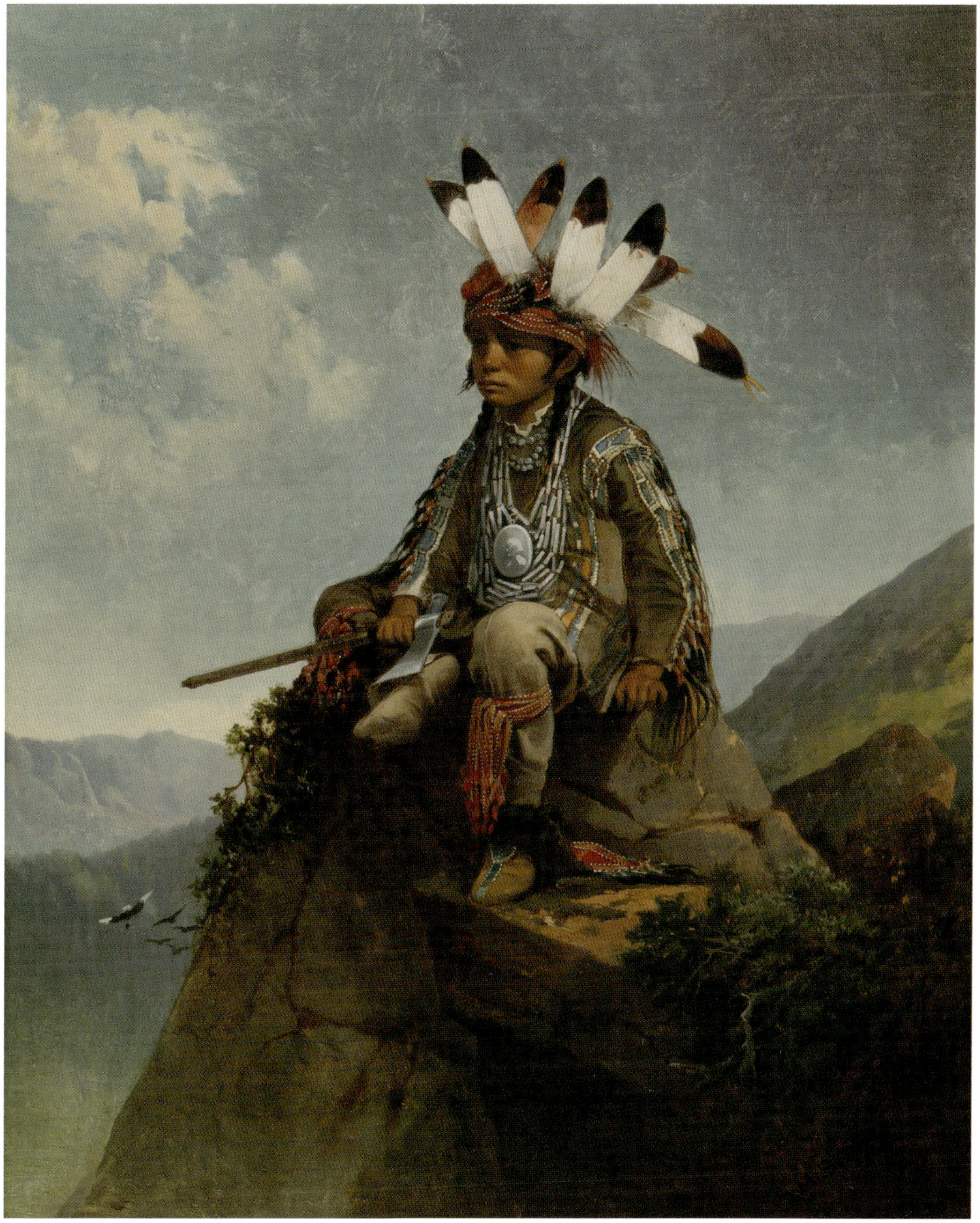

FIG. 1.6.
John Mix Stanley, *Young Chief*, 1868. Oil on canvas; 20 × 16 in. (50.8 × 40.6 cm).
Courtesy Haub Family Collection, Tacoma Art Museum, Washington,
gift of Erivan and Helga Haub, 2014

capitalize on their potential to be included in his exhibitions.[32] The only other markets that Stanley seems not to have tapped were the growing popular illustration press, such as *Harper's Weekly*, and the print market cultivated by the American Art-Union.[33] On the whole, however, Stanley nestled himself into a wide range of artistic venues that insatiably sought representations and

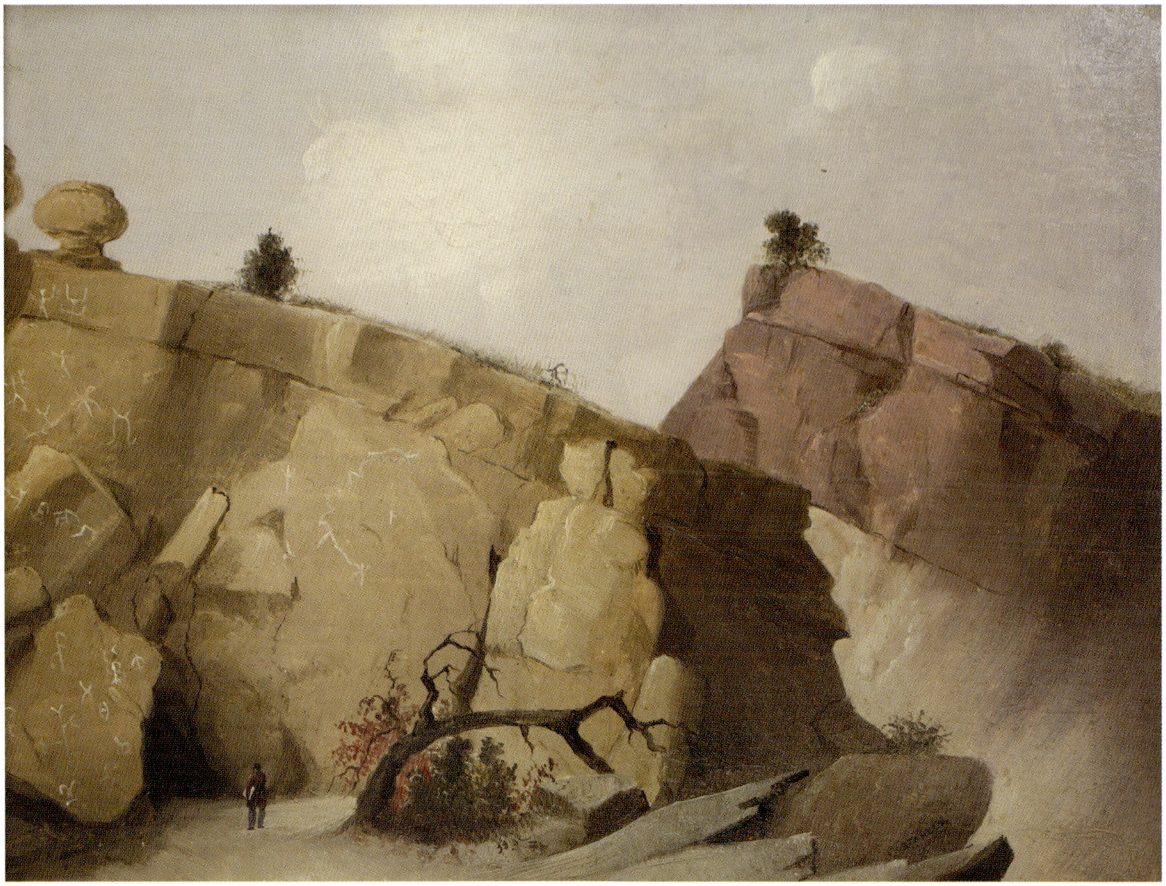

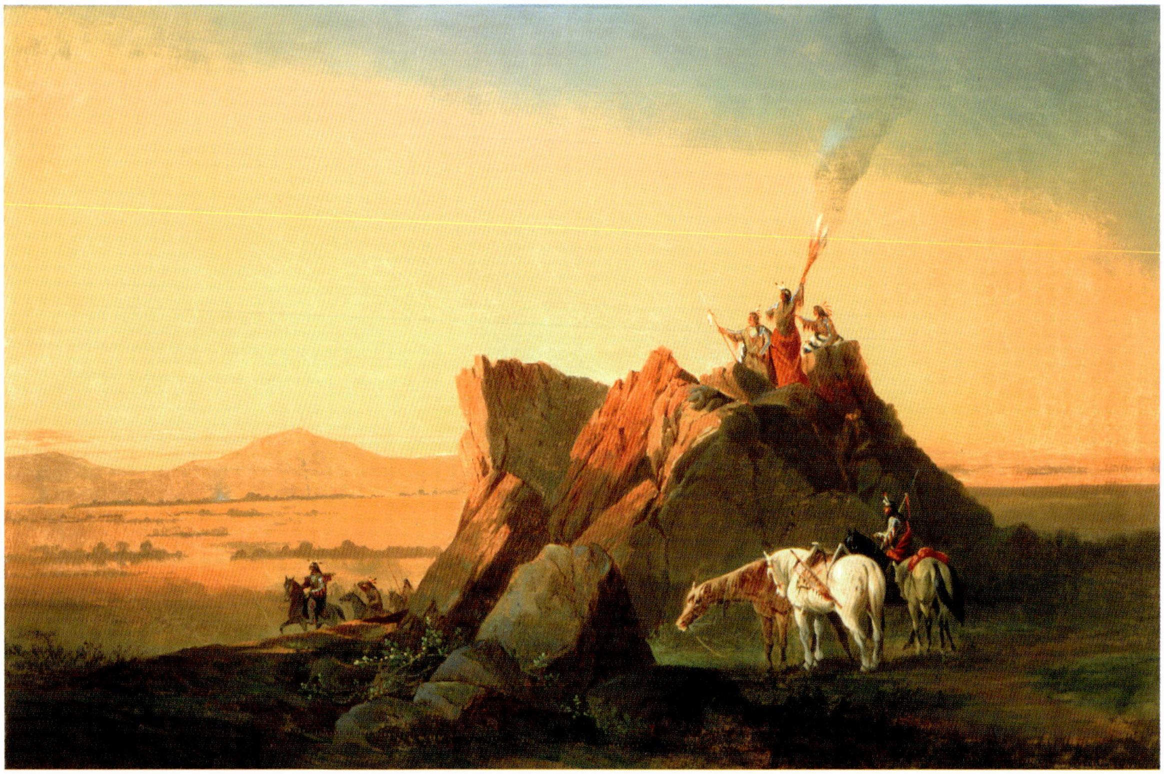

FIG. 1.7.
John Mix Stanley, *The Hieroglyphic Rocks on the Gila*, 1847. Oil on academy board; 10 × 12⅝ in. (25.4 × 32.1 cm). Courtesy Nelda C. and H. J. Lutcher Stark Foundation, Stark Museum of Art, Orange, Texas (31.23.3)

FIG. 1.8.
John Mix Stanley, *Indian Telegraph*, c. 1863. Oil on canvas; 21 × 31 in. (53.3 × 78.7 cm). Private collection; photograph courtesy Gerald Peters Gallery, Santa Fe, New Mexico

imaginations of American western landscapes and their inhabitants. With his malleable entrepreneurial strategies, he exemplifies the shifting relationship between art, spectacle, and mass culture just before and following the Civil War. His range of stylistic approaches and genres of art making bear the influence of his own peripatetic life, and the dissemination of his objects reveals his attempts to capitalize on interest in the West during a heightened period of expansion.

Stanley's paintings regularly enact ideas of their circulation through repeated themes of heightened observation and communication. For example, in *The Hieroglyphic Rocks on the Gila* (fig. 1.7, cat. no. 038), one of his survey representations from the mid-1840s that survives in two versions, Stanley silhouettes the figure of an artist, with sketchbook under arm, against a large rocky edifice, inspecting American Indian pictographs. In Stanley's reference to systems of American Indian communication and memory, the artist simultaneously implies his role as close observer and intercessor for the viewer. Likewise, in *Indian Telegraph* (fig. 1.8, cat. no. 178), a subject that Stanley also painted several times, he emphasizes the subject of communication through smoke signals across a long distance. A group of American Indian figures stand on top of a large rock waving a fiery bouquet of sticks to create a patterned wave of smoke in the sky. One critic argued that American Indians "can maintain intelligible communication on important matters by this means."[34] The title invokes the "telegraph," an electrical system of communication patented by Samuel F. B. Morse (1791–1872) in 1837, but applies it to a depiction of more "primitive" modes of contact.[35] This painting and title highlight Stanley's attempts to link his American Indian subjects with popular topics in a steadily modernizing America. These themes of looking and communicating across distance parallel the circulation of Stanley's paintings and chromolithographs across wide spaces and through eclectic communities.

"TOUCH THE HEART OF EVERY AMERICAN": WESTERN SPECTACLE AND STANLEY'S INDIAN GALLERY

In the idea to create an American Indian gallery of portraits and artifacts, art historian Julie Schimmel suggests that Stanley may have been motivated by encounters with Iroquois in his home region of upstate New York.[36] Stanley was also inspired by the success of Catlin's Indian gallery in the 1830s, and may have seen Catlin's gallery on display in Baltimore in the summer of 1838.[37] Stanley's business partner, Dickerman, was from Troy, New York, where he may have seen Catlin's gallery in 1837. Dickerman may have encouraged Stanley's idea to create a similar spectacle. It seems that while they traveled together briefly and were partners in the North

American Indian Gallery, Stanley produced the paintings, and Dickerman organized the venues and managed the distribution of information along with the exhibition.[38] Stanley also followed the course of other artist-explorers, such as the Canadian Paul Kane (1810–1871), who produced a collection of portraits of American Indians, and whom Stanley may have encountered in 1847 in Oregon Territory.[39] Setting off into the western territories, Stanley presumably possessed a spirit of adventure and entrepreneurship that paralleled these contemporaries. His itinerant lifestyle may have resulted from the vicissitudes of the art market, which forced him to seek patronage along multiple avenues concurrently.

Catlin, Kane, Dickerman, and Stanley all manipulated the popular press, using broadsides and critical reviews to market their American Indian galleries to a wide public audience.[40] Tellingly, one "anonymous" letter to the editor appeared almost verbatim in the Cincinnati press in 1846 and in the Troy press in 1850. It is possible that the press in Troy recycled the earlier letter to drum up interest, and indeed many reviews are repeated between the town newspapers, but it is also plausible that Stanley or Dickerman circulated the same letter as a marketing attempt to cultivate certain perceptions of their exhibition and its merits as both art and document. Both articles repeat the comment that American Indian "hunting grounds, but little more than half a century ago, included the spot where their representatives are now exhibiting."[41] The two venues in question were Washington Hall in Cincinnati, Ohio, and Concert Hall, Morris Place, in Troy, New York. This odd repetition coalesces two different histories of U.S.–American Indian contact as a single narrative.

Although Stanley did not write directly about his motivations, the reception of his Indian Gallery partly mirrored that of Catlin's project as an attempt to document a so-called vanishing race.[42] Catlin consistently emphasized the documentary nature of his project and was outspoken about his concern with the possibility of American Indian extinction. Stanley likewise combined paintings with American Indian artifacts in the vein of ethnography; one visitor described "a great number of Portraits, Landscapes, Sketches, &c. nearly covering the walls of the large Hall—also many interesting curiosities properly arranged about the room."[43] Similarly, Stanley's accompanying text argued that he was collecting representations from a wide range of American Indian tribes for posterity and offered anecdotal observations about each community. Public reception, however, did not usually distinguish the distinctive features of each tribe.

Many mid-nineteenth-century viewers embodied what later critics have categorized as "imperialist nostalgia"; influential anthropologist Renato Rosaldo has noted that settler colonialism often resulted in a paradoxical response on the part of the conquerors, or "agents of colonialism." As they acknowledged their power in altering a culture, many white viewers also longed for the cultural characteristics that were lost in that process.[44] During this period, as many scholars have considered, exploration was tightly intertwined with expansion. Artistic representations were often complicit in these settler colonialist projects. For example, when Stanley went to Hawaii for over a year in 1848, the artist's presence paralleled broader "signs of progress in the humble little country of our adoption" with "civilization and improvement at work at their ancient landmarks."[45] During this period, Hawaii experienced both a transition to a constitutional monarchy and an attempt to reconsolidate land ownership.[46] As a better-trained artist than others in Hawaii before him, according to the article, Stanley was a harbinger of an approaching "civilization," though one of his major projects was to paint portraits of the Hawaiian king and queen (cat. nos. 060 and 061). The idea of civilization fails to

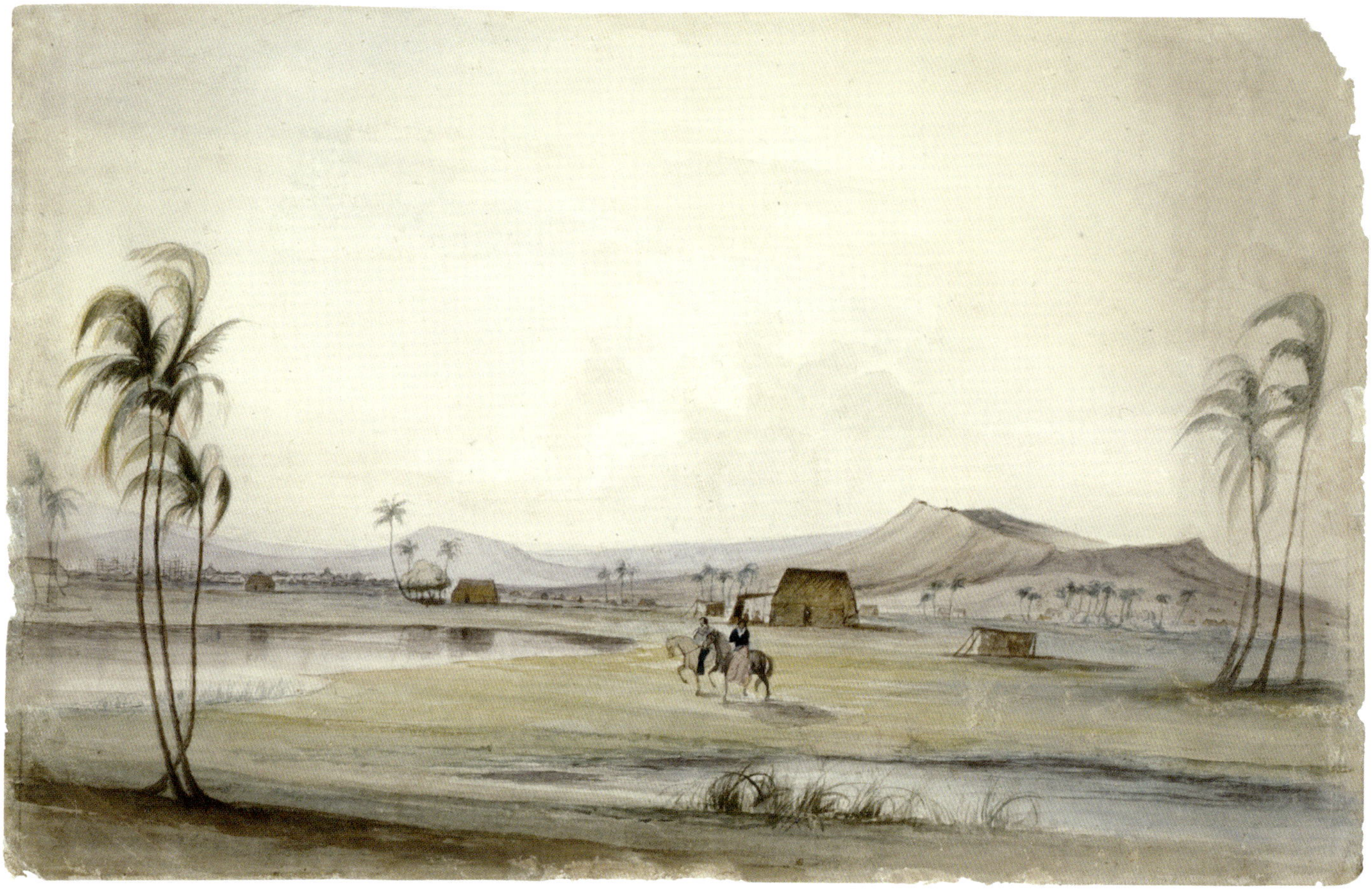

FIG. 1.9.
John Mix Stanley, *View from Waikiki*, c. 1849. Watercolor on paper; 8¼ × 12½ in. (21.0 × 31.7 cm). Courtesy Honolulu Museum of Art, bequest of Patches Damon Holt, 2003 (27388)

come to mind in a watercolor, *View from Waikiki* (fig. 1.9, cat. no. 063), from Stanley's travels to Hawaii. Here, the artist emphasizes the investigations of a couple on horseback taking in a wide open landscape framed by palm trees blowing in the wind, and with only a few rudimentary buildings dotting the horizon. This open landscape seems ripe for exploration and growth.

As cultural historian Shari Huhndorf has argued, mythologies of U. S. history tended to claim the figure of the American Indian as the original American only after actual American Indians' minimal role in contemporary American politics seemed secured.[47] Although Huhndorf applies her argument largely to the period after Custer's Last Stand in 1876, some of the language around Stanley's exhibitions in Cincinnati suggests that this concept can also be applied to the 1850s in areas where American Indians had already been relocated or assimilated by the Indian Removal Act of 1830. One review of Stanley and Dickerman's Indian Gallery in Cincinnati began with the pronouncement, "We are proud to say, that we have not an Indian in our borders." The author implied the injustice of the policies of American Indian removal but offered only to "breathe one last sigh over these wild children," engaging with Stanley's representation of their "remains" as a document for posterity.[48] Another visitor described the ethnographic objects alongside the paintings as "mementos of a people who are fast fading away before the rapid strides of civilization."[49] Letters to the editor in Cincinnati and in Albany celebrated these figures, "whose genius would have done honor to any nation," claiming Stanley's American Indian sitters as ancestral Americans and encouraging projects that "preserve such memorials as we can of their existence."[50] One visitor to the exhibition summarized in this vein that Stanley and Dickerman's gallery "should touch the heart of every American, for we should at least feel an interest in the original owners of this vast country" as part of the "antiquity and history of this great and glorious republic."[51] These comments suggest that in some parts of the United States during the 1840s and 1850s, indigenous populations were already being assimilated as the noble ancestors of white America.

In their subject matter, Stanley's paintings and exhibition frequently raised questions of time for visitors. One Louisville critic likened the ephemerality of Stanley's exhibition to that of the subjects of his paintings. He encouraged the public to "catch a fleeting glance at the rapidly retreating race who were lords of the soil of North America."[52] The dynamism of Stanley's spectacle paralleled the naturalized language of Manifest Destiny. Yet the paintings also offered viewers the idea of timelessness; one visitor to Stanley's and Dickerman's Indian Gallery in Troy described the time Stanley "spent among the living pictures, transferring them to the deathless canvass [*sic*]," canvases that were presumed to exist indefinitely.[53] Viewers read Stanley's paintings as material traces that would remain for posterity even as indigenous populations purportedly receded. Stanley's turn to chromolithography at the end of his career raised this same desire for durability. These tensions between the presumed transience of the American Indian along with the ephemeral exhibitions and the intended permanence of these representations themselves resurfaced in the critical reception to the touring gallery.

Stanley's Indian Gallery engages with the cultural conversation around American Indian removal, a subject that participated in a rising tide of American cultural nationalism. By the 1860s, critics like Henry Theodore Tuckerman (1813–1871) wrote that American artists should seek cultural uniqueness by depicting western subjects. "It is in our border life alone that we can find the materials for national development, as far as literature and art are concerned," he wrote.[54] While Stanley was not privileged among the artists Tuckerman discussed as examples, other contemporary critics invoked a parallel nationalistic celebration through Stanley's paintings. The reason for visiting the exhibition, for one New York City writer, was twofold: "Pay your respects to the Native Americans, and the genius of American enterprise and talent."[55] One Cincinnati critic highlighted the display of "the fading remnants of this doomed race," but also argued that visitors "will testify their interest in the arts, as well as their national pride in American subjects, portrayed by American talent."[56] These comments pictured Stanley as an archetypal American entrepreneur. A Van Buren, Arkansas, reviewer concurred: "Why not a great American, as well as an Italian artist? Why not Stanley as well as Ruben [*sic*]?"[57] Many critics sought to distinguish Stanley as a uniquely U.S. artist. A Washington, D.C., observer registered these concepts of nationalism in Stanley's paintings, writing:

> As works of art his pictures are equal to any thing of the kind to be found in Europe. There is no flashy, dawdy coloring here to catch the eye: no unnatural positions to create wonder: no over-wrought delineations to mystify and amaze. Here art in its simplicity and candor unfolds, in all the truthfulness of Nature, the characters, persons,

habits, virtues, and peculiarities of the 'red man.' Here the lover of art feels pride at the triumph of American genius fully employed in American subjects.[58]

This writer suggested that European representations use trickery to dazzle the viewer, but Stanley cultivated a perceived honesty of representation that the author sees as part of an American pragmatism. Stanley's lack of European artistic pedigree became an asset to many of his viewers.

U.S. critics coalesced their notion of Stanley's privation, as constructed by his self-portrait (fig. 1.1, cat. no. 073), into their reading on the national value of his representations as worthy of public attention. One writer in 1846 noted Stanley's "perilous and arduous task in collecting these pictures" in the survey expedition, which had "enough . . . privation, toil, fatigue, and personal risk, to make it, in the main, anything but agreeable."[59] In order to obtain such representations, another critic agreed, "artists must *live* themselves," applying "indomitable energy" to their artistic endeavor.[60] Another reporter purportedly quoted from Stanley himself, who emphasized the labor and danger in his project: "If I had known the extent of the task I had assumed, the adversity, the privations and the fatigues to which I was to be exposed, and the frequent despondencies that were to come over me, I would no longer have prosecuted the work upon which I had embarked."[61] The notion of labor and adversity enhanced intrigue and public interest in Stanley's project. This rhetoric only increased over time; an 1850 exhibition of the larger gallery in Troy, New York, was read as "the fruit of eight years' unceasing toil and perilous adventure through the vast wilds and deserts."[62] In addition to Stanley's production of these 150-odd paintings, the physical demands on their transit to these destinations became part of the spectacle. In their celebration of Stanley's adversity, critics upheld him as a model for other Americans "to encourage others to emulate the zeal and perseverance, amid toil, privations, and danger."[63] In recounting his traversing of dangerous landscapes, the press cast Stanley as the ideal frontiersman who faced risk to produce his art. This nationalist narrative became a marketing strategy to sell Stanley's project to public audiences.

Critics occasionally noted Stanley's unique versatility in depicting such a wide range of subjects that crossed genre categories. One writer explained, "Whatever he may undertake—whether a wild Western prairie or mountain scene, an Indian dance, a buffalo hunt, or a portrait, his drawing seems equally strong, his perception of form equally accurate, and his treatment of color equally judicious and effective."[64] Writing in 1855, an anonymous critic expanded this discussion of Stanley's tremendous range: "Sketches of this kind call for the development of a varied skill, which few have ever well combined." This reviewer connected Stanley's flexibility of approach to his peripatetic lifestyle: "Mr. Stanley's experience through years of toil, privation, and dangers, in forest and prairie, seems to have emancipated his mind from the thralldom of artificial standards of taste, and his works happily attest the benefit of this emancipation."[65] For this critic, Stanley had eschewed stylistic requirements of any artistic school, allowing his painting approach to be uniquely dictated by its subject.

As a result of Stanley's purported detachment from his subjects and from conventions of representation, writers celebrated his lack of "the customary humbuggery."[66] Many writers claimed a truth factor in his art and insisting on its didactic role in creating "transcripts from the great book of Nature."[67] As Stanley and Dickerman may have pointedly written about their project, the North American Indian Gallery "scorn[ed] all those accessions of Humbug, which bring throngs to a vile caricature, and counterfeit presentment of a subject which should be sacred from trickery."[68] This pronouncement was perhaps offered in comparison with other American Indian galleries, including Catlin's, which enhanced the sense of spectacle by having live, costumed American Indian performers on display with the objects.[69] The *Troy Daily Whig* scornfully noted that at Stanley and Dickerman's gallery, "no one goes away disappointed, except in two or three cases, when the unsophisticated visitors supposed the exhibition consisted of live Indians."[70] Some writers sought to differentiate Stanley's exhibition from "'catch penny' affair[s]" and "the thousand monkey shows that are of no interest but to amuse for an hour," and to insist that Stanley's art marked an unmediated representation of the American West that served a didactic function.[71]

Yet, these comments about humbuggery suggest that the exhibition occupied an uneasy terrain between middlebrow and lowbrow culture. Indeed, some of Stanley's paintings were displayed in the epicenter of humbuggery in the mid-nineteenth century: P. T. Barnum's American Museum in New York City.[72] In their production and reception, Stanley's paintings exhibit a constant tension between a modern desire for spectacle and the claims of documentation, or between "entertainment and instruction."[73] Indeed, as one critic wrote, "while these paintings [are] works of art . . . they especially commend themselves to the simple taste of the mass" because of the eclectic selection of imagery and the American Indian artifacts. This reviewer concluded, "This is not only a collection of portraits, but of far west scenery, and of incidents in Indian life. It is an exhibition of costume and character, and a museum of specimens of art and fancy work."[74] While some reviewers noted the spectacular qualities of Stanley's oeuvre, enhanced by venues like Barnum's museum, claims to the objects' authenticity rang louder in the popular press.

STRATEGIES OF DIFFERENTIATION: STANLEY AND CATLIN

Although Stanley's North American Indian Gallery is indebted to Catlin's ethnographic display, Stanley also tried to transform his project into a distinct enterprise through several key strategies of differentiation. These attempts did not necessarily separate his projects from Catlin's in practice; many parallels existed between them, as Brian W. Dippie has addressed. Yet, press clippings—at least those that were pasted into Stanley's scrapbooks—carefully sought to clarify the distinctions between the two projects. Stanley may have attempted to fill the vacuum created when Catlin took his Indian gallery to Europe in 1840.[75] Stanley's critics emphasized the development of his artistic practice in a wider variety of genres than Catlin attempted, especially after the 1840s. Early in his career, Stanley made American Indian portraits in the tradition of Catlin, Charles Bird King (1785–1862), and Henry Inman (1801–1846).[76] He also produced scenes that seem intended to document American Indian life from an ethnographic perspective, such as *International Indian Council* of 1843 (cat. no. 014), which depicts a crowd of American Indian figures from many tribes gathered beneath a wooden-framed structure to discuss intertribal politics. This painting was accompanied by a series of published notes containing Stanley's descriptions of being present at the event.[77]

Stanley's Indian Gallery also included landscapes that exoticized the American West, such as the idealized *Chain of Spires along the Gila* (cat. no. 130), which some critics celebrated over the American Indian portraits.[78] Reviewers highlighted Stanley's interest in landscape as unique, though Catlin also painted avidly in this genre. As Julie Schimmel has considered, one

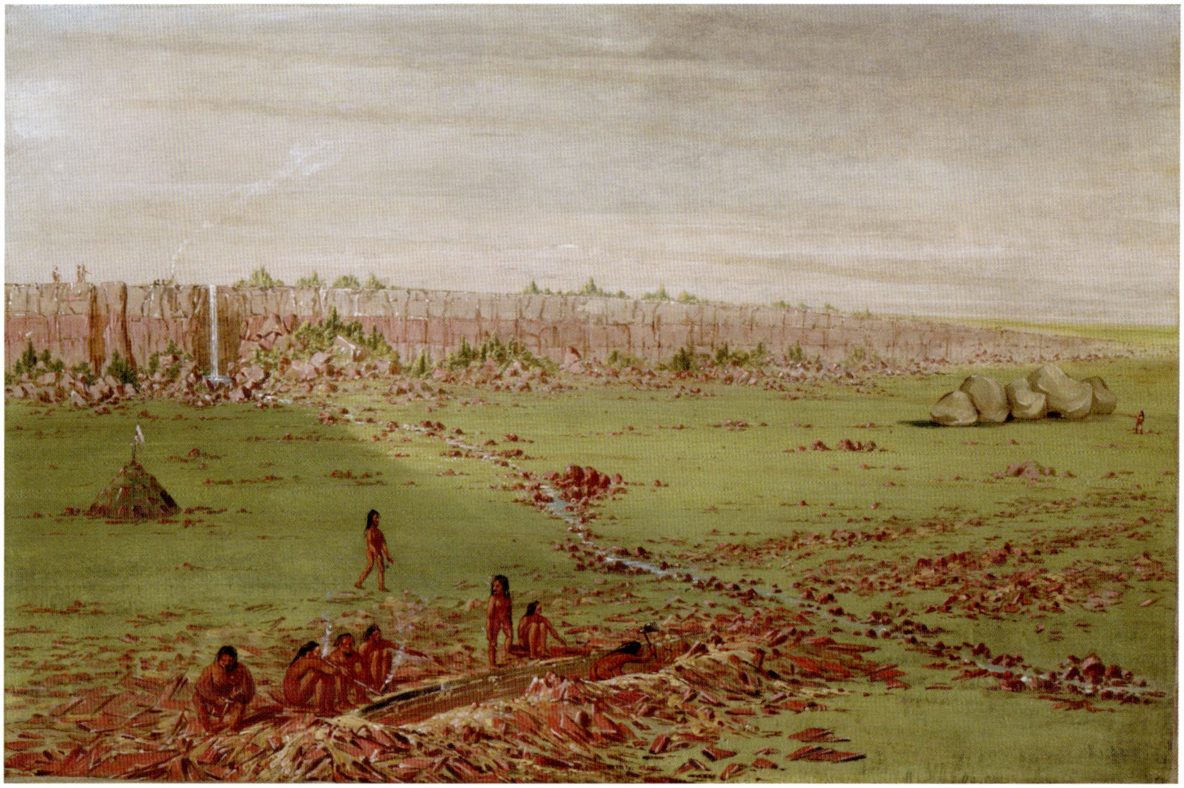

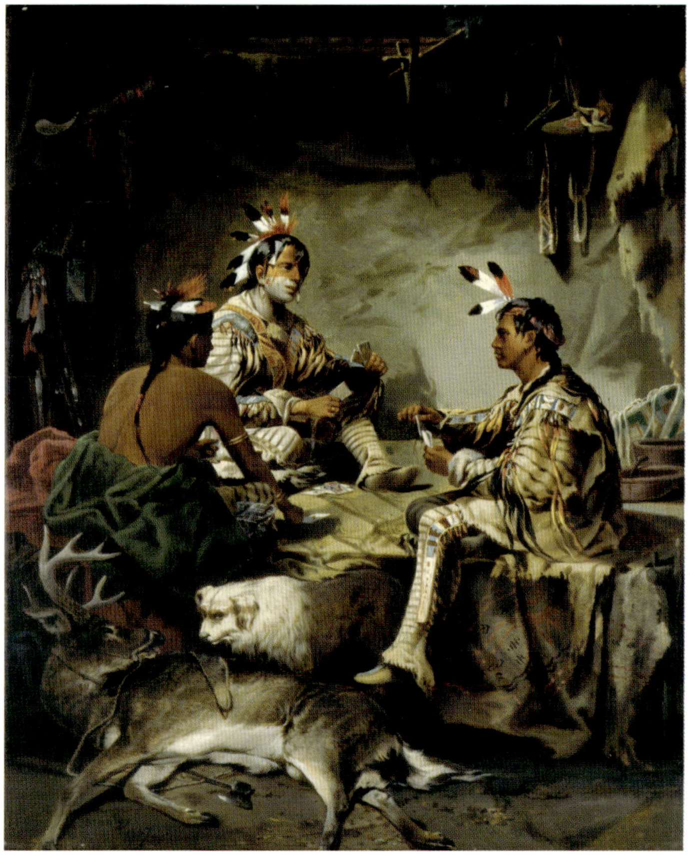

FIG. 1.10.
George Catlin, *Pipestone Quarry on the Coteau des Prairies*, 1836–1837. Oil on canvas; 19½ × 27¼ in. (49.5 × 69.2 cm). Courtesy Smithsonian American Art Museum, Washington, D.C., gift of Mrs. Joseph Harrison, Jr. (1985.66.337)

FIG. 1.11.
John Mix Stanley, *Gambling for the Buck*, 1867. Oil on canvas; 20 × 15⅞ in. (50.8 × 40.3 cm). Courtesy Nelda C. and H. J. Lutcher Stark Foundation, Stark Museum of Art, Orange, Texas (31.23.11)

of Stanley's additional contributions to art history has been his interest, likely inspired by Hudson River School painting, in depicting atmosphere in large-scale landscapes, seen in *Mount Hood from the Dalles* (cat. no. 223), and in his view of *Oregon City on the Willamette River* (cat. no. 066) from c. 1852, which offered a view overlooking a growing town on a lake, with the pastoral inclusion of American Indian figures in the foreground of the town.[79] According to some of Stanley's contemporaries, this multiplicity of genres broadened the appeal of Stanley's gallery through a more eclectic range of imagery.

Over time, Stanley evolved his portraits into genre scenes that imagined anecdotes of American Indian episodes in daily life, such as communication and gambling.[80] Documentation gave way to narrative, perhaps as a result of the lack of a buyer for Stanley's Indian Gallery or changing market pressures. Compared with Catlin's more ethnographic studies, which imagine tribal ritual and work, such as *Pipestone Quarry on the Coteau des Prairies* (fig. 1.10), Stanley's later genre scenes, such as *Gambling for the Buck* (fig. 1.11, cat. no. 206), of 1867, offered more monumental, European-inspired compositions in which the figures become characters in a story rather than ethnographic types.[81] In *Gambling for the Buck*, three carefully posed figures play cards, wagering on the large buck at the lower left of the composition. The figures are arranged in a triangular central grouping in which gesture and costume move the viewer's eye

FIG. 1.12.
John Mix Stanley, *Kidnapped*, 1853. Oil on canvas; 30 × 41½ in. (76.2 × 106.7 cm). Courtesy Denver Art Museum, William Sr. and Dorothy Harmsen Collection (2001.454)

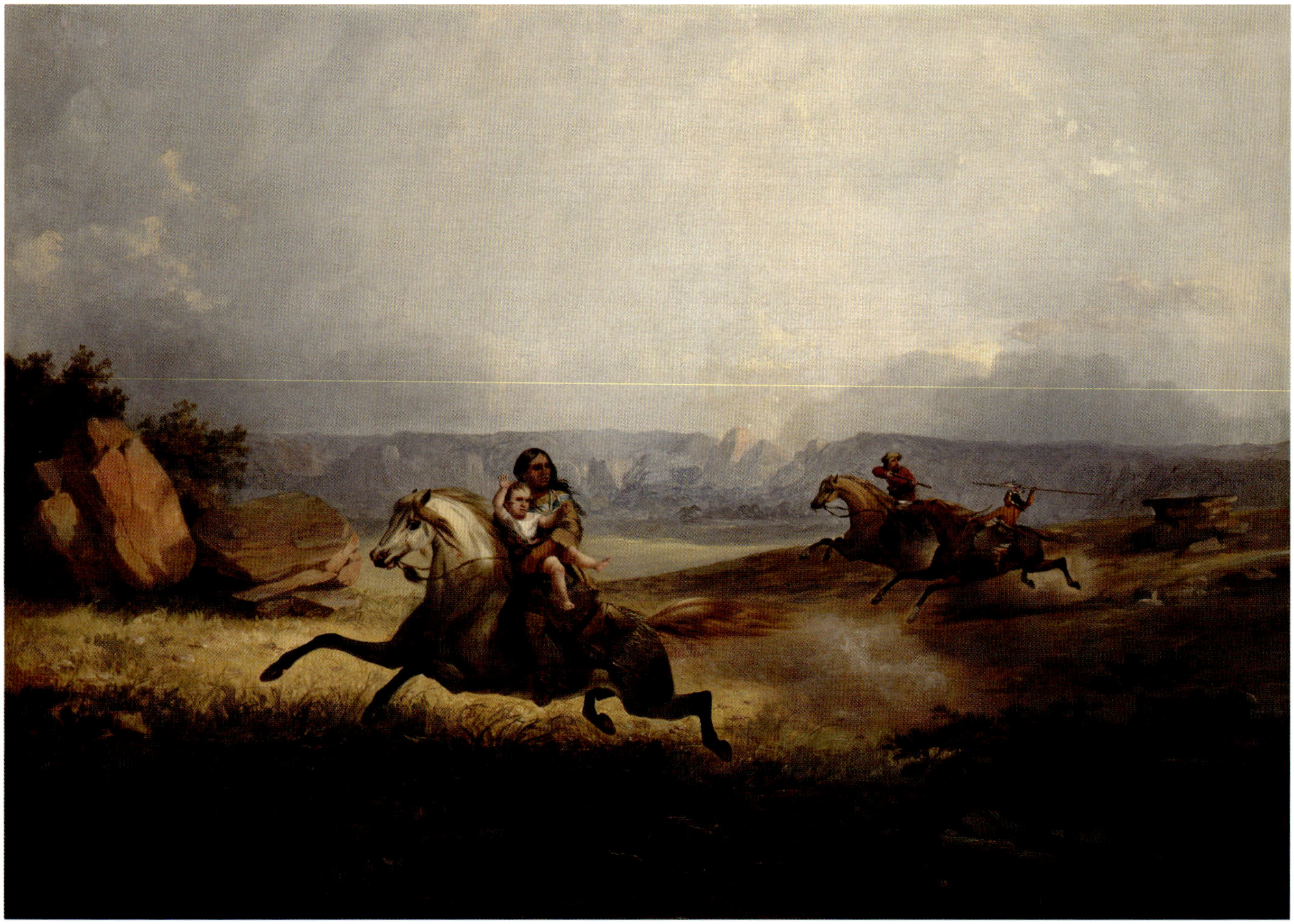

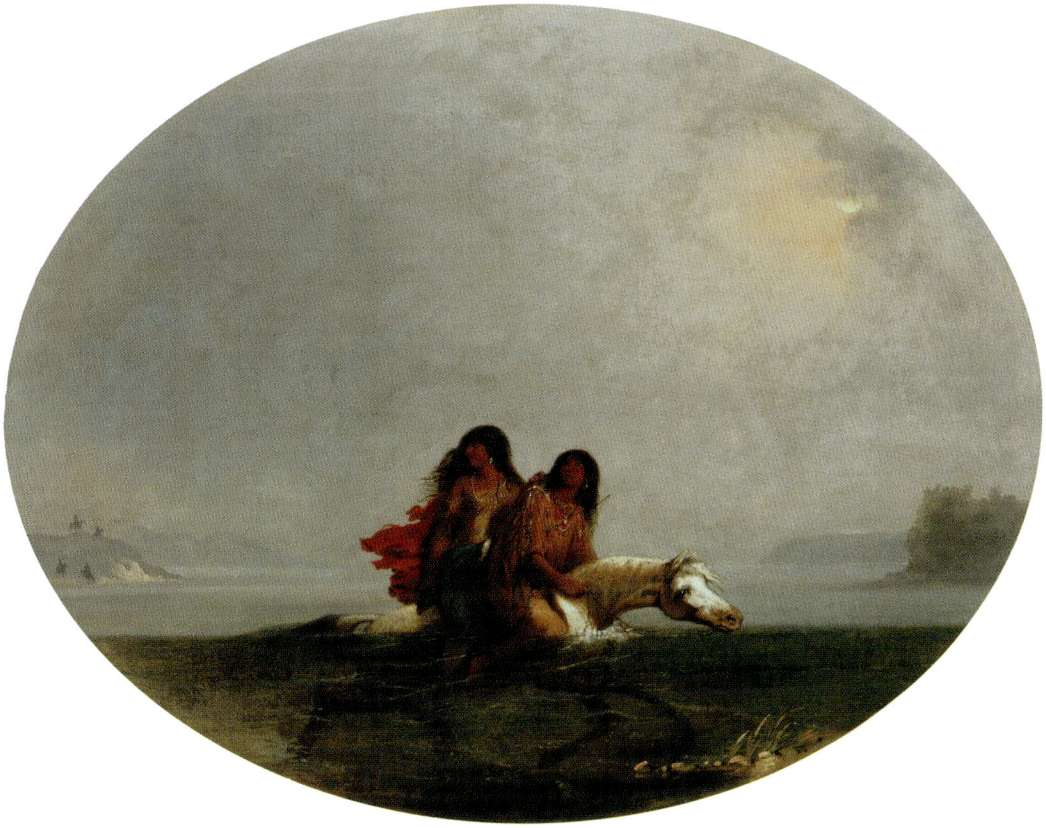

FIG. 1.13.
Alfred Jacob Miller, *Indian Elopement*, 1852. Oil on canvas; 30¼ × 36¼ in. (76.8 × 92.1 cm). Courtesy Buffalo Bill Center of the West, Cody, Wyoming

around the painting. Stanley draws from his ethnographic studies but applies them to a narrative. While Catlin's representations of American Indian landscapes, such as *Pipestone Quarry* (fig. 1.10), framed a wide-angled representation that distanced the viewer from the subjects, Stanley focused on the figures rather than the setting. In *Gambling for the Buck* (fig. 1.11, cat. no. 206), the figures are pressed to the front of the picture plane, and their environment seems like a stage set, revealing Stanley's studies of American Indian artifacts, which surround the card players.

Stanley's brushstrokes, such as those in *Gambling for the Buck,* are tighter, more subtle, and more academic than Catlin's. With imperceptible layers of glaze, Stanley's paintings align with genre painting of his day, and one reviewer noted "the high finish of the paintings, their depth of expression, and the bold and striking air of life and reality," even in the portraits in the Indian Gallery.[82] Another commentator on his style described its "truthful yet bold effect, and subdued taste in coloring withal, which might shame many of our much extolled artists."[83] Stanley also employed brighter and more saturated colors than his counterpart, who often used a more limited palette of muted greens, browns, and tans (fig. 1.10), which one critic, probably thinking of Catlin, described as "Spanish brown daubs, usually presented to the public as portraits of Indians."[84]

In Stanley's color choices and greater concern with pyramidal compositions, he drew from romantic idealizations of American Indian characters in the genre paintings of Alfred Jacob Miller (1810–1874), William T. Ranney (1813–1857), and Charles Deas (1818–1867).[85] For example, Stanley's *Kidnapped* of 1853 (fig. 1.12, cat. no. 139) seems closely related to Miller's *Indian*

FIG. 1.14.
John Mix Stanley, *Crossing the Milk River*, c. 1855. Oil on canvas; 30½ × 42 in. (77.5 × 106.7 cm). Courtesy Autry National Center, Los Angeles, California (88.108.33)

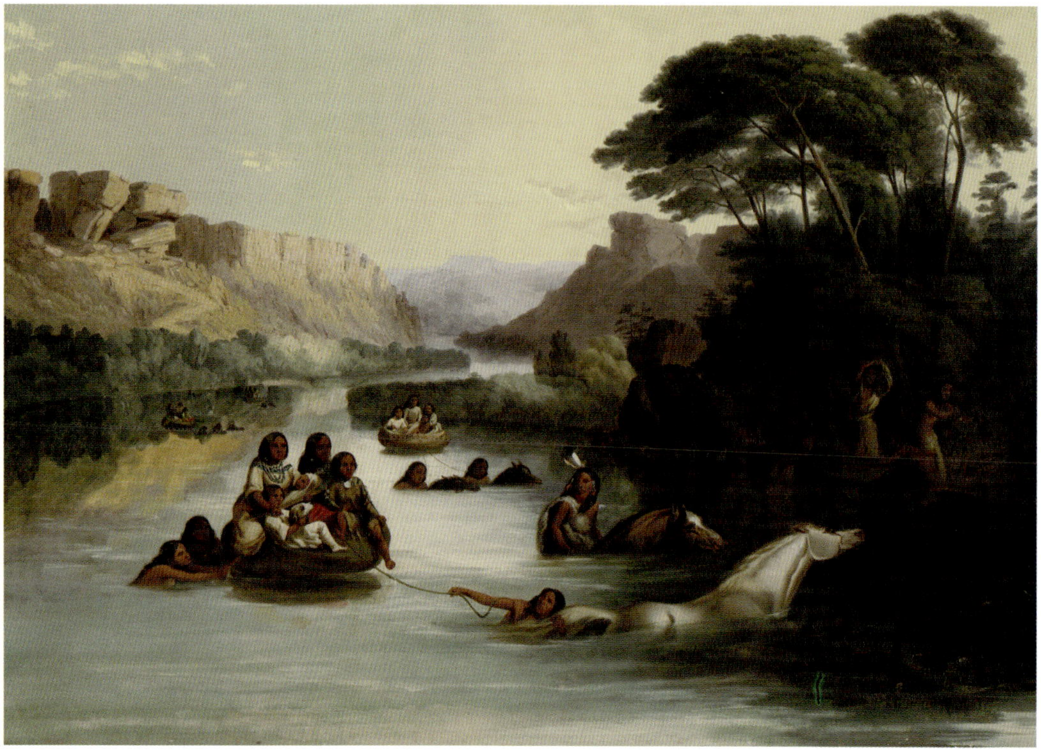

FIG. 1.15.
William Tylee Ranney, *Crossing the Ferry–Scene on the Peedee*, c .1846. Oil on canvas; 28⅛ × 42⅛ in. (71.4 × 107.0 cm). Courtesy Morris Museum of Art, Augusta, Georgia (1993.006)

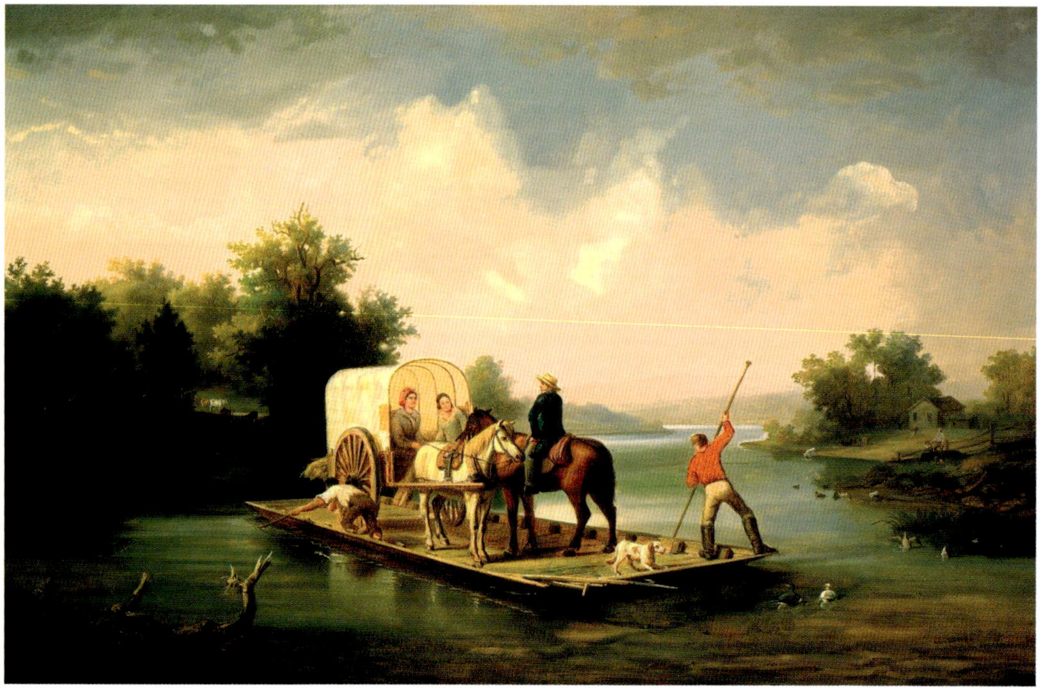

Elopement (fig. 1.13) of the previous year.[86] Both artists favor the romantic narrative within a landscape, use a similar palette, and engage an analogous depiction of light and shadow. These scenes transform Catlin's discourse of ethnographic documentation into a different genre targeted at different audiences. Like Ranney, who emphasized representations of trappers, Stanley's idealizations of scouts, such as *Scouts along the Teton River* (cat. no. 131), naturalized the scouts' dominion over the landscape, as the figures are silhouetted against the evening sky.[87] Stanley's *Crossing the Milk River* (fig. 1.14, cat. no. 140), from c. 1855, also recalls the composition and color of Ranney's *Crossing the Ferry—Scene on the Peedee*, from c. 1846 (fig. 1.15).

Stanley's engagement with genre painting seems to draw from European academic compositional strategies. This seems surprising, since the artist did not travel to Europe until 1868. Yet he would have developed his knowledge of academic painting from prints; viewing paintings on exhibition in cities such as Washington, D.C., as Lisa Strong discusses in her essay in this volume; and from the work of other American genre painters, such as Miller and George Caleb Bingham (1811–1879), who did train overseas.[88] In addition, portraitist James Bowman (1793–1842), who was one of Stanley's early teachers, traveled to Rome and London for study.[89]

Catlin and Stanley had a slightly different relationship with photography in their production of images of American Indians.[90] Catlin used photography while touring with Ojibwe Indians in Europe in the 1840s, but this technology was not available to him when he was beginning his projects of documenting American Indians in the West. Beginning in 1842, the production of daguerreotypes became a central part of Stanley's narrative of encounter. Stanley allegedly made duplicate daguerreotypes in each sitting, keeping one for his portfolio and leaving one with the sitter.[91] As Martha A. Sandweiss has pointed out, when Isaac Stevens recalled Stanley's use of the daguerreotype during the 1853 survey, he looked with a primitivizing gaze on the American Indian sitters who were "delighted and astonished to see their likenesses produced by direct action of the sun. They worship the sun, and they consider that Mr. Stanley was inspired by their divinity, and he thus became in their eyes a great medicine man."[92] According to these accounts, Stanley used his photographic equipment as a tool to elevate his status among his sitters, and then drew from his imagery as he developed his gallery of American Indian portraits.

While Catlin's scenes of tribal dances sought to establish ethnographic distance by tending to avoid white figures, Stanley's narrative paintings heighten the drama of encounter, as in *An Osage Scalp Dance* (cat. no. 025), where a white woman and child are at the center of the grouping.[93] This type of scene suggests a kind of imagined narrative of encounter that Catlin tended to avoid expressing directly. In addition to such dramatic genre scenes, Stanley also approached the language of history painting in some of his representations.[94] In *The Last of Their Race* (cat. no. 159), for example, the scale of the painting and the placement of the figures against a backdrop like a stage set draws from the stylistic tropes and grand narrative of academic history painting, but applied to an American subject.[95] One critic highlighted the "execution of this painting [which] is very smooth and faultless, while the conception and design are bold and original."[96] *The Trial of Red Jacket* (cat. no. 212), of 1868, seems similarly the heir to the tradition of Benjamin West (1738–1820).[97] Stanley's contemporaries argued that he was able to combine all genres of painting into this piece, with its one hundred individuated figures and inclusion of landscape and still life with "stereoscopic" perspective. This reviewer also appreciated Stanley's academic finish as "finely and smoothly executed . . . in finish unsurpassed by any large painting in this country."[98] By this late period, Stanley sent paintings such as this one to Chicago and

FIG. 1.16.
George Catlin, *Collection in the Salle de Séance*, 1848. Engraving; 4¼ × 2¼ in. (10.8 × 5.7 cm). From Catlin, *Notes of Eight Years' Travels and Residence in Europe*, 1848. Courtesy McCracken Research Library, Buffalo Bill Center of the West, Cody, Wyoming

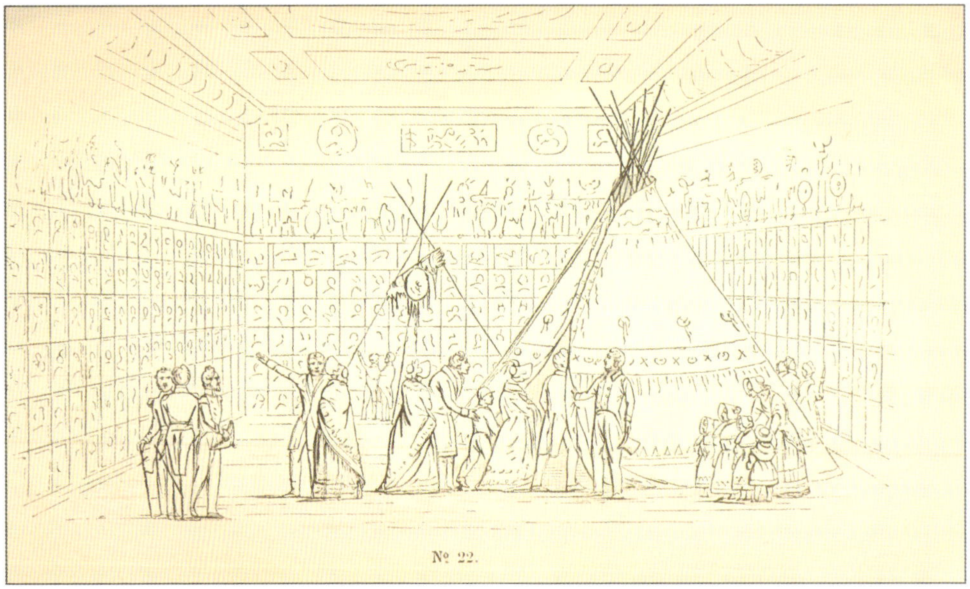

Buffalo on single-object tours or hung them in the windows of shops in Washington, D.C., and Detroit. In a letter to his wife, Stanley describes a single room for "Red Jacket" shown draped with curtains and surrounded by gas light in the tradition of Hudson River School single-painting exhibitions.[99] These venues were perhaps less cumbersome and less risky than sending out his entire gallery, which had been largely destroyed in 1865.

While Catlin's scenes exoticized his subjects, Stanley's genre paintings, perhaps unwittingly, humanized American Indian characters into scenes that could be more readily imagined from the perspective of white U. S. culture. Stanley's paintings occupy a middle ground between the exotic costumes and makeup of his figures and their everyday activities. There was approachability, or what one critic called a "gentleness of the scenes he usually selects," that made Stanley's paintings participate in a domestication of the western wilderness as they circulated in the American East and Midwest.[100] As art historian Elizabeth Johns has noted, many genre scenes of the American West in the 1840s were meant to construct the accessibility of the West for eastern audiences, such as those who encountered Stanley's work.[101] Likewise, Julie Schimmel has argued that Stanley's "transition to more reflective scenes of daily life paralleled the decreasing threat of the Indian to western expansion."[102] Indeed, viewers during the height of Catlin's popularity were different from those during Stanley's; notions of Manifest Destiny were not as assimilated into the popular imagination as they would be by the 1840s and 1850s. Thus, Stanley seems less engaged with a preservation ethic than Catlin because Stanley's images spoke to an audience with a different mindset about his subjects. *Indian Telegraph* (fig. 1.8, cat. no. 178) normalized American Indian communication through the lens of contemporary technology, and *Gambling for the Buck* (fig. 1.11, cat. no. 206) showed American Indian figures exoticized through dress but performing an act recognizable to white observers, for whom card playing was also popular. The effect, perhaps inadvertent, of these paintings was to stabilize exoticism and difference through the use of quotidian representations that emphasized similarities and accessibility, rather than difference.[103] These genre paintings play out the discourse noted above in which Stanley's generation expressed greater belief in the possibility of American Indian assimilation than Catlin's.

Stanley's American Indian display tactics subtly differed from Catlin's. Stanley's tour visited some midwestern and southeastern towns, like Cincinnati and Louisville, that Catlin's tour, which circulated mainly in the American East and in Europe, did not reach. Both artists used American Indian artifacts to offer context to the paintings and claim the authenticity of tribal contact. But, in the surviving photograph of Stanley's Smithsonian gallery (fig. 1.2), the variety of sizes and frames set the objects apart from the more taxonomic representation of Catlin's display, as illustrated in Paris in the mid-1840s (fig. 1.16). Catlin's illustration implies that paintings all of the same size were organized like a catalogue, as in Charles Willson Peale's Philadelphia Museum during the early republic. By the time Stanley's collection was displayed in Washington, D.C., the numbers of American Indian artifacts may have been reduced.[104] Stanley's frames hung forward from the wall in varying sizes, tilted toward the viewer, and revealed his more eclectic range of subjects. Arranged salon-style, the paintings designed a tapestry from threads of an imagined American West. The objects were treated as both individual works of art and a collective experience. His contemporary viewers—increasingly accustomed to viewing popular entertainment by this period—treated them simultaneously as art, document, and spectacle.

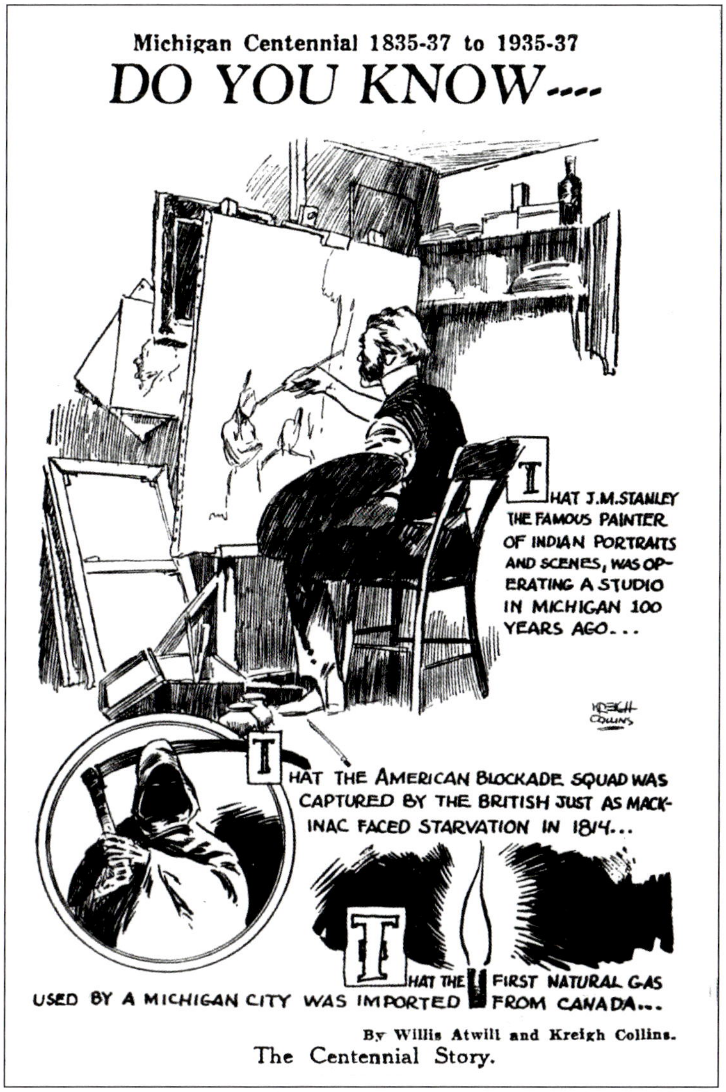

FIG. 1.17.
Willis Atwill and Kreigh Collins, "Michigan Centennial 1835–37 to 1935–37," *Saginaw News*, c. 1937. John Mix Stanley Papers, 1830–1973, Archives of American Art, microfilm copy, reel 687, Smithsonian Institution, Washington, D.C.

POSTERITY

In the 1930s, the *Saginaw News* in Michigan (fig. 1.17) remembered Stanley far differently from his 1850s self-construction inside his tent (fig. 1.1, cat. no. 073). A regular centennial series recalled that in 1835–37, "J. M. Stanley the famous painter of Indian portraits and scenes was operating a studio in Michigan." This article recalls a twenty-one-year-old Stanley, ironically in advance of any of his western forays. Here, paired with comments about the War of 1812, illustrated with a grim reaper, and the development of natural gas, Stanley is depicted as a bearded artist in his studio interior, making paintings of American Indians amidst canvases and bare walls as though the source for his art had been merely his imagination. The only remnant of Stanley's "prairie home" is the large paint box at his side. Although the image is a far cry from the trope of the artist-explorer that Stanley cultivated during his day, the article's homage to the artist still celebrated the role of travel and circulation: "every place to which he journeyed became a subject for his art and a background upon which he painted the native peoples." The article also highlighted Stanley's history paintings as well as images of "Indian character."[105] Perhaps the moment recalled here is more likely Stanley's return to Detroit at the end of his life, where he used his "portfolio" from his earlier travels to engage in "filling out his sketches of Indian life."[106] In this late period, he focused on paintings that approach the level of grand manner history painting, such as the massive *The Trial of Red Jacket* (cat. no. 212), which he toured in addition to reproducing in chromolithograph. He also instructed at least a few art students in Detroit.[107]

Julie Schimmel has summarized his work: "Diversity characterized Stanley's art production."[108] Indeed, Stanley's significance to the history of nineteenth-century American art comes through his adaptable style and the variety of fields in which he marketed his art: to ethnography, to government survey, to history and genre paintings, to portraiture, and to the popular imagination through panoramas and chromolithography. His peripatetic life was mirrored in the eclecticism of his style and iconography. On the eve of the explosion of the mass-market illustrated press, Stanley sought a wide market for his representations through various means. He represents the character of a mid-nineteenth-century artist directing his work to many audiences simultaneously and walking a line between document and spectacle in his constant awareness of his objects' circulation. Thus, understanding the trajectory of Stanley's career through the surviving reviews of his work enables us to define the subtle cultural differences between Catlin's experience in the American West, earlier in the nineteenth century, and Stanley's, which straddled the middle of the century. Stanley's projects visually expressed distinct ideas about expansion and assimilation and more directly engaged with the culture of spectacle through his carefully packaged western subjects.

I am grateful to Peter Hassrick, Mindy Besaw, Jaclyn Rubino, and Emily Wilson for sharing their knowledge and research materials on Stanley. Thanks to William Truettner, Brian Dippie, and Melanie Mallon for their comments on this essay and to Chloë Courtney and Anna Dubbins for research assistance.

NOTES

1. "Washington News," *Nashville Union*, April 26, 1853, 2.

2. For more on Stanley's engagement with United States–Indian relations through his paintings, see the essays by Lisa Strong and Scott Manning Stevens in this volume.

3. "Stanley's Portrait of General Scott," undated clipping, unknown newspaper, c. 1860, John Mix Stanley Papers, 1830–1973, owned by Stanley descendants, reel 687, Archives of American Art, Smithsonian Institution, Washington, D.C. (hereafter Stanley Papers).

4. Brian W. Dippie, "'Far Superior to Catlin's': Stanley and His Indian Gallery," in *Catlin and His Contemporaries: The Politics of Patronage* (Lincoln: University of Nebraska Press, 1990), 265–317. William H. Truettner, *The Natural Man Observed: A Study of Catlin's Indian Gallery* (Washington, D.C.: Smithsonian Institution Press, 1979); and George Gurney and Therese Thau Heyman, eds., *George Catlin and His Indian Gallery* (New York: Norton, 2002).

5. "Indian Portrait Gallery," *Ohio Union*, February 26, 1846, Stanley Papers.

6. "Indian Portraits," *Cincinnati Advertiser*, c. February 1846, Stanley Papers. See also J. H. C., "Indian Portraits," *New York Sunday Times*, December 5, 1850, Stanley Papers.

7. *Portraits of North American Indians with Sketches of Scenery, Etc., Painted by J. M. Stanley* (Washington, D.C.: Smithsonian Institution, 1852). Only 7 of the more than 150 paintings survived. On the fire, see John Mix Stanley scrapbook, 1843–1868, pp. 49–53, reel OAM, Archives of American Art, Smithsonian Institution, Washington, D.C. (hereafter Stanley scrapbook); Dippie, "Far Superior to Catlin's," 314–17; Herman J. Viola, with H. B. Crothers and Maureen Hannan, "The American Indian Genre Paintings of Catlin, Stanley, Wimar, Eastman and Miller," in *American Frontier Life: Early Western Painting and Prints*, ed. Ron Tyler (Fort Worth, Tex.: Amon Carter Museum, 1987), 142–43; Julie Schimmel, "John Mix Stanley and Imagery of the West in Nineteenth-Century American Art" (Ph.D. diss., New York University, 1983), 143–46; Christine Buckman, "Fire in the Museum," undated clipping, unknown newspaper, Stanley Papers; and Joseph Henry to John Mix Stanley, March 11, 1865, Stanley vertical file, Smithsonian American Art Museum and National Portrait Gallery Library (hereafter Stanley file).

8. On constructions of the American West in mid-nineteenth-century representation, see William H. Truettner, ed., *The West as America: Reinterpreting Images of the Frontier, 1820–1920* (Washington, D.C.: National Museum of American Art and Smithsonian Institution Press, 1991); Jules David Prown et al., *Discovered Lands, Invented Pasts* (New Haven, Conn.: Yale University Press, 1992); William H. Goetzmann and William N. Goetzmann, *The West of the Imagination*, 2nd ed. (Norman: University of Oklahoma Press, 2009); Richard Slotkin, *The Fatal Environment: The Myth of the Frontier in the Age of Industrialization, 1800–1890* (Middleton, Conn.: Wesleyan University Press, 1985); Joni L. Kinsey, *Plain Pictures: Images of the American Prairie* (Washington, D.C.: Smithsonian Institution Press, 1996); William H. Truettner, *Painting Indians and Building Empires in North America, 1710–1840* (Berkeley: University of California Press, 2010); Stephanie Mayer Heydt, Mindy N. Besaw, and Emma L. Hansen, *Art of the American Frontier from the Buffalo Bill Center of the West* (Atlanta: High Museum of Art, 2013); and Sarah E. Boehme, "Frozen in Time: Euro-American Portrayals of Indians," in *Powerful Images: Portrayals of Native America*, by Sarah E. Boehme et al. (Seattle: Museums West and University of Washington Press, 1998), 35–62.

9. A sketchbook microfilmed in the Stanley Papers suggests that Stanley made coastal observations of El Salvador and Guatemala along Central America as well.

10. Recountings of Stanley's biography and travels can be found in Schimmel, "John Mix Stanley and Imagery"; Viola, Crothers, and Hannan, "American Indian Genre Paintings," 137–44; Julie Schimmel, "John Mix Stanley (1814–1872)," in *Artists of Michigan from the Nineteenth Century*, ed. J. Gray Sweeney (Muskegon, Mich.: Muskegon Museum of Art, 1987), 39–40, 49–54; Andrew J. Cosentino and Henry H. Glassie, *The Capital Image: Painters in Washington, 1800–1915* (Washington, D.C.: Smithso-

nian Institution Press, 1983), 97–101; David I. Bushnell, Jr., "John Mix Stanley, Artist-Explorer," in *Annual Report of the Board of Regents of the Smithsonian Institution* (Washington, D.C.: Government Printing Office, 1925), 507–12; W. Vernon Kinietz, *John Mix Stanley and His Indian Paintings* (Ann Arbor: University of Michigan Press, 1942); Robert Taft, "John M. Stanley and the Pacific Railroad Surveys," in *Artists and Illustrators of the Old West, 1850–1900* (New York: Scribner, 1953), 1–21; David C. Hunt, "John Mix Stanley: Survey Artist and Indian Painter," *American Scene* 12, no. 4 (1971): 1–20; Charles H. Sawyer, *John Mix Stanley: A Traveller in the West* (Ann Arbor: University of Michigan Museum of Art, 1969); Nellie B. Pipes, "John Mix Stanley, Indian Painter," *Oregon Historical Quarterly* 33, no. 3 (September 1932): 250–58. See also Stanley Papers; Stanley scrapbook; and Stanley file.

11. On Dickerman, see Schimmel, "John Mix Stanley and Imagery," 34–36; Dippie, "Far Superior to Catlin's," 267–68; and Viola, Crothers, and Hannan, "American Indian Genre Paintings," 138.

12. David L. Nicandri, "Isaac I. Stevens and the Expeditionary Artists of the Northern West," in *Encounters with a Distant Land: Exploration and the Great Northwest*, ed. Carlos A. Schwantes (Moscow: University of Idaho Press, 1994), 133–48.

13. The Stanley Papers include letters of introduction dated August 17, 1842, from Secretary of War John C. Spencer (1788–1855) and T. H. Crawford (1786–1863) of the Bureau of Indian Affairs in support of Stanley and Dickerman's documentary project "to visit the different tribes of Indians for the purpose of taking the portraits of the most prominent chiefs among them."

14. On earlier nineteenth-century American expedition imagery, see Kenneth Haltman, *Looking Close and Seeing Far: Samuel Seymour, Titian Ramsay Peale, and the Art of the Long Expedition, 1818–1823* (University Park: Pennsylvania State University Press, 2008); William H. Goetzmann, *Army Exploration in the American West, 1803–1863* (New Haven, Conn.: Yale University Press, 1959); William H. Goetzmann, *Exploration and Empire: The Explorer and the Scientist in the Winning of the American West* (New York: Knopf, 1966); Peter H. Hassrick, "Artists Employed on United States Government Expeditions to the Trans-Mississippi West before 1850" (master's thesis, University of Denver, 1969); and William M. S. Rasmussen, "Art of the Nineteenth-Century Government Explorations in the West: Changing Concepts of the Western Landscape" (master's thesis, University of Delaware, 1975).

15. Castle McLaughlin, *Arts of Diplomacy: Lewis and Clark's Indian Collection* (Cambridge, Mass.: Peabody Museum of Archaeology and Ethnology, Harvard University, 2003). For more on Stanley's participation in western expeditions, see the essay by Peter Hassrick in this volume; and Robert Taft, "The Pictorial Record of the Old West. XV. John M. Stanley and the Pacific Railroad Reports," *Kansas Historical Quarterly* 20, no. 1 (February 1952): 1–23.

16. "Notes," *Indian Notes* 6, no. 3 (July 1929): 327.

17. Stanley's collection of at least fifty American Indian artifacts was acquired from his widow by the father of American painter Gari Melchers (1860–1932). Melchers later gave the collection to the Museum of the American Indian. See "Notes"; and Frederick Webb Hodge, "A Proposed Indian Portfolio by John Mix Stanley," *Indian Notes* 6, no. 4 (October 1929): 360.

18. Schimmel, "John Mix Stanley and Imagery," 258.

19. On the rising importance of spectacle in American culture and its implications, see Lawrence Levine, *Highbrow, Lowbrow: The Emergence of Cultural Hierarchy in America* (Cambridge, Mass.: Harvard University Press, 1988).

20. Both may have been moving panoramas. See Erkki Huhtamo, *Illusions in Motion: Media Archaeology of the Moving Panorama and Related Spectacles* (Cambridge, Mass.: MIT Press, 2013), 266–67; Martha A. Sandweiss, "The Public Life of Western Art," in Prown et al., *Discovered Lands, Invented Pasts*, 118; Dippie, "Far Superior to Catlin's," 290–95; Schimmel, "John Mix Stanley and Imagery," 117–20, 130–35; and Kinsey, *Plain Pictures*, 216n80. See also Stephan Oettermann, *The Panorama: History of a Mass Medium* (New York: Zone Books, 1997), 313–44; and Bernard Comment, *The Painted Panorama* (New York: Abrams, 1999). An ongoing dissertation on moving panoramas in antebellum America is by Christopher Oliver, "Civic Visions: The Panorama and Popular Amusement in Ameri-

can Art and Society, 1845–1870" (Ph.D. diss., University of Virginia, forthcoming).

21. Quoted from the *Boston Post*, August 12, 1862, on a *Broadside for Stanley & Conant's Polemorama! Or Gigantic Illustrations of the War*, August 1862, Archives of Americana, American Broadsides and Ephemera Series 1.

22. See, for example, William H. Emory, *Notes of a Military Reconnoissance, from Fort Leavenworth, in Missouri, to San Diego, in California, including part of the Arkansas, Del Norte, and Gila Rivers* (Washington, D.C.: Wendell and Van Benthuysen 1848); and Isaac I. Stevens, *Narrative and Final Report of Explorations for a Route for a Pacific Railroad, near the Forty-seventh and Forty-ninth Parallels of North Latitude from Saint Paul to Puget Sound*, vol. 12, book 1 of *Reports of Explorations and Surveys, to Ascertain the Most Practicable and Economical Route for a Railroad from the Mississippi River to the Pacific Ocean* (Washington, D.C.: Thomas H. Ford, 1860).

23. See "Chromo-Lithography," *Detroit Free Press*, c. 1868; and "Mr. Stanley's Chromos," *Detroit Free Press*, April 19, 1869, Stanley Papers. On the rise of chromolithography, see Joni L. Kinsey, *Thomas Moran's West: Chromolithography, High Art, and Popular Taste* (Lawrence: University Press of Kansas, 2006); and Michael Clapper, "'I Was Once a Barefoot Boy!': Cultural Tensions in a Popular Chromo," *American Art* 16, no. 2 (2002): 16–39.

24. "Art Matters," *Detroit Daily Post*, April 28, 1868, Stanley Papers.

25. Ibid. See also Peter C. Marzio, *The Democratic Art: An Exhibition on the History of Chromolithography in America, 1840–1900* (Fort Worth, Tex.: Amon Carter Museum of Western Art, 1979), 80; Kinietz, *John Mix Stanley*, 28; and Schimmel, "John Mix Stanley and Imagery," 153–56.

26. On the German fascination with the American West, see Pamela Kort and Max Hollein, eds., *I Like America: Fictions of the Wild West* (Munich: Prestel, 2006); and H. Glenn Penny, *Kindred by Choice: Germans and American Indians since 1800* (Chapel Hill: University of North Carolina Press, 2013), though Stanley is not mentioned directly in either.

27. These included *On the War Path* and a portrait. See "New Chromo," undated clipping, *Detroit Tribune*, c. 1872; "'On the War Path': Completion of the Chromo of one of Stanley's Best Paintings," *Detroit Tribune*, August 5, 1872; and "Stanley's 'On the War Path,'" *Detroit Free Press*, August 4, 1872, Stanley Papers; Marzio, *Democratic Art*, 80–81; and Schimmel, "John Mix Stanley and Imagery," 140.

28. Impressions of *Uncas, the Young Chief; The Trial of Warpath;* and *On the Warpath* survive in the collection of the Amon Carter Museum in Fort Worth, Texas. Other advertisements highlighted the availability of chromolithographs of *The Trial of Red Jacket* (cat. no. 212) and *Snake in the Grass* (cat. no. 214).

29. Marzio, *Democratic Art*, 80; and Schimmel, "John Mix Stanley (1814–1872)," 50. See "Indian Telegraph and the Deer Slayer Just Published," *Detroit Free Press*, September 14, 1869; and "On the War Path—Mr. Stanley's Last Great Painting," *Detroit Free Press*, May 6, 1871, Stanley Papers.

30. "John M. Stanley," *New York Times*, April 14, 1872, 2. See also "Death of Stanley, the Artist," *Detroit Free Press*, April 10, 1872; "Death of J. M. Stanley," *Detroit Daily Post*, April 11, 1872; "A National Loss," *Grand Rapids Eagle*, April 12, 1872; and "Stanley, the Artist," *Washington Sunday Gazette*, April 21, 1872, Stanley Papers.

31. Kinietz, *John Mix Stanley*, 19–20; Schimmel, "John Mix Stanley and Imagery," 147–49; and Hodge, "Proposed Indian Portfolio," 359–67.

32. Martha A. Sandweiss, *Print the Legend: Photography and the American West* (New Haven, Conn.: Yale University Press, 2002), 111.

33. On *Harper's* and representations of the West, see Claudine Chalmers, *Chronicling the West for Harper's: Coast to Coast with Frenzeny and Tavernier in 1873–1874* (Norman: University of Oklahoma Press, 2013). On the American Art-Union, to which many of Stanley's fellow painters of the American West did submit images, see Patricia Hills, "The American Art-Union as Patron for Expansionist Ideology in the 1840s," in *Art in Bourgeois Society, 1790–1850*, ed. Andrew Hemingway and William Vaughan (Cambridge and New York. Cambridge University Press, 1998), 314–39; and

Amanda Lett, Patricia Hills, Peter John Brownlee, and Randy Ramer, *Perfectly American: The Art-Union and Its Artists* (Tulsa, Okla.: Gilcrease Museum, 2011).

34. "Indian Telegraph," *Detroit Daily Post*, April 28, 1868, scrapbook, p. 55, Stanley Papers.

35. On the role of circulation and the telegraph on American art in visual culture, see Jennifer Roberts, *Transporting Visions: The Movement of Images in Early America* (Berkeley: University of California Press, 2014).

36. Schimmel, "John Mix Stanley and Imagery," 26. See also the Stevens essay in this volume.

37. Goetzmann and Goetzmann, *West of the Imagination*, 47; and Truettner, *Natural Man Observed*, 37–39.

38. See "Stanley's Indian Gallery," *Hartford Times*, April 14, 1851, Stanley Papers.

39. On Kane, see Kenneth R. Lister, *Paul Kane, the Artist: Wilderness to Studio* (Toronto: Royal Ontario Museum Press, 2010); Paul Kane, *Paul Kane's Frontier; Including Wanderings of an Artist among the Indians of North America, by Paul Kane*, ed. J. Russell Harper (Austin: University of Texas Press, 1971); Dippie, "Far Superior to Catlin's," 273–76; and Schimmel, "John Mix Stanley and Imagery," 32–33.

40. Stanley also sent letters to the press from the field to raise interest in his project. See, for example, "Letter from J. M. Stanley," c. May 13, 1846; "Interesting from California: Letters from John M. Stanley," January 24, 1847; and "The Indian War in Oregon," c. January 8, 1848, clippings, unknown newspapers, Stanley Papers.

41. [An Admirer of Art and Friend to Modest Merit], "Communicated," *Cincinnati Enquirer*, February 12, 1846, Stanley Papers; and "Stanley & Dickerman's North American Indian Portrait Gallery," *Northern Budget*, September 13, 1850, Stanley Papers.

42. Brian W. Dippie, *The Vanishing American: White Attitudes and U.S. Indian Policy* (Middletown, Conn.: Wesleyan University Press, 1982).

43. "Stanley's Indian Gallery," *Hartford Times*, April 22, 1851, Stanley Papers.

44. Renato Rosaldo, *Culture and Truth: The Remaking of Social Analysis* (Boston: Beacon Press, 1993), 69, 87.

45. "Fine Arts in Honolulu," *Polynesian*, April 14, 1849, p. 190. On Stanley in Hawaii, see David W. Forbes, *Encounters with Paradise: Views of Hawaii and Its People, 1778–1941* (Honolulu: Honolulu Academy of Arts, 1992), 93, 130–33.

46. See Jonathan Kay Kamakawiwo'ole Osorio, *Dismembering Lāhui: A History of the Hawaiian Nation to 1887* (Honolulu: University of Hawaii Press, 2002), 44–50; and Jon J. Chinen, *The Great Mahele: Hawaii's Land Division of 1848* (Honolulu: University of Hawaii Press, 1958). See also Gary L. Fitzpatrick, *The Early Mapping of Hawai'i* (Honolulu: Editions Limited, 1986), 116–17; and *Maps and Illustrations of the American Board of Commissioners for Foreign Missions, September 1846* (Boston: Board of Commissioners for Foreign Missions, 1846) for maps and illustrations of the "Sandwich Islands" during this period.

47. Shari Huhndorf, *Going Native: Indians in the American Cultural Imagination* (Ithaca, N.Y.: Cornell University Press, 2003), 21.

48. "Our Indians: Stanly [*sic*] & Dickerman's Exhibition at Washington Hall," *Cincinnati Evening Journal*, February 21, 1846, Stanley Papers. See also Schimmel, "John Mix Stanley and Imagery," 91.

49. O.P.Q. "Stanley & Dickerman's Indian Portrait Gallery," *Troy Daily Whig*, September 11, 1850, Stanley Papers. See also "Indian Portrait Gallery," *Troy Family Journal*, September 7, 1850, Stanley Papers.

50. B. St. J. F., "Stanley & Dickerman's Gallery of Indian Portraits," *Cincinnati Herald*, February 19, 1846; and "The Indian Portrait Gallery," *Albany Evening Journal*, October 12, 1850, Stanley Papers.

51. "Stanley's Indian Gallery," undated clipping, unknown newpaper, c. 1851, p. 36, Stanley Papers.

52. "The Gallery of Paintings at the Apollo Rooms," *Louisville Daily Journal*, March 7, 1846, Stanley Papers.

53. "For the Troy Daily Post," *Troy Daily Post*, September 13, 1850, Stanley Papers.

54. Henry T. Tuckerman, *Book of the Artists: American Artist Life, Comprising Biographical and Critical Sketches of American Artists: Preceded by an Historical Account of the Rise and Progress of Art in America* (New York: Putnam, 1867), 424. See also Nancy K. Anderson, "'Curious Historical Artistic Data': Art History and Western American Art," in Prown et al., *Discovered Lands, Invented Pasts*, 1–2.

55. "Stanley's Indian Gallery," *New York Sunday Times*, June 1851, Stanley Papers.

56. "Indian Portrait Gallery—No. 1," *Cincinnati Enquirer*, February 24, 1846, Stanley Papers. See also Schimmel, "John Mix Stanley and Imagery," 88–89.

57. "The Fine Arts," *Van Buren Intelligencer*, c. 1844, Stanley Papers.

58. *Daily National Intelligencer*, March 3, 1852, p. 3, cited without a title in Schimmel, "John Mix Stanley and Imagery," 88.

59. "Indian Portrait Gallery," *Ohio Union*, February 26, 1846, Stanley Papers. See also "Indian Portrait Gallery," *Albany State Register*, October 8, 1850, Stanley Papers.

60. [Admirer of Art], "Communicated," Stanley Papers.

61. "Stanley's Indian Gallery," *National Intelligencer*, undated clipping, scrapbook, p. 41, Stanley Papers. Also cited in Schimmel, "John Mix Stanley and Imagery," 86–87.

62. "The North American Indian Portrait Gallery," undated clipping, unknown newspaper, c. 1850, Stanley Papers.

63. "Our Troy Correspondence," *New York Herald*, September 6, 1850, Stanley Papers.

64. "Art Gossip," undated clipping, unknown newspaper, c. 1865, p. 51, Stanley Papers.

65. "Prairie Landscapes," *National Intelligencer*, March 6, 1855, 2.

66. See also "Stanley's Indian Gallery," *State Register*, October 31, 1850; and "The Indian Portrait Gallery," *Cincinnati Commonwealth*, February 27, 1846, Stanley Papers, which insisted, "There is no *humbug* in this matter."

67. "Gallery of Indian Portraits," *Cincinnati Herald*, February 27, 1846; and [Admirer of Art], "Communicated," Stanley Papers.

68. "Stanley & Dickerman's North American Indian Portrait Gallery," *Northern Budget*, September 13, 1850, Stanley Papers.

69. However, at least one newspaper reporter noted that George Copway (1818–1869), an Ojibwe writer, gave a lecture in the New York City venue. "Stanley's Indian Gallery," *New York Sunday Times*, May 19, 1851, Stanley Papers.

70. "Indian Gallery," *Troy Daily Whig*, September 7, 1850, Stanley Papers.

71. "Stanley's Indian Gallery," *Hartford Courant*, April 22, 1851; and "The Indian Gallery," *Cincinnati Evening Journal*, February 20, 1846, Stanley Papers.

72. On the cultural discourses around humbuggery in this period, see Michael Leja, *Looking Askance: Skepticism and American Art from Eakins to Duchamp* (Berkeley: University of California Press, 2004), 46–54. See also Neil Harris, *Humbug: The Art of P. T. Barnum* (Boston: Little, Brown, 1973); and James W. Cook, "The Architect of the Modern Culture Industry," in *The Colossal P. T. Barnum Reader: Nothing Else Like It in the Universe*, ed. James W. Cook (Urbana and Chicago: University of Illinois Press, 2005), 1–8. Stanley's paintings here were destroyed in another fire in 1865.

73. Untitled clipping, *Mineral and Tradesman Journal*, January 29, 1851, Stanley Papers.

74. "Gallery of Indian Portraits," [illegible] *Advertiser*, February 28, 1846, Stanley Papers. Quotations from this article were also reprinted in "Indian Gallery, at the Gallery of Fine Arts," *Albany Argus*, October 10, 1850, Stanley Papers.

75. Truettner, *Natural Man Observed*, 41–59.

76. On King, see Andrew J. Cosentino, *The Paintings of Charles Bird King (1785-1862)* (Washington, D.C.: Smithsonian Institution Press, 1977); Herman J. Viola, *The Indian Legacy of Charles Bird King* (Washington, D.C.: Smithsonian Institution Press, 1976); and Robert J. Moore, Jr., *Native Americans: A Portrait: The Art and Travels of Charles Bird King, George Catlin, and Karl Bodmer* (Edison, N.J.: Chartwell Books, 2002). On Inman, see Herman J.

Viola, *Indians of North America: Paintings by Henry Inman from the D. Harold Byrd, Jr. Collection* (Cody, Wyo.: Buffalo Bill Historical Center, 1983); and Heydt, Besaw, and Hansen, *Art of the American Frontier*, 47, 169.

77. "Lost Pages of History: John Mix Stanley in Indian Territory," undated clipping, unknown newspaper, Stanley Papers. See also the Stevens essay in this volume.

78. "Stanley's Indian Gallery," *Troy Daily Whig*, September 10, 1850; and "Indian Gallery of Paintings," *National Intelligencer*, undated clipping, c. 1860, Stanley Papers.

79. On *Mount Hood*, see "A Picture of Mount Hood," *National Intelligencer*, 1866, Stanley Papers. On *Oregon City*, see Albert Boime, *The Magisterial Gaze: Manifest Destiny and American Landscape Painting c. 1830–1865* (Washington, D.C.: Smithsonian Institution Press, 1991), 117; Elizabeth Johns, "Settlement and Development: Claiming the West," in Truettner, *West as America*, 208–209; Schimmel, "John Mix Stanley and Imagery," 252–56; and William Cronon, "Telling Tales on Canvas: Landscapes of Frontier Change," in Prown et al., *Discovered Lands, Invented Pasts*, 70. On Stanley in Oregon, see also David L. Nicandri, "John Mix Stanley: Paintings and Sketches of the Oregon Country and Its Inhabitants," *Oregon Historical Quarterly* 88, no. 2 (Summer 1987): 149–73.

80. On Stanley's gambling scenes, see Viola, Crothers, and Hannan, "American Indian Genre Paintings," 143; Goetzmann and Goetzmann, *West of the Imagination*, 50.

81. Schimmel, "John Mix Stanley and Imagery, 188–89, 222.

82. "The Indian Gallery," *Cincinnati Evening Journal*, February 20, 1846, Stanley Papers.

83. "Indian Portrait Gallery," *New York* [illegible], December 1851, Stanley Papers.

84. "Stanley's Indian Gallery," *New Haven Palladian*, March 7, 1851, Stanley Papers.

85. On Miller, see Ron Tyler, ed., *Alfred Jacob Miller: Artist on the Oregon Trail*, with a catalogue raisonné by Karen Dewees Reynolds and William R. Johnston (Fort Worth, Tex.: Amon Carter Museum, 1982); and Lisa Strong, *Sentimental Journey: The Art of Alfred Jacob Miller* (Fort Worth, Tex.: Amon Carter Museum, 2009). On Ranney, see Linda Bantel and Peter H. Hassrick, *Forging an American Identity: The Art of William Ranney, With a Catalogue of His Works* (Cody, Wyo.: Buffalo Bill Historical Center, 2006); and Estill Curtis Pennington, *Passage and Progress in the Works of William Tylee Ranney* (Augusta, Ga.: Morris Museum of Art, 1993). On Deas, see Carol Clark et al., *Charles Deas and 1840s America* (Norman: University of Oklahoma Press, 2009).

86. On *Kidnapped*, see Schimmel, "John Mix Stanley and Imagery," 228–30.

87. Patricia Hills, "Picturing Progress in the Era of Westward Expansion," in Truettner, *West as America*, 116.

88. Schimmel also links Stanley's development in composition and atmosphere to his time in Washington, D.C. See "John Mix Stanley and Imagery," 120, 165. Stanley met Bingham at least once in New York City in 1851. See untitled clipping, *New York Home Journal*, February 19, 1851, Stanley Papers.

89. On Bowman, see Schimmel, "John Mix Stanley and Imagery," 15–18, 197–98; and Kane, *Paul Kane's Frontier*, 10–11.

90. Bushnell, "John Mix Stanley," 509, 510; and Bertha Heilbron, "Frontier Artists: Before the Camera Brought Back an Authentic Picture of Pioneer Minnesota," *American Heritage* 1, no. 2 (Winter 1950): 13. See also Sandweiss, *Print the Legend*, 109–11; and Schimmel, "John Mix Stanley and Imagery," 104.

91. Viola, Crothers, and Hannan, "American Indian Genre Paintings," 140.

92. Cited in Sandweiss, *Print the Legend*, 109–10.

93. Julie Schimmel, "Inventing 'the Indian,'" in Truettner, *West as America*, 164–65; Schimmel, "John Mix Stanley and Imagery," 168–71; and Rena Coen, "David's *Sabine Women* in the Wild West," *Great Plains Quarterly* 2, no. 2 (Spring 1982): 69–71.

94. Schimmel, "John Mix Stanley and Imagery," 162.

95. Sarah Boehme, "Frontier America: The Artists' Environment," in *Frontier America: Art and Treasures of the Old West from the Buffalo Bill Historical*

Center, by Paul Fees and Sarah Boehme (New York: Abrams, 1988), 27–28; Schimmel, "John Mix Stanley and Imagery," 285–86; and Brian W. Dippie, "The Moving Finger Writes: Western Art and the Dynamics of Change," in Prown et al., *Discovered Lands, Invented Pasts*, 101–102. For more on this painting, see the essay by Mindy Besaw in this volume.

96. "The Great Sale of Paintings at St. Andrew's Hall," undated clipping, unknown newspaper, Stanley Papers.

97. Schimmel, "John Mix Stanley and Imagery," 239. See also the essay by Stevens in this volume.

98. "Stanley's Great Painting: 'The Trial of Red Jacket,'" *Detroit Free Press*, December 13, 1868, 1.

99. Stanley to Alice English Stanley, April 24, 1871, Stanley Papers.

100. "Prairie Landscapes," *National Intelligencer*, March 6, 1855, 2.

101. Elizabeth Johns, *American Genre Painting: The Politics of Everyday Life* (New Haven, Conn.: Yale University Press, 1991), 3, 60–99. See also Sandy Harthorn and Kathleen Bettis, *One Hundred Years of Idaho Art, 1850–1950* (Boise, Idaho: Boise Art Museum, 1990), 19; and "Gallery of Indian Portraits," *Van Buren Intelligencer*, c. 1844, Stanley Papers.

102. Schimmel, "John Mix Stanley and Imagery," 240–41.

103. Eric Ames, "From the Exotic to the Everyday: The Ethnographic Exhibition in Germany," in *The Nineteenth-Century Visual Culture Reader*, ed. Vanessa R. Schwartz and Jeannene M. Przyblyski (New York and London: Routledge, 2004), 313–27.

104. One narrator of the Smithsonian fire noted that there had been "several curious specimens of the ingenuity and taste displayed by this untutored race" included in the Washington, D.C., display. See "The Smithsonian Institute Fire," undated clipping, unknown newspaper, Stanley Papers.

105. Willis Atwill and Kreigh Collins, "Michigan Centennial 1835–37 to 1935–37," undated clipping, *Saginaw News*, Stanley Papers.

106. "John M. Stanley," *New York Times*, April 14, 1872, 2.

107. "Stanley's Studio: Interesting Paintings Completed—a Historical Picture Proposed—Maxfield's Works," undated clipping, unknown newspaper, Stanley Papers; and Schimmel, "John Mix Stanley and Imagery," 152–53.

108. Schimmel, "John Mix Stanley and Imagery," 162.

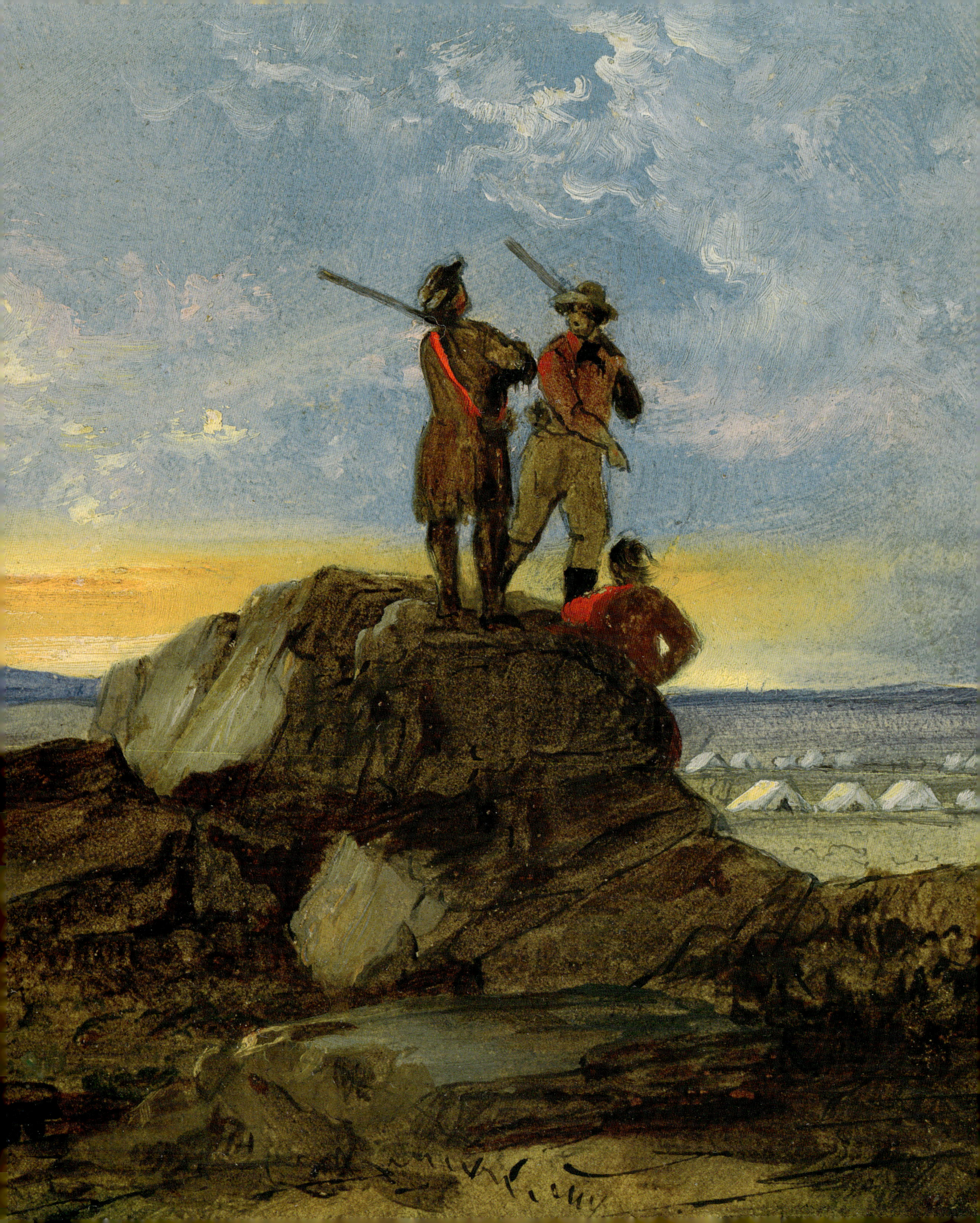

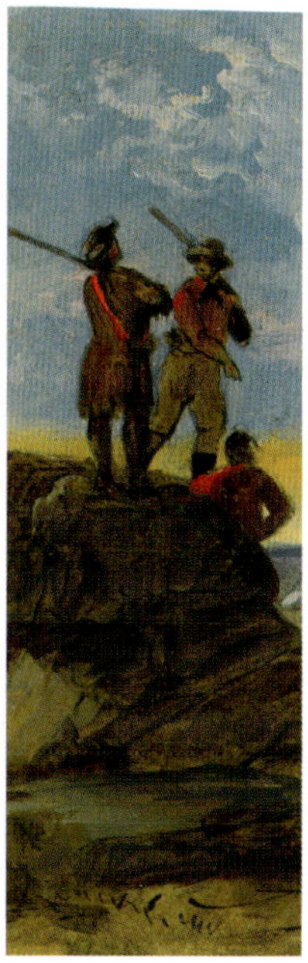

2

In War and Peace

John Mix Stanley's Western Expeditions with the U.S. Government

Peter H. Hassrick

The United States declared war on Mexico in mid-May 1846. It was the perceived military solution to fervent American demands for expanded western lands. Already "the spirit of 'Westward, Ho' is on the wing in all directions," wrote the author Josiah Gregg from Independence, Missouri, a few days before war started.[1] He foresaw vast numbers of immigrants crossing the plains from various embarkation points. Gregg himself was about to head for Santa Fe, and he actually started down the trail before diverting to Mexico with a military mission. The artist John Mix Stanley was part of that surge, but rather than searching for a new home, he was out to find fresh artistic subjects in the Southwest.

When Stanley embarked in June 1846 on this, the fourth of his western trips, he probably contented himself with the notion that he would get to Santa Fe, paint among the Pueblo Indians, and return with a portfolio of novel New Mexico images for his Indian Gallery. It would have been difficult for him to have imagined that he would be swept up by the Mexican War, pressed into service of the U.S. Army, and carried by the forces of destiny (his own and Manifest Destiny) to the Pacific shores of California.

In standard biographical accounts of Stanley issued at the time of his death, there is usually mention that he traveled to New Mexico during his first western trip in 1842.[2] No detailed accounts of how far into New Mexico he reached or what subjects he captured there have survived, but there is a hint that New Mexico had found his attention from an early date. In 1846, with his Indian Gallery attracting lofty reviews but disappointing attendance in places like

OPPOSITE

(detail) J. M. Stanley, *Untitled, Teton Valley Scene*, c. 1855 (cat. no. 132)

Louisville and Cincinnati, he and his partner, Sumner Dickerman, decided to close up shop for a while in mid-March. Ever the optimist, though, Stanley assumed that more variety would be better and thus made plans to head west again and revisit New Mexico.

At Independence, Stanley stopped to visit his friend Josiah Gregg, the first great writer of the Southwest, whose romantic inclinations and keen powers of observation mirrored Stanley's.[3] The two traveled with Colonel G. C. Owens's wagon train, which left Independence for Santa Fe at the end of June 1846. Although Gregg turned back shortly after their departure to join another expedition into Mexico, Stanley continued on to Santa Fe, arriving there about two months later, on the last day of August.

Although Gregg did not record the journey, the story of the Owens wagon train moving west was preserved in the diary of Susan Shelby Magoffin (see fig. 134.1, in cat. no. 134), wife of a veteran Santa Fe trader, Samuel Magoffin. Susan chronicled the high and low points of the two-month trek, including the loss of a baby she was carrying until their arrival at Bent's Fort. Her observations of the scenery near Council Grove (in present-day Kansas) being "truly magnificent" and, in its beauty, awaiting "the artist's pencil" caused her to remember, "We have one in our Company, Mr. Stanley rather celebrated for his Indian sketches."[4] She had not met him as yet, but she would, and Stanley documented the bond he eventually made with Susan and Samuel in his 1855 oil *Wagon Train: Break in the Journey* (fig. 2.1, cat. no. 134). The affectionate couple rides together into the foreground with the Arkansas River and the Owens's wagons pictured behind. Stanley, who retained this painting through his lifetime, presented Susan as a prairie Madonna—pure on her white horse, demure in demeanor, and rather overtly submissive to Samuel's attentions. The perceived sanctity of such shared matrimonial harmony and the westward movement was painted by other artists of the period, such as William Ranney, who produced his oil *The Pioneers* (fig. 2.2) in this period.

Exactly how Stanley occupied his time during the trip is uncertain. He seems to have painted none of the major subjects that passed before his eyes as the troop moved west, neither a vast herd of bison, Susan estimated them at "some thousands," nor bands of Arapaho and Cheyenne Indians who visited the travelers during the journey.[5]

No preliminary or field studies survive from Stanley's trip from Independence to Santa Fe in 1846. Besides *Wagon Train: Break in the Journey*, the only other known finished work by Stanley that resulted from his time on the Santa Fe Trail was an oil that carries the title today of *After the Hunt* (cat. no. 168). Two hunters, their dog, pack horse, and two mounts make up the prairie scene that follows the shooting of a large buck deer. Perhaps they are debating who shot the deer, a common theme in Stanley's later work, or simply recalling the hunt or discussing arrangements for the animal's distribution. Behind them are seen the wagons and domestic animals of the pioneers. Stanley was known as a skilled hunter himself, so such a scene, if not autobiographical, at least resonated with him. The two primary figures in the painting, as well as the fallen deer, seem to reappear in an 1862 Stanley work, an interior scene titled *Hunters and Traders* (cat. no. 172). Even the contrasting poses of the hunters, one standing and leaning on his rifle while the other reclines, suggests that the pieces are related and that *After the Hunt* was created in Stanley's Washington, D.C., studio well after his time in New Mexico.

Stanley reached Santa Fe in late August, about ten days after General Stephen Watts Kearny and his "Army of the West," as it was called, had triumphantly marched into the city on his way to conquer California. Among Kearny's entourage was a young lieutenant named Wil-

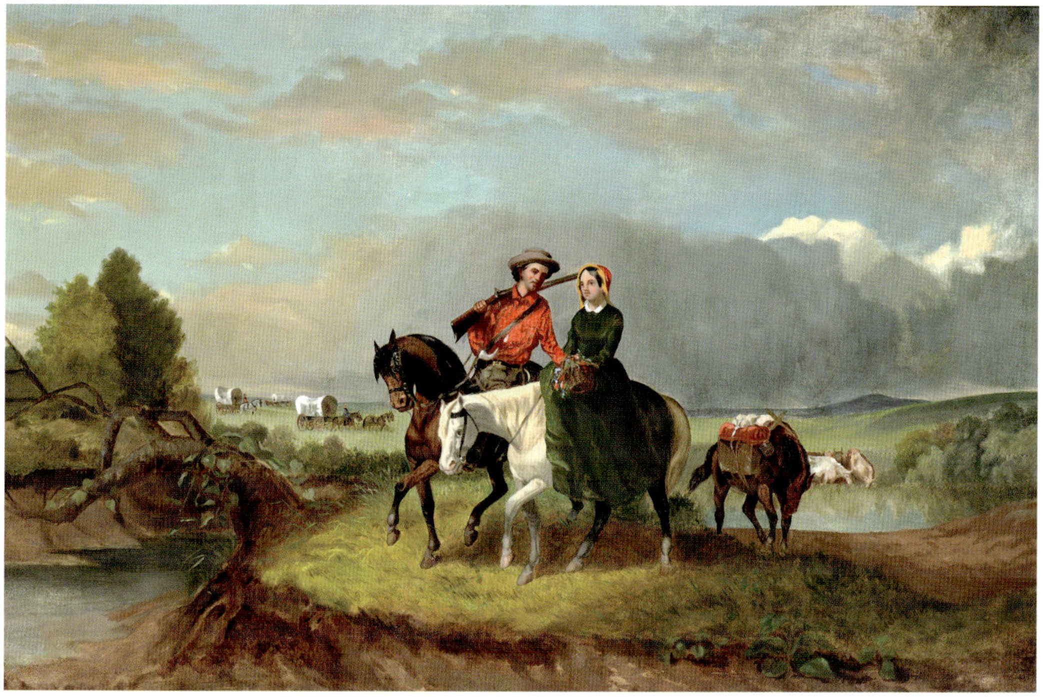

FIG. 2.1.
John Mix Stanley, *Wagon Train: Break in the Journey*, c. 1855. Oil on canvas; 30 × 44 in. (76.2 × 111.8 cm). Courtesy American Museum of Western Art–The Anschutz Collection, Denver, Colorado; photograph courtesy William J. O'Connor

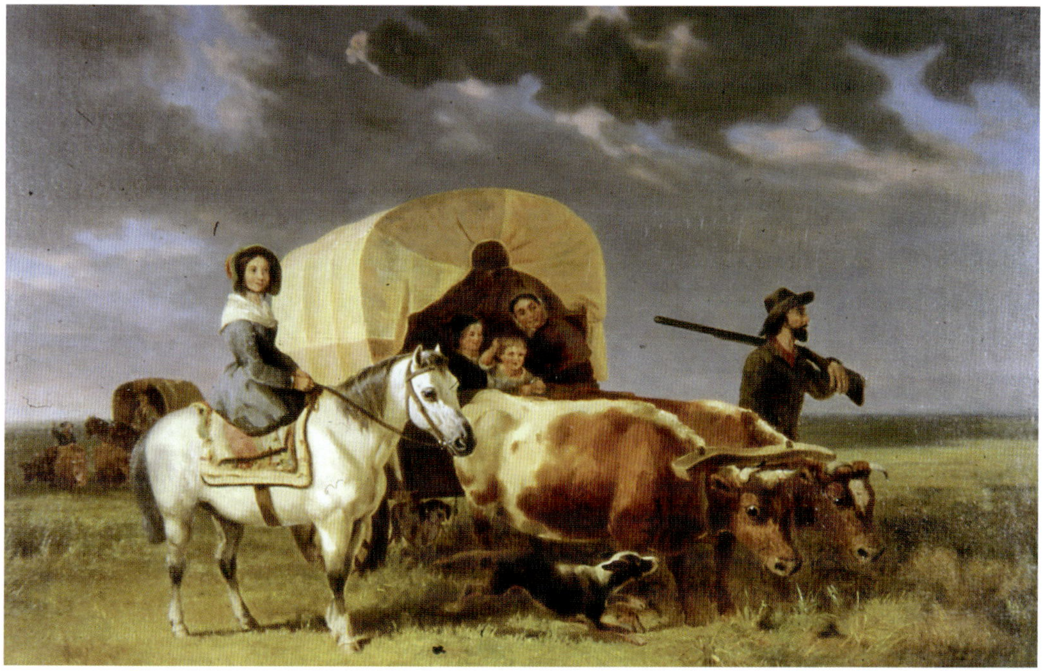

FIG. 2.2.
William Tylee Ranney, *The Pioneers*, c. 1850. Oil on canvas; 24 × 36 in. (61.0 × 91.4 cm). Private collection; photograph courtesy the Athenaeum, www.the-athenaeum.org

liam H. Emory. He served in the U.S. Army Corps of Topographical Engineers, an elite group that had been founded by George Washington to provide the military with scientific and logistical support information.[6] Its initial western experience had been with the government's sixth important trans-Mississippi expedition in 1820 under Major Stephen H. Long, an early member of the corps who had gathered a troop of scientists, soldiers, and two artists to run a survey up

FIG. 2.3.
John Mix Stanley, *San Felippe, New Mexico*, 1847. Oil on academy board; 10 × 12¾ in. (25.4 × 32.4 cm). Courtesy Nelda C. and H. J. Lutcher Stark Foundation, Stark Museum of Art, Orange, Texas (31.23.5)

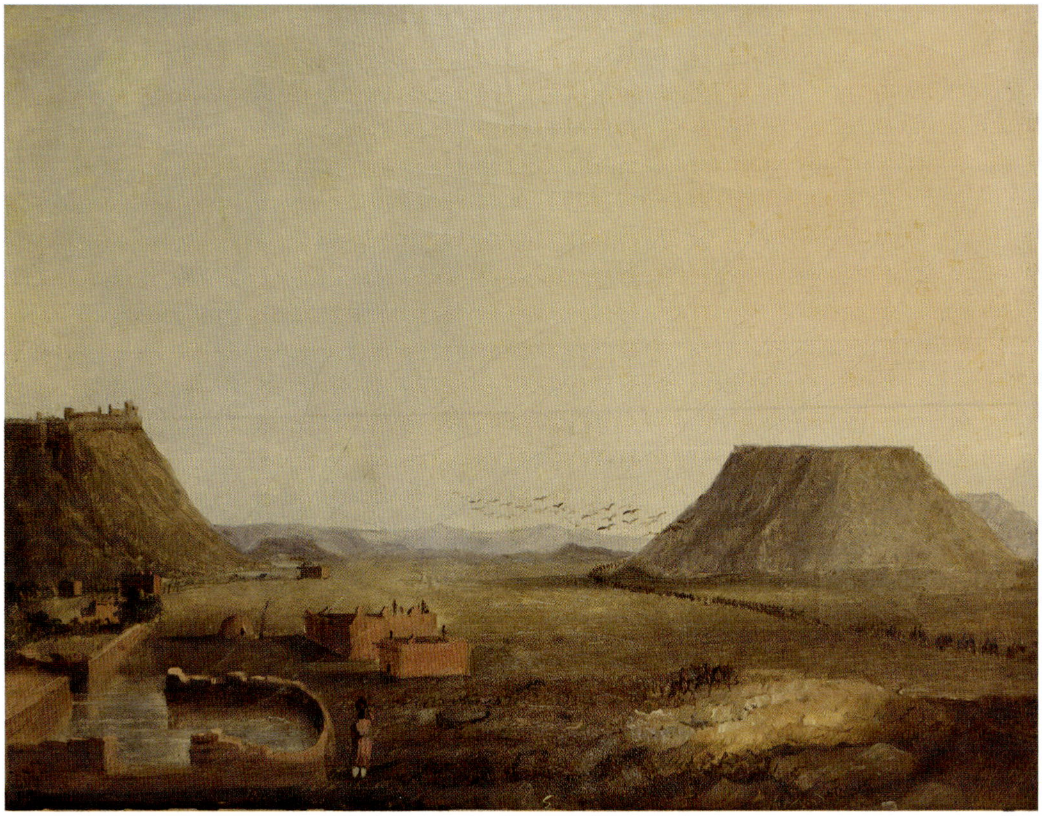

the South Platte River to the Rocky Mountains and then back down the Arkansas River. Emory also had in his ranks two artists, lieutenants William G. Peck and James W. Abert, whose father, Colonel John J. Abert, was commander of the corps. Under John J. Abert's direction, the corps had been reorganized in 1838 to focus primarily on the exploration and development of the western frontier.[7]

Emory found himself in rather desperate straits when he arrived in Santa Fe under Kearny's command. His force was severely diminished. James Abert, quite talented with brush and sketchbook, had been left dangerously ill at Bent's Fort, while William Peck, who had been trained as a field artist at West Point like Abert, fell sick shortly after the army settled in town, and he too would have to be left behind when the Kearny forces moved farther west. Abert was particularly gifted and had painted several landscape views as well as Cheyenne Indians along the way, but both artists would be sorely missed.[8] It was with considerable relief to Emory that Stanley arrived so serendipitously on the scene. By September 25, the day Emory recorded in his diary that he had received notice "the general was to march at 2, P.M., for California," Stanley was formally, though rather unceremoniously, entered in the roster as "draftsman," along with the fourteen other members of his small command.[9]

Stanley's facility for painting portraits and sketching topographical views was soon recognized as commendable if not rather extraordinary. His view of San Felipe Pueblo, for example, was quite a pictorial document, detailing not only the impressive scope of the Kearny forces as they paraded by, but the two churches of San Felipe and parts of the pueblo as well (fig. 2.3, cat.

no. 030). Emory, as if in complete aesthetic concert with the painter, described "the pretty village" as "overhung by a steep craggy precipice, upon the summit of which are the ruins of a Roman Catholic church, presenting in the landscape sketch the appearance of the pictures we see of the castles in the Rhine."[10] At Isleta Pueblo, south of Albuquerque, however, the harmony of vision was not so evident. Emory called on Stanley to paint a particularly beautiful Pueblo woman whom the mayor of the pueblo had summoned forth to represent his people. His profile likeness, in this case, received mixed reviews from the officer, who wrote, "Her first position was exquisitely graceful, but the light did not suit, and when Stanley changed her position, the charm of her attitude was gone." Sufficient allure must have endured, however, since Emory chose to include the resulting portrait, *A New Mexican Indian Woman* (fig. 2.4), in his published report.[11]

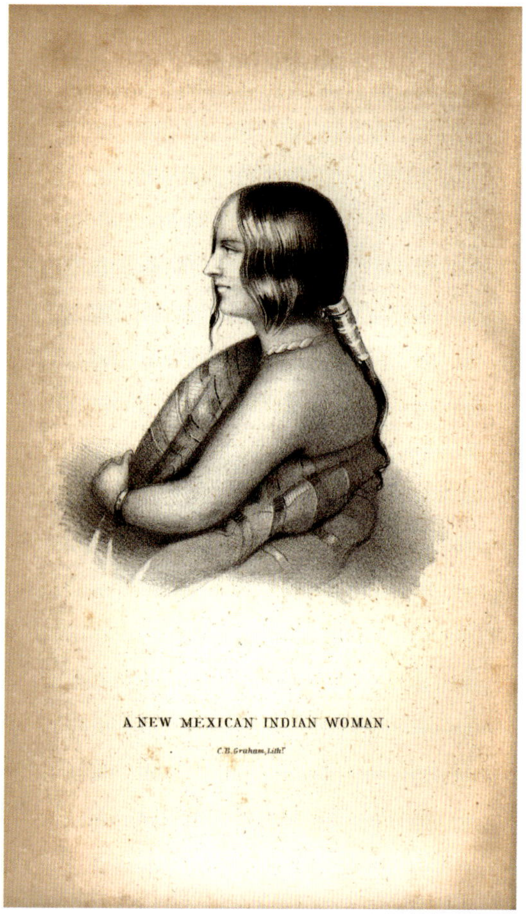

FIG. 2.4.
John Mix Stanley, *A New Mexican Indian Woman*, 1848. Lithograph; 2½ × 4½ in. (6.4 × 11.4 cm). From Emory, *Notes of a Military Reconnoissance*, opp. p. 37. Courtesy McCracken Research Library, Buffalo Bill Center of the West, Cody, Wyoming

Emory's group followed the Rio Grande from Albuquerque south past *Valencia, New Mexico* (cat. no. 031) and some exotic bluffs and rock formations, such as the *Butte on the Del Norte* (cat. no. 032), and then twenty days after departing Santa Fe, they turned west toward the Gila River. Here they left the wagons and proceeded on with only horses and mules. The Mimbres Valley, which they encountered several days later, provided the subject for several Stanley views. The Santa Rita del Cobre copper mines (cat. no. 035) afforded a record of foiled enterprise that had left the landscape scarred and the confidence of entrepreneurs shattered, as the Apaches had run off the initial prospectors. But the Sierra Mimbres contained multiple vistas that engaged Stanley's best skills as a landscapist (cat. nos. 032, 034, 036, and 041). It was these roughed hills that had provided harbor to the Apaches and now, after considerable anxiety and anticipation, revealed to the expedition the mercurial Native people who called them their home. On October 17, a few days before the Apaches revealed themselves, Stanley painted sketches for *Valley of the Mimbres* (cat. no. 029). It shows a mountain spire in the distance and a flat, verdant valley below, through which the expedition forces ride unobstructed. A large finished oil titled *Black Knife* (fig. 2.5, cat. no. 064) combines the feeling of this landscape with the sublime presence of one of the Apaches' leading military figures. It was one of only two paintings from the southwestern tour that ended up as part of Stanley's Indian Gallery, where it initially appeared on tour in 1850.

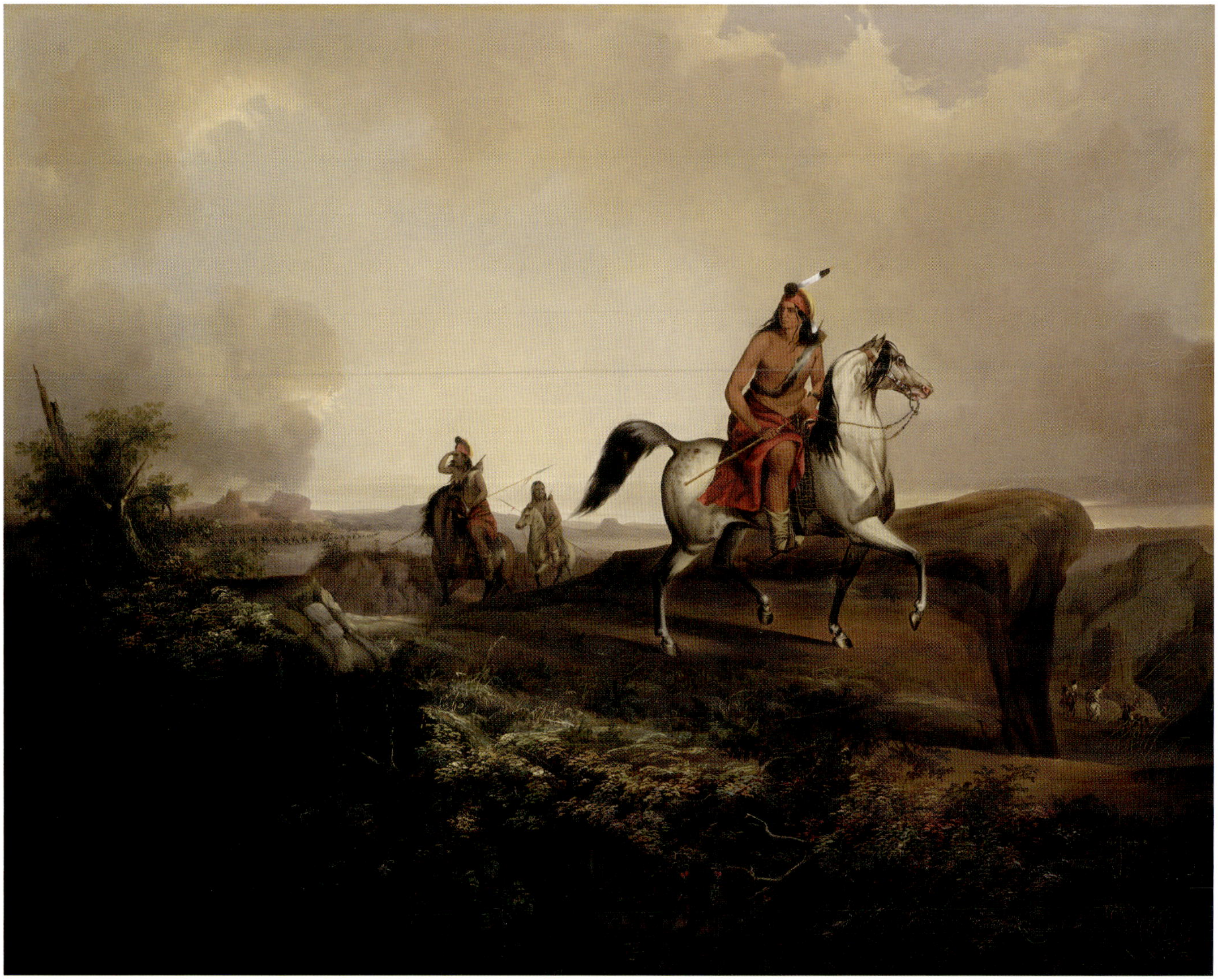

FIG. 2.5.
John Mix Stanley, *Black Knife, An Apache Chief on Horse Back, Reconnoitering Gen. Kearney's Command, Version I,* 1850. Oil on canvas; 42⅜ × 52 in. (107.6 × 132.1 cm). Courtesy Smithsonian American Art Museum, Washington, D.C., gift of the Misses Henry (1985.66.248.933)

Emory reported that the Apaches were first encountered on October 19, when arrangements were made for them to come into Kearny's camp to trade. That happened the next day when the Apache chief Red Sleeves and thirty of his men arrived. It was no doubt while the trading was going on that Stanley had a chance to make a portrait of Black Knife, known to the Mexicans as Cuchillo Negro, a Mimbres Apache chieftain who was second in command to Red Sleeves.[12] This was a critical moment for Kearny's mission, as he secured a number of fresh animals and the welcome, if only ephemeral, assurance of the Apaches' allegiance against the Mexican forces. As Captain A. R. Johnston of the First Dragoons reported, the Apaches "had promised perpetual friendship with the Americans; they seemed all anxious to conciliate to the Americans."[13] It is no accident, therefore, that Stanley, when he chose to render Black Knife cresting a hill and looking back over his shoulder at Kearny's troops moving along the Mimbres Valley toward their ultimate victory in California, chose to emulate a most famous pose from American art. In 1818 Thomas Sully had painted *The Passage of the Delaware* (fig. 2.6), a historical allegory of George Washington having just crossed the Delaware River on his way to the Battle of Trenton, which would ultimately determine the success of the American Revolution for the colonial forces.[14] Although the roles are somewhat altered, with Black Knife assuming the place and posture of General Washington, the message is clear. Kearny was now able to push his small Army of the West on to California and a hard-fought, often disputed, but seminal victory over the Mexican Army at the battle of San Pasqual. The dark cloud directly above Kearny's troop and the blighted tree on the left of the composition symbolize the hardships that were still to be faced.

FIG. 2.6.
Thomas Sully, *The Passage of the Delaware*, 1819.
Oil on canvas; 146½ × 207 in. (372.1 × 525.8 cm). Courtesy Museum of Fine Arts, Boston, gift of the Owners of the old Boston Museum

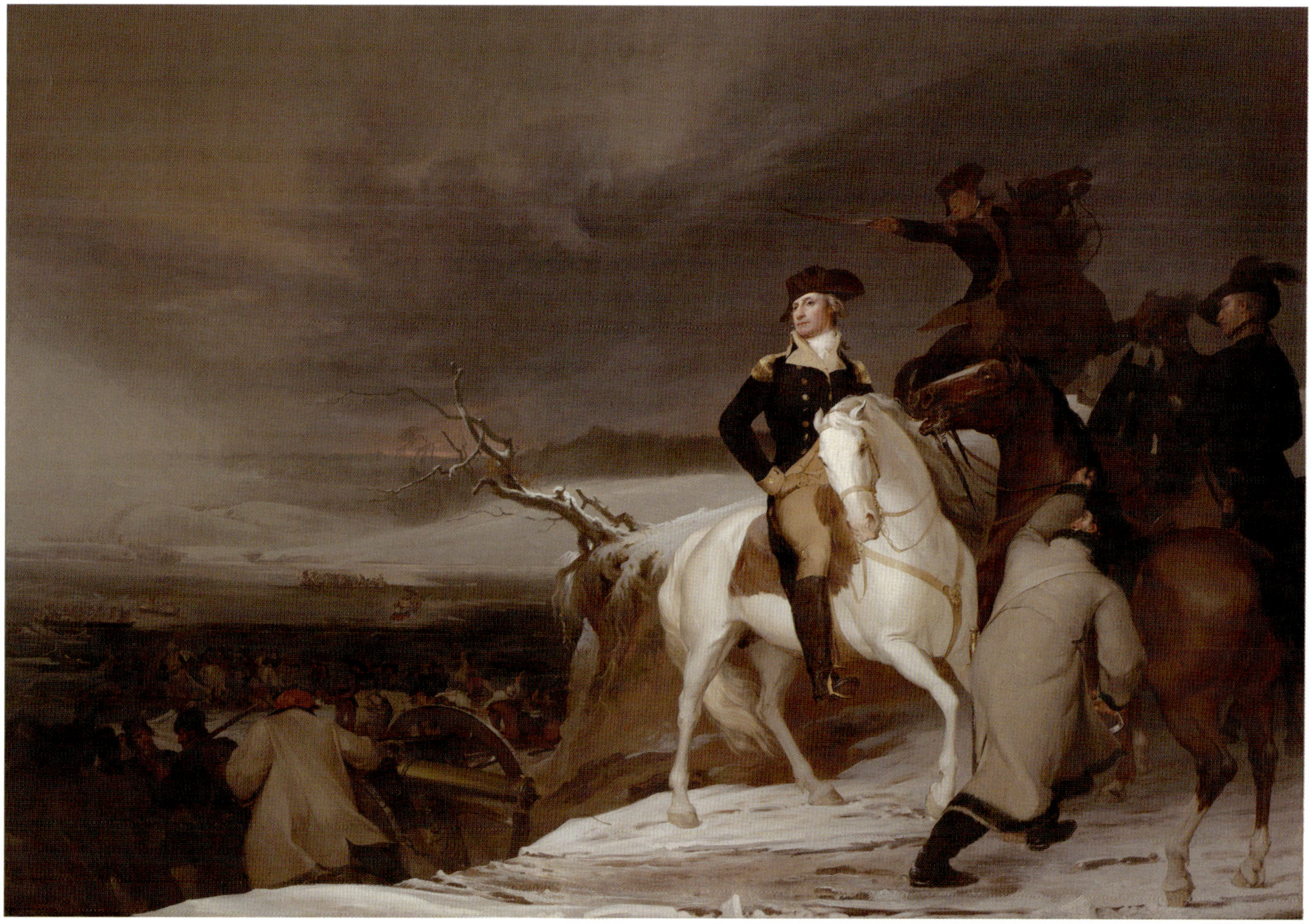

The war with Mexico was frequently equated with the American Revolution in American painting. For example, William Ranney's large tribute to the Continental Army's leader, *Washington Rallying the Americans at the Battle of Princeton* (Princeton University Art Museum), was painted in 1848 and exhibited at the National Academy of Design that year as a celebration of the close of the Mexican War. The winning of American freedom in 1776 and the conclusion of the battle for the American continent of 1846 were subtly wed in works of art like Ranney's and Stanley's paintings.[15]

Black Knife (cat. no. 064), was added to Stanley's Indian Gallery in 1850 and, over the next few months, became something of a sensation.[16] Special notice of it was made, for example, after the collection reached the Smithsonian Institution for an extended display in early 1852. A critic for the *National Intelligencer* who saw the exhibition commented, "Whilst there is probably no painting in the collection which is not good, some are truly exquisite." One of four that he then singled out as exceptional was *Black Knife*.[17]

The other major painting that resulted from the Kearny expedition and found its way into the Indian Gallery was also a strongly metaphorical work, *View on the Gila River*, of 1851. Known today only by a second version titled *Chain of Spires along the Gila* (fig. 2.7, cat. no. 130), dated 1855, it was showered with praise by the same *National Intelligencer* critic as a "ravishing view" whose exotic

FIG. 2.7.
John Mix Stanley, *Chain of Spires along the Gila*, 1855. Oil on canvas; 30¾ × 42⅜ in. (78.7 × 106.7 cm). Courtesy Phoenix Art Museum, museum purchase, 1968 (68.20)

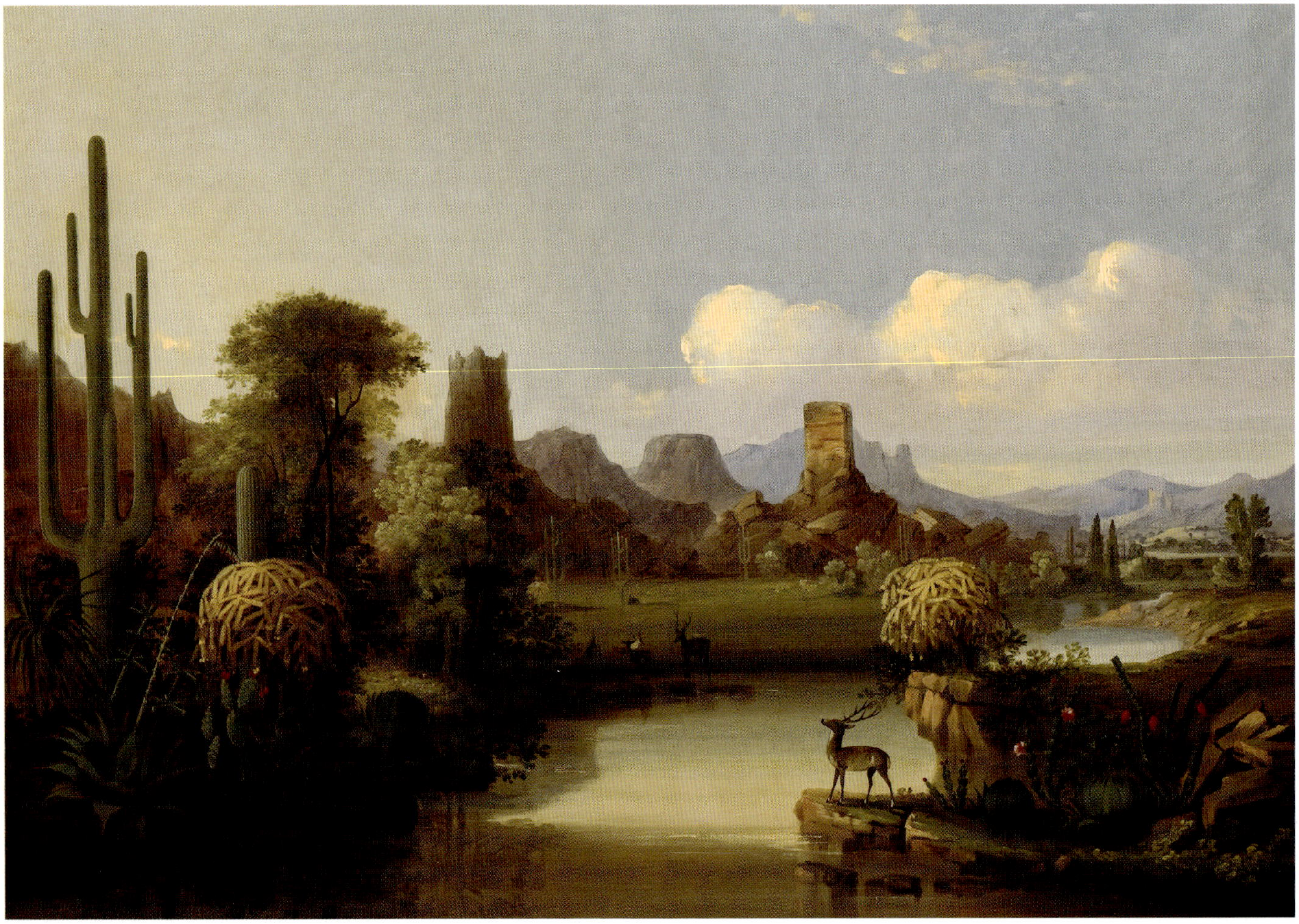

flora and topography filled viewers with wonder. It disclosed, he said, "an order of the vegetable kingdom and a style of geology as different from what prevail in our region of the continent as if they were the belongings of some other planet."[18] Being a purely Edenic idyll, it contrasted fundamentally with his portrayal of *Black Knife* (cat. no. 064) and suggested the complexity of Stanley's experience. *Chain of Spires along the Gila* (cat. no. 130) embraces a welcoming wonderland of pastoral beauty, while *Black Knife* presents the antithesis, a sublime and awesomely austere landscape that more credibly mirrors the Sonoran Desert through which Kearny and his soldiers passed.

Stanley's metaphor in *Chain of Spires along the Gila* is not the corporeal hope of future military victory but the spiritual promise of a land that could be settled by Americans and that for him was sanctified by the same divine hand that was said to support the concept of Manifest Destiny. From deep within the desert fastness, Stanley took this opportunity to deny the observations that had stood firmly for nearly thirty years, that the West was "the Great American Desert."[19] Although the painting was inspired by sketches of cactus and a valley camp scene, *Chain of Natural Spires on the Gila* (see fig. 130.1, in cat. no. 130), it may also associate with an 1828 work of Hudson River School founder Thomas Cole, *Garden of Eden* (fig. 2.8). Known to have been engraved at least once in the early 1830s, the Cole landscape of an imagined tropical jungle may have been familiar to Stanley.[20]

FIG. 2.8.
Thomas Cole, *Garden of Eden*, 1828. Oil on canvas; 38½ × 52¾ in. (97.8 × 134.0 cm). Courtesy Amon Carter Museum of American Art, Fort Worth, Texas (1990.10)

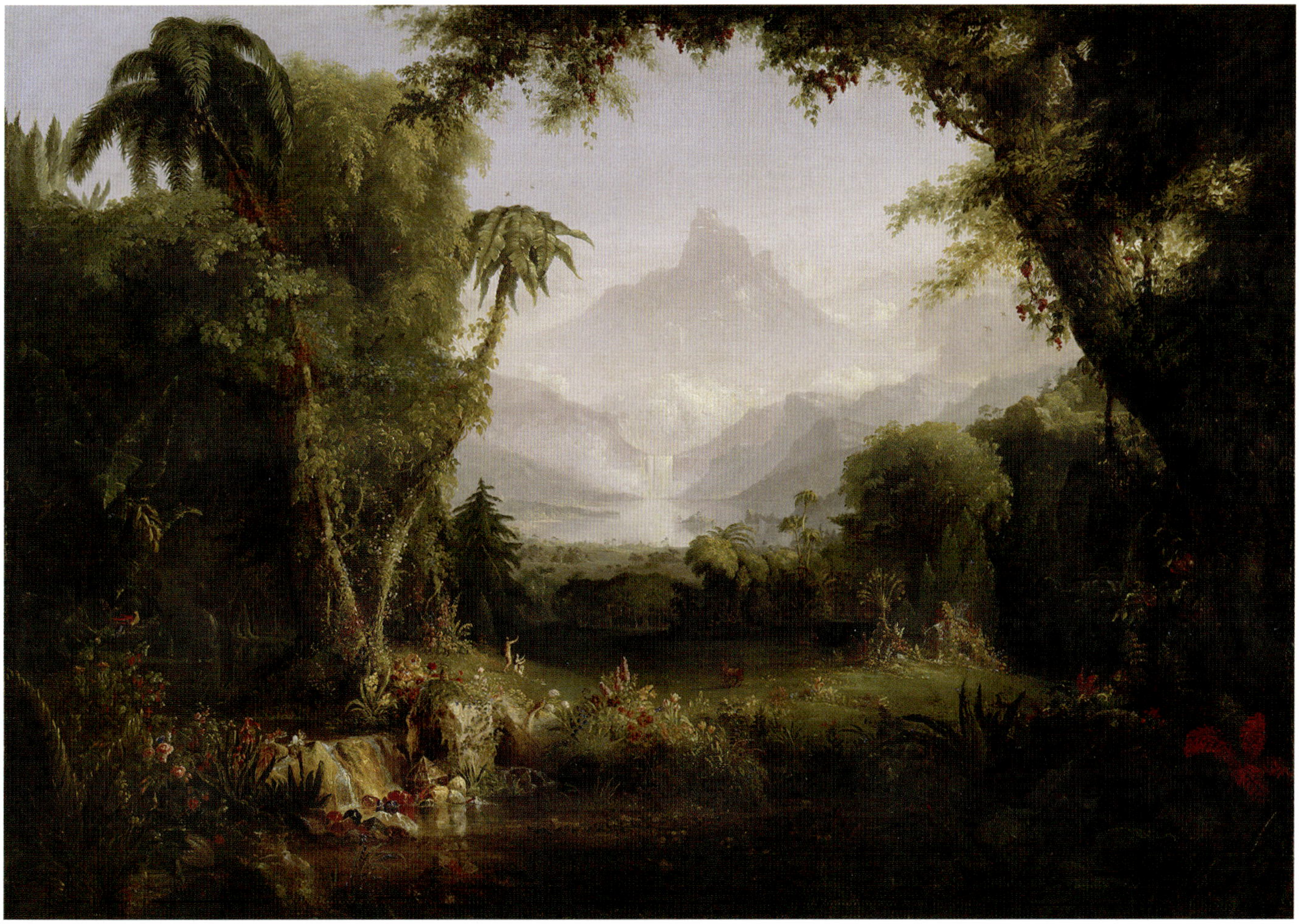

Despite Stanley's poetic image of the Gila River Valley, his vision was not shared with many of his fellow travelers. Emory reported on the scene in quite matter-of-fact geological terms, while another in the party, Captain Henry Smith Turner, an adjutant of the Army of the West, perceived the valley of the Gila as especially horrid. "I constantly feel as though I were in a dream," he wrote, "to be surrounded day after day with a wilderness, not one familiar object in nature except the sun, the moon and the stars—all else is wild and strange . . . to me, and I wish from the bottom of my heart I had seen the end of this toilsome march."[21] Yet relatively few probably ever read Emory's geological accounts, though ten thousand copies of the report were published, and no one but his wife would have seen Turner's grumblings. Thousands, however, would have stood spellbound before Stanley's large canvas in New York, Hartford, New Haven, and Washington, D.C., marveling at the natural glory of the Gila's treasures and the superlative artistry of the painting. The one thing that is a bit unsettling about the painting is that the sun appears to be setting on the new West, just as the region is being adopted into the American sphere. But perhaps the glow in the western sky represents not a passing day, but the discovery of gold in California, fresh news when Stanley started to paint this canvas and a sign for many that Manifest Destiny could pay off.

Although Stanley added three portraits from his southwestern adventure to his Indian Gallery in 1852, *Black Knife* (cat. no. 064) and the early version of *Chain of Spires along the Gila* (cat. no. 130) were the only large scenic canvases from the Kearny expedition that would ever enhance the display.[22] It is surprising that more were not adapted for the exhibition as these two were among the most popular works in the show. Perhaps if the Indian Gallery had sold to the Smithsonian Institution, Stanley might have added more of the southwestern scenes to the mix. Oddly, also, it appears that he never painted more than one Pueblo Indian while with Kearny. Not until 1852, two years after his return to the East, when a delegation of Pueblo Indians from New Mexico visited Washington, D.C., did he correct that omission. At that time he induced them to sit for their portraits, and the five resulting canvases were added to the Indian Gallery.[23]

By November 23, Stanley and the group had descended the Gila River to its junction with the Colorado River. Stanley traveled with Emory and another officer to this confluence, and there Stanley made several drawings. The illustration in the report titled *Junction of the Gila & Colorado Rivers* (see fig. 42.1, in cat. no. 042) does not picture the confluence at all, but was drawn some miles below it. By the time the Emory party had left the valley of the Gila and completed an eight-day trek across the desert to the Sierra Madres, Stanley had added considerable dimension to the American pictorial panorama. He had recorded in pencil and watercolor sketches the breadth of what is now southern New Mexico, Arizona, and California.[24] His subjects ranged from his favorites, Indian portraits, to skillful botanical sketches, landscapes, and views of the major points of travel and even copies of drawings inscribed on several canyon walls.

Before arriving at San Diego, Kearny's troops, exhausted and outnumbered, had several encounters with the Mexican Army, one of which was the battle of San Pasqual. Stanley did not witness the encounter since he had been left behind with a small group to guard the baggage.[25] As a consequence, there is no Stanley rendering of this critical confrontation between the U.S. and Mexican troops. In a subsequent engagement between the two forces, Stanley lost all his personal belongings but was able to save his most precious possessions, the sketches of the trip and the painting materials on which his life work depended.[26] By December 12, the Emory group ascended a small hill and looked for the first time on San Diego and the Pacific. The long trip was at an end. Stanley was invited to go aboard the U.S. Navy ship *Cyane*, then anchored in San Diego harbor, to begin converting his sketches into finished works.[27] He remained with this ship when it sailed to San Francisco in spring 1847. Here he delivered a number of small oil paintings to Emory. The lithographs for the report were taken from these paintings. Edwin Bryant, an American in San Francisco at this time, saw the Stanley oils and made the following flattering comment:

> Mr. Stanley, the artist of the expedition, completed his sketches in oil, at San Francisco; and a more truthful, interesting, and valuable series of paintings, delineating mountain scenery, the floral exhibitions on the route, the savage tribes between Santa Fe and California—combined with camp-life and marches through the desert and wilderness—has never been, and probably never will be exhibited. Mr. Stanley informed me that he was preparing a work on the savage tribes of North America, and of the islands of the Pacific, which, when completed on his plan, will be the most comprehensive and descriptive of the subject, of any that has been published.[28]

Still in California after finishing the oils, Stanley carried out one more service for the government. Traveling among the California tribes, he compiled a collection of Indian articles of dress and associated ethnological items for the Smithsonian. He was thus supplementing a collection already amassed by the artist-explorer Edward Kern. But, unfortunately, Stanley's collection was lost at sea on its way east, so his only enduring contribution was an artistic one.[29]

Stanley has received mixed reviews of his work with Emory. Twenty-four plates by Stanley appeared in Emory's published report, including views, portraits, and studies of fish and animals. An additional group of thirteen plant studies, some quite spectacular, was also illustrated. Over the years he has received less than laudatory commendation for these works. Ross Calvin, in editing a reprint of the Emory report in 1951, made the following criticism of the landscape views used as illustrations: "Some of the illustrations included in the body of the text itself, although they might have added antiquarian charm, are so inaccurate as to make it clear that the draughtsman never beheld the scenes he was attempting to depict."[30] This evaluation is overly harsh since Emory mentions the fidelity of at least some of Stanley's work, and those views related to the pictures of other artists are quite similar. A comparison of Stanley's and Abert's views of the ruins of Pecos Church in New Mexico reveals that Stanley was, if anything, more diligent in recording details than even Abert. However, there is always the possibility that some parts of Stanley's landscapes were fanciful. That a whole picture was a fabrication is doubtful since he was being hired expressly for the purpose of contributing accurate delineations of the scenes that the expedition passed.

Stanley scholar Julie Schimmel has critiqued the portraits and plant and animal studies as "rather poorly drawn," although the landscape views conform with Emory's descriptions for the most part. The only shortcoming, according to Schimmel, is that "they did not suggest the hardship endured by the expedition members."[31]

Stanley's words, however, delivered a different message than his pictures. He summarized his experiences with Kearny in two letters to his partner, Sumner Dickerman, both sent from San Diego in January 1847. "The march of General Kearney's [*sic*] command to this place was arduous," he started his account. Even when they traveled down the Gila River, "a fine mountain stream, about twenty yards wide, flowing through a valley, wide, fertile and well timbered," they suffered. It was especially hard going when they had to leave the river because of geological impediments. "Whenever this was the case," he wrote, "we were compelled to cross mountains of the most rugged character, and in some instances for fifty miles without water. I do assure you we paid a toll for our enjoyment of wild scenery." By his reckoning, once they arrived in San Diego, they had traversed "a distance of one thousand and ninety miles from Santa Fe."[32]

From San Francisco, Stanley's travels continued at his own expense. He journeyed as far north as Fort Vancouver and eastward along the Columbia River, where he painted landscapes and portraits of settlers and Indians. He narrowly escaped the Whitman massacre, which became the subject of a later oil painting. He sailed then to Hawaii, where he painted the portraits of prominent islanders, including King Kamehameha III (cat. no. 060) and his queen, Kalama (cat. no. 061), which still hang in the Iolani Palace at Honolulu.

Stanley did not return from his journeys until the spring of 1850, when he met up with Dickerman in Troy, New York, and settled down to add paintings to his Indian Gallery. The revised exhibit opened to rave reviews in September 1850. Encouraged in part by Stanley's reputation as a truly rare talent, and in part because of a perceived urgency to see the artist's renderings of "a people who are fast fading away before the rapid strike of civilization," crowds packed the galleries.[33] Such reactions to the exhibit and to Stanley as an artist persisted over the coming months as the Indian Gallery made a rambling tour through Albany, New York City, New Haven, and Hartford before coming to rest in Washington, D.C., in early 1852. Viewer numbers were impressive. "Thousands of our citizens daily visit this splendid collection of paintings," reported the *New York Sunday Era* when the show hung at the Alhambra Rooms on Broadway in that city.[34] And one of the most frequently made comments was about how Stanley's exhibition stacked up against his famous forerunner, George Catlin, whose Indian Gallery had been seen by many fifteen years before and was now in Europe. "As a collection of Indian paintings and curiosities," wrote one Albany paper about Stanley's exhibition, "it has no rival in the world. The paintings are superb and costly works of art."[35] Others were more direct. "In every respect it is superior to the far famed Catlin exhibition—whether we regard the size or finish of the paintings," observed another critic as he stood before the first version of Stanley's remarkable southwestern landscape, what he called "Scene on Gilla [*sic*] River."[36]

Stanley arrived in the nation's capital by February 1852. Once his Indian Gallery had been deposited and placed on display in the Smithsonian Institution, his hope abounded that Congress would appropriate funds for its purchase. Worthy advocates, other artists included, were beseeched to testify on behalf of such an outcome. A letter from Seth Eastman to Stanley, for example, expressed a contemporary opinion of Stanley's works compared with Catlin's.

> Washington, D.C.
> January 28, 1852
>
> Mr. Stanley,
>
> Dear Sir: Having been requested by you to express my opinion as to the comparative merits of yours and Mr. Catlin's Paintings of the Indians of this country, it affords me pleasure to say that I consider the artistic merits of yours far superior to Mr. Catlin's; and they give a better idea of the Indian than any works in Mr. Catlin's collection.
>
> Very respectfully, your obedient servant,
> S. Eastman[37]

Public opinion found even more articulate advocates. A visitor to the Indian Gallery, the travel writer and artist Charles Lanman (who referred to himself as simply "A WESTERN MAN"), offered perhaps the most eloquent and expansive testimony.

> I am intimately familiar with many of the scenes and personages in the gallery, and . . . at once recognized their truthfulness. It is the first thing of the kind, in my opinion, which really deserves the name of art, and dubs it an "American-Indian Gallery." The foliage, the nature of the soil, even to the formation of the country, its rocks and mineral properties, vegetation and atmosphere, are all to be found here. It is worth a hundred statistical reports as a means of useful information, and whether Congress has the constitutional power or not, or the inclination to purchase this gallery, it should never be allowed to leave the country. Such a glorious work, so useful, so new, and so instructive, is well worth the patronage not only of the Government, but of private taste in any one who has national pride.[38]

Stanley displayed his collection of Indian paintings in the Smithsonian Institution in 1852, at which time there were 152 oils. A full catalogue was published that December.[39] At the same time, Stanley formally petitioned Congress to purchase his collection. Yet, notwithstanding the favorable critique of Eastman and others, as well as the panegyrics of several western senators, his efforts came to naught. The decision, when it came on March 3, 1853, fell along sectional rather than party lines, with southerners unswervingly arguing that the government should have no role in supporting the arts.[40]

Stanley's disappointment was profound, but his choices for furthering his career were far from closed. The day before opting to refuse Stanley's petition, Congress passed a law authorizing a set of four federally funded surveys to spread across the West in search of the most favorable route for a transcontinental railroad.[41] Within a couple of months, some of the surveys were set to embark on their tasks. The largest and most complex of these expeditions selected a path traversing a route from Saint Paul to the Puget Sound. Under the command of Washington Territory's newly appointed governor, Isaac I. Stevens, a troop of about eighty men began to be assembled.

Stevens was a brilliant engineer. He had graduated first in his class from West Point in 1839 and won a commission in the prestigious Corps of Engineers, a fellow branch of the Army Corps of Topographical Engineers. He had studied under Seth Eastman and through that association had gained an appreciation and affection for art and learned the value of artists on expeditions. He probably consulted his mentor Eastman, who is thought to have subsequently recommended Stanley for the task.[42] By early May 1853 Stanley was hired at the highest wage of any of Stevens's employees ($125 per month) and was on his way west. He had visited Fort Snelling in 1837, and the *Washington Republican* reported that "Mr. Stanley has in past times traversed through that country" and knew the Indians of the Northwest well. The paper went on to say that, despite Stanley's long familiarity with Indian people, "the present expedition may be regarded as one of some peril."[43] Stanley wrote reassuringly from Saint Louis to his new fiancée, Alice English, addressing this latter point. "There is no doubt but we will have a large council of those northern Indians—and with the facilities in my power I will make many captives—on paper and plate—and dear one there will be no danger."[44]

Stanley and Stevens appeared to be very close from the start. They traveled together to begin the trip and were mutually supportive throughout. Because of his experience with Emory, Stanley was entrusted with several key assignments in Saint Louis to help with provisioning for the expedition. These included acquiring camp furniture and small stores for the eighty-member troop and, more important for his own duties, supplementing his artist supplies with a daguerreotype apparatus.[45] Stanley had probably been acquainted with the use of daguerreotypes for many years, maybe as far back as 1846, when he had traveled on the Santa Fe Trail with Josiah Gregg.[46] Now he was expected to make liberal use of the camera device in the execution of his responsibilities, and he proved his facility with the machine on several occasions, especially when recording portraits of Native people he met along the way.[47]

Stanley's equipment, however, was only partly responsible for his success in the field. His philosophical vision also guided him in important ways. His betrothed was quite religious, and he seems to have shared Alice's passion for things spiritual. In one of his letters to her at the beginning of the trip, he defined his mission and the wilderness that he was about to immerse himself in as something stretching well beyond the province of mere mortals. Perhaps remembering how he had equated the Gila River Valley with a Garden of Eden in *Chain of Spires along the Gila* (cat. no. 130), Stanley envisioned his new enterprise as a visit to God's sacred sphere. "When we get away—and over all the annoyances of preparation," he wrote her from Saint Louis, he would find himself "in the quiet solitude of Nature's garden, surrounded only by God's own work, as fresh as blooming, as when first born in Paradise."[48] Many of the scenes he began to collect and record would reflect this divine embrace.

Stevens's party assembled in Saint Paul and was ready to start the adventure by early June. There Stanley made his first recorded sketch, *Saint Paul M.T. (Minnesota Territory)* (cat. no. 086), one of sixty that would be illustrated as toned lithographs in the final Stevens report.[49] This watercolor (and thirty-seven others like it that are found in the present volume) is probably not the actual field study that Stanley made that day, rather a studio piece for the lithographers completed in 1854 or 1855 that was worked up from pencil and watercolor studies made on site.[50] Some of his field sketches were seen by a reporter in Saint Paul before the troop moved west, though, and they were startlingly brilliant. The reporter wrote, "I have already seen some of the Artist's work, and can promise the public when Gov. Stevens' Report is made up and given to the world, there will be something as pleasing to the eye as to the mind."[51] Stevens wanted in the most serious way to have Congress select the northern route, and his instructions to Stanley must have been to choose views that would be read as supportive of that perspective. His view of Saint Paul and Stevens's description started this perceptual partnership off on the right foot:

> St. Paul (see accompanying sketch) is beautifully located upon a high bluff on the east bank of the river, and is rapidly growing in size and importance. It is quite a business place, everything indicating vigor and activity. Among its prominent buildings are the territorial capitol, modeled after the Capitol at Washington, and several very fine churches.[52]

From this point forward, Stanley entered his wilderness paradise, a well-watered, accessible, nonthreatening place that would logically share in his mind God's natural garden with Stevens's railroad dream and America's expansionist agenda. For him, there was no paradox, only a natural synergy between the untrammeled forces of nature and the exigent promise of industry.

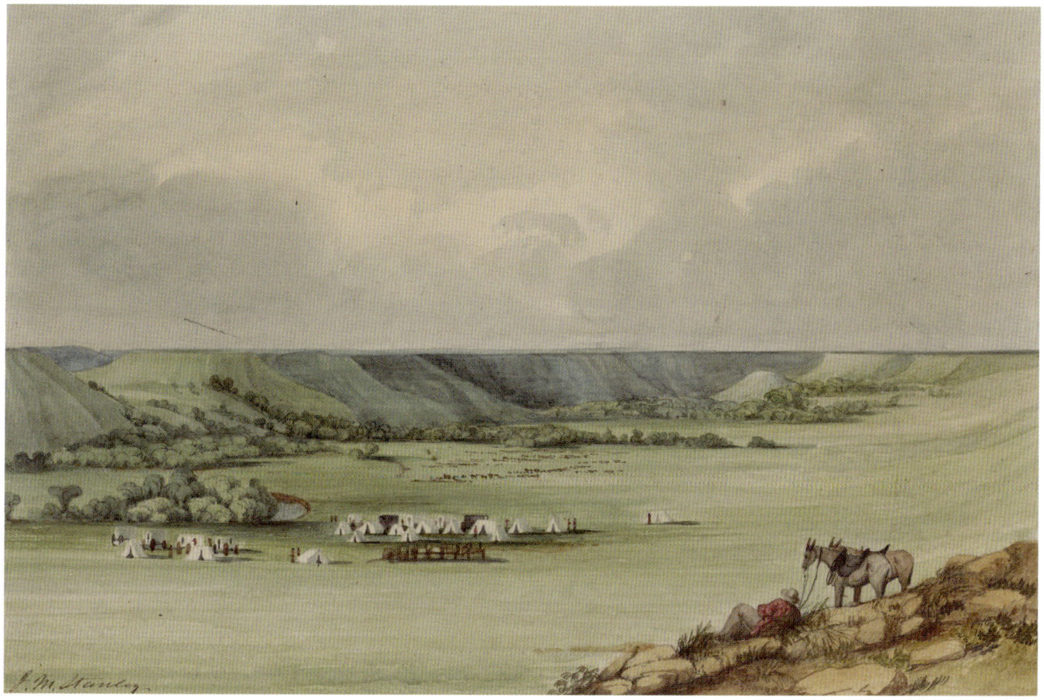

FIG. 2.9.
John Mix Stanley, *Sheyenne River*, 1854. Watercolor with graphite on paper; 8 9/16 × 11½ in. (21.7 × 29.2 cm). Courtesy Yale University Art Gallery, New Haven, Connecticut, gift of Paul Mellon, B.A. 1929, L.H.D.H. 1967, Collection (1982.39.6A)

Stevens and his group moved west with speed and precision. By early July they were halfway to Fort Union and the mouth of the Yellowstone River. As they intersected with the Sheyenne River (a tributary of the Red River), Stevens commented in his journals, "The country, thus far, is exceedingly favorable for a railroad, no grade over forty feet to the mile."[53] Stanley's idyllic vista of the scene (fig. 2.9, cat. no. 092), recorded on July 8, reinforced Stevens's assessment. Two days later, they encountered their first large herd of buffalo. Stevens estimated their number at two hundred thousand, while some in the group speculated higher, up to one million. "I had heard of the myriads of these animals inhabiting these plains, but I could not realize the truth of these accounts till to-day, when they surpassed anything I could have imagined."[54] Stanley, according to Stevens, captured the awesomeness of the scene, which was illustrated adjacent to the text in the lithograph *Herd of Bison, Near Lake Jessie* (see fig. 85.1, in cat. no. 85). Nature's bounty lay before him as seen by few white men before. Never could he have imagined that within thirty years, the bison would be nearly extinct in North America. This and most of his images of the prairies portray their munificence, in contrast with the reports of the other surveys that consistently regarded them as barren and fruitless.[55] Yet, unlike Catlin before him and William Jacob Hays less than a decade later, both of whom prophesied the bison's impending demise, Stanley was silent on the matter.[56] Even when this sight became one of the panels in his huge western panorama, *Scenes and Incidents of Stanley's Western Wilds*, 1854, he could only respond to the seemingly limitless numbers of animals, not their uncertain future.[57]

A camp of the Red River hunters that the Stevens party passed a few days beyond Jessie Lake proved to be a favorite theme for Stanley. His lithograph of the camp pictured the full sweep of Indian and mixed-blood life they encountered. More than one hundred buffalo hide lodges contained 1,300 people, "the whole presenting a very fine appearance," according to Stevens.[58]

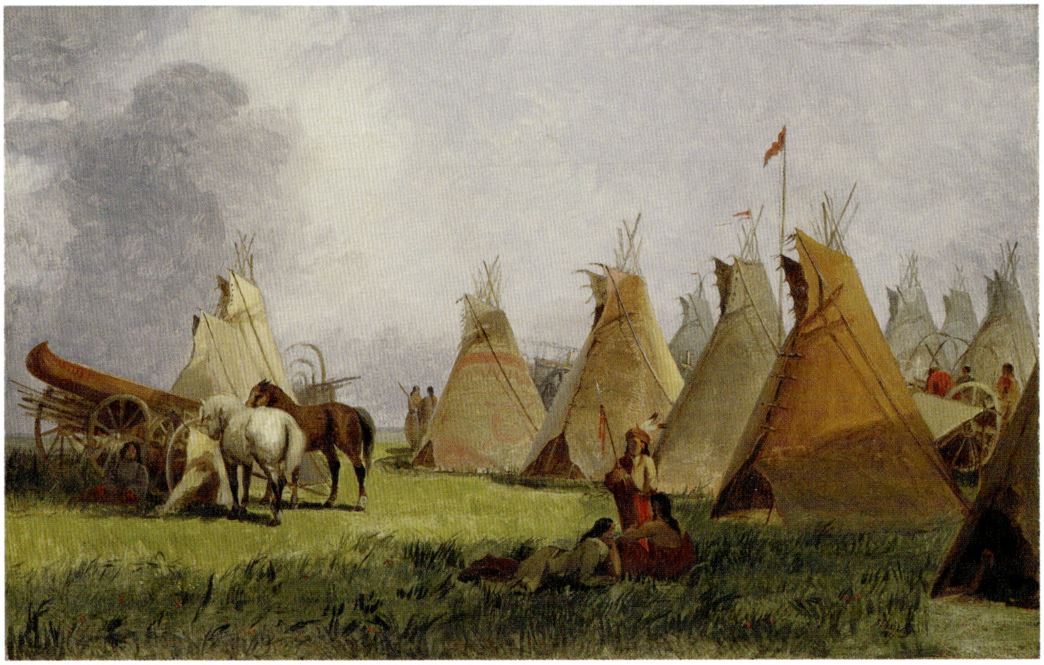

FIG. 2.10.
John Mix Stanley, *Camp of the Red River Hunters*, 1857. Oil on canvas; 13¾ × 21⅛ in. (34.9 × 53.6 cm). Courtesy Amon Carter Museum of American Art, Fort Worth, Texas (1966.52)

Stanley used this scene to illustrate one panel in his panorama and painted at least one independent work in 1857, *Camp of the Red River Hunters* (fig. 2.10, cat. no. 160), for a Detroit friend and patron, Alexander Hamilton Redfield (cat. no. 161). These hunters were residents of Stanley's paradise, comprising "many happy people" on a "sweet" prairie filled with sunlit lodges abreast a "smooth prairie."[59] Nothing could have made his long journey more gratifying, more confirming.

By early August, the Stevens party reached Fort Union. There they distributed goods among the Assiniboin Indians, as seen in a Stanley watercolor (cat. no. 094), and rested for a while. Stanley was busied with taking daguerreotypes of the Indians, an enterprise that was rewarded with jubilant reactions from the sitters. Sadly, none of Stanley's daguerreotypes have survived. He also made several drawings in pencil, one of Fort Union (cat. no. 075) and another of teepees near the fort (cat. no. 074). These rare drawings may provide insight into how Stanley primarily worked in the field, not with watercolor or oils but in pencil.

Stanley always remembered his time at Fort Union fondly. One of the panels of his panorama preserved an image of the twenty-year-old American Fur Company fort. In his panorama depiction he presented a sunset atmosphere. It was golden and "dream-like" with a group of three "wild and free" Indian riders racing before the walls, "glowing with hot joy and pride" as they darted "through the rushing air."[60] The energy of this scene, none of which is evident in the illustrations for the government report for political reasons, reveals the true measure of Stanley's elation at being among Indian people again. The plates in the book could only display a peaceable picture of Indian encampments and treaty gatherings, all scenes that in Stevens's mind might prejudice Congress to choose the northern route as an accommodating and welcoming option. Stanley had no such restraints with his panorama.

From Fort Union, the party moved west along the Missouri River, through Gros Ventres country and on to Fort Benton, crossing the beautiful Milk River along their way. They had with them Alexander Culbertson (cat. no. 080), a devoted friend and later patron of Stanley's, as well as the founder of Fort Benton, whose collaborative relationship with the Gros Ventres and Blackfeet was legendary. Stevens counted on Culbertson to set the stage for positive negotiations with both tribes, but especially with the traditionally combative Blackfeet. But he also had another tool with which to effect an affirmative outcome—John Mix Stanley. The artist was known for his ability to treat with Indians, and his talents were soon put to the test.

Stanley and two others, a lieutenant and the engineer Frederick W. Lander (who would later play an important role in surveying other portions of the West and working with artists like Albert Bierstadt), were assigned the task of performing a reconnaissance of the Bear Paw Mountains after they first reached the Milk River. It turned out to be a trying ordeal as the threesome, after the first day, somehow ran out of food and ammunition and feared for their safety. Stanley, the true hunter of the group, wasted their last bullet on a wily antelope that walked off unscathed after a faulty shot. They staggered into Fort Benton just as Stevens was about to send out a rescue party. The episode, slightly altered in detail, was recounted in Stanley's panorama.[61]

Such a misadventure did not apparently shake Stevens's faith in Stanley's abilities, as the artist was soon put in charge of another mission. After astonishing and delighting the Indians at Fort Benton with his daguerreotypes—they "considered that Mr. Stanley was inspired by their divinity (the sun), and he thus became in their eyes a great medicine man"—he was asked to take a party of six men north of the fort to treat with the Piegans, a branch of the formidable Blackfeet, and bring in some of their leaders to meet with Stevens. In this venture, Stanley was considerably more successful. He and his party rode north thirty-five miles to Three Buttes. He then moved farther north and west, where he interacted with a large camp of Piegans, organized and partook in a thrilling buffalo hunt, and brought back to Fort Benton a group of thirty-five of their "chiefs, braves and warriors" to treat with Stevens.[62] Stevens made it clear that Stanley had been most successful.

> In eleven days he had gone 160 miles and back, effected the business he was sent for, made a number of sketches of the country and the Indians, and collected a partial vocabulary. The accompanying sketch [see fig. 82.1, in cat. no. 82] is a view of the Three Buttes and the Blackfoot Indians engaged in the hunt, taken by Mr. Stanley on his return to Fort Benton.[63]

The hunt was commemorated in Stanley's panorama panel titled "A GRAND BUFFALO HUNT," which showed the artist participating in the chase, and the brochure rhapsodized that proudly mounted on his steed, he stops to "contemplate his own work, for to-day Stanley has been a mighty hunter."[64] An 1854 studio piece, *Buffalo Hunt* (cat. no. 082), preserves the same event.

But probably Stanley's proudest moment came when he rode into Fort Benton with the Piegan delegation at his side. In 1859 he memorialized that occasion in an oil painting known today as *Fort Benton Indians* (fig. 2.11, cat. no. 166). Compositionally derived from his watercolor sketch of *Fort Benton* (cat. no. 102), the painting amplified the scene with an array of figures moving toward the fort.[65] Stanley, as with *Buffalo Hunt*, may have painted himself into the canvas as part of the cavalcade. The horseman in the blue shirt gesturing toward the final destination may well be a self-portrait of the artist. Once again, the triumph was Stanley's, for the efficacious gathering of Stevens and the Piegans was deemed a seminal moment in the expedition's challenging efforts to placate the Native peoples of the region.

FIG. 2.11.
John Mix Stanley, *Fort Benton Indians*, 1859. Oil on canvas; 26½ × 38⅜ in. (67.3 × 97.4 cm). Courtesy American Museum of Western Art–The Anschutz Collection, Denver, Colorado; photograph courtesy of William J. O'Connor

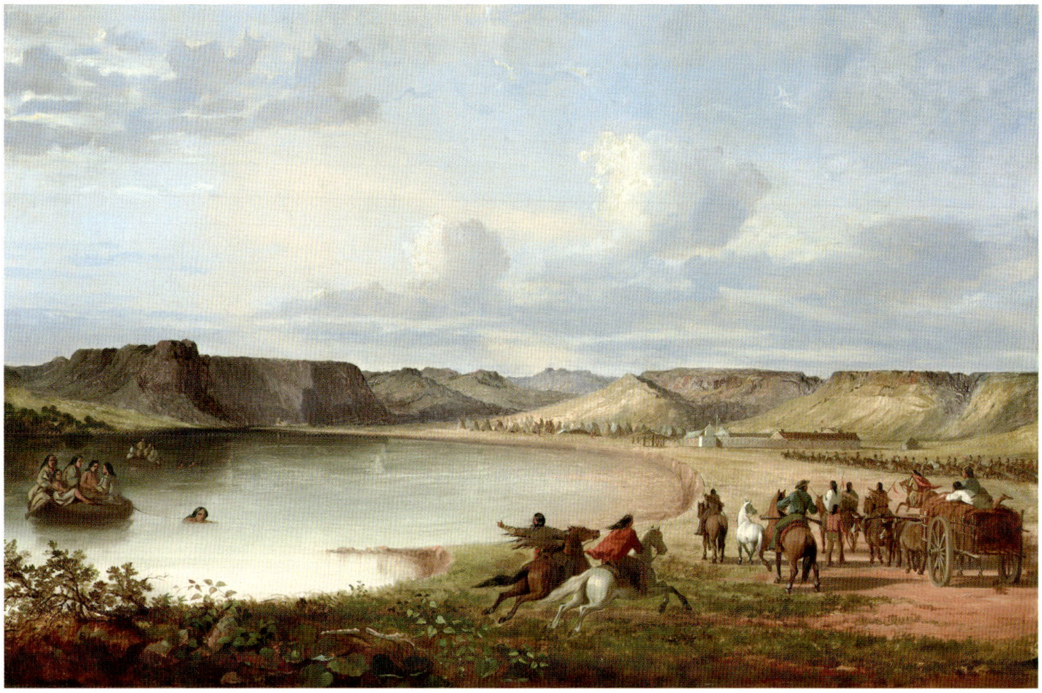

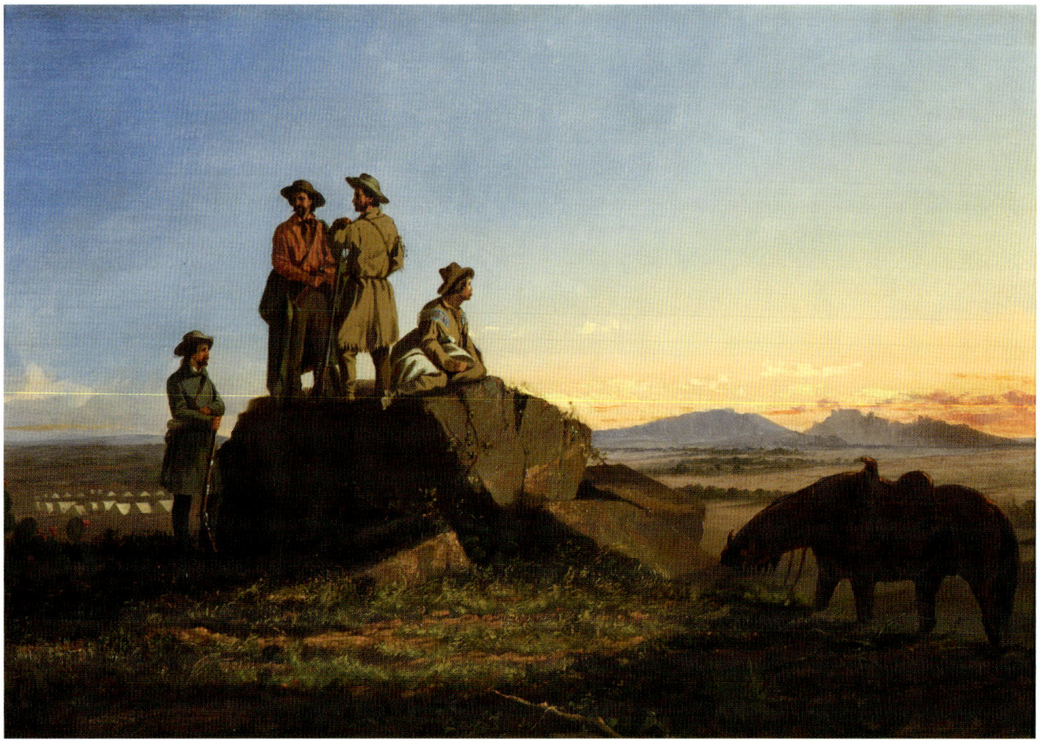

FIG. 2.12.
John Mix Stanley, *Scouts along the Teton River*, c. 1855. Oil on canvas; 24 × 34¼ in. (61 × 87 cm). Courtesy Gilcrease Museum, Tulsa, Oklahoma (0126.1143)

Just before Stevens pushed west from Fort Benton, on September 17, he wrote and sent down the river a brief description of the trip thus far. In it he took pains to praise Stanley for his service to the expedition. "J. M. Stanley, Esq., the artist of the expedition, has taken a great many sketches illustrative of the progress of the expedition, besides taking at various points on the way numerous daguerreotypes of Indians. His reputation, already so well established, cannot be enhanced by any reference to his satisfactory discharge of duty."[66]

Stevens's troop, including his most reputable artist, was soon on the move again. On September 22 and 23, they camped overlooking the Teton River, with the first spires of the Rocky Mountains in the distance. It was, according to Stevens, "exceedingly picturesque and suggestive."[67] Stanley's view from the bluffs looking into the Teton River Valley (cat. no. 105) was replicated as a plate, *Teton Valley*, in the Stevens report. Sometime shortly after Stanley returned to Washington, D.C., in 1854, he completed an oil that revisited this scene, one that turned out to be among the most compelling works of his later career, *Scouts along the Teton River* (fig. 2.12, cat. no. 131). A band of four men has topped a rocky outcrop overlooking the Teton River and their camp below. In the distance, the sun sets in crimson and gold layers of sky and clouds. Two of the men look in that direction, anticipating the party's coming ascent of the first passage through the Rockies, Cadott Pass, just south of where Lewis and Clark had crossed nearly a half century before. The other two peer back toward the camp, in the direction from which they have come. The fellow in the red shirt is Isaac Stevens. He naturally assumes an ascendant position in the composition, and the backward glance may reflect the satisfaction he enjoyed with the accomplishments of the expedition thus far. With this painting, Stanley introduced a new character into the pantheon of western heroes. Except for various interpretations of Daniel Boone and a rare monumental tribute to the pathfinder *John C. Fremont* (fig. 2.13), posed in front of the Wind River Mountains, by Stanley's contemporary George Peter Alexander Healy, few artists had celebrated the American explorer as an epic figure. Alfred Jacob Miller, of Baltimore, and William T. Ranney, of Hoboken, had elevated the mountain man to exalted national stature by this time, but the official explorer, including even the revered icons Lewis and Clark, had been left out. Stevens had achieved that standing in Stanley's estimation, however, and this painting deserves special art historical notice as a result.[68]

Stevens and his band of intrepid explorers have been placed on a natural stone pedestal. They survey America's new domain with what one scholar has called a "magisterial gaze."[69] With their engineering savvy, their scientific intellects and instruments, and their documentary artist, men such as these adventurers command and control all that they survey. Through their gaze, they metaphorically take possession of everything they can see. In sympathy with the popular dicta of Manifest Destiny, they represent not the roughed, individualistic, entrepreneurial, free spirit of the legendary mountain man, but the collective, expansive dream of a mostly Anglocentric nation that, with the benefit of evolving technologies such as the railroad, would soon conquer the continent, harness its resources, and subdue its Native people. Stanley, who viewed the western wilds as a paradise, seemed conflicted, though he probably saw only patronage rather than paradox when he painted this oil.

That being said, Stanley also placed Indians in similar poses and on equally magisterial plinths. These pyramidal compositions (early examples include *Blackfoot Indians*, 1854 [cat. no. 081] and *Halting to Smoke*, 1855 [cat. no. 128]) situate the Plains hunters and warriors, probably Blackfeet, in equally noble, controlling attitudes, as if looking back at the presumptuous

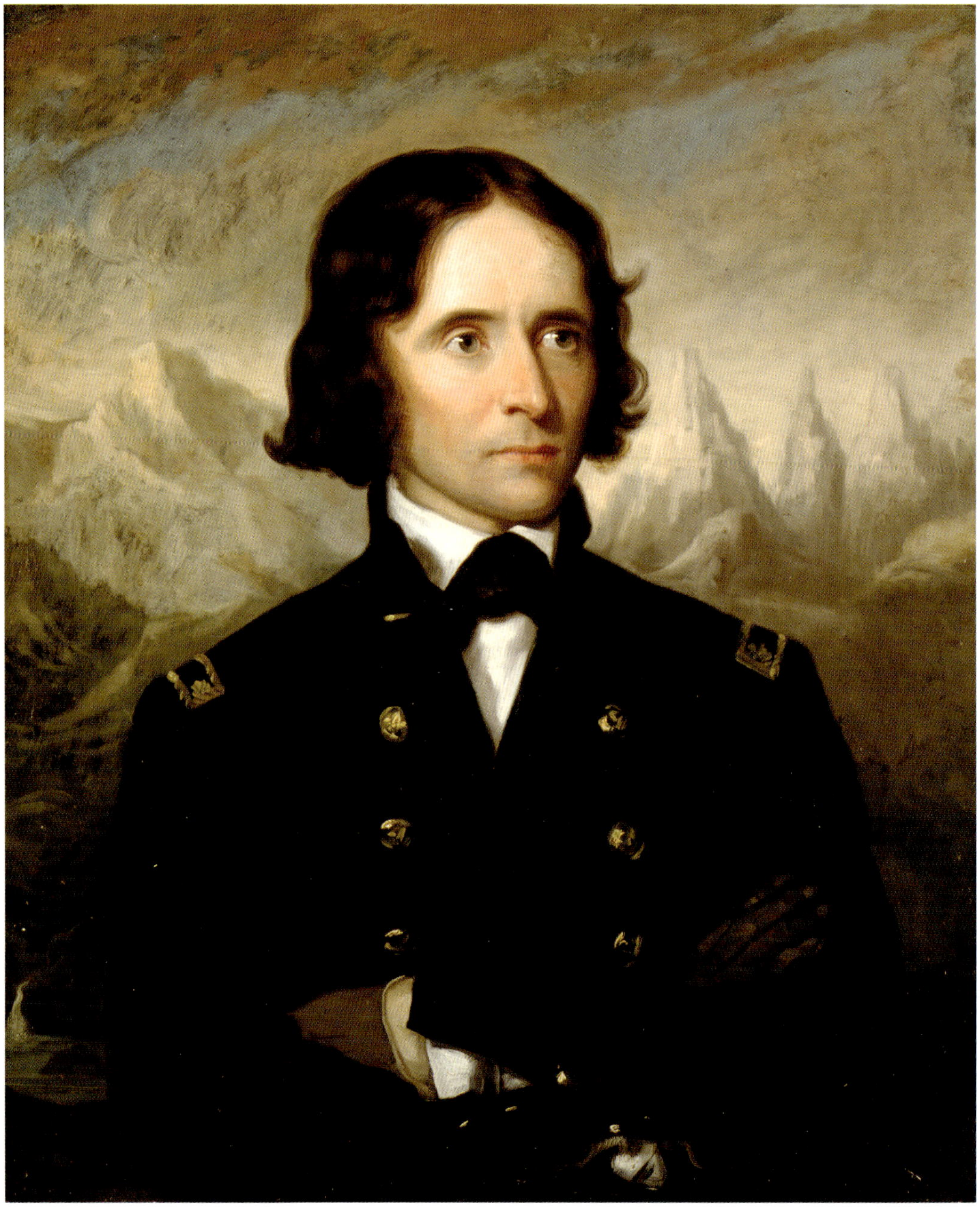

FIG. 2.13.
George Peter Alexander Healy, *John C. Fremont*, n.d. Oil on canvas; 30 × 25¼ in. (76.2 × 64.1 cm). Courtesy Union League Club of Chicago, Illinois

explorers with disdain, just as the Apache chief Black Knife had done. Their poses appear, in fact, more natural than the explorers' and situate the figures in a place that feels like home rather than an exotic, foreign land. Stanley thus distributed the motif with equal measure.

At the beginning of the northern survey, Stevens had split his troop in two. The second half of the expedition was led by Captain George B. McClellan, who had in his party two artists of some renown, Gustavus Sohon and James Graham Cooper.[70] McClellan had sailed around to the Columbia River and worked his way east as Stevens came west. Even though they met partway, Stevens decided to continue on to the Pacific and his new home, the Washington Territory. On the last leg of the journey, he took Stanley with him as his guide. Together they descended the Columbia River in a canoe.[71]

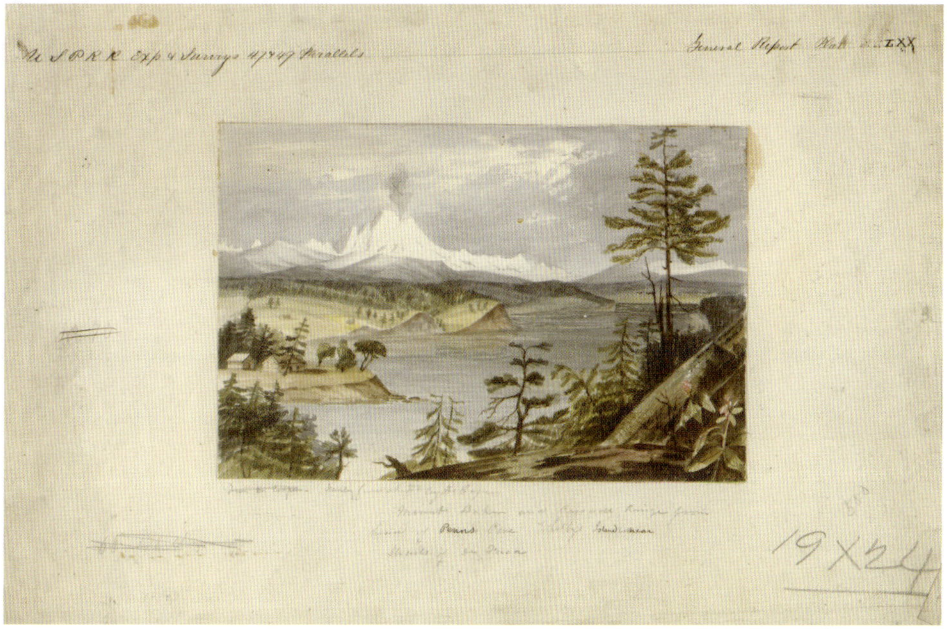

FIG. 2.14.
John Mix Stanley, *Mt. Baker and Cascade Range, from Whitby's Island*, 1854. Watercolor and pencil on paper; 5⅞ × 8¹¹⁄₁₆ in. (14.8 × 22.1 cm). Courtesy Yale University Art Gallery, New Haven, Connecticut, gift of Paul Mellon, B.A. 1929, L.H.D.H. 1967, Collection (982.39.41A)

Ten of the plates in the Stevens report are ascribed to Sohon, and several others as reworked by Stanley from Sohon originals. Three plates, *Mount Rainier Viewed from Near Steilacoom, Mt. Baker & Cascade Range from Whitby's Island*, and *Puget Sound and Mt. Rainier from Whitby's Island* (cat. nos. 126, 127, and 125), are attributed to Stanley after sketches by Cooper.[72] Cooper's studies are not known to exist, but Stanley's watercolors using them as a guide, such as his view of *Mount Baker* (fig. 2.14, cat. no. 127), are stunning. The Columbia River segment of the trip was familiar territory for Stanley, who had traveled much of its length in 1847 and 1848, following the southwestern expedition with Emory and Kearny. He had enjoyed painting many of the scenes previously, such as the sublime cascade *Pelous Falls* (cat. no. 114), and his view of Mount Hood in *Dalles of the Columbia [River] Looking Westward* (cat. no. 115).[73] Though topographical in spirit and function, they are gems of American landscape art that merit serious attention as paintings and prints.

Soon after Stanley and Stevens reached Fort Vancouver, the artist was released to return to the States. He was anxious to reconnect with his fiancée, Alice, and Stevens was happy to dispatch him to Washington, D.C., with a preliminary copy of his report of the survey. Stanley traveled through the isthmus of Panama and arrived in New York early January 1854. He was married on May 3 that year. In this safe return, as in his marriage, Stanley felt blessed.

On his way home, he heard of a colleague who had not enjoyed such good fortune. The news reached him of the demise of members from another Pacific Railroad Survey, under the leadership of Captain John W. Gunnison of the Corps of Topographical Engineers. Gunnison had been assigned the exploration of the 38th parallel and had left Fort Leavenworth in June 1853, just a few weeks later than Stevens departed from Saint Paul. Among his ranks was a friend and associate of Stanley's from Philadelphia, Richard H. Kern, an accomplished artist and explorer who had crisscrossed the West a number of times, beginning in 1848 with John C. Fremont's ill-fated assault on the Colorado Rockies. Together Kern and Gunnison lost their lives just west of the Wasatch Mountains in October 1853, through the treachery of Paiute Indians who, some said, had been stirred to murderous revenge by the Mormons.[74] Stanley wrote in his diary, when he heard the news, that Kern had "often told me the Black Feet would have my scalp . . . but a kind of providence has thus far saved my life—while he sleeps his last sleep I am in a wilderness."[75]

Within months after his return to Washington, D.C., Stanley was engaged in working up his own and a dozen of the surviving Kern sketches for the official published reports. Kern's sketches, as redrawn by Stanley, would find their way into volume 2 of the reports and Stanley's into book 1 of volume 12.[76] Stanley received a stipend of $125 per month for his continuing services, the same wages he earned while on the expedition. It was, according to Stevens, "a small compensation . . . in view of his ability and experience."[77] Within about a year of his return, Stanley had completed fifty-one Indian subjects, the same number of landscape views, and twenty-six drawings of trees and geological specimens.[78] Despite Stanley's ambitions as he embarked on his northwestern venture that he would supply "sketches of Indians [that] should be made and colored from life, [and] with care to fidelity in complexion as well as feature," none of the Indian portraits appear in the final volume.[79] Nor are any natural history subjects included. The only plates in the report are sixty landscapes and treaty scenes along with ten reworked views from Sohon. This difference in expectations between the artist and the Government Printing Office is thought to have caused the delay of several years for publication of the Stevens report. Although most of the other volumes were completed by 1855, Stevens's did not come out until 1859. In total, all the expeditions employed eleven artists, and despite the reduction of Stanley plates, he was still the most prolifically illustrated of the lot. Moreover, the works he produced, as sketches, lithographers' models, and indirectly as illustrations on the Stevens and the Emory expeditions, carried special significance for their sheer rigor as aesthetic expression and more. This perspective, articulated by historian David Nicandri, recognizes Stanley's exploration works as layered in importance, "not merely the documentation of particular sites at a point in time, not just representations of an artistic mode, but additionally, indications of the deepest currents of scientific interest and natural philosophy."[80]

Stanley's watercolors that were used in the Stevens report were essentially tailored to the mission of the expedition. They were inviting, nonthreatening, pleasant views that expose nothing antagonistic or inhibiting about the journey. As one student of the watercolors has observed, they were "nearly devoid of hints of the unknown, the hardships of a forbidding wilderness, or the threats of hostile societies." Their purpose was to foster a positive public view of the northern route for a railroad, and as such, they were a remarkable success.[81]

Stanley, who still waited and pleaded faithfully though fruitlessly for Congress to acquire his Indian Gallery, showed considerable entrepreneurial zeal in the months and years directly following his return to the States. His sketches from his trek with Stevens were re-employed as models for forty-two pictorial episodes in a huge panorama he called *Scenes and Incidents of Stanley's Western Wilds*, which opened in early September 1854 in Washington, D.C. According to one reviewer, it promised to be more "than usually interesting" and far superior to most panorama extravaganzas that were unrolled in that era before motion pictures. Being "illustrative of Indian life and Indian scenes," its pictures of the West were seen as "accurate sketches of the places represented, giving a truthful view of the country traversed, and the incidents in the life of those wild tribes . . . [as] portrayed from personal observation by the artist himself."[82] When it opened, the *Washington Daily Evening Star* splashed across one page the headline "Triumphant Reception of Stanley's Western Wilds." "The scenes," they wrote, were "exceedingly instructive."[83] When it traveled to Baltimore later in the fall, the panorama was effusively proclaimed "the most beautiful and instructive work of art ever seen there."[84] A brochure was

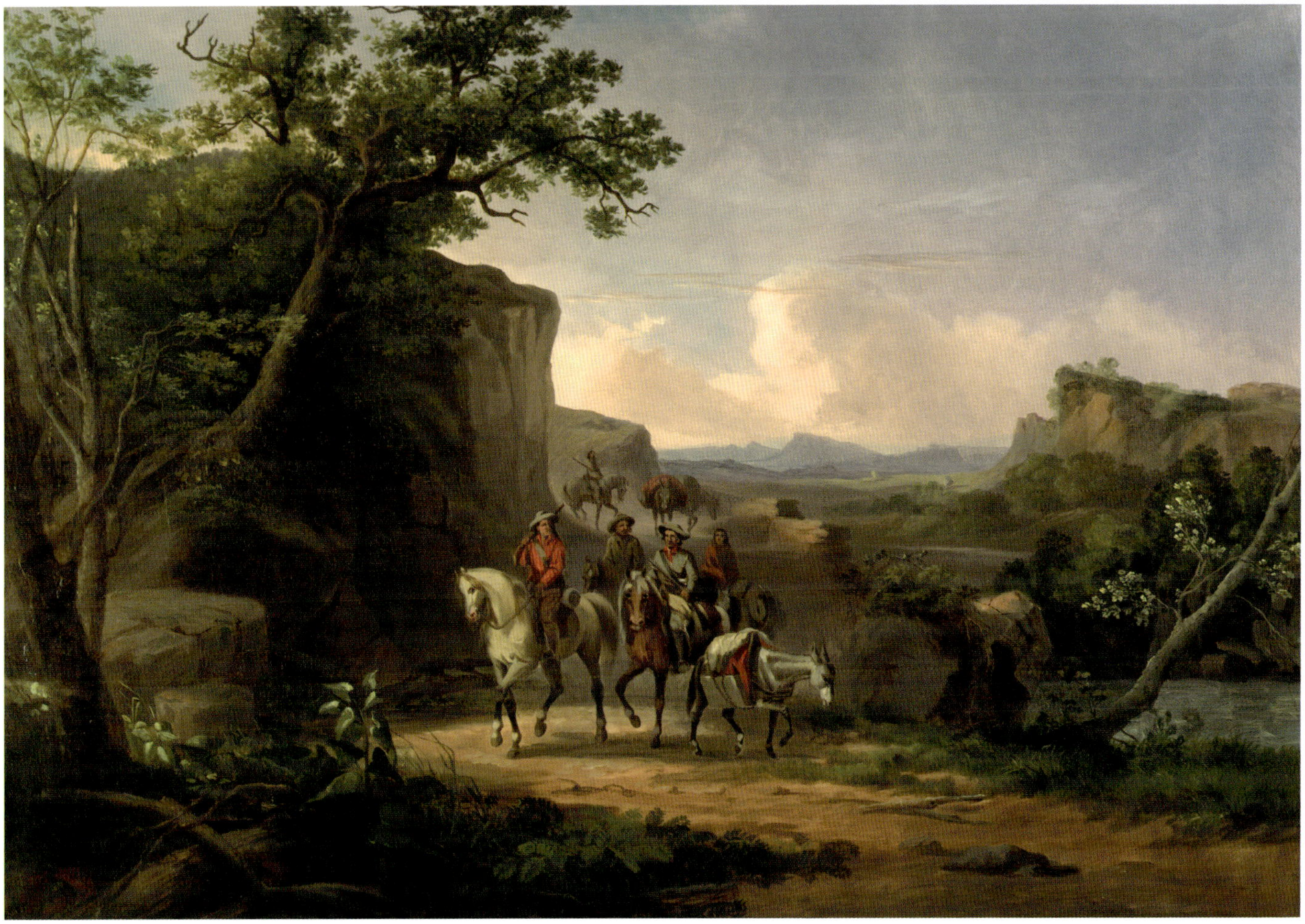

available for ten cents over the twenty-five cent admission. It carried a hyperbolic narrative, which, though inspired by Stanley, was written by a local dramatist and poet, Thomas Seaton Donoho.

The panorama was short lived, having run its course by early 1855. It is doubtful that Stanley saw much profit from it.[85] Yet, in addition to modest revenues from its audiences, Stanley garnered a number of important commissions for paintings adapted from scenes presented on the moving screens. For example, *The Buffalo Hunt*, 1855 (cat. no. 138), is thought to have derived from the panorama's episode titled *The Perils of the Chase*, and *Seeking a Home*, 1855 (cat. no. 129), follows the description of a panel titled *Halting on the Prairie*.

Beyond the panorama, other opportunities presented themselves as a result of his northwestern travels. One of them was securing new patrons. Isaac Stevens became one of his most supportive collectors over the years. He is thought to have purchased at least two large oils from Stanley in the mid-1850s, *Landscape with Deer* (cat. no. 164) and *Mounted Surveyors and Pack Animals* (fig. 2.15, cat. no. 084). The latter is thought to portray Stevens leading a party of explorers through a western ravine. Though lacking the epic monumentality of George Caleb Bingham's 1851 historic tableau of *Daniel Boone Escorting Settlers through the Cumberland Gap*

FIG. 2.15.
John Mix Stanley, *Mounted Surveyors and Pack Animals*, c. 1854. Oil on canvas; 35 × 46 in. (88.9 × 116.8 cm). Private collection; photograph courtesy Berry Hill Galleries, New York, New York

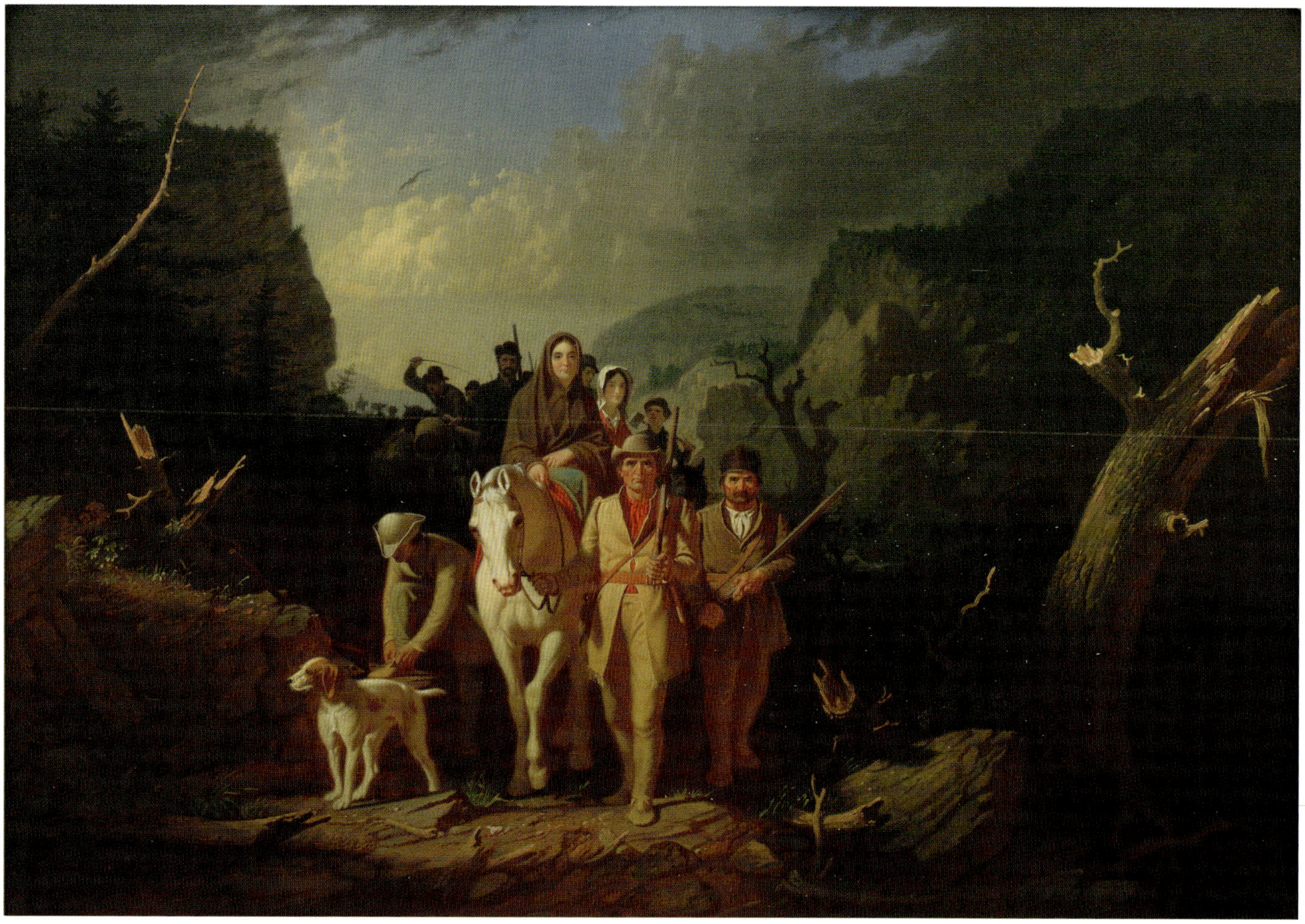

FIG. 2.16.
George Caleb Bingham, *Daniel Boone Escorting Settlers through the Cumberland Gap*, 1851–1852. Oil on canvas; 36½ × 50¼ in. (92.7 × 127.6 cm). Courtesy Mildred Lane Kemper Art Museum, Washington University, St. Louis, Missouri, gift of Nathaniel Phillips, 1890

(fig. 2.16), Stanley's painting essentially mirrors Bingham's theme of Anglo explorers entering the wilderness. Stanley's setting is open, sunlit, and promising rather than foreboding, shadowed and staged as with Bingham's, but the story of a promised land still prevails.

Stanley's *Landscape with Deer* (cat. no. 164) also blushes with pristine splendor, similar to his southwestern master landscape, *Chain of Spires along the Gila* (fig. 2.7, cat. no. 130). This northern variation records the same paean to nature's glory. Probably inspired by views taken on the upper Milk River or the Marias River, *Landscape with Deer* exalts the virgin, unimpeded vistas that were part of their daily fare as he and Stevens pushed westward in their quest. Stanley had found another Garden of Eden, this time on the prairie alongside the Missouri River.

Another Stanley patron from the railroad survey experience was Alexander Culbertson (cat. no. 080), the founder of Fort Benton whom Stevens had employed in Saint Louis to facilitate negotiations with the Assiniboin and Blackfeet Indians along the Upper Missouri. Culbertson and Stanley became close friends, and Culbertson later purchased as many as five major canvases from Stanley, including one version of his allegorical masterpiece *The Last of Their Race* (cat. no. 159), and a self-portrait of Stanley (cat. no. 167).[86] *The Last of Their Race* pictures Culbertson's wife, the Blood woman Natawista, and her brother Seen From Afar pushed to the brink of extinction on the shores of the Pacific. There is also strong suggestion that Culbertson once owned *Kidnapped* (cat. no. 139), as its provenance includes one of Culbertson's grandsons, Henry Clay Culbertson.

After his return to Washington, D.C., in early 1854 and his subsequent marriage to Alice, Stanley never ventured into the West again. He was ready to settle down. Stanley had crossed vast stretches of the frontier in the previous dozen years, probably more than any other artist of his time. In his years as an explorer-artist with Emory and Stevens, he had traversed the western part of North America twice. The government had provided him purpose and protection for a life of adventure in a land of promise. He in turn embellished the expeditions' reports and left finished studio paintings that are art treasures of unequaled significance today.

NOTES

1. Gregg to John Bigelow, May 8, 1846, quoted in Maurice Garland Fulton, ed., *Diary and Letters of Josiah Gregg: Southwestern Enterprises, 1840–1847* (Norman: University of Oklahoma Press, 1941), 190.

2. See, for example, "Death of J. M. Stanley," *Detroit Daily Post*, April 11, 1872. See also "Biographical Chronology," John Mix Stanley Papers, 1830–1973, Archives of American Art, Smithsonian Institution, Washington, D.C. (hereafter Stanley Papers).

3. The visit is alluded to in a letter from Gregg to Dr. George Engelmann, April 17, 1846, published in Fulton, *Diary and Letters of Josiah Gregg*, 188.

4. See Stella M. Drumm, ed., *Down the Santa Fe Trail and into Mexico: The Diary of Susan Shelby Magoffin, 1846–1847* (Lincoln: University of Nebraska Press, 1982), 19–20.

5. See, for example, Ibid., 49, 65.

6. See William H. Goetzmann, *Army Exploration in the American West, 1803–1863* (New Haven, Conn.: Yale University Press, 1959), 2–21, for a history of the corps.

7. See William H. Goetzmann, *Exploration and Empire: The Explorer and the Scientist in the Winning of the American West* (Austin: University of Texas Press, 1993), 231.

8. See John Galvin, ed., *Western America in 1846–1847: The Original Travel Diary of Lieutenant J. W. Abert, Who Mapped New Mexico for the United States Army* (San Francisco: John Howell, 1966). Abert and Peck both survived their ailments and were later assigned to perform a reconnaissance of New Mexico for the Corps of Topographical Engineers. Their findings were appended to Emory's report as J. W. Abert, *Report of Lieut. J. W. Abert of His Examination of New Mexico* (Washington, D.C.: Wendell and Van Benthuysen, 1848). This report was also published as 30th Cong., 1st Sess., S. Doc. No. 23 (1848), *Serial Set* 517.

9. William H. Emory, *Notes of a Military Reconnoissance, from Fort Leavenworth, in Missouri, to San Diego, in California, including part of the Arkansas, Del Norte, and Gila Rivers* (Washington, D.C.: Wendell and Van Benthuysen, 1848), 45. This report was also published as 30th Cong., 1st Sess., S. Doc. 7 (1848), *Serial Set* 517. Emory reported that Stanley was provided an assistant, Dabney Eustis, about whom nothing further is known. The *National Intelligencer*, November 14, 1846, reported on Stanley's appointment in an article, "Late from Santa Fe," saying that "Mr. Stanley [has been] employed in Santa Fe as the artist of the expedition."

10. Emory, *Notes*, 38.

11. Ibid., opp. 37.

12. *The Journal of Captain A. R. Johnston*, which is appended to Emory, *Notes*, 579, mentions three principal Apache chiefs who came to trade that day, Red Sleeves, Lasady, and Black Knife.

13. Ibid.

14. Stanley would have been familiar with Sully's masterpiece either by seeing the original or through prints like George S. Lang and William Humphrys' 1825 engraving after the painting. I am grateful to Meredith Crawford of the Museum of Fine Arts, Boston, for information about the prints.

15. See Linda Bantel and Peter H. Hassrick, *Forging an American Identity: The Art of William Ranney, With a Catalogue of His Works* (Cody, Wyo.: Buffalo Bill Historical Center, 2006), 45–48.

16. A checklist of *Stanley's Indian Gallery* printed for the New York showing at the Alhambra Rooms, early November 1850 to late February 1851, included this painting. When the display moved to Washington in 1852, a full catalogue was printed by the Smithsonian, *Portraits of North American Indians, with Sketches of Scenery, Etc., Painted by J. M. Stanley* (Washington, D.C.: Smithsonian Institution, 1852), which lists the painting as number 98 and having been painted in 1846, a most unlikely date for the work.

17. "Indian Gallery of Paintings," *National Intelligencer*, February 23, 1852.

18. Ibid.

19. See the map accompanying Edwin James, *An Account of an Expedition, from Pittsburgh to the Rocky Mountains* (Philadelphia: H. C. Carey and I. Lea, 1822). This is considered briefly in James Ballinger, "John Mix Stanley, A 'Hudson River' Painter in Arizona," *Phoebus: A Journal of Art History* 3 (1981): 70. Ballinger also discusses at

some length the connection of Stanley with the Hudson River aesthetic, and with Thomas Cole and Asher B. Durand in particular.

20. The 1831 engraving by James Smillie appeared in an edition of the Bible published in Boston by Gray and Bowen. I am grateful to Margi Conrads of the Amon Carter Museum for information about that engraving.

21. Dwight L. Clarke, ed., *The Original Journals of Henry Smith Turner with Stephen Watts Kearny to New Mexico and California, 1846–1847* (Norman: University of Oklahoma Press, 1966), 100–101.

22. The three portraits were listed as numbers 100–102 and titled *Pimo Chief, Pimo Squaw*, and *Maricopa Chief and Interpreter*. They probably relate to two illustrations in the Emory report, *The Interpreter of the Pimos, a Coco-Maricopa* (295), and *Juan Antonio—Pomo Head Chief* (297).

23. "The Pueblo Indians," *National Intelligencer*, September 7, 1852. The portraits are listed in the 1852 Smithsonian catalogue, *Portraits of North American Indians*, numbers 93–97, p. 56.

24. It is assumed here, since his later field sketches were in watercolor, that those done on the Emory tour were of a similar medium. None have survived, however.

25. Emory, *Notes*, 108. On January 24, 1847, he wrote his partner Dickerman, saying, "Captain Emory takes part of my sketches with him; as yet they have been confined to plants and are in watercolor. I have become quite proficient in this branch of the art." The letter was published in "Interesting from California: Letters from John M. Stanley," in an 1847 clipping, unknown newspaper, Stanley Papers.

26. Dwight L. Clarke, "Soldiers Under Stephen Watts Kearny," *California Historical Society Quarterly* 45 (June 1966): 140.

27. Ibid., 114. Clarke refers to these as watercolors, but the known finished works are all oils.

28. Edwin Bryant, *What I Saw in California: Being the Journal of a Tour by the Emigrant Route and South Pass of the Rocky Mountains, across the Continent of North America, the Great Desert Basin, and through California, in the Years 1846, 1847*, ed. Richard H. Dillon (Palo Alto, Calif.: Lewis Osborne, 1967), 435–36.

29. Benjamin P. Draper, "John Mix Stanley, Pioneer Painter," *Antiques* 61 (March 1942): 181.

30. Ross Calvin, ed., *Lieutenant Emory Reports: A Reprint of Lieutenant W. H. Emory's Notes of a Military Reconnoissance* (Albuquerque: University of New Mexico Press, 1951), 3–4.

31. Julie Schimmel, "John Mix Stanley and Imagery of the West in Nineteenth-Century American Art" (Ph.D. diss., New York University, 1983), 259–63.

32. "Interesting from California: Letters from John M. Stanley," Stanley Papers.

33. "Stanley and Dickerman's Indian Portrait Gallery," *Troy Daily Whip*, September 11, 1850.

34. "Stanley's Indian Gallery," *New York Sunday Era*, February 2, 1851.

35. "Indian Gallery," *Albany Kuick*, October 8, 1851.

36. "Stanley's Indian Gallery," *Albany Dutchman*, October 11, 1851.

37. Quoted in W. Vernon Kinietz, *John Mix Stanley and His Indian Paintings* (Ann Arbor: University of Michigan Press, 1942), 17.

38. Charles Lanman, "Stanley's Gallery," *Daily National Intelligencer*, March 3, 1852.

39. *Portraits of North American Indians*.

40. For a full account of Stanley's futile efforts to attract congressional patronage, see Brian W. Dippie, *Catlin and His Contemporaries: The Politics of Patronage* (Lincoln: University of Nebraska Press, 1990), 282–86. The rejection was reported in "Indian Appropriation Bill," *Congressional Globe*, March 3, 1853.

41. See Goetzmann, *Exploration and Empire*, 281–93, for a full discussion of these first four railroad survey expeditions.

42. Dippie, *Catlin and His Contemporaries*, 286.

43. For reference to Stanley's travels to Fort Snelling, see Charles Richard Tuttle, *General History of the State of Michigan* (Detroit: R. D. S. Tyler, 1873), 235–36. The *National Intelligencer*, April 9, 1853.

44. Stanley to Alice English, May 10, 1853, Stanley Papers.

45. Ibid.

46. Stanley helped Dr. George Engelmann equip Gregg in Saint Louis in 1846, with Stanley in charge of obtaining passports, and Engelmann assigned to purchase daguerreotype plates. See Fulton, *Diary and Letters of Josiah Gregg*, 188.

47. For an excellent account of Stanley's use of daguerreotypes during the Stevens expedition, see Martha A. Sandweiss, *Print the Legend: Photography and the American West* (New Haven, Conn.: Yale University Press, 2002), 108–11.

48. Stanley to Alice English, May 10, 1853, Stanley Papers.

49. Isaac I. Stevens, *Narrative and Final Report of Explorations for a Route for a Pacific Railroad, near the Forty-seventh and Forty-ninth Parallels of North Latitude from Saint Paul to Puget Sound*, vol. 12, book 1 of *Reports of Explorations and Surveys, to Ascertain the Most Practicable and Economical Route for a Railroad from the Mississippi River to the Pacific Ocean* (Washington, D.C.: Thomas H. Ford, 1860), 35. These reports were also published as 36th Cong., 1st Sess., S. Doc. No. 56 (1860), *Serial Set* 1054 and 1055.

50. Stevens hired a second artist in Saint Paul to assist Stanley on the trip, Max Strobel. His appointment as "the assistant artist to Mr. Stanley" was announced in a Saint Paul newspaper, July 20, 1853, and reprinted in "The Puget Sound Expedition," *New York Tribune*, August 3, 1853. Strobel quit the expedition early in the trip because of Stevens's imperious ways. He did, however, make a watercolor of Saint Paul that was published in 1853 (seven years before Stanley's view in the official report) as a lithograph. See I. N. Phelps Stokes and Daniel C. Haskell, *American Historical Prints* (New York: New York Public Library, 1933), 111.

51. "Puget Sound Railroad Survey," *New York Tribune*, June 3, 1853, from a story of May 26 in an unidentified Saint Paul newspaper.

52. Stevens, *Narrative and Final Report*, 35.

53. Ibid., 56.

54. Ibid., 59.

55. See Joni L. Kinsey, *Plain Pictures: Images of the American Prairie* (Washington, D.C.: Smithsonian Institution Press, 1996), 58.

56. For Catlin's 1830s commentary, see George Catlin, *Letters and Notes on the Manners, Customs, and Conditions of the North American Indians* (London: David Bogue, 1844), 1:262–63, and for a discussion of Hays's subsequent 1860s assessment, see Dawn Glanz, *How the West Was Drawn: American Art and the Settling of the Frontier* (Ann Arbor, Mich.: UMI Research Press, 1982), 98–100. Kinsey, *Plain Pictures*, 58–59, also has an interesting discussion of Stanley's image.

57. See program for the work, Thomas S. Donoho, *Scenes and Incidents of Stanley's Western Wilds* (Washington, D.C.: Evening Star Office, c. 1854), 5.

58. Stevens, *Narrative and Final Report*, 65.

59. *Scenes and Incidents*, 6.

60. Ibid., 7.

61. See Stevens, *Narrative and Final Report*, 103, and *Scenes and Incidents*, 7.

62. The reference to Stanley's skill as a photographer is found in Stevens, *Narrative and Final Report*, 103–104, and the account of his second independent trip on 114–15.

63. Ibid., 115.

64. *Scenes and Incidents*, 8.

65. *Fort Benton Indians* appears to have corrected what some modern critics have said about the illustration of *Fort Benton* in Stevens, *Narrative and Final Report*, that the teepees are disproportionately large in comparison to the fort. See Robert Taft, *Artists and Illustrators of the Old West, 1850–1900* (New York: Scribner), 18, for an example.

66. First published in the *Washington Union*, it was later reprinted as "Pacific Railroad. Northern Route," *Oregonian*, January 21, 1854.

67. Stevens, *Narrative and Final Report*, 118.

68. Stanley painted at least two canvases of the mountain man in 1851, listed in the 1852 catalogue *Portraits of North American Indians*, 40–41. These were listed under the heading of "Black-Foot" but were painted a couple of years before he met any

Blackfeet Indians. Their titles, *Flight of a Mountain Trapper* and *The Trapper's Escape*, suggest that he might have been familiar with Ranney's famous *Trapper's Last Shot*, 1859, and presaged Arthur Fitzwilliam Tait's *The Prairie Hunter—One Rubbed Out*, 1852.

69. Albert Boime, *The Magisterial Gaze: Manifest Destiny and American Landscape Painting c. 1830–1865* (Washington, D.C.: Smithsonian Institution Press, 1991), 154.

70. For information on Sohon, see Patricia Trenton and Peter H. Hassrick, *The Rocky Mountains: A Vision for Artists in the Nineteenth Century* (Norman: University of Oklahoma Press, 1982), 85–89; and for information on Cooper, see Dumas Malone, ed., *Dictionary of American Biography*, vol. 4 (New York: Scribner, 1930), 406–407.

71. Stevens, *Narrative and Final Report*, 154.

72. A thorough discussion of the different editions of Stevens, *Narrative and Final Report* and of the credit given to Cooper by the various lithographers can be found in Taft, *Artists and Illustrators*, 257.

73. See *Portraits of North American Indians*, 66–67, for mention of the earlier versions.

74. See Goetzmann, *Exploration and Empire*, 286–87; and David J. Weber, *Richard H. Kern: Expeditionary Artist in the Far Southwest, 1848–1853* (Albuquerque: University of New Mexico Press, 1985), 237–40.

75. Stanley diary, January 3, 1854, Stanley Papers.

76. For a full description of this work, see Taft, *Artists and Illustrators*, 254–78. According to Kern's biographer, David Weber, only one of the original Kern sketches survive, and this is not sufficient to ascertain how much Stanley altered the Kern sketches for the lithographers, but probably very little. See Weber, *Richard H. Kern*, 223.

77. Stevens to Captain A. A. Humphreys, September 26, 1854, Isaac Stevens letterbook, Office of Explorations and Surveys, Records of the Office of the Secretary of the Interior, National Archives, Washington, D.C.

78. This is recounted in Schimmel, "John Mix Stanley and Imagery," 112–13. A partial list of these is found in a letter from Stanley to Lieut. K. G. Warren, April 3, 1855, Stevens letterbook.

79. Quoted in Schimmel, "John Mix Stanley and Imagery," 103.

80. David L. Nicandri, "Isaac I. Stevens and the Expeditionary Artists of the Northern West," in *Encounters with a Distant Land: Exploration and the Great Northwest*, ed. Carlos A. Schwantes (Moscow: University of Idaho Press, 1994), 137. Nicandri credits Barbara Stafford's book, *Voyage into Substance: Art, Science, Nature and the Illustrated Travel Account* (Cambridge, Mass.: MIT Press, 1984), for these insights.

81. Robin Jaffee Frank, "John Mix Stanley and the Isaac I. Stevens Railroad Survey Expedition of 1853," in *Life, Liberty, and the Pursuit of Happiness: American Art from the Yale University Art Gallery*, ed. Helen A. Cooper (New Haven, Conn.: Yale University Press, 2008), 292.

82. Unidentified clipping from a Washington, D.C., newspaper of August 1854 in the Stanley Papers.

83. "Triumphant Reception of Stanley's Western Wilds," *Washington Daily Evening Star*, September 8, 1854.

84. "Stanley's Panorama," *Washington Daily Evening Star*, December 7, 1854.

85. See Dippie, *Catlin and His Contemporaries*, 294.

86. For a discussion of these works, see Lesley Wischmann, *Frontier Diplomats: Alexander Culbertson and Natoyist-Siksina' Among the Blackfeet* (Norman: University of Oklahoma Press, 2004), 275–76.

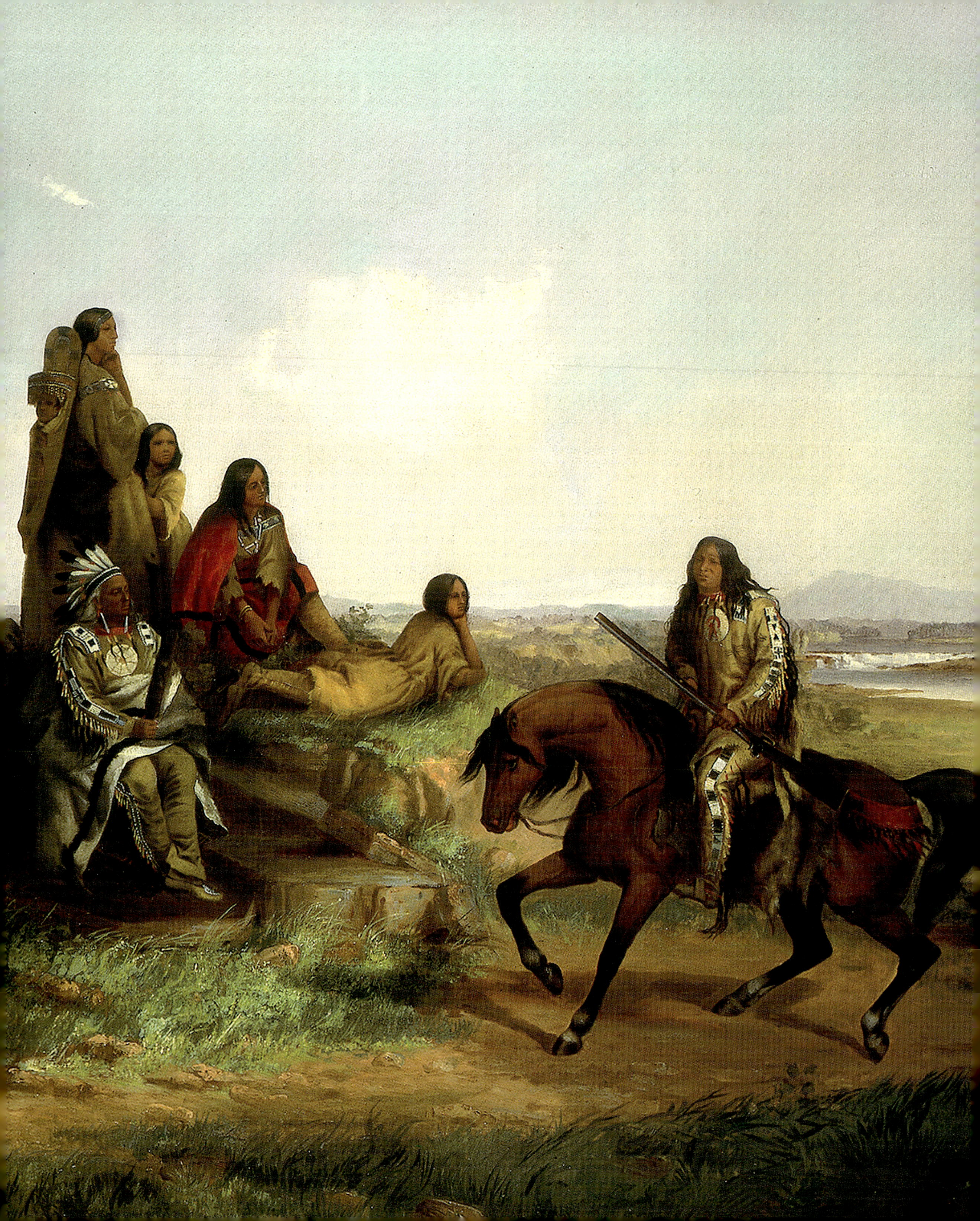

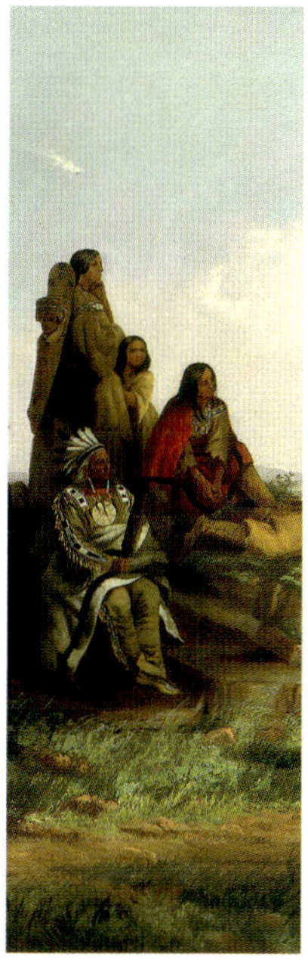

3

John Mix Stanley and the Peculiar Advantages of Washington

Lisa Strong

When John Mix Stanley arrived in Washington just after the new year of 1852, he came with the hope of selling his Indian Gallery to the U.S. government. The decade he had spent traveling and painting representatives of tribes from across North America had been a significant investment. He had traversed thousands of miles from Detroit west to California, as far north as Oregon Territory, and as far south as Texas, painting more than 140 portraits and genre scenes of what he had seen. He had paid out of his own pocket for photographic equipment that he used to make studies for his paintings as well as for artist's materials and framing and shipping, recouping precious little from admissions over six years of touring the show.[1] In an interview with a Washington newspaper, Stanley pointed to the first portrait he painted for the gallery, saying, "If I had then known the extent of the task I had assumed, the adversity, the privations, and the fatigues to which I was to be exposed, and the frequent despondencies that were to come over me, I should no longer have prosecuted the work upon which I had embarked."[2] The timing of Stanley's arrival in the city was surely calculated. His rival and predecessor George Catlin had just submitted a petition for the government to purchase his gallery of Indian portraits.[3] Stanley wasted no time, settling in the home of fellow Indian painter Charles Bird King and visiting Joseph Henry on January 27 to offer his gallery for exhibition at the Smithsonian.[4] By mid-February, Stanley's gallery was installed in the Library Room of the Smithsonian Institution (fig. 3.1), where papers claimed it was "daily crowded by multitudes of admiring spectators" and speculated that it would "probably become the property of the nation."[5] Fellow expedition-

OPPOSITE

(detail) J. M. Stanley, *A Family Group (Barter for a Bride; Indians in a Landscape)*, c. 1856 (cat. no. 145)

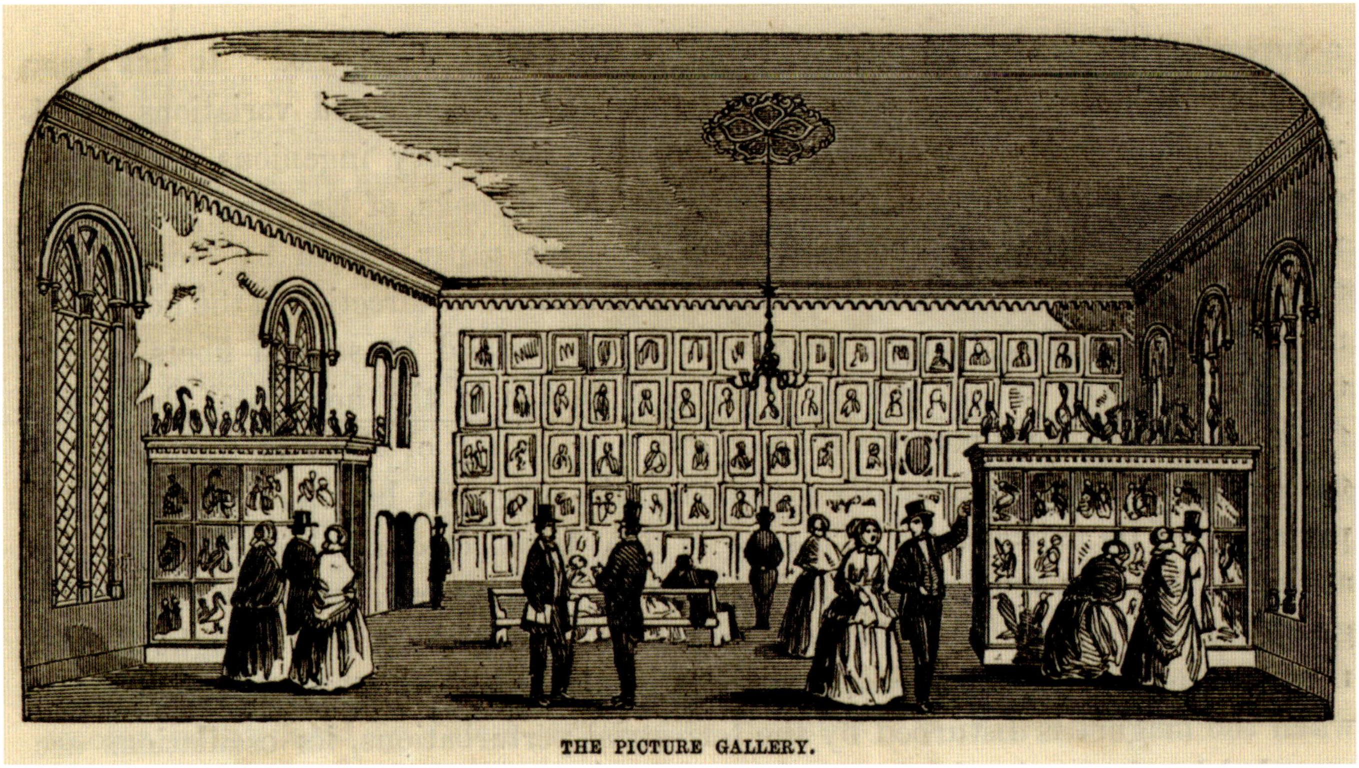

FIG. 3.1.
Unknown, *The Picture Gallery*, 1858. From Rhees, *An Account of the Smithsonian Institution*, 27.

ary artist Captain Seth Eastman proclaimed the artistry and accuracy of Stanley's gallery "far superior to Mr. Catlin's," and Brian Dippie has expertly documented Eastman's promotion of Stanley over Catlin in the rivals' bid for government patronage.

Despite his auspicious introduction, Stanley's biographers have detailed how his hopes in the city were dashed, first by the government's refusal to purchase the gallery in 1853, then by the Smithsonian's refusal to purchase in 1856, and finally by the tragic Smithsonian fire of 1865 that destroyed all but seven of the paintings in his Indian Gallery.[6]

Although his ten-year residence in Washington, D.C., has been presented as a period of professional disappointment, when, with one exception, he was neither exploring the West painting Indians nor enjoying the financial reward he would receive later when he settled in Detroit, Stanley's time in Washington was far from a lost decade. In the years he resided in the city, Stanley absorbed the lessons offered by what was then one of the premier sites for viewing contemporary American art. His style of rendering the human form matured, he experimented with greater and more complex narratives, and he built a solid base of government patronage. His residence with King and his participation in the Washington Art Association and the National Art Association, both as exhibitor and as treasurer for the organizations, speak to his success at building professional networks very early in his residence and capitalizing on them to gain commissions and find venues for the exhibition and sale of his artwork.[7] In focusing on Stanley's attempts to sell his Indian Gallery, scholars have discounted the significance of his Washington residence on his artistic development, and missed the effects of its sectional and professional politics on his paintings. In so doing, they have overlooked the extent to which some of his premier narrative paintings, such as *The Trapper's Cabin* (cat. no. 163), and *A Family Group (Barter for a Bride; Indians in a Landscape)* (cat. no. 145), are not just western scenes, but true Washington City pictures.

ART AND POLITICS IN ANTEBELLUM WASHINGTON CITY

The two decades preceding the Civil War were a golden period for the arts in what was then commonly called Washington City. The growing number of artist residents, private collections, and government patronage made Washington one of the nation's best destinations for public art viewing. Stanley's first host, Charles Bird King, lived and worked in Washington for four decades, operating a gallery and museum that became a touchstone for artists living in or traveling through Washington. There King exhibited his own artwork, along with plaster casts and prints by other artists, exceeding 250 pieces by 1848. Perhaps as important, his gallery was a venue for the temporary exhibition of work by other American artists, including Thomas Sully and William Dunlap, as well as contemporary European copies, such as Théodore Gericault's *The Raft of the Medusa*.[8] By 1855, the city was also graced by the growing collection of American and European artworks owned by William Wilson Corcoran, who opened his residence on Lafayette Square to the public several days a week.[9] In addition to Corcoran, there was Mayor Peter Force, whose portrait Stanley painted in 1857 (cat. no. 156), and possibly others, including Joseph Gales, the editor of the *National Intelligencer* whose portrait appears in Samuel F. B. Morse's *The House of Representatives,* 1822.[10] Washington also had the unique advantage of government commissions on view in the city. The Capitol rotunda contained eight well-known murals depicting American history by John Trumbull, John Gadsby Chapman, Robert Weir, John Vanderlyn, and William Powell, as well as sculpture programs in the pediment over the portico and on the doors. But the Capitol also contained hundreds of other works on temporary or permanent view in rooms around the rotunda. These included Vanderlyn's panorama of Versailles, Rembrandt Peale's "porthole" portrait of George Washington, a biblical scene by Thomas Rossiter, and a number of European paintings, including works by Ary Scheffer and Enrico Causici.[11]

The urban development of Washington also contributed to the flourishing of the arts in this period. In the 1850s, the city went through a spectacular physical transformation as streets were widened, regraded, and paved; gas lights and a major sewer system were installed; and low-lying areas were drained of swampy water and filled. In addition to improving the federal city, Congress passed appropriations bills that resulted in significant construction and expansion of federal buildings, including two new wings and a dome for the Capitol, a greenhouse and botanical gardens, a soldier's home, a hospital for the insane, and an expansion to the patent office (fig. 3.2).[12] With these new projects came a demand for monumental sculptures to decorate the exterior of the Capitol, as well as public parks and squares. Construction on the Capitol wings similarly resulted in commissions for interior paintings and murals to adorn the building.

The spate of government commissions both spoke to the country's maturation and offered an auspicious moment for American artists to pause and consider what a suitable decorative program for the nation's capital should comprise. The influential New York–based fine art journal *The Crayon* followed the artistic life of Washington with interest, particularly regarding this question. The editors opined, "No city in the country offers the peculiar advantages of Washington as a place for an artist to make himself known by his works, nor the like advantages as a field for the future development of national art."[13] Although they did not specifically define

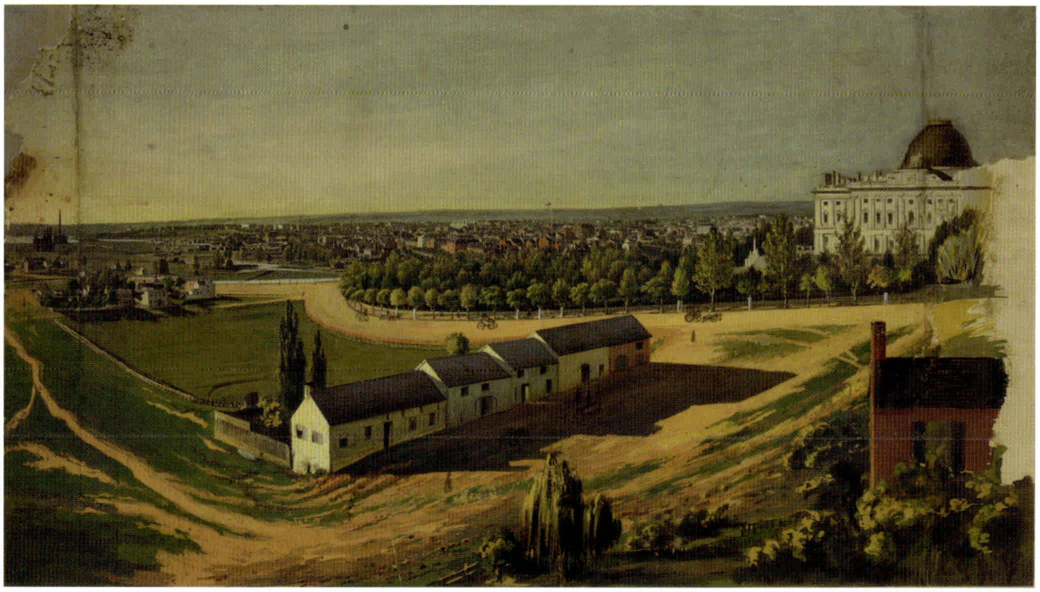

FIG. 3.2.
Augustus Kollner, *View of Washington Looking Northwest from Southeast of the U.S. Capitol*, c. 1846–1855. Watercolor and gouache on paper; 16¼ × 28⅛ in. (41.4 × 71.6 cm). Photograph by Will Brown, courtesy Library of Congress, Prints and Photographs Division.

a "national art," they repeatedly called for art in a contemporary style that depicted uniquely American subject matter. The journal was very critical of the design of the Washington Monument, for instance, because its classical form was an "unmeaning fabric," which suggested little about the life or achievements of George Washington.[14] A national art also needed to be steeped not just in significant historical events, but in a detailed knowledge of American culture. Speaking of the decoration of the Capitol, *The Crayon*'s editors wrote: "Familiarity with the implements of labor, as well as the character of the farmers, mechanics, etc. who use them; also the occupations and interest which the people in general are devoted to, renders the artist who has studied such material, the most suitable man of the time to make designs for the decoration of a national building."[15]

The frustration American artists felt over their marginalization at a time when they had so much to contribute led to the formation of the Washington Art Association. The association had a twofold mission: to support the development of art at the local (Washington city) and national levels.[16] The association made substantial progress on their first goal by mounting an annual exhibition and lecture series, and using proceeds from artworks sold to fund it. They furthered their second goal by sponsoring an annual art convention, which convened in Washington each winter from 1858 to 1860, and which, in turn, spawned the sister organization the National Art Association. The convention brought a small but influential number of artists to Washington, including John F. Kensett and George Caleb Bingham, to discuss the advancement of American art.[17] Much has been made over the National Art Association's success in persuading the government to establish a commission of three members to oversee decoration of the Capitol.[18] But the group's ambitions went beyond controlling the Capitol's decorative program. The association planned to establish a national art school to educate young artists in a comprehensive curriculum of material practice, theory, aesthetics, and science. The group succeeded in persuading the government to establish the U.S. Art Commission to oversee decoration of the Capitol, and in April 1859, Stanley, along with Horatio Stone, John Cranch, and J. G. Branch met with President James Buchanan to present him with the names of three nominees for the commission.[19] With greater control over the nation's artistic program, a thriving art association, and the promise of an official art school, American artists hoped to one day make Washington the nation's artistic capital, a city that could rival the great European art capitals of London and Paris. Stanley, thrilled with the possibilities, wrote sculptor Henry Kirke Brown shortly after the meeting with the president, saying Washington "is the place—this the theatre—*the Arena*—call it what you will: It is the fountain of our brightest hopes."[20]

JOHN MIX STANLEY IN WASHINGTON

Upon his arrival in Washington City, Stanley quickly established himself within the artistic milieu.[21] His first host, Charles Bird King, had spent much of his career in Washington painting, among other things, portraits of visiting Indian delegations for the Bureau of Indian Affair's Indian Gallery in the War Department. These portraits would join Stanley's at the Smithsonian in 1858, and suffer destruction in the fire in 1865. King knew Joseph Henry, as well as Seth Eastman, and likely helped broker introductions for his guest.[22] Stanley did not overstay his welcome with King but soon began renting a studio on Pennsylvania between 10th and 12th in the home of Seth L. Cole, a clerk for the census office.[23] This section of Pennsylvania Avenue was the center of Washington's entertainment and leisure in the period. Stanley's studio was a block and a half south of King's, and near to the homes and studios of other influential artists, including Eastman Johnson, John Cranch, William D. Washington, and Horatio Stone.[24] Stanley was also only blocks from the William Wilson Corcoran building on H and 13th, where the first meetings, lectures, and exhibitions of the Washington Art Association were held, and just across the street from its second location, on the north side of Pennsylvania between 10th and 11th.

Stanley's first major exhibition was, of course, the Indian Gallery, which was installed in the Smithsonian. Soon thereafter, Stanley gained an important commission to paint a portrait of General Winfield Scott (unlocated), who was then the Whig candidate for president. Commissioned by the Scott and Graham Club, an organization supporting Scott and his running mate, William A. Graham, the portrait must have helped Stanley to establish himself as a society portraitist, rather than just a specialist in Indian subjects. The painting was placed on exhibit in the window of his studio and announced in the paper. [25] Around that time, he also exhibited two new trapper scenes painted the previous year, *Flight of a Mountain Trapper*, 1851, and *The Trapper's Escape*, 1851 (both unlocated), in the window of Taylor and Maury's bookstore, located across the street from his studio.[26] These two paintings represented an attempt to expand his repertoire beyond Indian subjects and may well have been painted in response to the recent popularity of trappers as a subject. Charles Deas's *Long Jakes* made a splash at the 1845 Art-Union exhibition, and trapper imagery had grown so common by 1852 that one critic complained the subjects were "becoming painfully conspicuous in our exhibitions and shop-windows, [with their] glaring red shirts, buckskin breeches and very coarse prairie grass."[27] Stanley would have had an opportunity to view William Tylee Ranney's trapper scenes while he was in New York with his gallery in 1850–51. In June 1852, Stanley was at work on another new composition: *Black-Foot Indians in Ambush, Awaiting the Approach of an Emigrant Party* (unlocated), a scene of two Indian men "habited in the mountain costume, lying in wait with gun cocked and bowstring drawn for the approach of the mounted pioneer of an emigrant party."[28] He next took the

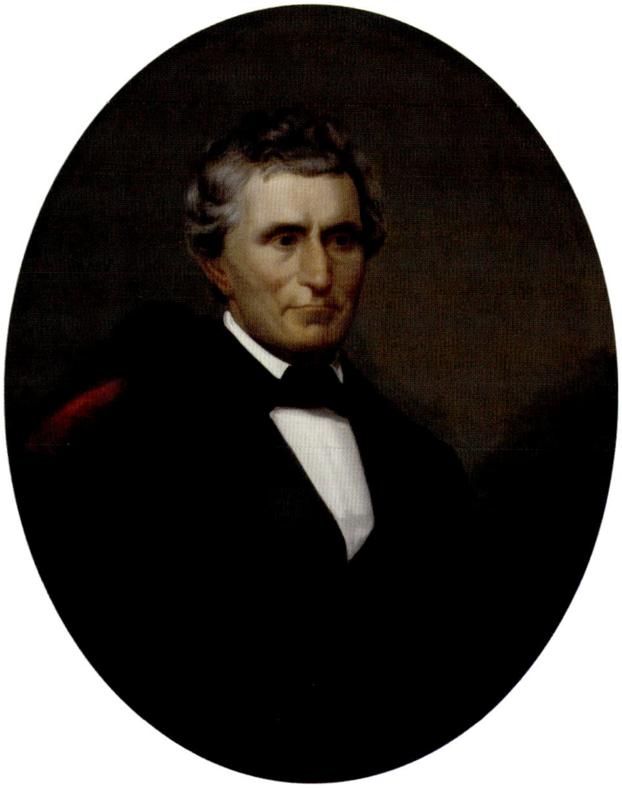

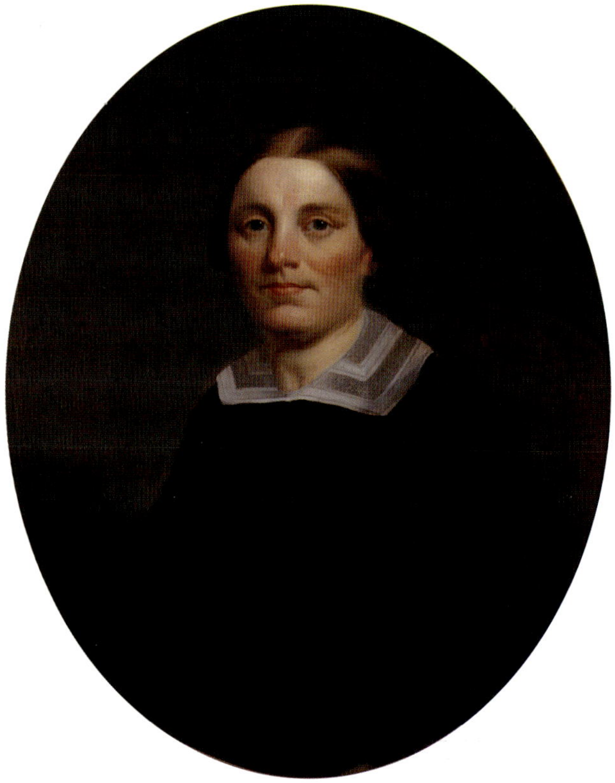

FIG. 3.3.
John Mix Stanley, *Berniah Willet*, c. 1853. Oil on canvas; 34⅛ × 26¾ in. (86.8 × 67.9 cm). Courtesy Smithsonian American Art Museum, Washington, D.C., gift of Dr. and Mrs. George A. Hass (1982.104.1)

FIG. 3.4.
John Mix Stanley, *Emeline Willet*, c. 1853. Oil on canvas; 34⅛ × 27⅛ in. (86.7 × 68.9 cm). Courtesy Smithsonian American Art Museum, Washington, D.C., gift of Dr. and Mrs. George A. Hass (1982.104.2)

opportunity to paint the five members of the Pueblo Tesuque delegation, who visited Washington in August 1852. He added all eight of these paintings to the Indian Gallery and included them in the catalogue the Smithsonian printed in December 1852, signaling his continued belief that a government purchase was his best avenue for patronage.[29]

After he prepared his first petition for government purchase of his portrait gallery in December 1852, Stanley prudently began to build a clientele for his non-Indian portraits. He capitalized on his location to garner a commission for what are probably his earliest located Washington pictures, portraits of Berniah and Emeline Willet, c. 1853 (fig. 3.3, cat. no. 069, and fig. 3.4, cat. no. 070). These, together with a portrait of Alice Caroline English and her brother, Morgan (fig. 3.5, cat. no. 071), inscribed to Ann Adeline Cole (wife of his landlord, Seth Cole) in 1853, present a good idea of Stanley's artistry upon his arrival, and offer a means of assessing his development in Washington. Stanley's portrait of Alice English, whom he would marry in 1854, and her brother, is unlocated. From a photograph, however, it is possible to see the result of Stanley's endeavors as a largely self-taught artist. Alice and Morgan's faces are rendered with great sensitivity. When compared to a photograph of Alice taken around the time of their marriage (fig. 6.3), Stanley's rendering is clearly a very good likeness. However, the portrait shows Stanley's difficulty in depicting anatomy. Alice's fingers, for instance, lack articulation, and her arms appear too long; Morgan's right arm is not convincingly foreshortened. Moreover, the figures each have a strong outline against a dark, uniform background, giving them a slightly flattened quality.

Some of the same characteristics are evident in the bust of Berniah Willet (fig. 3.3, cat. no. 069). The Willets were neighbors of Stanley's and could have passed the Cole's home on

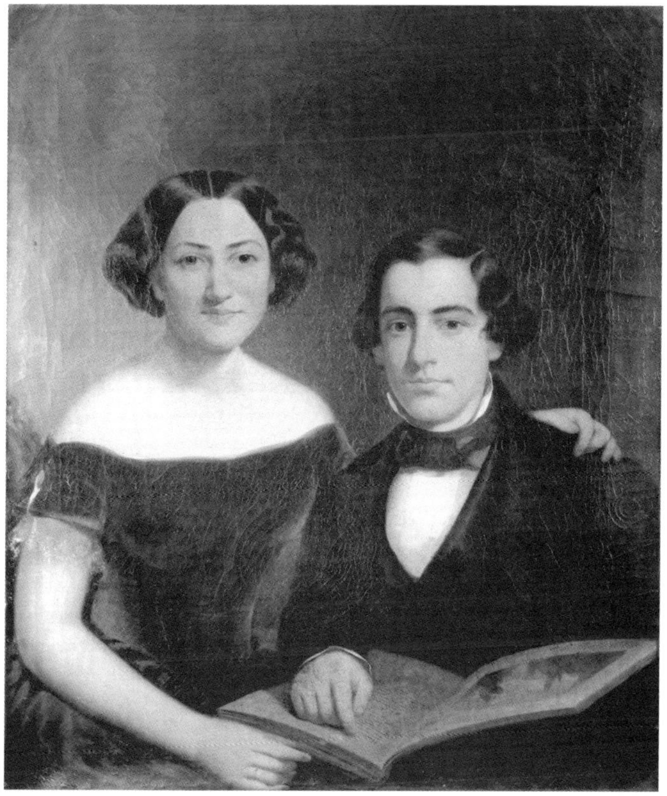

FIG. 3.5.
John Mix Stanley, *Alice Caroline and Morgan English*, 1853. Oil on canvas; 36 × 29 in. (91.4 × 73.7 cm). Private collection; courtesy Julie Schimmel Papers

their way to their carpentry shop each day. Berniah was said to have been a sober and learned man, and his portrait expresses as much.[30] He wears a proper black suit and a stern but thoughtful expression. Although his lapels have a satiny sheen, the rest of his jacket, the upholstery, and the carved wood frame of the chair appear relatively flat, with un-nuanced color. His face is rendered convincingly, particularly around his eyes, but the overly uniform beige coloring of his skin gives the painting a leaden quality akin to the work of early American self-taught portraitists Robert Wollaston or Robert Feke. Like John Singleton Copley before he traveled to London, Stanley never had the benefit of formal training, apart from his apprenticeship in Detroit. He did not have instruction in color theory, nor did he have access to life drawing classes. He traveled to Europe only after he had left Washington, and he spent much of his early career in Detroit or the Far West.[31] Stanley did tour his show in Troy, Baltimore, and New York City, each a developed art center. None of the cities, however, offered Washington's range of art on public display. In Washington, he could enjoy weekly, or even daily, access to the work of accomplished, European-trained portraitists. G. P. A. Healey exhibited in the Capitol rotunda in 1852, and there was, of course, King's outstanding collection of Indian portraits in the War Department as well as his own gallery, which included his own portraits and copies of portraits by Gilbert Stuart.[32] Sully's 1850 self-portrait was part of William Wilson Corcoran's collection, although it is not clear when Corcoran acquired it. These were in addition to complex figural compositions by Anton Raphael Mengs, Daniel Huntington, and Emanuel Leutze, as well as figurative sculptures that were on view within walking distance from Stanley's studio, in Corcoran's home.[33]

FIG. 3.6.
John Mix Stanley, *Senator Thomas Hart Benton*, 1857. Oil on canvas; 34 × 27 in. (86.4 × 68.8 cm). Courtesy Harry S. Truman Library and Museum, Independence, Missouri

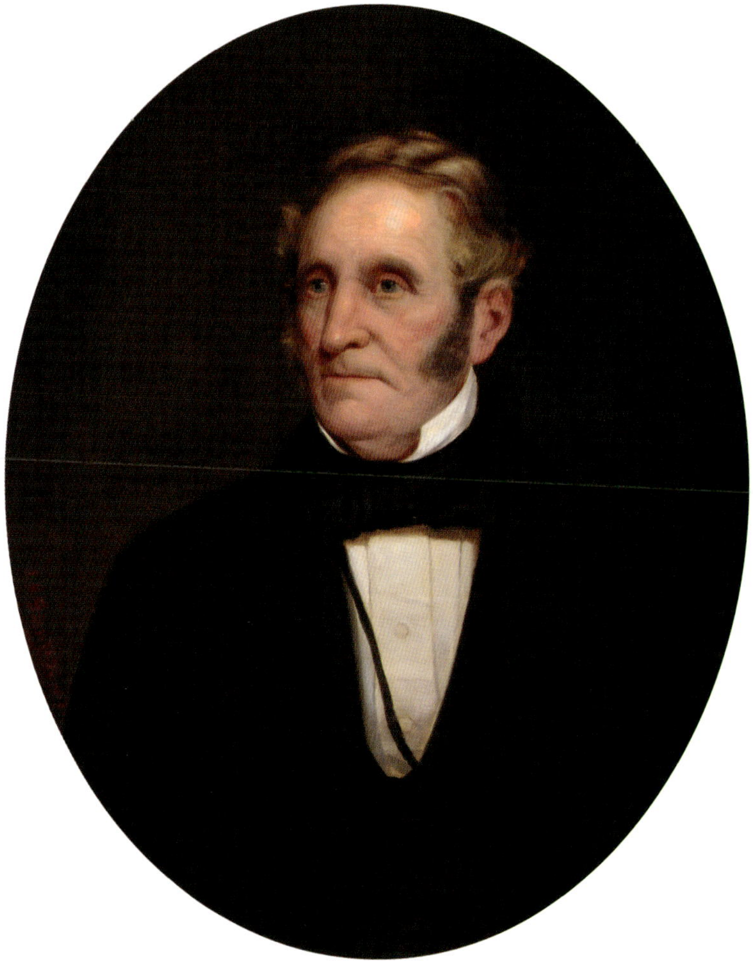

Stanley's portraiture showed a marked evolution during his stay in Washington, surely a result of his ability to study more sophisticated examples. In comparison to Berniah Willet, his portrait of Senator Thomas Hart Benton, painted in 1857 (fig. 3.6, cat. no. 157) and later exhibited at the Fourth Annual Exhibition of the Washington Art Association (1860), demonstrates the artist's maturation.[34] Stanley depicts more dramatic, directional lighting falling across Benton's face. His forehead shines, and a fleck at the end of his nose, a favorite conceit of Gilbert Stuart, enlivens his face. Stanley's use of color is much more sophisticated as well. Shades of brown, umber, and white model the folds of Benton's skin, while the sitter's cheeks flush with a highly modulated pink that is picked up in his ears. Stanley's official portrait of Secretary of the Interior Caleb Blood Smith, painted in 1861 (fig. 3.7, cat. no. 170), shows the artist's new skill in realizing the human form. Smith's pose is more relaxed and convincing as he leans back in his chair, his hands resting on the arms. His limbs are better proportioned than those of the Englishes, and his hands are fully articulated with convincing renditions of knuckles, fingernails, and veins. Dramatic lighting here falls across Smith's head and hands, throwing a shadow across the book on the table beside him. The dark green of the chair upholstery is worked into the black of the sitter's suit, illuminating an array of creases and folds, which adds interest to the otherwise dark planes.

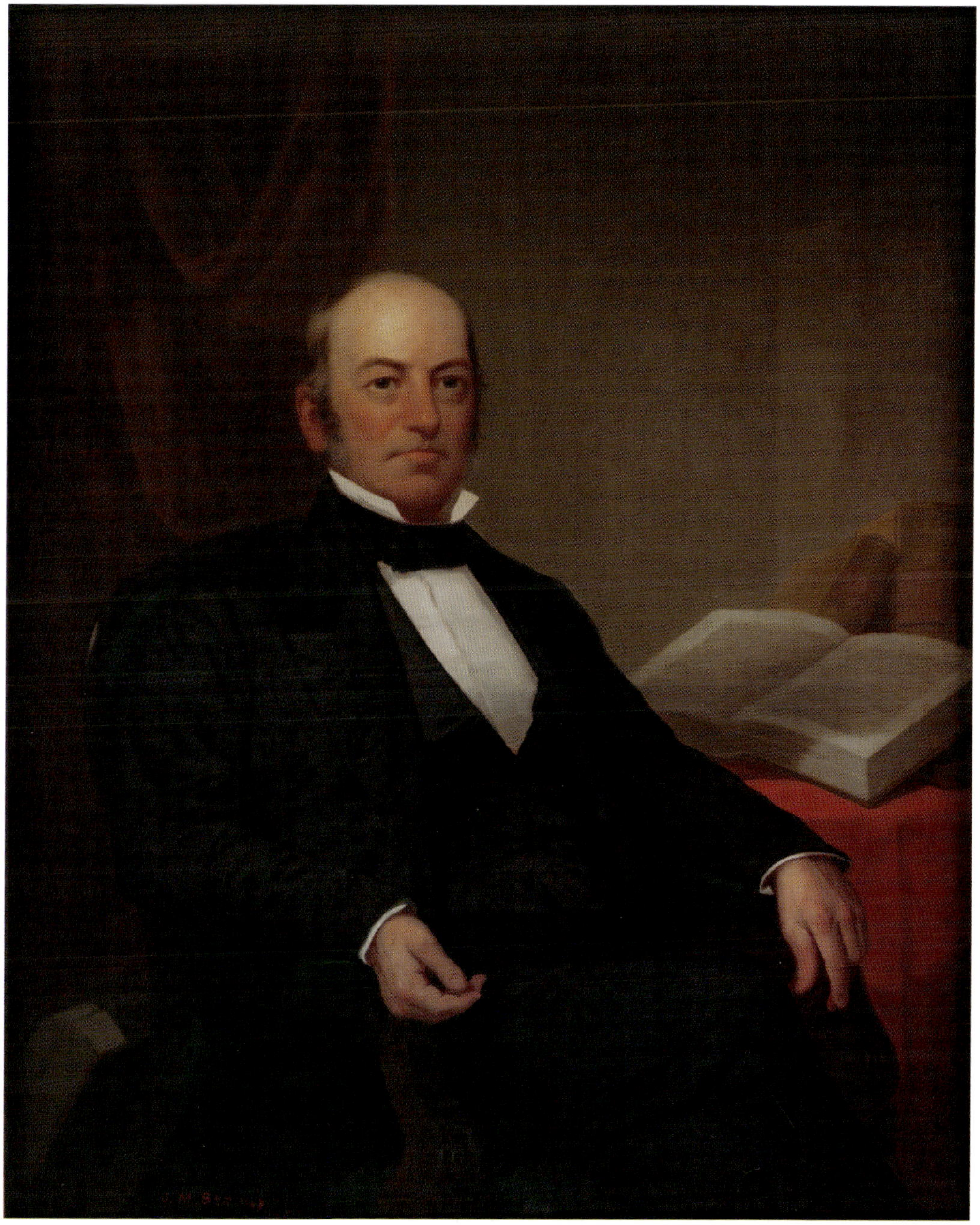

FIG. 3.7.
John Mix Stanley, *Caleb Blood Smith*, 1861. Oil on canvas; 50 × 40 in. (127.0 × 101.6 cm). Courtesy U.S. Department of the Interior, Washington, D.C.

Stanley's progress in his western genre was also marked. In about 1853, he painted a second version of a work in the Indian Gallery, *Black Knife, Apache War Chief Reconnoitering the Command of General Kearny On His March from Santa Fe to California, Version II* (fig. 3.8, cat. no. 072). He exhibited the painting at the Metropolitan Mechanics Institute, apparently in hopes of selling it outside of the Indian Gallery.[35] Its composition and dimensions are virtually identical to *Black Knife*, 1850 (cat. no. 064) one of the few surviving Indian Gallery paintings, suggesting the possibility that Stanley used a mechanical device or photographic means of reproducing the painting. However, there are important differences in the overall rendering of the

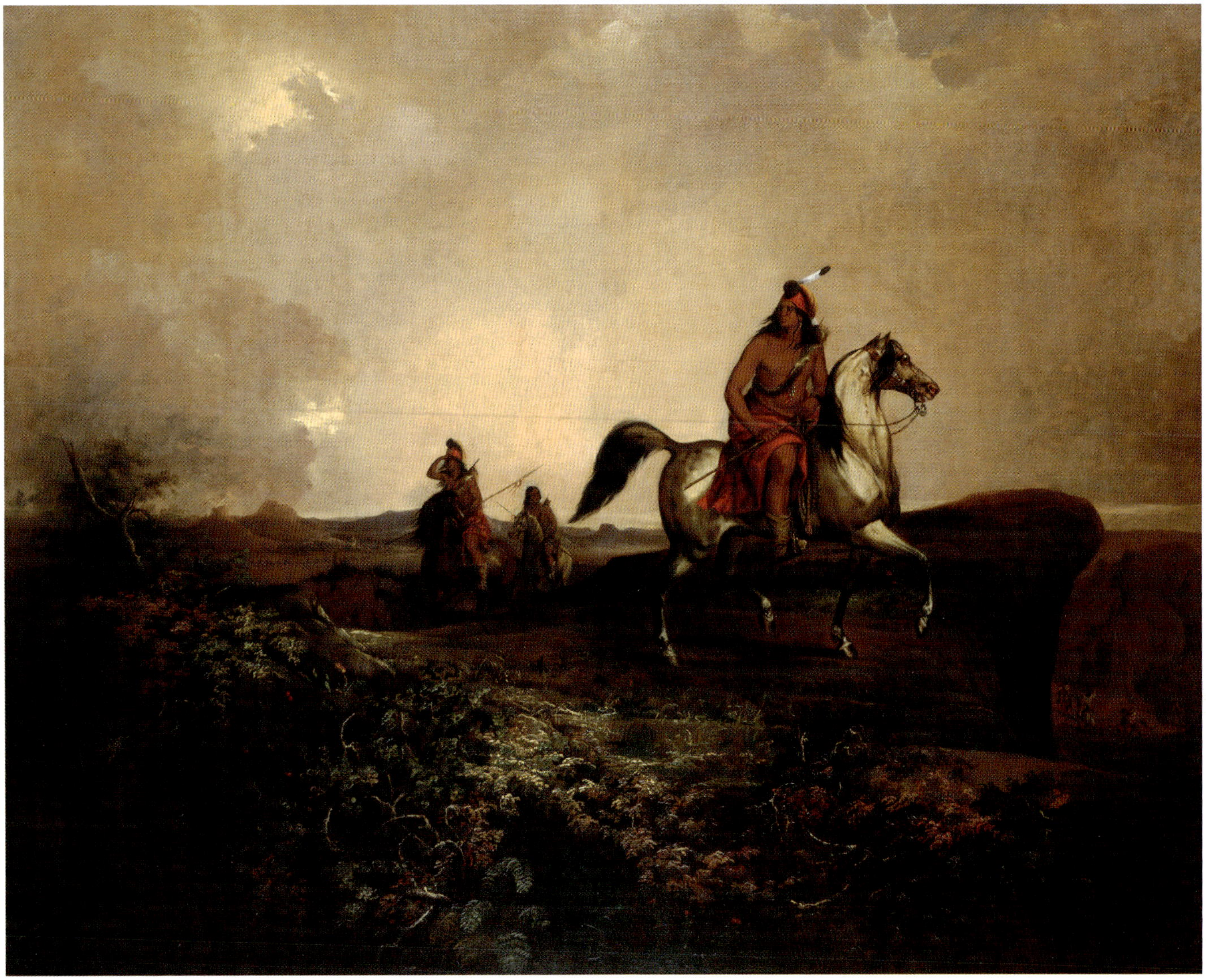

FIG. 3.8.
John Mix Stanley, *Black Knife, Apache War Chief Reconnoitering the Command of General Kearny On His March from Santa Fe to California, Version II,* 1853. Oil on canvas; 41½ × 50 in. (105.4 × 127.0 cm). Private collection; photograph courtesy Gerald Peters Gallery, Santa Fe, New Mexico

forms. Stanley has succeeded in softening the contours of the horse in the later version so that it does not stand out as starkly from the background. He also employs more tonal coloring, making the distant rock formation match the shade of brown in the foreground. Likewise, the two Indians on the rise behind Black Knife are now a more convincing light brown than the grayish shade he employed in the earlier painting. His foliage is also more elaborate and diverse, a quality seen in many of his paintings in the Washington period, perhaps a result of his study of numerous landscapes on view in the city. The effect of these changes is a more sophisticated and unified overall effect, which resulted in a more convincing evocation of three-dimensional space.

Stanley also began to devise more sophisticated compositions for his paintings, including composing genre scenes rather than simple portraits. The catalogue description of Stanley's Indian Gallery, as well as a surviving photograph (fig. 3.9) and engraving (fig. 3.1), all show that the majority of works in his Indian Gallery were bust-length portraits.[36] The narrative scenes and full-length portraits were fewer. Among these were the five salvaged from the fire and now in the collection of the Smithsonian: *International Indian Council*, 1843 (cat. no. 014); *Ko-rak-koo-kiss, a Towoccono Warrior*, 1844 (cat. no. 017); *A Buffalo Hunt*, 1845 (cat. no. 026); *An Osage Scalp Dance*, 1845 (cat. no. 025); and *Black Knife*, 1850 (cat. no. 064). Indeed, Stanley confessed to a reporter from the *Washington Sentinel* that he viewed his work on the Indian Gallery as incomplete and wished to expand his artistry beyond the confines of the portraits or "memorials." Stanley "had preserved the portraits of individuals of distinction, many of whom now traverse 'the happy hunting grounds in the spirit land,' but he desired to portray to the civilized world the Home of the Red Man, and his manner of life in that home."[37]

Stanley had been offered the opportunity to observe and record more facets of American Indian life when in 1853 he took a seven-month excursion from Washington to join the Isaac Stevens expedition for the Pacific Railroad Survey along the northernmost route between the 47th and 49th parallels. The trip had a profound impact on Stanley's work, providing him with a rich cache of subject matter, commissions, and inspiration for new projects, including a monumental forty-two panel panorama, *Scenes and Incidents of Stanley's Western Wilds*, that he undertook the spring following his return.[38] As Hassrick notes in this volume, the panorama gave him the opportunity to expand his narrative repertoire and allowed him to portray the Sioux, Blackfeet, and Flatheads he met on the trip as he chose, freed from the conventions of the Indian Gallery. His work on the panorama was followed by a commission from the government to prepare illustrations for several volumes of the Pacific Railroad Survey. The illustrations, which included landscape and genre scenes, also expanded Stanley's range of subjects.

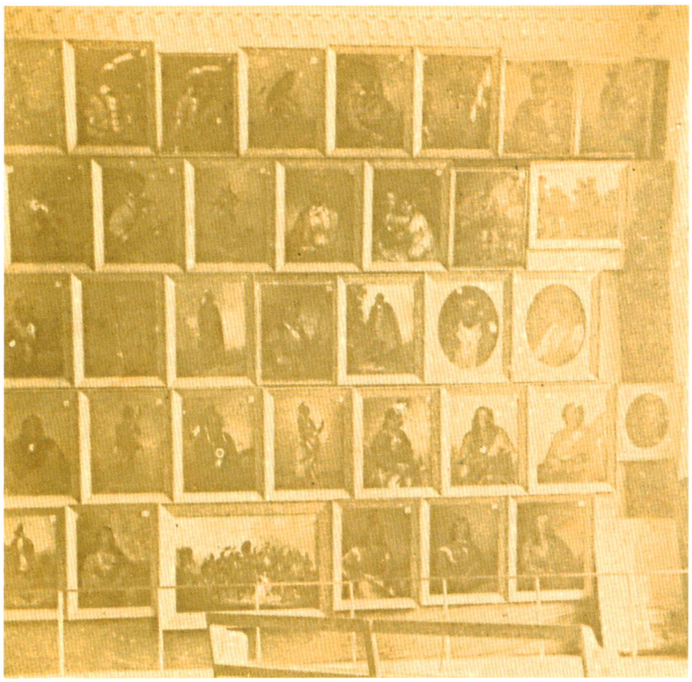

FIG. 3.9.
American Stereoscopic Co., Langenheim, Lloyd & Co., *[John Mix Stanley] Picture Gallery, Smithsonian Institute*, 1858. Albumen print mounted on cardboard; 3¼ × 6¾ in. (8.3 × 17.1 cm). Courtesy Smithsonian Institution Castle Collection, Washington, D.C. (SI.2004.021)

This spate of new and challenging work undertaken within the artistic milieu of Washington led to marked developments in his method of composition. His earlier *A Buffalo Hunt*, 1845 (fig. 3.10, cat. no. 026), for instance, is a simple arrangement with buffalo, horse, and rider oriented at a slight diagonal, but in two successive planes. The hunter's body is turned sharply to the side, so that the full of his back is in line with the horse's body. *The Buffalo Hunt*, 1855 (fig. 3.11, cat. no. 138), painted following the Stevens expedition, shows a more complicated grouping. Stanley portrays a bison charging diagonally from the lower left to gore a white horse, which lies on the ground facing diagonally outward. His rider struggles to free himself from his fallen mount, while his companion's horse rears behind him. A third mounted hunter is about to thrust his lance into the side of the bison, creating a variety of pose and action that heightens the drama of the scene.

BARTER FOR A BRIDE

Stanley also began to create more nuanced narratives in his paintings immediately following his return from the Stevens expedition. One such painting, *A Family Group (Barter for a Bride)* (fig. 3.12, cat. no. 145), is not signed or dated, but there are several reasons to believe it was executed sometime in 1854–57. First, it depicts the Blackfeet against the backdrop of Great Falls just west of Fort Benton in present-day Montana, an area Stanley first visited with Stevens in 1853.[39] The Blackfeet also became a focus for Stanley following the trip. He devoted about one-

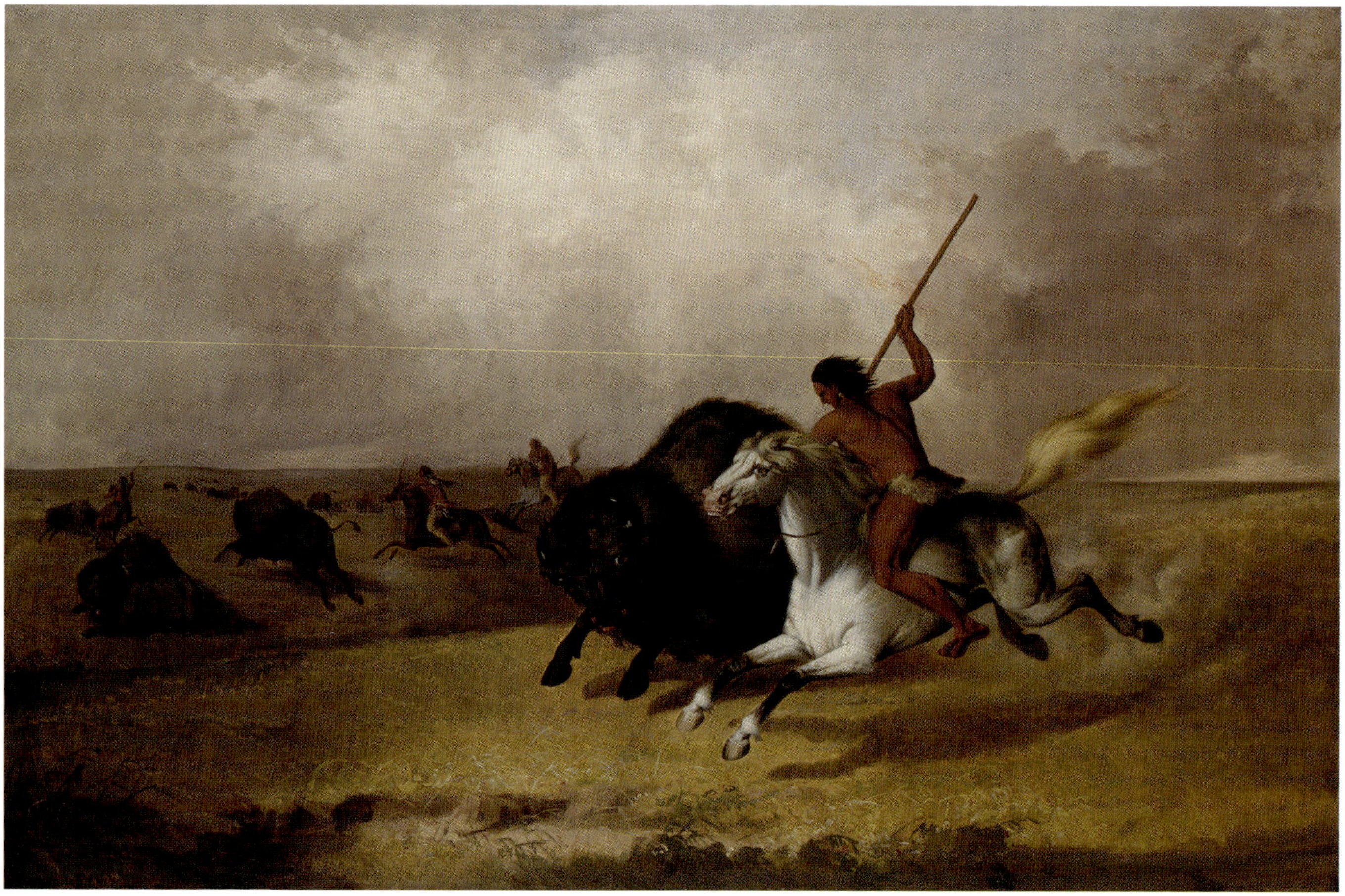

FIG. 3.10.
John Mix Stanley, *A Buffalo Hunt*, 1845. Oil on canvas; 40½ × 60¾ in. (102.9 × 154.3 cm). Courtesy Smithsonian American Art Museum, Washington, D.C., gift of the Misses Henry (1985.66.248.932)

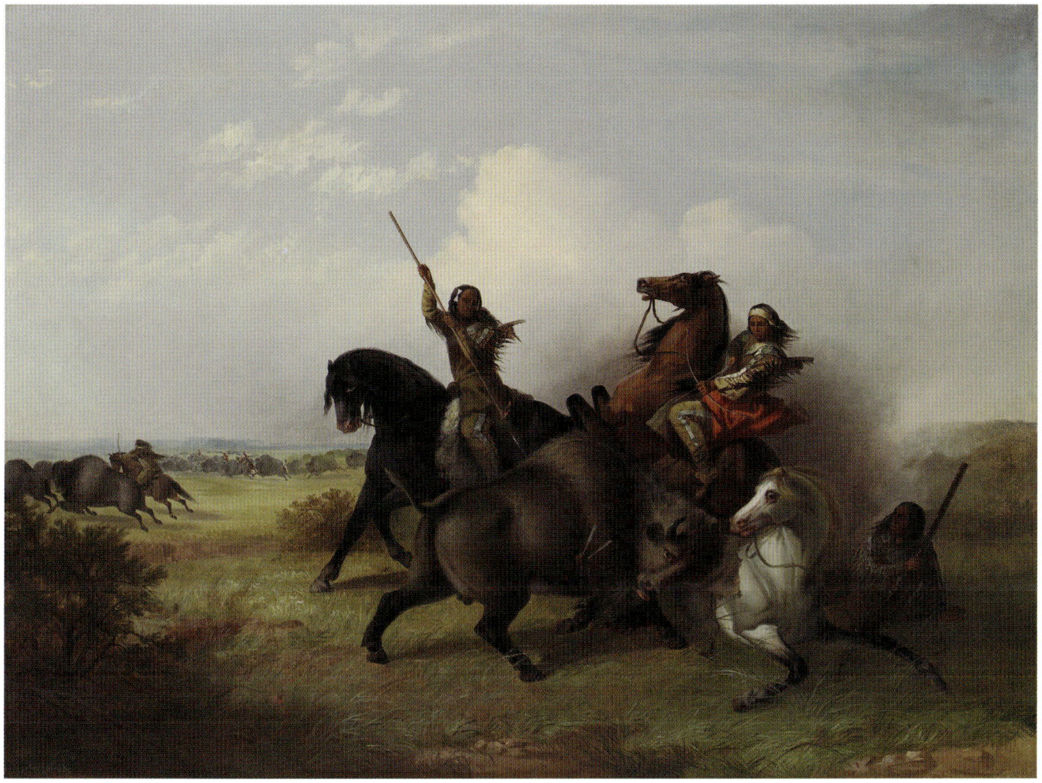

FIG. 3.11.
John Mix Stanley, *The Buffalo Hunt*, 1855. Oil on canvas; 29¾ × 39 in. (75.6 × 99.1 cm). Courtesy Crystal Bridges Museum of American Art, Bentonville, Arkansas

FIG. 3.12.
John Mix Stanley, *A Family Group, (Barter for a Bride)*, c. 1856. Oil on canvas; 40 × 63 in. (101.6 × 160.0 cm). Courtesy Diplomatic Reception Room, U.S. Department of State, Washington, D.C., gift of Morris and Gwendolyn Cafritz Foundation, 1965

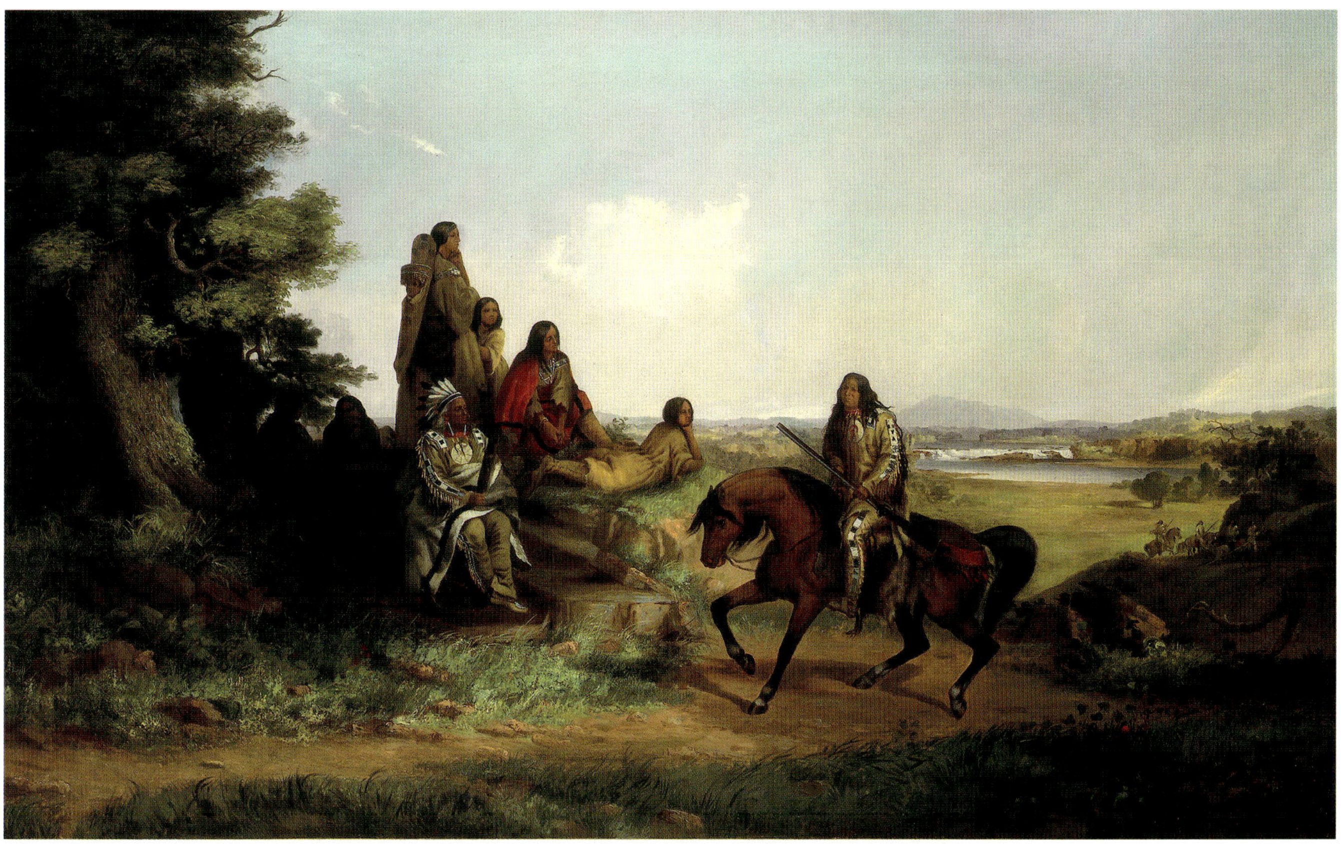

third of the panels of *Scenes and Incidents of Stanley's Western Wilds* to the Blackfeet and Fort Benton.[40] In addition, many of his watercolors for the railroad survey, most of which were executed in 1855, depict scenes related to the Blackfeet.[41] Stanley also embarked on three medium to large genre paintings of the Blackfeet in 1855, including *Crossing the Milk River* (cat. no. 140), *The Buffalo Hunt* (fig. 3.11, cat. no. 138), and *Halting to Smoke* (cat. no. 128). He spent most of 1856 painting portraits for the Department of the Interior and the Department of Justice, but three more canvases related to the Blackfeet appear in 1857, including *View on Milk River* (cat. no. 155) and *The Last of Their Race* (cat. no. 159). Finally, if the painting depicts a marriage negotiation, as I suggest below, Stanley had good reason to be interested in the subject of marriage during this period. Long a bachelor, the forty-year-old Stanley finally married Alice English in May 1854. His journal, and his extensive correspondence with Alice, show that marriage was very much on his mind during his travels with Stevens and certainly would have been in the years immediately following.[42]

In *A Family Group (Barter for a Bride)* (cat. no. 145), Stanley portrays what could be interpreted as a marriage negotiation unfolding against an expansive landscape. A Blackfeet man, dressed in elaborately quilled clothing that bespeaks his wealth, arrives on horseback before a family group. Coming up the hillside in the distance is a line of men on horseback, pulling travois packed with what are possibly gifts that would be exchanged as part of the proposal or claim of marriage. The presumed father of the bride sits on a rock in the foreground. He wears a headdress and holds an eagle wing staff, suggesting his status as a leader.[43] His hunting shirt, which includes a central sun-sign medallion and blue and white quill work along the arms, is based on one Stanley collected on his trip (see chapter 4, fig. 4.3).[44] Located behind him are women of varying ages, probably including his wife or sisters, who would have consulted on a marriage negotiation.

As noted above, the painting marks a significant shift in Stanley's oeuvre toward greater narrative complexity. Canvases such as *The Buffalo Hunt*, 1855 (fig. 3.11, cat. no. 138), or the earlier *Osage Scalp Dance*, 1845 (cat. no. 025), showing a woman defending herself and her child from club-wielding Osage, are narrative-driven paintings in which figures react to obvious and imminent threats. In *A Family Group (Barter for a Bride)*, however, the protagonists display a wide range of emotions that hint at characterizations and introduce ambiguity into the scene. The presumed bride, who lies on the ground, chin in hand, appears coy or disinterested in her suitor and his entourage. The elaborately dressed woman behind her, perhaps her mother, looks on with a tilted head as if to express sympathy or at least patience with her daughter. Behind her stands a young woman, perhaps the bride's older sister, with an infant in a cradleboard and a second daughter leaning against her. Standing calm and erect, she models the stability of the married state that could result from the young woman's assent, but her posture, chin in hand, also expresses suspense as to the outcome of the visit.

If the painting depicts an Indian marriage, it suggests the influence of another well-known painter of Indian genre and a contemporary of Stanley's, Alfred Jacob Miller (1810–1874). Miller painted a total of seven versions of his best-known composition *Trapper's Bride* between 1841 and 1857.[45] Stanley surely saw the 1852 version of the painting (fig. 3.13), depicting the marriage of an Indian woman and a white trapper, when it was exhibited with his portrait of *Black Knife* at the Metropolitan Mechanics Institute in Washington in February 1853, and he likely met Miller himself at one of the venues at which they both exhibited, if he had not already visited the artist in his studio in Baltimore.[46]

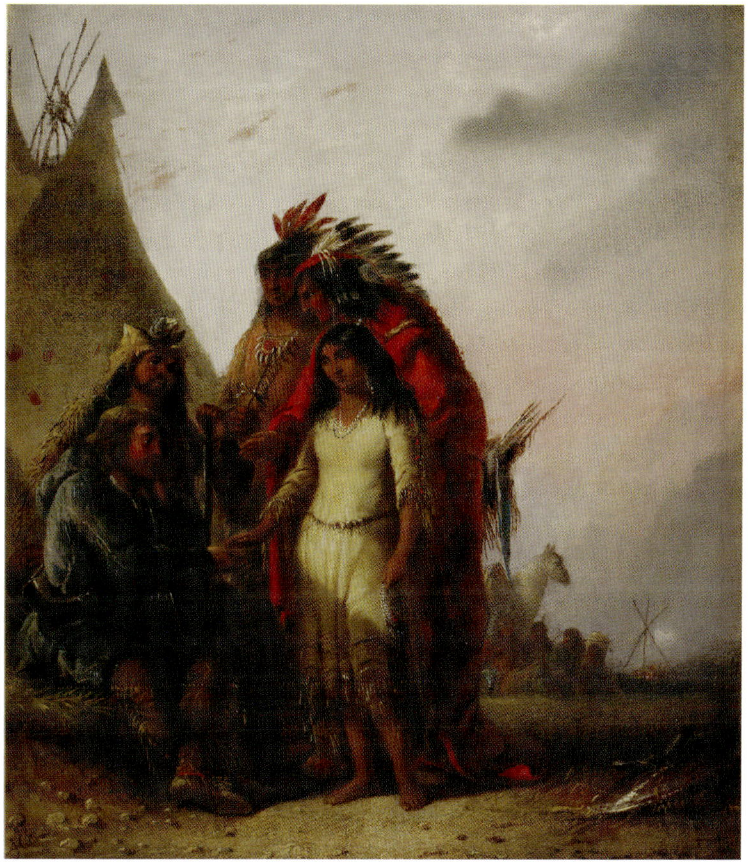

FIG. 3.13.
Alfred Jacob Miller, *Trapper's Bride*, c. early 1840s. Oil on canvas; 19 × 16 in. (48.3 × 40.6 cm). Courtesy Hunter Museum of American Art, Chattanooga, Tennessee, gift of Mr. and Mrs. Scott L. Probasco, Jr. (1991.24)

Miller's success with the subject of Indian marriage, as well as with other scenes depicting the human side of frontier life, such as romantic engagements, diplomatic negotiations, or sporting events, could not have been lost on Stanley. *Trapper's Bride* won a first diploma at the Mechanics Institute, and Miller had already sold four versions of the scene to patrons in Baltimore.[47]

Miller excelled at creating scenes in which characterizations drive the narrative. His watercolor *Indian Courtship*, c. 1858 (fig. 3.14) for instance, portrays a young woman shrinking from a suitor who presents a box full of beads and ornaments to her father. Miller communicates the woman's reluctance and modesty through her posture. She curls inward, her knees drawn up, her arm wrapped around her torso, and her eyes cast downward. The father's intense focus on the treasure and the suitor's confident posture contrast her fear and generate a conventional, sentimental narrative about the vulnerability of women.[48] In *A Family Group (Barter for a Bride)* (cat. no. 145), Stanley stops well short of the sentimentality Miller portrays. While the poses of the bride and the woman behind her introduce narrative complexity, and there is no obvious outcome signaled, the other figures nevertheless lack the expressive gestures of the figures in *Indian Courtship*. Without clearly identified villains and heroes, Stanley's painting is less melodramatic than Miller's, but it nevertheless remains more focused on the interior life of its protagonists than his earlier paintings were.

FIG. 3.14.
Alfred Jacob Miller,
Indian Courtship, c. 1858.
Watercolor on paper; 9 × 11 7/16 in. (22.9 × 29.1 cm).
Courtesy The Walters Art Museum, Baltimore, Maryland (37.1940.168)

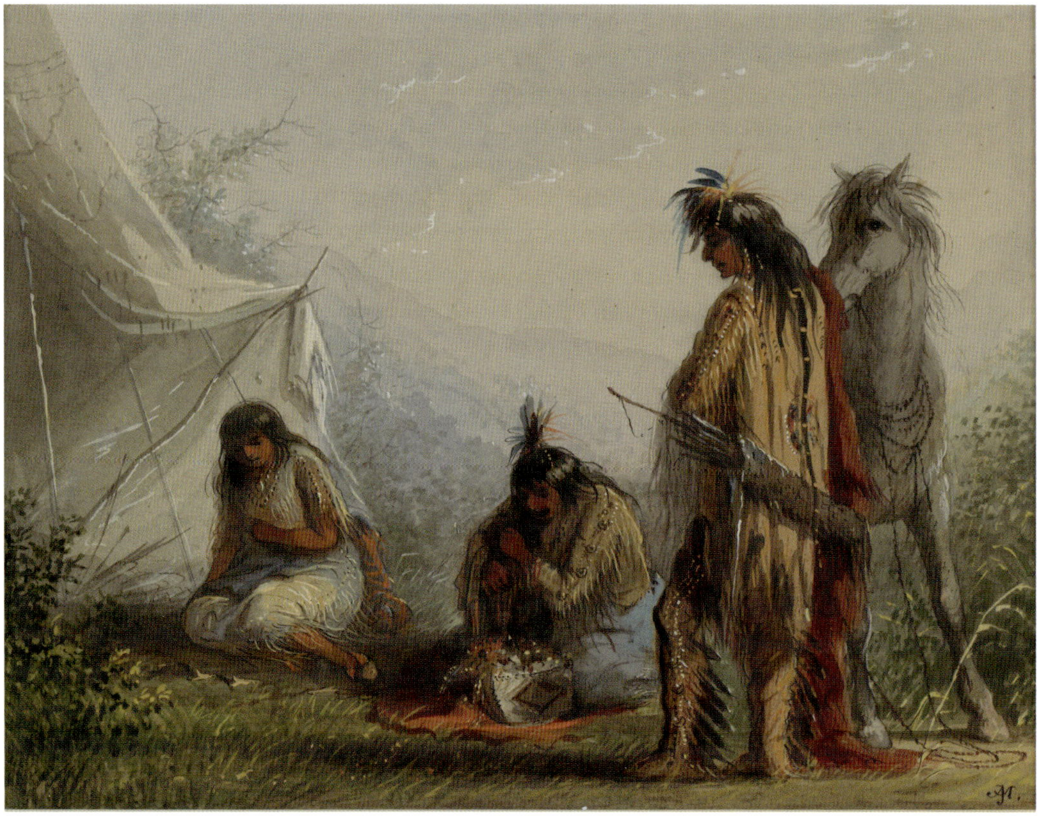

Lack of melodrama notwithstanding, the painting marks another significant moment in Stanley's career, when the artist began to move outside of the restrictive parameters of the Indian Gallery paintings to create Indian genre that engaged more directly with life and events in Washington, D.C. The period in which Stanley was executing his series of Blackfeet paintings was also a significant one for Blackfeet-U.S. relations. The Blackfeet had been in conflict with the United States since the Lewis and Clark expedition and had the reputation in Washington of being "predatory and intractable savages."[49] They had hitherto been known as the "neglected tribe" because few white Americans visited the region where they lived along the Upper Missouri River, in what is now north-central Montana. In 1853, they were one of the few Indian peoples not to have entered into a major treaty or enjoyed diplomatic relations with the U.S. government.[50] Although Stevens's mission was to locate a suitable railroad route along the 47th–49th parallel, no route would be viable if it could not be secured from attacks by the Blackfeet. In fact, in absence of a treaty, Stevens's party was itself in danger from the Blackfeet as it traveled from Fort Union to the Columbia River. Stevens, who also served as first governor of Washington Territory, understood the importance of good diplomacy, so before he embarked from Saint Paul, he stopped in Saint Louis to engage Alexander Culbertson, and then at Fort Union, Culbertson's Blackfeet wife Natoyist-Siksina' (Natawista).[51] Culbertson was a partner in the American Fur Company and a longtime agent to the Blackfeet. Together with Natawista, he had been instrumental in negotiating the establishment of Fort Benton in Blackfeet territory in 1847, as well as in the negotiation of the Fort Laramie Treaty of 1851. The couple was deeply invested in improving Blackfeet-U.S. relations and opening the Upper Missouri to the American fur trade.[52] Stanley himself played a crucial diplomatic role in gathering members of the Piegan (a sub-group of Blackfeet) and escorting them to Fort Benton to meet with Stevens, an experience he sketched during the excursion, described in a narrative for the government report, and documented in his panorama.[53]

Building on their diplomatic efforts at Fort Benton, Stevens asked Culbertson to come to Washington in spring 1854 (possibly with Natawista) to lobby Congress for an appropriation of $67,000 to $100,000 to cover gifts, transportation, and other costs of a major treaty council arranged for the following summer.[54] Although members of the Indian Appropriations Committee accused Stevens of lobbying on behalf of an appropriation that would bolster the fortunes of the northern railroad route, Stevens argued that a treaty with the Blackfeet was necessary to preserve peace among the western Indians, and thus the viability of all other Indian treaties, as well as to ensure the safety of Americans traveling overland to Washington Territory. Much of the debate centered on whether it would be prudent to enter into treaties with "wild" Indian tribes as opposed to more "civilized" groups who had closer contact with white Americans.[55] An editorial published in advance that supported the appropriation conceded that the Blackfeet were "the terrors of the mountains and the plains" and "as perfect specimens of the savage in his primitive condition as can be found on the North American continent." But the author, "R. S." claimed to have witnessed successful negotiations with them at Fort Benton: "They listened to [Stevens's] remarks with deep and marked attention. The system of revenge, robbery and warfare which had ever characterized their diplomacy, would not bear the scrutiny of clear-headed, intellectual reasoning." As a consequence of Stevens's negotiations, R. S. noted that the Piegan delegation called back two war parties en route to battle and pledged peaceful relations with neighboring Crows and Flatheads, leading the writer to conclude "by honest treaties, kept in good faith, between them and the whites, much good humanity can result."[56]

Given his participation in the expedition, Stanley was certainly aware of the debates about the Blackfeet in summer 1854. But a more direct reminder came in the form of a visit from his "old friend" Culbertson in August that year. In Stanley's studio, Culbertson saw the artist at work on a view of Fort Benton, a panel from the final third of the panorama. The artist asked Culbertson if he remembered it. "Remember!" Culbertson was said to have replied, "why it is my own home; the fort I built myself," adding wistfully, "you make me long to be off over the plains again."[57] Although the account gives no further information about their conversation, it is difficult to imagine that the two did not discuss Culbertson's efforts on behalf of the Blackfeet, particularly because Stanley played a role in setting up the council Culbertson sought to fund. Certainly the publicity around their meeting, described in the paper and included by the artist in his personal scrapbook, helped both men in their projects. Through association with Culbertson, Stanley gained publicity and a stamp of authenticity for his portrayal of the Blackfeet in his paintings and the panorama. Culbertson, in his turn, had the benefit of a positive visual portrayal of the terrain and people whose interests he promoted. Indeed, any visual information about the Blackfeet served to familiarize a Washington audience with them and helped to advance the case for funding their treaty council.

Stanley and Culbertson's interests in the Blackfeet certainly converged around *A Family Group (Barter for a Bride)* (cat. no. 145), which depicted Piegan people in the midst of their own successful negotiation of marriage. But their mutual interest is also evidenced by the painting itself. Stanley's model for the woman shown wrapped in the red striped blanket was Culbertson's wife, Natawista.[58] Stanley painted Culbertson's portrait (cat. no. 080) in 1854, probably during the trader's time in Washington. If Natawista accompanied Culbertson to Washington (her family recollected that the couple always traveled together), she could have sat for Stanley at that time, or he could have made studies of her the year previous.[59] Stanley also used Natawista and her brother, the prominent chief Seen From Afar, as models for the standing and seated figures at the far right in both versions of *The Last of Their Race* (cat. nos. 159 and 165).[60] Culbertson clearly endorsed the painting because he commissioned the second version of *The Last of Their Race* (fig. 4.2) for his newly built mansion in Peoria in 1859 and exhibited it at the Illinois State Fair.[61]

Natawista's presence in Stanley's painting signals its larger message about Blackfeet-U.S. diplomacy. *A Family Group (Barter for a Bride)* (cat. no. 145) shows Piegan people negotiating out in the open, instead of within the village, where such arrangements would actually have been conducted.[62] Stanley presents the meeting against the enticing backdrop of an abundant landscape, with its varied foliage, distant mountains, plateaus, and a dramatic waterfall. Like the landscape that is spread out before her, the bride is herself a kind of tabula rasa in her plain buckskin dress, leggings, and moccasins. Her clothing is not embellished with the elk's teeth or beads a successful Piegan hunter or white trader could offer her, nor does her dress contain the elaborate quillwork seen on her mother's. In the logic of Stanley's narrative, both the suitor and the white settler will engage in domesticating and embellishing the woman/landscape that lies before them. Appropriately, the men in the painting are far from the popular characterizations of Blackfeet marauders and horse thieves. The elder, seated chief is circumspect, demonstrating the kind of careful attention that R. S. saw in the Piegans at Fort Benton. Young, unmarried Blackfeet men were singled out in the press and in congressional debates as the main threat to successful treaties.[63] Here, however, the Piegan suitor in *A Family Group* (*Barter for a Bride)* behaves respectfully, his horse suitably reigned in and his gun pointed upward. He is accompanied not by false promises, but by tangible goods with which to demonstrate his respect for the chief's authority and to recognize the stature of his prospective family. Moreover, he has had significant accomplishments in battle that entitle him to wear his own embellished hunting shirt. As the editorial penned by R. S. counters the negative image of the Blackfeet, so too *A Family Group (Barter for a Bride)* presents us with an image of harmony and domesticity from a seasoned traveler with first-hand knowledge of this heretofore "neglected" people.

THE TRAPPER'S CABIN

Stanley was continuing to engage with politics, as well as with art interests in Washington, when he painted what would be his most successful Washington painting, *The Trapper's Cabin*, 1858 (fig. 3.15, cat. no. 163). Although the canvas was relatively small in comparison to *A Family Group (Barter for a Bride)* (cat. no. 145), Stanley's introduction of the painting at the newly opened exhibition space of Franklin Philp's Booksellers on Pennsylvania Avenue, followed by exhibition in Baltimore at the Maryland Institute for the Promotion of the Mechanic Arts, signaled his high ambitions for it.[64] A critic for the *Evening Star* called the picture, "the best thing so far coming off his easel. The time will arrive when, as a faithful and yet thoroughly artistic memento of American border life, it will sell for many times its weight in gold."[65] In December, the painting was purchased at auction by William Wilson Corcoran, who, in turn, loaned it to the Third Annual Exhibition of the Washington Art Association in 1859, the most celebrated of the institution's shows.[66]

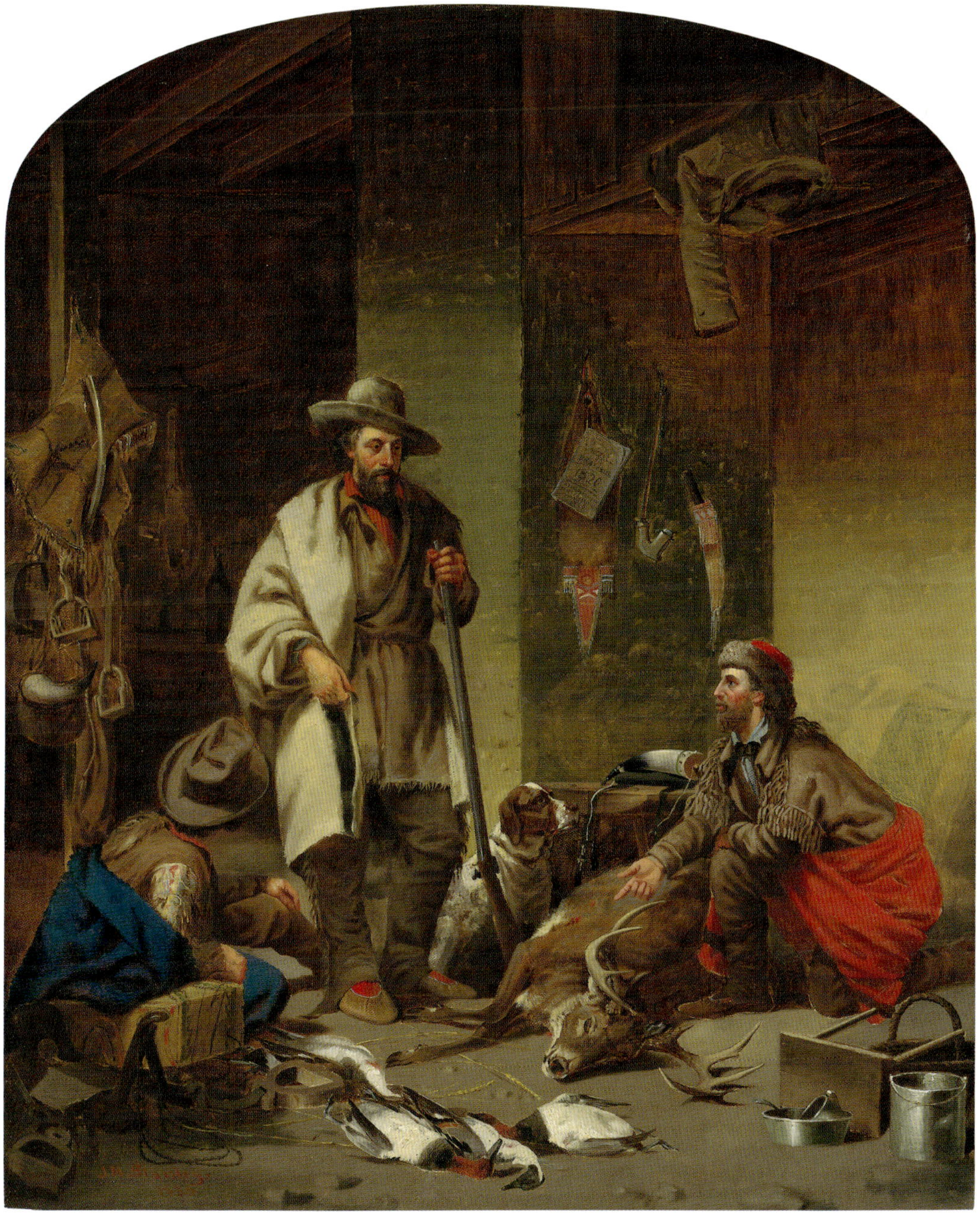

FIG. 3.15.
John Mix Stanley,
The Trapper's Cabin,
1858. Oil on canvas;
36 × 29 in. (91.5 × 73.5 cm).
Courtesy National Gallery
of Art, Washington, D.C.,
Corcoran Collection, gift of
William Wilson Corcoran

Although it is ostensibly a western scene showing three trappers and their game, the painting is a quintessentially Washington picture insofar as it deals with ideas of central importance to the city at the time. Stanley shows three figures in an interior, a setting that was uncommon for him and for scenes of trappers generally since most trappers were necessarily itinerant or spent the off-season in Native American villages.[67] Despite its title, it is more likely Stanley depicted a fort than a cabin. For trappers (who traveled the streams and rivers trapping beaver) and hunters (who were employed by the fur companies to provide meat for the fort), fur trade forts, not cabins, were the nexus of their activities. Moreover, the architecture, with its high ceilings and storage cupboards, resembles the construction of a fort. The pintail and scaup ducks shown on the floor in front of the hunters are native to the Great Lakes region, and the otter skin tobacco pouch hanging on the wall behind the standing figure is also characteristic of bags made by the Dakota who lived in the area, making it possible that Stanley referred to old studies or daguerreotypes from his time in Fort Snelling in 1839.[68] The three men are dressed in a typical frontier mix of fringed buckskin leggings and moccasins and Anglo-American cloth shirts and trade blankets. They are gathered around a large white-tailed deer and some ducks and surrounded by characteristic objects of western life: a tin mess kit at the lower right; a decorated buckskin case, saddle, and beaver trap along the left; and an elaborate otter skin bag, calumet, and knife sheath hanging on the wall above the kneeling figure on the right.

Stanley's detailed depiction of the objects such as the otter skin bag might at first seem to express the same ethnographic interest found in his Indian portraits. A contemporary reviewer noted the painting was "admirable in design, costume, and all the accessories, and with a minute attention to details not always followed by this artist."[69] The painting's title, however, points to a more complex, metaphorical meaning than the artist had heretofore attempted in his work. First called *The Trapper's Cabin* when exhibited at Philp's, the painting was retitled *Huntsman's Cabin* in Baltimore a few months later, and then *The Trapper's Cabin, or the Disputed Shot* when it was auctioned in the rooms of the Washington Art Association in December 1858. It was listed as *The Trappers* in the Washington Art Association catalogue, but when William Wilson Corcoran deeded it to the Corcoran Gallery of Art in 1869, it was known as *The Disputed Shot*, a title it retained for more than a century thereafter.[70]

A commentator writing a few years after the opening of the Corcoran clearly saw a depiction of a dispute: "Three hunters having returned to their cabin from the chase, have just assorted their game, consisting of a deer, ducks and various birds; and while two of them are apparently disputing as to whose shot brought down the deer, they are watched with grave dignity by a noble settler in the background."[71] Indeed the man kneeling to the right points at the deer while looking steadily at the man in the center as he makes his analogous rhetorical point. The man seated opposite also looks toward the standing figure, his head tilted up as if eager to gauge his reaction. The figure in the center, however, seems far from the disinterested observer the reviewer saw. He stands quietly looking down toward the disputed game with a grave expression that conveys his attentiveness as he listens to the argument. His erect posture, articulated by the line of his right leg and hand, and echoed by the gun in his left, as well as his location in the center of the painting also connote his role as arbiter. The heavy folds of his trade blanket give his figure a solidity that gains support from the heavy rectangular pylon that runs from floor to ceiling behind him. This sense of gravity, both physical and circumstantial, gives him the aforementioned dignity of a settler of arguments, rather than territory. Upon closer observation, however, Stanley hints at a gravitas beyond the surface narrative of a hunting dispute. The figure, bearded and wrapped in a thick blanket, holding his rifle as if it were a staff, and crowned with a broad brimmed hat, takes on the aspect of an Old Testament king meting out his justice.

Significantly, Stanley's overall composition bears some resemblance to established old master compositions of the parable of good adjudication, the judgment of King Solomon. The story, from 1 Kings 3:16–28, recounts how two women, each with a baby, came before the king. One of the infants had died and both women claimed to be the mother of the living one. Solomon tricked the women by threatening to cut the living baby in half, knowing the true mother would reveal herself by relinquishing her claim on the child. Paintings by Raphael (1483–1520), Peter

Paul Rubens (1577–1640), and Nicolas Poussin (1594–1665) show one or both mothers kneeling to either side of Solomon's throne, gesturing as they argued (fig. 3.16). Frequently, the dead child was laid out in the center foreground of the painting, its white skin providing both the visual focus and the narrative impetus of the dispute.

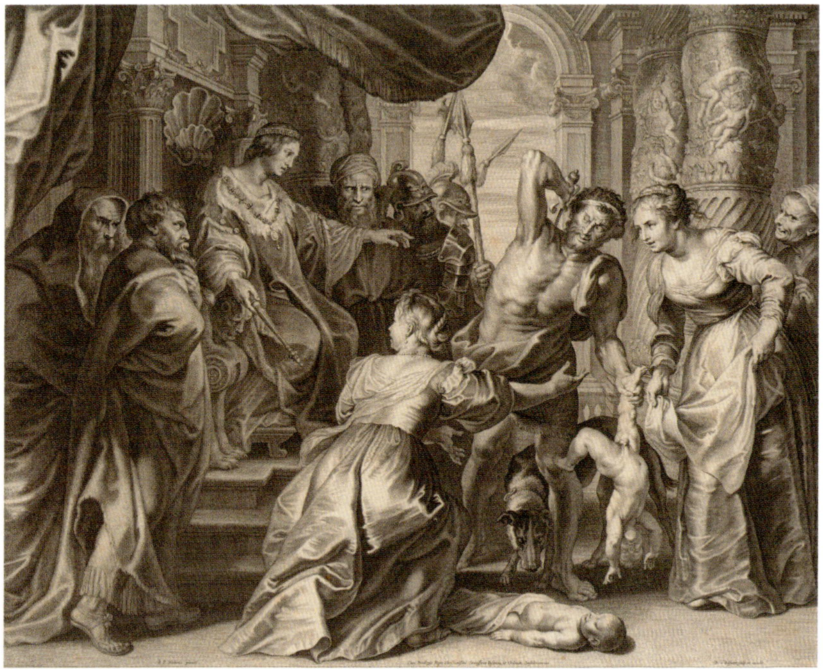

FIG. 3.16.
After Peter Paul Rubens, *The Judgment of Solomon*, n.d. Engraving; 17⁵⁄₁₆ × 20³⁄₁₆ in. (44.0 × 51.3 cm). Courtesy The Metropolitan Museum of Art, Elisha Whittelsey Collection, Elisha Whittelsey Fund (1951, 51.501.7016)

In Stanley's painting, the kneeling men, one gesturing toward the buck, provide the compositional correspondents to the mothers. The ducks, arranged in a line and placed face up to expose their glistening white breasts, take the place of the body of the dead infant.

Missing from Stanley's composition is a visual analog for the soldier who raises his sword to cleave the disputed child in half. There is, however, a startling conceptual analog to the violent partition of the infant in the presence of a pamphlet hanging over the otter skin bag and beside a calumet ("peace pipe") and a knife. With the exception of a faint "M" at the beginning of the longest word, the text is mostly illegible. The date, however, is clear: 1820, the year the Missouri Compromise was passed. The Missouri Compromise was an attempt to stave off sectional strife by balancing congressional power in the United States between slave and free states. Missouri entered the Union as a slave state and Maine as a free state, and slavery was prohibited in territories north of the 36th parallel, or the southern boundary of Missouri. The controversial bill was repealed by the Kansas-Nebraska Act in 1854, and in 1857, the year before (or perhaps during which) this work was completed, the Supreme Court declared it unconstitutional in the Dred Scott decision.

The Dred Scott decision, arrived at on March 6, 1857, had a profound impact on the country's history, but it is also a key for understanding the meaning of Stanley's painting. The decision marked only the second time that the Supreme Court had declared an act of Congress unconstitutional and marked a clear victory for supporters of slavery. The case exacerbated sectional tensions in the country and particularly in Washington, D.C., where sectional politics even found their way into the proceedings of the Washington Art Association. When its president, Horatio Stone, gave the inaugural address a month before the case was decided, he called for artists to do their part to preserve the Union. "With the facilities at our command we may do much to elevate, expand, and purify the national affection; much to silence the fearful words of disunion, which sometimes fall from high places, and from inconsiderate lips, by the illustration of what the union has done to make it sacred forever."[72] Preserving the Union was important to the mission of the organization in part because Stone understood that its power would come from the association's ability to unify and represent the interests of all the nation's artists across all regions. But Stone also saw the interests of art and the nation as "mutually dependent and inseparable."[73] Unlike the earlier Hudson River School, whose more idealistic nationalism consisted of portraying primeval America, the Washington Art Association was far more pragmatic. For Stone and his association, the core of American identity lay in the unique facets of its national sentiments, its history, and its way of life. Portraitists, genre painters, history painters, as well as landscapists should make the nation in all its facets (its citizens, its daily life, its history, and so on) their subject matter. In so doing, they both commemorated the pride and attainments of the nation and created better art. "Art must have something in its national history and home to revere, to cherish, and to hope for, or else to excellence it will never attain,"[74] Stone argued before the association assembly. "[Composing] the greatness of the past, and all the imaginable splendors of the future, into the woof of the passing time, is the high vocation of all whom the Muses inspire, and especially of the poets and artists—the illustrations of civilization—the fame-keepers of nations."[75] Stone argued that artists should serve an important role in shaping the course of their nation. If artists could only dress the nation with "all the adornments of science, literature, and art," he concluded in his address, "its beauty, if not its solid worth, shall save it from partition and alienation for all time."[76]

Stone's ideas about the role of artists in promoting the Union would certainly have been familiar to Stanley, who was an officer of the Washington Art Association and an active participant in its offshoot, the National Art Association. Indeed, Stanley's painting appears to meet the criteria Stone laid out in his address, as well as the earlier proscriptions for a national art given by the editors of *The Crayon*. In portraying western trappers or hunters and their accoutrements, he records the history of his nation's settlement. More important, the painting's narrative of a disputed shot being peacefully resolved in a western setting offered a hopeful metaphor of the West as a place for compromise between contending regional factions.[77] The trapper's calm and considered judgment may also stand as an implicit critique of the Dred Scott decision and its flawed judgment.

Although the Dred Scott case might seem at first to provide only a context for the painting, its connection is more explicit if we understand the setting of the painting to be Fort Snelling. The crux of Dred Scott's case concerned his claim that he was a free man as a consequence of living at Fort Snelling in Wisconsin Territory, where slavery was illegal.[78] Scott and his wife, Harriett, lived at Fort Snelling with their owner, army surgeon John Emerson, from 1836 to 1838, the year before Stanley arrived at the fort.[79] Harriett had formerly been the slave of Lawrence Taliaferro, Indian agent at Fort Snelling from 1820 to 1839 and the person to whom Stanley would have applied for permission to visit neighboring Indians. It is thus possible that Stanley knew of Dred Scott, if he did not actually overlap his time at the fort.

If Stanley intended to honor Stone's challenge in his painting by promoting compromise over division, and celebrating the West as a place where sectional conflicts could be alleviated, he found a sympathetic buyer in patron William Wilson Corcoran. As noted above, Corcoran purchased *The Trappers* soon after its completion. Although Corcoran would become a strong supporter of the South and states' rights following the outbreak of the Civil War, he had been a proponent of preserving the Union beforehand, serving as a behind-the-scenes lobbyist on behalf of the group of bills known as the Compromise of 1850.[80] Building on the model of the Compromise of 1820, the Compromise of 1850 negotiated a similar series of compromises for the territories that entered the Union following the Mexican-American War. Again, the legislation relied on the promise of the West as a place that could balance tensions between North and South and thus serve as a last, best hope of preserving the Union.

THE CIVIL WAR IN WASHINGTON AND STANLEY'S DEPARTURE

Stanley's participation in the Third Annual Exhibition of the Washington Art Association represented a high point for both his career and the arts in Washington City. The *Washington Daily Globe* proclaimed the exhibition to be "the largest, and in every respect the best collection of American paintings ever made, comprising about two hundred paintings of all descriptions by artists of all parts of the Union," adding, "[I]t is thus truly representational of American art as it now exists."[81] The claims were no mere expression of local pride. Papers in Baltimore, New York, and Boston also praised the exhibition. A reviewer for *The Crayon* called the show "magnificent—decidedly, in my opinion, the best exhibition of American works, which it has been my privilege to see in this country," and a local paper confided satisfaction when "told by two non--resident artists from different cities that there was not and perhaps never had been in the whole country so fine a collection of pictures in one gallery as was now on exhibition in the galleries of the Art Association."[82]

If the 1859 exhibition represented a high point for the arts in Washington, the outbreak of the Civil War cut short its promise. The art convention convened for last time late in 1860, in conjunction with the art association's fourth and last exhibition.[83] Thereafter, the group splintered. William D. Washington, an officer and driving force behind the organization, moved back to Virginia, where he joined the Confederate Army in 1860.[84] In 1861, Stone too left Washington to join the Union forces, serving as a doctor in prison hospitals throughout the north.[85] Stanley stayed through the initial unrest, the early battles, and the fortification of Washington. He opened an art school in the vacated offices of the art association and began taking students in 1860.[86] In 1861 he tried his hand at a second panorama depicting battles from the first year and a half of the war.[87] He toured with it briefly and then began looking for a new location to settle his family. After visiting Buffalo, he finally chose Detroit, where he and his family settled in 1863.[88]

During his decade in the nation's capital, Stanley's art evolved dramatically. He expanded his art enterprise from the Indian Gallery to political portraiture, genre scenes, and entrepreneurial panoramas. As his choice of subject matter became more ambitious, his compositions grew from simple, planar configurations to more complex arrangements of figures in space with convincing renderings of volume, movement, and color. And not least, in the milieu of Washington art organizations, he became more conscious of the artist's role in articulating the goals of a young nation. Rather than simply documenting what he believed to be a vanishing population, in paintings like *A Family Group (Barter for a Bride)*, he could locate the Blackfeet's specific interests within the broader fabric of the nation. And rather than merely depicting the romantic life of the trapper, *The Trappers* could point the way for western settlement to ease the sectional tensions that threatened the Union. In so doing, Stanley followed the proscription of Horatio Stone and the art association to make his art not just the exponent of national life, but "the means of its commemoration and development."[89] In Washington, he found inspiration to move beyond the narrow confines of his Indian Gallery and embrace the ambitions of a national artist.

NOTES

1. For Stanley's biography, see Julie Schimmel, "John Mix Stanley and Imagery of the West in Nineteenth-Century America" (Ph.D. diss., New York University, 1983), part 1, 7–139.

2. "Stanley's Indian Gallery," *National Intelligencer*, undated clipping, John Mix Stanley scrapbook, 1843–1868, reel OAM, p. 42, Archives of American Art, Smithsonian Institution, Washington, D.C. (hereafter Stanley scrapbook).

3. Brian W. Dippie, *Catlin and His Contemporaries: The Politics of Patronage* (Lincoln: University of Nebraska Press, 1990), 265–318. See also mention of Catlin in "Indian Gallery of Paintings," *National Intelligencer*, February 23, 1852, 4.

4. Virgil E. McMahan, *The Artists of Washington, D.C., 1796–1996*, vol. 1, *A Directory of Painters, Sculptors, and Engravers Born Before 1900* (Washington, D.C.: Artists of Washington, D.C., 1995), 206. Marc Rothenberg, ed., "Henry Desk Diary, Tuesday January 27th, 1852," in *The Papers of Joseph Henry*, vol. 8, *January 1850–December 1853: The Smithsonian Years* (Washington, D.C.: Smithsonian Institution, 1972), 281.

5. "Stanley's Historical Portrait Gallery," *National Intelligencer*, February 19, 1852, 3; untitled and undated clipping, *National Intelligencer*, Stanley scrapbook, p. 42. Other articles on the same page similarly noted that the gallery had attracted much attention: "The high popularity these pictures enjoy is demonstrated by the number of citizens and strangers who continually crowd to inspect them."

6. Schimmel, "John Mix Stanley and Imagery," 109–35; Dippie, *Catlin and His Contemporaries*, 280–317; W. Vernon Kinietz, *John Mix Stanley and His Indian Paintings* (Ann Arbor: University of Michigan Press, 1942), 8–10; Joseph Henry to John Mix Stanley, March 11, 1865, transcript in John Mix Stanley vertical file, Smithsonian American Art Museum and National Portrait Gallery Library, Washington, D.C.

7. Josephine Cobb, "The Washington Art Association: An Exhibition Record," in *Records of the Columbia Historical Society of Washington, D.C., 1963–65*, ed. Francis Coleman Rosenberger (Washington, D.C.: Columbia Historical Society, 1966), 135; *Proceedings of Annual Conventions of the National Art Association Held at Washington City, from 1858 to 1860, Inclusive* (Washington, D.C.: William H. Moore, 1860), 7, 20, 26.

8. Andrew J. Cosentino and Henry H. Glassie, *The Capital Image: Painters in Washington, 1800–1915* (Washington, D.C.: Smithsonian Institution Press, 1983), 39–40.

9. Unidentified clipping, William Wilson Corcoran scrapbook, vol. 1, 73, Corcoran Gallery and College of Art Archives, Washington, D.C.

10. Cosentino and Glassie, *Capital Image*, 69.

11. Ibid., 68.

12. Constance McLaughlin Green, *Washington Village and Capital, 1800–1878* (Princeton, N.J.: Princeton University Press, 1962), 201–203.

13. "The Exhibition of the Washington Art Association," *The Crayon* 4, no. 5 (May 1857): 156.

14. "Washington National Monument," *The Crayon* (June 21, 1855): 395.

15. "Sketchings," *The Crayon* 3, no. 10 (October 1856): 311.

16. Constitution and Bylaws of the Washington Art Association, Corcoran Gallery and College of Art Archives.

17. Cobb, "Washington Art Association," 122.

18. Cosentino and Glassie, *Capital Image*, 80.

19. *Proceedings of Annual Conventions*, 16.

20. May 20, 1859, Henry Kirke Bush-Brown Papers, 4:1058, Manuscript Division, Library of Congress, as quoted in Schimmel, "John Mix Stanley and Imagery," 125.

21. McMahan, *Artists of Washington, D.C.*, 206.

22. Cosentino and Glassie, *Capital Image*, 39–42.

23. Seth L. Cole was a witness to Stanley's will, prepared in advance of the artist's trip with Isaac Stevens in 1853; "John Mix Stanley, Last Will and Testament, May 4, 1853," John Mix Stanley Papers, 1830–1973, reel 687, Archives of American Art, Smithsonian Institution, Washington, D.C. (hereafter Stanley Papers). Cole's wife, Ann Adeline, is the Mrs. S. T. [*sic*] Cole to whom Stanley inscribed

his portrait of his fiancée, Alice English, and her brother, Morgan, cat. no. 071. See her obituary, *Evening Star,* June 2, 1853.

24. Mark Herlong, "Vernon Row: An Early Washington Art Community," unpublished manuscript, Corcoran Gallery of Art Curatorial Files, Washington, D.C. (hereafter CGA Curatorial Files). For studio locations, see Alfred Hunter, comp. and pub., *The Washington and Georgetown Directory, Strangers' Guide-Book For Washington, and Congressional and Clerks' Register* (Washington, D.C.: Kirkwood and McGill, 1853), full text available at *Making of America*, accessed August 20, 2014, http://name.umdl.umich.edu/AFJ8697.0001.001. See also, Cobb, "Washington Art Association," 131–36, Cosentino and Glassie, *Capital Image*, 78.

25. "Stanley's Portrait of General Scott," undated clipping, unknown newspaper, Stanley scrapbook, p. 41; and Hunter, *Washington and Georgetown Directory*.

26. "Works of Art," undated clipping, unknown newspaper, Stanley scrapbook, p. 41.

27. Elizabeth Johns, *American Genre Painting: The Politics of Everyday Life* (New Haven, Conn.: Yale University Press, 1991), 60–99; Carol Clark, "Charles Deas," in *American Frontier Life: Early Western Paintings and Prints*, ed. Alan Axelrod (New York: Cross River Press, 1987), 51–78; *Literary World,* May 1, 1852, 316, as quoted in Johns, *American Genre Painting*, 80.

28. "Fine Picture," *Daily National Intelligencer*, June 7, 1852, 3.

29. *Portraits of North American Indians, with Sketches of Scenery, Etc., Painted by J. M. Stanley* (Washington, D.C.: Smithsonian Institution, 1852), cat. no. 61, p. 41.

30. Berniah Willet portrait, "Luce Center Label," Smithsonian American Art Museum, accessed June 23, 2013, http://americanart.si.edu/collections/search/artwork/?id=22857.

31. Schimmel, "John Mix Stanley and Imagery," 8–23.

32. Cosentino and Glassie, *Capital Image*, 73.

33. Charles Lanman, *Catalogue of W. W. Corcoran's Gallery* (Washington, D.C., 1857).

34. *Catalogue of the Fourth Annual Exhibition of the Washington Art Association* (Washington, D.C.: Henry Polkinhorn, 1860), cat. no. 12.

35. *A Record of the First Exhibition of the Metropolitan Mechanics Institute, Held in the East Wing of the Patent Office, February–March, 1853* (Washington, D.C.: Henry Polkinhorn, 1853), 41. Stanley is also known to have copied another successful composition from the Indian Gallery, *View on the Gila River*. The first version was painted in late 1851 and added to the Indian Gallery, where it was destroyed in 1865. A critic for the *National Intelligencer* called it a "ravishing view" (February 24, 1852), and it was later positively compared to a second painting, *Indians Lying in Wait*, which was on view in his studio in June (*National Intelligencer*, June 7, 1852, 3) The second version, *Chain of Spires along the Gila River*, was painted in 1855, cat. no. 130, and is now at the Phoenix Art Museum.

36. *Portraits of North American Indians*.

37. "The Panorama and the Artist," *Washington Sentinel*, September 5, 1854, 3.

38. "J. M. Stanley, Esq.," *Evening Star,* May 11, 1859, 3.

39. John C. Ewers, "Barter for a Bride," *American West* 5 (November 1968): inside cover.

40. Thomas S. Donoho, *Scenes and Incidents of Stanley's Western Wilds* (Washington, D.C.: Evening Star Office, c. 1854).

41. Dippie, *Catlin and His Contemporaries*, 295–96. Schimmel, "John Mix Stanley and Imagery," 110.

42. Schimmel, "John Mix Stanley and Imagery," 109; Stanley Papers.

43. I thank C. Adrian Heidenreich, professor emeritus, Montana State University, Billings, for generous assistance in providing information and offering interpretation about the figures and scene Stanley portrayed. Professor Heidenreich also walked me through the 1858 treaty negotiations with the Blackfeet and provided context for Stanley and Stevens's activities during the 1853 expedition.

44. I thank C. Adrian Heidenreich for locating this shirt in the NMAI collection. The NMAI provides the following provenance: Formerly in the collection of Western artist John Mix Stanley (1814–

1872); possibly collected by him in 1853 during an expedition and survey of Blackfeet country, where he served as the expedition artist; inherited by his wife Alice C. (née English) Stanley (ca. 1836–ca. 1890); sold to sculptor Julius Theodore Melchers (1829–1903); inherited by his son, artist Gari Melchers (1860–1932); donated to NMAI in 1929.

45. Ron Tyler, ed., *Alfred Jacob Miller: Artist on the Oregon Trail*, with a catalogue by Karen Dewees Reynolds and William R. Johnston (Fort Worth, Tex.: Amon Carter Museum, 1982), cat. 191–191H.

46. *Record of the First Exhibition*, 62–63, 67; *The Book of the Exhibition: Seventh and Eighth Exhibition of the Maryland Institute for the Promotion of the Mechanic Arts* (Baltimore: Mills and Cox, 1854), cat. no. 1–151; Miller also exhibited two theatre scenes at the *Second Annual Exhibition of the Washington Art Association* (Washington, D.C.: Henry Polkinhorn, 1857), cat. nos. 20, 21. Miller is listed as a member of the organization; see Washington Art Association Letterbook, 1856–1857, MS 334, Archives and Manuscripts Collection, Historical Society of Washington, D.C.

47. *Record of the First Exhibition*, 67; Lisa Strong, *Sentimental Journey: The Art of Alfred Jacob Miller* (Fort Worth, Tex.: Amon Carter Museum, 2009), 124.

48. Marvin C. Ross, ed., *The West of Alfred Jacob Miller* (Norman: University of Oklahoma Press, 1968), plate 168.

49. Lesley Wischmann, *Frontier Diplomats: Alexander Culbertson and Natoyist-Siksina' Among the Blackfeet* (Norman: University of Oklahoma Press, 2004), 221–24.

50. Ibid., 231.

51. Ibid., 217–18.

52. Ibid., 230ff.

53. Schimmel, "John Mix Stanley and Imagery," 105–106. The sketch, "Blackfeet Indians [hunting buffalo] Three Buttes" is unlocated; see Robert Taft, *Artists and Illustrators of the Old West, 1850–1900* (New York: Scribner, 1953), 19, 274n54; *Scenes and Incidents*, 15.

54. Wischmann, *Frontier Diplomats*, 224–25.

55. "Indian Appropriation Bill, April 24, 1854," *Daily Union*, May 2, 1854, 1.

56. R. S., "Blackfeet Indians," *Daily Union*, April 14, 1854, 3.

57. "Incidents of Stanley's Western Wilds," undated clipping, unknown newspaper, Stanley scrapbook, p. 44. The newspaper account was repeated with added details in the panorama program, Donoho, *Scenes and Incidents*, 13–14; Stanley's progress on the panorama was closely followed by Washington City papers, including the *Sentinel*, the *Daily Union*, and the *Evening Star*. The *National Intelligencer* published articles on his progress almost daily from September 2 until it opened on September 11. Based on his rate of progress, Stanley was probably at work on section three by the beginning of August when Culbertson called.

58. Wischmann, *Frontier Diplomats*, 241, 274.

59. Ibid., 21.

60. "Works of Art at the Fair," *Peoria Daily Transcript*, December 1, 1859.

61. Ibid.

62. I thank C. Adrian Heidenreich for this observation.

63. "Indian Appropriation Bill, April 24, 1854," *Daily Union*, May 2, 1854, 1; Wischmann, *Frontier Diplomats*, 232.

64. "Philp's Gallery," *Evening Star*, August 21, 1858, 2; *The Book of the Exhibition: Eleventh Annual Exhibition of the Maryland Institute for the Promotion of the Mechanic Arts* (Baltimore: Samuel S. Mills Steam Press, 1858), 195.

65. "Philp's Gallery," *Evening Star*, August 21, 1858, 2.

66. "Sale of Choice Paintings," *Evening Star*, December 18, 1853, 3; *Catalogue of the Third Annual Exhibition of the Washington Art Association* (Washington, D.C.: William H. Moore, 1859), cat. no. 1.

67. Schimmel, "John Mix Stanley and Imagery," 187.

68. Joni L. Kinsey, "John Mix Stanley," in *The West as America: Reinterpreting Images of the Frontier, 1820–1920*, ed. William H. Truettner, 368 (Wash-

ington, D.C.: National Museum of American Art and Smithsonian Institution Press, 1991); Kinietz, *John Mix Stanley*, 4.

69. "Sale of Choice Paintings," *Evening Star*, December 18, 1858, 3.

70. *Book of the Exhibition: Eleventh*, 195, and untitled *Baltimore Sun*, November 3, 1858, 1; "Sale of Choice Paintings," *Evening Star*, December 18, 1858, 3. Stanley may have reverted to *Trapper's Cabin* so that the painting would be recognized by a Washington audience as the same work shown in August at Philp's. *Register of Paintings*, CGA Curatorial Files. Its title has recently been restored to *The Trapper's Cabin*, see change of title memorandum, CGA Curatorial Files.

71. "Our Washington Letter," *Forest and Stream: A Journal of Outdoor Life, Travel, Nature Study, Shooting* 9, no. 15 (November 15, 1877): 295.

72. Horatio Stone, *Addresses before the Washington Art Association, Feb. 24, 1857 and Feb. 10, 1858* (Washington, D.C.: Cornelius Wendell, 1858), 9.

73. Ibid., 5.

74. Ibid.

75. Ibid., 6.

76. Ibid., 10.

77. Art historian Patricia Hills has argued that the American Art-Union patronized western subject matter because it promoted a vision of America that was neither north nor south, thus appealing broadly to both. Patricia Hills, "The American Art-Union as Patron for Expansionist Ideology in the 1840s," in *Art in Bourgeois Society, 1790–1850*, ed. Andrew Hemingway and William Vaughan (Cambridge and New York: Cambridge University Press, 1998), 316.

78. Dred Scott v. Sandford [*sic*], 60 U.S. 393.

79. Kinsey, "John Mix Stanley," 368. See also Kinietz, *John Mix Stanley*, 4, and Charles Richard Tuttle, *General History of the State of Michigan* (Detroit: R. D. S. Tyler, 1873), 235–36, on Stanley at Fort Snelling.

80. Email correspondence with Mark Goldstein, Ph.D. candidate, University of Maryland, May 21, 2013. For more on Corcoran's views toward secession, see William Wilson Corcoran to J. Watson Webb, May 9, 1851, *Outgoing Letterbook* 30, no. 160, William Wilson Corcoran Papers, Manuscript Division, Library of Congress, Washington, D.C.; and Davira Taragin, *Corcoran* (Washington, D.C.: Corcoran Gallery of Art, 1976), 17.

81. "The News," *Washington, D.C., Daily Globe*, January 12, 1859, 1.

82. "Interesting Discourse on Art," *Baltimore Sun*, February 23, 1859, 3; "A Visit to Washington," *Boston Daily Evening Transcript*, February 2, 1859, 2; "Artist's Supper in Washington," *New York Tribune*, January 18, 1859, 2; "The Art Exhibition," *National Intelligencer*, February 2, 1859, 3.

83. "Fourth Annual Meeting of the Washington Art Association," *Daily National Intelligencer*, November 8, 1859, 3.

84. Cobb, "Washington Art Association," 128.

85. Ibid., 126.

86. "Drawing and Painting," *Daily National Intelligencer*, August 22, 1860, 3.

87. Schimmel, "John Mix Stanley and Imagery," 130–34.

88. Ibid., 135–36.

89. Horatio Stone, *National Art: An Address Delivered before the Washington Art Association, February 10, 1858* (Washington, D.C.: Cornelius Wendell, 1858), 16.

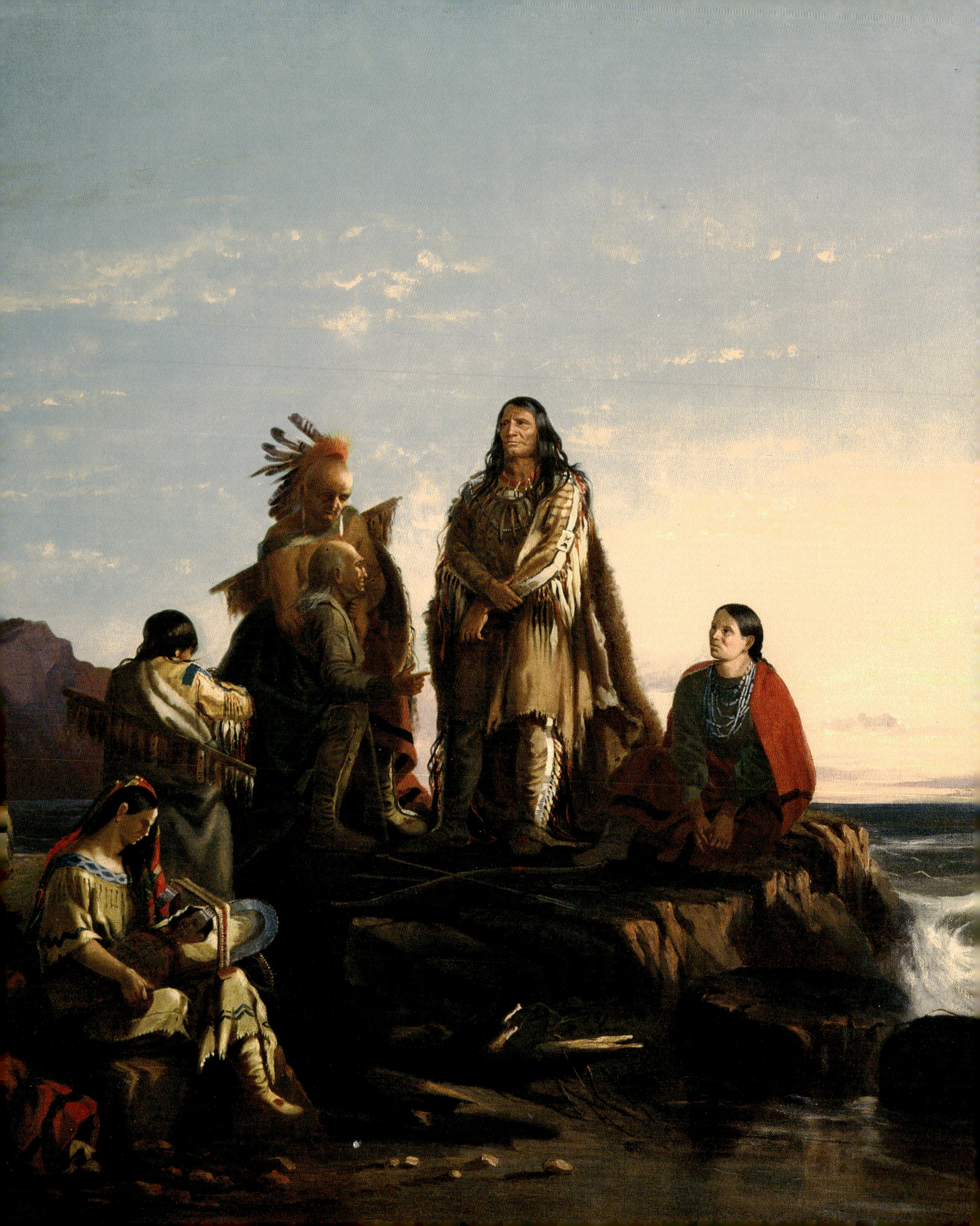

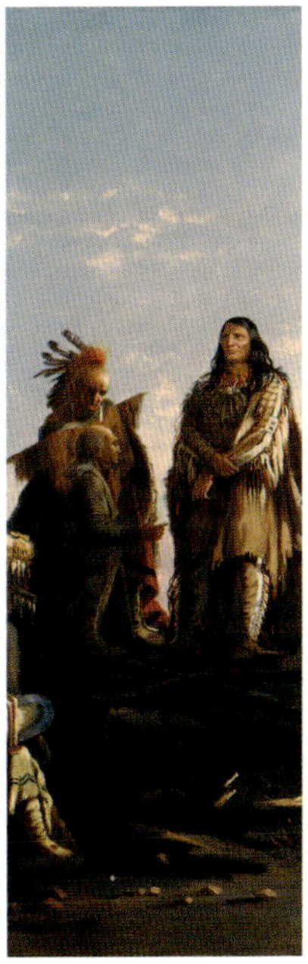

4
John Mix Stanley's *The Last of Their Race* and the "Doomed Indian" in American Culture

Mindy N. Besaw

The nation's unquestioning faith that America's Native tribes were doomed to disappear in the face of progress was pervasive in writing and images in the nineteenth century. "They will vanish like a vapour from the face of the earth," predicted Washington Irving of American Indians in 1814. "The places that now know them will know them no more forever."[1] As a powerful expression of the so-called doomed Indian, John Mix Stanley's *The Last of Their Race* (fig. 4.1, cat. no. 159) played an influential role in "concurrently forming, reflecting, and reinforcing attitudes toward the Indian."[2]

By 1857, when Stanley completed *The Last of Their Race*, the United States was growing rapidly. On his many journeys west in the 1840s and 1850s, Stanley experienced firsthand the dramatic effects of U.S. Indian policy and westward expansion on Native peoples. President Andrew Jackson's 1830 Indian Removal Act "to provide for an exchange of lands with the Indians residing in any of the states or territories, and for their removal west of the river Mississippi" resulted in the forced transplantation of nearly fifty thousand Native peoples from their homes in the eastern parts of the United States to Indian Territory in present-day Oklahoma, and subsequently the deaths of thousands.[3] The Removal Act allowed for American settlement in the southern states, but shortly thereafter, America looked west. Manifest Destiny, a term coined by newspaper editor John O'Sullivan in 1845 to describe America's belief in its divine obligation to stretch the boundaries of the nation to the Pacific Ocean, dominated the American attitude of the 1840s. As the United States rapidly added territory through upheaval and

OPPOSITE

(detail) J. M. Stanley, *The Last of Their Race*, 1857 (cat. no. 159)

FIG. 4.1.
John Mix Stanley, *The Last of Their Race*, 1857. Oil on canvas; 43 × 60 in. (109.2 × 152.4 cm). Courtesy Buffalo Bill Center of the West, Cody, Wyoming (5.75)

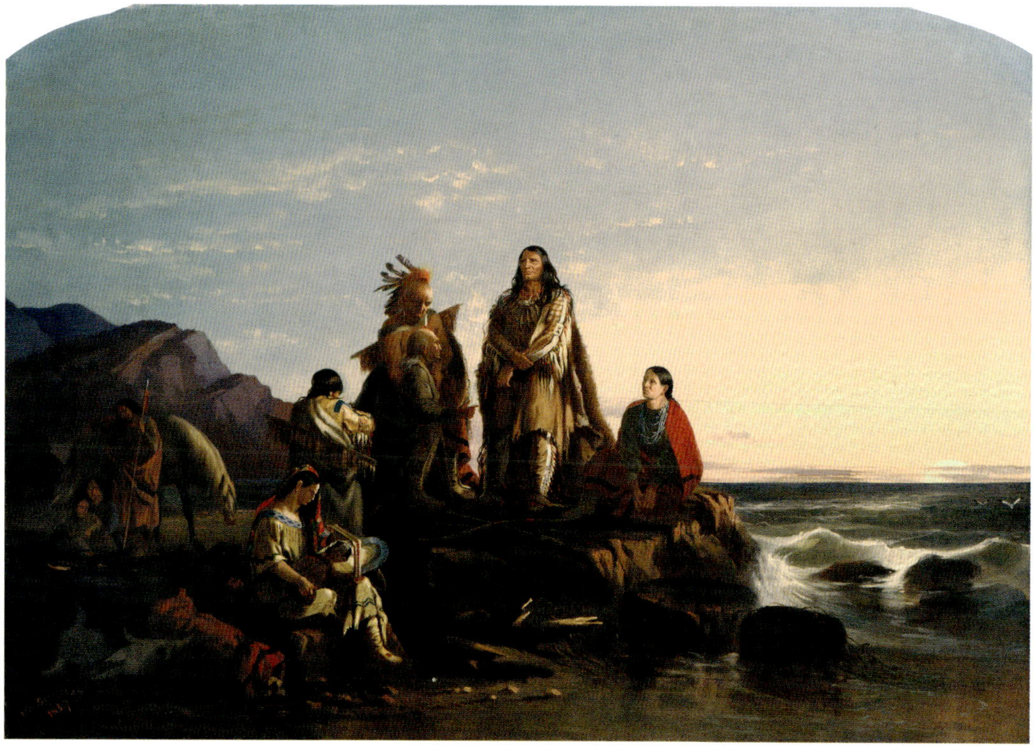

acquisitions, massive western migration ensued (in the 1840s alone, the United States added Texas, areas of the Southwest, Oregon, and California to its holdings). From the 1840s through the 1860s, the east-west wagon route of the Oregon Trail was used by hundreds of thousands of people. Also at the heart of Manifest Destiny was a belief in cultural and racial superiority, which encouraged and sanctified occupying land set aside for Native tribes and using extremes to subdue Native people. Americans poured west into Indian Territory and beyond, recalling what congressional member Oliver H. Smith told the House of Representatives in 1828: "We have seen them driven by whites, from river to river, from State to State, from hill to hill, from mountain to mountain, and from forest to forest; the tide of white emigration still flowing West, and still pressing close upon them; and if we continue the present policy, the time cannot be very far distant, when the last sound of the Indian must die on the Pacific."[4] In the 1850s, the Indian reservation system was on the verge of creation, and just a decade later, Ulysses S. Grant developed his "Peace Policy," which intended to protect and provide food and supplies to American Indians who moved to the reservations. The system, sadly, proved to be unfair and devastating, essentially restating the earlier 1830s policy of removal.[5]

The Last of Their Race is an allegory of the vanishing race, yet the painting is also a family portrait of sorts, presenting a sympathetic view and preserving the familiar types identified in the sitters. Stanley arranged a multigenerational group of American Indians on a rocky outcropping before a setting sun sitting low on the horizon. A centrally placed warrior, recognized as such from his decorated shirt, buffalo robe, and bear claw necklace, forms the apex of the group. A seated woman, an elder, another man, a boy facing away from the viewer, and a mother holding a child in a cradleboard flank the warrior. In the distance, a family, which includes a man, woman, and child, is clustered with their white horse. Bleached buffalo skulls in the foreground foreshadow their impending demise, as the Pacific Ocean laps at their feet. Legible details identifying clothing and accessories are representative of many tribes, contributing to the reading of the painting as symbolic of the collective race perishing at the edge of the ocean.

Close examination of Stanley's *The Last of Their Race* within his oeuvre and compared to other depictions of doomed Indians in nineteenth-century American art provides insight into Stanley's own attitude toward American Indians and American cultural values of the time. Painted at the height of his career, *The Last of Their Race* was so successful that Stanley also completed a second version with only a few variations from the first (fig. 4.2, cat. no. 165).

A poem by L. A. Christie, printed on the occasion of the exhibition of *The Last of Their Race* at the Washington Art Association in 1857, acted as a companion to the painting.

> But this is our last stand!
> And from this narrow rock, washed by the restless sea,
> Our lost, loved hunting-grounds, we bid farewell to thee!
> No more we'll draw the bow, for bleached skulls round us lie,
> Our game starved on this shore—and here we'll bravely die! [6]

The poem summarizes what had become, seemingly, an inevitable and necessary fact for American readers—Native peoples would vanish. Stanley echoed the sentiments of inevitable demise through the composition of *The Last of Their Race*.

FIG. 4.2.
John Mix Stanley, *The Last of Their Race*, c. 1859.
Oil on canvas; 35 × 52 in. (88.9 × 132.1 cm). Courtesy Nelda C. and H. J. Lutcher Stark Foundation, Stark Museum of Art, Orange, Texas (31.23/10)

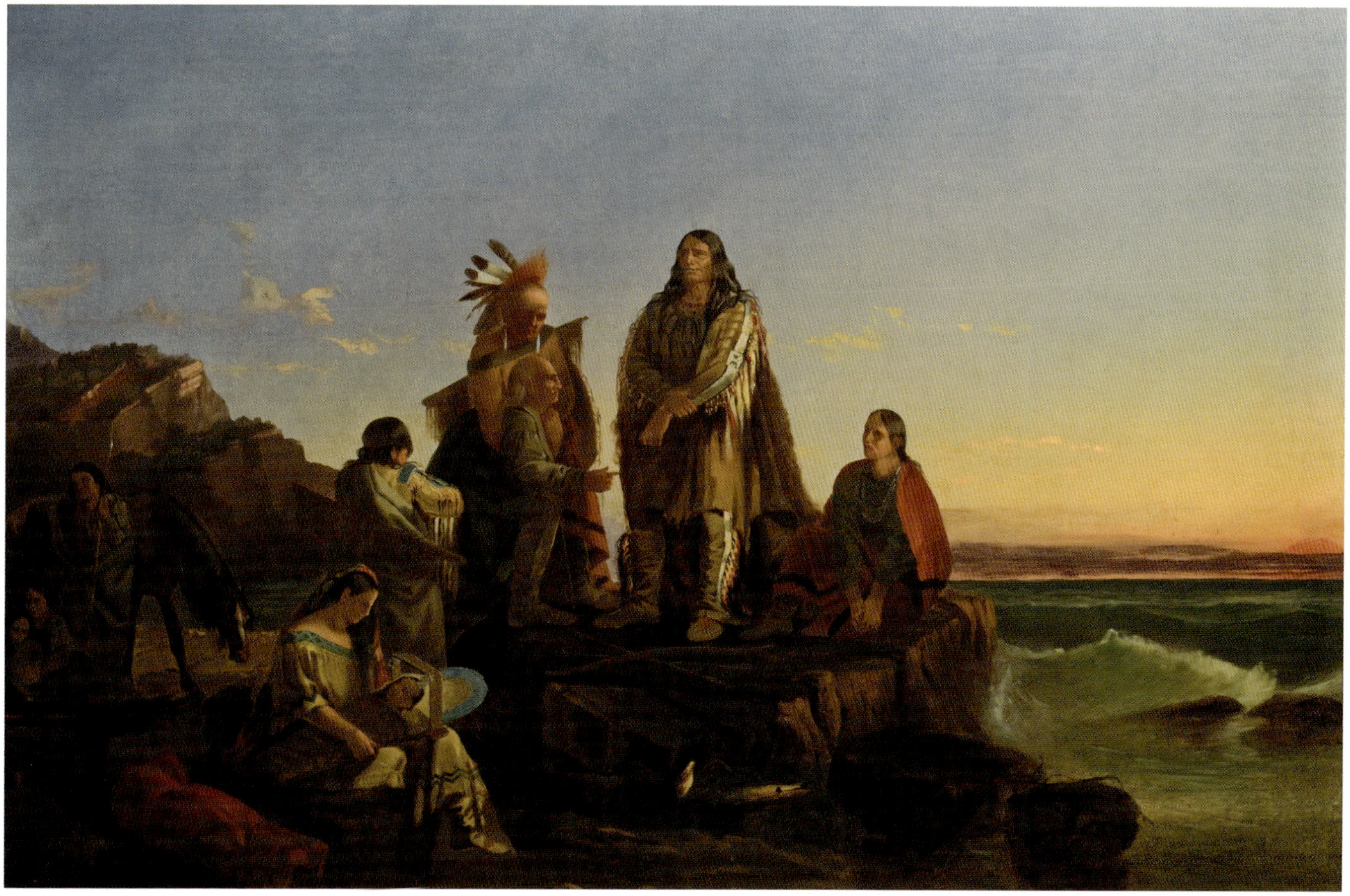

Stanley positioned his figures in a pyramid arrangement, a sturdy composition that has origins in Renaissance art. While the figures read as a unit due to the way they visually overlap, they do not connect through eye contact. Instead, each seems to be looking off into the distance or at another person who does not return the glance. Notably, no one meets the gaze of the viewer, inviting the viewer to look and linger freely. As art critic John Berger pointed out in his influential book, *Ways of Seeing*, when the subject turns away, she becomes a passive object for the active gaze of the viewer.[7] In this case, the American Indians in *The Last of Their Race* become objects of consumption for the (white) viewers. Visually, the composition ennobles the Indians, while nuances among the group undercut the strength of the figures and reinforce the notion that American Indians were inferior to Euro-Americans, a quality that was believed to have contributed to their demise.

The Last of Their Race won a silver medal and second place in the category of History Paintings at the Tenth Annual Exhibition of the Maryland Institute for the Promotion of the Mechanic Arts in Baltimore in 1857. The allegorical message in *The Last of Their Race* qualified it as a history painting, long considered the most prestigious type of painting in Europe. The painting is ambitious in scale, contains multiple figures, and conveys a message or moral. *The Last of Their Race* is a lament for the passing of a dignified and noble race, already interpreted in the past tense even though American Indians were not extinct. As one newspaper described the painting, only a decade after it was first exhibited,

> [*The Last of Their Race*] represents a group of Indians on the Pacific coast. . . . Their last ray of hope has died out. Over the prairies they have been driven, and through the rugged passes of the Rocky Mountains, on and on till not one foot of the land which was once all their own, is left for them. They dare not look out upon the ocean though its waves were liquid gold, for it tells them that their just hope is gone, their wild home is wrestled from them, and the life of their once proud race is flickering in the socket soon to go out forever. All that remains to them is memory, and they look to the east, toward their homes of better days.[8]

Stanley was actively exhibiting his Indian Gallery in the 1850s, a collection that had grown to nearly 150 American Indian portraits and scenes of everyday life.[9] For public consumption and ticket sales, the reception of Stanley's Indian Gallery certainly benefited from the perception that Native tribes were a vanishing race. As if drawn by the rare opportunity to see an endangered species, the paintings afforded audiences a glimpse of people and a way of life that had potentially already disappeared.[10] The urgency to view the Indian Gallery was conveyed on advertisements, like one that featured Thomas L. McKenney, the first director of the Bureau of Indian Affairs. "I consider it the last and best offering of this sort which will ever come to us from the wilderness home of this people," wrote McKenney, "Their destiny as a race is sealed. They will soon be lost to our sight forever."[11] A statement in the 1852 guide to the Indian Gallery once again reiterates what was thought to be the inevitable demise but also seems to encourage viewers to take an active part in preserving the Indian people: "Look at their portraits, and excite some desire that the memory, at least, of these tribes may not become extinct."[12]

The figures in *The Last of Their Race* allegorically symbolize all Native peoples collectively—one vanishing race that was "melting away . . . [into] oblivion."[13] From colonial times,

Euro-Americans spoke and wrote as if members of different tribes were interchangeable.[14] Stanley could certainly discern attributes of different tribes from his personal interaction with Native peoples through his travels in the West and his work painting portraits for his Indian Gallery. Yet, when depicting the American Indians for this painting, Stanley freely combined clothing and accessories from multiple tribes and regions.[15] Most of the recognizable items in the painting relate to the Plains tribes, such as the cradleboard and hide clothing with quillwork or beaded designs, but there are some important departures that point to other regions. The roach headdress with feathers worn by the standing man behind the elder is associated with eastern tribes and resembles the headdresses Stanley painted on Osage Indians in *An Osage Scalp Dance* (cat. no. 025). Further, some specific items in Stanley's collection of Native artifacts, now in the National Museum of the American Indian, likely inspired details in this painting. Stanley owned a Jicarilla Apache bow and arrows like those in the foreground, Mohawk moccasins and Comanche beaded boots with leggings similar to the footwear on the figures, a Blackfeet bear claw necklace like the one worn by the chief, and a Blackfeet hide dress with a blue beaded pattern along the bottom like the dress worn by the woman holding the cradle board.[16]

Even though Stanley relies on the symbolic interpretation of the whole race in his amalgamation of diverse tribes, the majority of the characteristics can be identified as Blackfeet. Stanley's use of Plains Indian attributes was also not unusual for his time. In the mid-nineteenth century, as Americans were moving west, artists adopted characteristics, clothing, and objects from the Plains tribes, such as eagle-feather bonnets, moccasins, hide shirts, and leggings, to symbolize all American Indians.[17] Stanley also had recent personal experience with the Plains tribes. He painted *The Last of Their Race* after he returned home to Washington, D.C., from his 1853 journey with Isaac Stevens as the expeditionary artist on the railroad survey.[18] While on this trip, Stanley encountered Blackfeet Indians at or around Fort Benton on the Upper Missouri and may have collected a number of Blackfeet items, like those already mentioned and a Pikuni Blackfeet (Piegan) shirt and leggings, used as reference for *The Last of Their Race*. The Blackfeet man's shirt appears as the shirt worn by the central figure in the painting, recognized by the quillwork medallion, ermine and hair fringe along the sleeves, and striped patterning on the upper half (fig. 4.3).[19]

FIG. 4.3.
Pikuni Blackfeet (Piegan) *Man's Shirt*, c. 1840. Leather, human and horse hair, quills, pigment, sinew; 44⅛ × 17¾ in. (112 × 45 cm). Courtesy National Museum of the American Indian, Smithsonian Institution, Washington, D.C. (16.5207)

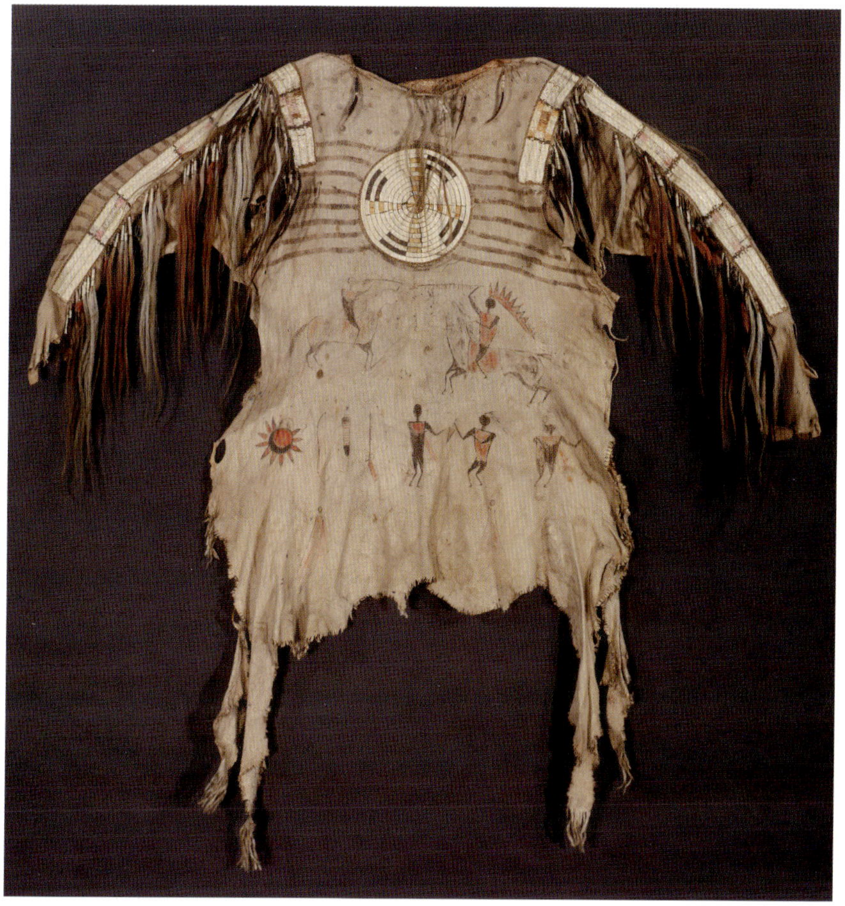

By retracing the provenance of both versions of *The Last of Their Race*, we can verify the identity of two of the sitters. It is thought that Isaac Stevens once owned the 1857 version of *The Last of Their Race* (fig. 4.1, cat. no. 159). The specificity of clothing may have especially appealed to Stevens, an experienced explorer who had many encounters with Plains Indian peoples. The second version of the painting (fig. 4.2, cat. no. 165) was painted expressly for Major Alexander Culbertson, the American Fur Company's chief trader on the Upper Missouri River and founder of Fort Benton in present-day Montana (cat. no. 080). Stanley met Culbertson in Saint Paul preceding the Stevens railroad survey in 1853 and spent time with him at Fort Union and at Fort Benton.[20] Culbertson was also a sophisticated viewer—one who could easily discern details related to various tribes.

The subject of Blackfeet Indians had particular relevance in the mid-nineteenth century, not only for Stevens and Culbertson, but also for Blackfeet-U.S. relations. As Lisa Strong discusses in this volume, Stevens had invited Culbertson to Washington in 1854 to lobby for appropriations to cover costs to hold a major treaty the following year.[21] While there, Culbertson visited his friend Stanley, and they reminisced about Fort Benton.

In 1853 at Fort Benton, Stanley would have met Major Culbertson's wife, Natawista, a Blackfeet Indian from the Blood tribe. Natawista was an active partner with her husband in the trade business, as historian Lesley Wischmann summarizes, "Without Natawista, Culbertson almost certainly would not have been as effective."[22] Stanley must have been taken with Natawista because he used her as a model for *The Last of Their Race*—seated at the right wearing a red trade blanket.[23] Visitors to Fort Benton described Natawista as "stunning," a reversal of commonly held attitudes of the time, especially toward female American Indians. Favorable comments about American Indians tended to focus on the men, who were often admired for their appearance, likened to classical Roman ideals. Even Stevens took note of Natawista's appearance and behavior, writing, "She presents the most striking illustrations of the high civilization which these tribes of the interior are capable of attaining."[24] Natawista sits calmly as an anchor to the compositional pyramid, wearing multiple strands of turquoise. Her gaze guides the viewer's eye to the central figure. The model for the standing figure in the center of the composition was Natawista's brother and chief of the tribe, Seen From Afar, likely also painted as a study while Stanley stayed at Fort Benton in 1853. Although general audiences would not have known about the sibling relationship between the models, Stanley conveyed a familial relationship through his composition.

Stanley adds impact to the allegorical message of the dying race by portraying a family—it is not only the end for a dying chief or elder, but for future generations as well. For a Euro-American audience, the idea of family was highly valued. Stanley's experience as a portrait painter, especially of children and families, informed *The Last of Their Race*, bringing together the values of the two cultures. In addition, Stanley had married Alice English in 1854, and they had their first child in 1855, which may have also contributed to his desire to paint a family group.

Natawista and her brother, Seen From Afar, were also used as models for *A Family Group (Barter for a Bride)* (cat. no. 145). Stanley placed Seen From Afar on a rock in the foreground, holding a staff and wearing what appears to be the same Blackfeet man's shirt with the quill medallion in the center from Stanley's collection (fig. 4.3). Natawista is seated nearby, once again with the red trade blanket. *A Family Group (Barter for a Bride)*, and many of Stanley's other paintings of multigenerational groups of Indians (such as *Crossing the Milk River*, c. 1855,

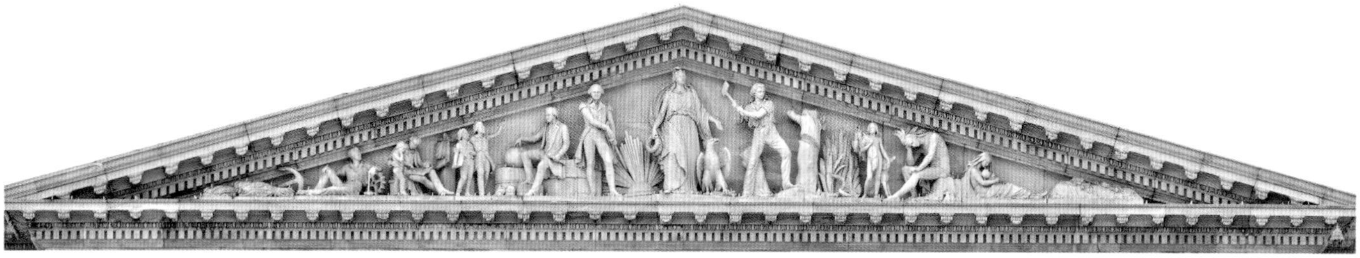

cat. no. 140, and *Seeking a Home,* cat. no. 129) provide a counterpart for interpreting *The Last of Their Race.* Less of an allegory, these paintings have characteristics of genre paintings, portraying scenes of everyday life. *Seeking a Home* and *A Family Group (Barter for a Bride)* are notable for their regenerative nature, highlighting families with promising futures. Images of American Indian children surrounded by extended families encouraged white audiences to identify with the subjects through associations with their own home life. Stanley's outdoor settings, however, especially featuring a migratory lifestyle, presented a noticeable difference between the domestic habits of American Indians and those of white viewers and provided a safe distance for appreciating Indian family imagery.[25] The multiple generations in *The Last of Their Race* encouraged viewers to identify with the individuals depicted, making the message of loss even more potent.

FIG. 4.4.
Thomas Crawford, *Progress of Civilization*, 1863. Marble; 80 × 12 ft. (24.4 × 3.7 m). Pediment, U.S. Capitol. Courtesy Architect of the Capitol (aoc.gov)

The extinction of the Indian in the face of progress was especially prominent in the nation's capital at mid-century, while Stanley was living in Washington, D.C. In 1850 Congress legislated the expansion of the U.S. Capitol, to be completed in a classical-revival style and adorned with numerous sculpture decorations. The pediment above the east entrance to the Senate wing featured "the struggle between civilized man and the savage, between the cultivated and the wild nature," a subject of current debate and relevance to the country's history.[26] *Progress of Civilization* was designed and created by American sculptor Thomas Crawford in 1854 (completed in 1863; fig. 4.4). In this allegorical grouping, America stands at the center of the pediment surrounded by an eagle and the rising sun. To her right is the future: a soldier, merchant, two children, a schoolmaster, and mechanic with sheaves of wheat. The past is to America's left: a pioneer, the stump of a tree (the taming of the wilderness), an Indian boy, an Indian chief, and an Indian mother and child lying near a grave.

The most striking of the figures is the American Indian chief, which Crawford also carved as a freestanding sculpture in the round, *The Dying Chief Contemplating the Progress of Civilization,* 1857 (fig. 4.5). The

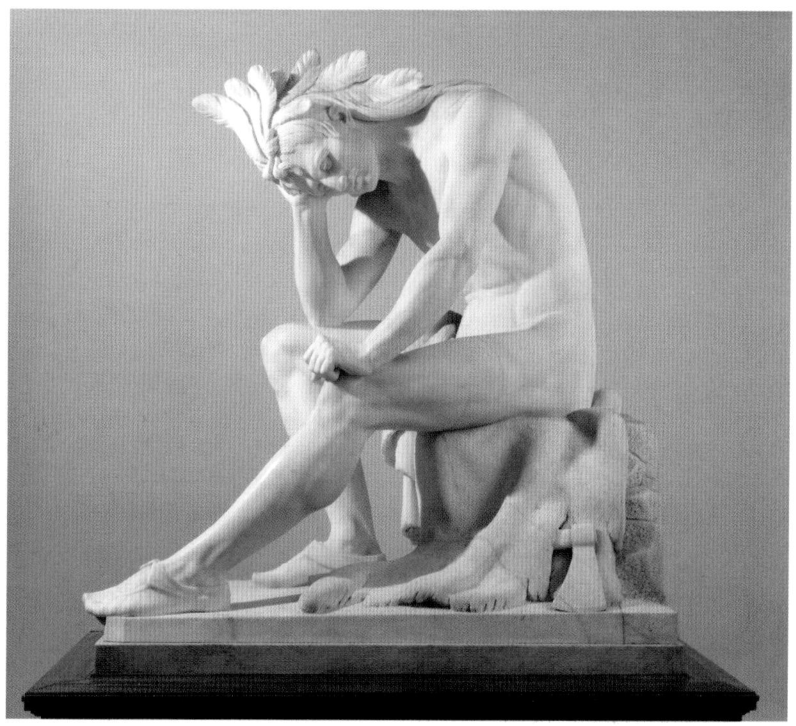

FIG. 4.5.
Thomas Crawford, *The Dying Chief Contemplating the Progress of Civilization*, 1857. Marble; 60 × 55½ × 28 in. (152.4 × 141.0 × 71.1 cm). Courtesy New York Historical Society, gift of Edwin W. Orvis (1931.1)

seated Indian, wearing a feathered war bonnet and moccasins, rests on a rock with an animal skin wrapped around his leg and lap. An ax, partially covered by the animal skin, leans against the rock. The chief's melancholy pose, with his whole body bent forward, head resting on his right hand, signifies despair. As one contemporary critic interpreted, "the weary chase of life is over, he is dying. . . . His tribe has disappeared, he is left alone, the solitary off-shoot of a mighty race."[27]

The dying chief's pose bespeaks discussions happening within the Capitol. In 1853, James L. Orr, the chairman of the House Committee on Indian Affairs, proclaimed, "The whites can no longer be kept out of Indian country. . . . The plains and prairies to the Rocky mountains have nearly ceased to echo the lowing of the buffalo; the crack of the emigrant's whip, the merry jest and joyous laugh of the Caucasian man, now ring through the vast wilderness."[28] The pediment supported statements like this, building the expectation that the country's Native peoples *must* perish in the face of progress. Whether spoken as a lament or a strategy, the end result was always the same, and American Indians were doomed.

The Dying Chief is not alone in the "inevitable fate awaiting its race" but is accompanied by a young boy and a mother cradling an infant.[29] Especially when the American Indian family is juxtaposed with the two boys and schoolmaster on the opposite side of the pediment, the message is clear: the future of America belongs to white youth. The boys, guided by schooling and discipline, ensure the continuation of the young nation, while the presence of Indian children make the demise of the race even more tragic. In the nineteenth century, "representing Indian children was a potential problem for artists," noted art historian Claire Perry, "because they testified to the persistence of people who were supposed to be on their way out." Therefore, depictions of American Indian children "were often framed by narrative devices that diffused any idea of a resurgent population."[30] The baby, literally cradled near the grave, is doomed in the face of progress, just as the infant and children in Stanley's *The Last of Their Race* face a similar fate.

Tompkins H. Matteson's widely circulated painting *The Last of the Race* portrays a similar subject of multiple generations of American Indians pushed to the Pacific (1847, fig. 4.6). An elder stands on an outcropping of rocks with his back to the viewer, contemplating the ominous clouds and setting sun on the horizon of the sea. Near him, a young woman reclines with her face hidden, and to his other side, a young man looks down. A woman with a child placed in the center of the composition is the only one to face the viewer. Matteson's painting was distributed as a print through the American Art-Union in 1847, suggesting that the romantic fading of Indian life was a popular subject in the East, and indeed, nationally.[31] As art historian Elizabeth Johns points out, the directors of the Art-Union looked for pictures that would satisfy popular taste, and the images purchased for distribution typically had three qualities: "They were arguably national in implication, they were easily readable by a minimally experienced audience, and they *appeared* at least to be high-toned in content."[32] Matteson's image fit the requirements and, in turn, further encouraged the widespread belief of the doomed Indian in the mid-nineteenth century.

Matteson produced another "Last of the Race" image for *The Odd-Fellows' Offering for 1848*, where it was accompanied by a poem of the same title by F. J. Otterson (fig. 4.7). The poet described the scene of a multigenerational group of American Indians, poised "along the rocky shore,"

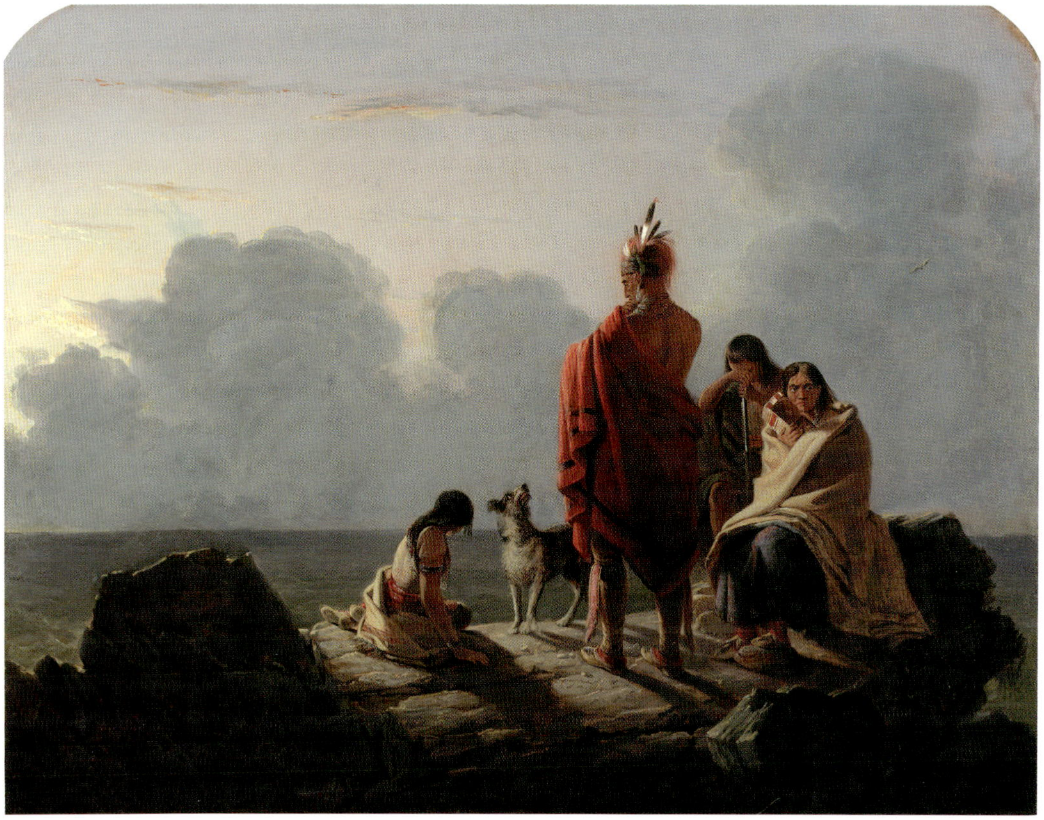

FIG. 4.6.
Tompkins H. Matteson,
The Last of the Race, 1847.
Oil on canvas; 39¾ × 50 in.
(101 × 127 cm). Courtesy
Collection of New-York
Historical Society, gift of
Edwin W. Orvis (1931.1)

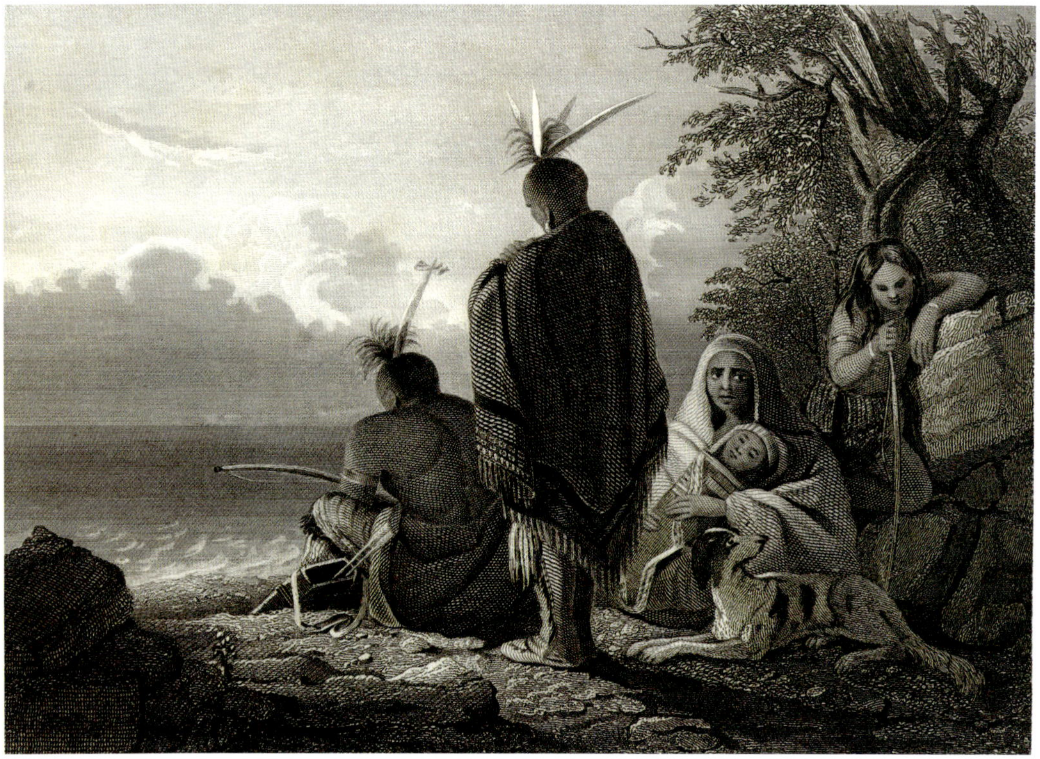

FIG. 4.7.
Tompkins H. Matteson,
The Last of Their Race.
Lithograph; 3¼ × 4½ in.
(8.26 × 11.43 cm). From
Ridgely and Donaldson,
The Odd-Fellows' Offering for 1848. Courtesy
McCracken Research Library,
Buffalo Bill Center of the
West, Cody, Wyoming

And down the rocks, where ocean oozed,
He hunted for a grave;
Around him ranged the little group—
The mother and the bride—
Upon their knees their heads they droop,
And wait the flowing tide.[33]

The stanzas convey a visually powerful narrative of the chief crying out his last laments while standing on the "utmost western verge" of the continent. It is likely Stanley saw at least one, if not both, Matteson pictures through a printed version sometime in the decade prior to painting his version. Stanley was a member of Order of the Odd-Fellows, an organization he joined early in his painting career as a way of finding clients for his portraiture (see *Daniel Wann*, 1838; cat. no. 003).

Within Stanley's oeuvre, allegorical depictions of the passing of American Indians were infrequent, although he addressed the subject again around 1870 with *Young Chief Uncas*, notably fixed as a child (cat. no. 210). Stanley painted two versions and had one made into chromolithographs that were marketed to a wide audience. The title refers to the main character of Uncas in James Fenimore Cooper's 1826 novel, *The Last of the Mohicans*. Cooper's popular portrayal of a dying race resonated with audiences in the early part of the century, but paintings of the subject continued to capture American artists' and audiences' imaginations for decades following. In Stanley's version, Uncas sits in a melancholy pose on a rocky outcropping in the wilderness, reflecting the passage in the book when Uncas is introduced. His father, Chingachgook, laments the demise of his tribe: "Where are the blossoms of those summers? Fallen, one by one. So all of my family departed, each in his turn, to the land of spirits. I am on the hilltop and must go down into the valley; and when Uncas follows in my footsteps, there will no longer be any of the blood of the Sagamores, for my boy is the last of the Mohicans."[34]

Stanley was certainly not the first artist to portray Uncas—Thomas Cole, for example, painted a series about the subject soon after the publication of the book (Thomas Cole, *Last of the Mohicans*, 1827, Wadsworth Athenaeum, Hartford, Connecticut). By mid-century, Hudson River School painter Asher B. Durand painted *The Indian's Vespers* (1847, also once known as "Last of the Mohicans"), with a solitary American Indian standing at the edge of a path, bathed in yellow and pink light from the setting sun, peering into the distance with his hands raised (fig. 4.8).[35] Durand's painting was the result of an American Art-Union commission for a landscape, but Durand added the American Indian into the composition to evoke the wild state of nature and man in his pure form in America's past. Stanley was similarly drawn to the wilderness, and in a letter to his fiancée, Alice English, in 1853, Stanley remarked how he found himself "in the quiet solitude of Nature's garden, surrounded only by God's own work, as fresh as blooming, as when first born in Paradise."[36] But Stanley's depiction of Uncas is atypical. Uncas is a young boy, not the mature man of Cooper's novel, and his war shirt and eagle-feather bonnet identifies him not as a Mohican Indian from the East, but as a Plains Indian from the West. Stanley's Uncas surpasses the literary figure and instead is a symbolic "last Indian." Stanley evokes sympathy for the young chief through the boy's saddened expression and slumped posture, which bears the weight of a tribal past and his imminent future demise. The storm clouds brewing overhead emphasize impending doom.

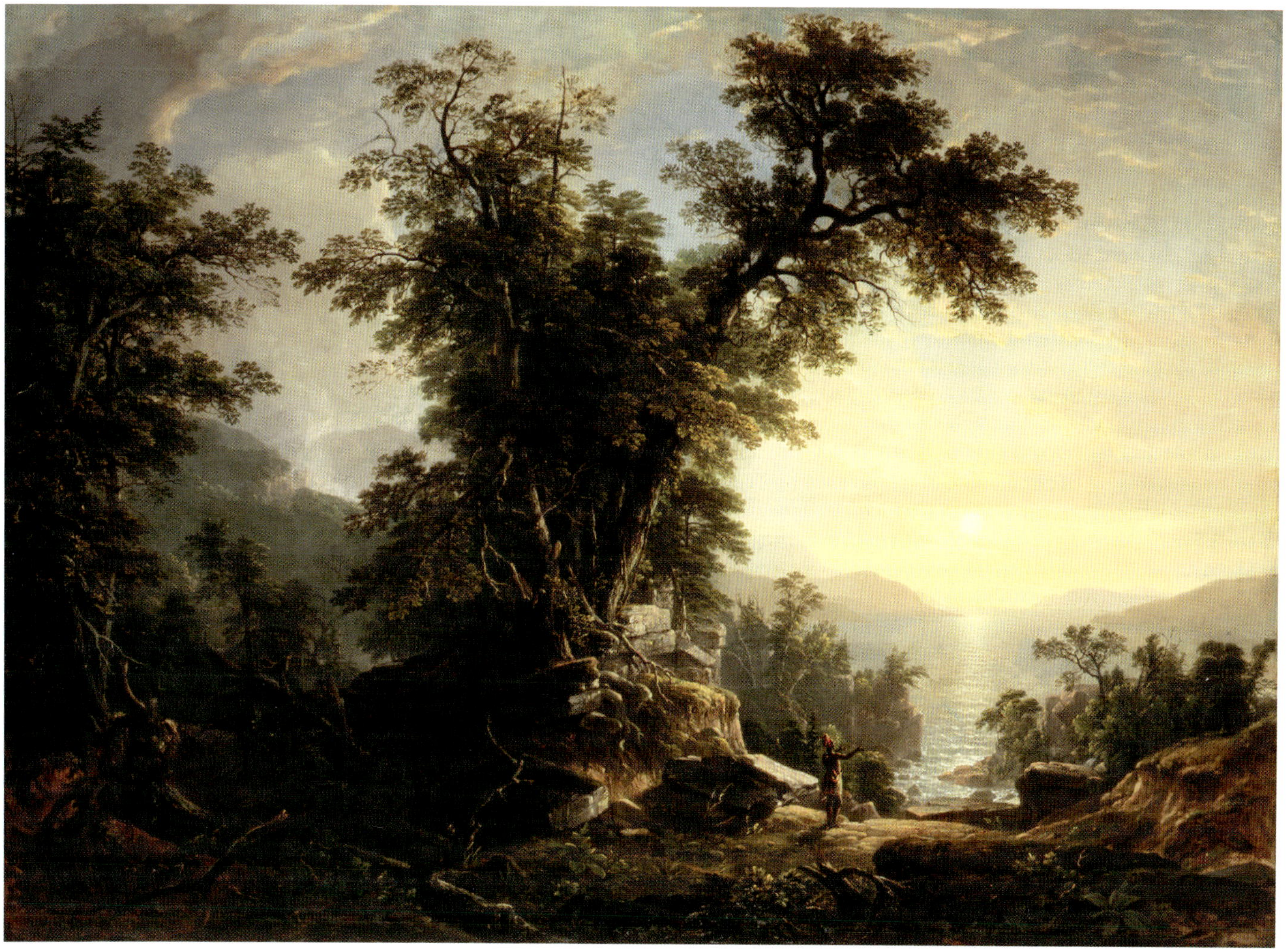

FIG. 4.8.
Asher B. Durand, *The Indian's Vespers*, 1847. Oil on canvas; 46⅛ × 62¼ in. (117.2 × 158.1 cm). Courtesy White House Historical Association, White House Collection, Washington, D.C.

Critical reviews of *The Last of the Mohicans* in the early nineteenth century were quick to point out that the portrayal of Uncas was unbelievable, primarily because Cooper brought a personal element into the character, giving him emotions and generosity that readers could identify with.[37] The natural virtue of Uncas complicated the common understanding of the doomed Indian, who was childlike, simple, and incapable of sympathies, feelings, and complex personalities. In time, especially by the 1880s, reference to Cooper and Cooper's Indians in popular literature and journals was a code for easterners who were sentimental and sympathetic to Indians, which was judged as an anti-progress viewpoint.[38]

During Stanley's mature career, the most influential mid-nineteenth-century literary work about American Indians was Henry Wadsworth Longfellow's epic poem, *The Song of Hiawatha* (1855). True to the common perception, at the end of the poem, the Indian hero Hiawatha has a vision of the demise of his tribe in the face of white expansion, "Saw the remnants of our people/ Sweeping westward, wild and woful," and in the concluding verse, Hiawatha walks off into the setting sun.[39] *The Song of Hiawatha* sold an estimated fifty thousand copies by 1857, further embedding the image of American Indians as vanishing people. Hiawatha's actions imply that whites and American Indians would never live together, which was a fate that befell Major

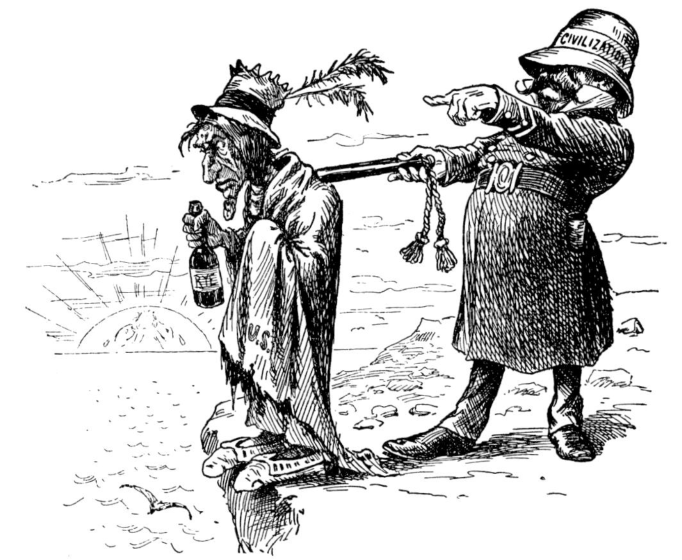

MOVE ON, MAROON BROTHER, MOVE ON!

FIG. 4.9.
Frederick Opper, "Move On, Maroon Brother, Move On!" From Bill Nye's *History of the United States* (London, 1894).

Culbertson and his Blackfeet bride, Natawista. In 1869, Culbertson declared bankruptcy and was forced to sell everything, including *The Last of Their Race*. The following year, Natawista moved back to the West from their home in Peoria, Illinois, to live with the Blood tribe on the reservation, where she remained for the rest of her life.[40] The circumstances of Culbertson's family bespeaks of the uncertainty of the time.

In the late 1860s and early 1870s, the popularity of the doomed Indian image declined, perhaps, observed Julie Schimmel, "because during those years the Plains Wars reached a frantic pitch and no artist could afford to lament the passing of the Indian."[41] But the image reappeared in the 1890s after the Wounded Knee Massacre, a tragic battle where more than three hundred Lakota men, women, and children were killed. Occasionally, a depiction of American Indians pushed to the edge of the continent addressed the cause of the demise of the race. Frederick Opper's "Move On, Maroon Brother, Move On" is a satirical drawing of a policeman with a baton literally jabbing a haggard and tattered Red Man to the edge of a precipice over the ocean, with the requisite sunset in the distance (fig. 4.9). Opper's illustration literally places blame by including a white figure with the Indian. However, because the Indian is not ennobled, but rather stereotyped as drunk and dirty, Opper does not garner sympathy for his subject. Other vanishing race images were used to incite national sympathy and preserve Native peoples. The reservation system had been instituted by this time, and the plight of the American Indian was even more desperate.

A more poetic and symbolic rendering of the American Indian at the edge of the continent is James Earle Fraser's *End of the Trail*, an image still popular today (fig. 4.10). A forlorn warrior, a muscular classical nude, sits slumped forward on his pony. His moccasined feet dangle loosely below a buffalo robe—his whole posture echoes the metaphoric weight of his fate. By 1915, when the sculpture was exhibited at two and one-half times life size at the Panama-Pacific International Exposition in San Francisco, American perception was that the "Indian problem" had been solved. As one guidebook proclaimed, "The Indian has ridden for many a weary day . . . but alas! . . . His trail is now lost and on the edge of the continent he finds himself almost annihilated."[42] Fraser was sympathetic to the plight of the Plains Indians who lived near his home in the Dakotas and intended his artwork to call attention to the pathetic conditions of reservations and Indian life. However, years of written and pictorial images of the demise of the American Indian framed this image so that it was interpreted instead as a memorial to the past. Fraser's ultimate vision for the sculpture was to cast it in bronze and place it overlooking San Francisco Bay, literally at the edge of the continent.

Visual images are powerful reflections and enforcers of beliefs. Americans have been exposed to images of the "doomed" Indian for nearly two hundred years, and Stanley's *The Last of Their Race* was one of many nineteenth-century images that both reflected and perpetuated

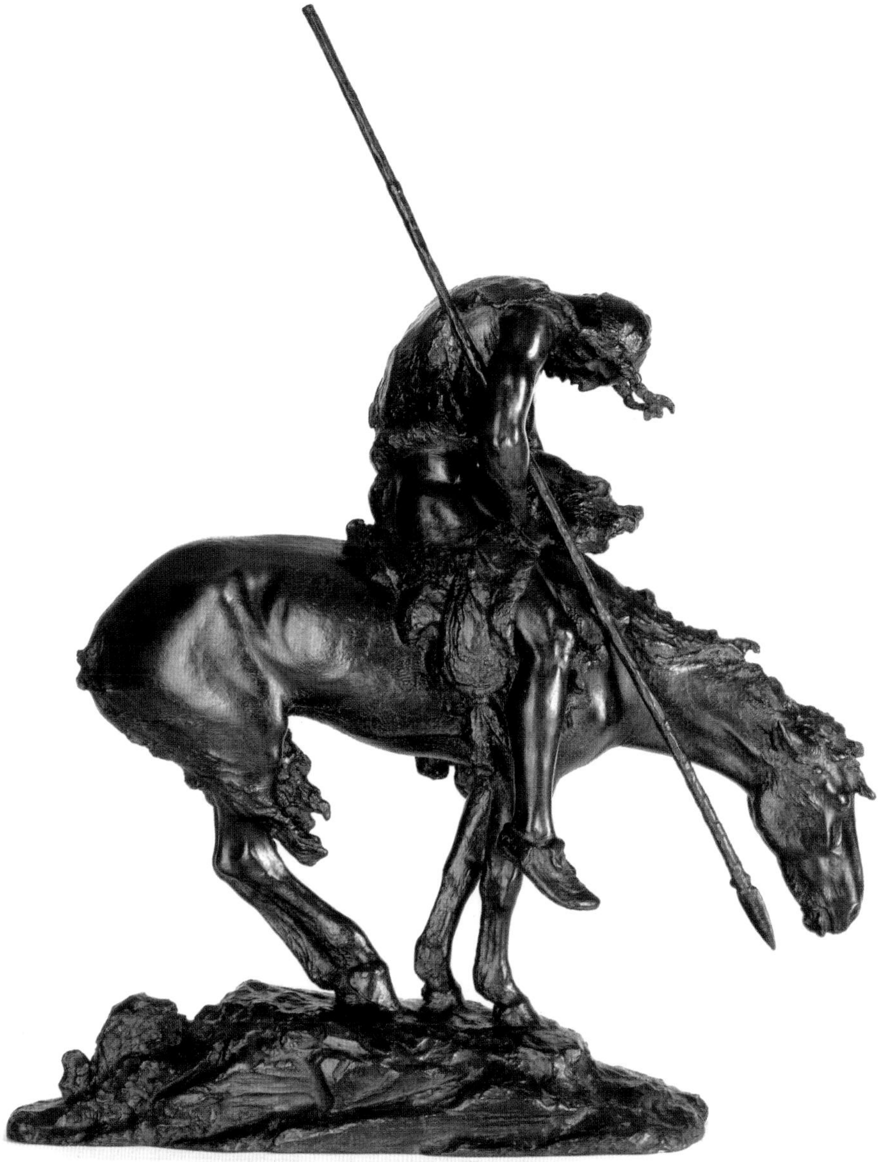

FIG. 4.10.
James Earle Fraser, *End of the Trail*, 1894. Bronze; 33¾ × 26 × 8 in. (85.7 × 66.0 × 20.3 cm). Courtesy Buffalo Bill Center of the West, Cody, Wyoming (112.67)

the belief that the race had perished. This message was so strong that it overwhelmed what was known to be true. Before the Indian Removal Act, for example, Cherokee Indians had established farms, adopted European dress, and developed professional careers as lawyers and teachers in the South. Cherokee behavior, however, did not fit the common perception that Indians were unteachable and different from Euro-Americans, which in part encouraged removal and isolation. Stanley had traveled in the West and was no doubt aware of the true conditions, difficult as they were; American Indians were not dying out, but struggling to adapt. Notwithstanding Stanley's experience, *The Last of Their Race* presents an ambivalent message, seemingly answering the prophecy of William Cullen Bryant, who defined the fate of the American Indian in his 1824 poem, "An Indian at the Burial-Place of His Fathers":

They waste us—aye—like April snow
  In the warm noon, we shrink away;
And fast they follow, as we go
  Towards the setting day,—
Till they shall fill the land, and we
  Are driven into the western sea.[43]

Yet, the American Indian race had not been defeated and had not been pushed into the Pacific Ocean in Stanley's lifetime, nor is it a prophecy that materialized in the twentieth century. "There must have been an inner strength in our ancestors that supported them through the difficult times when their economies, their cultures, and their very lives were threatened," recalls Emma I. Hansen, scholar and member of the Pawnee Nation. "They respect and celebrate the tribal heritages, histories, and traditions . . . [and] they also actively innovate and create their own futures on reservations and in small towns and cities throughout North America."[44] Stanley's *The Last of Their Race* presented a powerful allegory of an end, reflecting nineteenth-century American cultural beliefs, but even today, Native peoples continue to endure.

NOTES

1. [Washington Irving], "Traits of Indian Character," *Analectic Magazine* 3 (February 1814): 23. For an in-depth discussion of the social and political implications of the "Vanishing American" concept, see Brian W. Dippie, *The Vanishing American: White Attitudes and U.S. Indian Policy* (Middletown, Conn.: Wesleyan University Press, 1982).

2. Julie Schimmel, "John Mix Stanley and Imagery of the West in Nineteenth-Century American Art" (Ph.D. diss., New York University, 1983), 269. I am grateful to Julie Schimmel for sharing her research related to the "doomed Indian," for inspiring insight and ideas through her dissertation, and for providing valuable feedback on this essay.

3. Figures vary on the number of people from eastern tribes who were forced west. This statistic is from, "Indian Treaties and the Removal Act of 1830," *U.S. Department of State: Office of the Historian*, accessed March 12, 2014, https://history.state.gov/milestones/1830-1860/indian-treaties.

4. Oliver H. Smith, as quoted in Dippie, *Vanishing American*, 219.

5. Julie Schimmel, "Images of the Dispossessed," in *Henry Farny Paints the Far West* (Cincinnati, Ohio: Cincinnati Art Museum, 2007), 26.

6. The poem appeared in the newspaper during the Washington Art Association's exhibition of *Last of Their Race*. L. A. Christie, ["Doomed Race"], *National Intelligencer*, March 18, 1857, 1.

7. Berger defined the viewer's gaze as masculine, especially when the subjects were women. This idea could also be applied to a subject-viewer relationship marked by different races, in this case the white viewer and American Indian subject. See John Berger, *Ways of Seeing* (New York: Viking, 1972), 45–64.

8. Untitled clipping from [Detroit paper?] December 19, 1867, John Mix Stanley scrapbook, 1843–1868, reel OAM, Archives of American Art, Smithsonian Institution, Washington, D.C. (hereafter Stanley scrapbook).

9. For an in-depth conversation about Stanley's Indian Gallery, see Brian W. Dippie, "Far Superior to Catlin: Stanley and His Indian Gallery," in *Catlin and His Contemporaries: The Politics of Patronage* (Lincoln: University of Nebraska Press, 1990), 265–318. George Catlin, notably, was another artist-explorer who created an Indian Gallery.

10. For a discussion on "imperialist nostalgia" and mythologies of American history, see Emily C. Burns, "The Itinerant John Mix Stanley and the Circulating Public Spectacle of the West in Mid-Century America," in this volume.

11. Advertisement for Indian Gallery of John Mix Stanley, ca. 1850, Stanley Papers.

12. John Mix Stanley, "Preface," *Portraits of North American Indians, with Sketches of Scenery, Etc., Painted by J. M. Stanley* (Washington, D.C.: Smithsonian Institution, 1852).

13. [John Mix Stanley], "The Memorial of John M. Stanley of the State of New York," petition to Washington, January 12, 1863, as quoted in Kathryn S. Hight, "The Frontier Indian in White Art, 1830–1876: The Development of a Myth" (Ph.D. diss., University of California, Los Angeles, 1987), 263.

14. For a deeper discussion about this topic, see Robert F. Berkhofer, Jr., "The Idea of the Indian: Invention and Perpetuation" in *The White Man's Indian: Images of the American Indian from Columbus to the Present* (New York: Knopf, 1978), 25–31.

15. Scholars generally agree that the painting represents multiple tribes. W. Vernon Kinietz describes the painting as a generic group of Indians sitting at the promontory. Kathryn Sweeney Hight calls these "not tribe specific," in Hight, "The Frontier Indian in White Art," 264. Lesley Wischmann describes *Last of Their Race* as an "allegorical painting [that] depicted nine Indians, dressed in the style of different tribes." See Lesley Wischmann, *Frontier Diplomats: The Life and Times of Alexander Culbertson and Natoyist-Siksina'* (Spokane, Wash.: Arthur H. Clark, 2000). 275. Sarah Boehme interprets the figures as members of diverse tribes in Sarah E. Boehme et. al, *Powerful Images: Portrayals of Native America* (Seattle: Museums West and University of Washington Press, 1998), 40.

16. A collection of Stanley's artifacts is now in the National Museum of the American Indian, gift of Gari Melchers. Melchers had inherited the collection from his father, sculptor Theodore Melchers,

who had purchased the collection from Stanley's widow, Alice. See records for Jicarilla Apache bow and arrows, 165216 & 165217; Mohawk moccasins, 165218; Comanche man's boots/leggings, 165221; Pikuni Blackfeet bear claw necklace, 156203; and Pikuni Blackfeet woman's dress, 165205.

17. John C. Ewers, "The Emergence of the Plains Indian as the Symbol of the North American Indian," *Annual Report of the Smithsonian Institution for 1964* (Washington, D.C.: Government Printing Office, 1965), 530–44.

18. For a detailed account of Stanley's journey with the Stevens expedition, see Peter H. Hassrick's essay in this volume.

19. John C. Ewers questions this attribution, and suggests the shirt might be Assiniboin, rather than Blackfeet. Either way, it relates to the Plains tribes from the Upper Missouri region. See John C. Ewers, "Artists' Choices," *American Indian Art Magazine* 7, no. 2 (Spring 1982): 45.

20. Isaac I. Stevens, *Narrative and Final Report of Explorations for a Route for a Pacific Railroad, near the Forty-seventh and Forty-ninth Parallels of North Latitude from Saint Paul to Puget Sound*, vol. 12, book 1 of *Reports of Explorations and Surveys, to Ascertain the Most Practicable and Economical Route for a Railroad from the Mississippi River to the Pacific Ocean* (Washington, D. C.: Thomas H. Ford, 1860), 34, 85, 96.

21. See Lisa Strong's essay in this volume for a detailed examination of the Blackfeet-U.S. tensions and discussions in Washington during 1854–1855 with Culbertson and Stevens.

22. Wischmann, *Frontier Diplomats*, 21.

23. The identity of Natawista and her brother, Seen From Afar, is confirmed by an account in the *Peoria Daily Tribune*, December 1, 1859, which mentions that the models for the painting were Blackfeet Indians "taken from life." The article also states that the Culbertsons valued the painting for the family ties to the models.

24. Isaac I. Stevens to Alexander Culbertson, September 21, 1853, as quoted in Wischmann, *Frontier Diplomats*, 20.

25. Claire Perry, *Young America: Childhood in 19th-Century Art and Culture* (New Haven, Conn.: Yale University Press, 2006), 161.

26. Captain Montgomery Meigs served as the financial and engineering supervisor of the extension, under then secretary of war Jefferson Davis, who was appointed by President Pierce to oversee administrative responsibilities. Meigs often took the initiative to suggest subjects for the sculpture commissions and routinely chose European artists for the commissions, much to the anger of American artists in Washington, D.C. See Vivien Green Fryd, *Art and Empire: The Politics of Ethnicity in the United States Capitol, 1815–1860* (New Haven, Conn.: Yale University Press, 1992), 109–12.

27. "Crawford and His Last Work," *The Crayon* 1, no. 11 (March 14, 1855): 168.

28. James L. Orr, quoted in Dippie, *Vanishing American*, 73. Numerous accounts from this period reflect the inevitable disappearance of the American Indians, after literally being pushed farther west. For example, see Samuel G. Drake, *Indian Captivities; or, Life in the Wigwam* (Auburn, N.Y.: Derby and Miller, 1853), 6–7. Newspaper accounts and poems from the mid-nineteenth century about the "interesting, but doomed race of mankind" abound. See, for example, "The American Indians," *Maine Farmer*, August 2, 1849, 17.

29. "Crawford and His Last Work," 168.

30. Perry, *Young America*, 152.

31. Julie Schimmel, "Inventing 'the Indian,'" in *The West as America: Reinterpreting Images of the Frontier, 1820–1920*, ed. William H. Truettner (Washington, D.C., and London: National Museum of American Art / Smithsonian Institution Press, 1991), 169.

32. Elizabeth Johns, *American Genre Painting: The Politics of Everyday Life* (New Haven, Conn.: Yale University Press, 1991), 76.

33. James L. Ridgely and Paschal Donaldson, eds. *The Odd-Fellows' Offering for 1848* (New York: Edward Walker, 1848), 238, 240.

34. James Fenimore Cooper, *The Last of the Mohicans: A Narrative of 1757*, reprint ed. (Franklin Center, Pa.: Franklin Library, 1982), 28.

35. Interim owners generated the title of *Last of the Mohicans*, and the painting was published with that title in 1964. William Kloss, *Art in the White House: A Nation's Pride* (Washington, D.C.: White House Historical Association, 1992), 275, entry 112n1.

36. Stanley to Alice English, May 10, 1853, Stanley Papers.

37. Dippie, *Vanishing American*, 23.

38. Ibid., 134.

39. Henry Wadsworth Longfellow, *The Song of Hiawatha and Other Poems*, Reader's Digest ed. (Pleasantville, N.Y.: Reader's Digest Association, 1989), 166.

40. Wischmann, *Frontier Diplomats*, 311, 336–37.

41. Schimmel, "Inventing 'the Indian,'" 169. Robert F. Berkhofer further surmises that the Indian in literature declined in the decade before the Civil War because the romantic movement also waned. Berkhofer, *The White Man's Indian*, 86.

42. Juliet Helena Lumbard James, *Sculpture of the Exposition Palaces and Courts; Descriptive Notes on the Art of the Statuary at the Panama-Pacific International Exposition, San Francisco* (San Francisco: H. S. Crocker, 1915), 34.

43. William Cullen Bryant, "An Indian at the Burial-Place of His Fathers" (originally published 1824) in *The Poems of William Cullen Bryant*, ed. Louis Untermeyer (New York: Heritage Press, 1947), 67–68.

44. Emma I. Hansen, *Memory and Vision: Arts, Cultures, and Lives of Plains Indian People* (Seattle: University of Washington Press, 2007), 253.

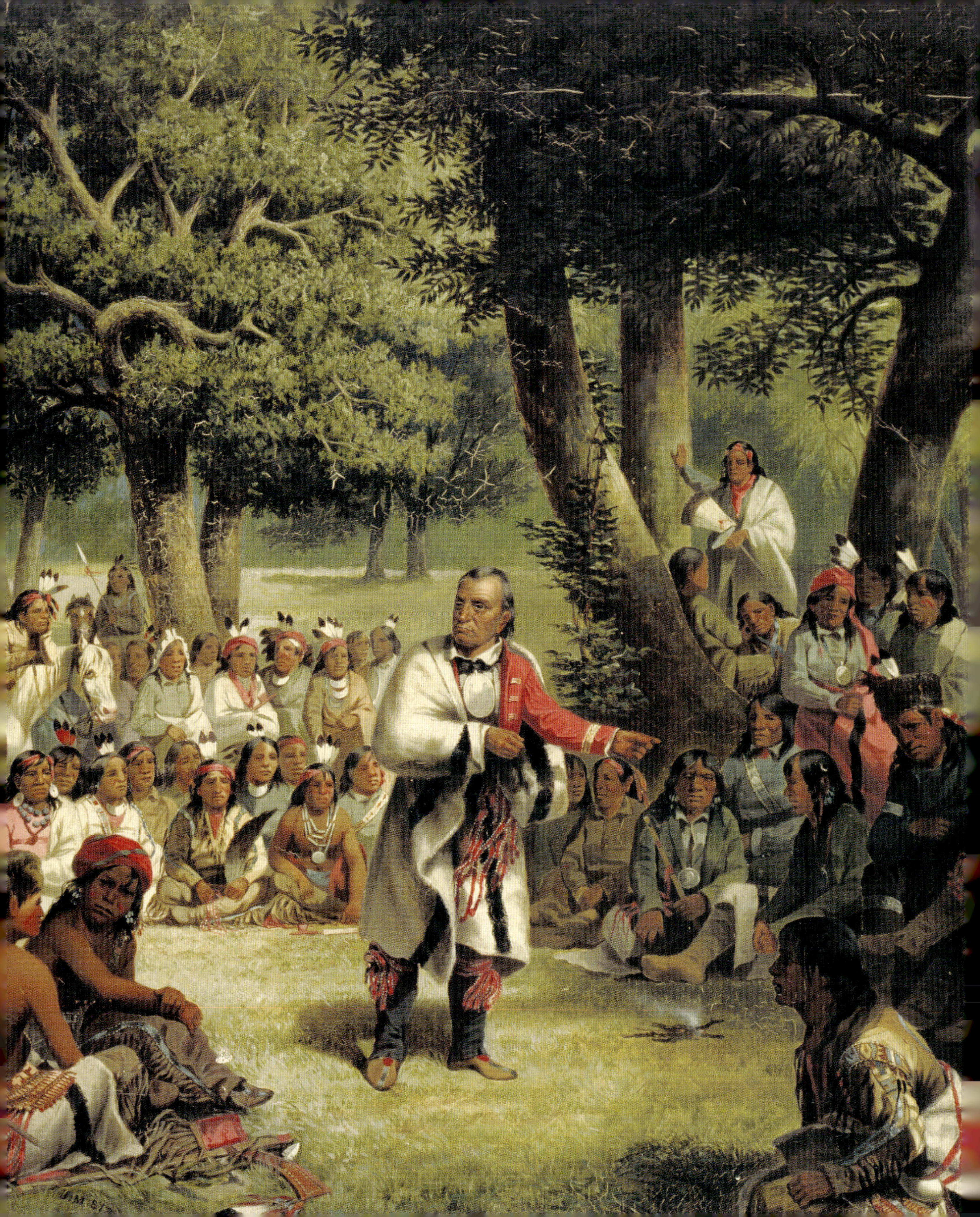

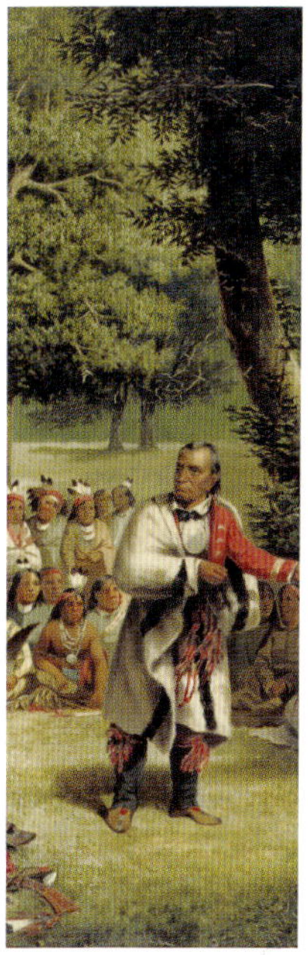

5

Witnessing History, Staging History

The American Indian Paintings of John Mix Stanley

Scott Manning Stevens

Like many contemporary Native Americans, I am keenly aware of the traces of my people's history submerged within the master narrative of the United States. Coming from an oral tradition, the Mohawk Nation in my case, that left no written records of our own before the eighteenth century, I have become accustomed to teasing out the voices of my ancestors from the colonial archive. Finding an accurate representation of a Mohawk perspective in the early documentary record is a study in frustration, as one attempts to read through the deeply prejudiced descriptions of Indian life found among the colonial chroniclers or the often dismissive observations of Christian missionaries. One learns to read both between the lines and outside the written record, the latter being expressed in Native oral accounts that continue to survive, archaeological evidence, and material culture (artifacts) that help fill in the record of our frequently contested past. This proves a similar challenge with visual materials as well. If we now recognize that the much-admired photographs of a figure such as Edward Curtis were often staged with costumes and props, how are we to trust the earlier pen or paintbrush to supply us with accurate historical and ethnographic information? But if we were to ignore the rich visual record left by the likes of George Catlin, Charles Bird King, or John Mix Stanley we would lose an invaluable archive of the Native American past.

John Mix Stanley is a figure whose works straddle two quite different, though complementary, traditions that developed in American art. His works, almost uniquely focused on the lives of the indigenous nations of this continent, can be said to represent both the documentary and

OPPOSITE

(detail) J. M. Stanley, *The Trial of Red Jacket*, 1869 (cat. no. 213) the historical painting genres popular in the early republic. Stanley was born into the dynamic era that marked the struggles between Native peoples and American settlers throughout the course of the century in which he lived. His birth in Canandaigua, New York, in 1814 meant he was born in the midst of the War of 1812, in a year when the fighting was happening alarmingly close, on the Niagara Frontier between Canada and New York State. The town of his birth was of course historically significant in its own right as the site of the 1794 Treaty of Canandaigua, between the United States and the Haudenosaunee (or Iroquois) Confederacy, of whom the Mohawks are one of the six constituent nations. This treaty attempted to resolve lingering issues following the American Revolution and independence. The majority of the Haudenosaunee, except for the Oneida and Tuscarora nations, maintained their alliance with Great Britain and fought against the Americans, realizing that an American victory would mean the loss of our own independence. Following the British defeat, the Haudenosaunee Confederacy was in a state of disarray as American settlers poured into our lands. The conference at Canandaigua was meant to resolve some of these issues, especially as they regarded territory. The statesman Timothy Pickering, along with several other American officials, represented President Washington, and the resulting treaty is recognized by the United States government to this day.

Though Stanley's family moved from Canandaigua to Buffalo, New York, when he was still a small child, he could hardly have been unaware of the significance of his birthplace, living as he now did adjacent to the Seneca territory of the Buffalo Creek Reservation. It was here that one of the most famous Native Americans in his day, and a participant in the negotiations at Canandaigua, still lived when Stanley was a boy, the Seneca leader Sagoyewahta, better known as Red Jacket—to whom I shall return later. Settlers in the recently founded town of Buffalo, New York, had coveted the Seneca lands proximate to their community since before the completion of the Erie Canal in 1825. In 1819 an attempt to extinguish Indian title to that land had been successfully thwarted by Red Jacket and his allies, but with the leader's death in 1830 and the inception of the U.S. federal Indian removal policy, the days of the reservation were numbered, and in 1838 the Treaty of Buffalo Creek sealed the fate of the Senecas living on that land. By that point, John Mix Stanley had already left the Buffalo region following the death of his parents. At fourteen he was living back in the Finger Lakes region of his birth, now in Naples, New York, where he was an apprentice coach maker and sometime sign painter. After moving to Detroit in 1834, then still very much a frontier town, he began his painting career in earnest.

It is during this same period that Stanley would have been exposed to American Indian life on the frontier. We know he also lived for a brief period in points west of Detroit, such as Galena, Illinois, and Fort Snelling, between 1838 and 1839. Galena, in the northeast corner of Illinois, was in the midst of the region where the Black Hawk War of 1832 had taken place, and Fort Snelling was a key U.S. military outpost between Dakota and Ojibwe territories. As had been the case in his youth, Stanley lived in a region where Indian and settler conflicts were either a very recent memory or were ongoing. In this atmosphere, it is hardly surprising that the aspiring artist turned to American Indians as his subject matter. As numerous art historians have pointed out, the American Indian was one of the truly incontrovertibly American subjects to which artists could turn if they wished to establish a visual tradition independent of European themes and genre painting. This was a matter of a considerably self-conscious effort during the years following independence. The writings of James Fenimore Cooper had established the interactions and conflicts between Indians and settlers as an archetypal theme in American letters in the 1820s, and visual artists embraced similar subjects. In the case of landscape painters, an easy shorthand to distinguish an American vista from a European one was the inclusion of a group of Native Americans or evidence of one of their communities in the scene.

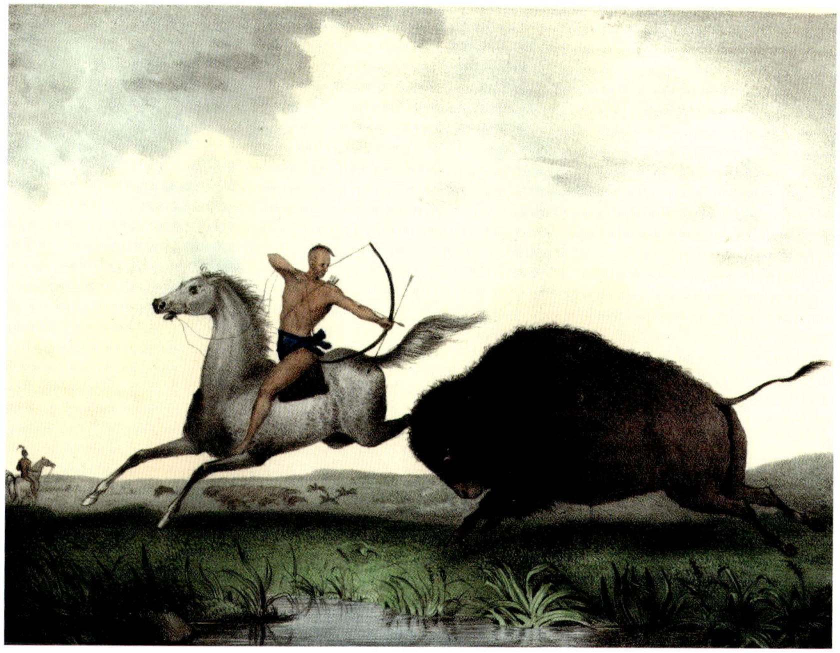

FIG. 5.1.
Titian Ramsay Peale, *American Buffaloe* [1830]. Engraving; 11 × 9 in. (27.9 × 22.9 cm). From *The Cabinet of Natural History and American Rural Sports*, vol. 1 (Philadelphia: J. and T. Doughty, 1830). Courtesy Rare Book and Special Collections Division, Library of Congress, Washington, D.C.

Also during the early 1830s, a young George Catlin (1796–1872) embarked on his western journeys to visit the indigenous nations of that region and begin the work that would make up his famous Indian gallery. Catlin, self-taught and of uneven artistic skills, would have encountered keen competition in his quest to become a successful portrait artist in a period when several refined painters had established careers in the urban centers of Boston, New York, and Philadelphia. His imagination and ambition, like those of others to follow, were instead fired by the unknown frontier and the indigenous nations who occupied it. Catlin would travel routes similar to those first visited by the American explorers Lewis and Clark just two decades earlier. In fact, Catlin befriended William Clark, now the territorial governor in St. Louis, and visited Clark's Indian Museum before embarking on his journey up the Missouri. Catlin would make several separate journeys through the upper Midwest and Plains in 1832, 1834, 1835, and 1836. It was also during this period that another artist who would make a name for himself recording Indian life was traveling in the Upper Missouri River region as well, the Swiss artist Karl Bodmer (1809–1893), who had been hired by Prince Maximilian von Wied und Neuwied (1782–1867) to make a visual record of Bodmer's patron's journey into the North American hinterlands. Catlin was not the first to paint the Indians of this region. Titian Ramsey Peale (1799–1885) had recorded a Plains buffalo hunt several years earlier (fig. 5.1), and John Neagle (1796–1865) and Charles Bird King (1785–1862) had begun painting the portraits of Native diplomatic representatives visiting Philadelphia and Washington, D.C., a full decade earlier than Catlin. One could say there was a vogue for Indian portraits, or at least a curiosity among easterners, who now mostly encountered Indians of the original thirteen colonies as acculturated and disenfranchised peoples, descended from once feared Native nations. The so-called wild Indians of the frontier loomed large in their imaginations as the United States set its sights ever westward.

John Mix Stanley was likely as interested as these other artists in the romance of traveling into Indian country and the possibility of making a career for himself recording through his art the various Natives of this continent. As the scholars William Truettner (1979, 119–25) and Brian Dippie (1990, 265–66) have demonstrated in their respective studies of the art and career of George Catlin, he was profoundly concerned with securing patronage through ceaseless self-promotion. Art was, after all, a business, too, and Stanley now was entering into this competitive art world almost a full decade after Catlin had come to prominence. Having spent three

FIG. 5.2.
John Mix Stanley, *Indian Council, Tehuacana Creek, Texas,* 1843. Oil on canvas; 17 × 24 in. (43.2 × 61.0 cm). Courtesy private collection

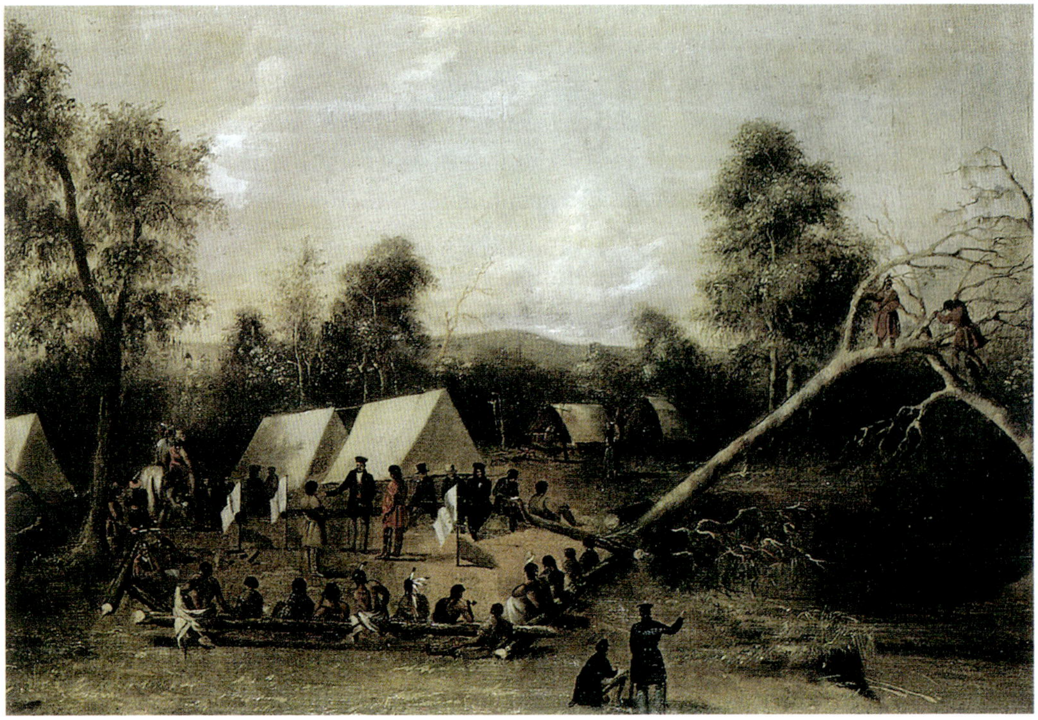

years as an itinerant portrait painter in the Northeast, Stanley went west again, this time to Fort Gibson in Indian Territory (present-day Oklahoma) in late 1842. The next year, Stanley was able to accompany Pierce M. Butler, the dashing former governor of South Carolina, who now acted as a commissioner in negotiations with the tribes living in the borderlands between the Republic of Texas and U.S. territories. It was on this diplomatic mission that Stanley began documenting the lives of American Indians through his artistic works. One of his earliest representations is of an actual Indian council that occurred at Tehuacana Creek near the current location of Waco, Texas.

This painting, titled simply *Indian Council, Tehuacana Creek, Texas* (fig. 5.2, cat. no. 008), is remarkable for the absence of narrative drama. Rather, we are presented with a, most likely idealized, representation of frontier diplomacy. The activity is depicted from a respectful distance and might at first glance seem more closely related to landscape painting than to a portrayal of an actual event. But upon closer inspection, we find a group consisting of Euro-Americans and various Indians sitting in a council circle on newly felled logs—all attending to the figures in the center of the circle, one of them presumably Pierce Butler. The viewer's eye is drawn to the light army tents in the background and the three white flags of peace within the council space itself. The three figures standing in the middle of the circle most likely represent the spokesmen for the United States, the Republic of Texas, and the Indian groups present. Stanley gives us not so much a snapshot of the actual proceedings but a depiction of the formal and decorous atmosphere, which he chose to emphasize. The flags of truce and relatively static actors in the scene help create an atmosphere of diplomatic exchange and mutual recognition rather than the usual conflicts we have come to expect on the frontier. This is underscored by the fact that Stanley would paint portraits of several participants from the Tehuacana council for his Indian Gallery and include some portions he had recorded from their translated speeches in the gallery guide, published by the Smithsonian some ten years later.[1] I find in such a painting not objective documentary evidence, but a desire on the artist's part to emphasize a legal and diplomatic aspect of what will still ultimately amount to the appropriation of Indian lands. Like Catlin before him, Stanley could deeply sympathize with the Indians while never questioning the logic of Manifest Destiny.

Equally significant is Stanley's choice to paint from a documentary perspective rather than the romantic one we see so clearly in the works of his contemporary Alfred Jacob Miller (1810–1874); nor at this point did Stanley adopt the style of grand history painting still highly admired in his day. As with Catlin and Bodmer, both Native American and non-Native viewers can turn to Stanley's works for the ethnographic and historical documentation they provide. This is not to say that aesthetic considerations were not paramount for these artists, but we know they were judged then and now for the accuracy of their portrayals. This aspect of the critical reception of the art of the American West has not waned. Scholar Nancy Anderson has noted that from the beginning, depictions of the western frontier were judged as frequently on the accuracy of their portrayals as they were on aesthetics. She writes, "Perhaps in no other area of American painting did artists so ardently declare themselves purveyors of accurate information" (1992, 5). Stanley's attachment to official diplomatic missions and later expeditions made it all the more likely that he strove for accuracy when recording events.

But Stanley's work is not merely the reportage of a courtroom artist or the images drawn by a scientific illustrator. We can also parse the complex intercultural relations that marked life in the American West. Moments in which our collective histories intertwined often appear in Stanley's works because he actually witnessed life in the regions that he depicted. He, like other artists who traveled to the West, was determined to record this frontier world within the artistic idioms of his day. The aesthetics of history might be easily ignored if we were to remain completely dependent on the textual records of the archive. Perhaps it is my own sense of the subjectivity and one-sidedness of that written record that makes me keen to refer to as much data as possible—whether or not it is produced by Native Americans. Just as oral history may contribute to our notions of past events, so too the visual record contributes greatly to a more holistic sense of that contested history.

Stanley's 1843 depiction of the *International Indian Council* (fig. 5.3, cat. no. 014) is an excellent example of just this phenomenon. Several written accounts, including one by Stanley, describe this important month-long meeting of some sixteen Indian nations, consisting of three to four thousand persons, and several representatives from the U.S. government, convened in Tahlequah, the capital of the Cherokee Nation in Indian Territory. Just five years after the forced removal of many Indian nations from east of the Mississippi, Cherokee leader John Ross called these representatives together so that "here in the west" they could engage in "the ancient talk of our fathers, perpetuating for ever the old fire and pipe of peace brought from the east, and . . . extending from nation to nation" (1985, 165). The leaders of various Native nations no doubt hoped that such a meeting would address the tensions caused by displacing so many peoples from the East into the traditional homelands of the Osage, Caddo, Kiowa, and others. Stanley was present as an observer, in attendance with other U.S. dignitaries, such as General Zachery Taylor and Pierce Butler, and he was purported to have with him a novel device—a daguerreotype camera. This apparatus was new on the scene of portraiture and of considerably more limited utility than later cameras. Stanley doubtless wished to collect images on site that would later be transformed into formal painted portraits.

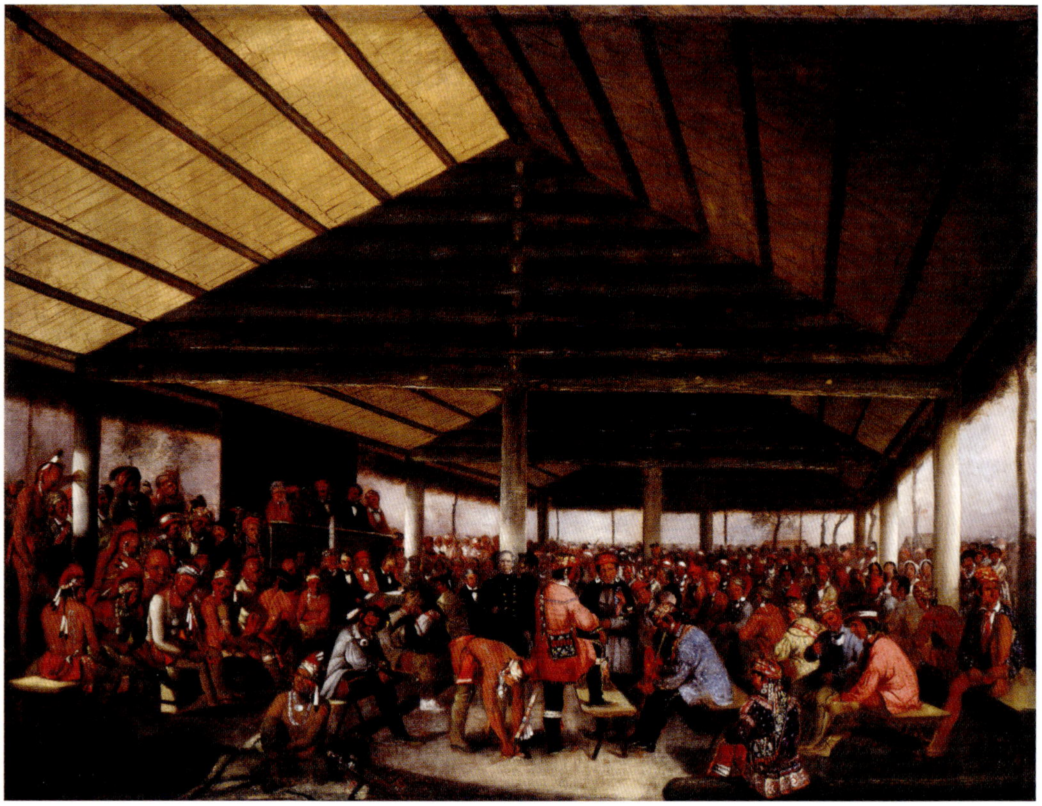

FIG. 5.3.
John Mix Stanley, *International Indian Council*, 1843. Oil on canvas; 31½ × 40½ in. (80.0 × 102.9 cm). Courtesy Smithsonian American Art Museum, Washington, D.C., gift of the Misses Henry (1985.66.248.934B)

One scholar has even attributed the somewhat static composition of Stanley's *International Indian Council* (cat. no. 014) to the influence of the daguerreotype—possibly used in this instance to record the features of General Taylor, who stands at the center of the painting, facing the viewer (Power 2007, 114). Although we know that Stanley did produce several daguerreotype portraits during his stay, and later portraits of the Ross family, he could not have relied on that cumbersome equipment for his *Indian Council* piece. Daguerreotypy typically required subjects to sit still for almost ten minutes in order to capture their image. This surely would have been impossible to do with a scene like the one depicted in the *Indian Council* painting. Here we see how superior an artistic and documentary medium the canvas could still be. Stanley represents hundreds of delegates with a profusion of color and sartorial detail. No early photographic depiction could compete with the sheer scale and diversity that appears in Stanley's tableau. If it is static in composition, the reasons may be similar to those I posited for his *Tehuacana Creek* painting.

These paintings occupy a space between documentation and the grand genre of history painting, whose primary goal is to provide a moral lesson anchored in some past action. Though a historical event is at the center of both paintings, they contain none of the drama and action of the much-revered history genre. Such paintings were meant to instruct and inspire by capturing the unfolding of significant events. Notable in the evolution of that genre were the works of the colonial American painter Benjamin West (1738–1820), whose famous *The Death of General Wolfe* (fig. 5.4) would revolutionize history painting by placing the action in its actual setting rather than turning to classical allegorizing to elevate its significance. Stanley was not yet

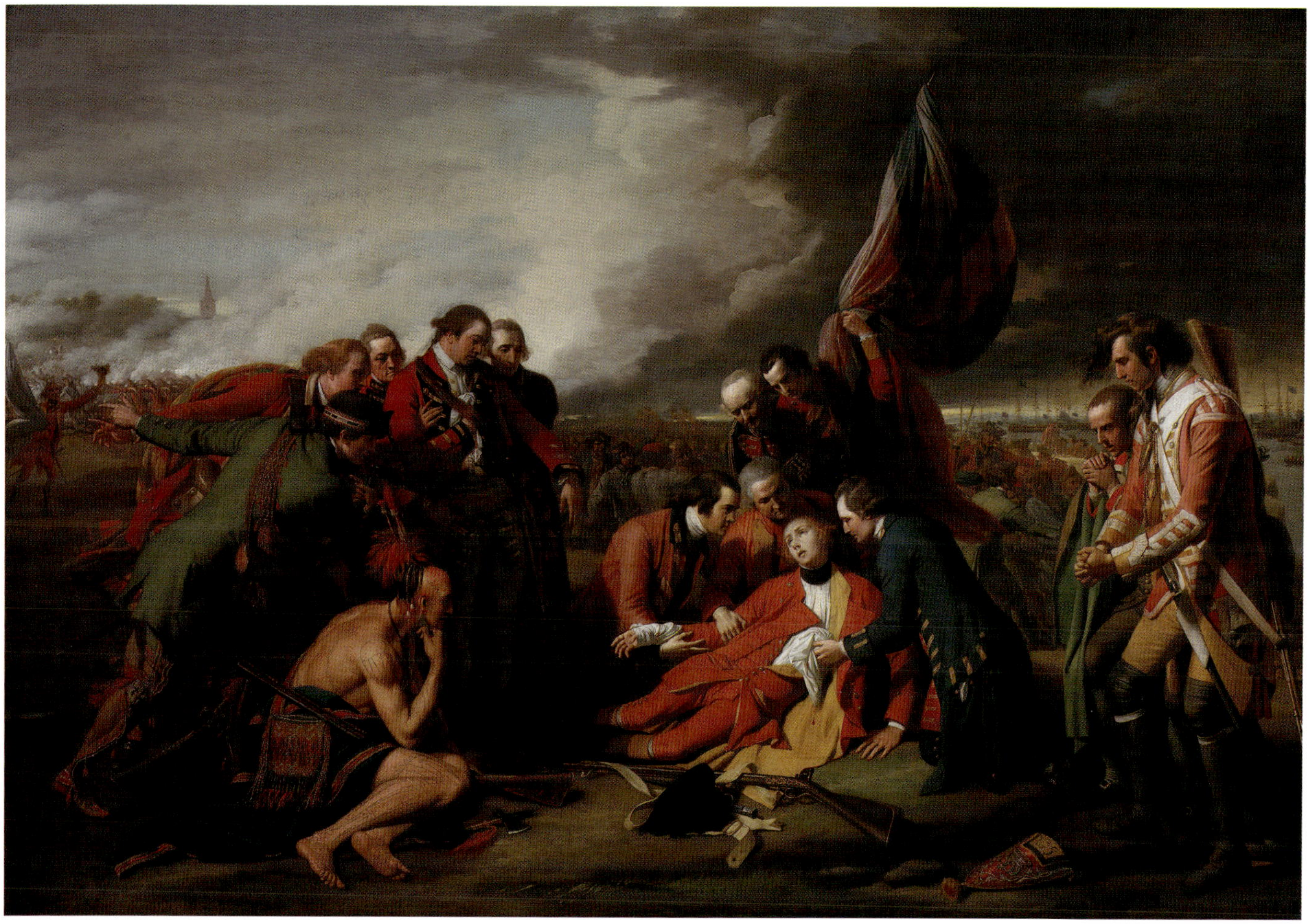

FIG. 5.4.
Benjamin West,
The Death of General Wolfe,
1770. Oil on canvas; 60 × 84½ in. (152.6 × 214.5 cm). Courtesy National Gallery of Canada, Ottawa, transfer from the Canadian War Memorials, 1921, gift of the 2nd Duke of Westminster, England, 1918

attempting anything that would approach the drama of such history paintings, though we might find an analog in West's equally famous *Penn's Treaty with the Indians* (fig. 5.5). This is a relatively static composition for a history tableau, but as with Stanley's, the subject here is that of a treaty, so considerable attention is placed on balance rather than action.

Many Native American viewers are likely to focus on another element in Stanley's *International Indian Council*—a crowded diplomatic council called together *by* Native people *for* Native people. What no daguerreotype could ever hope to capture or relate to the viewer is the scale and vibrancy of such a meeting. In an age that was beginning to wax elegiac about the imminent disappearance of the American Indian, here was a gathering of thousands of indigenous peoples at a single site. By some estimates, anywhere from four to ten thousand people attended the month-long council (Garrison 2013, 54). Stanley would have surely been impressed by the sheer size of such a gathering and could not help but see the proceedings as a powerful manifestation of American Indian political agency. Both this painting and the earlier council at Tehuacana Creek show that Stanley's initial interaction with the indigenous peoples of the West was at a nation-to-nation level. The "vanishing race" notion that artists like Catlin subscribed to was becoming popular in the post-Removal East, but here in the West was living proof against it. For Native viewers, Stanley provides a record of an event too little known in the chaotic decades

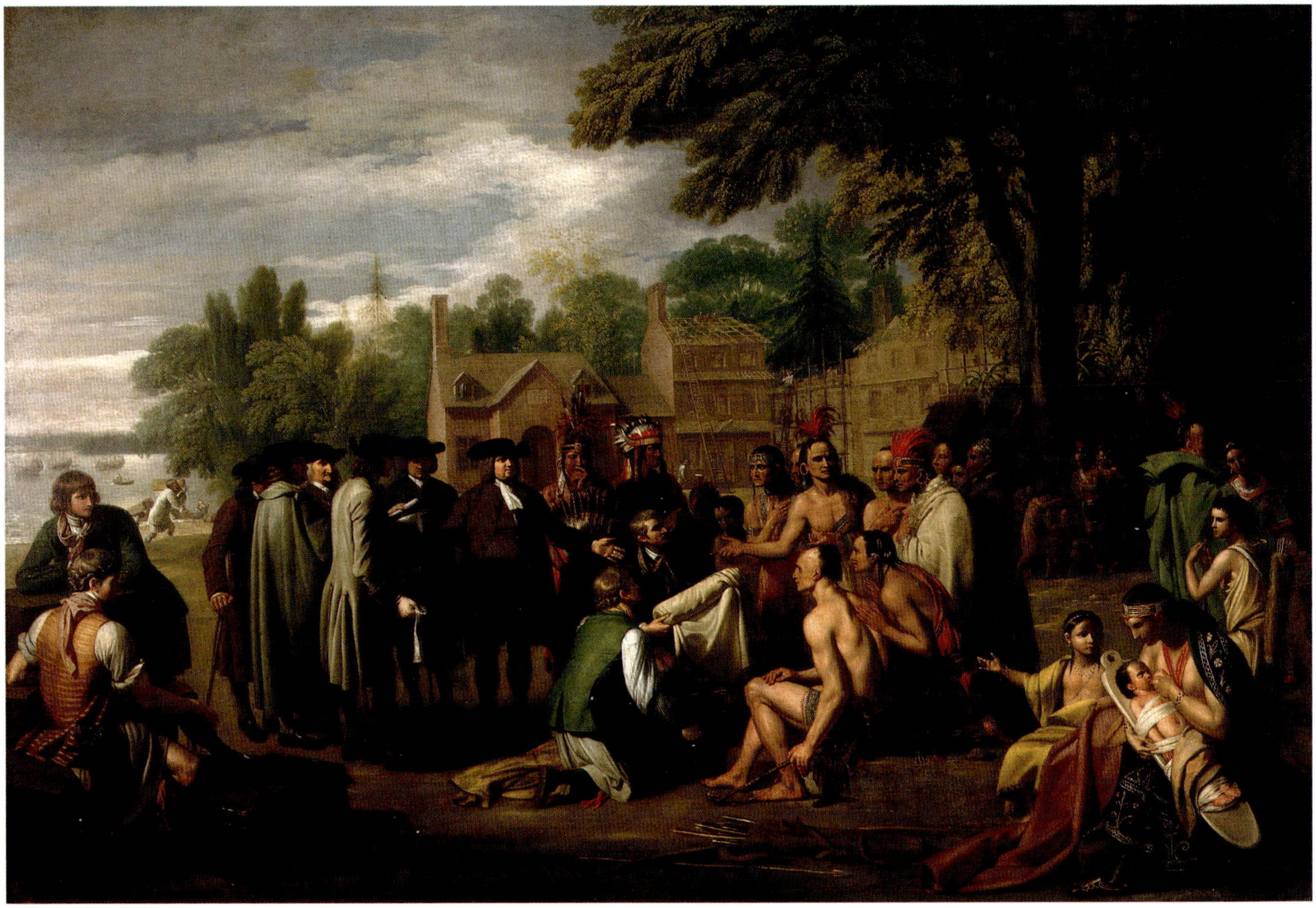

FIG. 5.5.
Benjamin West, *Penn's Treaty with the Indians*, 1771–1772. Oil on canvas; 75½ × 107¾ in. (191.8 × 273.7 cm). Courtesy Pennsylvania Academy of Fine Arts, Philadelphia, gift of Mrs. Sarah Harrison (Joseph Harrison, Jr., Collection)

of the antebellum period in Indian Territory. Historians may turn to several accounts of what occurred at this council in 1843, including those by the editor of the *Cherokee Advocate*, William Potter Ross (cat. no. 020); the Methodist missionary William H. Goode; the Indian agent Pierce Butler; and Stanley himself, but none of these documents would provide the visual context that Stanley's painting does, nor allow us a sense of the atmosphere of such an event.

Stanley would go on to complete several portraits of notable Cherokee citizens whom he met at the 1843 council, including Chief John Ross, George Lowery, Stan Watie, and Charles McIntosh—but these paintings, like most of his 200 or so paintings displayed in the Smithsonian Institution, were destroyed in the fire of 1865. We are fortunate that other paintings were not present or that a handful were saved, but we can never fully comprehend the loss. In the years between these councils and the tragic fire, the artist had continued to build his Indian Gallery in hopes of securing government patronage. At some point early on in this era marked by the notion of Manifest Destiny, Stanley began to describe his Indian Gallery as depicting a people whose populations and cultures were fast on the wane. Such assertions about the rapid decline of the Indians and their traditional ways of living may have been in part a strategy for shoring up the value and urgency of Indian galleries as records of observations on indigenous life in the United States. Stanley knew all too well that his exhibited portraits of the more urbane figures such as John Ross or George Lowery met with only tepid interest from the public.

He was in search of the "wild Indians" that both attracted the interest of early ethnographers and fueled the imaginations of dime novelists.

Stanley plunged into almost a decade of travel and genuine adventure in the Far West. His journey along the Santa Fe Trail in 1846 allowed him to join an expedition led by General Stephen Watts Kearny from Santa Fe to San Diego. This trek not only provided Stanley firsthand experience of Pueblo culture, but it also placed him near the battle of San Pasqual between Kearny's troops and Mexican lancers in December 1846, the Mexican-American War having broken out in July of that year. Stanley had been recording their journey through sketches that would later become illustrations in William Emory's *Notes of a Military Reconnoissance, from Fort Leavenworth, in Missouri, to San Diego, in California,* published in 1848. From California Stanley made his way to Oregon Territory and remained there for some five months before he traveled into the interior near Fort Walla Walla, narrowly avoiding the Whitman Massacre in November 1847. All through this period, he continued to sketch Native peoples along the way in preparation for his Indian Gallery. After some anxious winter months, Stanley resolved to leave via a sea route rather than risk travel overland. His voyage home was a circuitous one, taking him first to Hawaii, where he painted members of the Hawaiian royal family and the court, before returning to the East Coast via the isthmus of Panama in the fall of 1849.

Stanley had an uncanny knack for being present at historic events, and his experience of American hegemony's swift march toward the Pacific seems to have made him accept the notion of the inevitable decline of Native America. His petition to the U.S. Congress urging them to purchase his Indian Gallery took up the now-familiar refrain of a people "silently retreating or melting away before the pace of civilization like exhalations from the sunlight" (Dippie 1990, 283). Like Catlin before him, Stanley would meet with continued frustration at the hands of Congress. What looked promising in one session was defeated in the next, and his gallery remained in a sort of limbo. Without prospects for a definite sale, Stanley departed once again for the West, this time with the Pacific Railroad Survey led by Isaac Stevens, for whom the artist would serve as a draftsman and illustrator. Their route led from Saint Paul toward Fort Union, at the confluence of the Missouri and Yellowstone rivers, and from there on to Fort Benton, and eventually Spokane. Stanley encountered people from the Assiniboin and Piegan (or Blackfeet) nations and filled his sketchbooks with their images–perhaps with a mind to supplement the stalled sale of his Indian Gallery. In the end, these sketches would prove more lucrative as illustrations in the published railroad surveys and would indeed help support Stanley and his young family.

Stanley depended on various schemes for supporting himself through his art; he painted a Western panorama, genre scenes, and society portraits to support his family throughout the late 1850s and into the Civil War period. The bulk of his Indian Gallery had hung in the halls of the Smithsonian since 1851, and it was in the Smithsonian Castle that his collection was destroyed by the fire that tore through the galleries on January 24, 1865. With only seven paintings saved from the blaze, Stanley had lost a lifetime of work. Unable to recoup his losses in any commensurate manner, the artist could only continue to paint. At the time of the fire, now living in Detroit, Stanley was at work on a painting of a different type for him—a grand-style history painting. The subject would still be an American Indian one, but this time depicting an event that had taken place before his birth and that he would render on a huge scale. His painting *The Trial of Red Jacket* (fig. 5.6, cat. no. 212) was to cover a six-by-nine-foot canvas and feature the famed Seneca leader Sagoyewatha, known as Red Jacket (c. 1758–1830).

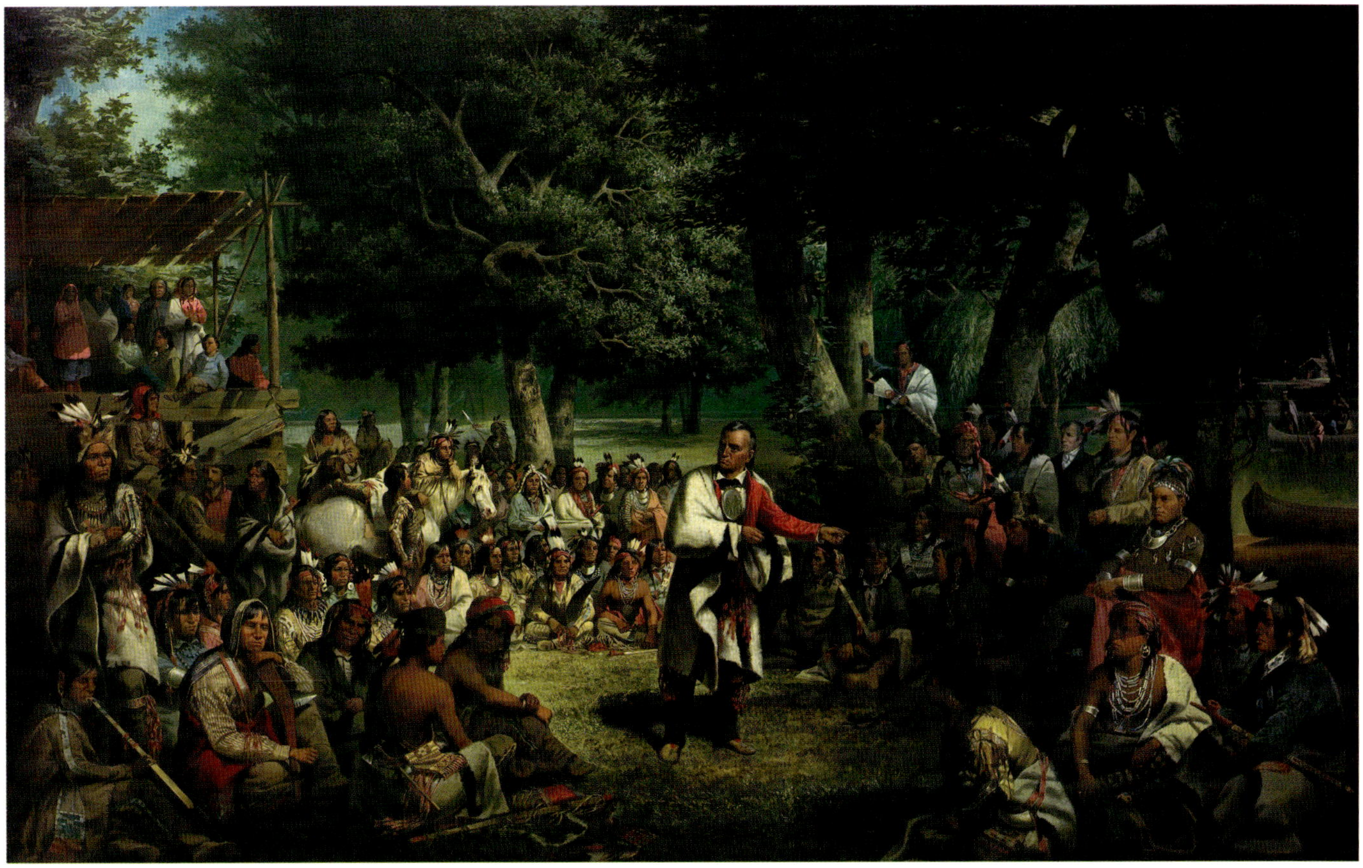

FIG. 5.6.
John Mix Stanley, *The Trial of Red Jacket*, 1868. Oil on canvas; 66 × 108 in. (167.6 × 274.3 cm). Courtesy The Buffalo History Museum, Buffalo, New York

Red Jacket had long been celebrated for his rhetorical skills; one of his famous speeches was translated and published in 1809—over two decades before his death. The Seneca leader had gained fame for his oratory style and was celebrated as a symbol of indigenous American eloquence. The play here is on the word indigenous. The Euro-Americans who lionized Sagoyewatha's oratory skills did so as the presumptive heirs to that tradition. Witham Marshe, the colonial representative from Maryland, had likewise praised the Onondaga leader Canassatego for his powerful oratory skills, which Marshe had witnessed at the 1744 Treaty of Lancaster; Canassatego's speech was soon thereafter printed by Benjamin Franklin. When Abbe Raynal asserted, "America has not yet produced one good poet," Thomas Jefferson rebutted him by pointing to Native eloquence and quoting the now famous words of the Mingo chief known as Logan. Jefferson held that such natural oratorical skill equaled the eloquence of Demosthenes and Cicero and was in fact "native" to America. Co-opting so-called good Indians, even those who had opposed Euro-American "civilization," became a popular means of extending America's heroic history into its recently appropriated indigenous past. Americans could speak with pride of "our Indians." As the scholar Gordon Sayre has pointed out, figures of Indian resistance could thus be viewed as tragic heroes in the drama of American history (2005, 1–41). Tecumseh and Black Hawk could be admired and memorialized once they were defeated.

We should also note that Red Jacket was a special favorite of the early painters of Indian portraits. Artists such as Charles Bird King, Henry Inman, John Neagle, Robert Weir, Seth Eastman, and George Catlin all painted portraits of Red Jacket—though several of these were based on King's portraits rather than drawn from life (da Costa Nunes 1980, 4–20). Sagoyewatha appealed to romantic ideas of the Indian who was nobly resistant to Euro-American civilization but ultimately doomed to be overwhelmed by it. Thomas McKenney, former head of the Indian Department in Washington, had commissioned Charles Bird King's more than 120 portraits of Native chiefs for an Indian gallery at the War Department. These images were often painted in Washington, when delegations of chiefs came to negotiate with the U.S. government, and almost all are bust-length portraits whose cumulative effect may seem somewhat formulaic. McKenney undertook much of the research necessary for the collection and then tasked his co-editor James Hall with writing the 121 biographical entries for the figures depicted by King and several other artists. The editors originally published these essays in folio-sized editions with hand-colored lithographs that appeared in parts as they became available. Later a handsome three-volume octavo series was issued in hopes of gaining a greater audience. *Red Jacket* (fig. 5.7) is one of only four Iroquois entries in the collection, but his biography takes pride of place by being the first one in the entire work. Hall's introductory remarks on Sagoyewatha are indicative of his concept of Iroquois history as a whole:

> The swelling tide has passed over and settled around them; and a little remnant of that once proud and fierce people, remains broken and dispirited, in the heart of a civilized country, mourning over the ruins of savage grandeur, yet spurning the richer blessings

FIG. 5.7.
Charles Bird King, *Sagoyewatha ("Known as Red Jacket")*, c. 1828. Oil on canvas; 17½ × 13¾ in. (44.5 × 34.9 cm). Courtesy Collection of the Albright-Knox Art Gallery, Buffalo, New York; gift of the Seymour H. Knox Foundation, Inc. (1970:11); image courtesy Art Resource, New York, New York

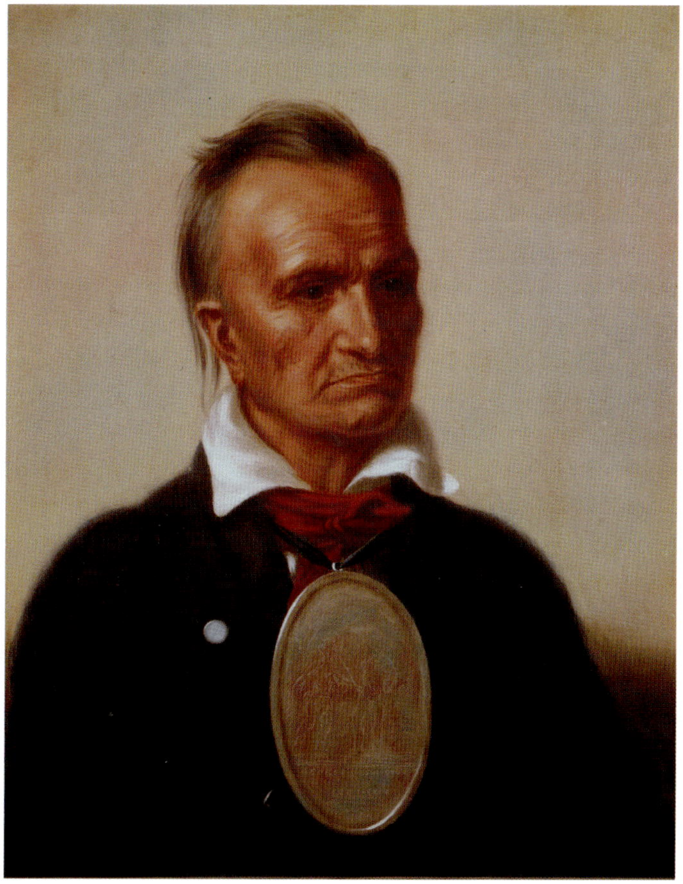

> enjoyed by the civilized man and the Christian. A few have embraced our religion, and learned our arts; but the greater part have dwindled away under the blasting effects of idleness, intemperance and superstition. Red Jacket was the last of the Senecas: there are many left who may boast the aboriginal name and lineage, but with him expired all that had remained of the spirit of the tribe. (1849, 6; emphasis in original)

The message was clear; though the descendants of the original inhabitants of this land may survive, they lack the essential and defining characteristics of their forebearers. It was thus possible to honor Natives of the past while discrediting and diminishing all those of the present.

We cannot be certain how Stanley came to choose the subject of his history painting. It may be that at this point in his life, his imagination turned back to the history of the region in which he was raised. Born as he was in Canandaigua (the name itself derived from a Seneca word meaning "the chosen place"), the site of a famous treaty at which Red Jacket had spoken during the negotiations, Stanley could hardly have failed to be aware of those celebrated events. As a child living in Buffalo, New York, while Red Jacket was still alive and a local figure of note, Stanley would have heard varying accounts of the man's character. But the artist would later recount to friends that his father knew Red Jacket when they lived in Buffalo and that the great chief was even said to have occasionally held young Stanley on his lap. It is also worth noting that when George Catlin made up his mind to leave the practice of the law in favor of seeking fame as an artist, he chose to travel to the Buffalo Creek Reservation in order to paint a portrait of Red Jacket. It was as though this were a necessary entry point into his career as a painter of American Indians. Sagoyewatha, his Seneca name meaning "He keeps them awake," had an almost mythic status at this point, and Catlin himself had heard of the great orator from his father, Putnam Catlin, who had been present at Canandaigua in 1794 for those famous negotiations. Three of Catlin's depictions of Red Jacket survive and provide evidence of an artist still very much in his apprenticeship. Only one (fig. 5.8) of these bears any resemblance to other portraits of Sagoyewatha painted from life. But Catlin had long considered Red Jacket the appropriate subject for a major work. In a letter to his father from 1823, Catlin uncannily presages Stanley's later impulse to portray Red Jacket; Catlin asks his father if he recalls details of the orator at the Canandaigua negotiations, because the aspiring artist believes this scene would make a worthy subject for a history painting (Haberly 1948, 27). While his father provided him with details, his father's friend and lead American representative at the negotiations, Timothy Pickering, claimed the event not worthy of such artistic treatment; Catlin seems to have abandoned his ambitions as a history painter thereafter.

Stanley would not likely have known of Catlin's plans since they were recorded in an unpublished letter, but the similarity between the impulses is telling. For both men, who desired to make their way as professional artists, the category of the history painter must have seemed among the most elevated, but both men staked their careers on the portrayal of North American Indians, and though their works brought each recognition, neither achieved the wealth or stability they had hoped to gain. Stanley had been forced to acknowledge that his Indian Gallery may never turn a profit and turned to other means of supporting his family through his art—though none of these could have satisfied his aspirations as an artist. This is perhaps why at a late date, he turned to the notion of a grand-style history painting. It had become clear to some entrepreneurs in the arts and in publishing that American history sold. Barbara Mitnick has noted that

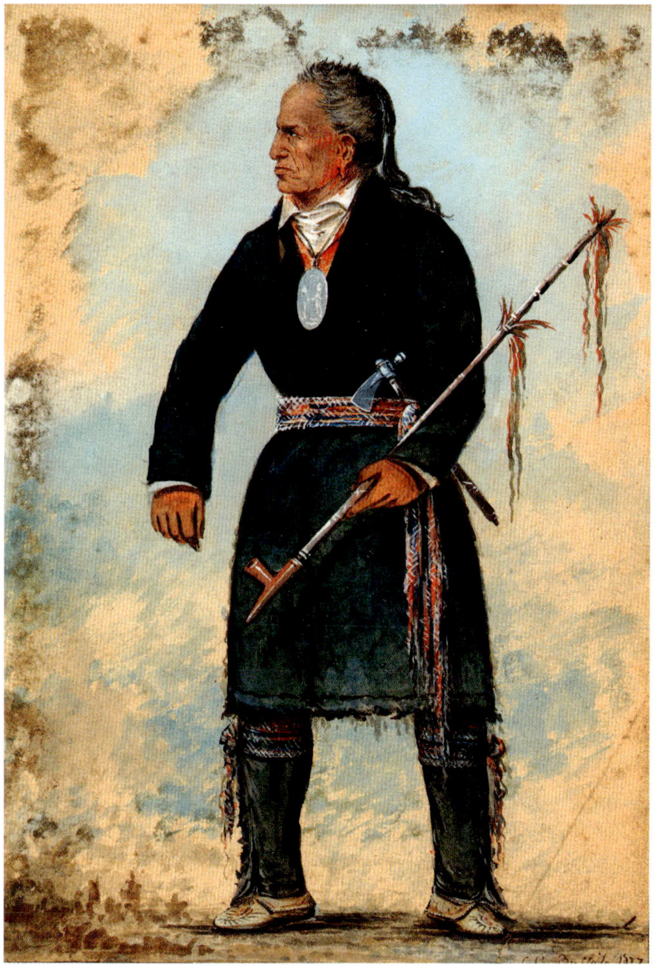

FIG. 5.8.
George Catlin, *Red Jacket, Seneca*, 1827. Watercolor on paper on card; 11¼ × 7½ in. (28.6 × 19.1 cm). Courtesy Gilcrease Museum, Tulsa, Oklahoma

after the tremendous popular success of Emanuel Leutze's *Washington Crossing the Delaware*, which toured several East Coast cities in 1851, and the commercial success of engravings of John Trumbull's *Declaration of Independence* in the same period, it became apparent that government was not the sole audience for the consumption of history paintings (Mitnick 1993, 164). Perhaps despairing of the possibilities for his Indian Gallery, Stanley turned to the idea of an Indian history painting as a last attempt to capitalize on both nationalist sentiment and nostalgia.

That nostalgic turn in Stanley's mind may be signaled by his 1857 portrayal of an Indian family group, in *The Last of Their Race* (cat. no. 159), as representative of the declension narrative that seems to have overcome Native American history. Stanley then chose to focus on a figure of Native heroism, and one from the region of his birth to create a fitting monument to the people he had spent so many years portraying. His painting of a family group in Plains clothing standing at the edge of what is likely the Pacific, complete with buffalo skulls at their feet, is a graphic depiction of the deadly logic of Manifest Destiny. It could not help but draw comparisons with another painting from a decade before, Tompkins Matteson's *The Last of the Race* (fig. 4.6), painted in 1847. That painting stages a similar scene, with a group of Natives looking forlornly over a vast stretch of land, perhaps their lost homelands, seemingly marooned by history. Painted at a time when many Native nations were still in control of their lands, these paintings may strike us as aspirational. But both Matteson and Stanley had elsewhere expressed their sympathy for the Indians, so we must in some ways accept these paintings as fatalistic or at best elegiac.

Stanley may well have known Matteson's work—if not this painting in particular, some of his others. Matteson, also from central New York, was born in Peterboro in 1813, and he went on to study at the National Academy of Design in New York City under William Sidney Mount. Unlike Stanley, Matteson was dedicated to the genre of history painting for most of his career (Groeschel 1985, 1–15). He tended toward early American scenes, such as the *Founding of the Colony of Maryland, George Washington at Valley Forge,* the *First Sabbath of the Pilgrims,* and so on. He also painted scenes from American fiction, such as a scene from the *Scarlet Letter* and another from the story of Rip van Winkle. Matteson was popular enough that the art dealer William Schaus commissioned a painting from him in 1853 of the *Signing of the Compact on Board the Mayflower* so that he could have mezzotint copies made for sale (Mitnick 1993, 164). Such manifestations of early America's political roots and ideals would doubtlessly resonate in the politically turbulent 1850s, though the story of America's Puritan roots was predictably more popular in the North, while the story of Jamestown was favored in the South. Matteson was ecumenical enough to agree also to paint an imagined scene of the *First Celebration of the Sacrament* for his Episcopalian clients. But it was the New England scenes that seemed to resonate most, and Matteson went on to produce two famous images taken from accounts of the Salem witchcraft trials. The first of these, *The Examination of the Witch,* was painted in the same year as the Mayflower painting and was followed by another, *The Trial of George Jacobs* (fig. 5.9) in 1855. Such paintings may not have been comparable to the level achieved by Trumbull or Leutze, but they clearly made Matteson a popular painter among middle-class patrons.

We might consider Stanley's *The Trial of Red Jacket* (fig. 5.6, cat. no. 212) within this commercial context. Discouraged by the failure of Congress to purchase his gallery, Stanley had turned to genre painting and portraits, and now he would attempt a history painting in hopes that this would provide the recognition and financial stability he so earnestly sought. The disastrous loss of his gallery made the success of this project (*The Trial of Red Jacket* was only half finished when the fire occurred) even more critical. Clearly the notion of a dramatic history painting, that would also be the basis for a trade in printed copies, was made even more appealing by the loss of so much of his work, of which almost no copies existed. Like Matteson in his *The Trial of George Jacobs,* Stanley also chose a moment when the hero of his painting is defending himself from an accusation of witchcraft. Knowledge of this event was popularized by William Leete Stone's 1840 biography of Red Jacket. Stone had written a popular biography of the Mohawk leader Joseph Brant, then turned to Red Jacket as another famous Indian figure who played a part in early American history. Most of Stone's account of the trial was drawn from Governor DeWitt Clinton's remarks on this incident in Red Jacket's life. Sagoyewatha was said to have been accused of witchcraft, a capital offense among his people, by the Seneca prophet Handsome Lake, half-brother to Red Jacket's political rival Cornplanter. At the trial Red Jacket was said to have delivered a three-hour rhetorical tour-de-force in which he successfully exonerated himself. Clinton had praised this event as the triumph of reason over Native superstition, and Stone contextualized it similarly. We cannot know if this is the same sentiment that drew Stanley to depict this moment of Ciceronian drama, but I am tempted to believe that it is rather his admiration of American Indian eloquence on its own terms. Having been present at several

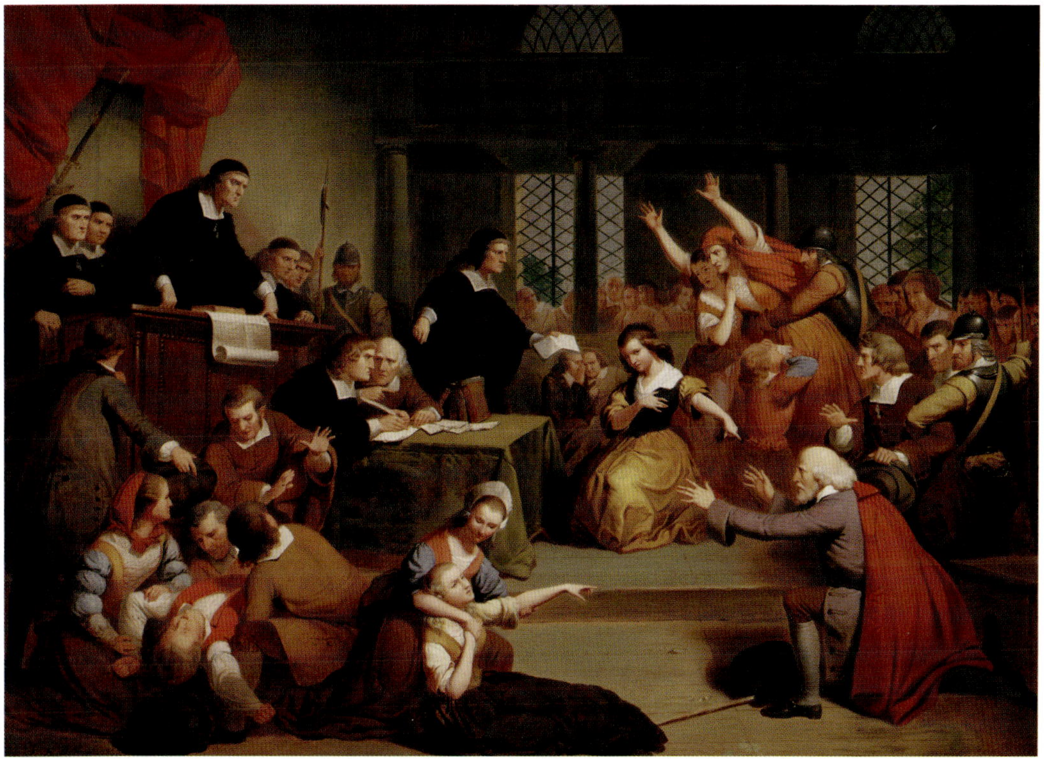

FIG. 5.9.
Tompkins H. Matteson, *The Trial of George Jacobs, August 5, 1692*, 1855. Oil on canvas; 39¾ × 50 in. (101 × 127 cm). Courtesy Collection of the Peabody Essex Museum, Salem, Massachusetts, gift of R. W. Ropes (1859.1246) © 2006 Peabody Essex Museum; photograph by Mark Sexton and Jeffrey Dykes

Indian councils and diplomatic meetings during his time in the West, and having recorded the solemnity of Native oratory in his written account of the International Indian Council of 1843, I see Stanley as celebrating the figure of the orator who relies on the persuasive power of words over force.

Scholars have tended to read Stanley's earlier painting *An Osage Scalp Dance* (fig. 5.10, cat. no. 025), in which a warrior, possibly the chief, wearing a peace medal, spares the lives of a captive white mother and her child, as an example of the "noble savage" whose associations to a supposedly more advanced civilization are made clear by the detail of the peace medal. This may in fact have been Stanley's intent, and the painting itself may be a cynical gesture at the type of sensationalism he hoped would sell, but if we look at his earlier works, which seem to honor gestures of mutual accommodation over those of inevitable conflict, we might argue for another reading of this work.[2] By the post–Civil War period, as the Indian Wars were beginning throughout the West, Stanley may have despaired of any lasting peace between Natives and settlers. His turn toward the past thus begins to make sense. Stanley's staging of history, in the manner of other painters in this genre, retains his usual focus on Native America and celebrates the life of a figure whose reputation grew as Americans began to look back at their earlier history with a sense of increasing pride. Red Jacket, who had so clearly rejected Euro-American culture, was now embraced by it.

Stanley's portrayal of Red Jacket, wearing a blanket draped over his shoulder much in the way a Roman senator might have worn his toga, presents us not with a sensational scene of accusation and recrimination, such as we have in Matteson's witchcraft paintings, but rather a stately moment of the oratorical sublime. Sagoyewatha holds forth, standing between his two

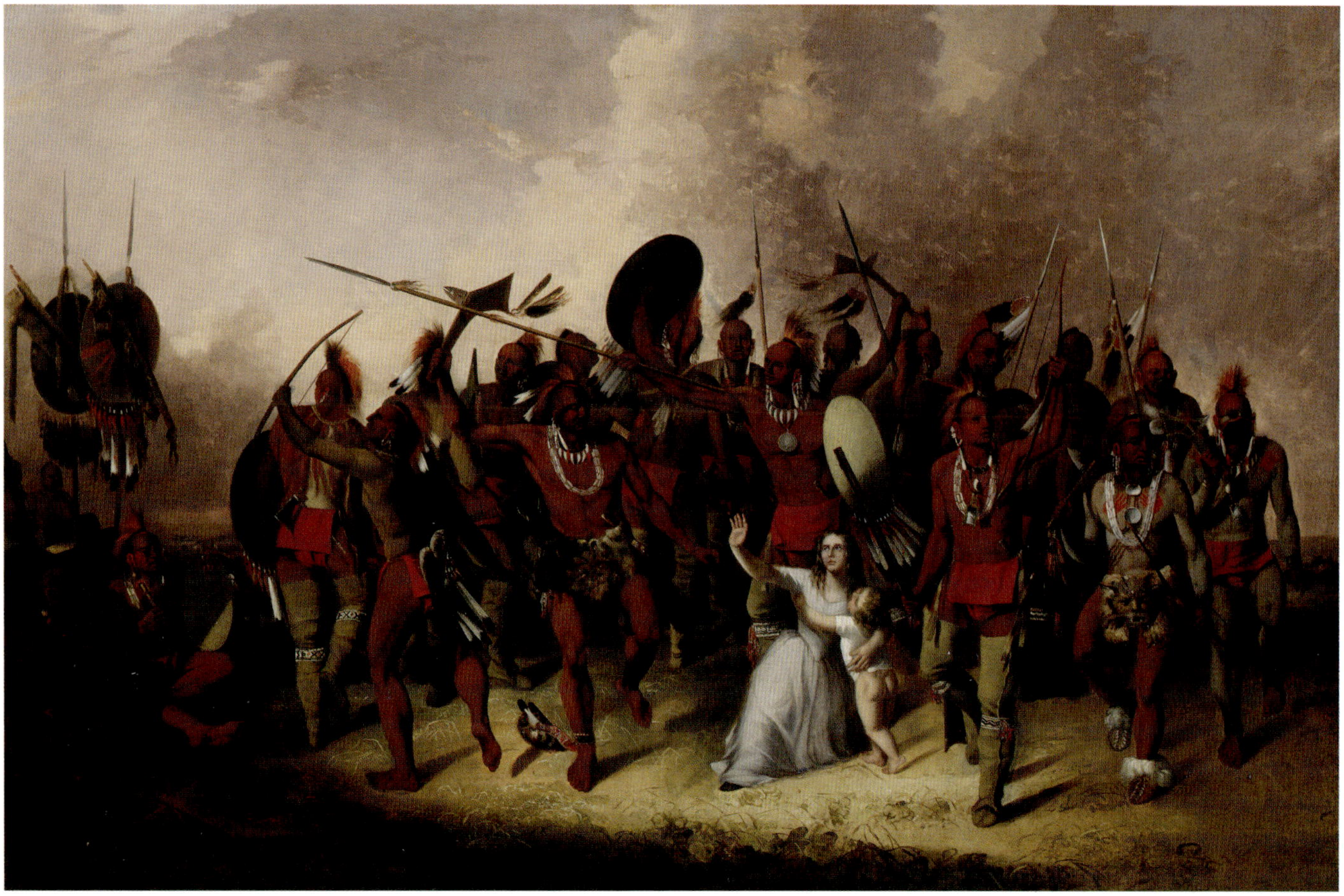

FIG. 5.10.
John Mix Stanley,
An Osage Scalp Dance,
1845. Oil on canvas;
40¾ × 60½ in. (103.5 ×
153.6 cm). Courtesy
Smithsonian American Art
Museum, Washington, D.C.,
gift of the Misses Henry
(1985.66.248.930)

seated accusers, Handsome Lake on the left and Cornplanter on the right. The crowd of some eighty figures wearing a kaleidoscopic range of colors and styles harkens back to Stanley's depiction of the International Indian Council over twenty years before. As with other history paintings, scholars cringe at the details. The clothing worn by the figures in the crowd are more typical in detail of Plains clothing and that of the peoples living in Indian Territory when he traveled there in the 1840s than of Iroquois clothing at the outset of the nineteenth century. The head of Red Jacket is clearly based on Charles Bird King's image of the orator popularized by the McKenney and Hall volume and chromolithograph prints—he even wears the Washington peace medal that appears in most images of him. Speculation as to the identity of others in the crowd, including two white men in attendance, has led some to conclude that the missionary Samuel Kirkland is portrayed standing among the trees on the right, and that the other white figure in the crowd on the left may even be Stanley. None of these suggestions can be definitively substantiated, but the details of the crowd encourage scrutiny.

As Brian W. Dippie has chronicled, the painting was an immediate success and toured several cities to large crowds of admirers (1990, 410–15). Papers dwelt on the hackneyed idea of the vanishing race even as they praised the vitality of the depiction. The rich detailing and huge scale impressed those viewers who may have been wholly ignorant of the event or individuals being portrayed. Stanley had finally found a commercial and critical success. Within several months of the debut of Stanley's masterpiece in 1868, the artist was making plans to have some of his remaining Indian paintings copied as chromolithographs to capitalize on his newfound popularity. This proved a success as well, Stanley having contracted the highly regarded lithographers Storch and Kramer in Berlin to produce prints for sale in the United States. He also painted a reduced-scale version of *The Trial of Red Jacket* and had chromos made of it that brought him unprecedented sales in 1869. Whether or not he was conceding to the realities of the market, we know some of his most popular images were his studio work and not those based on scenes he had actually witnessed. Take, for example, his *Young Chief Uncas* (fig. 5.11, cat. no. 210), a sentimental painting of a Plains Indian child based on a studio portrait by Saint Paul photographer

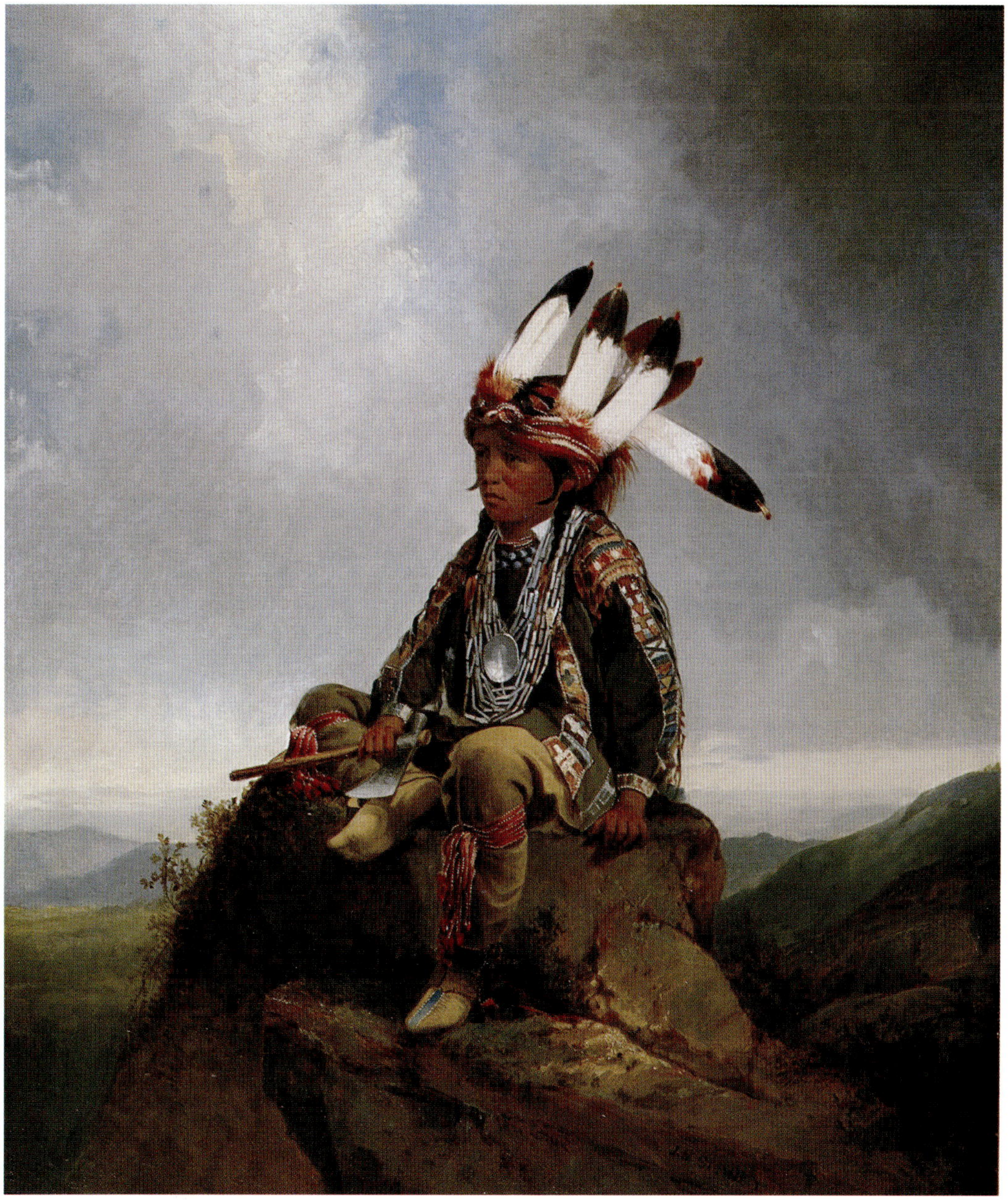

FIG. 5.11.
John Mix Stanley, *Young Chief Uncas*, c. 1868. Oil on canvas; 24 × 20 in. (61.0 × 50.8 cm). Courtesy Autry National Center, Los Angeles, California (88.108.10)

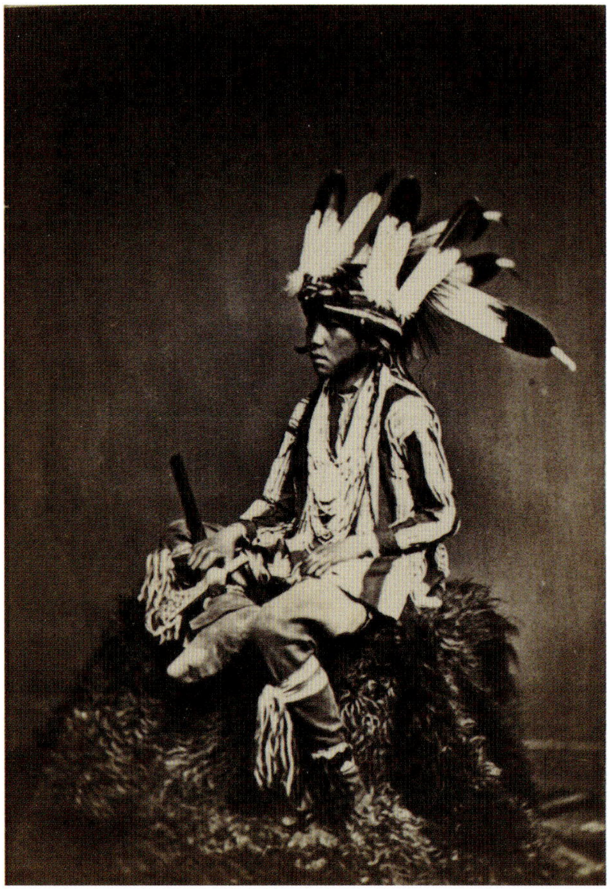

FIG. 5.12.
Joel Emmons Whitney, *Ma-Za-Oo-Nie (Little Bird Hunter)*, 1862. Photograph; 4 × 2 2/5 in. (10.2 × 6.0 cm). Courtesy Minnesota Historical Society, St. Paul, Minnesota

Joel Emmons Whitney (fig. 5.12). The photo poses a young boy in full Plains regalia, complete with the addition of a peace medal, none of which would have been suitable for a child of that age. Stanley must have recognized the sentimental appeal of the photograph and painted a version of it with the child now seated on a rock overlooking a mountainous landscape. The title makes the image even more unlikely, drawn as it was from Cooper's fictional eighteenth-century Mohican warrior. But viewers were not looking for ethnographic accuracy in these images—Indians had themselves become storybook figures and colorful myths. The lithograph of the boy would prove to be one of Stanley's most popular.

What I see when looking at Stanley's images of American Indians is the evolution of our history as a people, from his interest in our nations as political entities to the formulation of Native life in stereotypes and nostalgia. Stanley knew all too well the fickle interest of his audiences when it came to his chosen subject matter. Indian life was a curiosity to some, but a curiosity easily sated. As America's focus was almost monomaniacally on the future, white Americans had a hard time attending to a people they so resolutely associated with the past. The early moments of face-to-face diplomacy on the western frontier that Stanley had depicted in his first works now must have seemed like an embarrassing delay in America's march across the continent. Stanley's work also implicitly called attention to the fact of Indian life and behind it the history of dispossession and conflict in the face of American "progress." We are fortunate that we have what paintings of Stanley's we do, because their insistence about the presence of American Indians in the history of the United States remains a subject we cannot ignore.

NOTES

1. See Stanley entries for PA-CON-DA-LIN-QUA-ING, or Roasting Ears (entry 47) and KA-KA-KAT-ISH or Shooting Star (entry 79). *Portraits of North American Indians, with Sketches of Scenery, Etc., Painted by J. M. Stanley* (Washington, D.C.: Smithsonian Institution, 1852). Stanley refers to this council as having occurred on the Brazos River in Texas. This is the same spot where the Tehuacana Creek flows into the Brazos, so the painting refers to the Tehuacana, and the same council is referred to as having occurred on the Brazos.

2. Stanley was himself an active participant in securing peace at a moment when hostilities seemed imminent. We should note his diplomatic mission to the Piegan Blackfeet near Benton, Montana. See Taft (1993, 18–19).

REFERENCES

Anderson, Nancy K. 1992. "'Curious Historical Artistic Data': Art History and Western American Art." In *Discovered Lands, Invented Pasts: Transforming Visions of the American West*, by Jules David Prown et al., 1–35. New Haven, Conn.: Yale University Press, 1992.

Bowes, John. 2007. *Exiles and Pioneers: Eastern Indians in the Trans-Mississippi West*. Cambridge: Cambridge University Press.

da Costa Nunes, Jadviga. 1980. "Red Jacket: The Man and His Portraits." *American Art Journal* 12, no. 3 (Summer): 4–20.

Dippie, Brian W. 1990. *Catlin and His Contemporaries: The Politics of Patronage*. Lincoln: University of Nebraska Press.

Garrison, Tim Alan. 2013. "Pan-nationalism as a Crisis Management Strategy: John Ross and the Tahlequah Conference of 1843." In *Between Indigenous and Settler Governance*, edited by Lisa Ford and Tim Rowse, 48–58. New York: Routledge.

Groeschel, Harriet H. 1985. "A Study of the Life and Art of the Nineteenth-Century Genre Artist Tompkins Harrison Matteson." Master's thesis, Syracuse University.

Haberly, Loyd. 1948. *Pursuit of the Horizon: A Life of George Catlin, Painter & Recorder of the American Indian*. New York: MacMillan.

Hall, James. 1849. *History of the Indian Tribes of North America, with Biographical Sketches and Anecdotes of the Principal Chiefs*. Edited by Thomas McKenney and James Hall. Philadelphia: D. Rice and J. G. Clark.

Mitnick, Barbara. 1993. "Paintings for the People: American Popular History Painting, 1875–1930." In *Picturing History: American Painting, 1770–1930*, edited by William Ayers, 157–175. New York: Rizzoli.

Newhall, Beaumont. 1982. *The History of Photography: From 1839 to the Present*. New York: Museum of Modern Art.

Power, Susan C. 2007. *Art of the Cherokee: Prehistory to the Present*. Athens: University of Georgia Press.

Ross, John. 1985. *The Papers of Chief John Ross*. Vol. 2, edited by Gary Moulton. Norman: University of Oklahoma Press.

Sayre, Gordon M. 2005. *The Indian Chief as Tragic Hero: Native Resistance and the Literatures of America, from Moctezuma to Tecumseh*. Chapel Hill: University of North Carolina Press.

Stone, William Leete. 1840. *The Life and Times of Red Jacket or Sa-Go-Ye-Wat-Ha*. New York: Wiley and Putnam.

Taft, Robert. 1953. *Artists and Illustrators of the Old West, 1850–1900*. New York: Scribner.

Truettner, William H. 1979. *The Natural Man Observed: A Study of Catlin's Indian Gallery*. Washington, D.C.: Smithsonian Institution Press.

A NOTE TO THE READER

This catalogue represents a checklist of selected known extant works by John Mix Stanley. The entries are arranged chronologically, as best could be determined. Dimensions are given in inches and centimeters, height before width. Signatures, dates, inscriptions, labels, and canvas stamps have been described, again as best could be determined. Under PROVENANCE, parentheses indicate an auction house, dealer, or agent. When known, LIFETIME EXHIBITIONS are listed. Entries were authored by Peter H. Hassrick, unless otherwise noted with initials following the entry. Melissa Speidel authored entries that end with the initials M. S., and the Jacquelyn Sparks entry is indicated by her initials, J. S.

John Mix Stanley

A Select Catalogue of Known Works

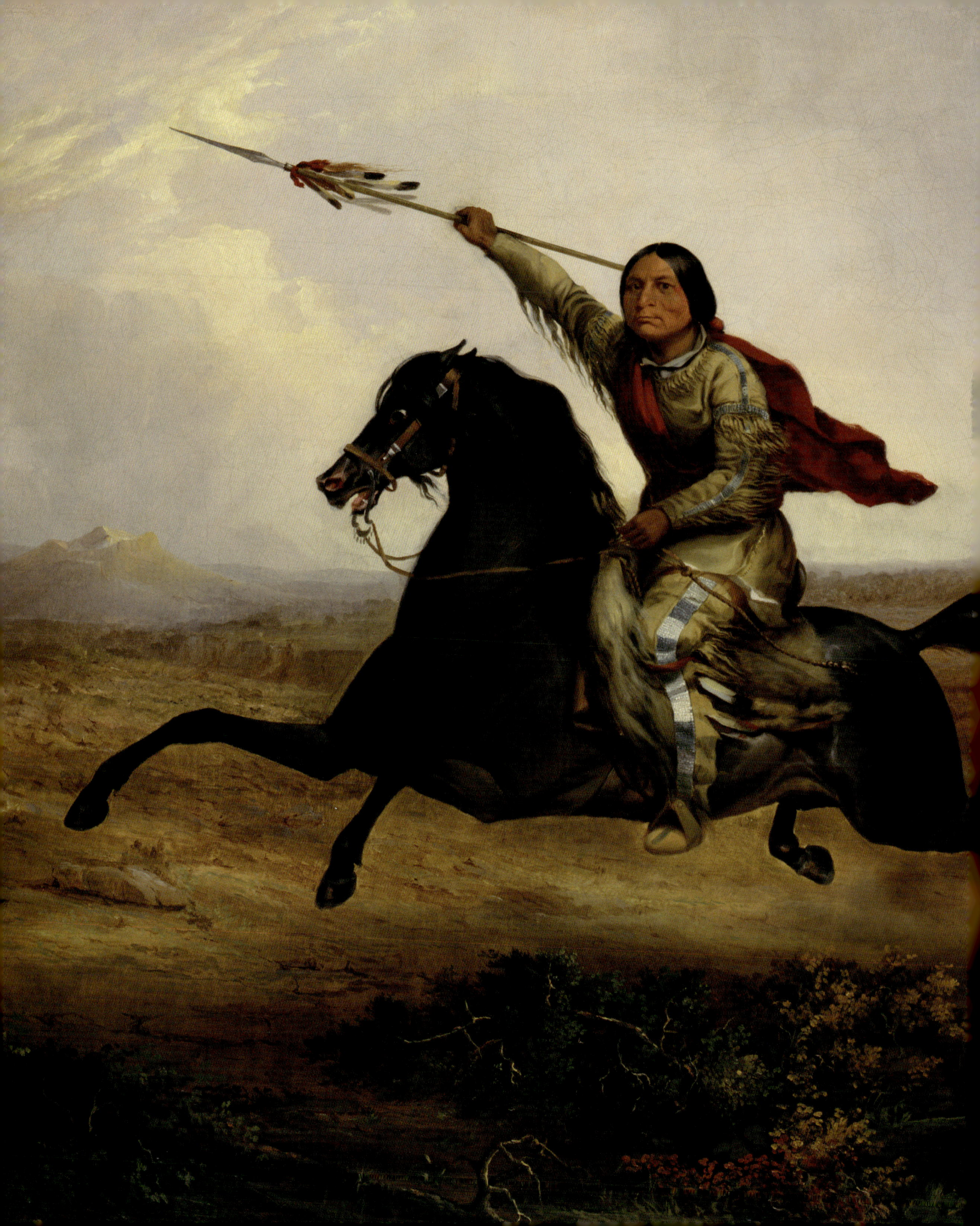

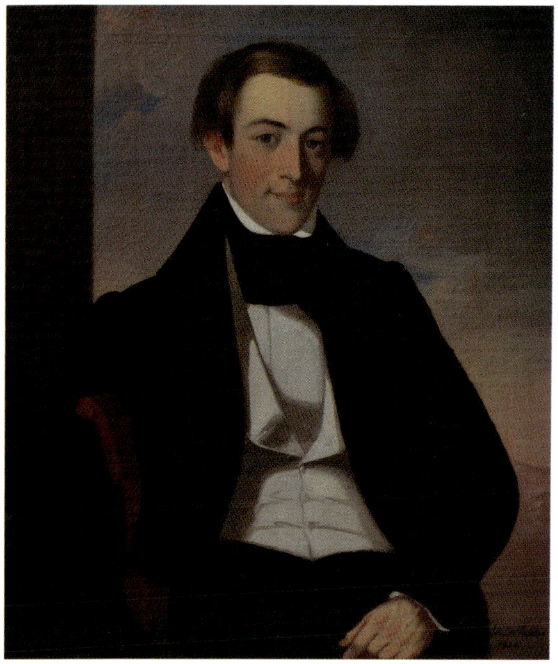

001

Le Grand Morehouse, 1838

Portrait of Captain LeGrand Morehouse

Oil on canvas, 35½ × 28¾ in. (90.2 × 73.0 cm)

INSCRIBED LOWER RIGHT: John M. Stanley / 1838; INSCRIBED VERSO: John M. Stanley / 1838

PRESENT COLLECTION: Muscatine Art Center, Muscatine, Iowa, gift of Mrs. Ralph Reuling and Mrs. A. R. Tipton, Muscatine, grandchildren of Captain Morehouse, 1968.75

PROVENANCE: The artist; Captain Le Grand Morehouse, Galena, Illinois; by descent to his granddaughters, Mrs. Ralph Reuling and Mrs. A. R. Tipton, Muscatine, Iowa; by gift to present owner

When Stanley met Le Grand Morehouse in Galena, Illinois, in 1838, he found a kindred spirit. Stanley was an itinerant painter, and Morehouse, a young man starting out in business. They were both genuinely gracious men, both ambitious and interested in art, one as a creative force and one as a patron. In Morehouse's obituary, published fifty years later, an old friend of the deceased claimed that he had never known a "kinder and more honorable man."[1] Stanley had observed this as well, and he was able, despite his relatively unpracticed hand, to present the visage of a character embodying those attributes.

Stanley arrived in Galena in February 1838. Morehouse had been a resident there for a couple of years, working for an uncle. A few years later, he embarked on a career in the river steamboat business, beginning as a clerk and quickly rising to the position of captain and owner. In a shipping career that lasted from 1842 to 1853, he mastered and often owned six different steamboats that plied the Mississippi River.

1. "The Late Capt. Morehouse," *Buffalo Blade*, May 24, 1889.

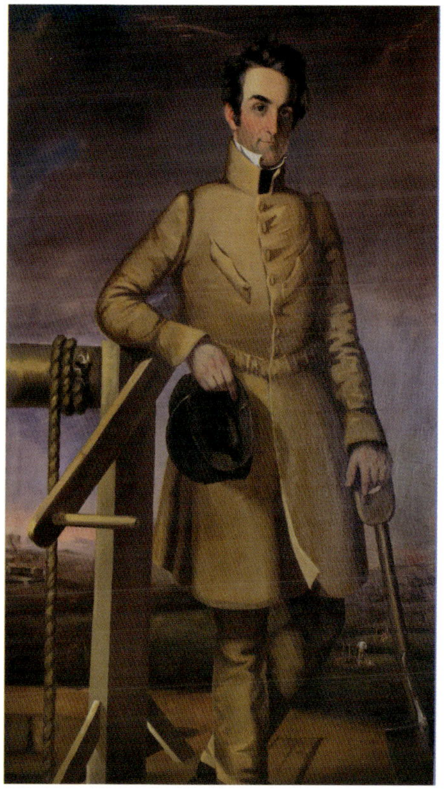

002

Hezekiah Gear, 1838

Oil on canvas, 86 × 57 in. (218.4 × 144.8 cm)

INSCRIBED VERSO: J. M. Stanley / 1838

PRESENT COLLECTION: Galena and U. S. Grant Museum, Galena, Illinois, 1938.249.01

PROVENANCE: The artist; Hezekiah Gear, Galena, Illinois; by gift to Miner's Lodge no. 273 A. F. and A. M., Galena, Illinois, 1874; on loan to present collection, 1938

Stanley started his painting career in Chicago and Galena, Illinois, painting portraits of wealthy residents.[1] By the time he reached Galena in early 1838, there were several quite affluent citizens to pick from and flatter. Among the most prosperous members of this famous mining community was Captain Hezekiah H. Gear, who had been there for almost a dozen years by the time Stanley reached the area.

Gear had arrived in Galena penniless in 1827. A man of "irrepressible energy," he built a modest log cabin for his family and began farming and scratching the surface of the land for galena (lead) crystals. One spot on his small farm looked promising enough to sink a hand-dug shaft in search of more abundant reserves of the mineral. Unlike many such enterprises, Gear's efforts struck pay dirt. Having uncovered one of the largest deposits of lead ever discovered in the region, he converted what was once a one-man operation into a vast empire overnight. By 1838 he could well afford a full-length portrait, showing him beside his original mine with a landscape view from what was called his "Council Hill diggings," to include the blast furnace he used to smelt the ore.[2]

Gear gave the painting to Galena's Miner's [Masonic] Lodge in 1874, and they eventually put it on permanent loan to the Galena history museum. He was reported to have paid Stanley $500 for the portrait.[3]

1. See Charles Richard Tuttle, *General History of Michigan* (Detroit: R. D. S. Tyler, 1873), 235–36.

2. Richard Gear Hobbs, *Glamorous Galena and Jo Daviess County: The Little Switzerland of Illinois* (Galena: Gazette Print, 1939), 30–32.

3. "Presentation of a Portrait," *Weekly Galena Gazette*, July 31, 1874.

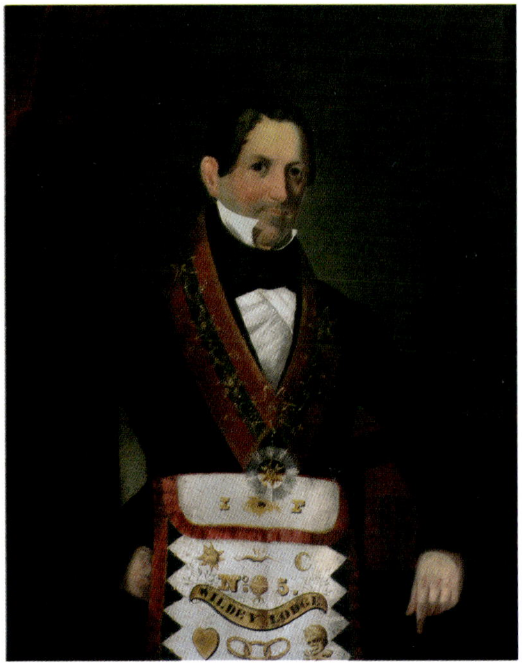

003

003

Daniel Wann, 1838

Oil on canvas, 44 × 34 in. (111.7 × 86.4 cm)

PRESENT COLLECTION: Galena and U. S. Grant Museum, Galena, Illinois, 1938.055.01

PROVENANCE: The artist; Galena Independent Order of Odd-Fellows Lodge, Galena, Illinois; by gift to present owner, 1938

Daniel Wann hailed originally from Bel Air, Maryland, where he was born in 1800. He had grown up there and entered the mercantile business in his twenties. In 1829 he left Maryland for the burgeoning town of Galena, Illinois. He brought with him a generous stock of dry goods and prospered in that business over the next twenty years.[1] Galena was a major hub on the Mississippi River and flourished in the mid-nineteenth century because of its lead mines and its central location between Saint Louis and Saint Paul as a trade center. Wann served as mayor of Galena for one term and as alderman for several more, so he was engaged in more than the commercial side of the town's life.

One of his true passions was his membership in the local Galena Independent Order of Odd-Fellows (IOOF), a fraternal organization. It was here that he met John Mix Stanley, who had arrived in Galena in 1838 and was formally welcomed into the order the next year. The artist portrayed Wann in his official IOOF regalia, with his starched wing collar, a special apron for the IOOF no. 5 Wildey Lodge, and a decorated medallion. Wann looks out at the viewer with a proud stance and expression.

1. For biographical information, see H. F. Kett, *The History of Jo Daviess County, Illinois* (Chicago: H. F. Kett, 1878), 654.

004

William Hempstead as a Boy, 1839

Oil on canvas, 48¼ × 38⅛ in. (122.6 × 94.3 cm)

INSCRIBED VERSO, UPPER RIGHT: J. M. Stanley / 1839

PRESENT COLLECTION: Nelda C. and H. J. Lutcher Stark Foundation, Stark Museum of Art, Orange, Texas; gift of Mildred Hempstead Proctor and Miles Proctor

PROVENANCE: The artist; Charles and Eliza Hempstead, Galena, Illinois; William Hempstead, Galena, Illinois; by descent to Clark Hempstead, Minneapolis, Minnesota; by marriage to Clara Newhall Hempstead, 1952; bequeathed to Mildred Hempstead Proctor, Santa Ana, California, 1970; H. J. Lutcher Stark, Orange, Texas, 1965; by gift to present owner, 1986

William Hempstead was the son of Charles and Eliza Hempstead. Born in Galena, Illinois in 1835, he was four years old when Stanley was invited to paint his portrait. Charles, a founder and the first mayor of Galena, had already been so flattered by American portraitist Chester Harding. Now it was his son's turn.

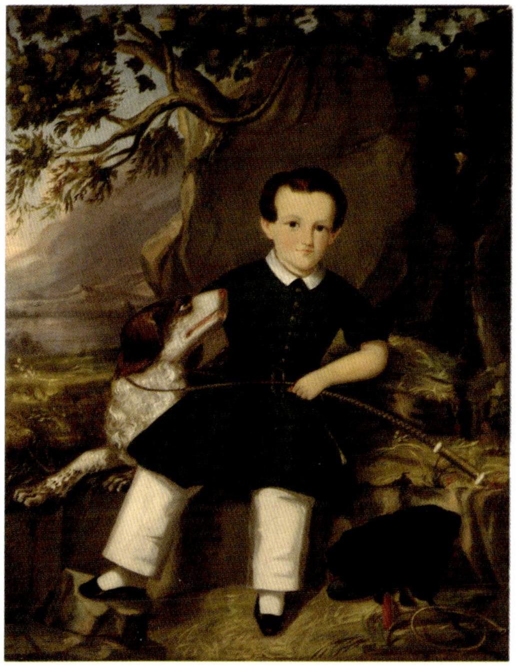

004

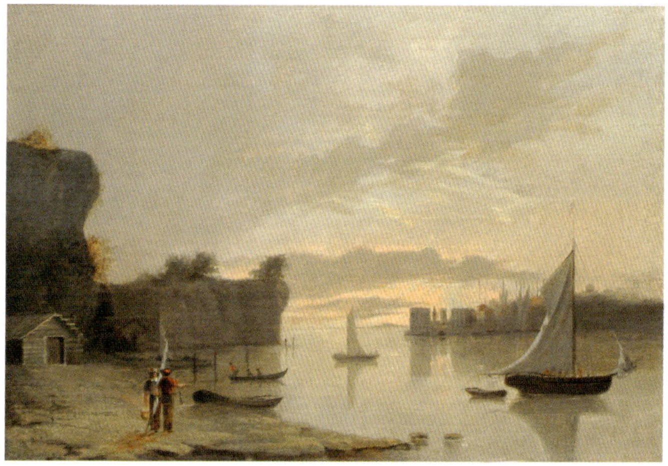

005

PRESENT COLLECTION: Private Collection, photograph courtesy of Vose Galleries, Boston, Massachusetts

PROVENANCE: (Edward Eberstadt and Sons, New York, New York); Mrs. Dean (Alice Stanley) Acheson, Washington, D.C.; (Kennedy Galleries, New York, New York, 1985, 1993) [?]; present collection

Stanley's portrait of William, though rather complex in depiction of the landscape surrounding the young boy, is a very rudimentary figural treatment. The likeness may have been suitable for his parents' approval, but the boy's costume and physical attributes, such as his arm and hand, are underdeveloped. The planar simplicity of the forms is typical of most naive painters of the period, though Stanley adds to the portrait's shortcomings with the sitter's awkward seating, tipped as he is to the right. The painting's merit is restored, however, by the pure charm of William's glance and the deferential gaze directed his way by his loyal setter. The whip as lasso, however, rather mitigates that blissful appraisal with the suggestion that loyalty has not been gained simply by gracious means.

William died in Minneapolis in 1897. He was known to have been one of the truly amiable men of his time and had enjoyed a career in the insurance business for several years before his death. He was buried beside his father in Galena.[1]

1. "In Native Earth," *Minneapolis Tribun*e, November 3, 1879.

005

Untitled, Harbor Scene, 1842

View of Troy, New York

Oil on canvas, 17 × 23¾ in. (43.2 × 60.3 cm)

INSCRIBED LOWER LEFT: STANLEY; INSCRIBED VERSO: J. M. Stanley pinx. / Troy 18[42] / photographed

Early views of upstate New York by Stanley are rare. This oil has been said to picture the city of Troy silhouetted against an evening sunset sky. Such a designation has probably come from the fact that the painting is inscribed on the back "J M Stanley / Troy 1842." Close observation of the landmarks and architectural elements suggest, however, that this is not true.[1] Though probably painted in Troy, where he was living in 1842, it is more likely a fanciful landscape done in the aesthetic of mid-seventeenth-century Dutch paintings by artists like Aelbert Cuyp. Wherever it may be set, though, this small painting is filled with joyful sentiment. Two fishermen furl their sail for the day and discuss perhaps a plan for the morrow. In the distance a boat makes for the near shore. There is a hush that pervades and a golden sense of harmony and promise as well.

In Troy, Stanley was primarily engaged in painting portraits. Troy is also where Stanley met Sumner Dickerman with whom he concocted the idea of going west to paint among the Indians and return with a gallery of images that would bring them both fame and fortune. Perhaps the sun setting in the west was a metaphor for the success that Stanley hoped to find beyond the shores of the Hudson River.

1. I am grateful to Stacy Pomeroy Draper, curator of the Rensselaer County Historical Society in Troy, and Craig Williams of the New York State Museum in Albany for confirming that the location is neither Troy nor Albany.

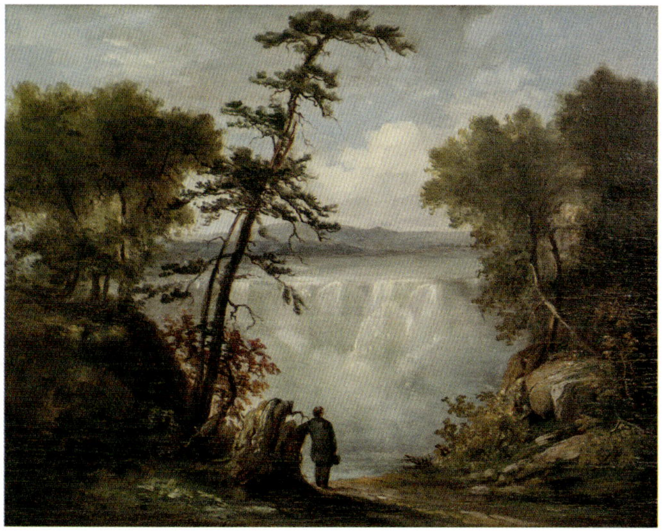

006

Cohoes Falls, 1842

Oil on board, 11½ × 14 in. (29.2 × 35.6 cm)

INSCRIBED VERSO: Presented to Isaac Strohm / with the compliments / of the artist / J. M. Stanley. January 1853 / Cohoes Falls / 1842

PRESENT COLLECTION: Private collection

PROVENANCE: The artist; Isaac Strohm, Cincinnati, Ohio, 1853; Mrs. Dean (Alice Stanley) Acheson, Washington, D.C., c. 1952; by descent to present owner

Cohoes Falls was one of America's sublime wonders and a repeated subject for artists beginning in the eighteenth century.[1] Situated on the lower Mohawk River, these falls are wider than and nearly as high as Niagara Falls and were the impetus in the 1820s for digging the Erie Canal. Stanley painted Cohoes Falls in 1842 while he was living in Troy, New York.

As with many Hudson River School paintings of the period, such as Thomas Doughty's *In Nature's Wonderland* of 1835 (Detroit Institute of Arts), the Stanley view pictures a small solitary figure, centered forefront in the composition and gazing into the awe-inspiring glory of a paradisiac wilderness. By including the figure, artists could better convey a sense of the grand scale of the surrounding landscape. The breathtaking falls are framed by trees and cliffs, which at once visually contain them and accentuate their majesty.

In 1853, Stanley gave this painting to a close personal friend of his, Isaac Strohm, who had been helpful in securing congressional attention to his Indian Gallery.[2]

1. See, for example, Thomas Pownall's engraving, *A View of the Great Cohoes Falls, on the Mohawk River*, 1761, in Hugh Honour, *The European Vision of America* (Cleveland: Cleveland Museum of Art, 1976), no. 162.

2. Several letters from Stanley to Strohm are preserved in the archive collections of the Cincinnati Museum Center.

007

The Williamson Family, c. 1842

Oil on canvas, 27 × 22 in. (68.6 × 55.9 cm)

PRESENT COLLECTION: The Metropolitan Museum of Art, gift of George H. Danforth III, 1976

PROVENANCE: The artist; James A. Williamson, New York, and Wyoming, New Jersey, 1897; by descent to John Q. Aymar Willamson, Jersey City, New Jersey, 1917; by descent to George H. Danforth III, New York, New York, 1976; by gift to present owner

Pursuant to a stint as an itinerant portrait painter in the Midwest during the late 1830s, Stanley moved east to try his hand along the Atlantic Coast. In addition to Philadelphia and Baltimore, Stanley plied his craft in New York City, where the young James Abeel Williamson family enthusiastically agreed to pose for a group portrait. James Williamson was a merchant. He stands behind his small family, Mary Louisa Hardenbergh and their toddler son, John Q. Aymar Williamson, surrounded by a cozy room filled with the furnishings of a prosperous Manhattan couple. Light beams in on the group from a window on the left, brightly illuminating the threesome and revealing other elements of their life together,

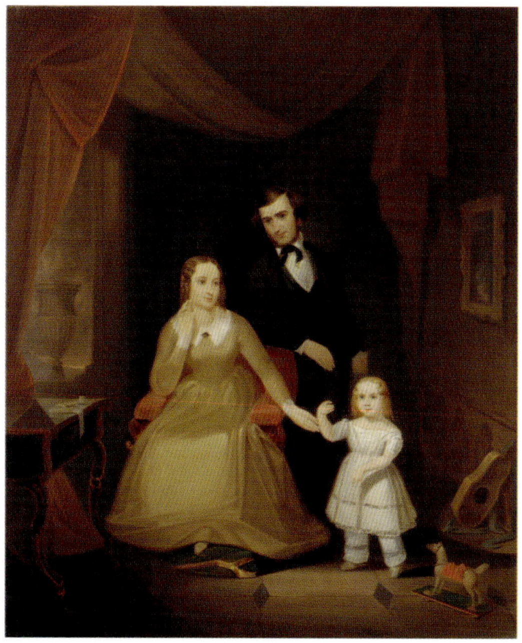

007

such as a toy horse for the child, a mandolin and some sewing for the lady of the house, and a marble urn and empire table to suggest their level of formal sophistication in taste and style. A framed painting hangs on the wall opposite the window, perhaps an ancestor portrait from Williamson's family. The work is delightfully cheery and carefully, even lovingly, designed and delineated. Young John looks out at the viewer, beckoning us to enter the room and join the comfortable scene. James, propped gently on the chair and projecting a sense of relaxed savoir faire, is equally welcoming.

008

Indian Council, Tehuacana Creek, Texas, 1843

Tehuacana Creek Indian Council

Oil on canvas, 17 × 24 in. (43.2 × 61.0 cm)

INSCRIBED VERSO: John M. Stanley / Texas March 20 1843

PRESENT COLLECTION: Private collection

PROVENANCE: The artist; Pierce Mason Butler, Fort Gibson, Indian Territory; by descent to Pierce Butler, Nashville, Tennessee, c. 1992

One of Stanley's first patrons in the West was Pierce Mason Butler, the ex-governor of South Carolina and then agent for the Cherokee tribe from Fort Gibson. He invited Stanley to attend an Indian council hosted by him in March 1843, where he intended to help resolve problems among the Republic of Texas, the U.S. government, and such tribes as the Caddos, Delawares, Wacos, Tawakonis, Lipan Apaches, and Tonkawas. Butler had been sent to Texas at the behest of President John Tyler. Given this painting's provenance back to Butler, this may well have been a commissioned work, one documenting the diplomat's role in bringing peace to the region.

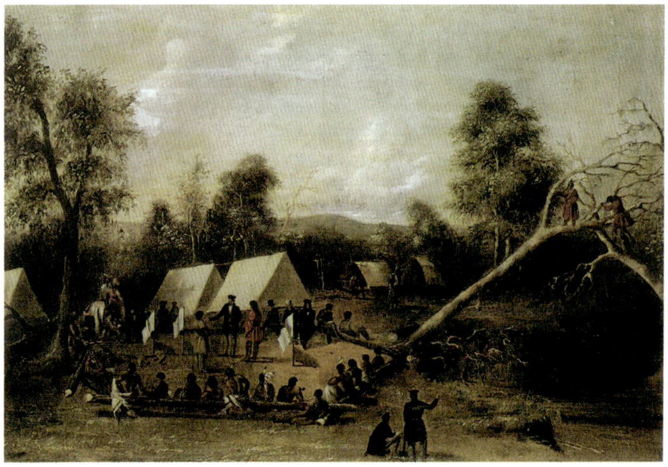

008

For Stanley, fresh from the East and in search of an array of American Indian faces in the Southwest, this was a bonanza. He had painted a number of Indian portraits at Fort Gibson the previous winter, where he had arrived in December 1842. Now his horizon expanded exponentially with Indians assembled from across the Texas frontier. Among the Caddos alone, he painted four portraits that would find space in his Indian Gallery: the principal chief, Bin-tah (*Bin-Tah, The Wounded Man*, cat. no. 015), a subchief, his wife, and a warrior.[1] Stanley concluded that by the end of the council, he had "succeeded in painting pictures of all the most distinguished men in Council."[2]

Stanley's painting of the council and his written account following the occasion all point to an exceptionally cordial gathering. Stanley reported that the Indians and Anglo members of the council had ridden into the camp together. "We were all intermingled," he wrote, and the social and formal gatherings that ensued were more than "pleasant."[3] Both Indians and Anglos planted flags of truce in the middle of the council grounds, and the representatives of all groups seem to share equal stature in the picture. This was quite the opposite from treaty scenes painted by the Long expedition's artist, Samuel Seymour. His works, such as *Pawnee Council* (Yale Collection of Western Americana, Beinecke Rare Book and Manuscript Library), structurally emphasized the confrontational nature of U.S. government negotiations with Plains people some twenty years earlier.[4]

1. This portrait of Bin-tah is an alternate portrait, not the one that was part of the Indian Gallery.

2. *Portraits of North American Indians, with Sketches of Scenery, Etc., Painted by J. M. Stanley* (Washington, D.C.: Smithsonian Institution, 1852), 48–49.

3. Stanley, "Indian Scenes, &c," from Fort Gibson, May 31, 1843, reprinted in an unidentified newspaper in the Stanley Papers.

4. See Kenneth Haltman, *Looking Close and Seeing Far: Samuel Seymour, Titian Ramsay Peale, and the Art of the Long Expedition, 1818–1823* (University Park: Pennsylvania State University Press, 2008), 92–96.

009

John Conner, 1843

Jim Connor [part-Delaware]

Graphite on paper, 9 1/16 × 11 3/8 in. (23.0 × 28.9 cm)

INSCRIBED LOWER LEFT: Stanley; INSCRIBED LOWER CENTER: Low. loose. Jim. Connor; INSCRIBED LOWER RIGHT: 38 / Texas March 21st 43—

PRESENT COLLECTION: The Metropolitan Museum of Art, New York, New York, gift of James C. McGuire (26.216.2)

PROVENANCE: James C. McGuire by descent; present owner, 1926

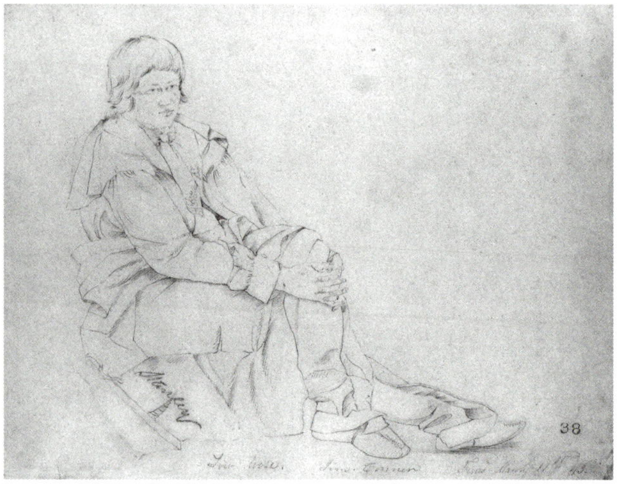

009

Although this pencil sketch is inscribed "Jim Connor," it is actually a portrait of John Conner, a distinguished member of a Delaware Indian contingent that was brought together in March 1843 to open friendly dialogue between the Republic of Texas and the southwestern Plains tribes, especially the bellicose Comanches. Under contract with President Sam Houston and with the assistance of Pierce M. Butler, a U.S. federal agent for the Cherokees, Conner and Jim Shaw (cat. no. 013) served as emissaries in an effort to cajole the Comanche leaders to assemble at Tehuacana Creek (near present-day Waco) and come to a truce as part of larger peace negotiations that were planned.[1]

1. For details, see William W. Newcomb, Jr., *German Artist on the Texas Frontier: Friedrich Richard Petri* (Austin: University of Texas Press, 1978), 41. See also H. Allen Anderson, "The Delaware and Shawnee Indians and the Republic of Texas, 1820–1845," *Southwestern Historical Quarterly* 94 (October 1990): 247.

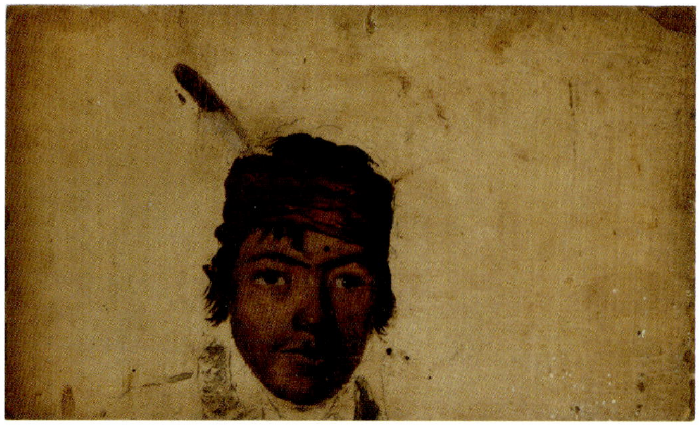

010

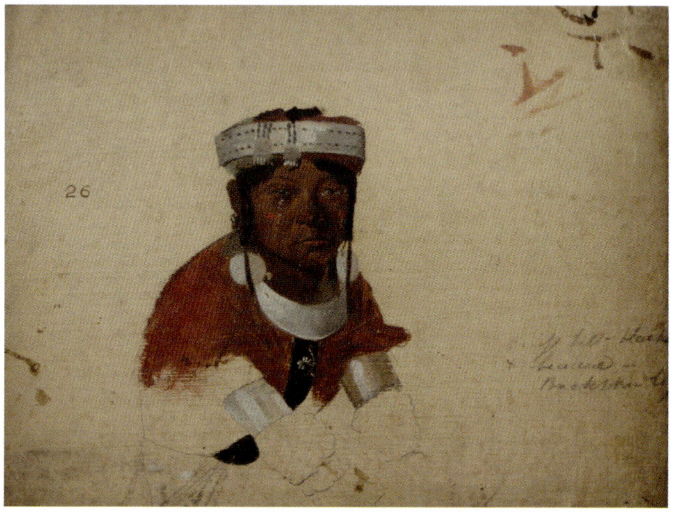

011

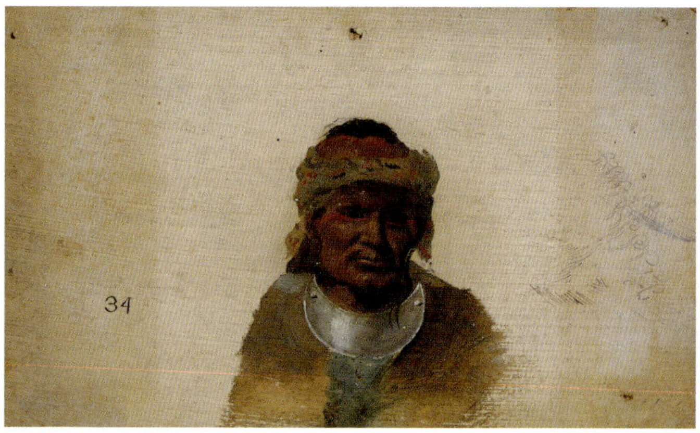

012

010

Unidentified Indian Man, 1843

Oil on paperboard, 5¼ × 8⅝ in. (13.3 × 21.9 cm)

INSCRIBED VERSO: [Recorded at Smithsonian as] 42 848 B

PRESENT COLLECTION: Stark Museum of Art, Orange, Texas (31.23.14)

PROVENANCE: The artist; by descent to Mrs. Dean (Alice Stanley) Acheson, Washington, D.C.; H. J. Lutcher Stark, Orange, Texas, 1965; present owner

011

Unidentified Indian Man "26", 1843

Oil on board, dimensions unknown

INSCRIBED MIDDLE RIGHT: craft belt-black / beaded / buckskin leg;

INSCRIBED MIDDLE LEFT: 26

PRESENT COLLECTION: Private collection

PROVENANCE: The artist; Jane Caroline Stanley; by descent to present owner

012

Unidentified Indian Man "34", 1843

Oil on board, 6⅜ × 6½ in. (16.2 × 16.5 cm)

INSCRIBED MIDDLE LEFT: 34

PRESENT COLLECTION: Private collection; photograph courtesy Christie's New York and Bridgeman Images, New York

PROVENANCE: Mrs. Dean (Alice Stanley) Acheson, Washington, D.C.; (Christie's, New York, New York, December 1996); present owner

Stanley took advantage of two peace gatherings in March and June 1843 to paint a substantial number of small portraits of southwestern Plains tribal members. The first meeting was convened at the behest of Texas Republic president Sam Houston near present-day Waco, Texas. The second, and larger, congregation took place in Tahlequah, in present-day eastern Oklahoma. It was organized by the Cherokee leader John Ross (whom Stanley painted the next year for his Indian Gallery, along with members of his family).[1] About twenty tribes were represented at the councils, including, among others, delegates from the Caddos, Wacos, Delawares, Senecas, Cherokees, Anadarkos, Shawnees, and Comanches.

These three portrait sketches of unidentified sitters resulted from one of those two councils. Two of these sketches have numbers written or stenciled in the margin (as does the portrait *Jim Shaw, Deleware,* cat. no. 013). This may relate to an inventory log the artist kept that is now lost.

1. See *Portraits of North American Indians*, 15.

013

Jim Shaw, Delaware, 1843

Oil on board, 6⅜ × 6⅜ in. (16.2 × 16.2 cm)

INSCRIBED UPPER LEFT: Jim Shaw / Delaware; INSCRIBED MIDDLE LEFT: 37

PRESENT COLLECTION: Private collection; photograph courtesy Christie's New York and Bridgeman Images, New York

PROVENANCE: The artist; Mrs. Dean (Alice Stanley) Acheson, Washington, D.C.; (Christie's, New York, New York, December 4, 1996); private collection; (Christie's, New York, New York, 2014); present owner

In Stanley's completed Indian Gallery, as it was shown at the Smithsonian Institution in 1852, there were six portraits of notable Delaware Indians. He had met them in Texas in 1843 when he was appointed by the Republic's president, Sam Houston, to take part in a peace delegation among the southern Plains tribes. Although Jim Shaw (also known as Bear Head) was one of the most celebrated and influential of their ranks, Stanley never completed a large portrait of him. Only this sketch survives.

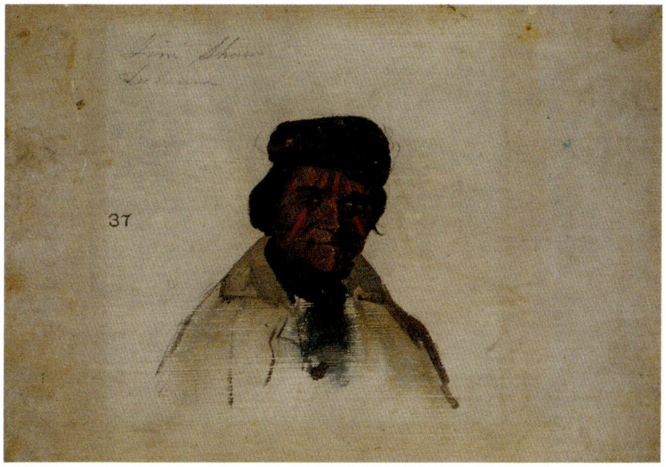

013

Shaw enjoyed a long history of facilitating Indian-white relations. He had served as a guide for John C. Fremont, spoke English and at least two Indian languages, and was considered a skilled diplomat.[1] He was also highly respected by his own people. When Stanley set about his task of recording members of the Delaware and eight other tribes, he was required to paint Jim Shaw and two of his compatriots first. "If they would consent to sit, and no hurt came to them," as a result of allowing their likenesses to be taken, the other "head Chiefs" would grant permission to have Stanley paint them.[2] This sketch of Shaw thus enabled Stanley to proceed with the portraits that he wanted in his Indian Gallery.

1. Roy D. Holt, *Heap Many Texas Chiefs* (San Antonio: Naylor Press, 1966), 184.

2. John Mix Stanley, "Indian Scenes, &c," from Fort Gibson, May 31, 1843, reprinted in an unidentified newspaper, John Mix Stanley scrapbook, 1843–1868, reel OAM, Archives of American Art, Smithsonian Institution, Washington, D.C. (hereafter Stanley scrapbook).

014

International Indian Council, 1843

International Indian Council, at Tahlequah, Cherokee Nation, held during month of June, 1843, 10,000 Indians in attendance; Indian Council of 1843 at Tellequah Indian Territory

Oil on canvas, 40½ × 31½ in. (102.9 × 80.0 cm)

PRESENT COLLECTION: Smithsonian American Art Museum, Washington, D.C., gift of the Misses Henry (1985.66.248.934B)

PROVENANCE: The artist; Joseph Henry, Washington, D.C., 1865; Mrs. Joseph Harriet A. Henry and daughters Caroline, Helen, and Mary Henry, 1878; Smithsonian Institution, Washington, D.C., 1908, by gift of the daughters

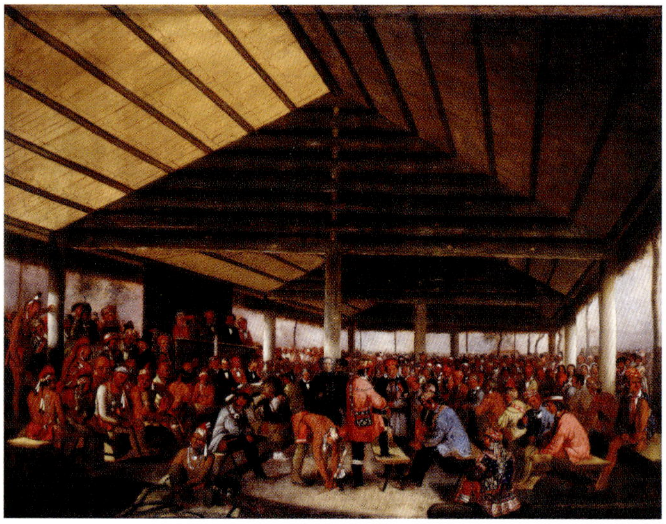

014

LIFETIME EXHIBITIONS: *Stanley's Indian Gallery*, Gallery of Fine Arts, Albany, New York, 1850; Alhambra Rooms, New York, New York, 1850–1851; City Hall, Hartford, Connecticut, 1851; *Portraits of North American Indians*, Smithsonian Institution, Washington, D.C., 1852–1865; Seventh Annual Exhibition of the Maryland Institute, Baltimore, Maryland, 1854

In June 1843, just a couple of weeks after attending the council with Pierce Butler at Tehuacana Creek in Texas, Stanley moved his portable studio north to the Cherokee Nation at Tahlequah, in Indian Territory (present-day Oklahoma). There John Ross, the Cherokee leader, organized another, even larger gathering known as the International Indian Council. About sixteen tribes and several thousand individuals convened there, and it lasted four weeks. Stanley busied himself during this time sketching and photographing principal figures from many of the tribes. He would eventually produce finished portraits for his Indian Gallery of about half of the most prominent men who attended.[1]

As was common by now with Stanley, the scene in this painting is remarkably egalitarian. Although General Zachary Taylor attended briefly, representing the U.S. government and pictured center stage, he is placed in the middle ground, with several of the Indian figures commanding more prominence. Compared to the pageantry of the scene, the brilliant color and variety of costumes worn by the Indians, Taylor's is a dour, marginalized presence indeed.[2]

1. A list of the sixteen tribes and thirty-eight principal men in attendance was published in "Indian Council," *Arkansas Intelligencer*, June 20, 1843.

2. For a full description of the council and Stanley's role in it, see Grant Foreman, *Advancing the Frontier: 1830–1860* (Norman: University of Oklahoma Press, 1933), 205–13.

015

Bin-Tah, The Wounded Man, 1843

Portrait of an Indian

Oil on wood, 8⅝ × 6¾ in. (21.9 × 17.1 cm)

PRESENT COLLECTION: Yale University Art Gallery, New Haven, Connecticut, gift of de Lancey Kountze, B.A. 1899 (1942.251)

PROVENANCE: De Lancey Kountze; present owner by gift, 1942

Stanley was among the Caddos in the Texas Republic during the summer of 1843. He painted at least four portraits at that time: the principal chief, Bin-Tah, a second chief and his wife, as well as a Caddo warrior. These four portraits appeared in the Indian Gallery as representatives of what was then a dwindling tribe of southern Plains people. In the mid-1830s, the Caddos had been unceremoniously pushed out of the United States and into Texas, where they banded together with several other tribes, including the Anadarkos, whom Stanley also painted. When Stanley visited them during the second administration of Sam Houston, life was relatively peaceful. Houston sought to accommodate Indians within his borders, contrary to others who had preceded him in power.[1]

The small size and inscription on this portrait would suggest that this may be the original field study for a larger portrait of Bin-Tah that appeared in the Indian Gallery. The catalogue for the Indian Gallery described Bin-Tah, the Wounded Man, saying that "he derived his name from the fact of his having been wounded in the breast by an Osage; he wears a piece of silver suspended from his nose, as an ornament."[2] George Catlin had visited the Caddo

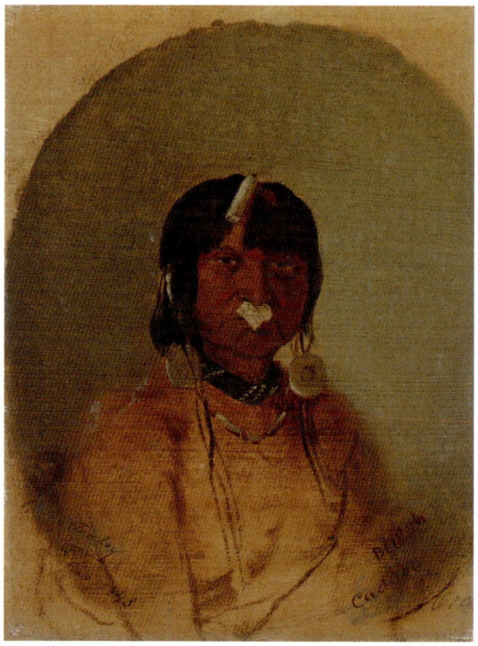

015

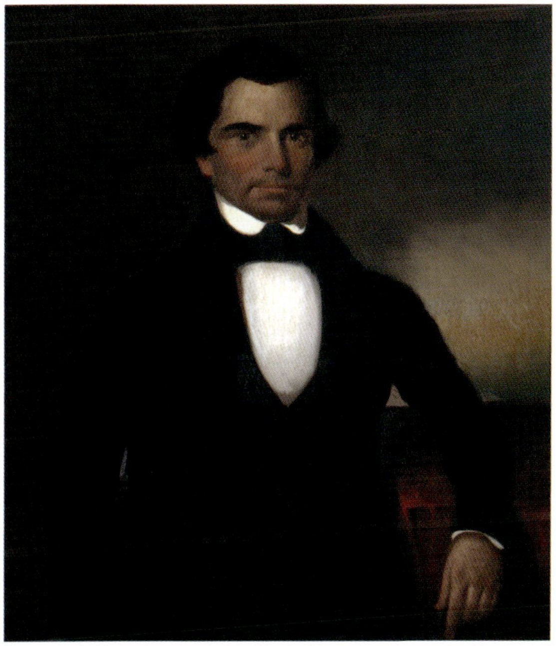

016

Indians in 1834 and painted several scenes of Caddo life, but no known portraits have survived.

1. John R. Swanson, *Source Material on the History and Ethnology of the Caddo Indians* (Washington, D.C.: Smithsonian Institution, Bureau of American Ethnology, 1942), 95–97.

2. *Portraits of North American Indians*, no. 74.

016

Peter Hanger, c. 1844

Oil on canvas, 36 × 30 in. (91.4 × 76.2 cm)

PRESENT COLLECTION: Private collection, Arkansas

PROVENANCE: The artist; Peter Hanger, Van Buren, Arkansas; through descent to present owner

Over the spring of 1844, Stanley spent time in Van Buren, Arkansas. He traveled there strictly to paint portraits of local citizens, and he promoted himself as a portraitist in the local newspaper.[1] He advised the populous that he was prepared to stay as long as a month and noted that his "studio is in the Hanger House [hotel]."[2] Peter Hanger was a noted merchant who operated freight and mail services in the region. Stanley was provided with lodging accommodations as well as studio space by Hanger. In exchange, he apparently painted this portrait of his host.

This is the only known surviving Arkansas painting.[3] Four other landscape scenes and one Indian portrait from Arkansas were added to his Indian Gallery, but all were destroyed in the Smithsonian fire of 1865.

1. "Portrait Painting," *Arkansas Intelligencer*, March 11, 1844.

2. Quoted in Swannee Bennett and William B. Worthen, *Arkansas Made: A Survey of the Decorative, Mechanical and Fine Art Production in Arkansas, 1819–1970*, vol. 2 (Fayetteville: University of Arkansas Press, 1990), 169.

3. Ibid.

017

Ko-rak-koo-kiss, a Towoccono Warrior, 1844

Tawakoni; Ko-rak-koo-kiss, Towoccono Warrior

Oil on canvas, 25 × 30¼ in. (63.5 × 76.8 cm)

PRESENT COLLECTION: Smithsonian American Art Museum, Washington, D.C., gift of the Misses Henry (1985.66.248.931)

PROVENANCE: The artist; Joseph Henry, Washington, D.C., 1865; Mrs. Joseph (Harriet A.) Henry and daughters Caroline, Helen, and Mary Henry, 1878; Smithsonian Institution, Washington, D.C., by gift of the daughters; by transfer to present owner, 1985

LIFETIME EXHIBITIONS: *Stanley's Indian Gallery*, Gallery of Fine Arts, Albany, New York, 1850; Alhambra Rooms, New York, New York, 1850–1851; City Hall, Hartford, Connecticut, 1851; *Portraits of North American Indians*, Smithsonian Institution, Washington, D.C., 1852–1865; Seventh Annual Exhibition of the Maryland Institute, Baltimore, Maryland, 1854

This is one of the first known equestrian portraits of an Indian. Although the format dates back to ancient Greek art, the artists before Stanley had used the static bust or, less frequently, full figure presentation.[1]

The Indian depicted is Ko-rak-koo-kiss, a Towoccono Indian whom Stanley sketched in November and December 1843, at the

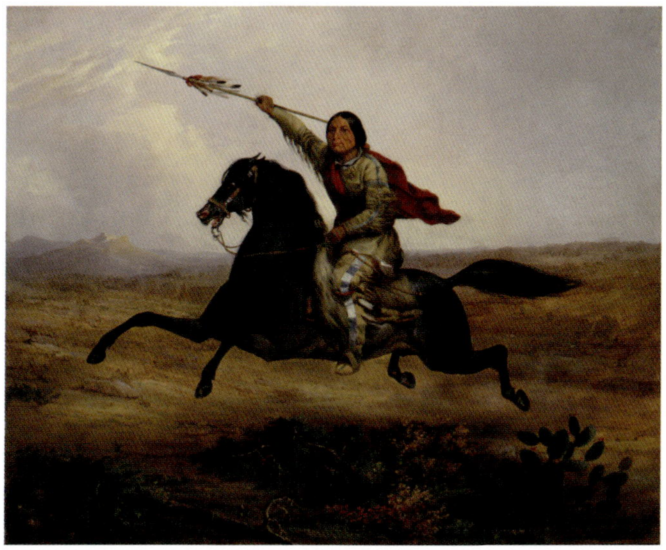

017

peace council held at Cache Creek, in Indian Territory, Oklahoma. After the council, Stanley returned to Fort Gibson, located in the northeastern corner of present-day Oklahoma, where in 1844 he painted this finished portrait and seventeen others, all intended for his Indian Gallery. Ko-rak-koo-kiss was not the most important Towoccono Indian at the council, but his portrait was the only one of the group to survive the 1865 fire that destroyed all but seven paintings in Stanley's Indian Gallery collection.[2]

In the catalogue for his Indian Gallery, Stanley explained that Ko-rak-koo-kiss gained the respect of his tribe as a warrior by attempting to steal horses from Fort Milan in Texas.[3] It is this proud and heroic moment that Stanley chose to capture. Speed is conveyed by the fluttering red blanket as well as the horse's streaming tail and wide stride. This stance, the essence of a galloping horse, was regularly used by artists until 1878, when Eadweard Muybridge's stop-action photography showed that the only time a running horse has all four legs off the ground is when they are collected beneath him, not splayed as depicted here.[4] If the calliope-like pose of the horse bothers modern audiences, so too must the variations in scale. The proportions in the artwork are imprecise (Ko-rak-koo-kiss's head is too large, the horse too small); however, this was painted very early in Stanley's thirty-year career as an artist. Eleven years later, in 1855, he duplicated this horse, changing only the color, in his painting *Kidnapped* (cat. no. 139). M. S.

1. For examples, see *Petelesharro* (Generous Chief), c. 1822, by Charles Bird King, and *Máh-to-tóh-pa (Four Bears, Second Chief in Full Dress)*, 1832, by George Catlin, both in the collection of the Smithsonian American Art Museum.

2. Two Towoccono Indians attended the 1843 Cache Creek Indian Council, Ko-rak-koo-kiss and Keeche-Ka-Rooki, or The Man Who Was Named by the Great Spirit, the tribe's principal chief as well as that of all the allied tribes of Texas, as described by Stanley in the exhibition catalogue.

3. *Portraits of North American Indians*, 52.

4. The photograph, *The Horse in Motion*, was first published in 1877.

018

John Golden Ross, 1844

Oil on canvas, 38 7/8 × 31 1/8 in. (98.7 × 79.1 cm)

INSCRIBED VERSO: Stanley / 1844

PRESENT COLLECTION: Gilcrease Museum, Tulsa, Oklahoma (0126.1149)

PROVENANCE: Shorey and Elisa Ross; Thomas Gilcrease, Tulsa, Oklahoma, 1944; present owner by gift

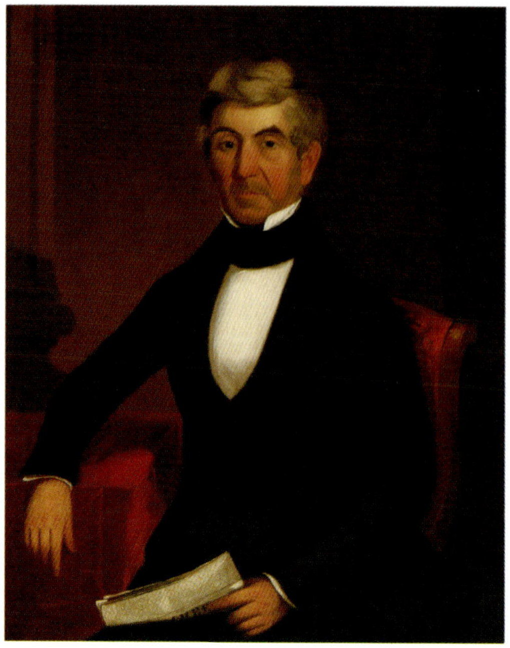

018

In fall 1843, Stanley and his partner, Sumner Dickerman, were, as the Van Buren *Arkansas Intelligencer* reported, "indefatigably engaged in the Indian country, taking portraits, sketches, and scenery." The community of Van Buren, situated across the Arkansas River from Indian Territory, hoped that the two would pause in their city on their way back east after their fieldwork was completed and remain long enough for the artist to work up his sketches into finished oils. "Besides," the paper's editor wrote, "many of our citizens would like to avail themselves of an opportunity of having their 'images and likenesses' transferred to canvas by Mr. Stanley's magic pencil."[1]

Stanley must have stayed into the next year, as one of the local citizens, John Golden Ross, prevailed on him in 1844 to paint half a dozen portraits of him and his family. John Golden Ross was of Scottish descent and a trader by profession. He not only was the patriarch of his family but was prominent in the Cherokee Nation, having married the sister, Elizabeth (cat. no. 019), of the principal Cherokee chief, John Ross (no relation). John and Elizabeth lived in Arkansas. He was close friends with the other John Ross and served as liaison with the Cherokee tribe in the chief's absence. John is posed in a straight-backed chair, attired in formal coat and cravat, and positioned next to a symbol of power, a fluted column. He holds a copy of the *Cherokee Advocate*, a newspaper that was edited by his eldest son, William Potter Ross (cat. no. 020).

1. *Arkansas Intelligencer*, September 23, 1843.

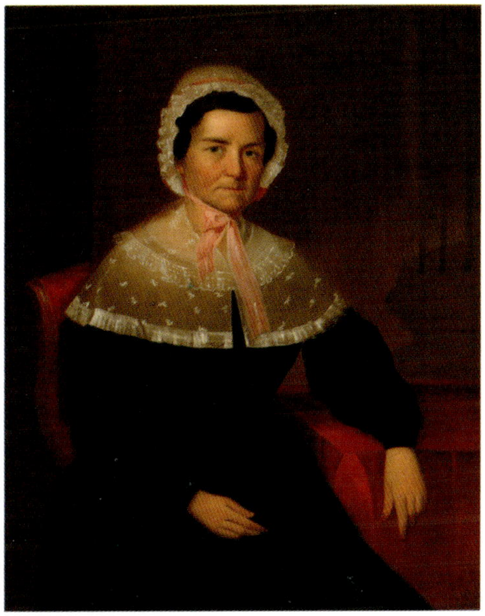

019

Elizabeth Ross, 1844

Oil on canvas, 39⅝ × 31½ in. (100.6 × 80.0 cm)

INSCRIBED VERSO: Stanley / 1844

PRESENT COLLECTION: Gilcrease Museum, Tulsa, Oklahoma (0126.1141)

PROVENANCE: Shorey and Eliza Ross; Thomas Gilcrease, Tulsa, Oklahoma, 1944; present owner by gift

Stanley's portrait of Elizabeth Ross (often referred to as Eliza) was obviously painted as a companion to that of her husband John (cat. no. 018). It would appear, from the details of the composition, that the paintings were intended to be hung back to back rather than facing one another. The fluted column and the placement and position of the hand resting on the table precisely mirror John's, and the two sitters look out at the viewer with identical force. There is no suggestion of the male patriarchy as in the 1853 portraits of Berniah and Emeline Willet (cat. nos. 069 and 070). The Rosses are presented as absolute equals.

Eliza was part Cherokee, being born in the Old Cherokee Nation in 1789. She was married to John Golden Ross (no relation to her family) in 1819 and traveled west with him to the new Cherokee Nation in 1839. She is said to have kept house there for her brother John Ross, the principal chief of the Cherokee.[1] It appears that Eliza was also in charge of the children's education, and her eldest son, William, was exemplary of her skill at guiding them. He graduated first in his class from Princeton and became the tribe's principal chief after his uncle stepped down.

1. Biographical information comes from W. Vernon Kinietz, *John Mix Stanley and His Indian Paintings* (Ann Arbor: University of Michigan Press, 1942), n.p.

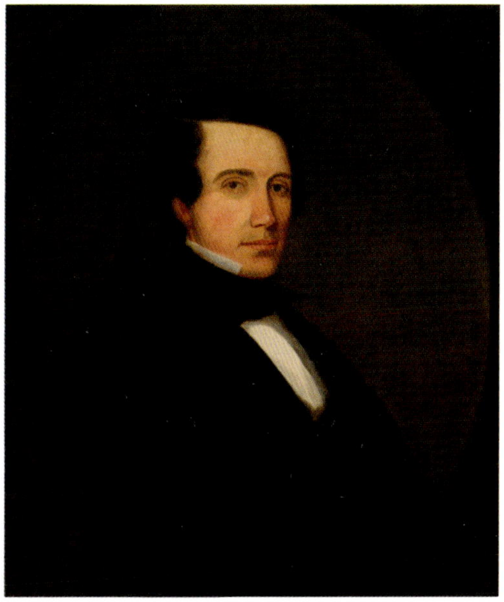

020

William Potter Ross, 1844

Oil on canvas, 30¼ × 25 in. (76.8 × 63.5 cm)

PRESENT COLLECTION: Gilcrease Museum, Tulsa, Oklahoma (0126.1147)

PROVENANCE: The artist; William Potter Ross; by descent to Mrs. Howard B. Upton, Tahlequah, Oklahoma; by gift to present owner

William Potter Ross was known as Will. He was born in 1820, the eldest son of John Golden and Elizabeth Ross (cat. nos. 018 and 019). He was taught to read by his mother and subsequently sent to Presbyterian Mission School in Alabama and preparatory school in New Jersey. If he looks a bit self-satisfied in the Stanley portrait, he should have been. In 1842, just two years before he sat for Stanley, he had graduated from Princeton, the first in his class of forty-four men.[1]

When Stanley visited the Ross family, Will was the editor of the *Cherokee Advocate*, a weekly newspaper that had recently been established by the Cherokee tribe. He later found employment as a lawyer and a merchant, and for eight years, between 1849 and 1857, he served in the Cherokee Senate. Will was elected principal chief of the Cherokee Nation in 1866, and despite his fervent allegiance to the southern cause in the Civil War, his first actions were to delete any reference to slavery in the Cherokee constitution and guarantee full citizenship rights to all former slaves. He was principal chief for five years and then returned to pursue the professions of lawyer and businessman.

1. For biographical details, see John Bartlett Meserve, "Chief William Potter Ross," *Chronicles of Oklahoma* 5 (March 1937): 21–29.

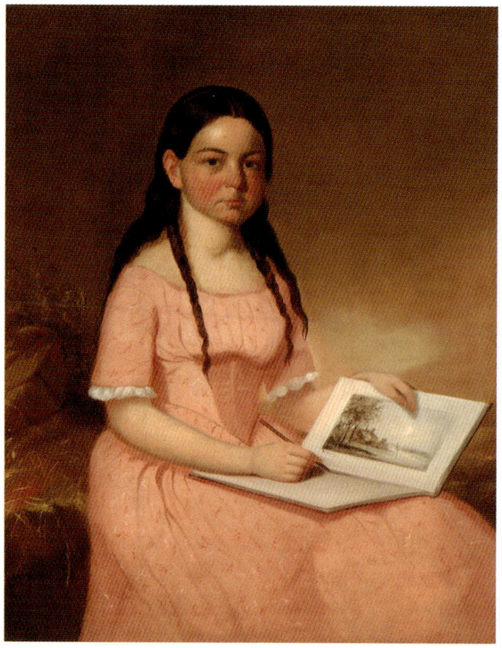

021

Eleanora C. Ross, 1844

Oil on canvas, 38½ × 30½ in. (97.8 × 77 cm)

INSCRIBED VERSO: J. M. Stanley—1844 Park Hill C.[herokee] N.[ation]

PRESENT COLLECTION: Gilcrease Museum, Tulsa, Oklahoma (0126.1148)

PROVENANCE: Shorey and Eliza Ross; Thomas Gilcrease, Tulsa, Oklahoma, 1944; present owner by gift

This portrait of John Golden and Elizabeth Ross's daughter Eleanora provides some indication of how Stanley operated as an artist in the field. The beautifully dressed and carefully coiffed young woman sits erect in three-quarter pose. She holds a pencil or pen in her right hand and cradles a book of sketches with her left hand and arm. The sketches appear to be watercolors, and the visible image carries Stanley's signature. It pictures a pastoral river scene with sailboats and a welcoming shoreline. The landscape was probably painted near Troy, New York, where Stanley was living at the time.

Stanley was known to offer lessons in art over the course of his career. Using his paintings to inspire young talent was rewarding for him, and it may be that Eleanora was preparing to make a copy of the Stanley landscape as part of some training. Girls of Eleanora's upbringing were encouraged to explore the arts, and Stanley may have grasped an opportunity to teach, as well as profit, from his patrons in this family. Carrying a book of sketches into the field no doubt enabled him to assert his prowess as a painter for possible patrons and to inspire creativity in them as well.

022

Lewis Anderson Ross, 1844

Oil on canvas, 40½ × 31⅝ in. (102.9 × 80.3 cm)

INSCRIBED VERSO: Stanley / 1844

PRESENT COLLECTION: Gilcrease Museum, Tulsa, Oklahoma (0126.1144)

PROVENANCE: Shorey and Eliza Ross; Thomas Gilcrease, Tulsa, Oklahoma, 1944; present owner by gift

Stanley's portrait of Lewis Anderson Ross, the youngest child of John Golden and Elizabeth Ross, is representative of the artist's penchant for and success with children as subjects, as well as his search for ways of presenting them that might best reveal their personalities (see *Boy with Birds*, cat. no. 027, as another example). Lewis is seated outside, in a natural, forested setting with his cap resting at his side. He seems intense, almost joyless, as he holds a small rabbit in his left hand and a bow and arrows in the other. The cradled rabbit exposes a potentially nurturing side of the sitter, while the bow and arrows suggest that he was also a stereotypical male of the period, equipped to persevere in the wilds. Or perhaps young Lewis has shot the parent of the bunny and intends to raise the survivor as a pet, a set of possibilities that would divulge a somewhat different character.

Not much is known about Lewis. He was, according to the curatorial records of the Gilcrease Museum, born in July 1834. He would have been ten years old when Stanley painted this portrait. Lewis came west with his parents in 1839. He married Nellie

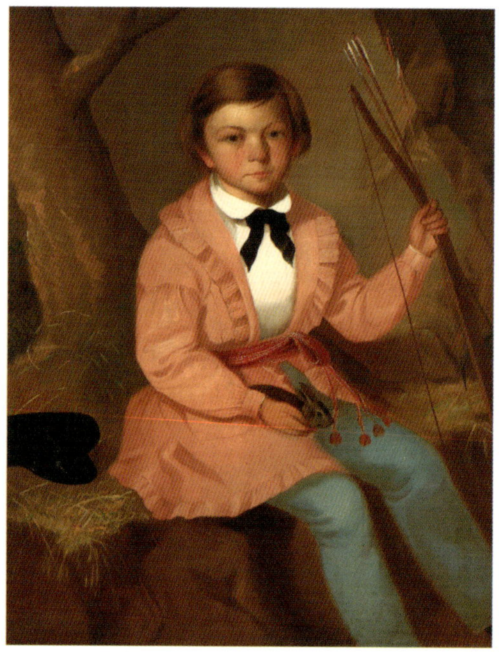

022

Potts in 1868 and served as a senator of the Cherokee Nation from the Tahlequah District for two terms after the Civil War.[1]

1. M. E. K., "Feature of the Month," *Curator* 3 (August 1975): 4.

023

Jane Ross Meigs and Her Baby Elizabeth, 1844

Oil on canvas, 39½ × 31½ in. (100.3 × 80.8 cm)

INSCRIBED: Stanley 1844

PRESENT COLLECTION: Anita Boudinot Pilkington

PROVENANCE: S. W. Ross, Park Hill, Oklahoma; Mrs. Annie Meigs Boudinot, Washington, D.C.; (Newman Galleries, Philadelphia, Pennsylvania, 2000); present owner

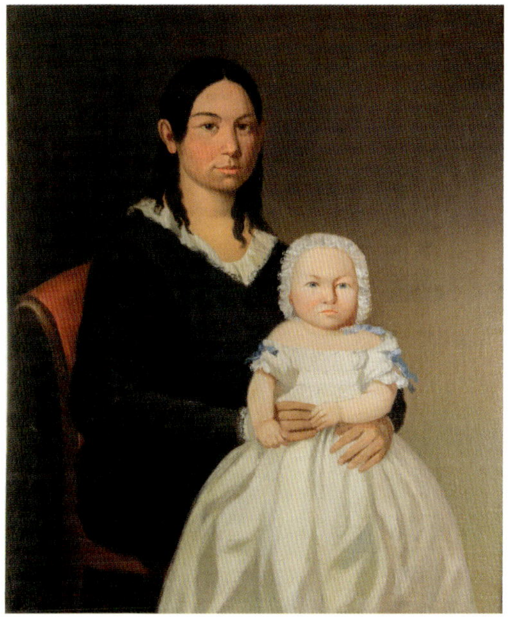

023

024

John Ross and Henry Clay Meigs, 1844

Oil on canvas, 39½ × 31½ in. (100.3 × 80.8 cm)

INSCRIBED: Stanley 1844

PRESENT COLLECTION: Private collection

PROVENANCE: S. W. Ross, Park Hill, Oklahoma; Mrs. Annie Meigs Boudinot, Washington, D.C.; present owner

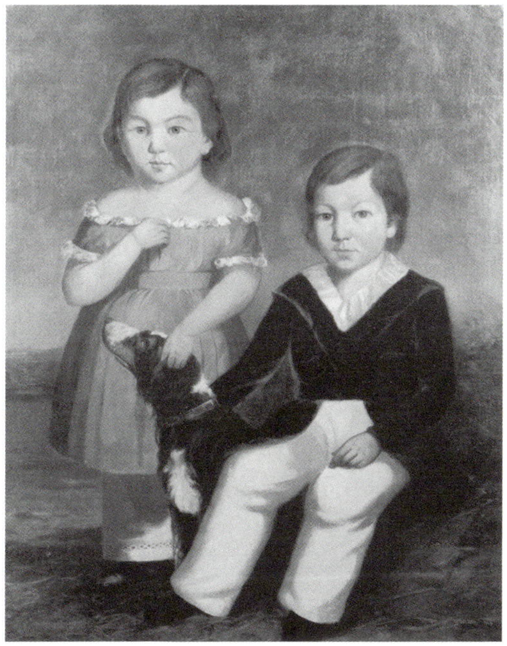

024

By 1844, Stanley was no stranger to painting the wealthy and affluent in Indian Territory. After making the acquaintance of John Ross, the principal chief of the Cherokee Nation, Stanley was commissioned to paint the majority of his extended family, including his daughter, Jane Meigs, and her three children. The four figures span two oil paintings, arranged to project "soft and bland manners" and the genteel domesticity of their patriarch.[1]

Jane is seated on a richly colored red chair, holding her third child, Elizabeth Grace Meigs. Clothed modestly in black, she wears no jewelry or other adornment, save for her elegantly coiffed hair. Jane sits erect in the chair, positioning her infant daughter to do the same. Her two older children mirror their pose in the facing painting, forming a complete family portrait. Henry Clay Meigs stands, right hand carefully clutched to his chest, as though in mid-gesture. John sits next to his younger brother, both resting a hand on their family dog, Carlo.[2] The dog does not point toward the boys or the viewer; rather it raptly gazes at young Elizabeth when the paintings are arranged as a set.

Unlike the painting of Lewis Anderson Ross, which was commissioned around the same time, these works are devoid of quivers of arrows and references to the natural world. This may be read as an incidental truth about the family or potentially as a political act, to demonstrate the education and civility of the family rather than show them with the trappings of "savagery."

Stanley would have been well acquainted with the political sensitivities of his clientele, as he spent much of the 1840s in Indian Territory. There he attended a large intertribal meeting in June 1843, where many leaders of tribes annexed by the federal government met to discuss their grievances and shared experiences in Tahlequah.[3] It was at this event that he met many of his early painting subjects, including the affluent Cherokee families that resided in nearby Park Hill.[4] Without a doubt, this led to his eventual commission by the Meigs family.

Henry's daughter, Annie Meigs Boudinot, inherited the paintings, and for a time they were housed at the Newman Gallery in Pennsylvania, where some restoration work was performed. In recent years, the museum returned the paintings by the request of the family. They are now in the collection of Mrs. Boudinot's grandchildren. J. S.

1. See *Portraits of North American Indians*, 15.

2. These details are outlined in "The Diary of Hannah Hicks," *American Scene* 13 (1972): 23.

3. Rev. William H. Goode, *Outposts of Zion with Limnings of Mission Life* (Cincinnati: Poe and Hitchcock, 1863), 69.

4. Letter dated August 4, 1843, Bayou Menard, Cherokee Nation, Stanley scrapbook, p. 4. *Van Buren Intelligencer*, date unknown.

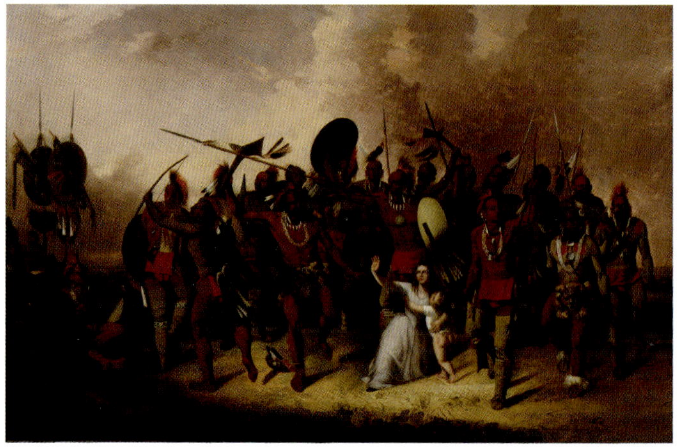

025

025

An Osage Scalp Dance, 1845

An Osage Scalp Dance around Their Captive

Oil on canvas, 40¾ × 60½ in. (103.5 × 153.6 cm)

PRESENT COLLECTION: Smithsonian American Art Museum, Washington D.C., gift of the Misses Henry (1985.66.248.930)

PROVENANCE: Joseph Henry, Washington, D.C., 1865; Mrs. Joseph (Harriet A.) Henry and daughters Caroline, Helen, and Mary Henry, 1878; Smithsonian Institution, 1908, by gift of the daughters; by transfer to present owner, 1985

LIFETIME EXHIBITIONS: *Stanley's Indian Gallery*, Gallery of Fine Arts, Albany, New York, 1850; Alhambra Rooms, New York, New York, 1850–51; City Hall, Hartford, Connecticut, 1851; *Portraits of North American Indians*, Smithsonian Institution, Washington, D.C., 1852–1865; Seventh Annual Exhibition of the Maryland Institute, Baltimore, Maryland, 1854

Painted in 1845, *An Osage Scalp Dance* was one of the earliest narrative pictures introduced into Stanley's Indian Gallery and certainly the most ambitious. It demonstrated to the public that he was more than an itinerant portrait painter or artist-explorer painting documentary pieces: he was a fine artist painting the life of the Indian.

His narrative scenes were historical, fantasy, or, like *An Osage Scalp Dance*, a combination of the two. Stanley had traveled to Osage country, present-day Oklahoma, as early as 1842, and although he may have seen Osage Indians, he never saw a scalp dance. His intention in this painting was not to record Indian culture for posterity, but to show his expertise as a painter and, through sensationalism, to attract and entertain visitors to his Indian Gallery.

Stanley made the imaginary scene more plausible by including accurate details, such as the weapons, clothing, and body painting. He omitted, however, the Native women and children, who traditionally danced in a ring around the men during scalp dances, and more pointedly, he included a white woman and her child about to be executed, an implausible action and one that had nothing to do with normal scalp dance ceremonies.

In doing so, Stanley acknowledged the work of contemporary American painters who depicted similar abduction themes and reinforced popular stereotypes of the Indian as savage and the Anglo as civilizer. The warrior behind the woman blocks the war club's blow with his spear to save their lives. Around his neck hangs a peace medal, an item given away by the government as a gesture of friendship to Indians who had pledged support to the United States. Stanley makes it clear that the Indians are wild but that interaction with whites civilizes them.[1]

The painting is skillfully painted and composed. Stanley's figures—monumental, sculptural, and idealized—add power to the scene but also demonstrate his awareness and mastery of current art trends being taught in European art academies, specifically the revival of classical art. Stanley used a shallow stage-like space to present the scene and spotlight the main event, reflecting the work of French neo-classicists such as Jacques-Louis David, whose art Stanley would have known through prints. Or, closer to home, *The Death of Jane McCrea* (1804, fig. 25.1) by John Vanderlyn could have provided a model. M. S.

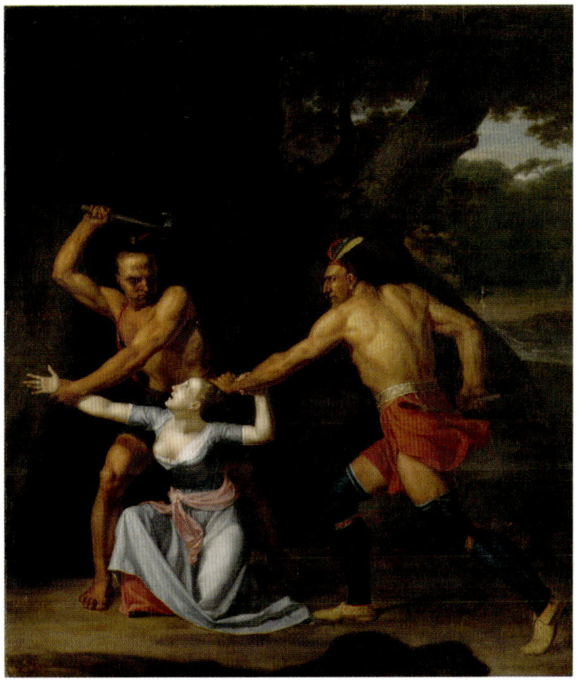

FIG. 25.1.
John Vanderlyn, *The Death of Jane McCrea*, 1804.
Oil on canvas; 32½ × 26½ in. (82.6 × 67.3 cm).
Courtesy Wadsworth Athenaeum, Hartford, Connecticut, and Art Resource, New York, New York (1855.4)

1. For a related discussion of the painting, see Julie Schimmel, "Inventing 'the Indian,'" in *The West as America: Reinterpreting Images of the Frontier, 1820–1920*, ed. William H. Truettner (Washington, D.C.: National Museum of American Art and Smithsonian Institution Press, 1991), 164–65.

026

A Buffalo Hunt, 1845

A Buffalo Hunt on the Southwestern Prairies;
A Buffalo Hunt on the South-western Prairies

Oil on canvas, 40½ × 60¾ in. (102.9 × 154.3 cm)

PRESENT COLLECTION: Smithsonian American Art Museum, Washington, D.C., gift of the Misses Henry (1985.66.248.932)

PROVENANCE: Joseph Henry, Washington, D.C., 1865; Mrs. Joseph (Harriet A.) Henry and daughters Caroline, Helen, and Mary Henry, 1878; Smithsonian Institution, Washington, D.C., 1908, by gift of the daughters; by transfer to present owner, 1985

LIFETIME EXHIBITIONS: Portraits of North American Indians, Smithsonian Institution, Washington, D.C., 1852

This oil, dated 1845, must be the first painting Stanley completed of the iconic Plains Indian buffalo hunt. It was a theme in American Anglo art of the West that was profoundly popular from its debut in *American Buffaloe*, a lithograph by Titian Ramsay Peale, published a dozen years earlier in the pages of the *Cabinet of Natural History and American Rural Sports* (fig. 5.1). Peale had traveled as an expeditionary artist with Stephen Long's tour of the south-central plains in 1819–1820. Peale, like Stanley, was an inveterate hunter, and as art historian Kenneth Haltman has observed, "his prowess as a hunter both underlay and predisposed his prowess as an artist."[1] Stanley's consuming fascination with the hunt bolstered his enduring interest in American Indian people.

The scene Stanley chose to reproduce was one he must have seen unfold among a small community of Texas Indians affiliated with the Waco and Wichita tribes, known as the Keechies.[2] It was exhibited originally under the title of *A Buffalo Hunt* in 1852. Despite this being one of his most dramatic pictures, he shared no commentary about it other than that the scene took place "on the South-western Prairies."[3] Even so, in its spirited action, its visceral depiction of nature's struggle, and its expansive prairie vista, the painting demonstrates Stanley's unwavering romantic vision. He would return to the theme, even inserting himself on more than one occasion as the "mighty hunter," at least a half dozen times over his career. For him, the buffalo hunt experience was "glory enough" for any artist, and as a painter, Stanley found no subject more sublime or engaging.[4]

1. Haltman, *Looking Close and Seeing Far*, 133.

2. *Portraits of North American Indians*, 52. This may be the same work, titled *Comanche Indians Hunting Buffalo*, that appeared in the exhibition *Stanley's Indian Gallery* at the Alhambra Rooms, New York, in 1850–1851.

3. Ibid.

4. Thomas S. Donoho, *Scenes and Incidents of Stanley's Western Wilds* (Washington D.C.: Evening Star Office, c. 1854), 15.

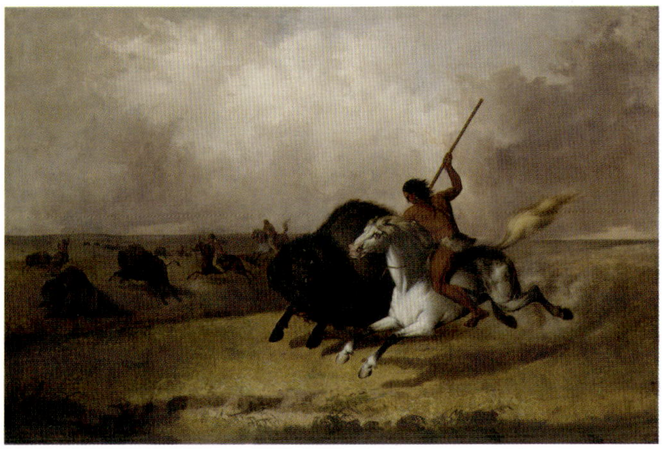

026

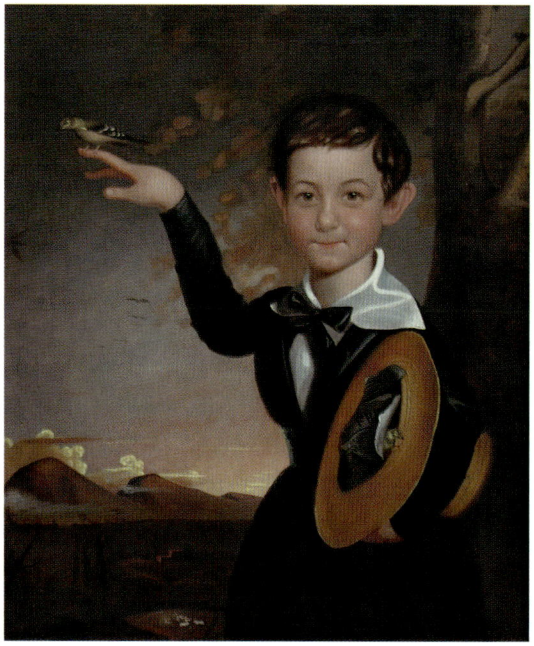

027

Boy with Birds, c. 1846

Boy (Said to be Son of the Printer, Abreu) Holding a Bird

Oil on canvas, 30 × 25 in. (76.2 × 63.4 cm)

INSCRIPTION: [Unsigned]

PRESENT COLLECTION: Private collection, Salt Lake City, Utah

PROVENANCE: (M. Knoedler and Company, New York, New York, c. 1959); Henry and Margaret S. Coe, Cody, Wyoming; Margaret S. Coe, Cody, Wyoming; present owner

This portrait of a small boy with two birds, though unsigned, has been attributed to Stanley since the late 1950s, when it was exhibited at the Whitney Gallery of Western Art's inaugural exhibition, *The Land of Buffalo Bill*, on loan from M. Knoedler and Company.[1] It pictures a smiling, cherub-faced lad in a bow tie. He holds a large hat under his left arm, in which one of the birds attempts to escape from beneath a wadded newspaper. The newspaper is clearly dated 1842. Its header, which includes the words "Free" and "Liberty," along with the boy's gesture of allowing the bird on his right forefinger to fly away if it desires has meaning well beyond the impish expression of the boy, who seems joyful at the proposition of releasing the birds back into nature.

It might be assumed that the date of 1842 had something to do with the date Stanley created the work. The distant landscape resembles the American Southwest, with the corralled sheep and an adobe building suggesting that this may have been painted with New Mexico in mind. He is said to have visited New Mexico that year, and again in 1845 and 1846.[2] The method of rendering the sitter's physiognomy recommends the latest date. The sophisticated modeling in the hand and face represents a more mature technique than seen in his portraits of the 1830s and early 1840s. In any event, Stanley enjoyed painting children's portraits at this time and, especially with boys, liked to show them posed with animals. For example, a credible thematic comparison can be drawn between this portrait and one of Lewis Anderson Ross of 1844 (cat. no. 022).

There is some evidence that suggests that this may be a son of Ramon Abreu, the man responsible for bringing the first printing press to New Mexico.[3] All of Abreu's newspapers, however, were printed in Spanish, and the one under the boy's arm is clearly English. Another possibility in the matter of identifying the sitter is that he is a son of Jesus Maria Baca, who actually operated the press for Ramon Abreu. That boy, who would have been about age eight in 1846, was named Luisiano Baca.[4] In either event, the birds that the boy holds are pine siskins, which are often seen in the Santa Fe area.

1. *The Land of Buffalo Bill: A Loan Exhibition of Paintings, Watercolors and Sculpture* (Cody, Wyo.: Buffalo Bill Historical Center, 1959), 5.

2. See G. B. Catlin, "John Mix Stanley," a typescript biographical sketch from information supplied by Stanley's son, Louis C. Stanley in 1924, in the Stanley Papers. See also Charles H. Sawyer, "John Mix Stanley—A Bibliographical Chronology," in *John Mix Stanley: A Traveller in the West* (Ann Arbor: University of Michigan Museum of Art, 1969), 10.

3. I am grateful to Jim Abreu of Las Vegas, New Mexico, for this insight.

4. I am grateful to Michael Stevenson, past president of the Historical Society of New Mexico, for this opinion.

028

The Ruins of Casa Grande, 1846

Pencil on paper, 15¾ × 8 in. (40.0 × 20.3 cm)

INSCRIBED: November 10, 1846

PRESENT COLLECTION: Peabody Museum of Archaeology and Ethnology, Harvard University, Cambridge, Massachusetts (41–72–10/481)

PROVENANCE: The artist; by descent to his son, Louis Crandall Stanley; by gift to David I. Bushnell, 1927; by descent to his mother, Belle Johnston Bushnell, 1941; by gift from the estate of Belle Johnston Bushnell to present owner, 1946

This drawing is the only example of Stanley's fieldwork identified as surviving from the Stephen Watts Kearny expedition. Scholars do not know exactly how Stanley worked in the field that year, whether he made only pencil drawings like this or also watercol-

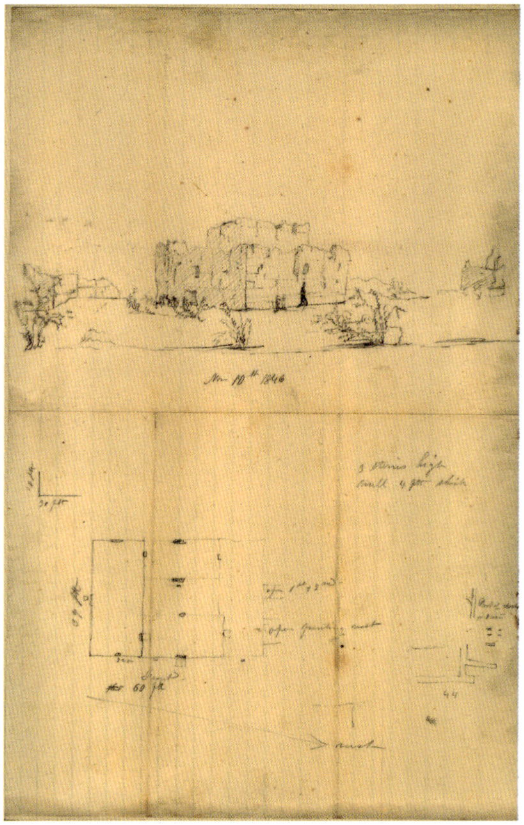

028

ors. The paintings in oil that survive and are associated with the 1846 trip, including the version of this scene (cat. no. 041), were painted in San Diego and San Francisco in 1847, completed some months after the journey had concluded.[1]

William H. Emory makes several references to Stanley's sketching along the way. For example, when they came upon this exciting archaeological discovery, Emory described it as follows: "It was the remains of a three-story mud house, 60 feet square, pierced for doors and windows. The walls were four feet thick, and formed by layers of mud, two feet thick." Then he concluded, "Stanly [*sic*] made an elaborate sketch of every part," thus describing this carefully articulated and annotated drawing, it is presumed.[2]

1. William H. Emory, *Notes of a Military Reconnoissance, from Fort Leavenworth, in Missouri, to San Diego, in California, Including Part of the Arkansas, Del Norte, and Gila Rivers* (Washington, D.C.: Wendell and Van Benthuysen, 1848), 114; and Edwin Bryant, *What I Saw in California: Being the Journal of a Tour by the Emigrant Route and South Pass of the Rocky Mountains, across the Continent of North America, the Great Desert Basin, and through California, in the Years 1846, 1847* (Palo Alto, Calif.: Lewis Osborne, 1967), 435–36.

2. Emory, *Notes*, 6–7.

029

Valley of the Mimbres, 1846

Oil on academy board, 9⅞ × 12¾ in. (25.1 × 32.4 cm)

INSCRIBED LOWER RIGHT: Stanley; INSCRIBED VERSO: To face journal of Oct. 17, 1846, 4 Oclock P.M.

PRESENT COLLECTION: Private collection, Washington, D.C.; Photograph courtesy of Gerald Peters Gallery, Santa Fe, New Mexico

PROVENANCE: David Alvey Reed, Washington, D.C.; (Sloans and Kenyon, Chevy Chase, Maryland, 2006); (Gerald Peters Gallery, Santa Fe, New Mexico); present owner

Captain Henry Smith Turner, an adjutant in Kearny's Army of the West, was called upon on October 17, 1846, to ride ahead of the troops and extend an invitation of council to Apache Indians who were reported to inhabit the area. He rode a good distance along the valley of the Mimbres River that day but was disappointed to find no Indians. The valley he described in straightforward terms as "generally interesting." The only thing that stirred his enthusiasm in the slightest was an abundance of brook trout he discovered in the stream.[1]

Emory's account and Stanley's pictorial record counter Turner's lack of fervor. Emory enjoyed the trout for sure, but he also found the valley and its stream to be "truly beautiful." It was endowed with "rich fertile soil, densely covered with cotton wood, walnut, ash, &c." And, he said, its stream, "rapid and dashing" in its descent, promised "sufficient water to irrigate its beautiful valley." The mountain that towered over the troop as they ascended the valley was named by Emory "the Dome."[2]

1. Dwight L. Clarke, ed., *The Original Journals of Henry Smith Turner with Stephen Walls Kearny to New Mexico and California, 1846–1847* (Norman: University of Oklahoma Press, 1966), 85.

2. Emory, *Notes*, 58.

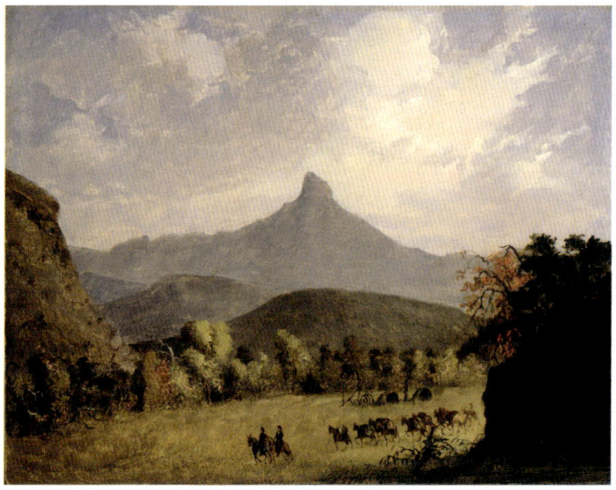

029

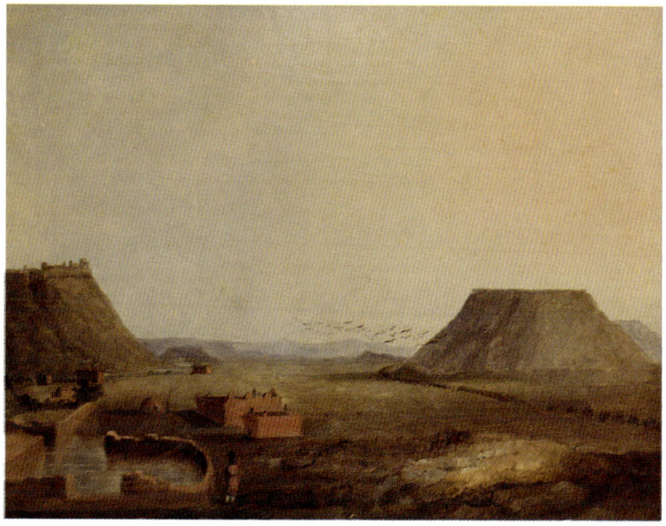

030

San Felippe, New Mexico, 1847

Oil on academy board, 10 × 12¾ in. (25.4 × 32.4 cm)

INSCRIBED LOWER RIGHT: STANLEY.; INSCRIBED VERSO: San Felippe—New Mexico / To face the journal of / Sept. 27th [actually the 2nd] 1846. ~~10 O'clock a.m~~

PRESENT COLLECTION: Nelda C. and H. J. Lutcher Stark Foundation, Stark Museum of Art, Orange, Texas (31.23/5)

PROVENANCE: The artist; William H. Emory; by descent to William Emory; by descent to Sarah Emory; by descent to William Emory III; Mrs. Dean (Alice Stanley) Acheson, Washington, D.C.; (Edward Eberstadt and Sons, New York, New York, 1957); H. J. Lutcher Stark, Orange, Texas, 1965; present owner

It is not known exactly what date Stanley was employed by William Emory to join his Corps of Topographical Engineers, but it was probably not until just before the troops pulled out of Santa Fe on September 25, 1846. Lieutenant W. G. Peck, a trained artist with the corps, had fallen ill when Emory first reached Santa Fe in early August. Peck was still convalescing on September 25 when Emory had to muster his troops to follow Kearny. Stanley was a last-ditch replacement, it seems, though an excellent one indeed.

Emory had visited San Felipe once with a small group on September 2, before Kearny began his march. Stanley's painting does not date until September 27, so it was created early in the army's subsequent journey south and west from Santa Fe. At that time, he portrayed a considerable force riding past the pueblo, which, according to Emory's count of Kearny's California-bound troop at that time, numbered three hundred mounted dragoons and five hundred Mormon Volunteer infantry.

Emory described the pueblo as a "pretty village . . . overhung by a steep craggy precipice, upon the summit of which are the ruins of a Roman Catholic church [the abandoned but original San Felipe church built in 1605] presenting in the landscape sketch the appearance of the pictures we see of the castles on the Rhine."[1] It was common practice for observers to equate exotic vistas in the American West with familiar scenes in Europe. Here Emory, by association, gives the West the veneer of continental grandeur.

1. Emory, *Notes*, 38. The 1605 church on the hill was named San Felipe. It was replaced in 1706 by another church of the same name, which was situated in the valley near the pueblo. Stanley included both churches in his painting. I am grateful to Rose Diaz, curator of the San Felipe Museum, for this information.

031

Valencia, New Mexico, 1847

Oil on academy board, 10 × 12¾ in. (25.4 × 32.4 cm)

INSCRIBED LOWER RIGHT: STANLEY; INSCRIBED VERSO: Valencia. New Mexico; To face the journal of / Oct. 1st 1846. ~~Near Valencia~~

PRESENT COLLECTION: Nelda C. and H. J. Lutcher Stark Foundation, Stark Museum of Art, Orange, Texas (31.23/4)

PROVENANCE: The artist; William H. Emory; by descent to William Emory; by descent to Sarah Emory; by descent to William Emory III; Mrs. Dean (Alice Stanley) Acheson, Washington, D.C.; (Edward Eberstadt and Sons, New York, New York, 1957); H. J. Lutcher Stark, Orange, Texas, 1965; present owner

The first day of October 1846, as Stanley's group passed what Emory called "the pleasant little village of Belen," south of Albuquerque, the artist encountered the setting for one of his most pastoral Southwest landscapes, *Valencia, New Mexico*. Emory found it difficult to restrain his emotions when he described what he saw as he emerged from his tent that morning. "The air was

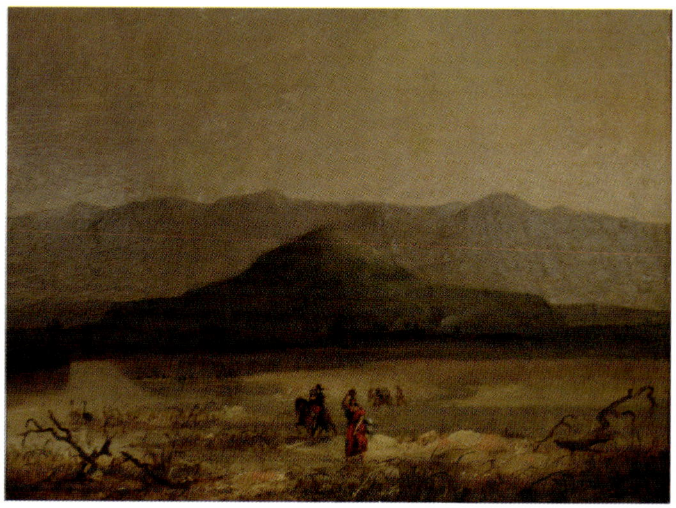

031

elastic, and fragrant with the perfumes of the wild sage from the adjacent hills," he wrote in his journal. "Everything was, in truth, *couleur de rose*; for the sun beamed out bright and red, infusing the same tint over the landscape, till near meridian."[1] Stanley captured the spirit of that account. The figures in the foreground set the tone of agreeable accommodation and quiet. The light is, as Emory described, suffused with a tint of rose. And the placid river, its limpid waters harboring a flock of ducks and a pair of sandhill cranes, flows peaceably by. The craggy trees in the foreground serve as *repoussoir* elements, reminiscent of Hudson River School landscape conventions. These, combined with the suffused atmosphere, suggest that such views were as much representative of Stanley's view of the West as a virgin American wilderness as they were documentary.

1. Emory, *Notes*, 48.

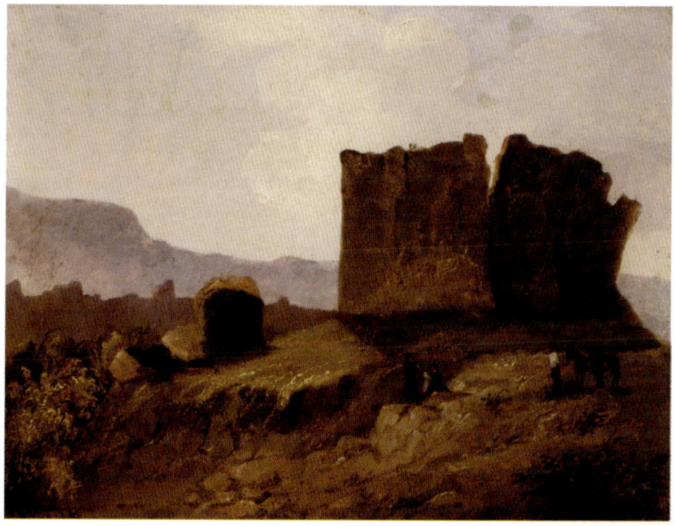

032

Butte on the Del Norte, 1847

Oil on academy board, 9⅞ × 12⅝ in. (25.1 × 32.1 cm)

INSCRIBED LOWER CENTER: STANLEY; INSCRIBED VERSO, IN DIFFERENT HANDS: [blue ink] 1846 Kearney; [red ink] John Mix Stanley; [black ink] To face the journal / Oct. 9th 1846—/ Butte on the Del Norte

PRESENT COLLECTION: Courtesy of the Eiteljorg Museum of American Indians and Western Art, Indianapolis, Indiana (1989.3.94)

PROVENANCE: Harrison Eiteljorg, Indianapolis, Indiana; by gift to present owner, 1989

A few days before the Kearny forces turned west off the Rio Grande and started their overland trek across the desert to the Gila River, Stanley stopped to paint this eccentric set of formations at the base of the Fra Cristobal Mountains. He recorded a couple of men, presumably from the Corps of Topographical Engineers, at work, perhaps engaged in recording some sample of geology or botany. Emory reported that a butte had been "seen in the distance, close to the river and surrounded by trees, which was at first taken for an adobe house, but the near approach showed it a conglomerate cemented by lime." At the base of this butte, Emory unearthed "some rare specimens of olivine set in lava."[1] The figures in the painting, therefore, may picture Emory himself holding one of the treasured rocks, with Stanley seated before him in the act of drawing the olive green gem, artist and officer united in the cause of science.

1. Emory, *Notes*, 55.

033

View in the Sierra Mimbres, 1847

Oil on academy board, 10 × 12¾ in. (25.4 × 32.4 cm)

INSCRIBED LOWER RIGHT: J. M. STANLEY; INSCRIBED VERSO: View in the Sierra Mimbres / To face the journal of Oct 18th 1846. Morning

PRESENT COLLECTION: Nelda C. and H. J. Lutcher Stark Foundation, Stark Museum of Art, Orange, Texas (31.23/7)

PROVENANCE:; William H. Emory; by descent to William Emory; by descent to Sarah Emory; by descent to William Emory III; Mrs. Dean (Alice Stanley) Acheson, Washington, D.C.; (Edward Eberstadt and Sons, 1957); present owner

Stanley records on the verso of this painting that it relates to a scene on the morning of October 18, 1846. A couple of the expedition's tents can be seen in the foreground, denoting that camp had not been broken as yet. The bivouac is towered over by an impos-

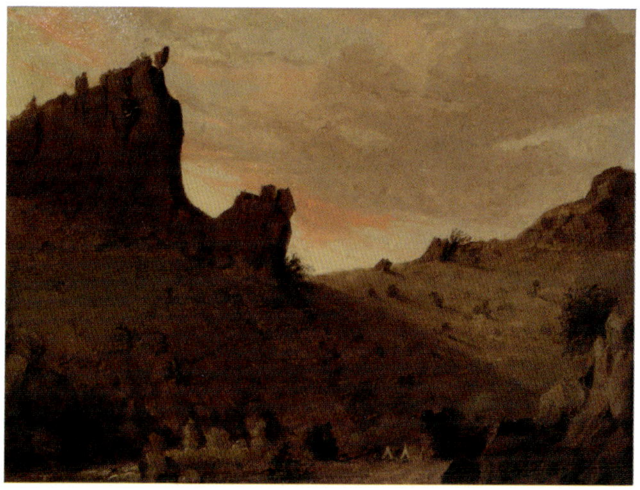

033

ing rock outcropping, which is capped by a precariously balanced boulder. This and the fiery sky add a dimension of sublime tension to the otherwise peaceful setting. Stanley was busy that day. It was the same date that he sketched *Ben Moore Mountain* (cat. no. 034).

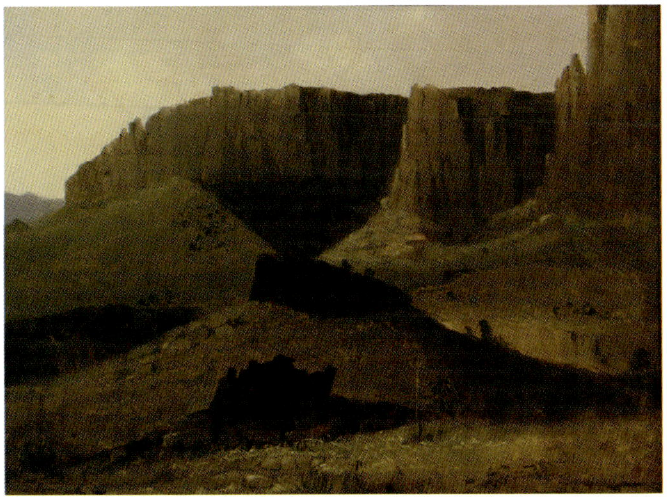

034

Ben Moore Mountain, 1847

Oil on academy board, 9⅞ × 12½ in. (25.1 × 32.7 cm)

INSCRIBED LOWER RIGHT: S[obliterated]LEY; INSCRIBED VERSO: To face the journal of / Oct 18th 1846; Ben More [*sic*] Mountain near HS/Summit

PRESENT COLLECTION: Nelda C. and H. J. Lutcher Stark Foundation, Stark Museum of Art, Orange, Texas (31.23.6)

PROVENANCE: (Edward Eberstadt and Sons, New York, New York); H. J. Lutcher Stark, Orange, Texas, 1965; present owner

Captain Benjamin Moore was in charge of the cavalry dragoons who accompanied General Kearny from Santa Fe to San Diego in 1846. He became a close friend of the man in charge of the small Corps of Topographical Engineers, Lieutenant William H. Emory. On October 18, as the troop passed through the rough country situated between the Rio Grande and Gila rivers, Emory elected to name one of the prominent features along the way Ben Moore Mountain. Emory wrote in his report the following account of the scene Stanley painted. "We passed at the foot of a formidable bluff of trap, running northwest and southeast, which I named Ben Moore, after my personal friend, the gallant Captain Moore, of the 1st dragoons."[1]

Neither the name of the mountain nor the "gallant Captain" would survive. Captain Moore was one of the first to perish in the initial engagement with Mexican troops in California in early December of that year.[2]

1. Emory, *Notes*, 58.

2. Ibid., 108.

035

View of the Copper Mine, 1847

Oil on academy board, 9⅞ × 12¾ in. (25.1 × 32.4 cm)

INSCRIBED LOWER RIGHT: STANLEY; INSCRIBED VERSO: View of the Copper Mine / To face the journal of / Oct. 18th 1846 / ~~Copper Mine~~

PRESENT COLLECTION: Nelda C. and H. J. Lutcher StarkFoundation, Stark Museum of Art, Orange, Texas (31.23.1)

PROVENANCE: The artist; William H. Emory; by descent to William Emory; Sarah Emory; by descent to William Emory III; Mrs. Dean (Alice Stanley) Acheson, Washington, D.C.; (Edward Eberstadt and Sons, New York, New York, 1957); H. J. Lutcher Stark, Orange, Texas, 1965; present owner

Shortly after the Emory party left the shadow of Ben Moore Mountain, the explorer reported that they "began to drop into the valley of what is supposed an arm of the Mimbres, where there are some deserted copper mines."[1] According to some specimens Emory collected, the talus revealed rich samples of gold as well. The early owners of the mines, long since abandoned when Emory and Stanley arrived, had evidently made a substantial fortune before they were scared away by the Apaches. Emory counted between twenty-five and thirty abandoned adobe houses that had once accommodated the miners.

In Stanley's painting, the troop winds its way toward the empty village. Autumn has started to come, and the post oaks are beginning to turn red.

1. Emory, *Notes*, 58.

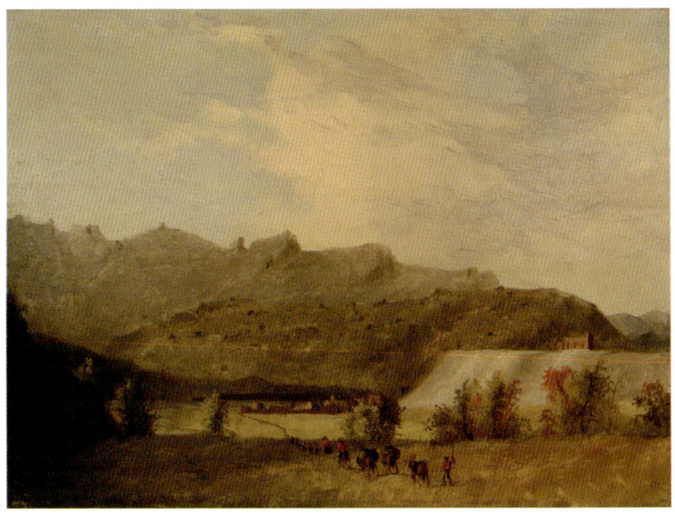

035

036

View in the Sierra Mimbres, 1847

Oil on academy board, 9⅞ × 12¾ in. (25.4 × 32.4 cm)

INSCRIBED LOWER LEFT: STANLEY; INSCRIBED VERSO: View in the Sierra Mimbres / To face the journal of / Oct. 20th 1846. ~~10 O'clock, a.m.~~

PRESENT COLLECTION: Nelda C. and H. J. Lutcher Stark Foundation, Stark Museum of Art, Orange, Texas (31.23.7)

PROVENANCE: The artist; William H. Emory; by descent to William Emory; by descent to Sarah Emory; by descent to William Emory III; Mrs. Dean (Alice Stanley) Acheson, Washington, D.C.; (Edward Eberstadt and Sons, New York, New York, 1957); H. J. Lutcher Stark, Orange, Texas, 1965; present owner

This painting documents the excitement that occurred on October 20, 1846, the first time the Kearny troop encountered a large group of Apaches. Their leader, Red Sleeves, had visited the camp briefly a few days before, but now he brought some thirty other Apaches to trade with the whites, mostly for horses and ropes. According to Emory, Red Sleeves "swore eternal friendship to the whites, and everlasting hatred to the Mexicans."[1] These were heartening words for the soldiers, though the expedition's guide, Kit Carson, did not trust such pledges.

Stanley pictures a couple of fleeting mounted figures galloping across the canvas, Apache warriors on their swift mounts. The rock spire in the distance, one of several "huge stone buttes shooting up into the sky" that Emory described in his journal, adds to the romantic sense of adventure that was shaped by the day's scenery and events.[2]

1. Emory, *Notes*, 60.

2. Ibid., 61.

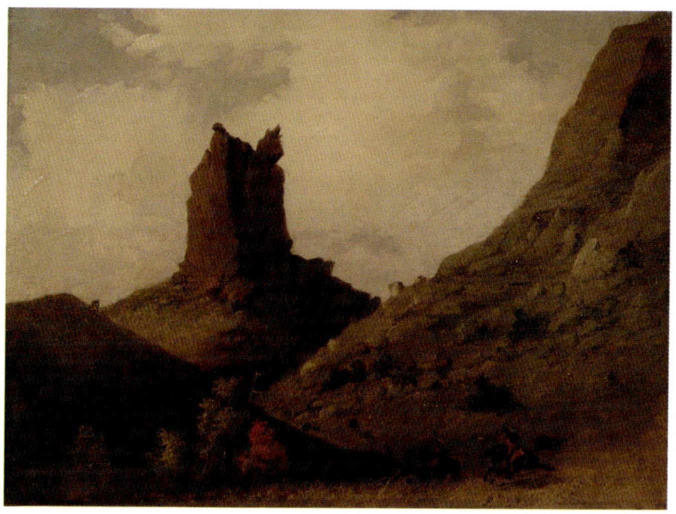

036

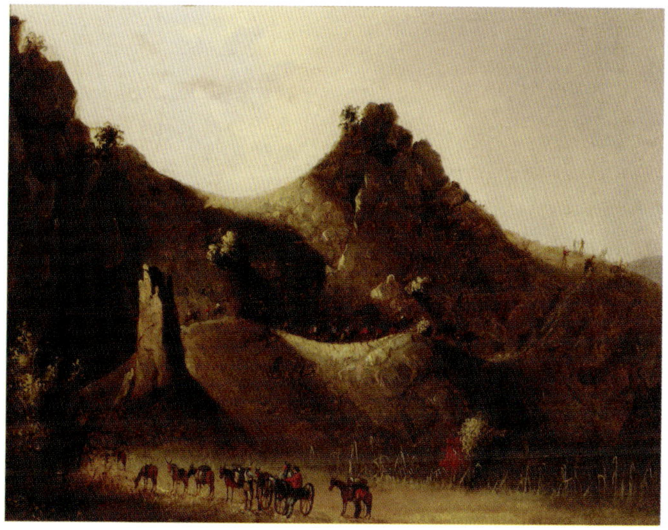

037

Passing an Obstruction: Mouth of Night Creek, 1847

Mouth of Night Creek

Oil on academy board, 9⅞ × 12¾ in. (25.1 × 32.4 cm)

INSCRIBED LOWER LEFT: STANLEY; INSCRIBED VERSO: To face journal of / Oct. 20th 1846 ~~11 O'Clock a.m.~~

PRESENT COLLECTION: Private collection. Photo courtesy of Thomas Nygard Gallery, Bozeman, Montana

PROVENANCE: The artist; William H. Emory; through descent to William Emory; by descent to Sarah Emory; by descent to William Emory III; Mrs. Dean (Alice Stanley) Acheson, Washington, D.C.; (Christie's, New York, New York, 1996); [?]; (Thomas Nygard Gallery, Bozeman, Montana, 2000); present owner

The trip west for the Kearny troop was as trying for the animals as for the men. At the high point on Night Creek, which they reached on October 20, 1846, the trail was so precipitous that Emory was uncertain if the mules and horses could continue. "We wended our way through the narrow valley of Night creek," he recorded in his report next to the lithographed copy of this painting. "On each side were huge stone buttes shooting up into the sky." The path became almost perpendicular at one spot, which caused him to conclude, as the pack mules ascended unimpeded, that "they could climb a wall as steep as a cat."[1]

Kearny's men had been marching for about a week without access to a substantial water source. The Gila River, which was their immediate destination, was just over the hill from this scene. It would be a welcome sight.

1. Emory, *Notes*, 61.

038

The Hieroglyphic Rocks on the Gila, 1847

Oil on academy board, 10 × 12⅝ in. (25.4 × 32.1 cm)

INSCRIBED LOWER RIGHT: STANLEY.; INSCRIBED VERSO: Hyeroglyphics [sic] / Seen Oct. 22nd 1846 ~~1 O'clock p.m.~~

PRESENT COLLECTION: Nelda C. and H. J. Lutcher Stark Foundation, Stark Museum of Art, Orange, Texas (31.23.3)

PROVENANCE: The artist, 1847; William H. Emory; by descent to William Emory; by descent to Sarah Emory; by descent to William Emory III; Mrs. Dean (Alice Stanley) Acheson, Washington, D.C.; (Edward Eberstadt and Sons, New York, New York, 1957); H. J. Lutcher Stark, Orange, Texas, 1965; present owner

A few days before the Kearny expedition reached the Gila River, they passed through a valley with a variety of side canyons. These dry arroyos revealed a series of petroglyphs that had been highlighted with white, spelling out a history of the early Native cultures of the region. Emory took a special interest in them, proposing that they might relate to "the ruins of the so-called Aztec towns" that their guide, Kit Carson, had suggested they were about to reach.[1]

Stanley took an opportunity to record the face of one of these cryptic stone curiosities. He pictured a man, with what appears to be a portfolio under his left arm, standing before a wall of mysterious symbols. Perhaps this is meant to be the artist himself, preparing for such a task. A lithographic plate in the Emory report, titled simply *Hyerogliphics* [*sic*], preserved the alluring scene for the author's enthusiastic reading public.

1. Emory, *Notes*, 63.

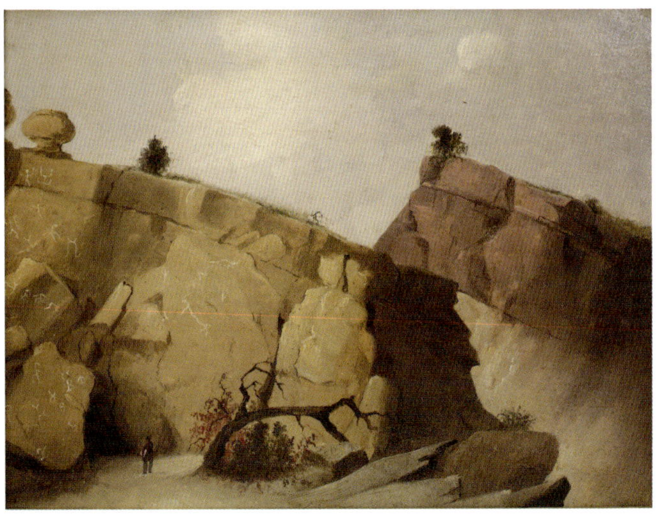

038

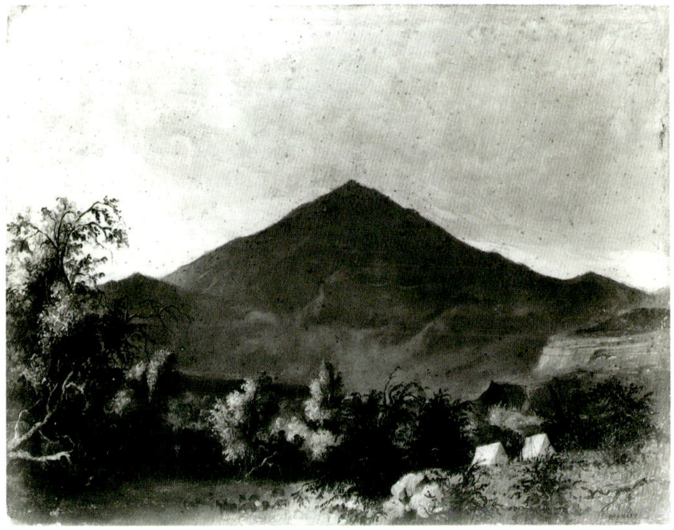

039

View of Mount Graham, 1847

Oil on academy board, 9⅞ × 12¾ in. (25.1 × 32.4 cm)

INSCRIBED LOWER RIGHT: STANLEY; INSCRIBED VERSO: In face the journal of / Nov. 1st [actually October 28] 1846 ~~Morning~~

PRESENT COLLECTION: Unlocated

PROVENANCE: Mrs. Dean (Alice Stanley) Acheson, Washington, D.C., c. 1981; present owner

Although Stanley recorded this vista as occurring on November 1, 1846, the Emory account describes it three days earlier. Part of the army's camp can be seen nestled beneath 10,700-foot Mount Graham, and a group of horses graze below. As bucolic as this scene appears to be, it belies the constant vigil that was required day and night now that the troop was amongst the Apaches. Neither party really trusted the other, so there seemed to be a constant state of alert for everyone.

040

A Tributary of the Gila, 1847

Oil on academy board, 9⅞ × 12¾ in. (25.1 × 32.4 cm)

INSCRIBED LOWER RIGHT: Stanley; INSCRIBED VERSO: A tributary of the Gila / To face the journal of / Nov, 5th 1846 11. Oclock _ a.m. [in Stanley's hand].

PRESENT COLLECTION: Private collection, Michigan

PROVENANCE:; Louis Crandall Stanley, Washington, D.C.; Jane Caroline Stanley, Detroit, Michigan; Sarah L'Estrange (Stanley) Frantz, Saginaw, Michigan; present owner, 1966

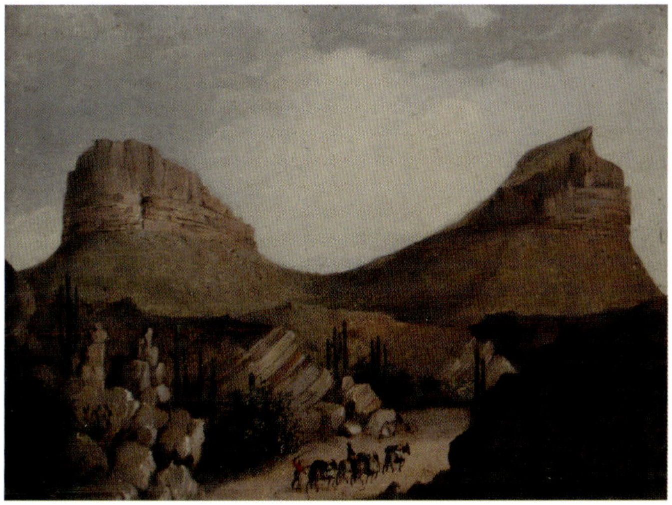

040

As the Kearny troop pressed westward along the Gila River in November 1846, they met with many spectacular sights. Described by Emory as presenting "an inhospitable look" geologically, the view was also filled with gorgeous plant life, as every "variety of cactus flourished in great luxuriance." Of special notice to Emory and Stanley was a mountain they called Saddle-Back, "an isolated peak of red sandstone," which provided a dramatic backdrop for Stanley's painting *A Tributary of the Gila*.[1]

Emory referred to the geology of this place as being especially confused, with many varieties of rock, from granite to sandstone, having multiple textures, irregular patterns, and multidirectional strata. Stanley's painting captures that complexity with the diverse bands and multiple orientations of the rock layers. The small genre scene that unfolds in the center of the composition, with the man at the rear whipping his pack mule, adds an unsettling aura to the scene.

1. Emory, *Notes*, 75.

041

Ruins of the Casa Grande, 1847

Oil on academy board, 9⅜ × 12¾ in. (23.8 × 32.4 cm)

INSCRIBED LOWER RIGHT: STANLEY; INSCRIBED VERSO: To face the journal of November 10, 1846 3 o'clock p.m. / The founders of which are unknown

PRESENT COLLECTION: Buffalo Bill Center of the West, Cody, Wyoming; gift of George M. Stanley (grandson of the artist) and family (1.99)

PROVENANCE: The artist; Col. W. H. Emory; purchased by Mrs. Dean (Alice Stanley) Acheson, Washington, D.C.; by gift to George M. Stanley, Fresno, California, 1952; by gift to present owner, 1999

One of the most curious sights witnessed by the Kearny expedition was a three-story adobe ruin of some ancient Sonoran Desert people that they came upon near a large village of Pima Indians on the Gila River. Referred to as the Casa Grande (cat. no. 028), it was studied by Emory, Stanley, and others in the group. One of the Pima chiefs, Juan Antonio Llunas, whom Stanley painted and who visited Emory's camp, explained that the ruins were part of a fanciful origin myth that his people cherished but that he, in fact, did not particularly believe.[1] Everyone came away from the scene uncertain about the history of the buildings, with Stanley inscribing on the back of his painting, "The founders of which are unknown." As the group moved on down the Gila River, though, Emory searched for additional ruins that might be associated with the Casa Grande, which he then referred to as Casa Montezuma, implying that they could be related to the famous sixteenth-century Aztec emperor. The ruins remain a mystery even to the present day.

Stanley described the ruins in a letter home to his associate Sumner Dickerman. "This building," he wrote, "is 60 feet by 45, three stories high, and is constructed of the adobe, similar to that used in the houses of New Mexico." Shards he found in the vicinity, "beautifully painted and ornamented," provided the "only clue which we had to the advancement of the builders in the mechanic arts."[2]

1. See Emory, *Notes*, 83, and Clarke, *Original Journals of Henry Smith Turner*, 107, for accounts of the origin myth.

2. Quoted in "Aztec Ruins," *Niles' National Register*, June 12, 1847.

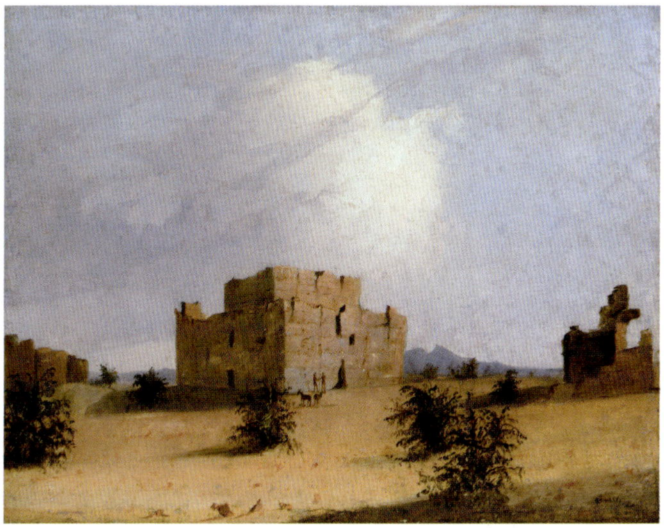

041

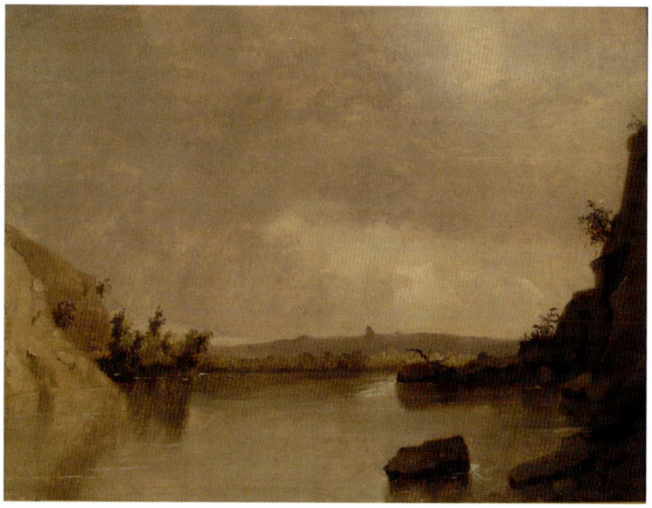

042

Junction of the Gila and Colorado Rivers, 1847

Oil on academy board, $9\frac{15}{16} \times 12\frac{3}{4}$ in. (25.2×32.4 cm)

INSCRIBED VERSO: Junction of the Gila and Colorado rivers; To face the journal / Nov 23rd, 1846 / ~~Rio Colorado & Hela [Gila]~~

PRESENT COLLECTION: Nelda C. and H. J. Lutcher Stark Foundation, Stark Museum of Art, Orange, Texas (31.23.2)

PROVENANCE: The artist; William H. Emory; by descent to William Emory; by descent to Sarah Emory; by descent to William Emory III; Mrs. Dean (Alice Stanley) Acheson, Washington, D.C.; (Edward Eberstadt and Sons, New York, New York, 1957); H. J. Lutcher Stark, Orange, Texas, 1965; present owner

On November 22, 1846, after two months of arduous travel, Kearny's troops arrived at a place a few miles from the junction of the Gila and Colorado rivers. Emory and Stanley were sent ahead the next day as scouts to reconnoiter. Emory remembered it as a stormy morning, with clouds of dust rising over the banks of the Colorado as they approached. "The Gila comes into it nearly at right angles," he wrote, "and the point of junction . . . is the hard butte through which, with a united force they cut a cañon." Stanley's painting of the scene captures the tempestuous, overcast sky with the powerful forces of the two rivers merging. Emory noted that the "sea-green waters" of the Gila were "lost in the chrome colored hue of the Colorado" as they joined to flow south to the Gulf of California.[1]

Stanley's illustrated depiction of the *Junction of the Gila & Colorado Rivers* (fig. 42.1), which appears as a lithograph on page 95 of the Emory report, pictures tents and soldiers camped on a high meadow above the rivers. Emory had brought in several captured Mexican men the evening before, and Kearny had decided to remain in the camp while he interrogated them. Their leader turned out to be Colonel Jose Maria Leguna, who was transporting horses north for the Mexican Army.

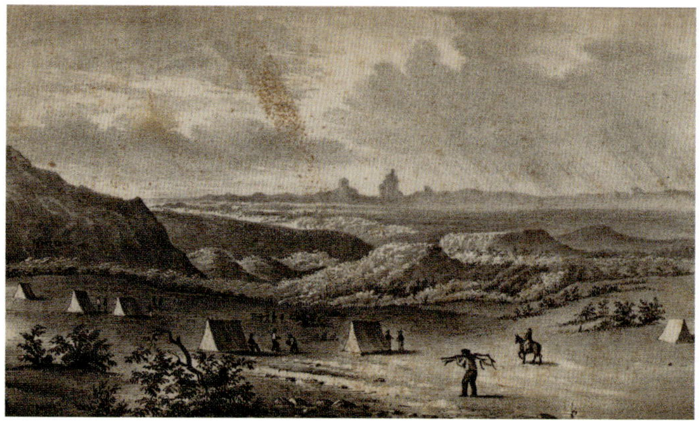

FIG. 42.1.
G. B. Graham after John Mix Stanley,
Junction of the Gila & Colorado Rivers, 1848.
Lithograph; $4 \times 6\frac{1}{4}$ in. (10.2×15.9 cm). From Emory, *Notes of a Military Reconnoissance*, 150. Courtesy McCracken Research Library, Buffalo Bill Center of the West, Cody, Wyoming

1. Emory, *Notes*, 95.

043

The Abduction, 1847

Indian and the Virgin on Horseback; Indian and Virgin

Oil on academy board, $12\frac{1}{2} \times 17\frac{1}{2}$ in. (31.8×44.5 cm)

INSCRIBED LOWER LEFT: Stanley / 1847 / California; INSCRIBED VERSO: Presented to Parson Price / with / the compliments of the artist / J. M. Stanley [illeg] / April 7, 47 / San Francisco, California

PRESENT COLLECTION: Property of the Westervelt Collection and displayed in The Tuscaloosa Museum of Art, Tuscaloosa, Alabama.

PROVENANCE: The artist; Parson Price, San Francisco, California; [?]; Lee B. Anderson, New York, New York, 1961; (Hirschl and Adler Galleries, New York, New York, 1973–1978); (Kodner Gallery of Fine Arts: Gallery of the Masters, Saint Louis, Missouri, 1977); Gordon Fraser, Minneapolis, Minnesota; (Kennedy Galleries, New York, New York, 1978); Jack Warner, Tuscaloosa, Alabama; [?]; present owner

This painting was completed in San Francisco while Stanley was stationed there putting final touches on his illustrations for Emory's report. It was painted for a Parson Price, who is yet to be identified, and is reminiscent of incidents that Stanley had heard about during his travels through Apache country in Arizona.

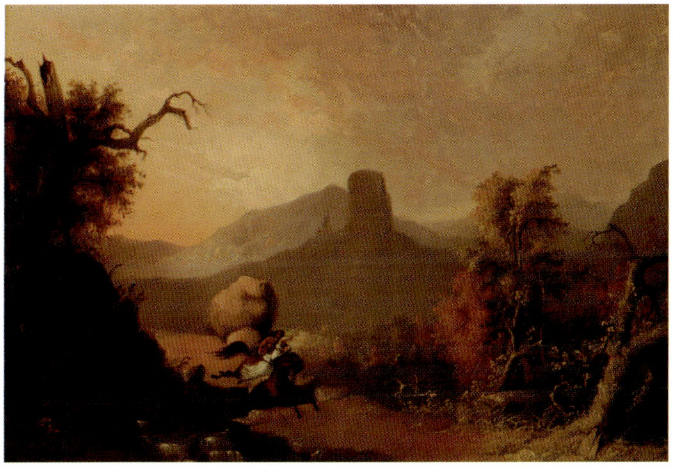

043

The background, with its prominent phallic spire physically and psychologically dominating the scene, suggests the view from the expedition's camp on the Gila River on November 8, 1846 (fig. 130.1). Emory described this protrusion, on the north side of the river, as a seam "of igneous rock, shooting up in irregular spires and turrets, one or two thousand feet in height."[1]

The Apaches, as with the Navajos, were famous for their plundering of the Mexican and Pueblo settlements. "The Mexicans are rascals," boasted one Apache chief to Emory. "We hate and will kill them all."[2] One of the common Apache and Navajo depredations against the Mexicans was abducting women and children for forced betrothal and enslavement.[3]

As a literary trope, captivity scenes were popular in the eighteenth century, but their appeal had waned somewhat by Stanley's time. Nonetheless, in American painting, as exemplified in Asher B. Durand's *Indian Rescue* (1846, American Museum of Western Art, Denver) and Carl Wimar's *The Abduction of Daniel Boone's Daughter by the Indians* (1853, Mildred Lane Kemper Art Museum, St. Louis), the motif was still in demand.

1. Emory, *Notes*, 127.

2. Ibid., 100.

3. Ibid., 48. Susan Shelby Magoffin describes in her diary, written in Santa Fe a short time before Kearny arrived, that a band of Navajos had come into Santa Fe and "carried off some twenty families." See Stella M. Drumm, ed., *Down the Santa Fe Trail and into Mexico: The Diary of Susan Shelby Magoffin, 1846–1847* (Lincoln: University of Nebraska Press, 1982), 68.

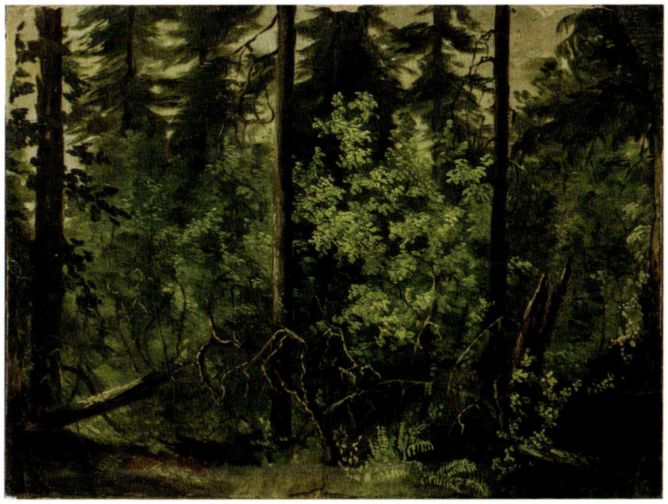

044

Sketch from Nature, Willamette Valley, 1847

Oil on paper, 9¼ × 12 in. (23.5 × 30.5 cm)

INSCRIBED VERSO: Sketch from Nature / Willamette Valley / 1847 / J. M. Stanley

PRESENT COLLECTION: Nelda C. and H. J. Lutcher Stark Foundation, Stark Museum of Art, Orange, Texas (31.23.16)

PROVENANCE: Mrs. Dean (Alice Stanley) Acheson, Washington, D.C.; H. J. Lutcher Stark, Orange, Texas, 1965; present owner

Oregon City's newspaper, the *Oregon Spectator*, which had marked the birth of journalism on the West Coast of North America less than two years earlier, announced the arrival of John Mix Stanley on July 8, 1847. It reported the welcome appearance of "a young American artist, Mr. J. M. Stanley, who visits our territory for the purpose of transferring to canvas some portions of the beautiful and sublime scenery with which our country abounds."[1]

Stanley busied himself painting portraits of Clackamus and Willamette Falls Indians, both considered by Stanley as "remnant" members of once prosperous tribes. He also, as the newspaper noted, took time to paint the local scenery and, later, Oregon City.[2] His new environment kept him busy until fall. Among the studies he made was one he inscribed as "Sketch from Nature, Willamette Valley, 1847." Its verdant tangle of foliage, rich palette, and somber tone reveal his fascination with the lushness of the Northwest, a remarkable contrast to the tawny void of the Arizona desert through which he had so recently trekked with Emory and Kearny. His Indian Gallery, as it took shape in 1850 upon his return to the United States, comprised 134 works. The paintings of the Northwest, thirty-three in number, were listed as "SKETCHES," suggesting that small works like this may have been temporarily exhibited until larger, more finished paintings were produced over the next two years.[3]

1. *Oregon Spectator*, July 8, 1847. In a letter written from Oregon City eight months later, March 7, Stanley stated that he had actually come to town in late June 1847. See "Letter from Oregon," undated clipping, unknown newspaper, from the Stanley scrapbook.

2. *Portraits of North American Indians*, 61–62.

3. *Stanley's Indian Gallery* (1850), 1. This flyer was printed for Stanley's exhibition in New York City, which ran from November 1850 to February 1851.

045

Abigail Walker, 1847

Oil on board, 14 1/16 × 11 1/2 in. (35.8 × 29.3 cm) (sight)

INSCRIBED LOWER LEFT: J. M. Stanley. Oregon. 1847—

PRESENT COLLECTION: Elkanah and Mary Richardson Walker Papers, Manuscripts, Archives, and Special Collections, Washington State University Libraries

PROVENANCE: Ruth Karr McKee; by gift to present owner

From his earliest work as a portraitist, Stanley relished painting children. During his fated journey up the Columbia River in fall 1847, he visited the Tshimakain Mission near present-day Spokane, Washington. The Congregational mission was run jointly by Cushing and Myra Eells and Elkanah and Mary Walker. Stanley had planned to spend only a couple of days at the mission, but bad weather and a severe cold impeded his travels. According to one account, "in order to pass the time," though certainly at the behest of the Walkers, Stanley paused to paint the missionaries' second child and only daughter, the enchanting seven-year-old Abigail Boutwell Walker.[1]

Stanley began the portrait in late October 1847, but in the process of working on it, Abigail fell sick with measles. Stanley decided that he would finish it later and set off for what was known then as Fort Colville to the north. When he returned on November 19, Abigail had recovered, and he completed his work in short order. So pleased were the parents with Stanley's efforts that they commissioned him to paint a companion portrait of the family patriarch, *Elkanah Walker* (cat. no. 046).[2]

1. Clifford Merrill Drury, *Elkanah and Mary Walker, Pioneers among the Spokanes* (Caldwell, Idaho: Caxton Press, 1940), 201. A note on the reverse of a photograph of the portrait (in the curatorial files of the Smithsonian American Art Museum), written by one of Abigail's grandsons, says she was seven when the painting was completed.

2. Ibid.

046

Elkanah Walker, 1847

Portrait of the Rev. Elkanah Walker

Oil on paper, 8 11/16 × 7 1/16 in. (22 × 18 cm)

INSCRIBED: [J.] M. Stanley, Oregon—1847

PRESENT COLLECTION: Beinecke Rare Book and Manuscript Library, Western Americana Collection, Yale University, New Haven, Connecticut (WA.MSS.440)

PROVENANCE: Frederick W. Skiff, Portland, Oregon; William Robertson Coe, New York, New York; present owner

The Tshimakain Mission northwest of today's Spokane, Washington, was one of several Protestant missions to be opened on the Oregon frontier in the 1830s. Its founders, Elkanah and Mary Walker, were from Maine. He was an ordained minister of the First Congregational Church and she, well educated and intellectually curious, was a serious student of geology and natural history. Far from zealots, they embraced a role of working with the Spokane Indians rather than merely converting them. Elkanah was especially interested in their language and published a lexicon of the Flathead tongue.

Stanley visited the mission in October and November 1847. He first painted a portrait of their only daughter, Abigail (cat. no. 045), and then was asked to preserve a likeness of Abigail's father.

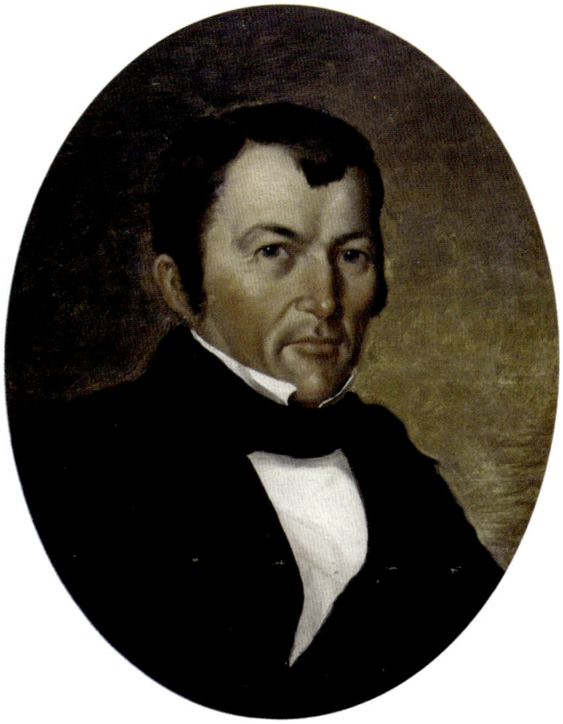

046

Elkanah recorded in his diary that Stanley began on November 18 and worked through the 22nd. By the second day of sitting, he wrote that the "work was much improved. I think Mr. Stanley a fine artist & executes his work well."[1] Stanley wrote with similar ardor that being in the gracious "society" of the Walkers and long "reminded of their kindness" had made him forget that he "was so far from any civilized community."[2]

After the Whitman massacre, the Walkers moved to Oregon City with the family and eventually settled north of Portland. They were known for establishing schools along the way. (See cat. nos. 052 and 053 for more information on the Whitman massacre.)

1. Quoted in Drury, *Elkanah and Mary Walker*, 201–202.

2. "Letter from Oregon," undated clipping, unknown newspaper, Stanley scrapbook. The letter quoted in the article is dated March 7, 1848.

047

Tin Tin Malikin, 1847

(Strong Breast [Spokane]; Tin-Tin-Ma-Li-Kan, or Strong Breast)

Oil on canvas on academy board, 11 × 8 in. (27.9 × 20.3 cm)

INSCRIBED LOWER LEFT: J. M. Stanley; ab: Tin Tin Malikin–or Strong Breast / Leggins [illegible] deer skin.

PRESENT COLLECTION: Detroit Institute of Arts, Detroit, Michigan, gift of Dexter M. Ferry, Jr. (38.103); photograph courtesy Bridgeman Images

PROVENANCE: Dexter M. Ferry, Detroit, Michigan; Dexter M. Ferry, Jr., Detroit, Michigan; present owner by gift

Only two things are known about Tin Tin Malikin—that his name translates to Strong Breast and that he was a significant figure among the Spokane Indians on the upper Columbia River, whom Stanley visited in the winter of 1847.

Stanley painted a large finished version of this field study some time between late 1850 and late 1852, when it appeared as a title in his catalogue *Portraits of North American Indians*, published by the Smithsonian Institution.[1] The sketch was retained by Stanley as part of his studio collection, while the larger work was destroyed by fire at the Smithsonian in 1865. Under what circumstances the sketch was acquired by Dexter M. Ferry, one of Detroit's most prominent businessmen, is not known. Ferry was recognized as an advocate for the arts and served for a time as a trustee of the Detroit Institute of Arts.

1. *Portraits of North American Indians*, 71. The published checklist, Stanley's Indian Gallery, which was available to visitors at his 1850 showing of the exhibition at the Alhambra Rooms in New York, does not list this portrait.

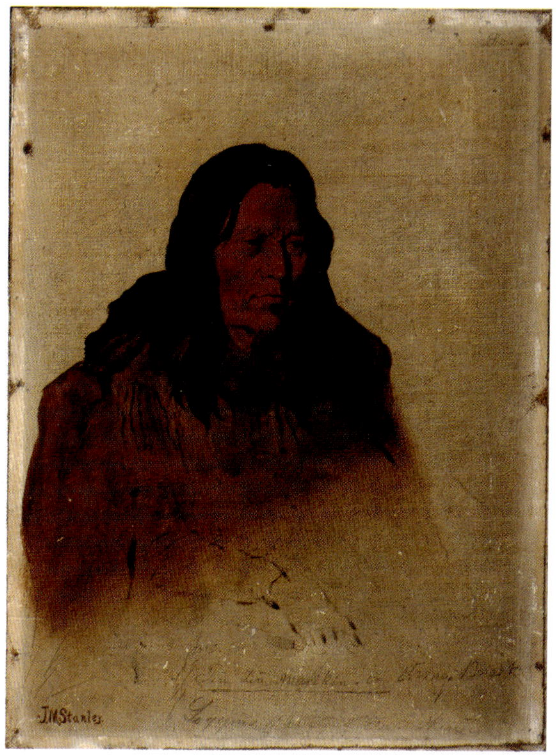

047

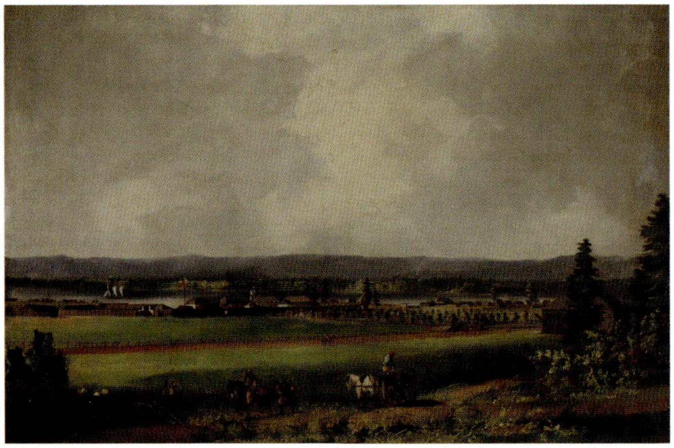

048

Fort Vancouver, c. 1847

Fort Vancouver, Columbia River

Oil on canvas, 15½ × 23⅝ in. (39.5 × 60.0 cm)

INSCRIPTION: [Unsigned]

PRESENT COLLECTION: Yale Collection of Western Americana, Beinecke Rare Book and Manuscript Library, New Haven, Connecticut

PROVENANCE: Sir George Simpson; by descent to Francis Ramsey Simpson; [?]; (Edward Eberstadt, New York, New York); William Robertson
Coe, New York, New York; present owner by gift

LIFETIME EXHIBITIONS: U.S. Capitol rotunda, Washington, D.C., 1854

Stanley first reached Oregon from California in early July 1847.[1] He visited Oregon City, painted Indians in the area of the Willamette Falls, and then proceeded north and west into the interior of the newly acquired U.S. territory and present-day Washington State.[2] On the way he passed the old Hudson's Bay Company outpost of Fort Vancouver on the Columbia River. It is suspected that it was during this trip that he painted this view of the fort.

This painting is unsigned and came into the collections of Yale University as a gift from William Robertson Coe.[3] At that time it was ascribed to the Canadian painter Paul Kane, who worked in the area at the same time as Stanley (see fig. 48.1). Since then, attributions have been less certain. John A. Hussey, in his 1957 monograph, *The History of Fort Vancouver*, referred to it as being painted by an unknown artist. Kane's biographer J. Russell Harper refused to include it in Kane's body of work in his 1971 seminal edited volume *Paul Kane's Frontier*.[4] C. P. Wilson, who wrote about the painting in 1949, attributed it to the British explorer-artist Lieutenant Henry Warre.[5] Yet Warre expert Ben Huseman of the University of Texas, Arlington, disclaims any connection with that artist. Partly, then, by process of elimination and partly as a function of connoisseurship, this painting should be considered as a work by Stanley. Certainly the landscape treatment, as well as the quality of light and the figural groups, conform to known Stanley landscapes of the period.

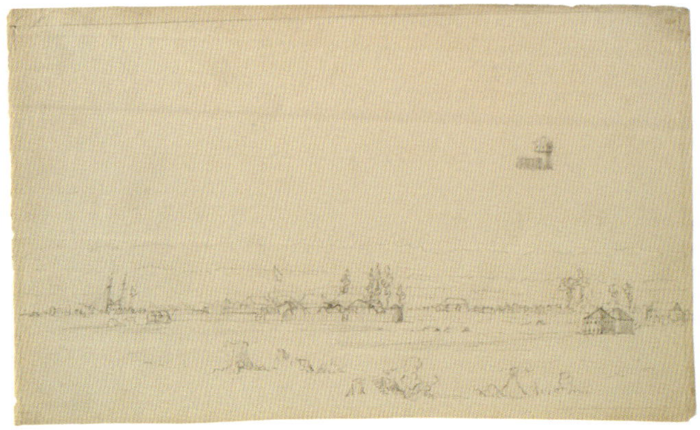

FIG. 48.1.
Paul Kane, *View of Fort Vancouver*, 1847. Pencil on paper; 15½ × 9 in. (39.4 × 22.9 cm). Courtesy Royal Ontario Museum, Toronto

1. *Oregon Spectator*, July 8, 1847.

2. See Nellie B. Pipes, "John Mix Stanley, Indian Painter," *Oregon Historical Quarterly* 33, no. 3 (September 1932): 251.

3. Mary C. Withington, *A Catalogue of Manuscripts in the Collection of Western Americana Founded by William Robertson Coe* (New Haven, Conn.: Yale University Press, 1952), 155.

4. Paul Kane, *Paul Kane's Frontier; Including Wanderings of an Artist among the Indians of North America, by Paul Kane*, ed. J. Russell Harper (Austin: University of Texas Press, 1971), 298; and John A. Hussey, *The History of Fort Vancouver* (Tacoma: Washington State Historical Society, 1957), xvii.

5. C. P. Wilson, "Early Western Paintings," *Beaver* 280 (June 1949): 12–13.

049

Peter Skene Ogden, c. 1848

Oil on canvas, 38 × 29 in. (96.5 × 73.7 cm)

INSCRIBED VERSO: Stanley, Oregon, 1848. Mrs. McKinlay with compliments of the artist.

PRESENT COLLECTION: Unlocated

PROVENANCE: The artist; Mrs. Susan Ellen McKinlay, 1848; British Columbia Provincial Museum, on loan to the provincial Archives of British Columbia, Canada; private collection

Peter Skene Ogden was serving as chief factor of Fort Vancouver in 1847 when Stanley first visited there. Ogden wrote a letter to artist Paul Kane in September speaking of Stanley and saying that he was "in quest of scenery" and that the Indian chiefs were "in great demand with him."[1] It may have been at this time, or in early 1848, when Stanley returned to Fort Vancouver following the Whitman massacre, that this portrait was made (see cat. nos. 052 and 053 for more information on the Whitman massacre). Ogden was personally responsible for negotiating the freedom of forty-seven women and children held ransom by the Cayuse Indians after the massacre, an act that won for him great praise from the American settlers.[2]

Americans were not always Ogden's admirers. As a British fur trader in the 1820s and 1830s, his assignment was to put the rival American fur companies out of business. His reputation for expansive exploration and ruthless competitive tactics was legendary. His "scorched earth" policy swept beaver nearly clean from territories as far away from the Northwest as present-day Utah (the city of Ogden is named for him) and California.[3] His last years saw him overseeing the demise and breakup of the venerable Hudson's Bay Company's operations in the Oregon country. His expression in the Stanley portrait would suggest that he was as resolute at that task as with any before. As with Stanley's portrayal of John Golden Ross (cat. no. 018), the artist posed Ogden in a formulaic posture of dominance with a fluted column at his side to imply power.

1. Quoted in Kane, *Paul Kane's Frontier*, 24.

2. Jeff Lalande, "Peter Skene Ogden (1790–1854)," *Oregon Encyclopedia*, accessed August 20, 2014, www.oregonencyclopedia.org/articles/ogden_peter_skene.

3. William H. Goetzmann, *Exploration and Empire: The Explorer and the Scientist in the Winning of the American West* (New York: Knopf, 1966), 92–101.

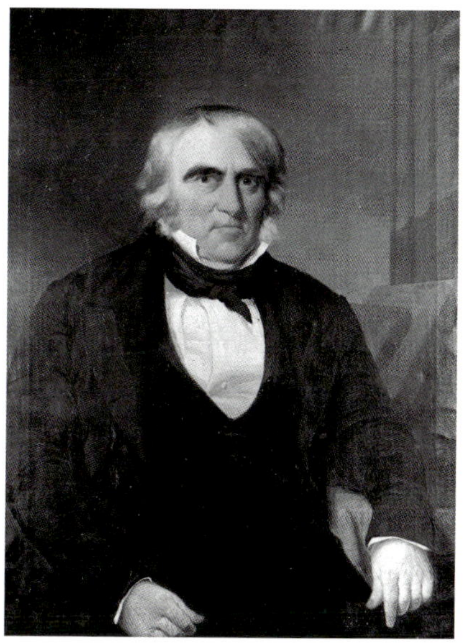

049

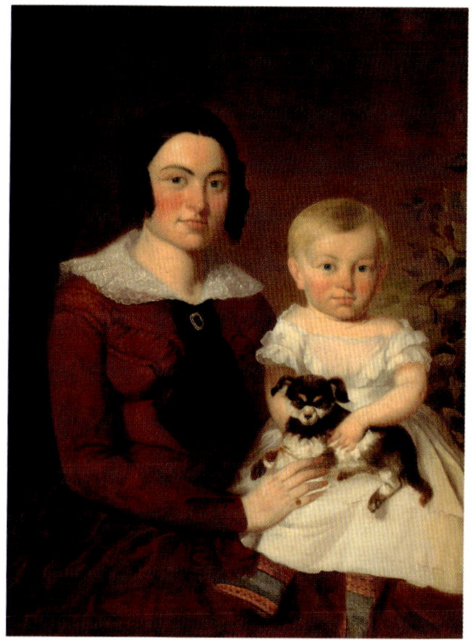

050

Mrs. Forbes Barclay and Son, 1848

Oil on canvas, 39 × 28 in. (99.1 × 71.1 cm)

INSCRIBED VERSO: J. M. S. Fort Vancouver, 1848

PRESENT COLLECTION: Oregon Historical Society, Portland, Oregon

PROVENANCE: Charlotte Pratt Miles; Dr. and Mrs. Franz R. Stenzel, Portland, Oregon; (Sotheby Parke Bernet, Los Angeles, California, 1980); present owner

Following Stanley's close shave with the Cayuse and the Whitman massacre, he returned to the sanctuary of Fort Vancouver in early 1848, where he painted several portraits, including one that is thought to be of the company's doctor, Forbes Barclay, and another of the doctor's wife, Maria, and a child.[1] Barclay family history held that the child was the Barclays' second son, Peter Thomas.[2] Maria, the daughter of one of the fort's chief traders, Pierre Chrysologue Pambrun, and Catherine Humpherville, was born in 1826. She spoke little English, coming from a French family, and enjoyed minimal education, but was known for her beauty.

Forbes and Maria had seven children, and Peter, who was born in April 1847, would have been over a year old when Stanley departed for Hawaii in August 1848. The child in this portrait looks to be about that age.[3]

1. Pipes, "John Mix Stanley," 254. The portrait of Forbes Barclay (Oregon Health and Science University, Portland) is attributed to Stanley, although sufficient information does not exist to make a firm attribution.

2. M. Leona Nichols, "Fine Old Mansion Storehouse of Treasures," *Portland Oregonian*, March 20, 1932.

3. For an account of the Barclay children, see Fred Lockley, *History of the Columbia River Valley* (Chicago: S. J. Clarke, 1928), 436–37.

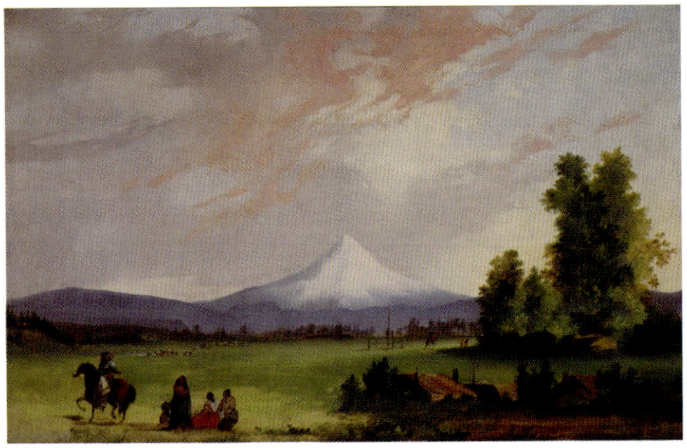

051

Mount Hood, 1848

Oil on canvas, 16¼ × 24½ in. (41.3 × 62.2 cm)

INSCRIBED VERSO: Presented to Dr. Forbes Barclay with the compliments of the artist / Oregon 1848

PRESENT COLLECTION: Floyd D. Gottwald, Jr.

PROVENANCE: The artist; Dr. Forbes Barclay, Fort Vancouver, 1848; by descent to Kate Barclay, Oregon City, Oregon, 1984; John Eulich Collection, Dallas, Texas, 1984; (Rosenstock Arts, Denver, Colorado, 1986); Jerry Blank, Sun Valley, Idaho, 1986; (Gessner Fine Arts, Key Largo, Florida); (Gerald Peters Gallery, Santa Fe, New Mexico); Vantage Collection of American and Western Art, Dallas, Texas; (Gerald Peters Gallery, Santa Fe, New Mexico); private collection, Miami, Florida; present owner

Stanley gave this painting to Forbes Barclay, the physician who ministered to the needs of Fort Vancouver in the 1840s. Trained and credentialed at the Royal College of Surgeons in Edinburgh, Scotland, Barclay played a vital role in Oregon frontier history. He commissioned Stanley to paint two portraits, one of himself (for which only a photograph remains; fig. 51.1) and another of his wife with a child (cat. no. 050). In return, the artist presented him with this lyrical view of Mount Hood from the outskirts of Fort Vancouver.

One of the doctor's daughters, Andrina Catherine Barclay, later remembered the landscape and particularly one of its prominent figures, the mounted Indian in the left foreground. His name, she said, was John Thomas, and he became a day laborer in Oregon City after he and the Barclays moved there in 1850.[1]

The Canadian artist Paul Kane, who was visiting the area, produced a similar view from a similar vantage point, *Mount Hood from West End* (Stark Museum of Art, Orange, Texas). The two artists may have met when Stanley first arrived at the fort in 1847. They certainly had similar aspirations of becoming famous through the creation of Indian galleries. Kane wanted his to include one hundred works offering a panorama of Canadian Indian life and western scenery from the Great Lakes to the Pacific. He embarked on his enterprise as soon as he returned to his hometown, Toronto, in 1848.[2]

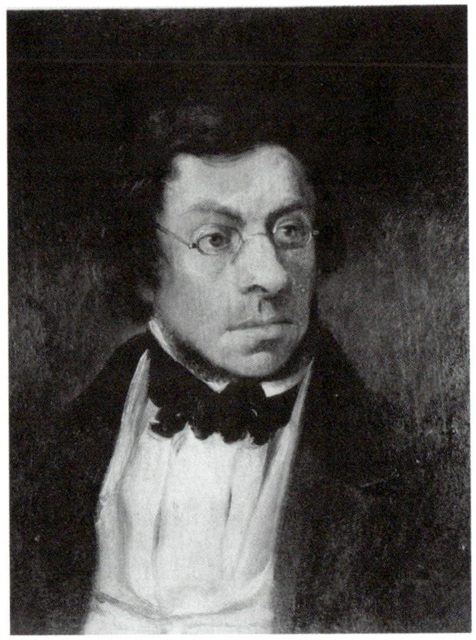

FIG. 51.1.
Unknown [possibly John Mix Stanley],
Portrait of Dr. Forbes Barclay, 1848.
Oil on canvas. Reproduction provided by the Oregon Health and Science University, Historical Collections and Archives, Olaf Larsell Papers, 1999–011.

1. M. Leona Nichols, "Fine Old Mansion Storehouse of Treasures," *Portland Oregonian*, March 20, 1932.

2. Kane, *Paul Kane's Frontier*, 32–33.

052

Shu-Ma-Hici, 1848

*Shu-Ma-hic-sie, or Painted Shirt; Painted Shirt [Cayuse]*Oil on paper, 9 × 6½ in. (22.9 × 16.5 cm)

INSCRIBED CENTER RIGHT: Shu ma hici / or / Painted Shirt / Edward / son of / Telocoit /Cay

PRESENT COLLECTION: Private collection

PROVENANCE: Neil Reisner, Scarsdale, New York, 1979; (Sotheby's, New York, New York, 1993); present owner

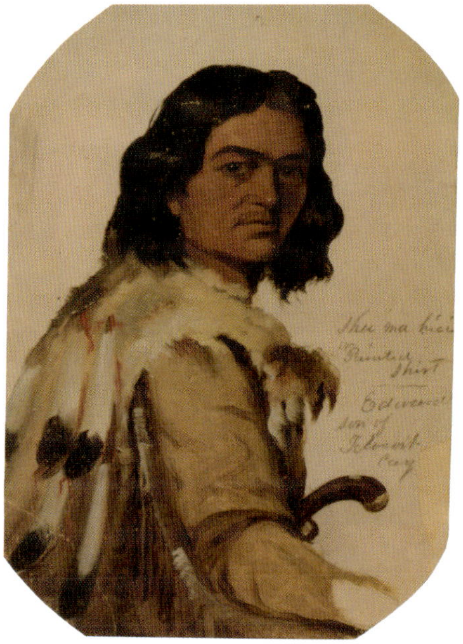

052

053

Waie-Cat, 1848

(Waie- Cat- One that Flies [Cayuse])

Oil on paper, 9 × 6½ in. (22.9 × 16.5 cm) (irregular)

INSCRIBED UPPER RIGHT: Waie.e.cat / Son of Tum [cut canvas] one that flies / Cayuse

PRESENT COLLECTION: Private collection

PROVENANCE: (Sotheby's, New York, New York, 1993); present owner

In late November 1847, Stanley was headed toward the Whitman Mission at Wailetpu when he learned of an Indian attack on the Marcus and Narcissa Whitman family and others at the mission. Stanley made a hasty retreat downriver and survived the onslaught. He wrote of it about a month later in the safety of Fort Vancouver: "The Cayuse Indians have recently perpetrated a most inhuman butchery of the family of Dr. Whitman and twelve of our countrymen, residing with him, and I narrowly escaped sharing their fate myself."[1]

Many of the perpetrators of the attack were arrested and brought to trial in Oregon City, where this and a companion portrait of another Cayuse man, *Waie-Cat* (cat. no. 053), were probably painted in spring 1848. Prior to the attack, Shu-Ma-Hici had been a close friend of the Whitman family and was named Edward after Narcissa Whitman's brother. According to the artist, he was also the son of Te-Lo-kikt, of whom Stanley also painted a portrait. Te-Lo-kikt was the principal chief of the Cayuse and one of the primary instigators among the Whitman assailants. He was hanged in 1859 for his role in the massacre.

This small oil is a field study for a larger portrait that was displayed beside one of Te-Lo-kikt in Stanley's Indian Gallery, both of which were lost in the Smithsonian's fire of 1865.[2] Shu-Ma-Hici's commanding pose, with the sitter looking directly at the viewer over his right shoulder, is a departure for Stanley, who tended to portray sitters in a fully frontal view.

1. "The Indian War in Oregon," undated clipping, unknown newspaper, quoting a letter from Stanley, Fort Vancouver, January 8, 1848, Stanley scrapbook.

2. See *Portraits of North American Indians*, 65.

This is a study for a finished portrait of a Cayuse Indian man who participated in the Whitman attack of November 29, 1847. Stanley painted him first in Oregon City in spring 1848, after he had been arrested and incarcerated. The artist recalled him as having an English name, One That Flies, and discussed him at some length in his Indian Gallery catalogue as the son of "the great ringleader and first instigator of the Wailetpu massacre," Tum-Suc-Kee.[1]

Although Waie-Cat was, according to Stanley, "an active participant in the massacre of Dr. Whitman, and committed many atrocities on the defenseless captives," he escaped punishment. His father, however, was not so fortunate; he was hanged in June 1850.

Much has been written about the Whitman affair, some of which lays the primary blame on the whites rather than the Indians. The whites brought diseases like measles to the Cayuse tribe, against which the Indians had no immunities. Marcus Whitman tried to minister to them but was essentially unsuccessful. Then

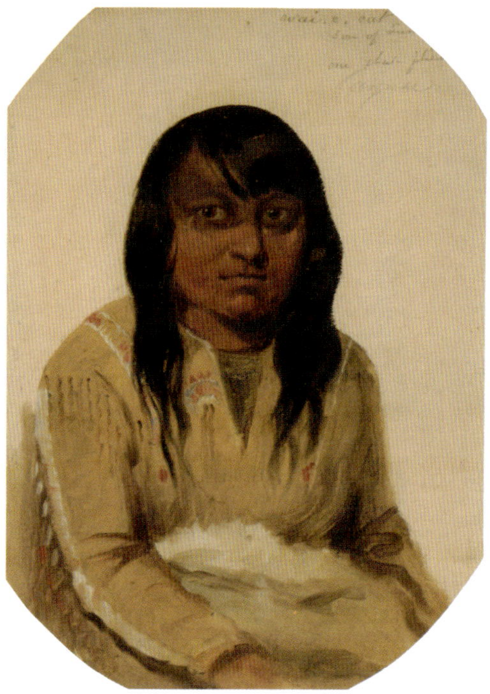

053

a disgruntled pioneer named Joe Lewis spread word among the Cayuse that Whitman had purposely spread the illness through their population. The result was a historical disaster, the Cayuse War, which raged for many months and concluded as one of the most tragic examples of cultural conflict in the early West. Though blame has been spread among all participants, Stanley chose to side with the settlers, very possibly because he was almost killed in the affair.

1. *Portraits of North American Indians*, 66.

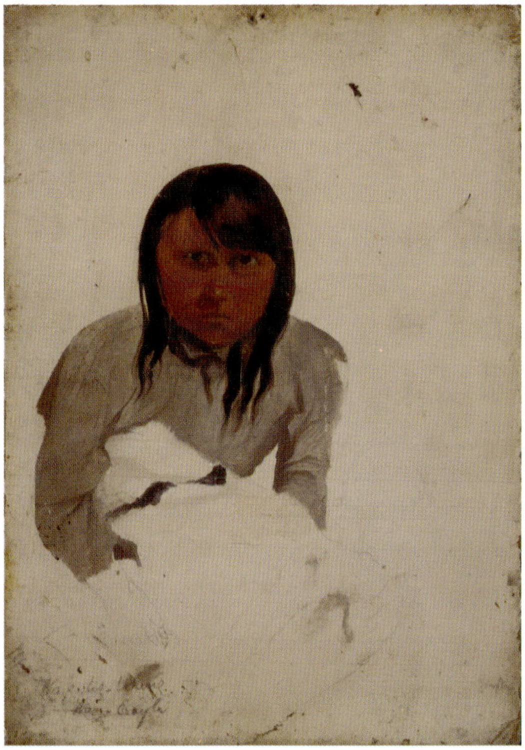

054

Wap-Tis-Tokene, 1848

Wap-Tis-Tokene, War Eagle (Indian Man)

Oil and pencil on academy board, 12¾ × 9⅛ in. (32.4 × 23.2 cm)

INSCRIBED LOWER LEFT: Wap tis-tokene / War-Eagle; INSCRIBED LOWER RIGHT: Wapt [oke]

PRESENT COLLECTION: Nelda C. and H. J. Lutcher Stark Foundation, Stark Museum of Art, Orange, Texas (31.23.12)

PROVENANCE: The artist; Louis Crandall Stanley, Detroit, Michigan; Mrs. Dean (Alice Stanley) Acheson, Washington, D.C.; H. J. Lutcher Stark, Orange, Texas, 1965; present owner

Prior to the attack on the Whitman Mission in 1847, the Cayuse Indians were, according to Stanley, "not only above want but the wealthiest tribe in Oregon." They had, under the leadership of Marcus Whitman, successfully "cultivated large fields of corn, wheat, potatoes, and other vegetables, which, with the fish that annually visit the streams watering their country, enabled them to live in comparative affluence."[1] What Whitman was not able to do, despite his training as a medical doctor, was shield the Indians against white man's diseases, so their prosperity was severely compromised when measles took hold. The Cayuse War of 1848 was the result of the cultural conflict that ensued.

This young Cayuse man was probably painted in Oregon City in the spring of 1848 along with *Shu-Ma-Hici* (cat. no. 052) and *Waie-Cat* (cat. no. 053), who were implicated in the murders of the Whitman family and others at the mission and were being held prisoner. It is not known whether Wap-Tis-Tokene had taken part in the incident or not, or whether he was prosecuted, but likely, given his sullen expression, he was being held against his will. Affluence had come to naught.

1. *Portraits of North American Indians*, 65.

055

Jean Baptiste Dorion, 1848

(Cayuse Man)

Oil on paper, 9⅛ × 12⅞ in. (23.2 × 37.7 cm)

INSCRIBED LOWER LEFT: sorrel / white stripe face; INSCRIBED LOWER RIGHT: Baptiste Dorion / Oregon City

PRESENT COLLECTION: Nelda C. and H. J. Lutcher Stark Foundation, Stark Museum of Art, Orange, Texas (31.23.15)

PROVENANCE: Mrs. Dean (Alice Stanley) Acheson, Washington, D.C.; H. J. Lutcher Stark, Orange, Texas, 1965; present owner

This portrait has had a mixed history in terms of the identity of the sitter. First mentioned by Stanley scholar Julie Schimmel in 1983 as a Cayuse man, it fit with a group of surviving small oil paintings on paper from Stanley's time on the upper Columbia River in 1847 and 1848.[1] Historian Brian W. Dippie later associated it with a large equestrian portrait of a Texas Towoccono warrior, *Ko-rak-koo-kiss* (cat. no. 017), painted in 1844 and part of the artist's Indian Gallery.[2] Historian and biographer Lesley Wischmann suggested that it was a portrait of Alexander Culbertson's brother-in-law, the Piegan chief Seen From Afar, whom Stanley met in 1853 and who is featured in several of Stanley's large genre and history paintings, such as *The Last of Their Race* (cat. no. 159).[3]

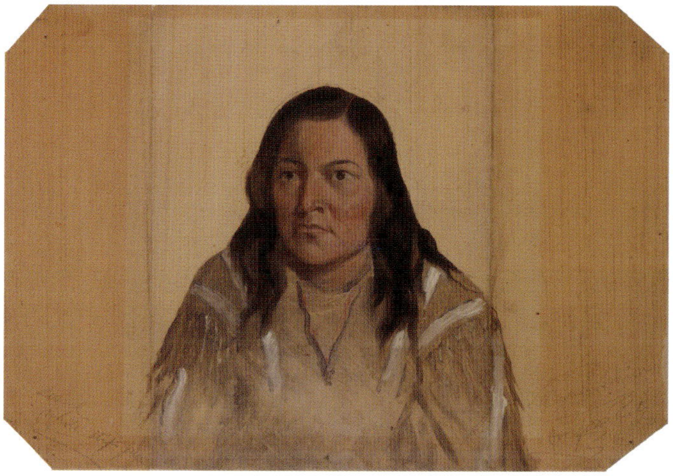

055

Turns out, nobody had it right. The painting compares favorably in medium, support, and trimming with two Cayuse portraits, *Waie-Cat* (cat. no. 053) and *Shu-Ma-Hici* (cat. no. 052), painted in 1848. But part of the inscription mentions Oregon City and Jean Baptiste Dorion, a famous Metis trader, guide, and interpreter who was married to a Cayuse woman and took part alongside the Anglo forces in the Cayuse War that ensued after the massacre of the Marcus Whitman family. The sitter is therefore most likely none other than Jean Baptiste Dorion, son of Pierre Dorion and Marie L'Aguivoise Aioe, an Iowa woman.[4] If the inscription on the painting is considered further, the portrait was probably made in Oregon City in 1848, where Stanley retreated after his ill-fated, abbreviated trip up the Columbia River.

1. See Schimmel, "John Mix Stanley and Imagery of the West in Nineteenth-Century American Art" (Ph.D. diss., New York University, 1983), 79, 390.

2. Brian W. Dippie, *Catlin and His Contemporaries: The Politics of Patronage* (Lincoln: University of Nebraska Press, 1990), 282–83.

3. Lesley Wischmann, *Frontier Diplomats, Frontier Diplomats: Alexander Culbertson and Natoyist-Siksina' Among the Blackfeet* (Norman: University of Oklahoma Press, 2004), 238, 242.

4. For this insight, I am grateful to Chalk Courchane of East Wenatchee, Washington.

056
Asa Lawrence Lovejoy, 1848

Oil on canvas, 30 × 25 in. (76.0 × 63.5 cm)

PRESENT COLLECTION: Oregon Historical Society, Portland, Oregon

PROVENANCE: Unknown

Stanley is thought to have painted this portrait of Oregon pioneer Asa Lovejoy in 1848, after the artist returned to Oregon City in retreat from the anguish of the Whitman massacre. Lovejoy had been a close friend of Whitman, having traveled across the plains to and from Oregon twice with him in the early 1840s. Lovejoy, a lawyer by profession and a politician by preference, had run unsuccessfully for territorial governor in 1845 and 1846; served as mayor of Oregon City; and in 1846 and 1848 attended the provisional legislature. When Stanley met him in 1848, he had been elected supreme judge of the territory and had made a fervent effort to recruit forces to track down and bring to justice the Cayuse and Anglo perpetrators of the attack on Whitman's mission.[1] A number of the women and children of the mission had been captured and held for ransom immediately following the tragedy. When they were eventually freed, Lovejoy and his wife accepted one of the newly orphaned girls, Mary Marsh, into their family.

Railroads were one of Lovejoy's great interests, and in his role as a provisional legislator, he chaired a committee in 1847 to persuade the U.S. Congress to construct a transcontinental railroad. The 1853 Isaac Stevens survey employed Stanley to document scenes and scenery along a possible northwest route and thus once again brought the artist into the Northwest.

1. Biographical information on Lovejoy is drawn primarily from Dumas Malone, *Dictionary of American Biography*, vol. 11 (New York: Scribner, 1933), 433–34.

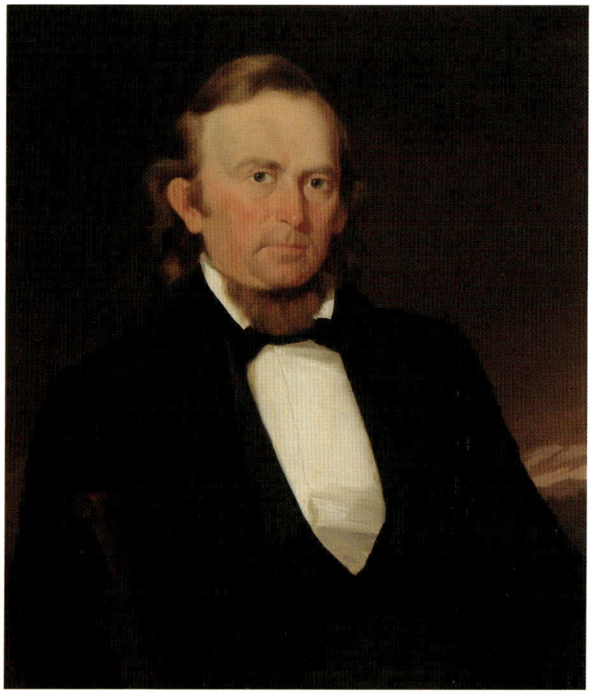

056

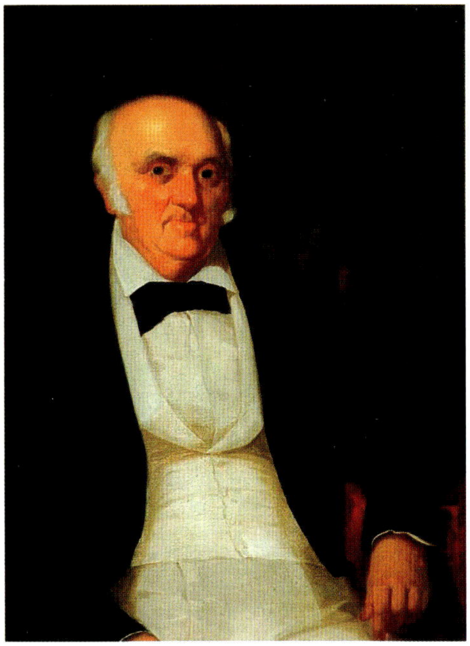

057

Captain Stephen Reynolds, 1848

Oil on canvas, 35 × 24¾ in. (88.9 × 62.9 cm)

INSCRIBED VERSO: Presented to Stephen Reynolds Esq / with the complements / J. M. Stanley / Honolulu / 1848

PRESENT COLLECTION: Peabody Essex Museum, Salem, Massachusetts (M3831)

PROVENANCE: The artist; Stephen Reynolds, 1848; Stephen Willard Phillips; Arthur Reynolds Wilmarth, Boston, Massachusetts, by 1920; present owner, 1932

Stanley had been in Hawaii less than three months when he wrote a letter to a friend in Canandaigua, New York (his birthplace), offering his impressions of his new surroundings. He did not mention the beauty of the islands or the charm of the city of Honolulu. Rather, he focused on the economic prosperity. "This is a place of much business," Stanley started out. "There are now in port not less than sixty sail, mostly whale ships. The commerce with California is very great, that market being supplied from this place and since the discovery of the Gold mines, the merchants here have been making money rapidly."[1]

One of the merchants who prospered greatly by this surge in commerce was Captain Stephen Reynolds. He commissioned Stanley to paint his portrait shortly after the artist arrived in August 1848. By late September the likeness was complete, and Reynolds hosted a special ball, inviting local worthies as well as international guests, like foreign ministers and fellow ship captains, to admire the portrait. This they did with alacrity, many judging "the likeness to be the most perfect production they had ever witnessed." Reynolds was so pleased that he later opened his home to visitors to "call at his residence without ceremony" to view the painting.[2] He also made great efforts to promote Stanley within the upper crust of Hawaiian society.

1. Letter from Stanley in Honolulu to a friend in Canandaigua, New York, November 6, 1848, quoted in an unidentified Canandaigua newspaper in the Stanley Papers.

2. "Sandwich Island News," *Polynesian*, September 21, 1848.

058

Mrs. Benjamin Pitman, 1849

High Chieftess Kinool-O-Liliha

Oil on canvas, 29¾ × 24 in. (75.6 × 61.0 cm) (oval)

PRESENT COLLECTION: Peabody Essex Museum, Salem, Massachusetts

PROVENANCE: The artist; Mrs. Benjamin Pitman, Hilo, Hawaii; [?]; Charles D. Childs, 1966; by gift to present owner, 1966

Mrs. Pitman, Kinoole-O-Liliha, was known for her beauty and her royal stature. Born in 1825, she was the hereditary high chieftess of Hilo on the island of Hawaii, being a descendant of the first Hawaiian king. Her father controlled vast tracts of land in Hilo and Puna, and the king of her generation, Kamehameha III, held her in high esteem.

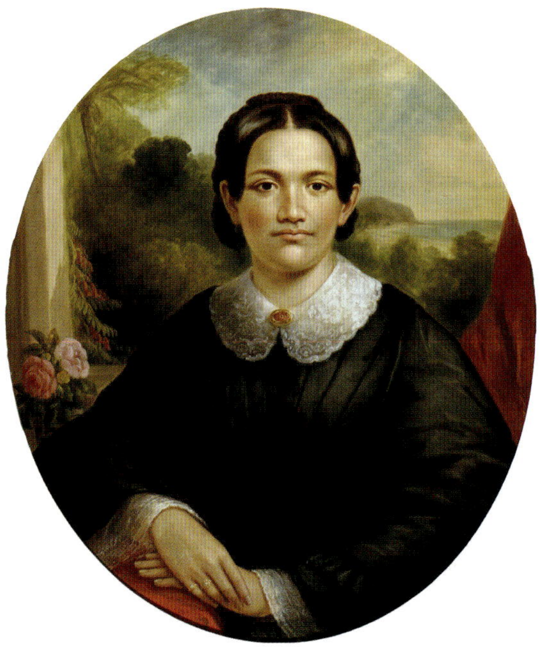

058

Kinoole Pitman and her American husband, Benjamin, lived in Hilo but frequented Honolulu, where they may have met Stanley. Benjamin's father had been a friend and business associate of Stephen Reynolds in the 1820s, and Reynolds probably provided an introduction. Stanley posed Kinoole on an open balcony with a lush tropical landscape unfolding in the distance. He thus connected her with a Hawaiian natural setting, much like his treatment of Queen Kalama (cat. no. 061). The pink roses in a vase at her side are said to be a reflection of her delicacy and beauty, while her pleated black silk gown, gold brooch, and regal countenance offer an aura of dignified, formal elegance.[1]

1. David W. Forbes, *Encounters with Paradise: Views of Hawaii and Its People, 1778–1941* (Honolulu: Honolulu Academy of Arts, 1992), 130.

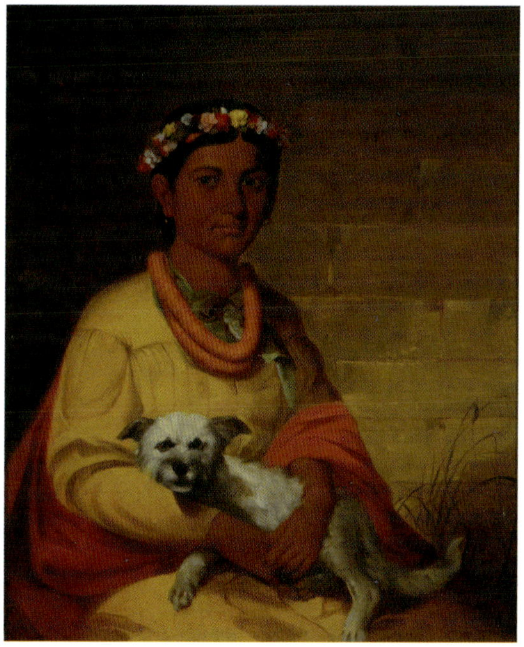

059

Hawaiian Girl with Dog, 1849

Hawaiian Woman with Dog; Queen Kalama

Oil on canvas, 36 3/16 × 28 13/16 in. (92.0 × 73.2 cm)

INSCRIBED VERSO: J. M. Stanley Honolulu, 1849

PRESENT COLLECTION: Bernice Pauahi Bishop Museum, Honolulu, Hawaii (MT no. 224 [SXC 103913])

PROVENANCE: Mrs. H. D. Young, London, England; (Unknown London dealer); Donald Angus, Tangier, Morocco, 1963; Mrs. Frances Damon, New York, New York; by gift to present owner, 1964

It took Stanley only a few weeks to set up a studio after he arrived in Hawaii in mid-August 1848. By September 21, he had painted at least one prominent citizen, the merchant Stephen Reynolds (cat. no. 057), and attracted the favorable notice of the press. *The Polynesian* boasted that they were proud to have made the acquaintance of such an important artist, and they found him "a very agreeable gentleman." The paper called on the well-to-do members of society to consider patronizing the painter. "If any of the residents desire to have their likenesses taken, they will never have a better opportunity than the present, nor find a person more competent to do it than Mr. Stanley."[1]

The sitter in this painting, a teenage Hawaiian girl, accepted that invitation the next year. Her identity is unknown, but she is quite obviously part of the affluent set. The multicolored floral lei that crowns her head, her yellow dress (called a *holoku*), accented with a red shawl and a double stranded *ilima* lei, all connote the status of a chiefly, some have even suggested royal, individual.[2] Other, less lofty interpretations of the sitter suggest that she may be one of Reynolds's wards. In his diary for February 11, 1849, Reynolds mentions that he and some of his young charges visited Stanley's studio "to see a portrait of Alakepa—a native girl—be painted.[3]

1. "The Fine Arts," *Polynesian*, September 21, 1848.

2. Mary Cooke, "Collection Reveals Royal Find," *Honolulu Star-Bulletin and Advertiser*, March 17, 1963.

3. Forbes, *Encounters with Paradise*, 133.

060

King Kamehameha III, 1849

Oil on linen, 50½ × 37½ in. (128.3 × 95.3 cm)

INSCRIBED VERSO: Painted Honolulu Oct. 20 1849, J. M. Stanley 'Iolani Palace. Honolulu, Hawaii

PRESENT COLLECTION: Hawaii State Archives. Photograph courtesy of the Friends of Iolani Palace; from the collection of the Hawaii State Archives

PROVENANCE: The artist; present owner, 1848

Stanley had originally thought he would stay in Hawaii for only a few months. He remained well over a year. One of the circumstances that might have delayed him was negotiating to paint formal portraits of the king and queen of the islands. This portrait was completed in October 1849, just a month before the artist sailed for the States.

As a monarch, Kamehameha III was considered Hawaii's great inspired national benefactor. He helped the islands evolve from an absolute to a constitutional monarchy. He orchestrated the

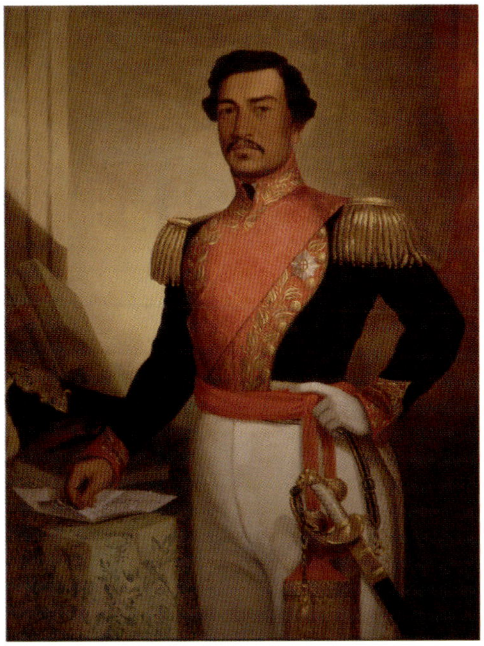

060

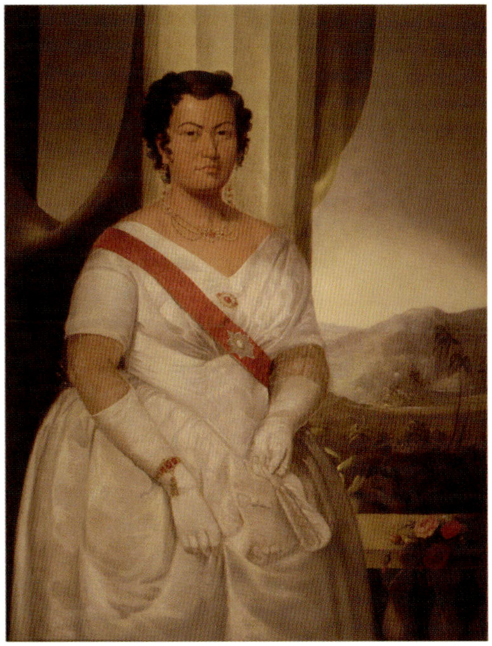

061

country's first constitution, adopted in 1840, and shaped its future as a modern nation with laws, basic human rights, stable governance, and sovereign authority.[1]

Stanley was offered the commission to paint the king with special instructions that he follow the design and pose of a portrait of the French monarch Louis Philippe by Franz Xaver Winterhalter ('Iolani Palace, Honolulu). The painting *Louis Philippe* is twice the size of the Stanley canvas and full length rather than three-quarter length. It had been a gift from Philippe to Kamehameha in 1848, just before the French ruler was forced to abdicate his throne. Kamehameha considered himself the Pacific island equivalent to Louis Philippe, who was known in his heyday as the people's king. By charter of a popularly elected Chamber of Deputies in 1830, Louis Philippe was originally granted his right to rule. In the Winterhalter portrait, his right hand may be resting on a copy of that charter. Kamehameha's right hand holds down an important document, perhaps a copy of his enlightened declaration of human rights from 1839 or what was called the Great Mahele of 1848, with which he redistributed land among the Hawaiian people.

1. See Rhonda E. A. Hackler, *Royal Portraits of Hawai'i in 'Iolani Palace* (Honolulu: 'Iolani Palace, 1982), 8–9.

061

Queen Kalama, 1849

Oil on linen, 50½ × 37½ in. (128.3 × 95.3 cm)

INSCRIBED VERSO: J. M. Stanley, 1849

PRESENT COLLECTION: Hawaii State Archives. Photograph courtesy of the Friends of Iolani Palace; from the collection of the Hawaii State Archives

PROVENANCE: The artist; present owner, 1849

In fall 1849, presumably directly after he completed the portrait of King Kamehameha III, Stanley painted a companion work of the queen, Kalama Kahakaleleponi, for the royal family. The three-quarter-length portrait hung comfortably next to the king's from that moment on. Now belonging to the State of Hawaii, the two portraits initially cost the Kingdom $500 and were a handsome climax to the artist's stay in the islands.

Kalama was born in 1817 to a family of considerably lesser stature than her husband. She led a sheltered life and bore two children, neither of whom reached adulthood. In 1845 Laura Fish Judd, wife of Kamehameha's minister of finance, Gerrit P. Judd, wrote a description of Kalama: "The queen is fine-looking, but has had few advantages of improvement. She was married to her royal husband very young, and he has always kept her close. . . . My daughters assist in arranging her wardrobe. She has laid aside her glowing reds and high colored shawls, of which she was fond, and looks very pretty in straw-colored satin, with hat, feathers, ribbons, flowers, and gloves to match."[1] Stanley painted her in this westernized manner. Her favored attire, probably rather like the *Hawaiian Girl with Dog* (cat. no. 059), was altered by the fashion dictates of the Judds' daughters in order to make her look regal.

1. Quoted in Hackler, *Royal Portraits*, 8.

062

Portrait of Princess Manaiula Tehuiarii, Wife of High Chief William Kealaloa Kahanui Sumner, c. 1849

Oil on canvas, 36⅛ × 26⅛ in. (91.7 × 66.3 cm)

PRESENT COLLECTION: Honolulu Museum of Art, gift of Myrna Anne Kamamoajualii Kauapiiokamakaala Kekuiapoiwa Buffandeau Topolinski in memory of her grandmother, Victoria Kualii Sumner Ellis Buffandeau, 2003 (12.708.1)

PROVENANCE: The artist; Manaiula and William K. Sumner; High Chieftess Nancy W. Sumner Ellis; Mrs. Victoria K. Sumner Ellis Buffandeau; Eugene Derwille Buffandeau I; Mrs. M. Anne K. Buffandeau Topolinski; present owner

At about the same time that Stanley was painting the portraits of the king and queen of Hawaii, he is thought to have produced this charming and welcoming portrait of another member of the island's royalty, Princess Tehuiarii. When she sat for the artist, the princess was married to part-Hawaiian High Chief William Keolaloa Kahānui Sumner. The princess was the daughter of a Tahitian protestant missionary, Prince Tute Tehuiarii, who had brought her to Hawaii as a girl in 1827. Her father was the appointed court chaplin to King Kamehameha III.[1]

Princess Tehuiarii's pose, though slightly abbreviated, resembles that of Stanley's portrait of Queen Kalama. Her arms are bowed toward the viewer as if to suggest an ample embrace, and her confident smile provides an air of poised self-assurance.

1. This biographical information comes from the Julie Schimmel Research Papers (Gerald Peters Gallery, Santa Fe, New Mexico) as part of an inquiry sheet on the painting filled out in the 1970s by John R. K. Topolinski, husband of a fifth-generation descendant of the princess.

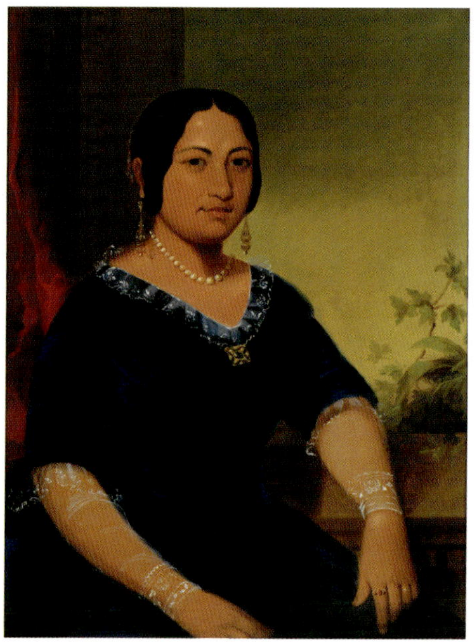

062

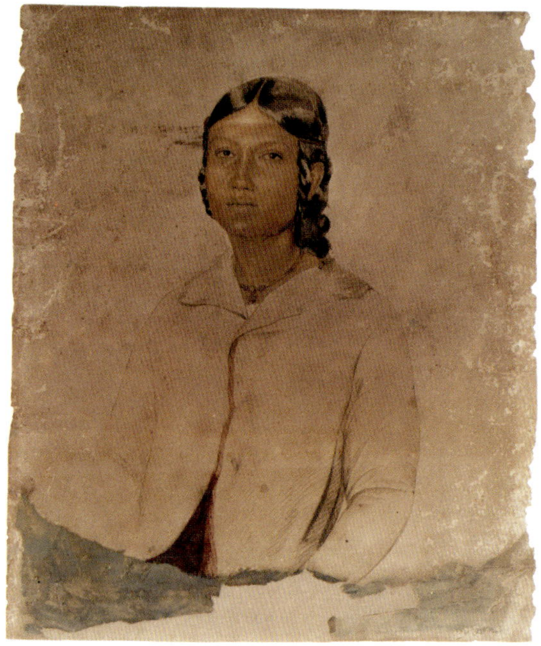

062.1

Uwaikikilani Halstead, 1849

Mrs. W. J. Halstead; Mrs. John Joseph Halstead

Watercolor on paper, 12¼ × 9⅞ in. (31 × 25 cm)

PRESENT COLLECTION: Bernice Pauahi Bishop Museum, Honolulu, Hawaii (1974.216 [SCX 114066])

PROVENANCE: Artist; Uwaikikilani Halstead, Maui; by descent to Mrs. Eleanor Kilani W. Carney, great-granddaughter of subject; by gift to present owner, 1974

This rather straightforward portrait has long been attributed to Stanley. It pictures Uwaikikilani, the wife of a whaling ship captain John Joseph Halstead of Maui. Uwaikikilani was a young woman of the chiefess class and the granddaughter of Isaac Davis, commander of the Royal Artillery in King Kamehameha's army.[1] It is thought that she sat for this unfinished portrait watercolor in 1849, during the late part of Stanley's stay in Hawaii.

This image is essentially a field study or sketch, probably intended for a finished oil painting. The technique of completing the face but sketching in the garment was common, preliminary practice for Stanley (see cat. no. 078), as was the use of underlying parallel, diagonal pencil hatching for shading (see cat. no. 077). These technical similarities to Stanley's work do not prove that he was the artist involved in its production, but they help suggest that the attribution to him is not too far-fetched.

1. I am grateful for this information that has been provided by Leah Caldeira of the Bernice Pauahi Bishop Museum Archives, Honolulu, Hawaii.

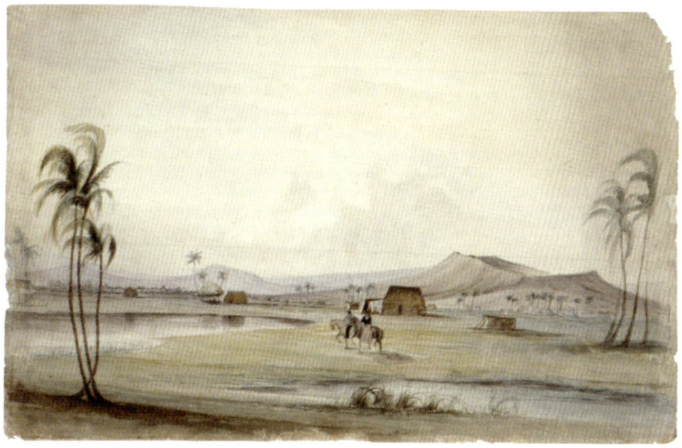

063

View from Waikiki, c. 1849

Looking Toward Honolulu from Waikiki; Waikiki

Watercolor on paper, 8 5/16 × 12 7/8 in. (21.1 × 32.7 cm)

INSCRIBED VERSO: signed

PRESENT COLLECTION: Honolulu Museum of Art, bequest of Patches Damon Holt, 2003 (27388)

PROVENANCE: (Sotheby Parke Bernet, New York, New York, 1970); John H. Garzoli, San Francisco, California; [?]; Patches Damon Holt, 2003; present owner, by bequest

What Stanley saw in Hawaii was quite different from what he had experienced in the Northwest. Sparse foliage along sandy beaches in dazzling sunlight provided a stark contrast to the rich arbor of trees and vines he had lived among in Oregon in 1847 and 1848. This watercolor pictures a man and a woman riding along Waikiki Beach with grass huts scattered behind. In the distance to the left can be seen the city of Honolulu and the masts of numerous whaling and trade ships in the harbor.

Stanley, unlike some of his fellow artists in Hawaii—such as American painter and illustrator Jules Tavernier—did not seek to sensationalize the island's landscape. Tavernier, who fled to Hawaii in 1884 to escape American creditors, became famous for his vivid views of Hawaii's volcanoes. He is known to have painted such scenes over fifty times.[1] Stanley, as was his penchant, picked a prospect from daily life set against a charming rather than overwrought vista. This is his only known surviving Hawaiian landscape.

1. Marjorie Arkelian, *Tropical: Tropical Scenes by the 19th Century Painters of California* (Oakland, Calif.: Oakland Museum, 1971), 46.

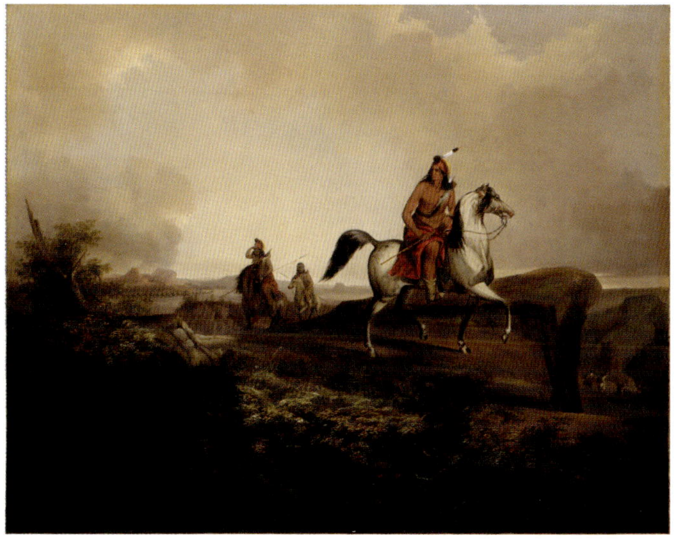

064

Black Knife, An Apache Chief on Horse Back, Reconnoitering Gen. Kearney's Command, Version I, 1850

Oil on canvas, 42 3/8 × 52 in. (107.6 × 132.1 cm)

PRESENT COLLECTION: Smithsonian American Art Museum, Washington, D.C., gift of the Misses Henry (1985.66.248.933)

PROVENANCE: The artist; Joseph Henry, Washington, D.C., 1865; Mrs. Joseph (Harriet A.) Henry and daughters Caroline, Helen, and Mary Henry, 1878; Smithsonian Institution, Washington, D.C., 1908, by gift of the daughters; by transfer to present owner, 1985

LIFETIME EXHIBITIONS: *Stanley's Indian Gallery*, Gallery of Fine Arts, Albany, New York, 1850; Alhambra Rooms, New York, New York, 1850–1851; City Hall, Hartford, Connecticut, 1851; *Portraits of North American Indians*, Smithsonian Institution, Washington, D.C., 1852–1865; Seventh Annual Exhibition of the Maryland Institute, Baltimore, Maryland, 1854

In this painting Stanley depicts Black Knife and his men scrutinizing General Stephen Kearny and his army, barely visible in the far left distance. In 1846, Stanley traveled with Kearny and his troops through the Valley of the Mimbres River and over the Sierra Mimbres, territory that was home to Apache Indians.[1] Although Stanley may have met Black Knife during this trip, the scene is a fictitious one rather than an event he witnessed.

To nineteenth-century Americans, the Indian was a savage, and the Apache was considered particularly brutal. Stanley shared this attitude and at times rendered his Indian subjects as formidable warriors to appeal to the public. In this painting he portrays Black Knife, who was second in command of the Chiricahua Apaches, as an intimidating fighter, spear in hand. At the same time the artist lends an element of dignity and pride to his subject by using a traditional format long popular for depicting military leaders, the equestrian portrait.[2] The similarity of Black Knife's pose to that of George Washington in Thomas Sully's huge 1819 equestrian portrait of the general (fig. 2.6) is unmistakable and reinforces the notion that painting was imagined and not documentary.

Stanley added *Black Knife* to his Indian Gallery in 1850. It was one of only seven paintings to survive the 1865 fire that destroyed the rest of the collection. It is also one but a few paintings of which Stanley is known to have created a second M. S.

1. Stanley was serving as the artist for the U.S. Army Corps of Topographical Engineers under the command of Lt. William H. Emory.

2. Schimmel, "John Mix Stanley and Imagery," 274.

065

Scene on the Columbia River, 1852

Oil on canvas, 17⅛ × 21⅛ in. (43.5 × 53.7 cm)

INSCRIBED VERSO: Scene on the Columbia River / By J M Stanley / Presented to A. B. Moore / August 9th 1852

PRESENT COLLECTION: Tacoma Art Museum, Haub Family Collection, promised gift of Erivan and Helga Haub, 2014

PROVENANCE: The artist; Abel B. Moore, 1852; by descent to Mrs. Claiborne Bates, Schenectady, New York; [Unidentified antique dealer, Albany, New York]; (Kennedy Galleries, New York, New York, 1972); Amon Carter Museum, 1972; (Zaplin-Lambert and Gerald Peters Gallery, Santa Fe, New Mexico, 2003); The Haub Family, Wiesbaden, Germany; present owner by gift, 2014

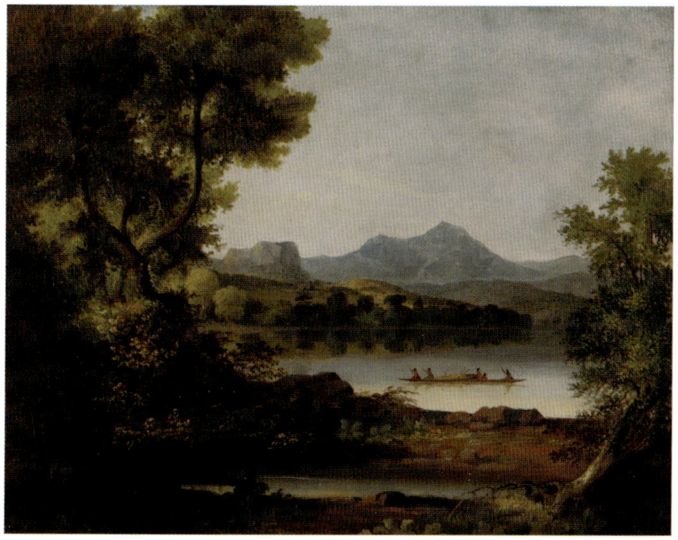

065

In the Indian Gallery that Stanley developed upon returning east in 1850 from travels to the Southwest, the Northwest, and Hawaii, he included two landscapes titled *View on the Columbia River* under the category of "Sketches."[1] The specific location of those scenes is not discussed, but they were most likely vistas along the river east of Fort Vancouver. This work may be the same or similar to one of those sketches. The verdure would suggest that it was painted during the summer, and according to his own account, Stanley left Oregon City in late August to begin moving upstream by boat toward Fort Walla Walla.[2]

Five Indians paddle a canoe through an idyllic western landscape. They are seen as if through a window framed by luxuriant foliage, which afforded the artist a momentary glimpse of nature's unspoiled denizens. His masterful portrayal of the crisp air and light-filled, shimmering leaves was a signature element in Stanley's early landscapes.

This painting was given to a fellow artist, Abel B. Moore of Troy, New York, in 1852. Moore had been Troy's foremost portrait painter since the mid-1830s.[3] The gift was probably an exchange for a portrait of Stanley that Moore produced around 1850 for inclusion in Stanley's Indian Gallery, a work that was destroyed in the 1865 fire.[4]

1. *Stanley's Indian Gallery* checklist (1850), nos. 126 and 127. These paintings appeared again in his larger, finished Indian Gallery of 1852. See *Portraits of North American Indians*, nos. 133, 134.

2. "Letter from Oregon," an undated clipping, unknown newspaper, Stanley scrapbook.

3. For a full biographical account of Moore, see Samuel Rezneck, "Moore Became Famous Portrait Painter," *Troy Record,* June 13, 1970.

4. *Stanley's Indian Gallery* checklist (1850), no. 98.

066

Oregon City on the Willamette River, c. 1852

Oil on canvas, 26½ × 40 in. (67.3 × 101.6 cm)

PRESENT COLLECTION: Amon Carter Museum of American Art, Fort Worth, Texas (1979.17)

PROVENANCE: Private collection, Philadelphia (1935–1973); (M. Knoedler and Co., New York, New York, 1973–1975); Mimi D. Bloch Collection, New York, New York; private collection, Lynn, Massachusetts; (Steven Straw Co., Newbury Port, Massachusetts, 1979); present owner, 1979

Stanley arrived in Oregon City in June 1847 and happily stayed two months, encouraged by opportunities to sketch local Indians and scenery, before departing for points north and west. He later returned to Oregon City in February 1848 and stayed in the area

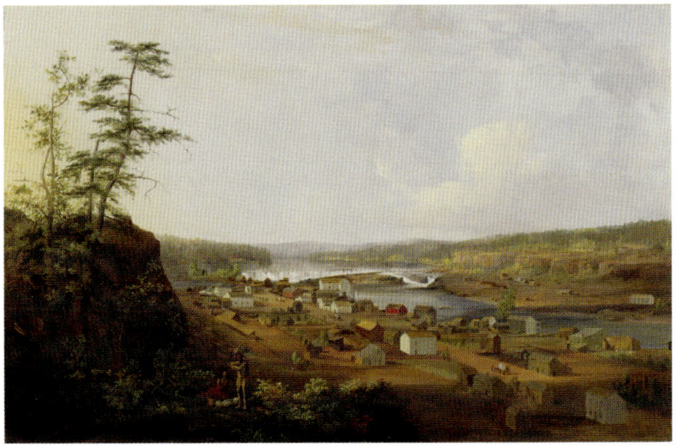

066

into August of that year. Stanley's time there, though bifurcated, provided him the chance to reflect on the pulse of the burgeoning community and its cultural and historical essence.

Stanley's subsequent pictorial rendition of the town is a complex metaphor for the changes on the frontier that were unfolding before his eyes. An Indian couple is presented in the foreground of the painting. They appear somewhat dejected and are cast in shadow, as if to announce that they are not part of the scene of progress behind them. The sunny town and the Willamette Falls speak to the alternate vision, Anglo aspirations to exploit the rich environment, the surrounding forests (Oregon City would supply lumber for the California gold camps), and the falls for industrial power. The fertile farm lands nearby made this, the terminus of the Oregon Trail, a suitable center for realization of the American agrarian dream.

An earlier version of this scene appeared in a painting of the same title dated 1848, which was part of Stanley's expanded Indian Gallery of 1852. This later work may have been painted as a commission for someone who, after seeing the gallery, wanted a pictorial remembrance of nascent Oregon City.

067

Sisters, c. 1852

Oil on canvas, 36 × 32 in. (91.4 × 81.3 cm)

INSCRIBED: [Said to be signed and dated]

PRESENT COLLECTION: Private collection

PROVENANCE: (Chapman Art Gallery, Sylvania, Ohio); present owner

This is thought to be Alice English and her younger sister, Delia, painted in Washington, D.C., just a year before Alice married Stanley. They make a charming, if slightly somber, duo. The portrait was perhaps painted at the request of the English family before

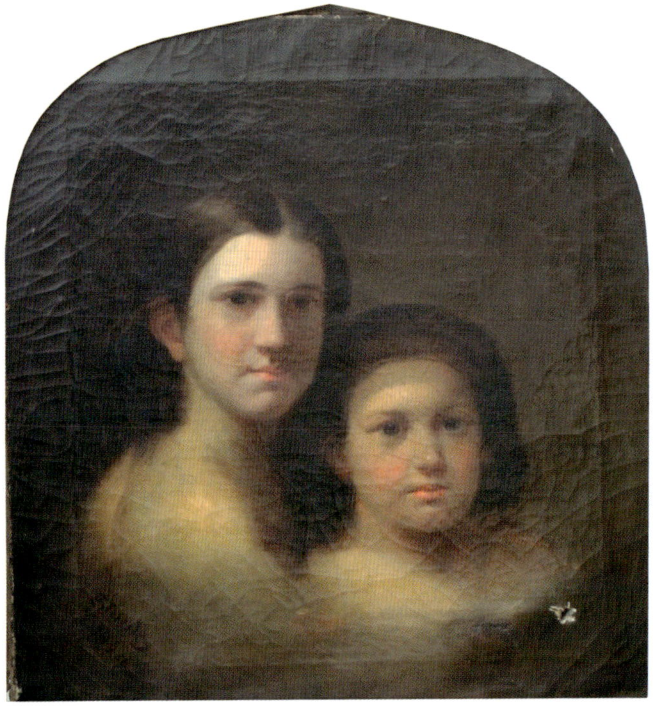

067

Stanley developed an attraction for the older sister—maybe this was his introduction to the family. In a slightly later portrait of Alice, where she sits with her brother Morgan (cat. no. 071), she appears noticeably more mature and contented. By the date of that second portrait, she wears a broad smile and a slightly coquettish dress, attesting to her affection for the man behind the easel who was making her portrait.

068

A Pueblo Chief on His Favorite Buffalo Horse, 1853

A Puebla [sic] Chief on His Favorite Buffalo Horse; Buffalo Hunt

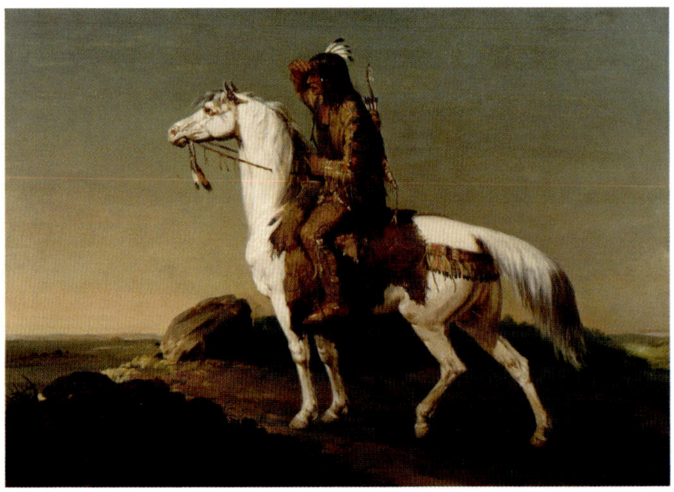

068

Oil on canvas, 18⅛ × 24⅛ in. (46.0 × 61.3 cm)

INSCRIBED LOWER RIGHT: Stanley

PRESENT COLLECTION: Private collection, Philadelphia

PROVENANCE: Mr. Harold Bennett, Hutton Heights, New Jersey c. 1930; by descent to [?]; (Thomas Nygard Gallery, Bozeman, Montana, 1995); present owner

LIFETIME EXHIBITIONS: First Annual Exhibition of the Metropolitan Mechanics Institute, Washington, D.C., 1853

Stanley had traveled among the Pueblo Indians in 1846 when he visited New Mexico. He made studies of their adobe villages and of certain of their citizens as well. Even so, it was not until 1852 that he incorporated Pueblo portraits into his Indian Gallery, and these were the result of a visiting delegation to Washington, D.C., whom he cajoled into sitting for him.[1] Five portraits soon appeared in his Indian Gallery. All were tragically burned in the 1865 fire.

One other painting is thought to have resulted from his exposure to the Washington troop of Pueblo men. In February 1853, at the First Exhibition of the Metropolitan Mechanics Institute in Washington, D.C., Stanley submitted five paintings. Included in this selection was a work titled *A Puebla [sic] Chief on His Favorite Buffalo Horse*.[2] Despite the fact that the Indian's costume looks more Northern Plains than Pueblo, this painting is thought to be that work.

1. "The Pueblo Indians," *National Intelligencer*, September 7, 1852.

2. *A Record of the First Exhibition of the Metropolitan Mechanics Institute, Held in the East Wing of the Patent Office, February–March, 1853* (Washington, D.C.: Henry Polkinhorn, 1853), 41, no. 1217.

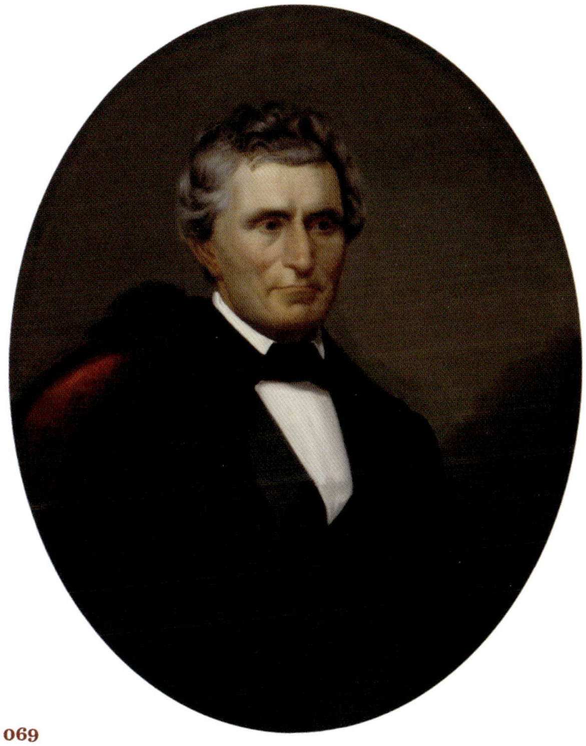

069

069

Berniah Willet, c. 1853

Oil on canvas, 34⅛ × 26¾ in. (86.8 × 67.9 cm)

PRESENT COLLECTION: Smithsonian American Art Museum, Washington, D.C., gift of Dr. and Mrs. George A. Hass (1982.104.1)

PROVENANCE: The artist; Mr. and Mrs. Berniah Willet, Washington, D.C.; [?]; Dr. and Mrs. George A. Haas, by 1982; by gift to present owner, 1982

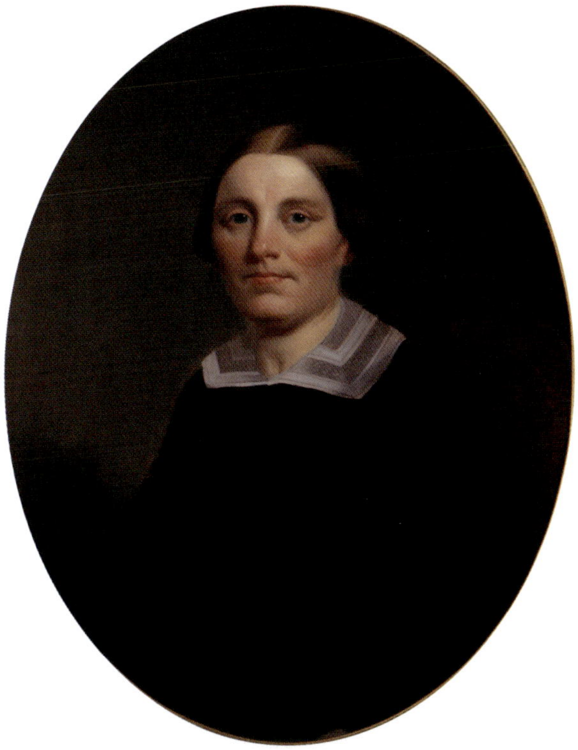

070

070

Emeline Willet, c. 1853

Oil on canvas, 34⅛ × 27⅛ in. (86.7 × 68.9 cm)

PRESENT COLLECTION: Smithsonian American Art Museum, Washington, D.C., gift of Dr. and Mrs. George A. Hass (1982.104.2)

PROVENANCE: The artist; Mr. and Mrs. Berniah Willet, Washington, D.C.; [?], Dr. and Mrs. George A. Haas, by 1982; by gift to present owner, 1982

For about a decade, from 1853 to 1863, Stanley resided in Washington, D.C., with a busy atelier on Pennsylvania Avenue. One couple who lived in his neighborhood, Berniah and Emeline Willet, befriended him early on and must have visited the artist in his studio. There Stanley produced a matching pair of portraits that, while not picturing the twosome together, were intended to be hung side by side. This reveals in a formal way the bond between husband and wife that would endure with only two frames separating them.

Berniah, a carpenter by profession, managed a shop near Stanley's studio as well. He was older than his spouse, Emeline, by perhaps ten years. His deportment is socially prescribed, his expression dour and, beyond the hint of a smirk, almost stern. Stanley presents Emeline as more obliging, gentle, and loving.

071

Alice Caroline and Morgan English, 1853

Oil on canvas, 36 × 29 in. (91.4 × 73.7 cm)

INSCRIBED VERSO: This picture is very respectfully presented to Mrs. S. T. Cole by the Artist 1853

PRESENT COLLECTION: Private collection

PROVENANCE: The artist; Mrs. S. T. Cole, by gift 1853; Frances Q. Bayles; Ruth Bayles, Oak Park, Illinois, 1957; (M. Knoedler and Co., New York, New York, 1962); [?]; (Kennedy Galleries, New York, New York, 1980); (Sotheby Parke Bernet, New York, New York, 1981); present owner

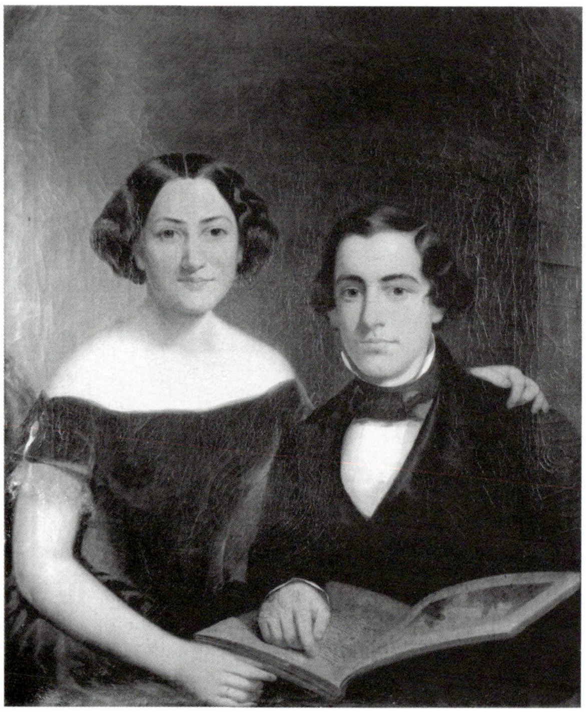

071

This portrait of Alice and Morgan English was probably painted in 1853 just before the artist departed for the Northwest and his many adventures with the Isaac Stevens expedition. Alice, who is thought to have been born about 1826, would have been twenty-eight years old, and her younger brother, Morgan, about nineteen at the time. They were two of the five children born to John C. and Adelia English. John is often referred to as Senator, but no proof of his attaining that office has yet been found. The pair appears to be looking at a book of essays or poems illustrated with landscape views, perhaps something Stanley would leave behind as a remembrance.[1] Stanley would marry Alice shortly after his return from his journeys in 1854.

The painting is inscribed on the reverse as a gift to Mrs. Seth Cole from the artist in 1853. Mrs. Cole may have been a grandmother of Alice and Morgan or an aunt; it is not known which. Morgan was an ensign in the U.S. Navy in 1860 and died in 1862, probably in the war. Alice survived Stanley by almost twenty years, dying in Detroit in 1891.

1. Stanley used this device in other portraits. See, for example, his portrait of Eleanora Ross of 1844 (cat. no. 021).

072

Black Knife, Apache War Chief Reconnoitering the Command of General Kearny On His March from Santa Fe to California, Version II, 1853

Apache War Chief Reconnoitering the Command of General Kearny on His March from Santa Fe to California

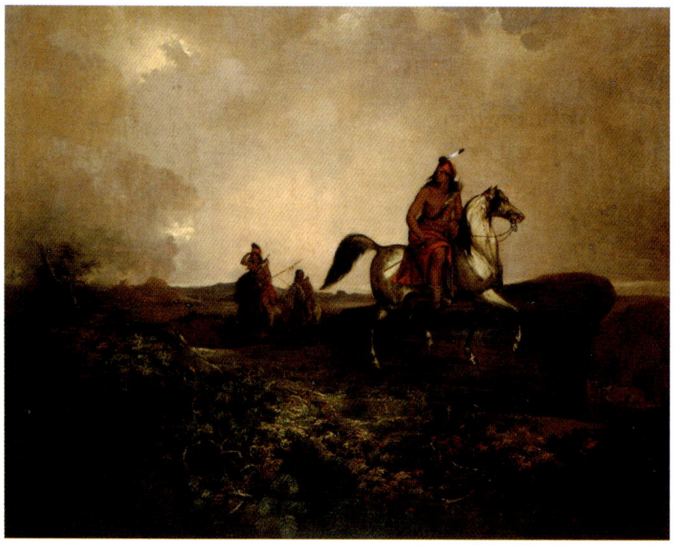

072

Oil on canvas, 41½ × 50 in. (105.4 × 127.0 cm)

INSCRIBED VERSO: Black Knife / Apache Chief. / Rio Gila / Darley ["Darley" inscription appears to be from the nineteenth century, but a later addition that led to misattribution]

PRESENT COLLECTION: Private collection; photograph courtesy Gerald Peters Gallery, New York, New York

PROVENANCE: Estate of William A. Burnett, Amherst, Maine; gifted by the Holyoke League of Arts and Crafts to Holyoke Public Library, Massachusetts, 1927; de-accessioned by Holyoke Library, 1989; (Winter Associates Auction, Plainville, Connecticut, December, 1996); (Gerald Peters Gallery, Santa Fe, New Mexico); present owner, 2002

LIFETIME EXHIBITIONS: First Annual Exhibition of the Metropolitan Mechanics Institute, patent office, Washington, D.C., 1853, as *Apache War Chief Reconnoitering the Command of General Kearny on His March from Santa Fe to California*. The painting was listed in the accompanying Exhibition Catalog of Paintings, no. 1217

This is the second of two almost identical versions that Stanley painted of Chief Black Knife and his men observing General Kearny's troops. The first mention of the painting was in 1853 when it was exhibited at the Metropolitan Mechanics Institute in Washington, D.C.[1]

Version one (cat. no. 064) was acquired by Joseph Henry directly from Stanley in 1865 as compensation for debts owed. At Henry's death in 1878, he left the painting to his daughters, who donated it to the Smithsonian in 1908. When the second version appeared in 1924 in the estate of William A. Burnett of Amherst, Massachusetts, it bore the signature of F. O. C. Darley, a prolific illustrator who was slightly younger than Stanley.

In 1927, the Holyoke League of Arts and Crafts purchased the painting from Burnett's estate and donated it to the Holyoke Public Library, which de-accessioned it in 1989. It was not until 1996 that the Darley signature was discovered to be fraudulent, and the painting was correctly attributed to Stanley.

There are small variations between the two paintings, but basically the paintings look alike.[2] The first version was part of Stanley's Indian Gallery, which he kept intact in the ardent hope that the Smithsonian would purchase the collection in its entirety. Maybe it was the painting's popularity with the public, perhaps a commission, or simply the impact that the encounter with Black Knife and the Apaches had made on Stanley that inspired him to paint the equestrian portrait twice. M. S.

1. As *Black Knife, Apache War Chief Reconnoitering the Command of General Kearney on His March from Santa Fe to California (In the Year 1846)*, in *Record of the First Exhibition*, no. 1217.

2. There are small variations in the foreground foliage and the clouds, and the second version is two inches narrower than the first.

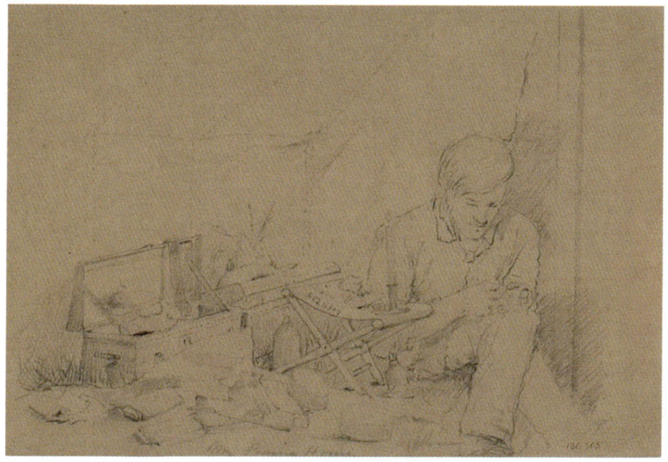

073

My Prairie Home, 1853

Pencil on brown paper, 6⅞ × 10 in. (17.5 × 25.4 cm)

INSCRIBED ON CANVAS STOOL, CENTER: Stanley; LOWER CENTER: My Prairie Home

PRESENT COLLECTION: National Anthropological Archives, Smithsonian Institution, Washington, D.C.

PROVENANCE: Unknown

Stanley made most of his field studies in pencil during the 1853 Isaac Stevens expedition, including this self-portrait in his tent, surrounded by his traveling furniture and artist materials. The drawing is fondly inscribed "My Prairie Home" and is signed on the canvas camp stool that supports a lighted candle by which he works. Though the setting is intimate, cozy, and rather endearing, the drawing exposes the challenging working and living conditions under which Stanley lived that year.

The Washington, D.C., newspaper *Daily National Intelligencer* suggested, as Stanley embarked on his trip, that the "expedition may be regarded as one of some peril."[1] Yet, he had reassuringly written his fiancée, Alice English, as he was starting on his journey west from Saint Louis, that there would be little danger ahead for him. He did not address what comforts, or lack thereof, he would be experiencing, however. This drawing illustrates that there were definitely few luxuries provided. Even so, it was Stanley who had been assigned to select camp furniture, so he had little to complain about.[2]

1. *Daily National Intelligencer*, April 18, 1853.

2. Stanley to Alice English, May 16, 1853, Stanley Papers.

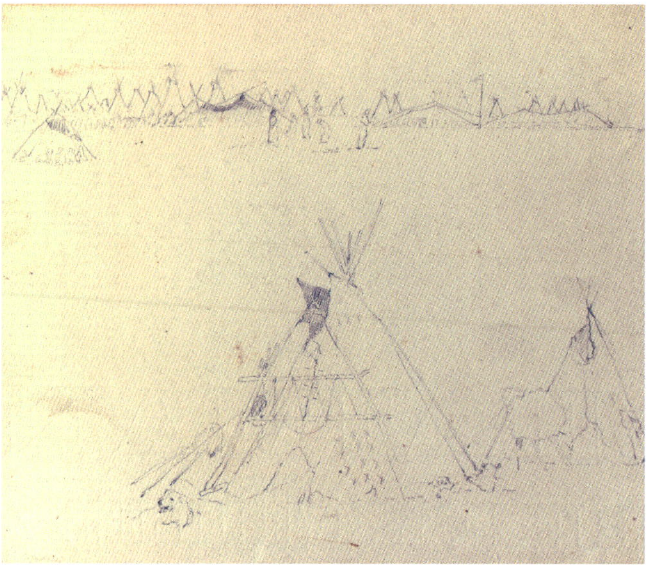

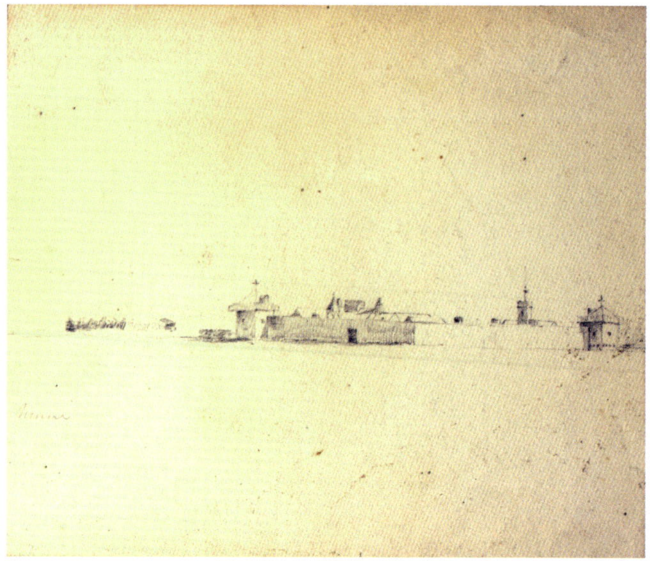

075

074

Untitled (teepees, dog and Fort Union), 1853

Pencil on paper, 8⅝ × 7¾ in. (21.9 × 19.8 cm)

INSCRIBED VERSO: sketch of Fort Union

PRESENT COLLECTION: Private collection

PROVENANCE: Robert Rockwell, Corning, New York, 1965; by descent to present owner

075

Untitled (Fort Union), 1853

Pencil on paper, 8⅝ × 7¾ in. (21.9 × 19.8 cm)

INSCRIBED VERSO: sketch of teepees

PRESENT COLLECTION: Private collection

PROVENANCE: Robert Rockwell, Corning, New York 1965; by descent to present owner

These pencil drawings are two of the scarce original field studies that survive from Stanley's trip west in 1853 with Isaac Stevens. His many daguerreotypes, for which he was duly celebrated by expedition members and Indians alike, have gone missing, and only a few of the original sketches exist today.[1]

Stanley produced these drawings in August on the banks of the Missouri River at Fort Union. Stevens described the fort as the primary supply depot for the American Fur Company. It was made of hewn timber, stood about 16 feet high and measured 250 feet square. It was managed by Stanley's and Stevens's mutual friend, Major Alexander Culbertson (cat. no. 080), and it accommodated the trading interests of the Assiniboin, Crow, and Gros Ventres Indians.[2]

These drawings of the fort were used by Stanley as models for his watercolor, *Fort Union, and Distribution of Goods to the Assiniboins* (cat. no. 096). The teepee in the foreground of one of the studies appeared in one of Stanley's last works, *Prairie Indian Encampment* (cat. no. 219) of about 1869, one of the paintings that he had hoped to include in his proposed large printed portfolio.

1. For an informed discussion of Stanley and his photographs, see Martha A. Sandweiss, *Print the Legend: Photography and the American West* (New Haven, Conn., and London: Yale University Press, 2002), 108–15.

2. Isaac I. Stevens, *Narrative and Final Report of Explorations for a Route for a Pacific Railroad, near the Forty-seventh and Forty-ninth Parallels of North Latitude from Saint Paul to Puget Sound*, vol. 12, book 1 of *Reports of Explorations and Surveys, to Ascertain the Most Practicable and Economical Route for a Railroad from the Mississippi River to the Pacific Ocean* (Washington, D.C.: Thomas H. Ford,1860), 86.

076

"Ah Dolle" Red Feathers, 1853

Watercolor and pencil on brown paper, 10 × 6⅞ in. (25.4 × 17.5 cm)

INSCRIBED LOWER LEFT: ah dolle / Red Feathers; INSCRIBED LOWER RIGHT: 130, 305; INSCRIBED VERSO: "Ah Dolle" / Red Feathers / by John M. Stanley / Cat. no. / 130. 350-Y / Stanley

PRESENT COLLECTION: National Anthropological Archives, Smithsonian Institution, Washington, D.C.

PROVENANCE: Unknown

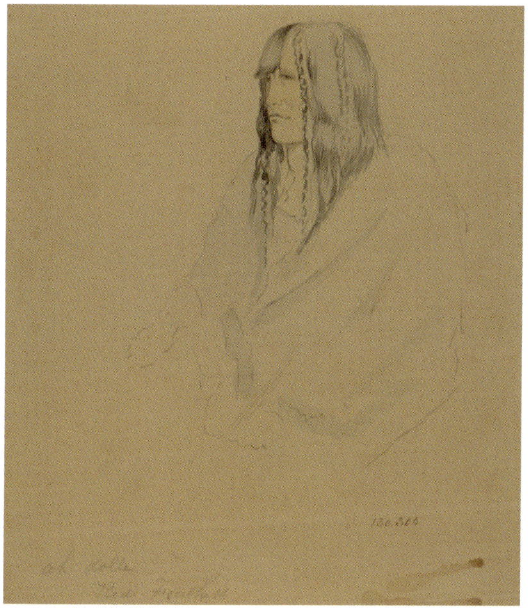

076

This is possibly an Assiniboin man drawn at Fort Union, or more likely, a Blackfeet or Piegan man sketched subsequently at Fort Benton. The hair style, with the extended bangs and the decorated braids, resembles that worn by males of those two tribes.[1] Both Karl Bodmer and George Catlin painted similarly quaffed Blackfeet men at Fort Union in the early 1830s. Of special note is Catlin's portrait of Iron Horn (Smithsonian American Art Museum, Washington, D.C.), a Blackfeet warrior whose likeness Catlin first painted in 1832 and then repeated on several occasions in later years.

Stanley was busy making portraits of the Indians around Fort Benton during the weeks that the Stevens expedition stopped there to treat with Piegan and Blackfeet representatives. "Ah Dolle" sits expressionless at three-quarter view, just like others Stanley sketched at the fort that fall (cat. no. 077).

1. The Smithsonian Institution's Archives, Manuscripts, Photographs Catalog refers to the sitter as Blackfeet.

077
Blackfoot-Piegan Man, 1853

Watercolor and pencil on brown paper, 9⅞ × 7 in. (25.1 × 17.8 cm)

INSCRIBED LOWER RIGHT: 130.305; INSCRIBED LOWER CENTER: Blackfoot-Piegan; INSCRIBED VERSO: blackfoot-piegan / by / john. m. stanley / cat no. / 130,305-X [in ink] / Black-Foot-/Piegan [Stanley's writing] / Stanley [in pencil]

PRESENT COLLECTION: National Anthropological Archives, Smithsonian Institution, Washington, D.C.

PROVENANCE: Unknown

This is one of several pencil drawings that Stanley made in the field during the Isaac Stevens expedition. Given the inscription and the fact that the unidentified sitter is posed in an armchair, it may be assumed that this portrait was made at Fort Benton in September 1853. Stanley had been praised by Stevens for the effectiveness of his daguerreotype portraits of the Indians around the fort.[1] Stevens wrote an open letter from the fort on the September 17 in which he mentioned that "J. M. Stanley, Esq., the artist of the expedition, has taken a great many sketches illustrative of the progress of the expedition, besides taking at various points on the way numerous daguerreotypes of Indians."[2] Since all the daguerreotypes are lost, portrait drawings like this are all that remain of the artist's efforts to document the Indians along the way.

When Stanley was preparing illustrations for the official Stevens report, he completed at least three portraits of Blackfeet to be included.[3] This could have been the preliminary study for one of those. Sadly, those were never published, and the finished watercolors, like the daguerreotypes, are lost.

1. Stevens, *Narrative and Final Report*, 103.

2. Letter from Stevens, September 17, 1853, quoted in "From the Washington Union. Pacific Railroad," *Oregonian*, January 21, 1854.

3. Stanley to Lieut. Warren, April 3, 1855, Isaac Stevens letterbook, Office of Explorations and Surveys, Office of the Secretary of the Interior, National Archives, Washington, D.C.

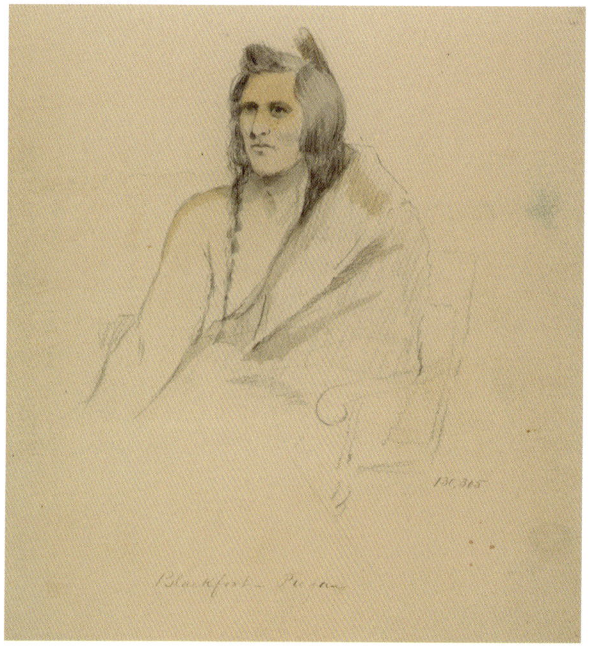

077

078

Indian Man, 1853

Watercolor and graphite on paper, $10\frac{1}{2} \times 8\frac{1}{4}$ in. (26.7 × 21.0 cm)

INSCRIPTION: [Unsigned]

PRESENT COLLECTION: Nelda C. and H. J. Lutcher Stark Foundation, Stark Museum of Art, Orange, Texas (31.23.13)

PROVENANCE: The artist; by descent to Mrs. Dean (Alice Stanley) Acheson, Washington, D.C.; present owner

This, the most finished of the sketches that survive from the Isaac Stevens expedition, provides the least amount of information about its sitter. Unsigned and lacking any inscription, it pictures a man wearing a rawhide shirt and cloaked in a robe or blanket. The shirt is fringed and decorated with a red tab. He sits at three-quarter view, but his head is turned in profile.

Stanley had hoped to paint likenesses of Native people in color during the expedition. None but this has survived. It reveals the working method of the artist. He appears to have been interested first and foremost in capturing the likeness and coloring of the sitter, with second in importance being clothing, then hands, and lastly background. Compositionally, little has changed since his work with the Emory survey in 1846. The pose resembles the lithograph of *The Interpreter of the Pimos* (fig. 78.1) that appeared as an illustration in the Emory report.

It is difficult or impossible to ascribe a tribal identity to the man, but the drawing was probably made at either Fort Union among the Assiniboin or at Fort Benton with the Piegan and Blackfeet.

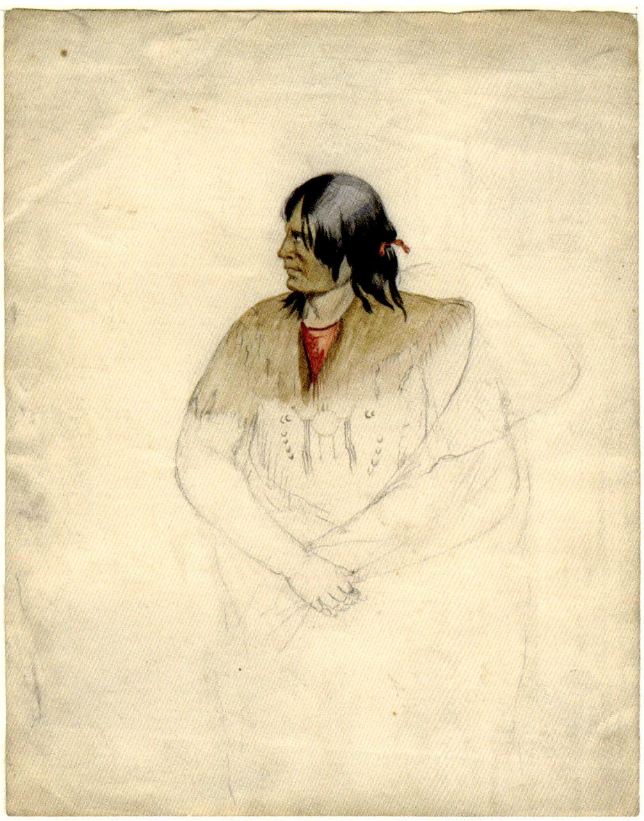

078

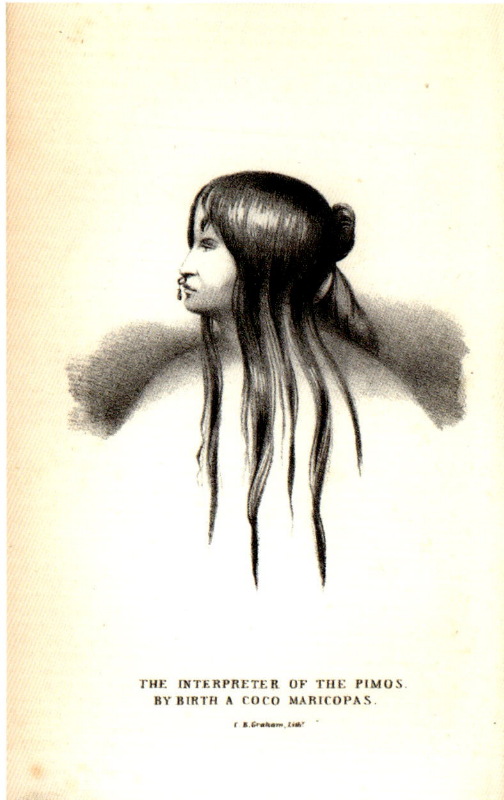

FIG. 78.1.
G. B. Graham after John Mix Stanley,
The Interpreter of the Pimos, By Birth a Coco Maricopas, 1847.
Lithograph; $6\frac{1}{4} \times 4$ in. (15.9 × 10.2 cm)
From Emory, Notes of a Military Reconnoissance, 132.
Courtesy McCracken Research Library, Buffalo Bill Center of the West, Cody, Wyoming

079

Wi-ti-my-hoy-she, Pelouse, 1853

Pelouse Man

Pencil on brown paper, $9\frac{7}{8} \times 7\frac{1}{8}$ in. (25.1 × 18.1 cm)

INSCRIBED LOWER LEFT: Pelous; INSCRIBED LOWER RIGHT: 130,305; INSCRIBED VERSO: [Drawing of peace medal with INSCRIPTION:] TH. JEFFERSON PRESIDENT OF THE US AD 1801; written in Stanley's hand beneath medal: opposite side clasped hands–/ cross pipes–. Peace & friendship

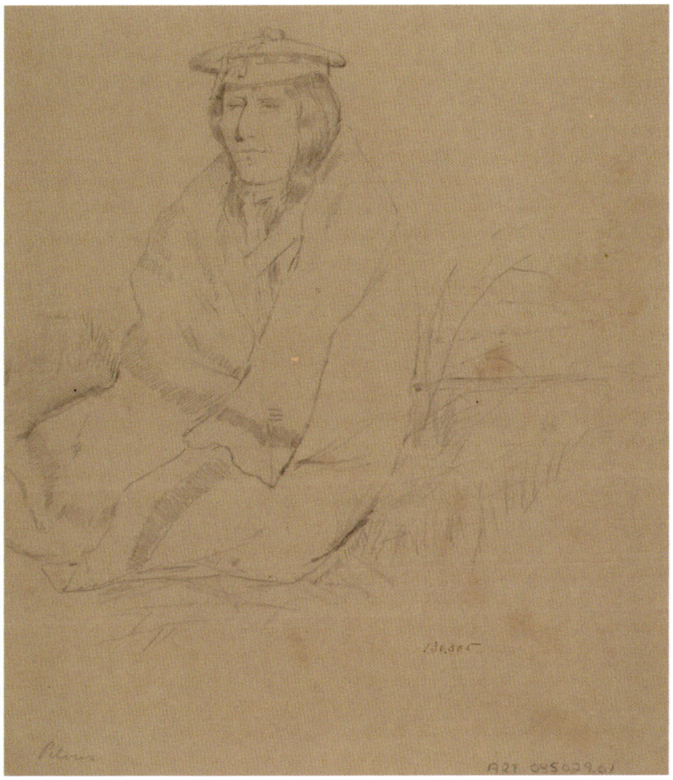

079

PRESENT COLLECTION: National Anthropological Archives, Smithsonian Institution, Washington, D.C.

PROVENANCE: Unknown

The Palouse River is a tributary of the Snake River, with their confluence in present-day southeastern Washington. The Isaac Stevens party reached this junction in early November 1853, on their way to Fort Walla Walla and the Columbia River. It was here that Stanley lingered for a couple of days to sketch the scenery and Indian people of the region. Stevens reported that after crossing the Snake River at the confluence, he "camped on its southern bank. . . . Several Peluse [sic] Indians [were] accompanying us, and among them a chief from a band but a few miles distant from our camp, Wi-ti-my-hoy-she."[1] The chief posed for Stanley wearing a tasseled tam-o'-shanter and a trade blanket. This is thought to be a portrait of that chief.

Stevens reported that Wi-ti-my-hoy-she proudly wore a Thomas Jefferson peace medal "dated 1801, given to his grandfather [Chief Kepowhan], as he alleges, by Lewis and Clark." On the verso of the Stanley drawing of this man is a sketch of that 1801 Thomas Jefferson peace medal (fig. 79.1).

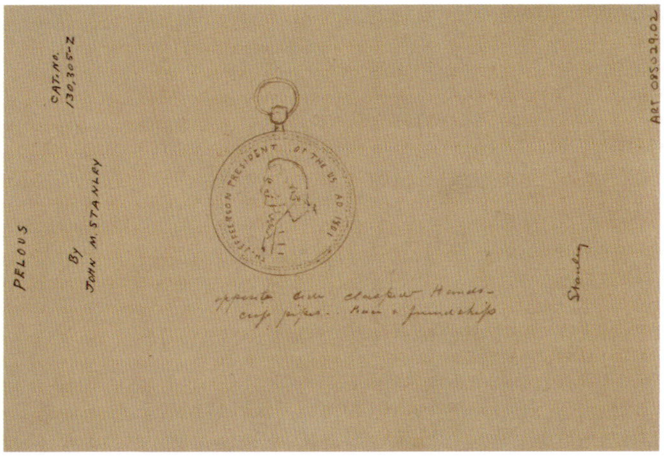

FIG. 79.1
John Mix Stanley, *Medal of Thomas Jefferson, 1801*, 1853.
Pencil on brown paper; dimensions unknown.
Sketched on back of *Wi-ti-my-hoy-she, Pelouse.*
Courtesy National Anthropological Archives,
Smithsonian Institution, Washington, D.C.

1. Stevens, *Narrative and Final Report*, 151. The Lewis and Clark journals mention the explorers giving several peace medals to chiefs and subchiefs in the area on October 10, 1805. See Gary E. Moulton, ed., *The Journals of the Lewis and Clark Expedition*, vol. 5 (Lincoln: University of Nebraska Press, 1988), 278.

080

Major Alexander Culbertson, 1854

Oil on canvas, 30 × 25 in. (76.2 × 63.5 cm)

INSCRIBED LOWER RIGHT: J. M. Stanley / 185(?)

PRESENT COLLECTION: Fort Benton Museums, Fort Benton, Montana

PROVENANCE: The artist; Major Alexander Culbertson; by descent to Alexander C. Roberts, Boise, Idaho; Mrs. George Taylor, Bethesda, Maryland, 1960; (Kennedy Galleries, New York, New York, 1966); [?], (John R. Howard Fine Art, Missoula, Montana, 2006); present owner

Alexander Culbertson was one of the most celebrated leaders of the western fur trade. He began his career on the upper Missouri River in the 1830s, becoming the chief trader for the American Fur Company by the end of that decade. He subsequently commanded Fort Union at the confluence of the Yellowstone and Missouri rivers, and by 1847 he had established his own outpost, Fort Benton, just below the terminus point of steamboat navigation, the Great Falls of the Missouri. When Stanley and Stevens embarked on their

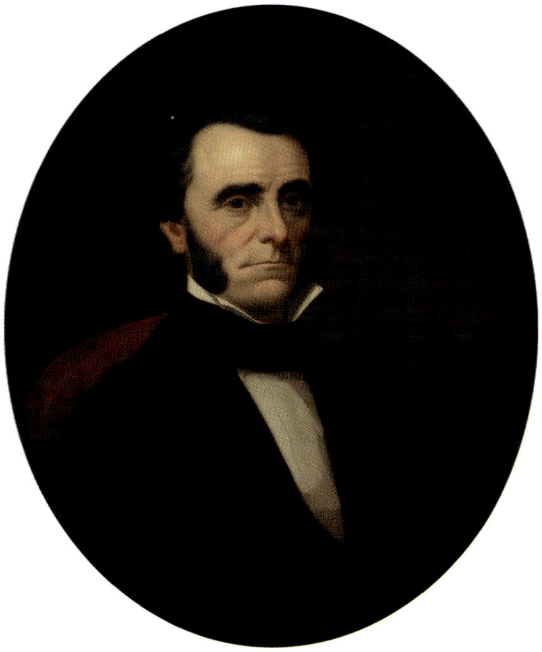

080

transcontinental railroad survey in 1853, Culbertson was engaged to serve as negotiator, appeaser, and translator among the Gros Ventres, Assiniboins and Blackfeet. He performed admirably.[1]

Stanley and Culbertson rendezvoused in Washington, D.C., in early 1854. Stanley had just returned from the Columbia River and had embarked on the production of a giant panorama with dozens of pictorial episodes, an artistic extravaganza he called *Scenes and Incidents of Stanley's Western Wilds*. Culbertson had come to entreat with various congressional committees on behalf of his beloved Blackfeet friends on the upper Missouri. The two came together one day when Culbertson stumbled upon Stanley's studio. Major Culbertson must have posed for this portrait that winter or early spring, for records show that he left the city for a return to the frontier in mid-May, and Stanley was preoccupied with his wedding to Alice English early that month.[2] Culbertson, who had accumulated substantial wealth over the years, later became one of Stanley's most loyal and ambitious patrons.

1. See Wischmann, *Frontier Diplomats*.

2. Stanley was married on May 3, 1854, and Culbertson left Washington on May 17, 1854. Ibid., 232–33.

081

Blackfoot Indians, 1854

Oil on academy board, 10 × 14 in. (25.4 × 35.6 cm)

INSCRIBED LOWER RIGHT: J. M. Stanley 1854

PRESENT COLLECTION: Private collection

PROVENANCE: The artist; by descent through the Stanley family; (Kennedy Galleries, New York, New York, c. 1958); Max and Carolyn William Family Trust, Dallas, TX, 1985–1993; The Lockwood Family Collection, Cincinnati, Ohio; (O'Meara Gallery, Santa Fe, New Mexico, 1982); (Mongerson-Wunderlich Gallery, Chicago, Illinois, 1994); (Gerald Peters Gallery, Santa Fe, New Mexico, 1995); present owner, 1996

The subject of this genre scene must have been something Stanley saw during his travels with Isaac Stevens through the Northwest. The Indians are probably Blackfeet, though the costume details are vague. The pyramidal composition lends strength to the narrative, the red highlights on the costumes provide powerful visual accent, and the open sky suggests a limitless expanse that these Indians control. The painting is a testament to Stanley's true embrace of American Indians as unique and lofty forces in nature.

Not since his painting *Black Knife* of 1850 (cat. no. 064) had a group of Indians been placed in such an ascendant position, as if to say they are in supreme command of their world. The horses that linger below them are strong steeds, mounts that seem poised and ready to carry them off to whatever tasks may confront them after their respite. This is one, if not the first, example of Stanley's standard, and soon to become somewhat formulaic, interpretation of Indian men resting on a rocky promontory looking out over a vast western landscape below.

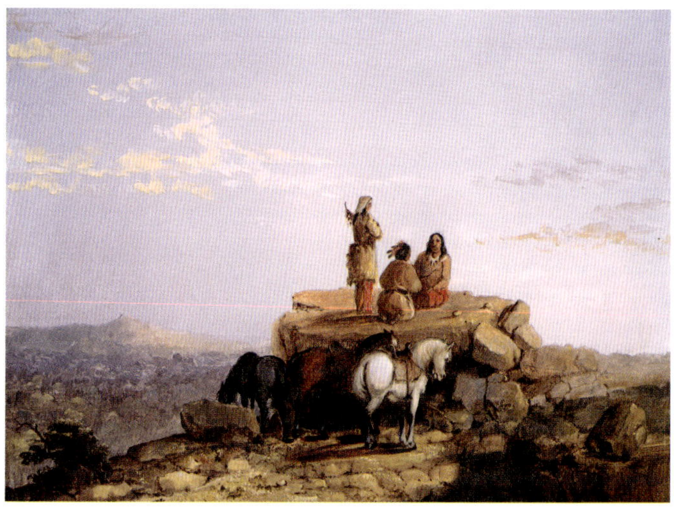

081

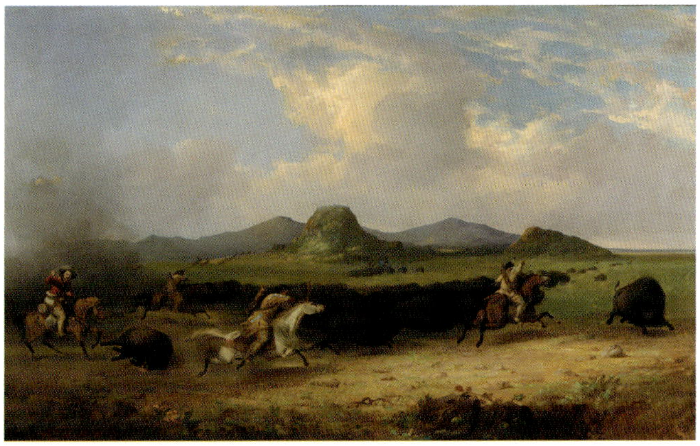

082

Buffalo Hunt, 1854

Oil on canvas, 39 × 61½ in. (99.1 × 403.4 cm)

INSCRIBED LOWER LEFT: J. M. Stanley 1854

PRESENT COLLECTION: Gilcrease Museum, Tulsa, Oklahoma (0126.1150)

PROVENANCE: A. G. Seaman, New York, New York; Robert J. McKeon, Chappaqua, New York; private collection, Kentucky; (Sotheby Parke Bernet, New York, New York, 1950); A. B. Adler, New York, New York; (M. Knoedler and Co., New York, New York, 1950); Thomas Gilcrease, Tulsa, Oklahoma; present owner

Almost immediately after returning to Washington, D.C., in January 1854, Stanley embarked on the production of his first of two grand panoramas, *Scenes and Incidents of Stanley's Western Wilds*. The vast canvas narrative comprised forty-two scenes and episodes. Among them was one panel titled *A Grand Buffalo Hunt*, which recounted a hunt he had organized among the Piegan Indians north of Fort Benton.[1] This painting, completed in the same year, is thought to have been sold to someone who saw the panorama and wanted a memento of Stanley's adventure.

Indeed, this painting is as much autobiographical as it is a record of Piegan hunting skills. The figure on the left of the picture is Stanley himself, who has just scored a kill. He recounted the occasion in the narrative of the panorama as follows: "One bold buffalo, wounded, turns at bay. . . . By him stops the Artist, on his steed—to contemplate his own work, for to-day Stanley has been a mighty hunter."[2] He was often a successful hunter but had lost his share as well. This enterprise was sufficiently successful to record twice for posterity.

A third variation of this scene, a tinted lithograph that appeared in the Stevens report, was titled *Blackfeet Indians—Three Buttes* (fig. 82.1). It replicates this composition but leaves out Stanley and his horse.

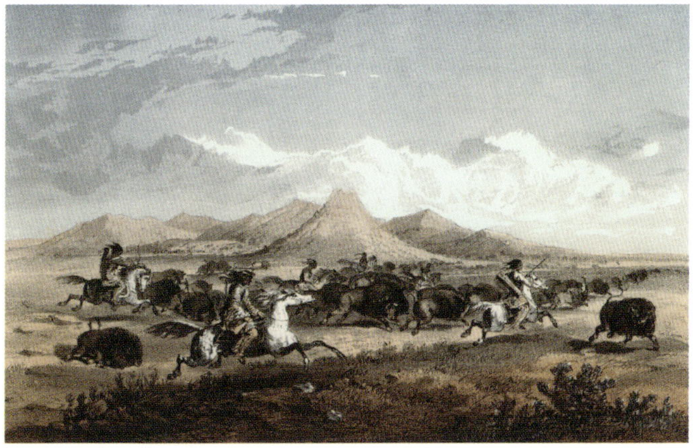

FIG. 82.1.
Sarony, Major, and Knapp after John Mix Stanley, *Blackfeet Indians–Three Buttes*, c. 1860.
Toned lithograph; 8½ × 11½ in. (21.6 × 29.2 cm).
From Stevens, *Narrative and Final Report*, opp. p. 115.
Courtesy McCracken Research Library, Buffalo Bill Center of the West, Cody, Wyoming

1. Donoho, *Scenes and Incidents*, 15.

2. Ibid.

083

Self-Portrait Sketching by a Stream, c. 1854

Oil on canvas, 19¼ × 15¼ in. (49 × 38.7 cm)

INSCRIPTION: [Unsigned]

PRESENT COLLECTION: Western Americana Collection, Beinecke Rare Book and Manuscript Library, Yale University, New Haven, Connecticut (Franz R. and Kathryn M. Stenzel Collection of Western American Art [WA.MSS.S-2368])

PROVENANCE: Isaac I. Stevens; Mrs. Helen Eskridge, Olympia, Washington; Dr. and Mrs. Franz Stenzel, Portland, Oregon; (Sotheby Parke Bernet, Los Angeles, 1980); present owner

This landscape with seated figure is unsigned and, until recently, unidentified. It has been attributed to Stanley over the years, and the treatment of the foliage certainly hints of his style. The provenance also suggests a strong connection with Stanley, as it was once owned by Isaac Stevens and descended through his family in Olympia, Washington. Whether it is a self-portrait or not is conjectural, though given that the Stevens family referred to it as such makes the assumption less speculative.

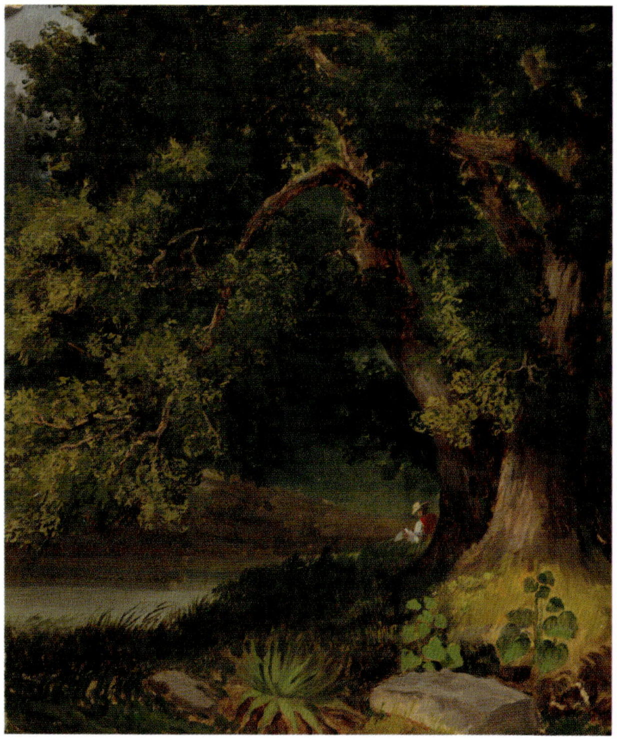

083

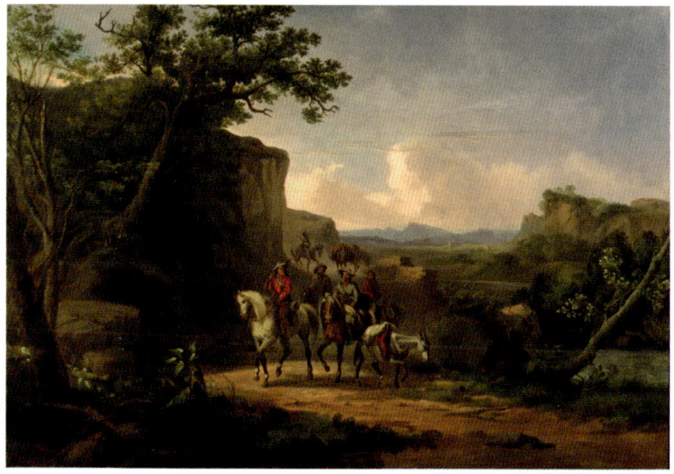

084

This is a charming example of Stanley as a landscape artist. The wooded interior dappled with sunlight, hushed by the slowly flowing stream and punctuated with a solitary, reposed figure provides a moment of quiet reverie. The century plant in the foreground suggests a southwestern scene, while the lushness connotes the Northwest. Perhaps this was intended to be a remembrance for Stevens of the glories of wild nature and the rewards of rest after a long day's work in the field.

084

Mounted Surveyors and Pack Animals, c. 1854

Oil on canvas, 35 × 46 in. (88.9 × 116.8 cm)

PRESENT COLLECTION: Private collection

PROVENANCE: Major Richard Stevens Eskridge, Olympia, Washington; (Berry-Hill Galleries, New York, New York, 2003); present owner

This painting, though it carries a rather generic title and might be thought to reveal Stanley's fascination with mountain men, is more probably a portrait of the artist's boss and cohort Isaac Stevens in the field. The provenance for this work is traced back to Stevens's family. It was probably bought or commissioned by him some time shortly after he and Stanley returned to Washington, D.C., in 1853. Given its provenance and strong visual relationship, the painting was probably produced a bit earlier than but as a companion piece to *Landscape with Deer* (cat. no. 164). *Mounted Surveyors and Pack Animals* may have traveled back to the newly established Washington Territory with Stevens in 1854, where he held the position of the territory's first governor.

Stevens was a brilliant man (graduating in 1839 the top of his class from West Point). He was also small in stature and quite handsome (fig. 84.1). He is thought to be the man in the blue shirt riding the bay horse at the center of the composition. The other riders, unidentifiable due to their more rudimentary physiognomic rendition, simply support the theme of exploration through an undisclosed scene in the wilds of the Northwest.

This work provided a chance for Stanley to express himself about the role of the Anglo explorer in the wilderness. Although it is not as closely related to the biblical story of Moses leading his people to the land of Canaan as George Caleb Bingham's *Daniel Boone Escorting Settlers through the Cumberland Gap,* 1851–1852 (Mildred Lane Kemper Art Museum, St. Louis), it does carry the same message. The sunlit explorers pass a dark rock cliff on their right and emerge from the shadows as protagonists in the divine metaphorical invention called Manifest Destiny. The riders' mission is entrepreneurially and nationally strategic as well as heavenly sanctioned.

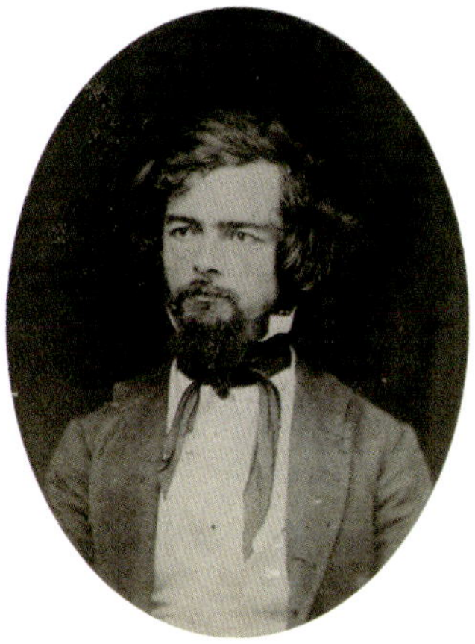

FIG. 84.1.
Unknown photographer, *Isaac Ingalls Stevens*, c. 1855. Photograph; 4¾ × 3½ in. (12.1 × 8.9 cm). Courtesy State Library Photograph Collection, 1851–1990, Washington State Archives–Digital Archives, www.digitalarchives.wa.gov

085

Western Landscape with Buffalo, c. 1855

Oil on canvas, 25⅜ × 35⅜ in. (64.5 × 89.9 cm)

PRESENT COLLECTION: Gilcrease Museum, Tulsa, Oklahoma (0126.1140)

PROVENANCE: The artist; John Carl Richberg, Knoxville, Tennessee; by descent to Donald R. Richberg, Charlottesville, Virginia, 1952; (Kennedy Galleries, New York, New York, 1957); Thomas Gilcrease, Tulsa, Oklahoma; present owner

On July 10, 1853, the Stevens expedition members crested a high hill in an area of what is today Lake Jessie, North Dakota. There they beheld such a vast herd of buffalo that Stevens was staggered by their numbers. He conservatively recorded having seen as many as two hundred thousand of the prairie monarchs.[1] In Stanley's open vista of the scene that lay before them, *Herd of Bison, Near Lake Jessie* (fig. 85.1), the artist created one of history's most captivating images of the immensity of animal life and the seemingly boundless expanse of territory where they thrived in the West during the mid-nineteenth century. Here the land and the wild animal blend into one sublime narrative.

In his painting, *Western Landscape with Buffalo*, Stanley introduced one additional exotic element, the Indian hunter. The painting engages the viewer not through its magnificent expanse, although that is effectively portrayed with the alternating light and dark areas in the composition, but more through the tension established between the highlighted hunter in the foreground and the unwary prey in the middle distance. The massive rock formation that hovers dramatically over the buffalo herd lends scale. George Catlin had employed a similar stalking narrative in at least one of his paintings, and Alfred Jacob Miller repeated it frequently, but none had such staged theatricality as Stanley's.[2]

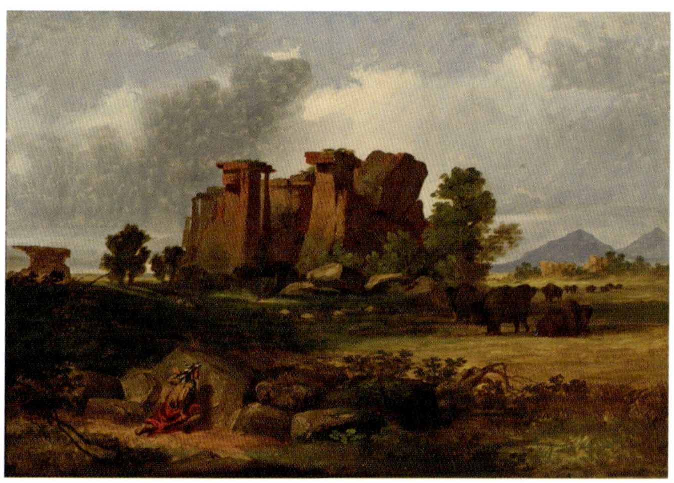

085

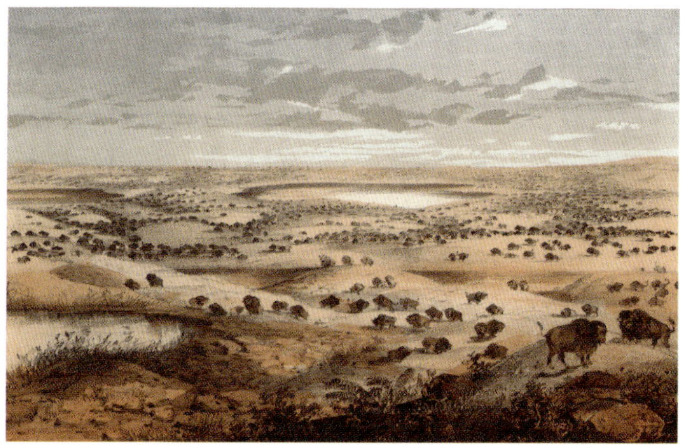

FIG. 85.1.
Sarony, Major, and Knapp after John Mix Stanley, *Herd of Bison, Near Lake Jessie*, c. 1860.
Toned lithograph; 8½ × 11½ in. (21.6 × 29.2 cm).
From Stevens, *Narrative and Final Report*, opp. p. 59. Courtesy McCracken Research Library, Buffalo Bill Center of the West, Cody, Wyoming

1. Stevens, *Narrative and Final Report*, 59.

2. Catlin pictured himself in such a pose in *Batiste, Bogard, and I, Approaching Buffalo on the Missouri* (1837–1839), Smithsonian American Art Museum, Washington, D.C., and Miller, who used the theme numerous times in his oeuvre, pictured his patron William Drummond Stewart as the hunter in *Approaching Buffalo under the Disguise of a Wolf* (c. 1837), Amon Carter Museum of American Art, Fort Worth, Texas.

Stevens Expedition Watercolors, Cat. Nos. 086–127

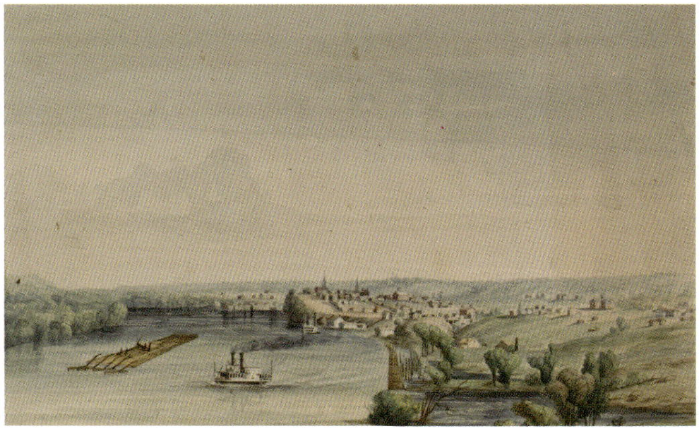

086

Saint Paul M.T. (Minnesota Territory), 1854–1855

Watercolor with graphite underdrawing, 9 1/16 × 13 1/4 in. (23.0 × 33.6 cm)

INSCRIBED ON SUPPORT LOWER LEFT: J. M. Stanley; INSCRIBED LOWER CENTER: Saint Paul M.T.

PRESENT COLLECTION: Yale University Art Gallery, New Haven, Connecticut, gift of Paul Mellon, B.A. 1929, L.H.D.H. 1967, Collection (1982.39.1A)

PROVENANCE: The artist; acquired by Thomas H. Ford [printer of *Pacific Railroad Survey Reports*, vol. 12, 1860]; [?]; Mr. and Mrs. Larry Fleishman, Detroit, Michigan; (Kennedy Galleries, New York, New York, by 1966); Paul Mellon, Upperville, Virginia, 1982; present owner, 1982

By December 1852 Stanley had strategically situated his Indian Gallery at the Smithsonian Institution in Washington, D.C. He felt comfortable about its new home and was ready by the end of the year to begin soliciting Congress to purchase the 152 paintings that composed the collection.[1] Over the next couple of months, the paintings drew much favorable attention. The landscape artist and travel chronicler Charles Lanman, writing for the *Daily National Intelligencer*, proclaimed the collection's merits in no uncertain terms. "As works of art his pictures are equal to any thing of the kind to be found in Europe," he wrote. Probably recalling Catlin's Indian Gallery, he continued, "There is no flashy, dawdy coloring here to catch the eye, no unnatural positions to create wonder, no over-wrought delineations to mystify and amaze. Here art, in its simplicity and candor unfolds, in all the truthfulness of Nature, the characters, persons, habits, virtues, and peculiarities of the 'red man.'"[2]

On the same day that Lanman's laudatory comments were published, March 3, 1853, the *Congressional Globe* announced that Stanley's petition to Congress had failed on a vote of 27 to 14.[3] Stanley must have been crushed, yet he was not one to languish in self-pity. He was already planning his next adventure and his future means of employment. Probably as a result of his Indian Gallery's critical success, his past experience with William Emory in the Southwest, and his personally persuasive manner, he was soon enlisted as official artist with Isaac Stevens for a survey of a possible transcontinental railroad route from St. Paul west along the 48th parallel to the Pacific shore. By May 15, Stevens announced that he and Stanley, "the artist of the exploration," had arrived in Saint Paul, ready to embark on their trip.[4]

Stanley was prepared to add to his Indian Gallery as he moved west. He told his future wife, Alice English, in a letter from St. Louis that he would "make many captives—on paper and plate."[5] Beyond his sophisticated knowledge of the daguerreotype camera that he would carry, Stanley was well equipped to document with drawings such subjects of natural history, the Native peoples, and the landscape through which the party of eighty men were to pass. In his instructions to himself, he made special mention of the importance of recording Indians and natural history specimens in color. Regarding the former group, he wrote, "Sketches of Indians should be made and colored from life, with care to fidelity in complexion as well as feature" (cat. no. 016 as an example). With regard to "drawings of their lodges, with their historical devices, carvings, &c.," he suggested only that "they be made with care."[6]

Just as Stanley and Stevens embarked on their journey from the upper Mississippi River to Puget Sound, a Saint Paul correspondent for the *New York Tribune* exclaimed about Stanley's sketches, "I have already seen some of the artist's work, and can promise the public when Gov. Stevens's Report is made up and given to the world, there will be something as pleasing to the eye as to the mind."[7] Most likely the correspondent saw Stanley's initial 1853 field sketch of Saint Paul, which was used a couple of years later to produce the finished watercolor *Saint Paul M.T. (Minnesota Territory)* Even so, the reporter's enthusiasm would suggest that the field study was striking on its own, especially in its verisimilitude and beauty. Stevens likewise was fervent in his praise of Stanley's fieldwork. When Stevens reached the upper Missouri at Fort Benton, he sent a letter back to Washington, D.C., extolling the value of his artist's labors. " J. M. Stanley, Esq., the artist of the expedition, has taken many sketches illustrative of the progress of the expedition, besides taking at various points on the way numerous daguerreotypes of Indians. His reputation, already established, cannot be enhanced by any reference to his satisfactory discharge of duty."[8]

Sadly, none of Stanley's daguerreotypes and very few of his field sketches survive today. The field sketches that are extant (cat. nos. 074 and 075 as examples) are pencil studies with no or just the slightest hint of coloring, with one exception, even when they portray important American Indian subjects. What does survive is a set of thirty-eight finished watercolors definitely by Stanley's hand, presented in this volume, that were painted in Washington, D.C., after the trip. They were presumably taken from his field sketches, to be used as models for the chromolithographers as they created plates for the final report of the Stevens expedition.

Stanley returned to Washington, D.C., in early January 1854. Stevens's report was not close to being ready, so the artist spent his first months at home preparing for his wedding to Alice in May; painting oils for sale from his studies and remembrances; and creating his monumental panorama *Scenes and Incidents of Stanley's Western Wilds*. In September 1854 Stevens wrote a letter to the chief of the War Department's exploration office, Captain A. A. Humphries, asking that Stanley be rehired. Stevens requested that the artist be reinstated at the salary he had enjoyed during the expedition, $125 per month, "a small compensation . . . in view of his ability and experience." He hoped that Stanley could "at once commence preparing his sketches for publication," and he was "desirous to bring out a complete Indian paper in connection with the exploration."[9]

Stanley was subsequently retained to work on the illustrations for the published reports, but before he could tend to the Stevens account, he was asked to redraw a set of sketches by his recently deceased colleague and friend Richard Kern from the ill-fated John W. Gunnison expedition through Utah. Both Kern and Gunnison had been killed by Paiute Indians, but Kern's field sketches and Gunnison's notes from their trek had been saved.[10] It was thus not until early 1855 that Stanley could fully devote himself to the Stevens illustrations. In April, he wrote to Lieutenant G. K. Warren, a noted western map maker who was in charge of the final volumes of the survey, that he had completed many of the images for the Stevens report and that they were ready for the "engraver." He told Warren that it would take him three more months to finish the "Natural Scenery" images and listed some thirty views, of which about half were ultimately selected. Stanley suggested that he was prepared to spend an additional two and a half months "for the Indian illustrations," twenty-seven in number, although none were included because the "Indian paper" that Stevens had proposed apparently never materialized.[11]

It is not known when Stanley finished his work for the Stevens volume of the U.S. War Department's *Reports of Explorations and Surveys* (vol. 12, books 1–2). There were two editions published, one in 1859 and a second in 1860, and there are slight variations in the plates between the two.[12] Of the seventy toned lithographs in the 1860 edition, fifty-four are ascribed solely to Stanley, three to Stanley after sketches by Gustavus Sohon, ten to Sohon alone, and three to Stanley after sketches by James Graham Cooper.

Sohon and Cooper were part of an auxiliary troop under Stevens's leadership. Stevens assigned them to accompany Captain George B. McClellan on a reconnaissance from the mouth of the Columbia River east through the Cascade Range, where they were slated to meet up with Stevens coming west. Cooper was the physician in McClellan's troop and was known for his superior work in the natural sciences, especially botany and zoology.[13] Sohon, a private in the Fourth Infantry, was a prized member of the military contingent. Stevens described Sohon a few years later, after a subsequent trip up the Columbia River with him, as having "shown great taste as an artist, and ability to learn the Indian language, as well as a facility in intercourse with the Indians."[14] The images by Sohon that relate most closely to Stanley's from the 1853 expedition appeared in a subsequent 1863 report, of a follow-up survey undertaken by Captain John Mullan of the potential railroad route between Fort Walla Walla and Fort Benton. Sohon again served as artist on this expedition and produced about a half dozen scenes that appeared in Mullan's report, including Sohon's view of *Fort Benton* (fig. 102.1), which has been favorably compared to Stanley's earlier rendition (cat. no. 102).[15]

Stanley's thirty-eight watercolors are presented here in the order of the route of the Stevens expedition as it moved west from the upper Mississippi River. The set begins with the above view of the embarkation point, Saint Paul, and ends with a vista of Mount Baker and the Cascade Range taken from east of the Pacific Coast on Whidbey Island, just north of present-day Seattle at the north end of Puget Sound (cat. no. 127). They are mostly landscapes showing the natural settings through which the explorers trekked, sometimes featuring Indians or the procession of explorers as adjuncts to the scene. Collectively, they are perhaps the loveliest and most engaging topographical studies produced by any of the many artist-explorers of the nineteenth century.[16] *Pelous Falls* (cat. no. 114), for example, embraces all the tenets of the Hudson River School artists. The watercolor is at once powerful and sublime in its effect while being intimate and charming in spirit. The crashing cascade and the small Indian figure reveal a tension between humble humankind and the splendor of raw nature. And when the human is an American Indian and the scene is the Far West, Stanley was able to add an unprecedented sense of the exotic, thus heightening the transcendent, spiritual connection between the corporeal and the divine worlds.

The set of thirty-eight Stanley watercolors pictured in this volume surfaced in the early 1960s and include mostly original compositions by Stanley, though some are indicated as having been painted after Sohon or Cooper originals. Where they came from has been a conundrum. The dealer Rudolph Wunderlich, of the Kennedy Galleries in New York, first told the artist's granddaughter Mrs. Dean (Alice Stanley) Acheson, of Washington, D.C., about them in 1966 and later told her that he had no idea where they had come from.[17] Wunderlich sold most of them to Paul Mellon of Upperville, Virginia, who subsequently donated them to the Yale University Art Gallery.[18] Two other examples (cat. nos. 090 and 101) from the set were purchased by Dr. and Mrs. Franz Stenzel of Portland, Oregon. He donated them to the Beinecke Rare Book and Manuscript Library at Yale University and with those came a hint of their previous ownership. Stenzel's records indicate that he had acquired them from Lawrence Fleischman of Detroit, a partner of Wunderlich's, and Fleischman had bought them from a descendant of Thomas H. Ford, the Washington, D.C., printer of volume 12 of the 1860 edition of the U.S. War Department's *Reports of Explorations and Surveys* (i.e., Stevens's *Narratives and Final Report*). It would appear, then, that Ford retained the watercolors after the railroad survey reports were completed, and if Fleischman's two watercolors came from this source, the Wunderlich watercolors probably did as well.

1. See "Stanley's Indian Gallery," *Congressional Globe*, December 28, 1852.

2. Charles Lanman, "Stanley's Gallery," *Daily National Intelligencer*, March 3, 1853.

3. "Indian Appropriation Bill," *Congressional Globe*, March 3, 1853.

4. Stevens, *Narrative and Final Report*, 34.

5. Stanley to Alice English, May 3, 1853, Stanley Papers.

6. J. M. Stanley, "Memoranda in Relation to Sketches in Natural History, Geology, Botany, and to Views of Scenery and Natural Objects," in Stevens, *Narrative and Final Report*, 7–8.

7. "Puget's Sound Railroad Survey," *New York Tribune*, June 3, 1853.

8. Quoted from the *Washington Union* in "Pacific Railroad. Northern Route. Governor Stevens' Exploring Expedition," *Oregonian*, January 21, 1854.

9. Stevens to Capt. A. A. Humphries, September 26, 1854, Stevens letterbook.

10. See David J. Weber, *Richard H. Kern: Expeditionary Artist in the Far Southwest, 1848–1853* (Albuquerque: University of New Mexico Press, 1985), 223, 262. The Stanley/Kern illustrations appeared in Isaac I. Stevens, *Route Near the Forty-Seventh and Forty-Ninth Parallels: Botanical Report*, vol. 12, book 2, of *Reports of Explorations and Surveys to Ascertain the Most Practicable and Economical Route from the Mississippi River to the Pacific Ocean* (Washington, D.C.: Thomas H. Ford, 1860). In the volume that I inspected, eight images were Stanley after Kern, two by Kern alone, and one Stanley after F. N. Eggloffstein. All were toned lithographs printed by A. Hoen and Co., Baltimore.

11. Stanley to Lieutenant G. K. Warren, April 3, 1855, Stevens letterbook.

12. See Schimmel, "John Mix Stanley and Imagery," 113; and Robert Taft, *Artists and Illustrators of the Old West, 1850–1900* (New York: Scribner, 1953), 255, for explanations of these differences.

13. See Dumas Malone, ed., *Dictionary of American Biography*, vol. 4 (New York: Scribner, 1930), 406.

14. Stevens, *Narrative and Final Report*, 198. The best biographical studies of Sohon appear in John C. Ewers, *Gustavus Sohon's Portraits of Flathead and Pend d'Oreille Indians, 1854*, Smithsonian Miscellaneous Collections, 110, no. 7 (Washington, D.C.: Smithsonian Institution Press, November 26, 1948), 1–68; and David L. Nicandri, *Northwest Chiefs: Gustav Sohon's Views of the 1855 Stevens Treaty Councils* (Tacoma: Washington State Historical Society, 1986).

15. See Capt. John Mullan, *Report on the Construction of a Military Road from Fort Walla-Walla to Fort Benton* (Washington, D.C.: Government Printing Office, 1863).

16. For a list and discussion of the western explorer-artists before 1850, see Peter H. Hassrick, "Artists Employed on United States Government Expeditions to the Trans-Mississippi West before 1850" (master's thesis, University of Denver, 1969); and for after 1850, Taft, *Artists and Illustrators*. An account of these artists as their works appeared in government documents is found in Katherine Karpenstein, "Illustrations of the West in Congressional Documents 1843–1863" (master's thesis, University of Rochester, 1953).

17. See Wunderlich to Acheson, May 20, 1966, and October 12, 1971, Stanley Papers.

18. Wunderlich gave the same message to Mellon that he did not know where the watercolors had come from. See letter from Mellon's curator, Willis Van Devanter, to Mrs. Acheson, August 24, 1971, Stanley Papers. A selection of these watercolors was published in William H. Goetzmann, "The Grand Reconnaissance," *American Heritage* 23 (October 1972): 44–59.

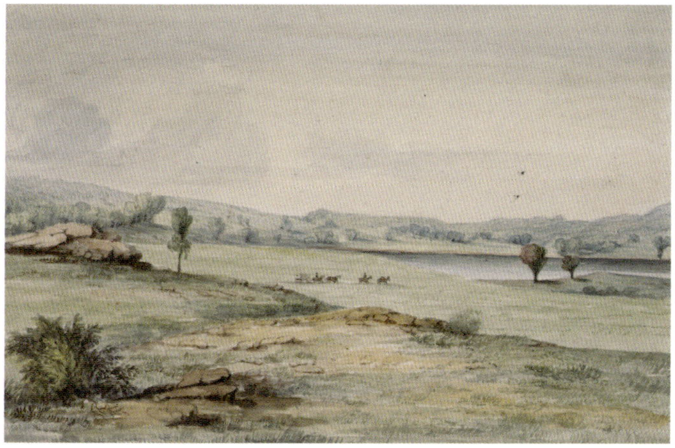

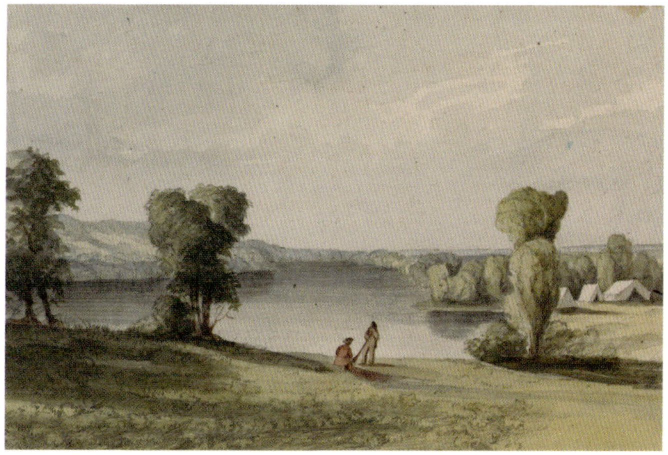

088

087
Sauk River, 1854–1855

Watercolor with graphite underdrawing on paper, 7⅝ × 11¼ in. (19.3 × 28.6 cm)

INSCRIBED ON SUPPORT LOWER LEFT: J. M. Stanley; INSCRIBED LOWER CENTER: Sauk River

PRESENT COLLECTION: Yale University Art Gallery, New Haven, Connecticut, gift of Paul Mellon, B.A. 1929, L.H.D.H. 1967, Collection (1982.39.2A)

PROVENANCE: The artist; acquired by Thomas H. Ford [printer of *Pacific Railroad Survey Reports*, vol. 12, 1860]; [?]; Mr. and Mrs. Larry Fleishman, Detroit, Michigan; (Kennedy Galleries, New York, New York, by 1966); Paul Mellon, Upperville, Virginia, 1982; present owner, 1982

088
Lightning Lake, 1854–1855

Watercolor with graphite underdrawing on paper, 5 13/16 × 8 9/16 in. (14.8 × 21.8 cm)

INSCRIBED ON SUPPORT LOWER LEFT: Stanley; inscribed on support lower center: Lightning Lake

PRESENT COLLECTION: Yale University Art Gallery, New Haven, Connecticut, gift of Paul Mellon, B.A. 1929, Hon. LLD 1967 1982.39.3A

PROVENANCE: The artist; acquired by Thomas H. Ford [printer of *Pacific Railroad Survey Reports*, vol. 12, 1860]; [?]; Mr. and Mrs. Larry Fleishman, Detroit, Michigan; (Kennedy Galleries, New York, New York, by 1966); Paul Mellon, Upperville, Virginia, 1982; present owner, 1982

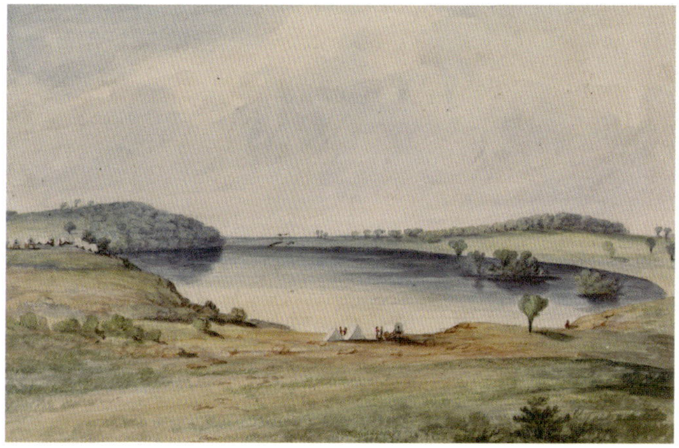

089
Pike Lake M.T., 1854–1855

Watercolor with graphite underdrawing on paper, 8 7/16 × 10⅞ in. (21.6 × 27.8 cm)

INSCRIBED ON SUPPORT LOWER LEFT: J. M. Stanley; INSCRIBED LOWER CENTER: Pike Lake M.T.

PRESENT COLLECTION: Yale University Art Gallery, New Haven, Connecticut, gift of Paul Mellon, B.A. 1929, L.H.D.H. 1967, Collection (1982.39.4A)

PROVENANCE: The artist; acquired by Thomas H. Ford [printer of *Pacific Railroad Survey Reports*, vol. 12, 1860]; [?]; Mr. and Mrs. Larry Fleishman, Detroit, Michigan; (Kennedy Galleries, New York, New York, by 1966); Paul Mellon, Upperville, Virginia, 1982; present owner, 1982

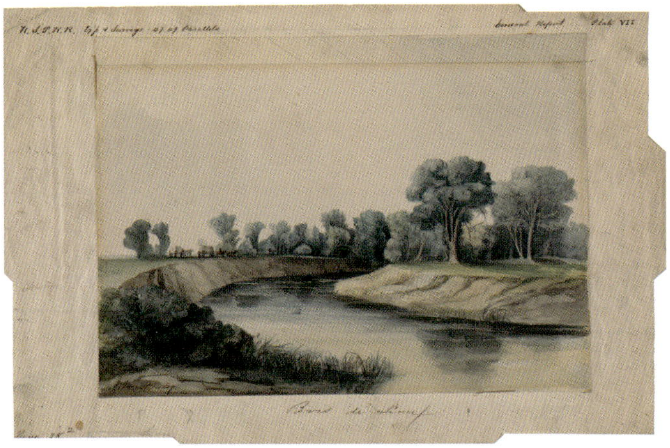

090

Bois de Sioux, 1854–1855

Bois de Sioux River

Watercolor with graphite underdrawing on paper, 8½ × 11½ in. (21.6 × 29.2 cm)

INSCRIBED ON SUPPORT: J. M. Stanley 1853

PRESENT COLLECTION: Beinecke Rare Book and Manuscript Library, Western Americana Collection, Yale University, New Haven, Connecticut (Franz R. and Kathryn M. Stenzel Collection of Western American Art Addition [WA.MSS.S-2601])

PROVENANCE: The artist; acquired by Thomas H. Ford [printer of *Pacific Railroad Survey Reports*, vol. 12, 1860]; [?]; Mr. and Mrs. Lawrence Fleishman, Detroit, Michigan; Franz R. and Kathryn M. Stenzel, Portland, Oregon; by bequest of Kathryn M. Stenzel to present owner, 2007

091

Maple River, 1854–1855

Watercolor with graphite underdrawing on paper, 5⅞ × 8⅝ in. (15 × 21.9 cm)

INSCRIBED ON SUPPORT LOWER LEFT: Stanley no. 9; INSCRIBED LOWER CENTER: Maple River

PRESENT COLLECTION: Yale University Art Gallery, New Haven, Connecticut, gift of Paul Mellon, B.A. 1929, L.H.D.H. 1967, Collection (1982.39.5A)

PROVENANCE: The artist; acquired by Thomas H. Ford [printer of *Pacific Railroad Survey Reports*, vol. 12, 1860]; [?]; Mr. and Mrs. Larry Fleishman, Detroit, Michigan; (Kennedy Galleries, New York, New York, by 1966); Paul Mellon, Upperville, Virginia, 1982; present owner, 1982

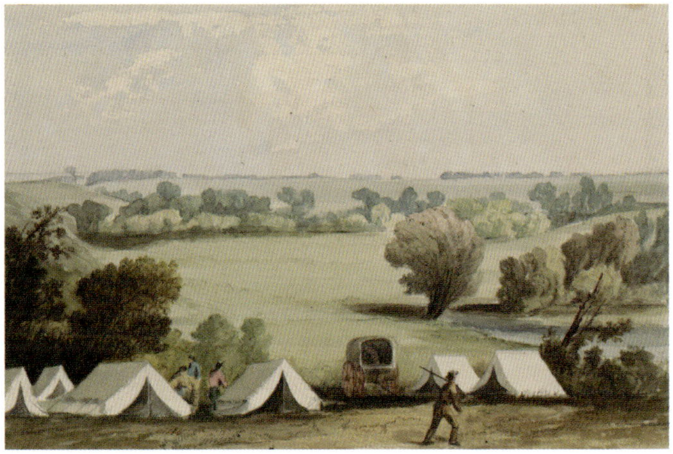

091

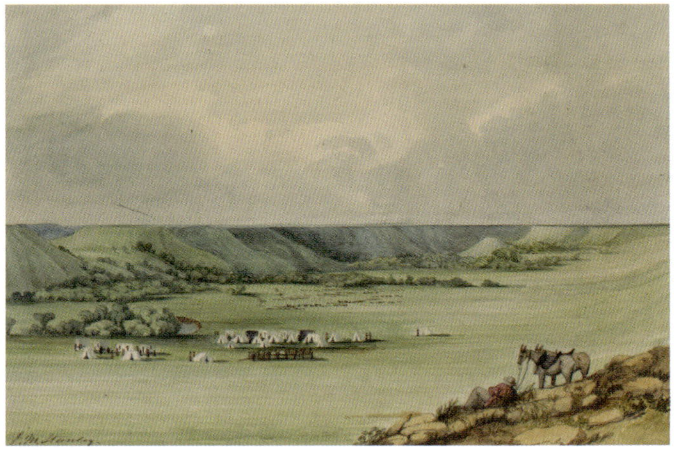

092

Sheyenne River, 1854–1855

Watercolor with graphite underdrawing on paper, 8 9/16 × 8¼ in. (21.7 × 29.2 cm)

INSCRIBED LOWER LEFT: J. M. Stanley; INSCRIBED ON MOUNT LOWER LEFT: July 8 2d; INSCRIBED ON MOUNT LOWER CENTER: Sheyenne River

PRESENT COLLECTION: Yale University Art Gallery, New Haven, Connecticut, gift of Paul Mellon, B.A. 1929, L.H.D.H. 1967, Collection (1982.39.6A)

PROVENANCE: The artist; acquired by Thomas H. Ford [printer of *Pacific Railroad Survey Reports*, vol. 12, 1860]; [?]; Mr. and Mrs. Larry Fleishman, Detroit, Michigan; (Kennedy Galleries, New York, New York, by 1966); Paul Mellon, Upperville, Virginia, 1982; present owner, 1982

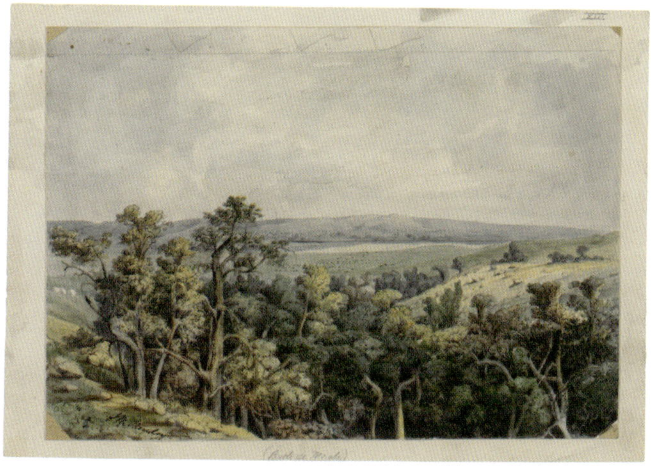

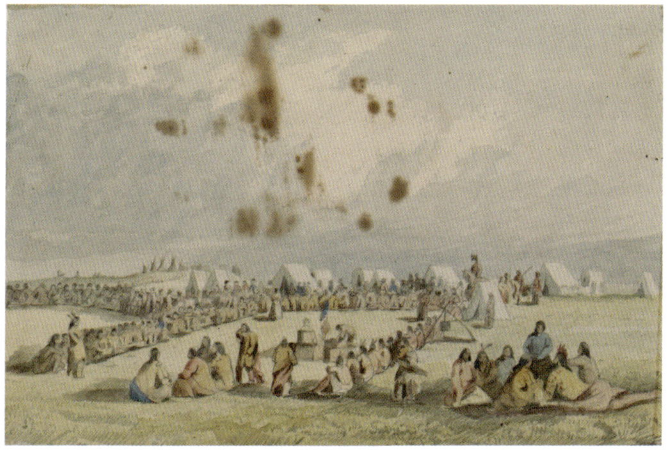

094

093

Butte De Morale, 1854–1855

Watercolor with graphite underdrawing on paper, $8\frac{3}{16} \times 11\frac{3}{16}$ in. (20.8 × 28.4 cm)

INSCRIBED LOWER LEFT: J. M. Stanley.; inscribed on mount, lower center: (Butte de Morale)

PRESENT COLLECTION: Yale University Art Gallery, New Haven, Connecticut, gift of Paul Mellon, B.A. 1929, L.H.D.H. 1967, Collection (1982.39.7A)

PROVENANCE: The artist; acquired by Thomas H. Ford [printer of *Pacific Railroad Survey Reports*, vol. 12, 1860]; [?]; Mr. and Mrs. Larry Fleishman, Detroit, Michigan; (Kennedy Galleries, New York, New York, by 1966); Paul Mellon, Upperville, Virginia, 1982; present owner, 1982

094

Distribution of Goods to the Assiniboins, 1854–1855

Watercolor with graphite underdrawing on paper, $5\frac{7}{8} \times 8\frac{11}{16}$ in. (15.1 × 22.1 cm)

INSCRIBED LOWER LEFT: 27; INSCRIBED ON MOUNT LOWER LEFT: Stanley; INSCRIBED ON MOUNT LOWER CENTER: ~~no. 16—Distribution of Goods to the Assinaboins~~

PRESENT COLLECTION: Yale University Art Gallery, New Haven, Connecticut, gift of Paul Mellon, B.A. 1929, L.H.D.H. 1967, Collection (1982.39.8A)

PROVENANCE: The artist; acquired by Thomas H. Ford [printer of *Pacific Railroad Survey Reports*, vol. 12, 1860]; [?]; Mr. and Mrs. Larry Fleishman, Detroit, Michigan; (Kennedy Galleries, New York, New York, by 1966); Paul Mellon, Upperville, Virginia, 1982; present owner, 1982

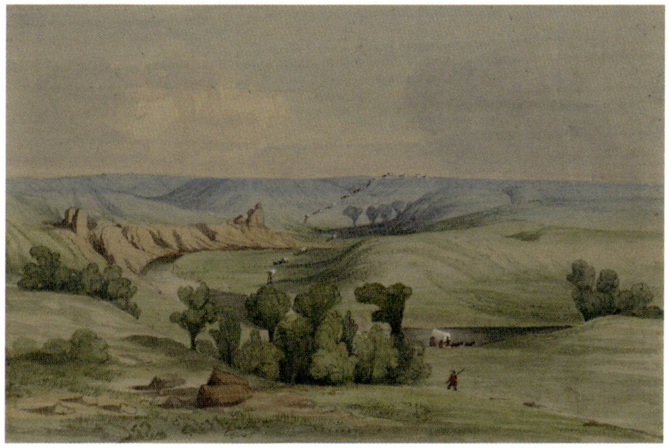

095

Near Mouse River, 1854–1855

Watercolor with graphite underdrawing on paper, $6\frac{15}{16} \times 9\frac{15}{16}$ in. (17.6 × 25.4 cm)

INSCRIBED ON MOUNT LOWER LEFT: J. M. Stanley / July 21st;
INSCRIBED ON MOUNT LOWER CENTER: Near Mouse River

PRESENT COLLECTION: Yale University Art Gallery, New Haven, Connecticut, gift of Paul Mellon, B.A. 1929, L.H.D.H. 1967, Collection (1982.39.9A)

PROVENANCE: The artist; acquired by Thomas H. Ford [printer of *Pacific Railroad Survey Reports*, vol. 12, 1860]; [?]; Mr. and Mrs. Larry Fleishman, Detroit, Michigan; (Kennedy Galleries, New York, New York, by 1966); Paul Mellon, Upperville, Virginia, 1982; present owner, 1982

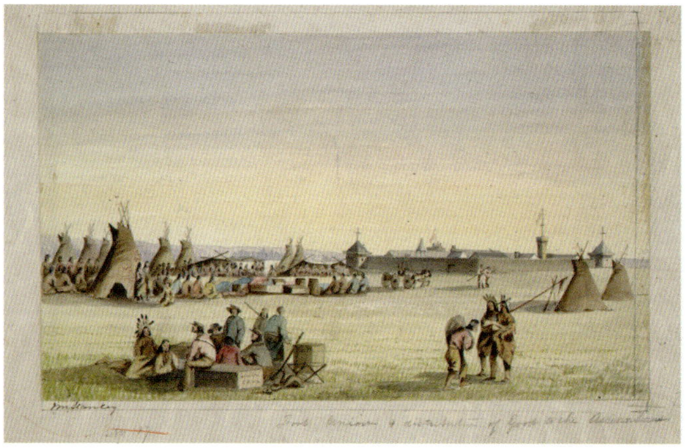

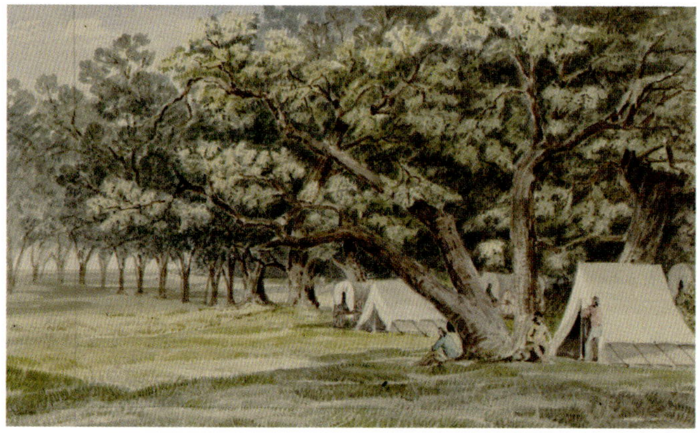

097

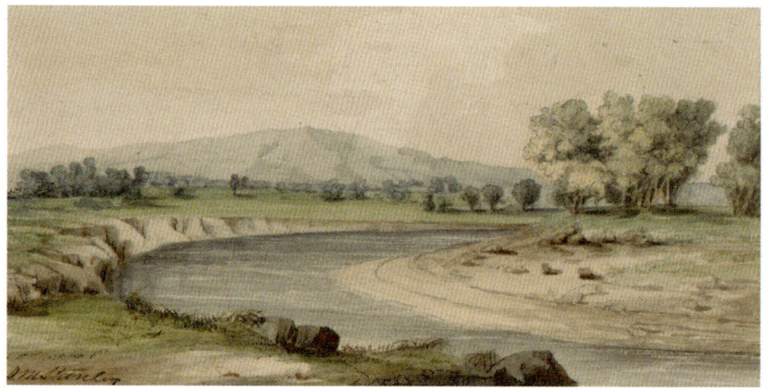

096

Fort Union, and Distribution of Goods to the Assiniboins, 1854–1855

Watercolor with graphite underdrawing on paper, 6 15/16 × 9 15/16 in. (16.4 × 27.1 cm)

INSCRIBED ON MOUNT LOWER LEFT: J. M. Stanley; INSCRIBED ON MOUNT LOWER RIGHT: Fort Union & distribution of Goods to the Assinniboinns [*sic*]; INSCRIBED ON MOUNT LOWER RIGHT: Fill up

PRESENT COLLECTION: Yale University Art Gallery, New Haven, Connecticut, gift of Paul Mellon, B.A. 1929, L.H.D.H. 1967, Collection (1982.39.10A)

PROVENANCE: The artist; acquired by Thomas H. Ford [printer of *Pacific Railroad Survey Reports*, vol. 12, 1860]; [?]; Mr. and Mrs. Larry Fleishman, Detroit, Michigan; (Kennedy Galleries, New York, New York, by 1966); Paul Mellon, Upperville, Virginia, 1982; present owner, 1982

097

A Cottonwood Grove, 1854–1855

Watercolor with graphite underdrawing on paper, 6 3/16 × 10 1/16 in. (15.7 × 25.4 cm)

INSCRIBED ON MOUNT LOWER CENTER: (A Cottonwood Grove)

PRESENT COLLECTION: Yale University Art Gallery, New Haven, Connecticut, gift of Paul Mellon, B.A. 1929, L.H.D.H. 1967, Collection (1982.39.11A)

PROVENANCE: The artist; acquired by Thomas H. Ford [printer of *Pacific Railroad Survey Reports*, vol. 12, 1860]; [?]; Mr. and Mrs. Larry Fleishman, Detroit, Michigan; (Kennedy Galleries, New York, New York, by 1966); Paul Mellon, Upperville, Virginia, 1982; present owner, 1982

098

Milk River and Panther Mountain, 1854–1855

Watercolor with graphite underdrawing on paper, 5 5/8 × 11 5/8 in. (14.3 × 29.5 cm)

INSCRIBED LOWER LEFT: J. M. Stanley; INSCRIBED ON MOUNT LOWER LEFT: August 12th 1883; INSCRIBED ON MOUNT LOWER CENTER: Milk River + Panther Mountain

PRESENT COLLECTION: Yale University Art Gallery, New Haven, Connecticut, gift of Paul Mellon, B.A. 1929, L.H.D.H. 1967, Collection (1982.39.12A)

PROVENANCE: The artist; acquired by Thomas H. Ford [printer of *Pacific Railroad Survey Reports*, vol. 12, 1860]; [?]; Mr. and Mrs. Larry Fleishman, Detroit, Michigan; (Kennedy Galleries, New York, New York, by 1966); Paul Mellon, Upperville, Virginia, 1982; present owner, 1982

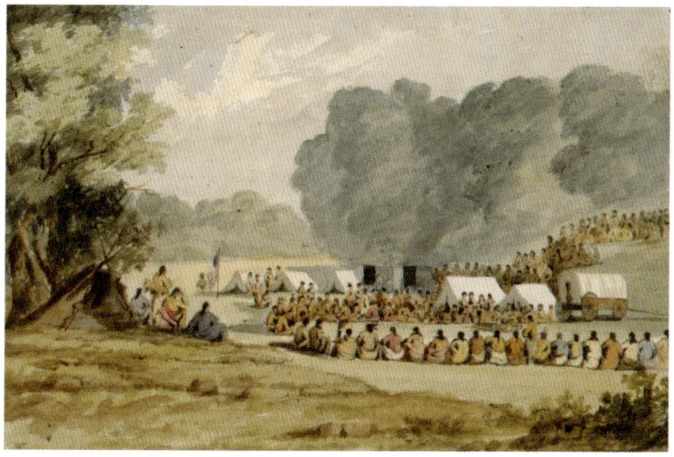

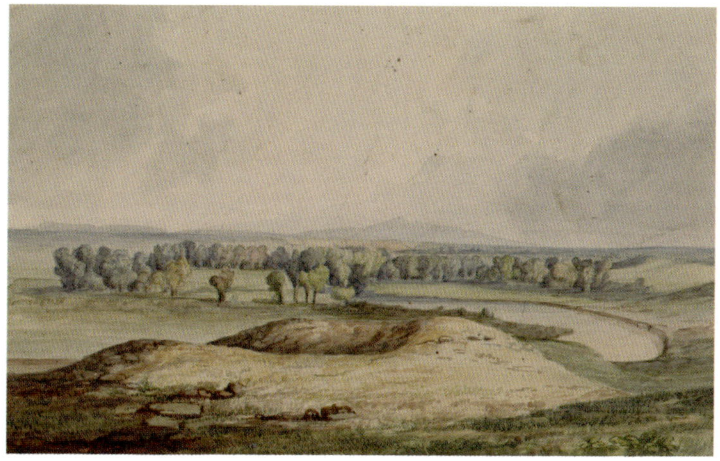

100

099

Distribution of Goods to the Gros Ventres, 1854–1855

Watercolor with graphite underdrawing on paper, $5\frac{7}{8} \times 8\frac{11}{16}$ in. (15 × 22 cm)

INSCRIBED ON MOUNT LOWER LEFT: Stanley; inscribed on mount lower right: Distribution of Goods to the Gros Ventres

PRESENT COLLECTION: Yale University Art Gallery, New Haven, Connecticut, gift of Paul Mellon, B.A. 1929, L.H.D.H. 1967, Collection (1982.39.13A)

PROVENANCE: The artist; acquired by Thomas H. Ford [printer of *Pacific Railroad Survey Reports,* vol. 12, 1860]; [?]; Mr. and Mrs. Larry Fleishman, Detroit Michigan; (Kennedy Galleries, New York, New York, by 1966); Paul Mellon, Upperville, Virginia, 1982; present owner, 1982

100

Milk River, Bear's Paw Mountains in Distance, 1854–1855

Watercolor with graphite underdrawing on paper, $7\frac{3}{16} \times 11\frac{11}{16}$ in. (18.2 × 29.7 cm)

INSCRIBED ON MOUNT LOWER CENTER: Bears Paw Mountain and Valley of Milk River [Valley of Milk River sliced through by edge; lost]; INSCRIBED ON MOUNT LOWER LEFT: August 2900 J. M. Stanley 23

PRESENT COLLECTION: Yale University Art Gallery, New Haven, Connecticut, gift of Paul Mellon, B.A. 1929, L.H.D.H. 1967, Collection (1982.39.14A)

PROVENANCE: The artist; acquired by Thomas H. Ford [printer of *Pacific Railroad Survey Reports,* vol. 12, 1860]; [?]; Mr. and Mrs. Larry Fleishman, Detroit Michigan; (Kennedy Galleries, New York, New York, by 1966); Paul Mellon, Upperville, Virginia, 1982; present owner, 1982

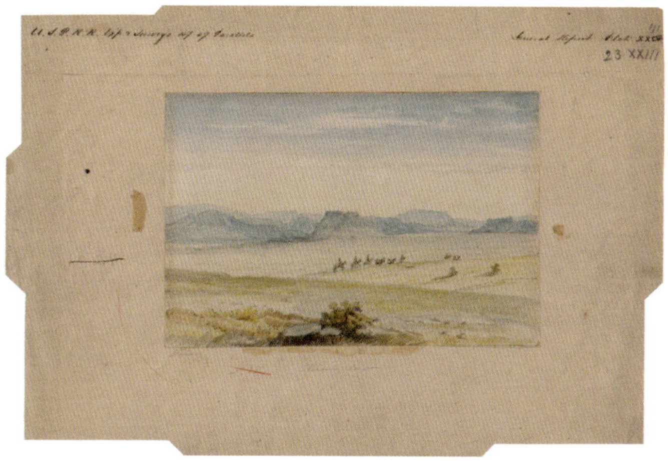

101

Bear's Paw, 1854–1855

Bear's Paw Mountains, Montana, August 30th 1853

Watercolor with graphite underdrawing on paper, $6\frac{1}{2} \times 8\frac{3}{4}$ in. (16.5 × 22.2 cm)

INSCRIBED ON MOUNT LOWER LEFT: Stanley; INSCRIBED ON MOUNT LOWER CENTER: Bears Paw

PRESENT COLLECTION: Beinecke Rare Book and Manuscript Library, Western Americana Collection, Yale University, New Haven, Connecticut (Franz R. and Kathryn M. Stenzel Collection of Western American Art Addition [WA.MSS.S-2601])

PROVENANCE: The artist; acquired by Thomas H. Ford [printer of *Pacific Railroad Survey Reports,* vol. 12, 1860]; [?]; Mr. and Mrs. Lawrence A. Fleischman, Detroit, Michigan; Dr. and Mrs. Franz Stenzel, Portland, Oregon; by bequest of Kathryn M. Stenzel to present owner, 2007

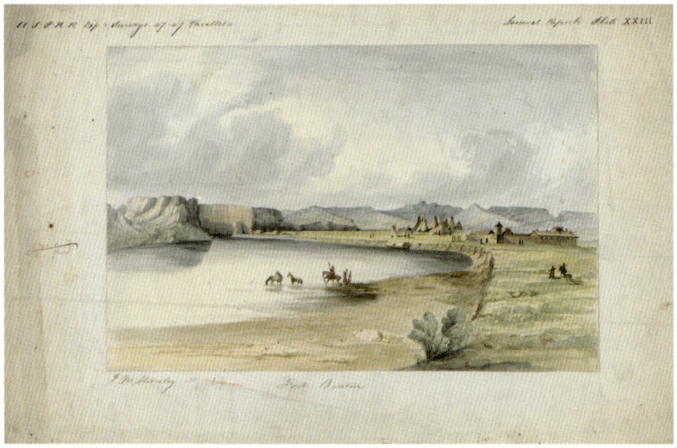

102

Fort Benton, 1854–1855

Watercolor with graphite underdrawing on paper, $7\frac{1}{2} \times 11\frac{1}{4}$ in. (19.1 × 28.6 cm)

INSCRIBED ON MOUNT LOWER LEFT: J. M. Stanley; INSCRIBED ON MOUNT LOWER CENTER: Fort Benton

PRESENT COLLECTION: Yale University Art Gallery, New Haven, Connecticut, gift of Paul Mellon, B.A. 1929, L.H.D.H. 1967, Collection (1982.39.15A)

PROVENANCE: The artist; acquired by Thomas H. Ford [printer of *Pacific Railroad Survey Reports*, vol. 12, 1860]; [?]; Mr. and Mrs. Larry Fleishman, Detroit, Michigan; (Kennedy Galleries, New York, New York, by 1966); Paul Mellon, Upperville, Virginia, 1982; present owner, 1982

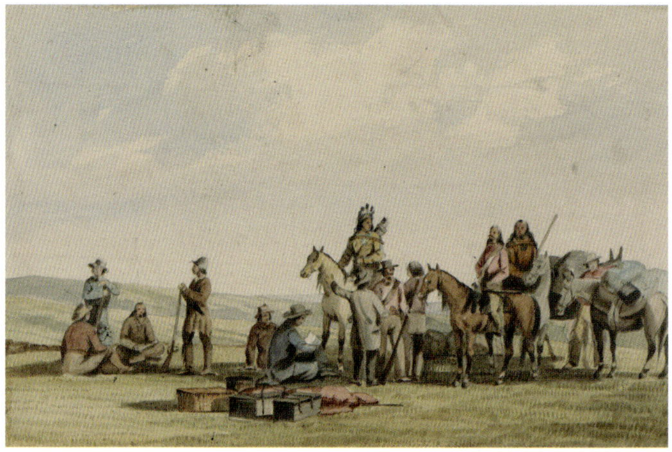

103

Lieutenant Grover's Dispatch—Return of Governor Stevens to Fort Benton, 1854–1855

Watercolor with graphite underdrawing on paper, $6 \times 8\frac{11}{16}$ in. (15 × 22 cm)

INSCRIBED ON MOUNT LOWER LEFT: Stanley

PRESENT COLLECTION: Yale University Art Gallery, New Haven, Connecticut, gift of Paul Mellon, B.A. 1929, L.H.D.H. 1967, Collection (1882.39.16A)

PROVENANCE: The artist; acquired by Thomas H. Ford [printer of *Pacific Railroad Survey Reports*, vol. 12, 1860]; [?]; Mr. and Mrs. Larry Fleishman, Detroit, Michigan; (Kennedy Galleries, New York, New York, by 1966); Paul Mellon, Upperville, Virginia, 1982; present owner, 1982

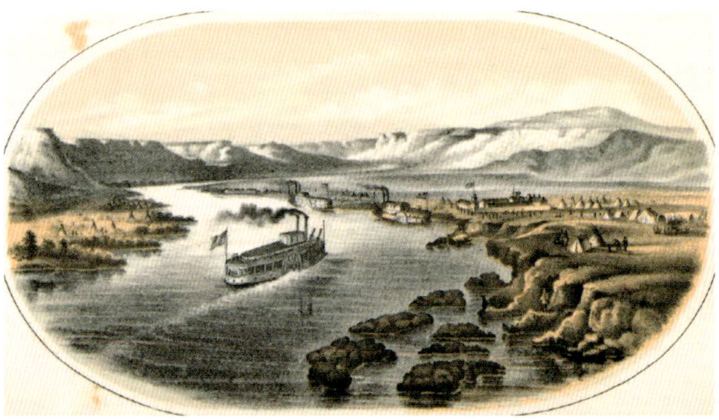

FIG. 102.1.
Gustavus Sohon, *Fort Benton—Head of Steam Navigation on the Missouri River*, 1863. Hand-colored lithograph; 9 × 6 in. (22.5 × 14.5 cm). From Mullan, *Report on the Construction*, between pp. 16 and 17. Courtesy Yellowstone Research Library

104

Marias River, 1854–1855

Watercolor with graphite underdrawing on paper, $6\frac{5}{8} \times 10\frac{9}{16}$ in. (16.9 × 26.9 cm)

INSCRIBED ON MOUNT LOWER LEFT: J. M. Stanley; INSCRIBED LOWER CENTER: Maria's River

PRESENT COLLECTION: Yale University Art Gallery, New Haven, Connecticut, gift of Paul Mellon, B.A. 1929, L.H.D.H. 1967, Collection (1982.39.17A)

PROVENANCE: The artist; acquired by Thomas H. Ford [printer of *Pacific Railroad Survey Reports*, vol. 12, 1860]; [?]; Mr. and Mrs. Larry Fleishman, Detroit, Michigan; (Kennedy Galleries, New York, New York, by 1966); Paul Mellon, Upperville, Virginia, 1982; present owner, 1982

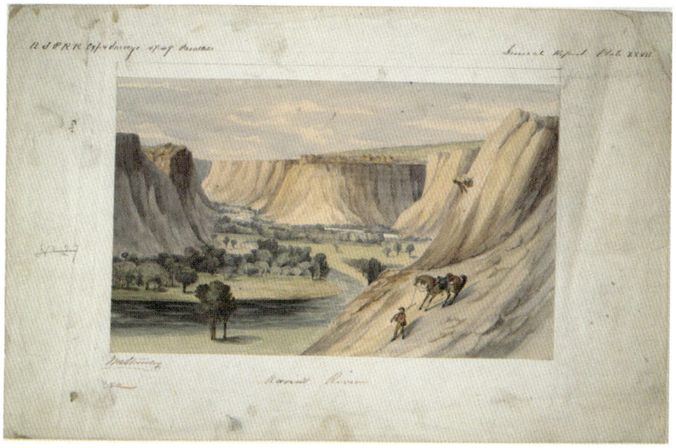

104

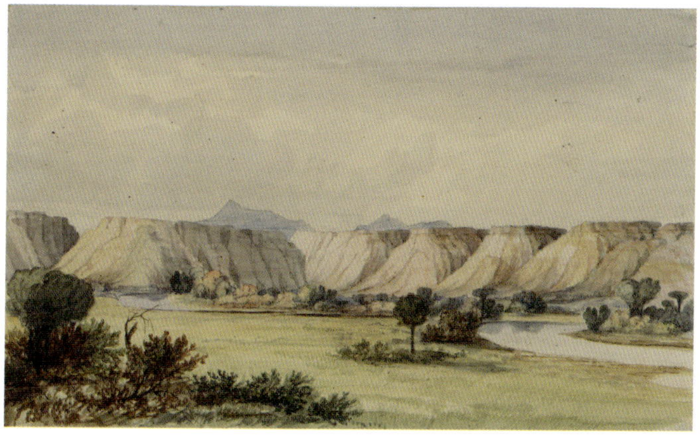

105

Teton Valley, 1854–1855

Watercolor with graphite underdrawing on paper, $6\frac{9}{16} \times 10\frac{9}{16}$ in. (16.7 × 26.9 cm)

INSCRIBED ON MOUNT LOWER LEFT: J. M. Stanley; INSCRIBED LOWER CENTER: Teton Valley

PRESENT COLLECTION: Yale University Art Gallery, New Haven, Connecticut, gift of Paul Mellon, B.A. 1929, L.H.D.H. 1967, Collection (1982.38.18A)

PROVENANCE: The artist; acquired by Thomas H. Ford [printer of *Pacific Railroad Survey Reports*, vol. 12, 1860]; [?]; Mr. and Mrs. Larry Fleishman, Detroit, Michigan; (Kennedy Galleries, New York, New York, by 1966); Paul Mellon, Upperville, Virginia, 1982; present owner, 1982

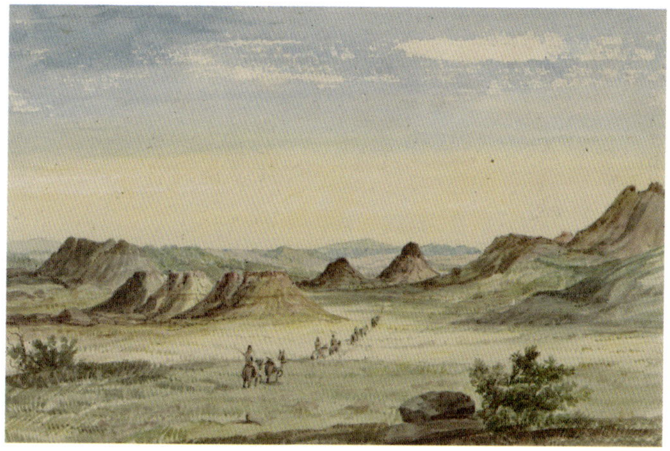

106

Approach to Cadotte's Pass, 1854–1855

Watercolor with graphite underdrawing on paper, $5\frac{7}{8} \times 8\frac{5}{8}$ in. (14.8 × 22.1 cm)

INSCRIBED ON MOUNT LOWER LEFT: Stanley del; INSCRIBED ON MOUNT LOWER CENTER: Approach to Cadotte's Pass / Approach

PRESENT COLLECTION: Yale University Art Gallery, New Haven, Connecticut, gift of Paul Mellon, B.A. 1929, L.H.D.H. 1967, Collection (1982.39.19A)

PROVENANCE: The artist; acquired by Thomas H. Ford [printer of *Pacific Railroad Survey Reports*, vol. 12, 1860]; [?]; Mr. and Mrs. Larry Fleishman, Detroit, Michigan; (Kennedy Galleries, New York, New York, by 1966); Paul Mellon, Upperville, Virginia, 1982; present owner, 1982

107

Victor's Camp—Hell Gate Ronde, 1854–1855

Watercolor with graphite underdrawing on paper, $5\frac{7}{8} \times 8\frac{11}{16}$ in. (14.9 × 22 cm)

INSCRIBED ON MOUNT LOWER LEFT: Stanley; INSCRIBED ON MOUNT LOWER CENTER: Victors Camp—Hell Gate Ronde

PRESENT COLLECTION: Yale University Art Gallery, New Haven, Connecticut, gift of Paul Mellon, B.A. 1929, L.H.D.H. 1967, Collection (1982.39.20A)

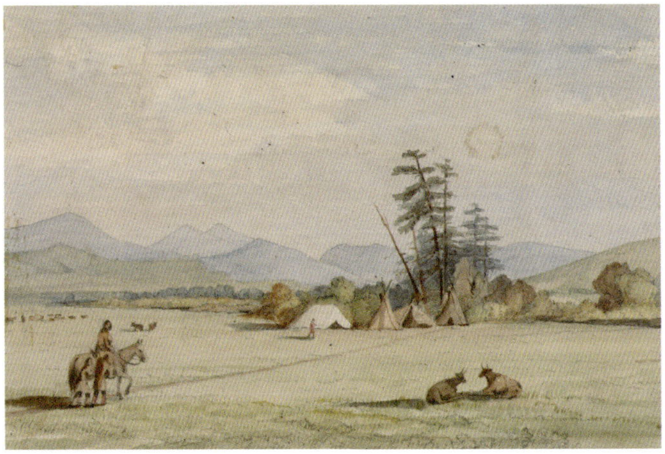

107

PROVENANCE: The artist; acquired by Thomas H. Ford [printer of *Pacific Railroad Survey Reports*, vol. 12, 1860]; [?]; Mr. and Mrs. Larry Fleishman, Detroit, Michigan; (Kennedy Galleries, New York, New York, by 1966); Paul Mellon, Upperville, Virginia, 1982; present owner, 1982

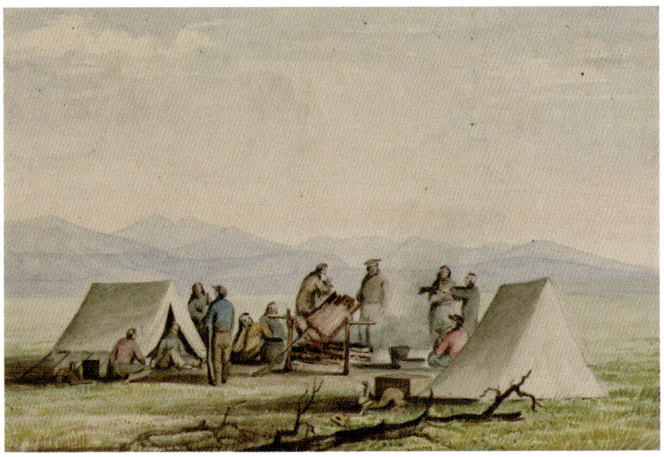

108

Awaiting the Return of Mr. Tinkham, 1854–1855

Watercolor with graphite underdrawing on paper, 5 7/8 × 8 11/16 in. (14.9 × 22 cm)

INSCRIBED ON MOUNT LOWER LEFT: Stanley; INSCRIBED ON MOUNT LOWER CENTER: Awaiting the Return of Mr. Tinkham

PRESENT COLLECTION: Yale University Art Gallery, New Haven, Connecticut, gift of Paul Mellon, B.A. 1929, L.H.D.H. 1967, Collection (1982.39.21A)

PROVENANCE: The artist; acquired by Thomas H. Ford [printer of *Pacific Railroad Survey Reports*, vol. 12, 1860]; [?]; Mr. and Mrs. Larry Fleishman, Detroit, Michigan; (Kennedy Galleries, New York, New York, by 1966); Paul Mellon, Upperville, Virginia, 1982; present owner, 1982

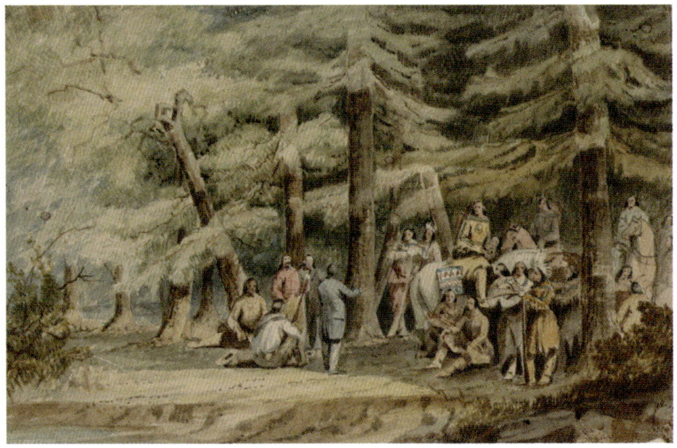

109

Nez Perces Indians, 1854–1855

Nez Perces

Watercolor with graphite underdrawing on paper, 5 7/8 × 8 5/8 in. (14.9 × 21.9 cm)

PRESENT COLLECTION: Yale University Art Gallery, New Haven, Connecticut, gift of Paul Mellon, B.A. 1929, L.H.D.H. 1967, Collection (1982.39.22A)

PROVENANCE: The artist; acquired by Thomas H. Ford [printer of *Pacific Railroad Survey Reports*, vol. 12, 1860]; [?]; Mr. and Mrs. Larry Fleishman, Detroit, Michigan; (Kennedy Galleries, New York, New York, by 1966); Paul Mellon, Upperville, Virginia, 1982; present owner, 1982

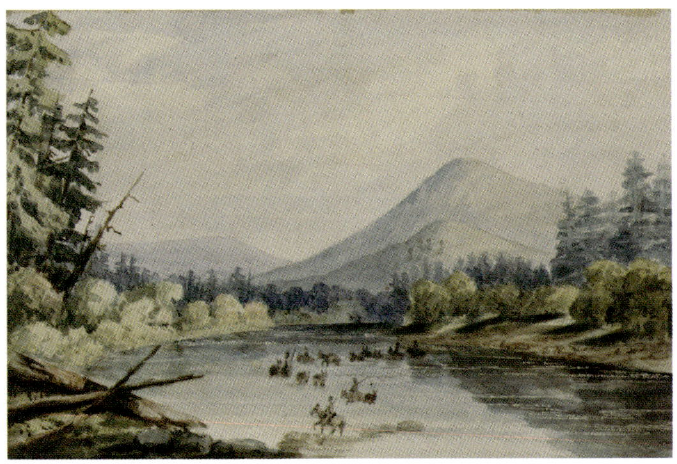

110

Crossing the Bitter Root, 1854–1855

Watercolor with graphite underdrawing on paper, 5 7/8 × 8 11/16 in. (14.9 × 22 cm)

INSCRIBED ON MOUNT LOWER LEFT: Stanley; INSCRIBED ON MOUNT LOWER CENTER: Crossing of the Bitter Root

PRESENT COLLECTION: Yale University Art Gallery, New Haven, Connecticut, gift of Paul Mellon, B.A. 1929, L.H.D.H. 1967, Collection (1982.39.23A)

PROVENANCE: The artist; acquired by Thomas H. Ford [printer of *Pacific Railroad Survey Reports*, vol. 12, 1860]; [?]; Mr. and Mrs. Larry Fleishman, Detroit, Michigan; (Kennedy Galleries, New York, New York, by 1966); Paul Mellon, Upperville, Virginia, 1982; present owner, 1982

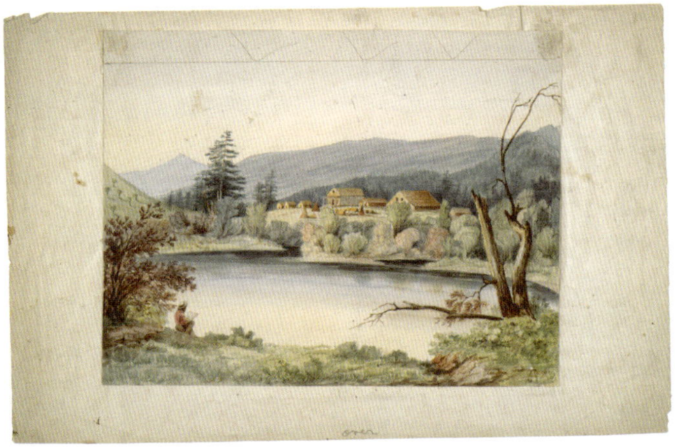

111

Coeur D'Alene Mission, St. Ignatius River, 1854–1855

Watercolor with graphite underdrawing on paper, $8\frac{5}{8} \times 10\frac{15}{16}$ in. (21.9 × 27.8 cm)

INSCRIBED ON MOUNT LOWER LEFT: J. M. Stanley; INSCRIBED ON MOUNT LOWER CENTER: Coeur D'Alene Mission / St. Ignatius River

PRESENT COLLECTION: Yale University Art Gallery, New Haven, Connecticut, gift of Paul Mellon, B.A. 1929, L.H.D.H. 1967, Collection (1982.39.24A)

PROVENANCE: The artist; acquired by Thomas H. Ford [printer of *Pacific Railroad Survey Reports*, vol. 12, 1860]; [?]; Mr. and Mrs. Larry Fleishman, Detroit, Michigan; (Kennedy Galleries, New York, New York, by 1966); Paul Mellon, Upperville, Virginia, 1982; present owner, 1982

112

Fort Okinakane, 1854–1855

Watercolor with graphite underdrawing on paper, $5\frac{13}{16} \times 8\frac{5}{8}$ in. (14.8 × 21.9 cm)

INSCRIBED ON MOUNT LOWER LEFT: Stanley / Fort Okinakane

PRESENT COLLECTION: Yale University Art Gallery, New Haven, Connecticut, gift of Paul Mellon, B.A. 1929, L.H.D.H. 1967, Collection (1982.39.25A)

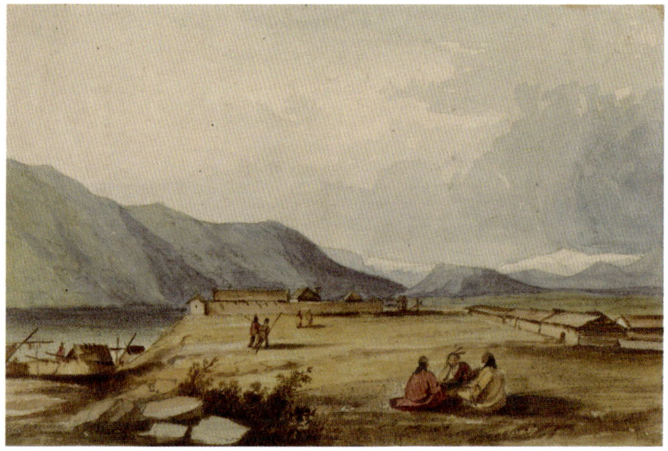

112

PROVENANCE: The artist; acquired by Thomas H. Ford [printer of *Pacific Railroad Survey Reports*, vol. 12, 1860]; [?]; Mr. and Mrs. Larry Fleishman, Detroit, Michigan; (Kennedy Galleries, New York, New York, by 1966); Paul Mellon, Upperville, Virginia, 1982; present owner, 1982

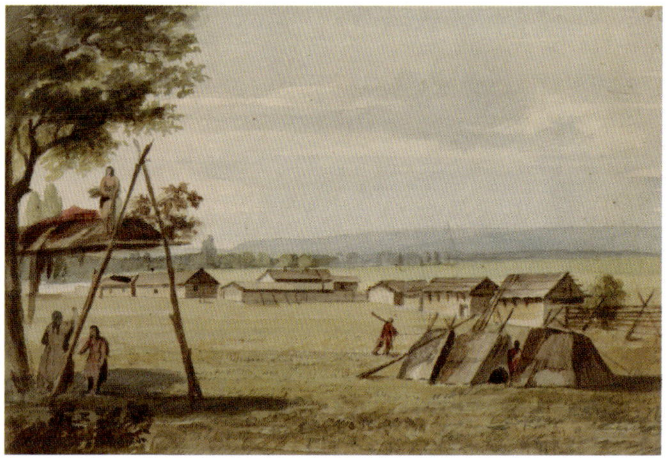

113

Tshimikaine Mission, 1854–1855

Chemakane Mission

Watercolor with graphite underdrawing, $5\frac{13}{16} \times 8\frac{9}{16}$ in. (14.8 × 21.8 cm)

INSCRIBED ON MOUNT LOWER LEFT: Stanley; INSCRIBED ON MOUNT LOWER CENTER: Tshimikaine Mission / ~~Chenikikame~~

PRESENT COLLECTION: Yale University Art Gallery, New Haven, Connecticut, gift of Paul Mellon, B.A. 1929, L.H.D.H. 1967, Collection (1982.39.26A)

PROVENANCE: The artist; acquired by Thomas H. Ford [printer of *Pacific Railroad Survey Reports*, vol. 12, 1860]; [?]; Mr. and Mrs. Larry Fleishman, Detroit, Michigan; (Kennedy Galleries, New York, New York, by 1966); Paul Mellon, Upperville, Virginia, 1982; present owner, 1982

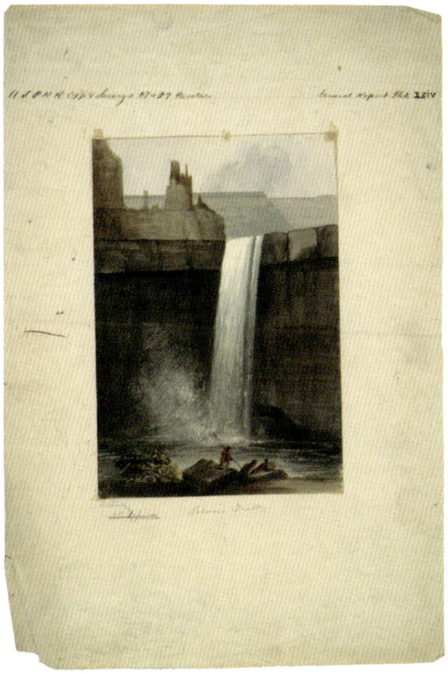

114

Pelous Falls, 1854–1855

Watercolor with graphite underdrawing on paper, 8 9/16 × 5 13/16 in. (21.9 × 14.5 cm)

INSCRIBED ON MOUNT LOWER LEFT: Stanley; INSCRIBED ON MOUNT LOWER CENTER: Pelous Falls

PRESENT COLLECTION: Yale University Art Gallery, New Haven, Connecticut, gift of Paul Mellon, B.A. 1929, L.H.D.H. 1967, Collection (1982.39.27A)

PROVENANCE: The artist; acquired by Thomas H. Ford [printer of *Pacific Railroad Survey Reports*, vol. 12, 1860]; [?]; Mr. and Mrs. Larry Fleishman, Detroit, Michigan; (Kennedy Galleries, New York, New York, by 1966); Paul Mellon, Upperville, Virginia, 1982; present owner, 1982

115

Dalles of the Columbia [River] Looking Westward, 1854–1855

Watercolor with graphite underdrawing on paper, 5 13/16 × 8 5/8 in. (14.7 × 21.9 cm)

INSCRIBED ON MOUNT LOWER LEFT: Stanley

PRESENT COLLECTION: Yale University Art Gallery, New Haven, Connecticut, gift of Paul Mellon, B.A. 1929, L.H.D.H. 1967, Collection (1982.39.28A)

PROVENANCE: The artist; acquired by Thomas H. Ford [printer of *Pacific Railroad Survey Reports*, vol. 12, 1860]; [?]; Mr. and Mrs.

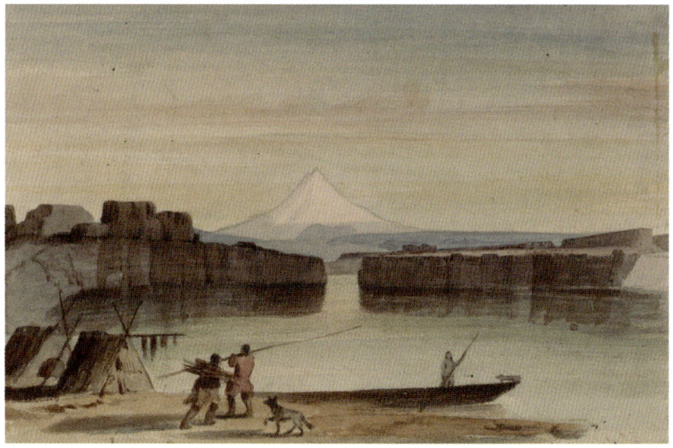

115

Larry Fleishman, Detroit, Michigan; (Kennedy Galleries, New York, New York, by 1966); Paul Mellon, Upperville, Virginia, 1982; present owner, 1982

116

Cascades of the Columbia River, 1854–1855

Watercolor with graphite underdrawing on paper, 6 1/8 × 10 3/4 in. (15.6 × 27.3 cm)

INSCRIBED LOWER LEFT: Stanley; INSCRIBED ON MOUNT LOWER CENTER: Cascades of the Columbia River

PRESENT COLLECTION: Yale University Art Gallery, New Haven, Connecticut, gift of Paul Mellon, B.A. 1929, L.H.D.H. 1967, Collection (1982.39.29A)

PROVENANCE: The artist; acquired by Thomas H. Ford [printer of *Pacific Railroad Survey Reports*, vol. 12, 1860]; [?]; Mr. and Mrs. Larry Fleishman, Detroit, Michigan; (Kennedy Galleries, New York, New York, by 1966); Paul Mellon, Upperville, Virginia, 1982; present owner, 1982

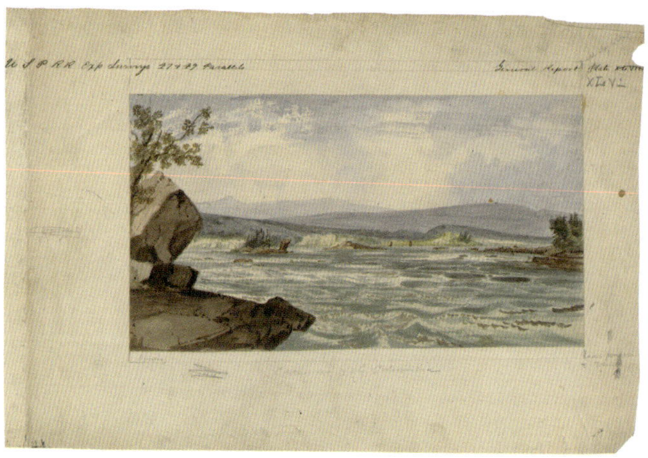

116

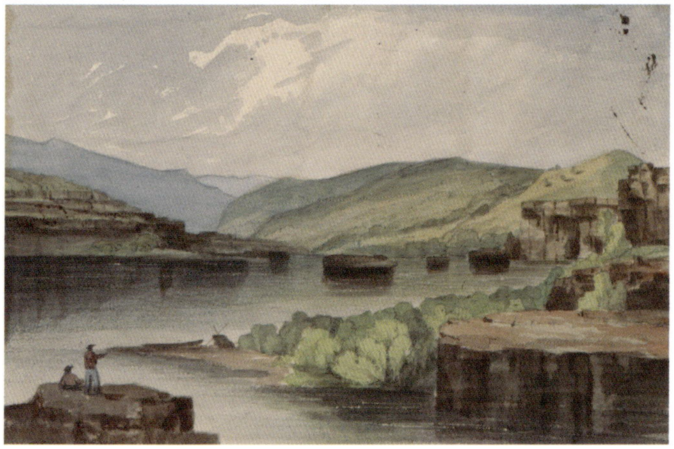

117

Cape Horn—Columbia River, 1854–1855

Watercolor with graphite underdrawing on paper, $5\frac{13}{16} \times 8\frac{11}{16}$ in. (14.8 × 21.9 cm)

INSCRIBED LOWER LEFT: Stanley; INSCRIBED ON MOUNT LOWER CENTER: Cape Horn—Columbia River

PRESENT COLLECTION: Yale University Art Gallery, New Haven, Connecticut, gift of Paul Mellon, B.A. 1929, L.H.D.H. 1967, Collection (1982.39.30A)

PROVENANCE: The artist; acquired by Thomas H. Ford [printer of *Pacific Railroad Survey Reports*, vol. 12, 1860]; [?]; Mr. and Mrs. Larry Fleishman, Detroit, Michigan; (Kennedy Galleries, New York, New York, by 1966); Paul Mellon, Upperville, Virginia, 1982; present owner, 1982

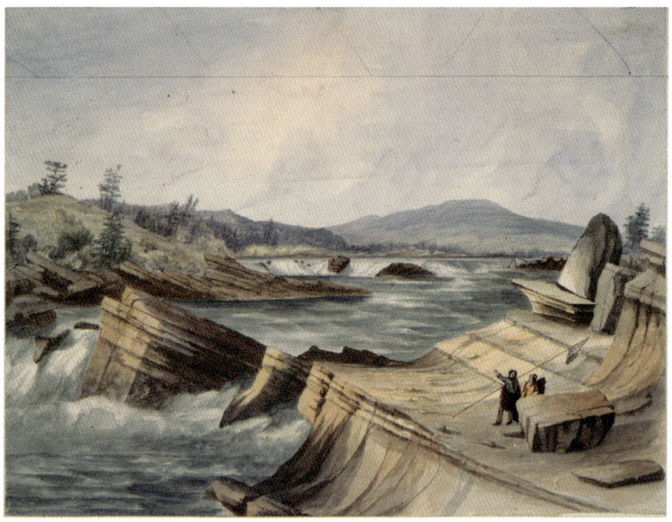

118

118

Kettle Falls, Columbia River, 1854–1855

Watercolor with graphite underdrawing on paper, $8\frac{9}{16} \times 11$ in. (21.7 × 28 cm)

INSCRIBED ON MOUNT LOWER LEFT: J. M. Stanley; INSCRIBED ON MOUNT LOWER CENTER: Kettle Falls Columbia River

PRESENT COLLECTION: Yale University Art Gallery, New Haven, Connecticut, gift of Paul Mellon, B.A. 1929, L.H.D.H. 1967, Collection (1982.39.31A)

PROVENANCE: The artist; acquired by Thomas H. Ford [printer of *Pacific Railroad Survey Reports*, vol. 12, 1860]; [?]; Mr. and Mrs. Larry Fleishman, Detroit, Michigan; (Kennedy Galleries, New York, New York, by 1966); Paul Mellon, Upperville, Virginia, 1982; present owner, 1982

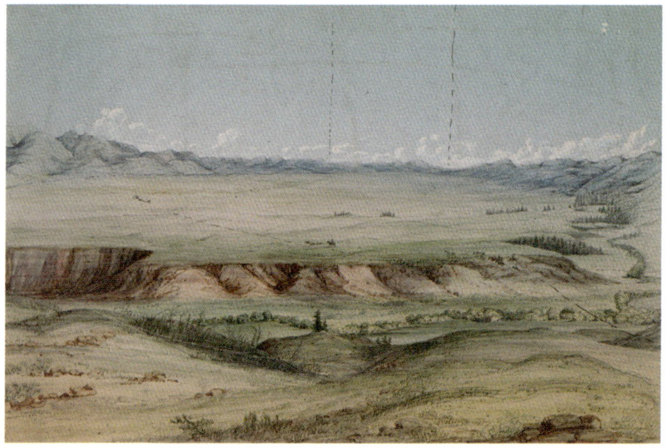

119

Big Hole Prairie from the North, 1854–1855

Watercolor with graphite underdrawing and ink on two-color scratchboard, $10\frac{1}{2} \times 15\frac{7}{8}$ in. (21.2 × 31.8 cm)

INSCRIBED ON MOUNT LOWER LEFT: J. M. Stanley; INSCRIBED ON MOUNT LOWER CENTER: Big Hole Prairie from the North

PRESENT COLLECTION: Yale University Art Gallery, New Haven, Connecticut, gift of Paul Mellon, B.A. 1929, L.H.D.H. 1967, Collection (1982.39.32A)

PROVENANCE: The artist; acquired by Thomas H. Ford [printer of *Pacific Railroad Survey Reports*, vol. 12, 1860]; [?]; Mr. and Mrs. Larry Fleishman, Detroit, Michigan; (Kennedy Galleries, New York, New York, by 1966); Paul Mellon, Upperville, Virginia, 1982; present owner, 1982

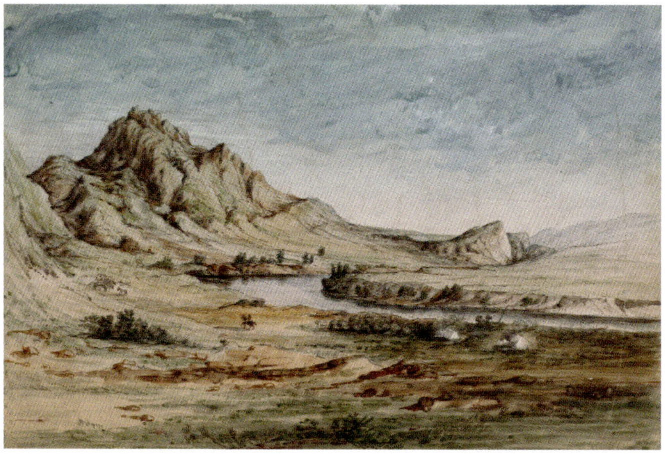

120

Bear's Teeth Missouri River Gate of the Mountains, 1854–1855

Watercolor with graphite underdrawing on paper heightened with white on coated colored paper, 8⅜ × 12¼ in. (21.3 × 31.1 cm)

INSCRIBED LOWER CENTER: Camp at the Bear's Teeth on the Missouri River

PRESENT COLLECTION: Yale University Art Gallery, New Haven, Connecticut, gift of Paul Mellon, B.A. 1929, L.H.D.H. 1967, Collection (1982.39.33A)

PROVENANCE: The artist; acquired by Thomas H. Ford [printer of *Pacific Railroad Survey Reports*, vol. 12, 1860]; [?]; Mr. and Mrs. Larry Fleishman, Detroit, Michigan; (Kennedy Galleries, New York, New York, by 1966); Paul Mellon, Upperville, Virginia, 1982; present owner, 1982

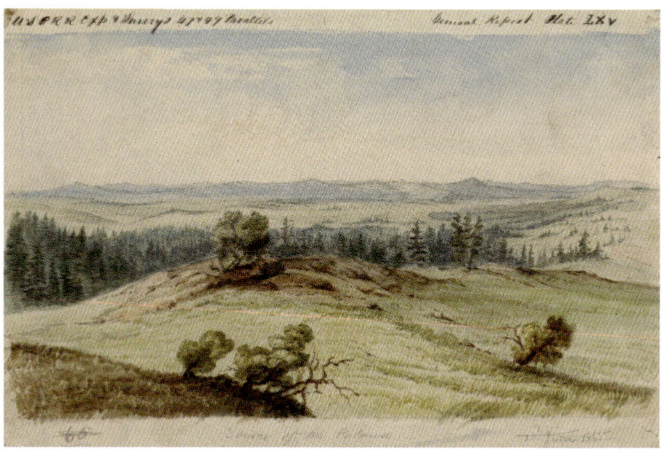

121

Source of the Peluse, 1854–1855

Watercolor with graphite underdrawing on paper, 6⅞ × 8⅞ in. (17.5 × 26.2 cm)

INSCRIBED ON MOUNT LOWER CENTER: Source of the Palouse; INSCRIBED LOWER LEFT: 21 June 1855

PRESENT COLLECTION: Yale University Art Gallery, New Haven, Connecticut, gift of Paul Mellon, B.A. 1929, L.H.D.H. 1967, Collection (1982.39.35A)

PROVENANCE: The artist; acquired by Thomas H. Ford [printer of *Pacific Railroad Survey Reports*, vol. 12, 1860]; [?]; Mr. and Mrs. Larry Fleishman, Detroit, Michigan; (Kennedy Galleries, New York, New York, by 1966); Paul Mellon, Upperville, Virginia, 1982; present owner, 1982

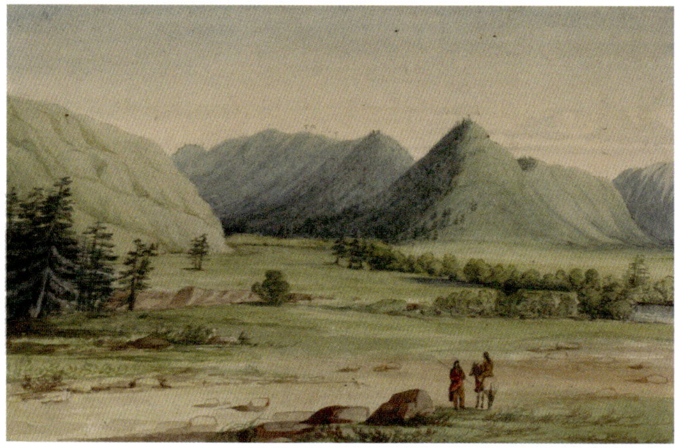

122

Hell Gate—Entrance to Cadotts Pass from the West, 1854–1855

Watercolor with graphite underdrawing on paper, 6¾ × 9¾ in. (17.2 × 24.7 cm)

INSCRIBED ON MOUNT LOWER LEFT: J. M. Stanley from sketch by T. Adams; INSCRIBED ON MOUNT LOWER CENTER: Hell Gate—Entrance to Cadotts [*sic*] Pass from the West; inscribed on mount lower left corner: The name of "hellgate" is given to this particular [?] of the Mts from the fact that it is the gap of the Mts through with the predatory bands of Indians drive the immense bands of horses that they steal from the friendly bands of Indians West of the Rocky range. J. M.

PRESENT COLLECTION: Yale University Art Gallery, New Haven, Connecticut, gift of Paul Mellon, B.A. 1929, L.H.D.H. 1967, Collection (1982.39.36A)

PROVENANCE: The artist; acquired by Thomas H. Ford [printer of *Pacific Railroad Survey Reports*, vol. 12, 1860]; [?]; Mr. and Mrs. Larry Fleishman, Detroit, Michigan; (Kennedy Galleries, New York, New York, by 1966); Paul Mellon, Upperville, Virginia, 1982; present owner, 1982

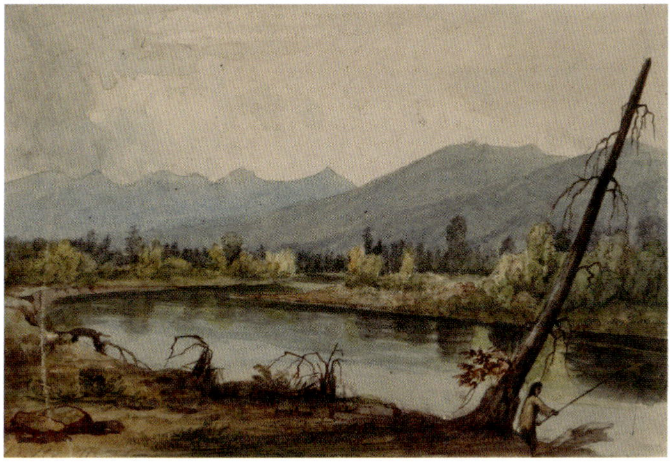

123

Bitterroot River near Fort Owen (St. Mary's Valley), 1854–1855

Watercolor with graphite underdrawing on paper, 6⅝ × 9½ in. (16.9 × 24.2 cm)

INSCRIBED LOWER LEFT: Bitter Root; INSCRIBED ON MOUNT LOWER LEFT: J. M. Stanley 30-A; INSCRIBED ON MOUNT LOWER CENTER: Bitterroot River near Fort Owen, St. Mary's [*sic*] Valley

PRESENT COLLECTION: Yale University Art Gallery, New Haven, Connecticut, gift of Paul Mellon, B.A. 1929, L.H.D.H. 1967, Collection (1982.39.37A)

PROVENANCE: The artist; acquired by Thomas H. Ford [printer of *Pacific Railroad Survey Reports*, vol. 12, 1860]; [?]; Mr. and Mrs. Larry Fleishman, Detroit, Michigan; (Kennedy Galleries, New York, New York, by 1966); Paul Mellon, Upperville, Virginia, 1982; present owner, 1982

124

Columbia River Mouth of Des Shutes, 1854–1855 *(Junction of Des Chutes)*

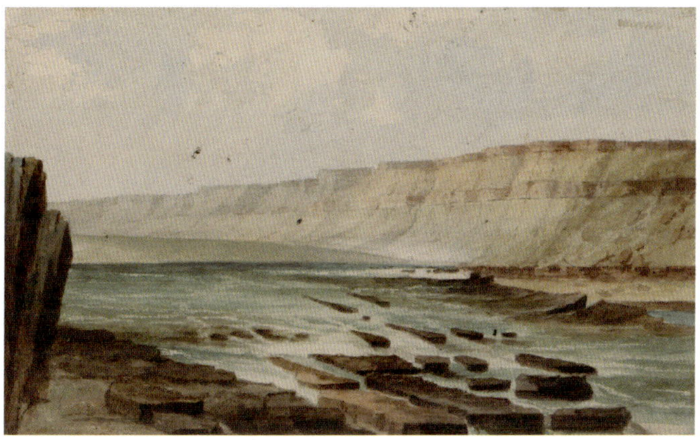

124

Watercolor with graphite underdrawing on paper, 5½ × 8¾ in. (14.0 × 22.1 cm)

INSCRIBED ON MOUNT LOWER LEFT: Stanley; INSCRIBED ON MOUNT LOWER CENTER: No 44—Columbia River Mouth of Des Shutes

PRESENT COLLECTION: Yale University Art Gallery, New Haven, Connecticut, gift of Paul Mellon, B.A. 1929, L.H.D.H. 1967, Collection (1982.39.38A)

PROVENANCE: The artist; acquired by Thomas H. Ford [printer of *Pacific Railroad Survey Reports*, vol. 12, 1860]; [?]; Mr. and Mrs. Larry Fleishman, Detroit, Michigan; (Kennedy Galleries, New York, New York, by 1966); Paul Mellon, Upperville, Virginia, 1982; present owner, 1982

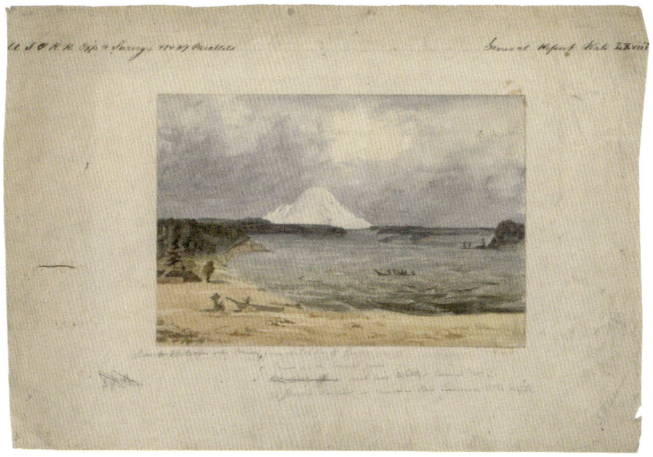

125

Puget Sound and Mt. Rainier from Whitby's Island, 1854–1855

Watercolor with graphite underdrawing on paper, 5¹³⁄₁₆ × 8¹¹⁄₁₆ in. (15.1 × 22.1 cm)

INSCRIBED ON MOUNT LOWER LEFT: From Dr. J. G. Cooper—by Stanley from sketch by Dr. Cooper View of the Sound from / Col. Abeys place west side Whitby's [*sic*] Island W. T. / Mount Rainier in New—Port Townsend to the right

PRESENT COLLECTION: Yale University Art Gallery, New Haven, Connecticut, gift of Paul Mellon, B.A. 1929, L.H.D.H. 1967, Collection (1982.39.39A)

PROVENANCE: The artist; acquired by Thomas H. Ford [printer of *Pacific Railroad Survey Reports*, vol. 12, 1860]; [?]; Mr. and Mrs. Larry Fleishman, Detroit, Michigan; (Kennedy Galleries, New York, New York, by 1966); Paul Mellon, Upperville, Virginia, 1982; present owner, 1982

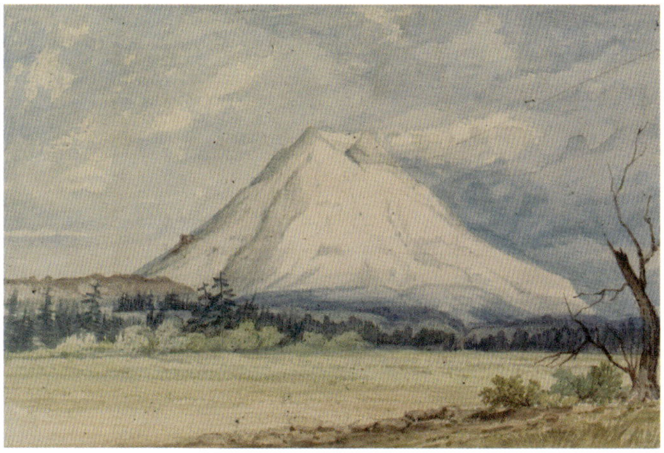

126

Mount Rainier Viewed from near Steilacoom, 1854–1855

Watercolor with graphite underdrawing on paper, $5\frac{7}{8} \times 8\frac{11}{16}$ in. (14.8 × 22.1 cm)

INSCRIBED ON MOUNT LOWER LEFT: Dr. J. G. Cooper—by Stanley from a sketch by Dr. Cooper; INSCRIBED ON MOUNT LOWER CENTER: Mount Rainier W. T. from near Steilacoom 15 miles distant

PRESENT COLLECTION: Yale University Art Gallery, New Haven, Connecticut, gift of Paul Mellon, B.A. 1929, L.H.D.H. 1967, Collection (1982.39.40A)

PROVENANCE: The artist; acquired by Thomas H. Ford [printer of *Pacific Railroad Survey Reports*, vol. 12, 1860]; [?]; Mr. and Mrs. Larry Fleishman, Detroit, Michigan; (Kennedy Galleries, New York, New York, by 1966); Paul Mellon, Upperville, Virginia, 1982; present owner, 1982

127

Mt. Baker and Cascade Range, from Whitby's Island, 1854–1855

Watercolor with graphite underdrawing on paper, $5\frac{7}{8} \times 8\frac{11}{16}$ in. (14.9 × 22.0 cm)

INSCRIBED ON MOUNT LOWER LEFT: from Dr. Cooper—Stanley from Sketch by Dr. Cooper; INSCRIBED ON MOUNT LOWER CENTER: No 70; INSCRIBED AT BOTTOM: Mount Baker and Cascade Range from / head of Penn's Cove Whitby's [*sic*] Island Near / Straights of de Fuca

PRESENT COLLECTION: Yale University Art Gallery, New Haven, Connecticut, gift of Paul Mellon, B.A. 1929, L.H.D.H. 1967, Collection (1982.39.41A)

PROVENANCE: The artist; acquired by Thomas H. Ford [printer of *Pacific Railroad Survey Reports*, vol. 12, 1860]; [?]; Mr. and Mrs.

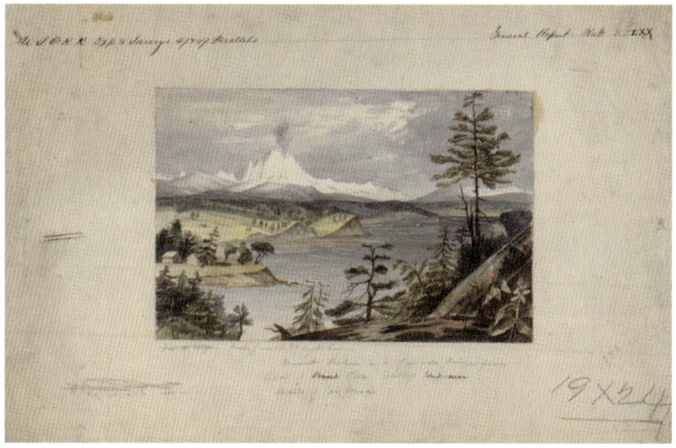

127

Larry Fleishman, Detroit, Michigan; (Kennedy Galleries, New York, New York, by 1966); Paul Mellon, Upperville, Virginia, 1982; present owner, 1982

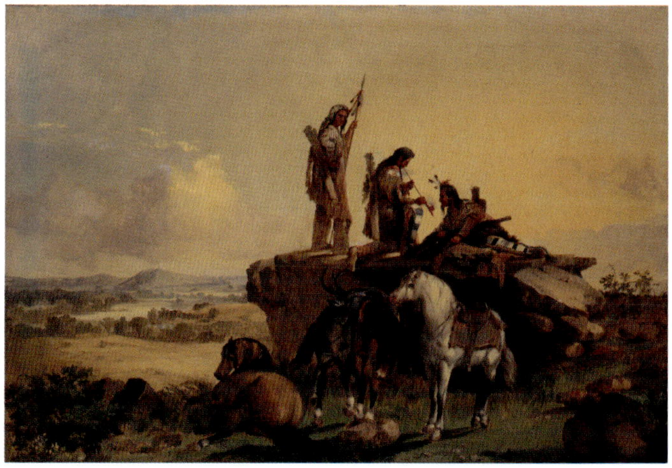

128

Halting to Smoke, 1855

Return of the Hunting Party

Oil on canvas, $28\frac{1}{8} \times 40$ in. (71.4 × 101.6 cm)

INSCRIBED LOWER RIGHT: Stanley / 1855

PRESENT COLLECTION: Nelda C. and H. J. Lutcher Stark Foundation, Stark Museum of Art, Orange, Texas (31.23.18)

PROVENANCE: Sandra Doane Turn, St. Petersburg, Florida; (Kennedy Galleries, New York, New York); (Browns Art Consultants, Omaha, Nebraska); H. J. Lutcher Stark, Orange, Texas, 1965; present owner

LIFETIME EXHIBITIONS: Second Annual Exhibition of the Metropolitan Mechanics Institute, Washington, D.C., 1855; J. M. Stanley's Studio, 159 Jefferson Avenue, Detroit, Michigan, 1867; Messrs. Galt and Brother Jewelry Store, Washington, D.C., March 16, 1855

In spring 1855, Stanley received laudatory notice for two of his recently completed paintings. One was a large painting hung in the shop of Messrs. Galt and Brother in Washington, D.C. Titled *Seeking a Home* (cat. no. 129), it was described as a "prairie scene" with a "group of Indians and their horses in the foreground."[1] The other painting, titled *Halting to Smoke*, had just been exhibited in the city with considerable commendation at the Metropolitan Mechanics Institute that winter. It had been awarded a first class medal as "a fine picture, with much to admire in its composition, and very fine drawing."[2]

This painting, which has borne the title of *Return of the Hunting Party* over recent years, is thought to be *Halting to Smoke*. Such a formal, pyramidal composition had taken form in Stanley's oeuvre only since his return in 1854 from travels among the Blackfeet on the upper Missouri River. His nascent effort with this motif had been painted that year, *Blackfoot Indians* (cat. no. 081), a small, less definitive work, which shared only theme and design with his 1855 version. The idea of positioning a group of Indian men above the horizon line on a rock outcrop pedestal, their horses resting below, and action reduced to idling their time over puffs of tobacco, caught on with Stanley's patrons. Over the next decade, he developed this arrangement with great success.

1. "Prairie Landscapes," *National Intelligencer*, March 16, 1855.

2. *A Record of the Second Exhibition of the Metropolitan Mechanics Institute* (Washington, D.C.: Henry Polkinhorn, 1855), 144.

129

Seeking a Home, 1855

Pawnees Looking Out for Enemies

Oil on canvas, 39¼ × 63 in. (99.1 × 160.0 cm)

INSCRIBED LOWER LEFT: Stanley

PRESENT COLLECTION: R. W. Norton Art Gallery, Shreveport, Louisiana

PROVENANCE: Senator Thomas J. Rusk, Washington, D.C.; by descent to Mary Cleveland and W. W. Barret; William M. Barret, Shreveport, Louisiana; Lola Belle H. Barret, Shreveport, Louisiana; by gift to present owner

LIFETIME EXHIBITIONS: Messrs. Galt and Brother Jewelry Store, Washington, D.C., 1855

"We have lately contemplated with much pleasure two very beautiful paintings from the easel of our talented townsman, J. M. Stanley," wrote a reporter for Washington's *National Intelligencer* on March 16, 1855. He had seen one of the paintings in the Galt and

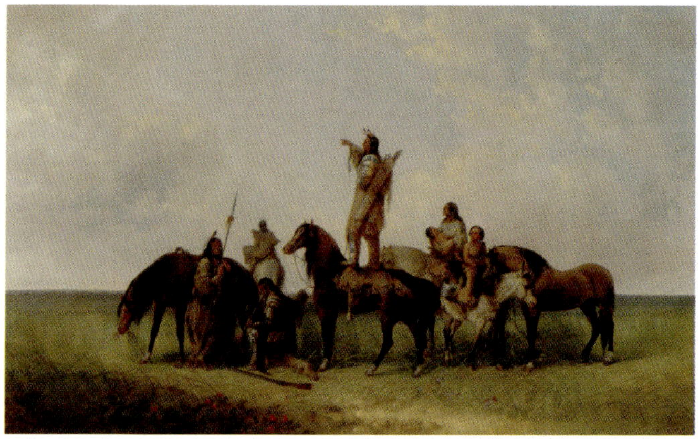

129

Brother gallery. It was titled *Seeking a Home*, and it was described as both "effective and pleasing." The reporter observed an "exquisiteness in the representation of the horses" that he had "seldom seen before." But it was the "grouping of men, women, children and animals" in the large picture that rendered it "remarkably natural, easy and true," and as representative of "the gentleness of the scenes he usually selects," it proved to be the antithesis of the ignoble Indian he presented in his abduction narratives, like *Kidnapped* (cat. no. 139) of that same year.[1]

By 1858, a few years after this work was painted and sold to Senator Thomas J. Rusk, Stanley began to feel he might be losing his grip on success. The U.S. art establishment seemed to be looking beyond him as America's premier artist of Indian subjects. *The Crayon* had recently proclaimed, instead of him, the Baltimore painter Alfred Jacob Miller as the most distinguished of the nation's Indian painters.[2] Stanley tried for a third time that year to interest Congress and the Smithsonian in purchasing his Indian Gallery. When these efforts were rebuffed, he vainly sought the attention, through the agency of John Bartlett, of the British Museum. This painting, with the more romanticized title of *Pawnees Looking Out for Enemies*, was published in April 1858 in the *Illustrated London News*. As part of a push for some serious notice abroad, however, it proved no more successful than his domestic efforts.[3]

Stanley is thought to have seen few if any Pawnees on his western treks. The figures in this painting are dressed, in fact, as Blackfeet. In any event, it closely resembles in composition a painting by genre and Indian painter Charles Deas, *Indian Group*, 1845 (fig. 129.1), which was owned by Philip Kearny, the nephew of Stanley's friend Stephen Watts Kearny.[4]

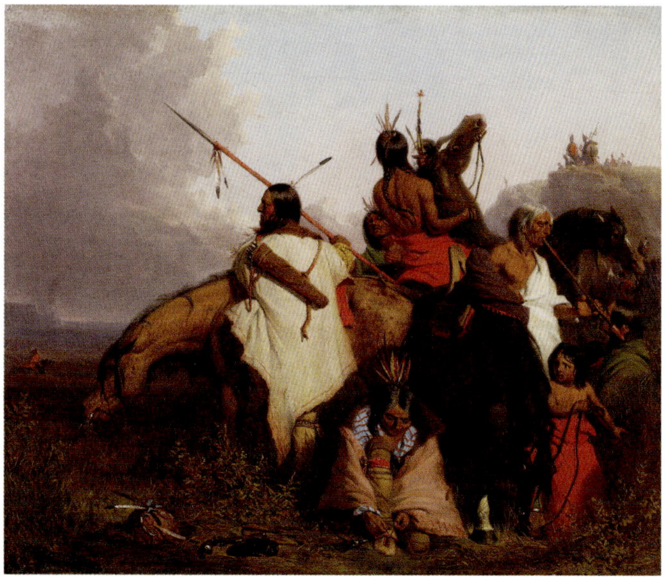

FIG. 129.1.
Charles Deas, *Indian Group*, 1845.
Oil on canvas; 14⅛ × 16½ in.
(35.9 × 41.9 cm). Courtesy Amon Carter Museum of American Art, Fort Worth, Texas (1980.42)

1. "Prairie Landscapes," *National Intelligencer*, March 16, 1855.

2. *The Crayon* 4 (June 1857): 187.

3. See Dippie, *Catlin and His Contemporaries*, 311.

4. See Carol Clark et al., *Charles Deas and 1840s America* (Norman: University of Oklahoma Press, 2009), 196.

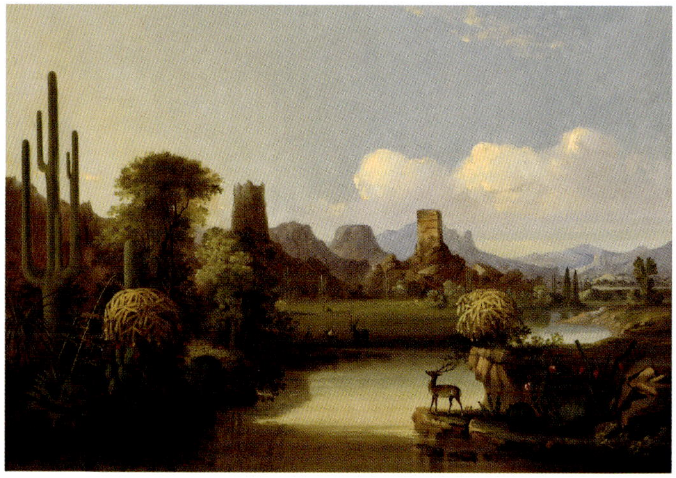

130

130

Chain of Spires along the Gila, 1855

View on the Gila; Scene on the Gila

Oil on canvas, 30¾ × 42⅜ in. (78.7 × 106.7 cm)

INSCRIBED LOWER RIGHT: STANLEY / 1855

PRESENT COLLECTION: Phoenix Art Museum, Arizona, museum purchase, 1968 (68.20)

PROVENANCE: Private collection, Boston, Massachusetts; (Harry Shaw Newman, The Old Print Shop, New York, New York); Kenneth M. Newman, New York, New York; (Caroline Smurthwaite, Phoenix, Arizona); present owner

On November 8, 1846, a bit over halfway along on their desert march from Santa Fe to do battle with the Mexican Army in southern California, General Stephen Watts Kearny's small force passed a particularly beautiful section of the Gila River. Stanley recorded the scene for Emory's report of the expedition and gave it the title of *Chain of Natural Spires along the Gila* (fig. 130.1).[1] That small illustration for the official report of the expedition became the genesis of this, one of Stanley's most renowned western landscapes. It transfigures the paradigm of the "great American desert" into a southwestern "garden of Eden," with its golden light and tranquil water, a revolutionary model for the times.[2]

The first large studio version of this oil, titled simply *View on the Gila River*, was painted in 1850 and found a prime place in Stanley's Indian Gallery and subsequent *Portraits of North American Indians* exhibitions.[3] It was a sensation among the press for its remarkable paint handling and its thematic novelty. One critic referred to it as "that ravishing view of the Gila, disclosing an order of the vegetable kingdom and a style of geology as different from what prevail in our region of the continent as if they were the belongings to some other planet."[4] This first version was destroyed in the 1865 Smithsonian fire. The second, 1855 version pictured here is thought to have been commissioned by someone beguiled by the Indian Gallery's piece *View on the Gila River*.

1. Emory, *Notes*, illustrated p. 96, with a description on p. 79.

2. See James Ballinger, "John Mix Stanley, A 'Hudson River' Painter in Arizona," *Phoebus: A Journal of Art History* 3 (1981): 70.

3. This painting, referred to as a "Scene on the Gila River," was noticed as "a gem" by an Albany, New York, reviewer in 1850. See "Stanley's Indian Gallery," *Albany Dutchman*, October 11, 1850. In his 1852 gallery catalogue, *Portraits of North American Indians*, he dates the painting 1851.

4. "Indian Gallery of Paintings," *National Intelligencer*, February 24, 1852.

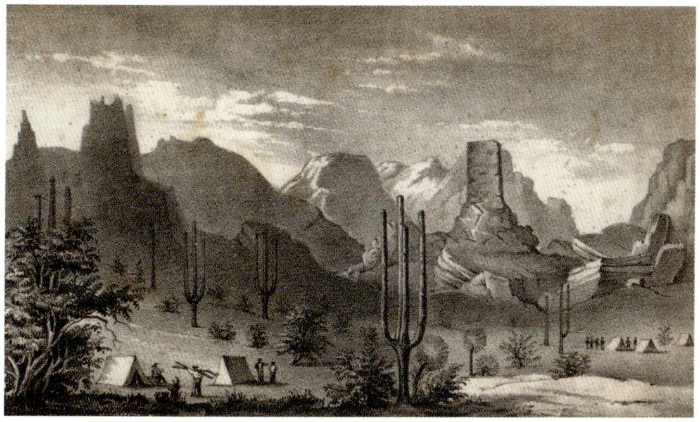

FIG. 130.1.
G. B. Graham after John Mix Stanley, *Chain of Natural Spires on the Gila*, 1848. Lithograph; 4 × 6¼ in. (10.2 × 15.9 cm). From Emory, *Notes on a Military Reconnoissance*, 96. Courtesy McCracken Research Library, Buffalo Bill Center of the West, Cody, Wyoming

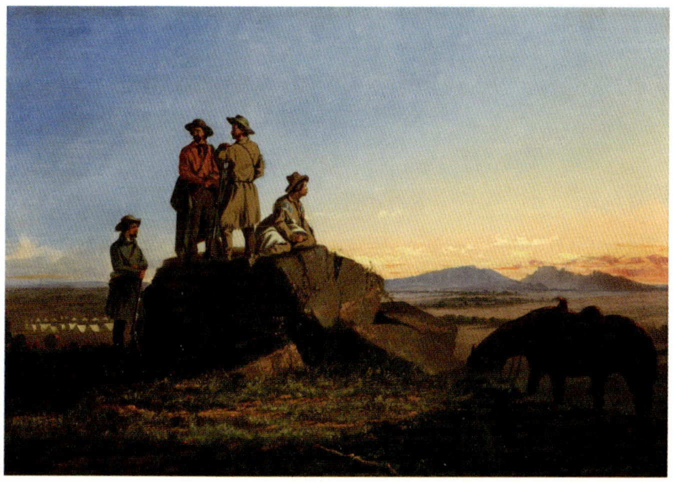

131

Scouts along the Teton River, c. 1855

Scouts in the Tetons; Encampment in the Teton Country

Oil on canvas, 24 × 34¼ in. (61 × 87 cm)

PRESENT COLLECTION: Gilcrease Museum, Tulsa, Oklahoma (0126.1143)

PROVENANCE: (M. Knoedler and Co., New York, New York, 1950); Thomas Gilcrease, Tulsa, Oklahoma; present owner

The Isaac Stevens expedition left the relative comforts of Fort Benton on the upper Missouri River in late September 1853 and headed west to confront the Rocky Mountains in quest of a northern route for a transcontinental railroad. This painting pictures a group from the exploring party posed near and atop a stony outcrop. Two of the men look west toward the setting sun and the two prominent peaks they are approaching, Ear Mountain on the left and Choteau Mountain on the right.[1] The man in the red shirt, probably Isaac Stevens (fig. 84.1), glances back toward the tents to his right.

In the expedition's report, Stevens described this scene as remarkable, one that he had embraced with wonder a couple of times before. "I have traveled over this plateau between the Teton and Sun Rivers on two other lines," he wrote, and "the view at almost any point of the plateau is exceedingly picturesque and suggestive."[2] Stanley was able to reflect that sense of marvel with the golden radiance that fills the distant sky and the raking light of evening that sheds so graciously across the figures enthroned on nature's pedestal. The men situated on the high lookout are steadfastly positioned to claim territory. Few other paintings by Stanley suggest so strongly the expedition's imperative of conquest as this does.

The pyramidal order of this composition, with its architectonic classicism, relates to figural genre paintings by George Caleb Bingham, one of Stanley's contemporaries.[3] Bingham's *Jolly Flatboatmen in Port* (1857, Saint Louis Art Museum) makes a strong formalist comparison. Yet while Bingham was paying reverence to the passing of the epic river boatmen, Stanley celebrated an ascendant moment, not many years past, of western explorers, in the present tense, seeking new paths into the wilds. The temporal parameters for the two artists were quite the opposite.

1. I am grateful to Jack Lepley and his staff at the Fort Benton Museums for helping to identify the geographical details in this painting.

2. Stevens, *Narrative and Final Report*, 118. This view does not appear in the Stevens report.

3. For a discussion of Bingham's classicism, see Barbara Novak, *American Painting of the Nineteenth Century* (New York: Praeger Publishers, 1976), 162.

132

Untitled, Teton Valley Scene, c. 1855

Oil on paper, 6 × 8¾ in. (15.2 × 22.2 cm)

INSCRIBED LOWER LEFT: J. M. Stanley / [illegible]

PRESENT COLLECTION: Buffalo Bill Center of the West, Cody, Wyoming, museum purchase from William E. Weiss Memorial Fund and Lakeside Foundation (1.14)

PROVENANCE: Private collection, Utah, 2013; present owner, 2014

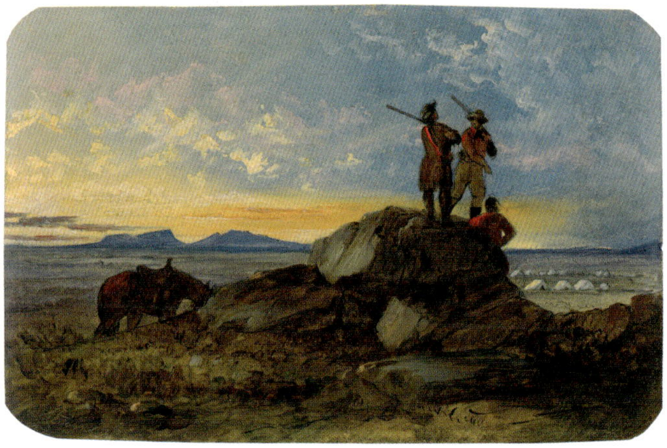

132

This small but strikingly brilliant oil painting is thought to be a preliminary study for Stanley's larger painting *Scouts along the Teton River* (cat. no. 131). Oddly, the scene is reversed in the sketch, with the tents on the right side and the horse and mountainous background on the left. Perhaps Stanley anticipated having this small version engraved. The figures in this study are also less identifiable than in the finished work.

This study accentuates the cloud effects, allowing the sun's rays to play through the yellow- and peach-highlighted puffs that fill the sky. There is a brooding, romantic quality of light that hovers over the explorers, a firmament that spells uncertainty for the ventures ahead as opposed to the clear sky with its glowing golden horizon that pervades the larger, finished piece.

133

Tepia Gatherers, 1855

Oil on canvas, 21 × 30¼ in. (53.3 × 76.8 cm)

INSCRIBED LOWER LEFT: J. M. Stanley, 1855; INSCRIBED VERSO: Indian picture—a true scene. By J. Mix Stanley $150 PRESENT COLLECTION: Gilcrease Museum, Tulsa, Oklahoma (0126.1142)

PROVENANCE: (M. Knoedler and Co., New York, New York, 1952); Thomas Gilcrease, Tulsa, Oklahoma; present owner

This painting was produced as one of two Stanley illustrations for Henry Rowe Schoolcraft's monumental treatise on America's Native people, *History of the Indian Tribes of the United States* (1851–1857). Schoolcraft's project involved six hefty, highly illustrated volumes, and by 1856 he was readying the sixth and final one. Over the years Schoolcraft had alienated at least two artists: George Catlin by refusing to consider him as an artist of merit; and Seth Eastman through poor treatment. He was now in search of a replacement for Eastman, and Stanley seemed appropriate as one of his options. Stanley viewed the job as a bright opportunity and sent Schoolcraft a couple of lengthy lists of possible subjects.[1] Schoolcraft ultimately selected only two, this work and a painting titled *Chinook Burial* (fig. 133.1, unlocated).

Stanley had included a similar tepia-harvesting subject in his 1854 panorama, *Scenes and Incidents of Stanley's Western Wilds*. The setting was near Fort Union on the upper Missouri River. He described a bright prairie, "mirror-like" lakes, and a group of women, one of whom is "digging teipsienna (tepia), a species of wild turnip, peculiar to this region, while another, standing by her side, has her hands filled with the white vegetable."[2] This painting no doubt derives from that section of the panorama, and provides a quiet genre subject in which women play a singularly important role. Schoolcraft, in his famously sanctimonious way, however, viewed such activities as barbaric and inefficient efforts at supplementing the Plains Indian primary diet of meat. After describing the scene, he concluded, "It is impossible to conjecture how these tribes can long survive the extinction of the race of quadrupeds [bison]."[3]

The companion illustration, *Chinook Burial* (fig. 133.1), provided a mixed message, at once a narrative of sadness and departure in the scaffolds but also one of hope and renewal with the mother and child below. The two works reveal the familial side of Stanley, as they focus specifically on women and children. Stanley's first child, a son named Louis, was born the year these paintings were completed, perhaps accounting for his attention to such themes.

1. See Dippie, *Catlin and His Contemporaries*, 299.

2. Donoho, *Scenes and Incidents*, 10.

3. Henry Rowe Schoolcraft, *History of the Indian Tribes of the United States: Their Present Condition and Prospects, and a Sketch of their Ancient Status* (Philadelphia: J. B. Lippincott, 1857), 6:553.

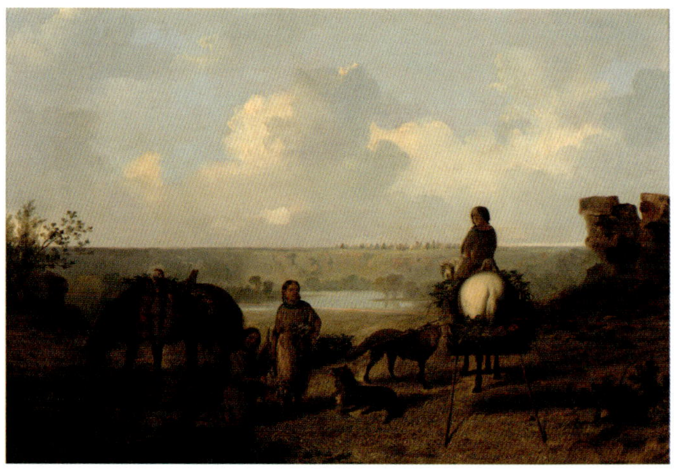

133

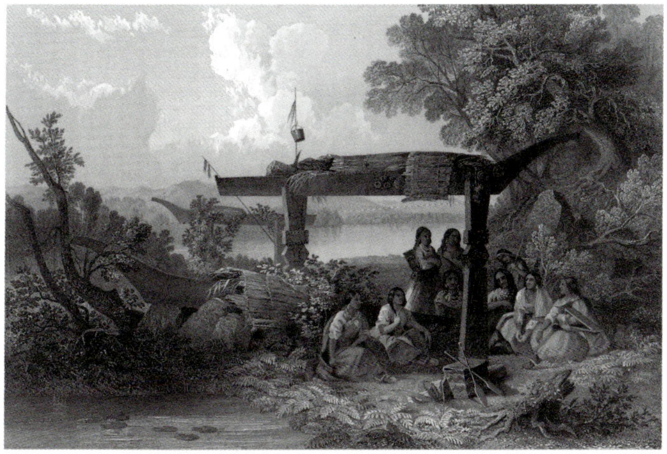

FIG. 133.1.
J. D. Smillie after John Mix Stanley,
Chinook Burial, c. 1855. Engraving; 5½ × 8 in. (14.0 × 20.5 cm).
From Schoolcraft, *History of the Indian Tribes of the United States*, vol. 6, opp. p. 552.
Courtesy McCracken Research Library, Buffalo Bill Center of the West, Cody, Wyoming

134

Wagon Train: Break in the Journey, c. 1855

Courtship on the Plains; Betrothal on the Plains

Oil on canvas, 30 × 44 in. (76.2 × 111.8 cm)

PRESENT COLLECTION: American Museum of Western Art—The Anschutz Collection, Denver, Colorado

PROVENANCE: The artist; by descent to Edith Stanley Bayles; (The Old Print Shop, New York, New York, 1963); (Kennedy Galleries, New York, New York, 1963); Alan Pensler, Washington, D. C; (Steve Good, Denver, Colorado); present owner, 2010

Stanley is known to have painted at least two finished studio oils in the mid-1850s remembering his weeks on the Santa Fe Trail in 1846, this work and *After the Hunt* (cat. no. 168). Although the painting has been known as *Betrothal on the Plains* and *Courtship on the Plains*, a close look at the work and the history of its primary subjects reveals that this is neither a courtship nor a betrothal scene. Rather, it portrays Samuel and Susan Shelby Magoffin (fig. 134.1.), his traveling companions that summer. The Magoffins had been married for about eight months when the journey began in June. Their courtship was long past, as was their betrothal. This view captures the couple, he thirty-three and she eighteen and much in love to be sure, somewhere along the Arkansas River.

Samuel Magoffin was a veteran Santa Fe trader who led the party west. Here, he holds his bride's hand as she embraces a basket containing a bouquet of flowers that he has perhaps collected for her. She was pregnant with their first child at the time. The baby was sadly lost at Bent's Fort sometime later.

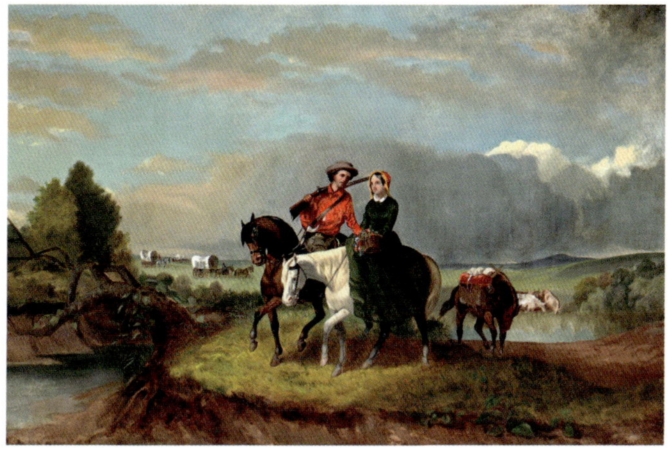

134

Susan kept a diary during the trip, and she mentioned Stanley as being "one in our Company," a gentleman "rather celebrated for his Indian sketches."[1] He in turn must have remembered the Magoffins fondly as the painting remained in the artist's possession throughout his lifetime. It was painted sometime after Stanley married Alice Caroline English in spring 1854 and probably reflected a personal sentiment of his own.[2]

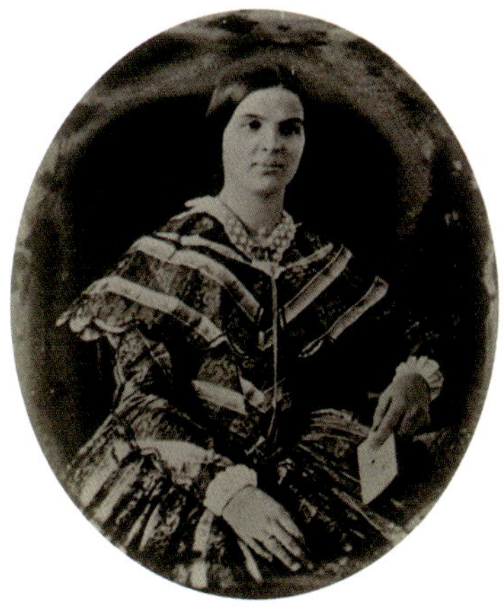

FIG. 134.1.
Unknown photographer, *Susan Shelby Magoffin*,
1845–1855. Daguerreotype; 7½ × 5 in. (17.8 × 12.7 cm)
Courtesy Missouri History Museum, St. Louis

1. Drumm, *Down the Santa Fe Trail*, 19–20. Howard Lamar's thorough foreword to the book provides a full accounting of the Magoffins and their lives before, during, and after the trip.

2. According to the *Kennedy Quarterly*, 4 (November 1963): 29, the painting's canvas bears a label of the Washington, D.C., art supply company C. S. Whittlesey, which was established in the city in 1855.

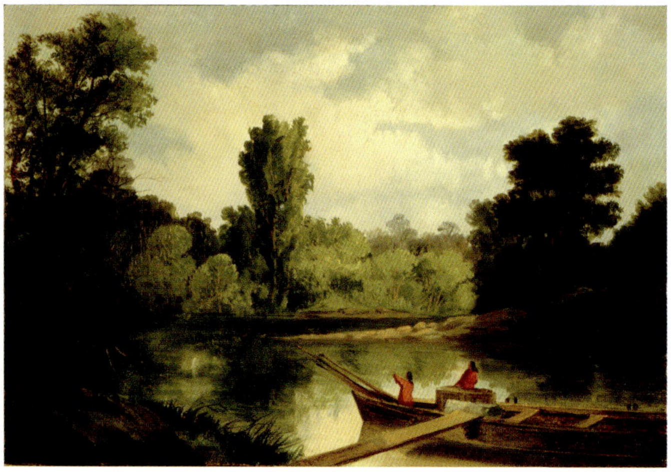

135

Chinook Indian Guides on the Clackamas River, c. 1855

Oil on paper mounted on canvas, 10¼ × 14⅜ in. (26.0 × 36.5 cm)

INSCRIBED LOWER LEFT: J. M. Stanley

PRESENT COLLECTION: Private collection

PROVENANCE: The artist; Isaac Stevens, Olympia, Washington; by descent to Major Richard Stevens Eskridge, Olympia, Washington; Dr. and Mrs. Franz R. Stenzel, Portland, Oregon, 1963; (Sotheby Parke Bernet, Los Angeles, 1980); (Fred Rosenstock, Denver, Colorado, 1980); (Gerald Peters Gallery, Santa Fe, New Mexico, 1980); present owner, 1983

Stanley painted several works for his friend and patron Isaac Stevens. This oil painting descended through the Stevens family and is thought to have been either commissioned or given to Stevens by the artist. Stanley and Stevens traveled down the Columbia River together in 1853 and may have witnessed or even participated in such a scene.

The painting was given a lengthy title by one of its owners, *Chinook Indian Guides on the Clackamas River*. It was also said to have been painted during Stanley's 1847 trip along the Columbia River. There is nothing on the painting or in the records of the work to corroborate the contention that the Indians are guides or that its setting is the Clackamas River. The long title has therefore been shortened to assume simply that the scene depicts Chinook Indians. The style of the painting, its generalized treatment of foliage, and its hasty rendition of the two human figures suggest a date more commensurate with the Stevens expedition than the artist's earlier adventures in the Northwest (as might be seen in *Scene on the Columbia River*, 1852, cat. no. 065).

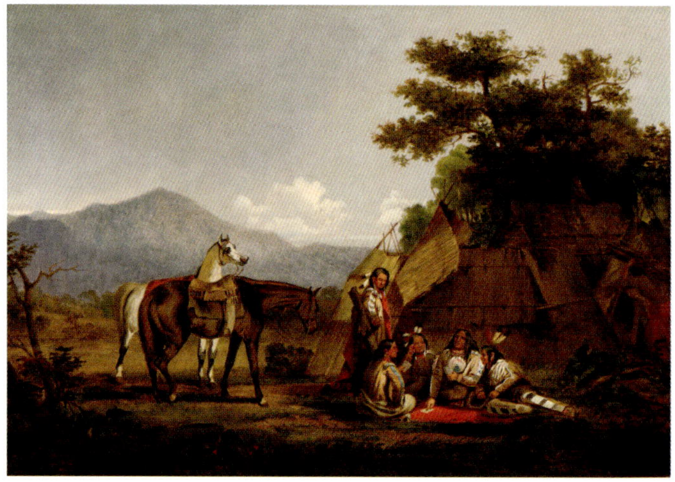

136

Game of Chance, c. 1855

Indians Playing Cards

Oil on canvas, 27⅕ × 38¾ in. (71.1 × 102.9 cm)

PRESENT COLLECTION: Gilcrease Museum, Tulsa, Oklahoma (0126.1137)

PROVENANCE: A. G. Seaman, New York, New York; Robert J. McKeon, Chappaqua, New York; (M. Knoedler and Co., New York, New York, 1952); Thomas Gilcrease, Tulsa, Oklahoma; present owner

Two men play cards on a red trade blanket. They sit beneath a shady arbor of trees with three onlookers and a camp of thatched and hide structures behind them. Two saddled horses look on from the left as if alert to the rules of the game. The older player points to an ace he has just put down. His expression is one of reserved confidence, as he watches his opponent study his own hand in hopes of an effective counter move.

It is not known why Stanley became so infatuated with the smoking and gambling habits of Plains Indian men. Nonetheless, he always selected men at cards, though women were inveterate gamblers as well, and he invariably dressed his players as warriors prepared for a major ceremony. This is one of a series of such card game pictures that he produced after his trip through the northern plains with Isaac Stevens. Perhaps his patrons were Anglo men of fashion who frequented their own men's clubs and perceived such scenes as culturally bonding with their exotic counterparts in the western wilds.

137

Buffalo Hunt, c. 1855

Indian Buffalo Hunt

Oil on canvas, 27¾ × 38¾ in. (70.5 × 98.4 cm)

PRESENT COLLECTION: Gilcrease Museum, Tulsa, Oklahoma (0126.1146)

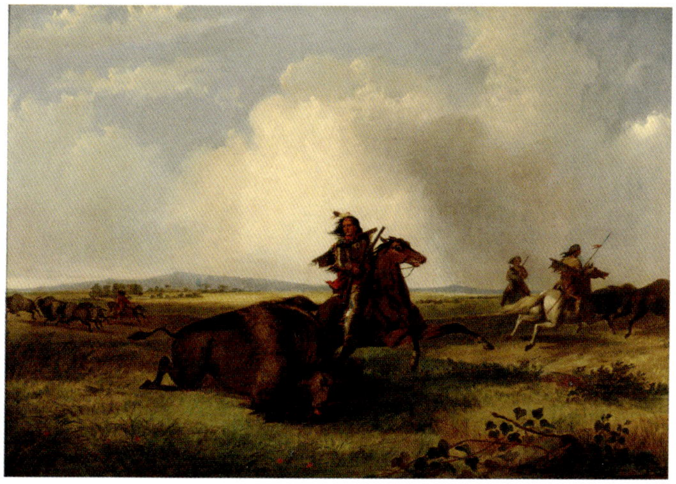

137

PROVENANCE: A. G. Seaman, New York, New York; Mr. Robert J. McKeon, Chappaqua, New York; (Kennedy Galleries, New York, New York); (M. Knoedler and Co., New York, New York, 1952); Thomas Gilcrease, Tulsa, Oklahoma; present owner

Stanley was an astute observer of works by other artists whose interests bent toward Indian subjects. His direct rivalry with George Catlin over which, if either, of their Indian galleries the government might elect to purchase was an epic, heartbreaking tale. Yet his connection with other artists was more felicitous, less competitive, and often venerating. This could likely be the case when he sat down in the mid-1850s to produce this version of the *Buffalo Hunt*.

Thomas L. McKenney and James Hall published their three-volume magnum opus on the *History of the Indian Tribes of North America* between 1836 and 1844, just as Stanley was starting his career as a painter. The McKenney and Hall volumes featured portraits of important Indian figures, paintings that were also in Charles Bird King's National Indian Portrait Gallery, which ultimately was exhibited beside Stanley's Indian Gallery in the Smithsonian and suffered the same tragic fate as Stanley's collection. The frontispiece in volume two of McKenney and Hall's *History of the Indian Tribes of North America* featured a watercolor by a deceased painter from Saint Louis, Peter Rindisbacher, titled *Hunting the Buffalo* (fig. 137.1).[1] Picturing a northern Plains chase, Rindisbacher's *Hunting the Buffalo* could easily have inspired Stanley to render this similar scene from life on the prairies some dozen years later.

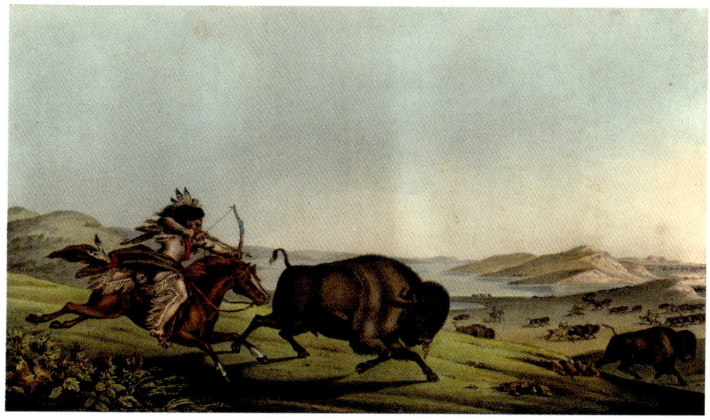

FIG. 137.1.
After Peter Rindisbacher, *Hunting the Buffalo*, c. 1837.
Chromolithograph; 13 × 17 in. (33 × 43 cm).
From McKenney and Hall, *History of the Indian Tribes of North America*, xx, frontispiece.
Courtesy McCracken Research Library, Buffalo Bill Center of the West, Cody, Wyoming

1. Thomas L. McKenney and James Hall, *History of the Indian Tribes of North America*, vol. 2 (Philadelphia: Frederick W. Greenough, 1838).

138

The Buffalo Hunt, 1855

Oil on canvas, 29¾ × 39 in. (75.6 × 99.1 cm)

INSCRIBED LOWER LEFT: J. M. Stanley / 1855

PRESENT COLLECTION: Crystal Bridges Museum of American Art, Bentonville, Arkansas

PROVENANCE: The artist; John Carl Richberg; by descent to Donald R. Richberg, Charlottesville, Virginia, 1957; O. Rundle Gilbert, Poughkeepsie, New York, 1958; (Kennedy Galleries, New York, New York, 1963); Bronson Trevor, New York, New York; (Hirschl and Adler, New York, New York, 1977); The Warner Collection of Gulf State Paper Corporation, Tuscaloosa, Alabama, 1980; (Gerald Peters Gallery, Santa Fe, New Mexico, 1982); William D. Weiss, Jackson, Wyoming, 1992; (J. N. Bartfield Galleries, New York, New York); The Petrie Collection, Denver, Colorado; (Sotheby's, New York, New York); present owner, 2005

Among the several paintings that likely resulted from showings of Stanley's monumental 1854 panorama *Scenes and Incidents of Stanley's Western Wilds* was this dramatic oil, known today as *The Buffalo Hunt*. As the action was portrayed in the panorama, it was

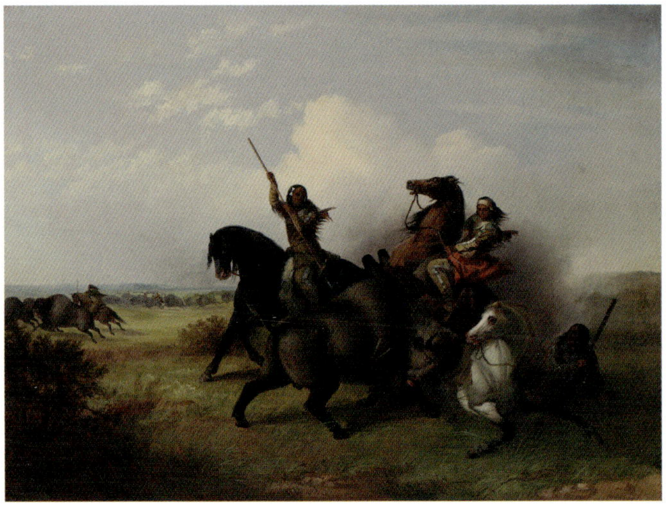

138

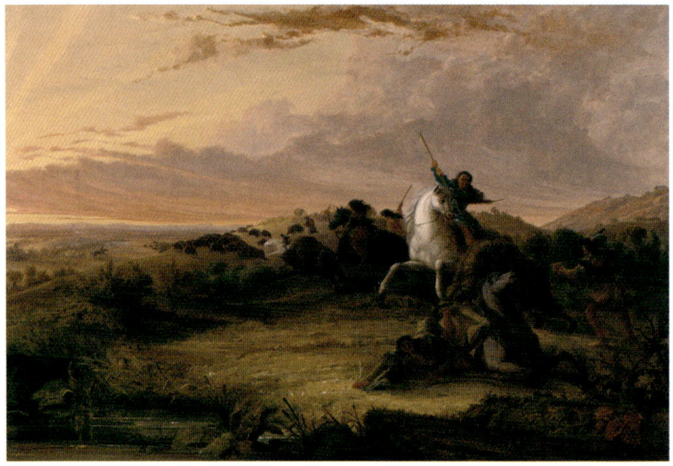

FIG. 138.1.
Seth Eastman, *Buffalo Hunt*, c. 1850.
Oil on canvas; 25 × 35 3/16 in. (68.5 × 89.3 cm).
Cincinnati Art Museum, Ohio,
Williams family gift in honor of William J. Williams;
photograph courtesy Bridgeman Images

titled *The Perils of the Chase* and included only two hunters, one fallen beneath an enraged bison and one attacking the wounded animal with a spear. The hunters in the panorama were Red River hunters, rather than Piegans, as pictured in this painting, but the narrative was essentially the same, with the ultimate outcome seeming to bode poorly for the dismounted man, the horse, and the wounded prey. As the panorama's program told it: "A wounded buffalo turns madly, on the hunter. Rider and horse are down, the horse falling on the rider, who looks up from the ground in most lamentable plight. . . . He cannot move; he can only look up for succor."[1] In the panorama version, the fallen rider survives.

Such scenes of danger in the pursuit of buffalo had been explored in paintings by George Catlin and Alfred Jacob Miller by this date. Stanley's variation on the theme was considerably more substantial in scale than Catlin's *Buffalo Chase, Bulls Making Battle with Men and Horses* (1832, Smithsonian American Art Museum) and more histrionic than Miller's *Buffalo Hunt* (c. 1838–1842, Amon Carter Museum of American Art).[2] But they were all breathtakingly intense. There may be a more probable connection between Stanley's *Buffalo Hunt* and a painting by his friend and supporter Seth Eastman that carried the same title (fig. 138.1). Eastman's version, thought to have been completed before 1850, pictures a similar melee with multiple human figures. The composition is strikingly similar to Stanley's, and it is certainly possible that Stanley might have seen Eastman's dramatic interpretation in his colleague's studio.[3] Stanley scholar Brian W. Dippie suggests a connection also between Stanley's histrionic brawl and a work by the French grand master painter Horace Vernet, *The Lion Hunt* (1836, The Wallace Collection), which would have been available for Stanley's perusal in one of two engraved versions.[4]

1. Donoho, *Scenes and Incidents*, 9.

2. Catlin's scene concludes in the same optimistic way; George Catlin, *Letters and Notes on the Manners, Customs, and Condition of the North American Indians* (London: David Bogue, 1844), 1:256–57.

3. Eastman's *Buffalo Hunt* is thematically similar to but dramatically enhanced in angst and action from his painting *Buffalo Chase* for Schoolcraft's *History of the Indian Tribes*, vol. 4 (1854), opp. p. 94.

4. Brian W. Dippie, "The Visual West," in *Oxford History of the American West*, ed. Clyde A. Milner II (New York: Oxford University Press, 1994), 686–87.

139

Kidnapped, 1853

Oil on canvas, 29 3/4 × 41 1/2 in. (76.2 × 106.7 cm)

INSCRIBED LOWER RIGHT: STANLEY 1853

PRESENT COLLECTION: Denver Art Museum, William, Sr., and Dorothy Harmsen Collection (2001.454)

PROVENANCE: The artist; probably Alexander Culbertson; by descent to either John or Joseph Culbertson; Henry Clay Culbertson, Cincinnati, Ohio; (Kennedy Galleries, New York, New York, 1959); William, Sr., and Dorothy Harmsen, Denver, Colorado, 1968; present owner by gift, 2001

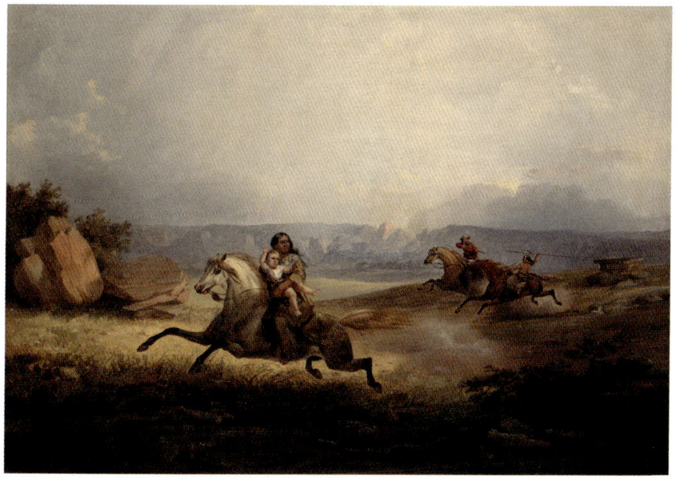

139

This scene, painted in 1853, during his first extended stay in Washington, D.C., might be reasoned to be a pictorial recounting of some earlier episode in Stanley's experience, either in Arizona or Oregon. One of the lost paintings in the Indian Gallery, completed before 1850 and titled *Abduction of Miss Bewley from Dr. Whitman's Mission*, would seem to be a reasonable source.[1] Yet that painting, if historically accurate, would have pictured a mature woman, since Ester "Lorinda" Bewley was in her early twenties when she was taken captive. She was later released and returned to her family.

The speculation about the painting's narrative has even led to the suggestion that the child being taken away here was Cynthia Ann Parker, who was abducted as a child by the Comanches in Texas. She became the mother of the famous chief Quanah Parker.[2] But Cynthia Ann was kidnapped in 1836 at age nine, so the toddler in the Stanley painting (who actually seems to be a boy) would not fit that supposition either.

Most likely this painting was created out of Stanley's imagination, to feed a prurient public appetite for savage abduction themes in the portrayal of Native people. Stanley had a penchant from time to time for such emotionally fraught scenes, suggested in the fact that this is at least the fourth such work in his oeuvre, the others being the Bewley painting mentioned above, *An Osage Scalp Dance*, 1845 (cat. no. 025), and his painting *The Abduction*, 1847 (cat. no. 043).

1. *Portraits of North American Indians*, 66.

2. See *Kennedy Quarterly* 1 (October 1960): 140.

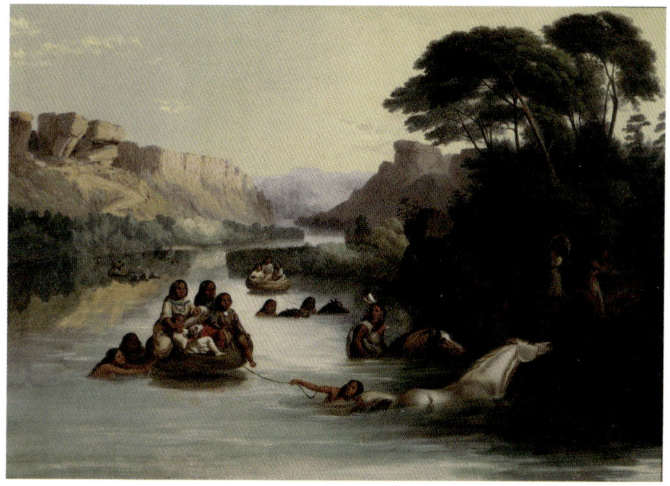

140

Crossing the Milk River, c. 1855

Oil on canvas, 30½ × 42 in. (77.5 × 106.7 cm)

PRESENT COLLECTION: Autry National Center, Los Angeles, California (108.88.33)

PROVENANCE: (Kennedy Galleries, New York, New York); Northern Natural Gas Company, Omaha, Nebraska; Enron Corporation, Houston, Texas; present owner

Stanley had passed beside and crossed the Milk River in present-day Montana several times during the 1853 Stevens expedition. This particular view must have come when he took a small special expeditionary force north from Fort Benton in mid-September that year. They were in search of a large camp of Piegan Indians, whom the artist was entreated to bring back to parley with Stevens at the fort. Along the way he came across three lodges of Piegans camped beside the river. They had just descended the river by boat, and they helped Stanley find the larger camp farther to the west. Stanley described the Milk River valley at that point as about a mile wide, "studded with groves of cottonwood" and "broken by ravines [that] look like the buildings and streets of some city."[1]

The scene of Indian women bathing and wringing out their clothes that unfolds on the right side of the composition is reminiscent of views of Indian bathers by Alfred Jacob Miller, published in New York in 1854, especially one titled *Toilet of the Indian Girls* (fig. 140.1).[2] Miller and Stanley exhibited together at the Washington Art Association, and were friendly competitors in the business of promoting Indians in art.

Stanley painted two versions of this scene, differing in certain details such as the landscape background and the arrangement of figures, but essentially the same theme. The other painting, *View on Milk River* (cat. no. 155), addresses the topic in a slightly smaller format. *Crossing the Milk River* was painted on a canvas supplied by George Jillard, who was active in the art supply business in Washington, D.C., from 1855 until 1863, so the date of the painting may be assumed to range from the mid to late 1850s.

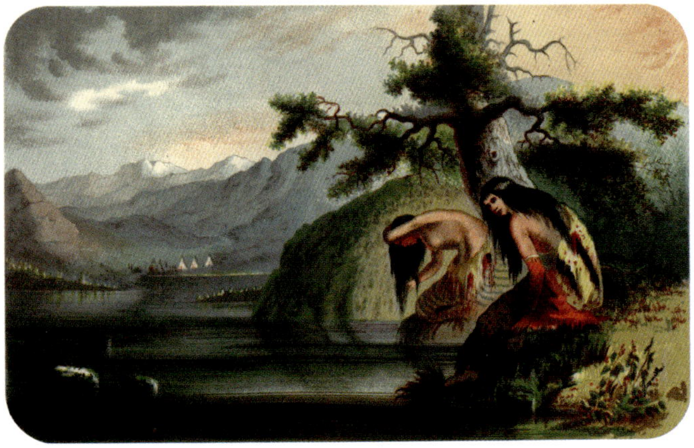

FIG. 140.1.
After Alfred Jacob Miller, *Toilet of the Indian Girls*, 1854.
Chromolithograph; 4⅞ × 7½ in. (12.2 × 19.0 cm).
From Webber, *Wild Scenes and Song-Birds*, opp. p. 144.
Courtesy McCracken Research Library,
Buffalo Bill Center of the West, Cody, Wyoming

1. Stevens, *Narrative and Final Report*, 114.

2. See Miller illustrations in Charles Wilkins Webber, *The Hunter Naturalist: Wild Scenes and Song-Birds* (New York: Putnam, 1854). Also, for discussion of Webber and the Miller illustrations, see Ron Tyler, ed., *Prints of the American West* (Fort Worth, Tex.: Amon Carter Museum, 1983), 64–65. For a later variation on Stanley's painting, see Gustav Sohon's *Mode of Crossing Rivers by the Flathead and Other Indians* in Mullan, *Report on the Construction*, between 50 and 51.

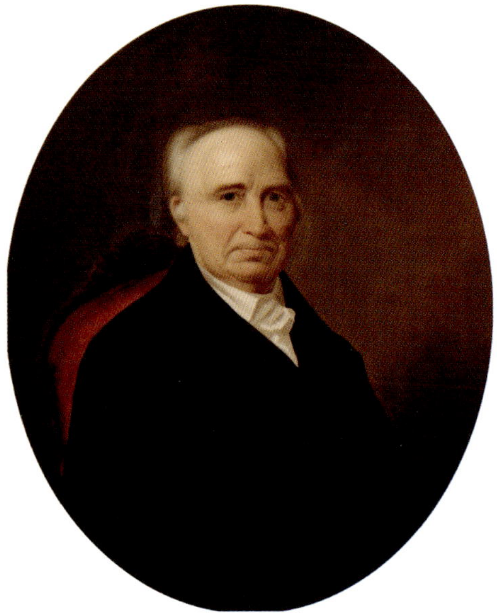

141

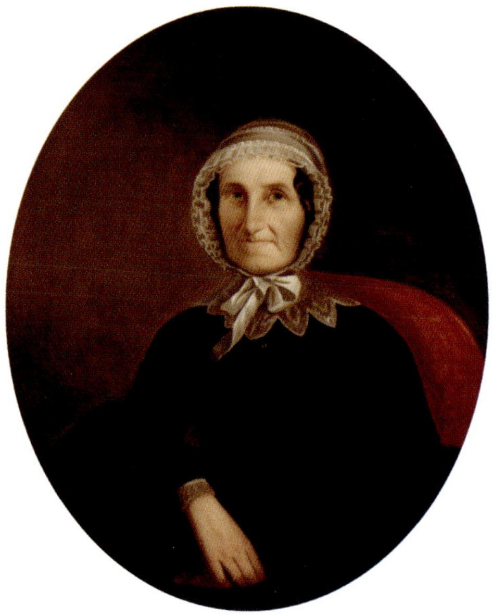

142

141, 142

Elisha Whittlesey and *Polly Whittlesey*, 1855

Oil on canvas, 34½ × 28 in. (86.6 × 71.1 cm) each

PRESENT COLLECTION: Western Reserve Historical Society, Cleveland, Ohio (40.1351 and 40,1352)

PROVENANCE: The artist; Elisha and Polly Whittlesey; through descent to Ralph K. Buckland; gift to present owner, 1940

In November 1855, Stanley wrote an old friend of his from Ohio, Isaac Strohm, that he had just "completed two very satisfactory portraits" of the first comptroller of the United States Treasury, Elisha Whittlesey, and his wife, Polly. Elisha was then in his early seventies. Stanley wrote Strohm, "The old gentleman says his wife['s] is the very best he ever saw—and that his friends are equally satisfied with his."[1] Stanley was much engaged with the business of portrait painting at the time, with his sizable commission from the Justice Department just getting under way.

How and why Stanley got connected with the distinguished Whittlesey family is not known. Whittlesey, a lawyer by training, had been a resident of Washington, D.C., since the mid-1830s. He was known as an art collector as well as being a sharp legal and financial mind. Both presidents Taylor and Lincoln highly valued his service with the Treasury.

Stanley wrote Strohm again in 1861 as the Civil War boiled into its early phase. The artist wanted some sort of an appointment with the government, one which Whittlesey wholeheartedly endorsed.[2] So far as we know, no appointment was forthcoming, so Stanley embarked on painting his Civil War panorama instead.

1. Stanley to Isaac Strohm, November 11, 1855, Schimmel Papers. Stanley also mentions portraits of Isaac Toucey (cat. no. 152) and Caleb Cushing (cat. no. 153) that were then in the works.

2. Stanley to Isaac Strohm, June 18, 1861, Isaac Strohm Papers, Archives of the Cincinnati Museum Center, Ohio.

143

Mrs. John Mix (Alice Caroline English) Stanley and Louis Crandall Stanley, 1856

Oil on canvas, 30 × 25 in. (76.2 × 63.5 cm)

PRESENT COLLECTION: Last known, Mrs. Dean (Alice Stanley) Acheson, Washington, D.C.

PROVENANCE: The artist; by descent to Mrs. Dean (Alice Stanley) Acheson, Washington, D.C.

John Mix Stanley married Alice Caroline English in Washington, D.C., on May 2, 1854. Their first child, a son named Louis, was born a year and a half later in November 1855. The artist painted this portrait of the two the next year. Though incomplete except for the sitters' heads, the baby's hands and arms, and the puppy, the portrait was proudly passed down through the family, eventually being owned and cherished by Louis's daughter, Alice Acheson of Washington, D.C. It was included in a Stanley exhibition that she organized with the Smithsonian Institution in 1944.[1]

Stanley had painted Alice prior to this, in 1853, just before he departed for the far Northwest and the railroad survey expedition. In that portrait (cat. no. 071) Alice is positioned in a similar pose, sitting beside her brother, Morgan English. Perhaps she favored such a pose, seated with a special family member.

1. *Exhibition of Paintings by John Mix Stanley (1814–1872), Jane C. Stanley (1863–1940), Alice Stanley Acheson* (Washington, D.C.: Smithsonian Institution, 1944), no. 30.

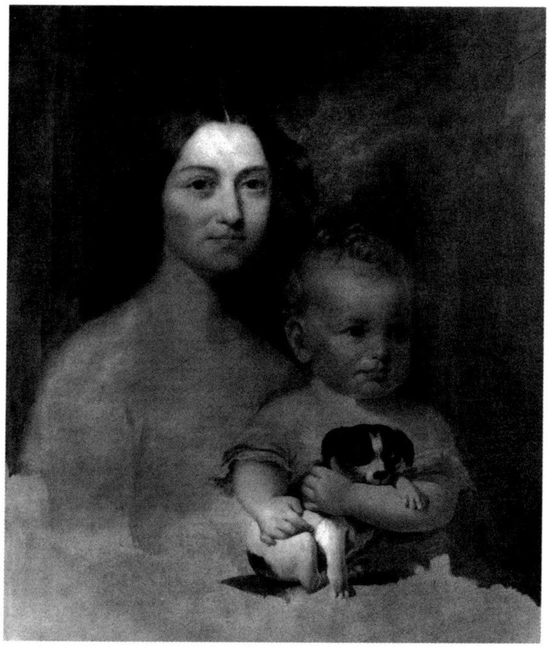

143

144

On the Snake River, c. 1856

Snake River, Idaho and Washington; Landscape on Snake River, Idaho and Washington

Oil on canvas, 36½ × 54 in. (92.7 × 137.2 cm)

PRESENT COLLECTION: Collection of Larry A. Sheakley

PROVENANCE: The artist; Isaac Stevens, Olympia, Washington; by descent to Major Richard Stevens Eskridge, Olympia, Washington; (Kennedy Galleries, New York, New York, 1966); [?]; (Kennedy Galleries, New York, New York, c. 1990); (Gerald Peters Gallery, Santa Fe, New Mexico, 2003); (Kennedy Galleries, New York, New York); (Scottsdale Art Auction, Scottsdale, Arizona, 2005); present owner

This is a particularly accomplished and prescient landscape. As part of the second-generation Hudson River School in the West, Stanley evinced a strong American aesthetic. He offered light-soaked skies and imposed a velvety glow to his landscape images, much in the spirit of the soft elegance championed by American luminist painters of the period. Unlike Albert Bierstadt's German-influenced, grandiose style and Thomas Moran's precise, English, Pre-Raphaelite persuasions, Stanley's work followed a far simpler program. He chose a path of unpretentious naturalism akin to that practiced by his contemporary Thomas Worthington Whittredge. As an important western landscape, *On the Snake River* sets the stage for all three painters: Bierstadt's first trip west was in 1859, Whittredge's in 1866, and Moran's in 1871.

This painting debuted in modern times at the Kennedy Galleries in New York as *Landscape of Snake River, Idaho and Washington* and was dated around 1853. Kennedy Galleries acquired it from Major Richard Stevens Eskridge, the grandson of the explorer

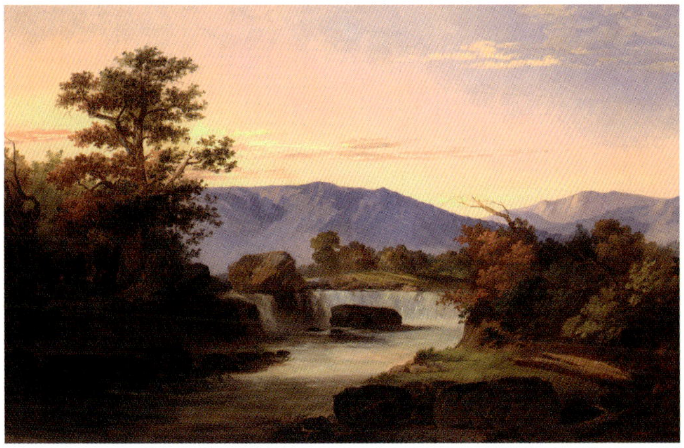

144

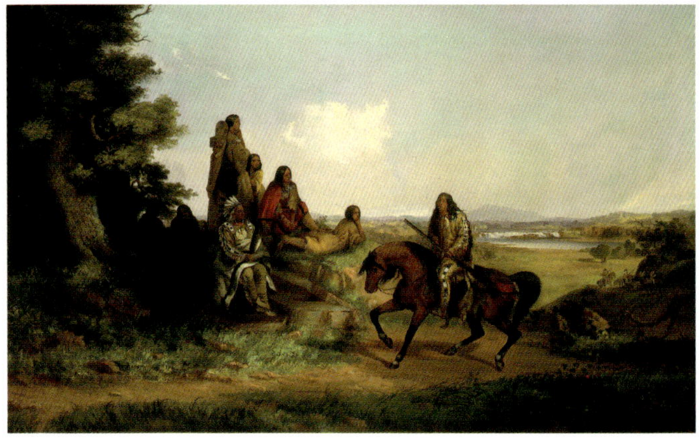

145

Isaac Stevens.[1] It was certainly produced as a result of scenes witnessed along the trail of the northern railroad survey, but there are no indications of the exact location, and the date of 1853 is impossible for such a large and finished work since Stanley was in the field throughout much that year.

The simple title *On the Snake River,* as later advertised in the *Kennedy Quarterly*, seems more reasonable. Yet no one acquainted with the Snake River has been able to identify the scene. It may simply be a fantasized landscape combining elements of northwestern scenery that Stanley and Stevens remembered.

1. Inventory record from Kennedy Galleries, Schimmel Papers.

145
A Family Group, c. 1856
(Barter for a Bride; Indians in a Landscape)

Oil on canvas, 40 × 63 in. (101.6 × 160.0 cm)

PRESENT COLLECTION: Diplomatic Reception Room, Department of State, Washington, D.C., funds donated by Morris and Gwendolyn Cafritz Foundation, 1965

PROVENANCE: The artist; probably directly to Colonel John K. Kilbreth; General J. William Kilbreth; Gertrude O. Barclay Kilbreth; (James Graham and Sons, New York, New York, 1963); present owner

LIFETIME EXHIBITIONS: Third Annual Exhibition of the Metropolitan Mechanics Institute, Smithsonian Institution Building, Washington, D.C., March 1857; Fourth Annual Exhibition, Washington Art Association, Washington, D.C., 1860

This painting has long been known as *Barter for a Bride*, a title that was given to it in the twentieth century, probably by one of its last owners before it was donated to the Department of State, where it resides today. It is with this title in mind that Lisa Strong discusses the painting in this volume. In the nineteenth century, however, it is thought to have been called *A Family Group*.[1] If that latter title is correct, it possibly pictures not a proposal for marriage but the simple gathering of a Blackfeet family, the sister and children of Seen From Afar, known personally to Stanley during his travels on the upper Missouri in 1853. The location is thought to be the Great Falls of the Missouri River, just west of Fort Benton, where the artist's close friend Alexander Culbertson ran operations.[2] Culbertson's wife, seated in a red blanket, was Natawista, Seen From Afar's sister. The identity of the older man seated to the left of Natawista is unknown but was probably her father. Natawista and Alexander visited Washington, D.C., in 1856, where Stanley painted his portrait (cat. no. 080) and perhaps an unlocated one of Natawista as well. He may have produced this genre scene at that time also.

Natawista and Seen From Afar are also prime figures in *The Last of Their Race* (cat. nos. 159 and 165), the latter version of which was acquired through auction in 1858 by Culbertson for his retirement home in Peoria, Illinois.[3]

1. Wischmann, *Frontier Diplomats*, 276.

2. Stanley is known to have painted the Great Falls of the Missouri River. He lists it as one of his suggested, though never published, plates for the Stevens report in his letter to Lieut. G. K. Warren, April 3, 1855, Stevens letterbook.

3. Wischmann, *Frontier Diplomats*, 276.

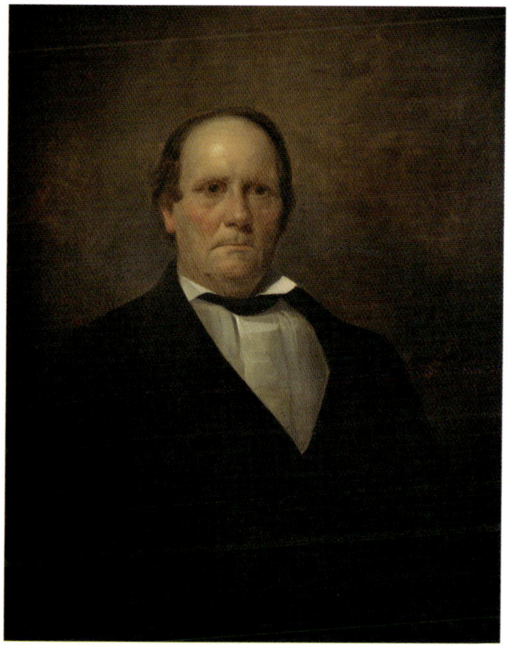

146

Secretary James Guthrie, 1856

Oil on canvas, 33⅛ × 26¼ in. (84.1 × 66.7 cm)

INSCRIBED LOWER CENTER: Stanley / 1856

PRESENT COLLECTION: U.S. Treasury Collection, Washington, D.C., Gifts and Bequests Fund (P.1998.001)

PROVENANCE: Caleb Cushing; by descent to the Christian family, Newburyport, New Hampshire; Newburyport Historical Society, 1950s; (North East Auctions, New Hampshire, August 1, 1998); present owner

LIFETIME EXHIBITIONS: First Annual Exhibition, Washington Art Association, Washington, D.C., 1857

When Franklin Pierce ascended to the highest office of the United States in 1853 as the fourteenth president, he was known as a moderate Democrat. He appointed several like-minded gentlemen to be the cornerstones of his cabinet, among them James Guthrie as secretary of the treasury. Although Pierce is commonly regarded as one of the worst presidents in U.S. history, his choice of Guthrie was inspired. A hard money Democrat, Guthrie pressed for a universal national currency supported by a singular gold standard. It was a particularly prescient decision, since gold pouring in from the West was in increasingly abundant supply, and as a consequence, the nation's treasury prospered and the national debt was substantially reduced.

Stanley painted this portrait not for the Treasury Department, but for one of Guthrie's fellow cabinet members, U.S. attorney general Caleb Cushing (cat. no. 153). Cushing also commissioned Stanley to render a likeness of the U.S. secretary of state, *William L. Marcy* (location unknown), at about the same time, between 1856 and 1857. The portrait of Guthrie descended through the Cushing family and was purchased by the Treasury Department in 1998. It is said to be the first lifetime portrait of a secretary in the department's collection.[1]

1. I am grateful to Merrill Lavine, registrar of the collections of the U.S. Department of the Treasury, for this information about the history of the Cushing commissions and of this painting in particular.

147

Reverdy Johnson, 1856

Oil on canvas, 32 × 25⅛ in. (81.3 × 63.8 cm) (oval)

INSCRIBED CENTER RIGHT: Stanley. / 1856

PRESENT COLLECTION: U.S. Department of Justice, Washington, D.C.

PROVENANCE: The artist; present owner, 1856

Stanley painted this portrait of Reverdy Johnson in 1856. It was one of a series of eight similar portraits of attorneys general that he executed between 1856 and 1858 for the Justice Department, one of the largest group commissions of the artist's career. During this period, Stanley was active in the life of the Washington, D.C., art community, and it may have been his elevated stature there that facilitated such a lucrative assignment.

Johnson served as the twenty-first attorney general under President Zachary Taylor, 1849 to 1850. He resigned that position

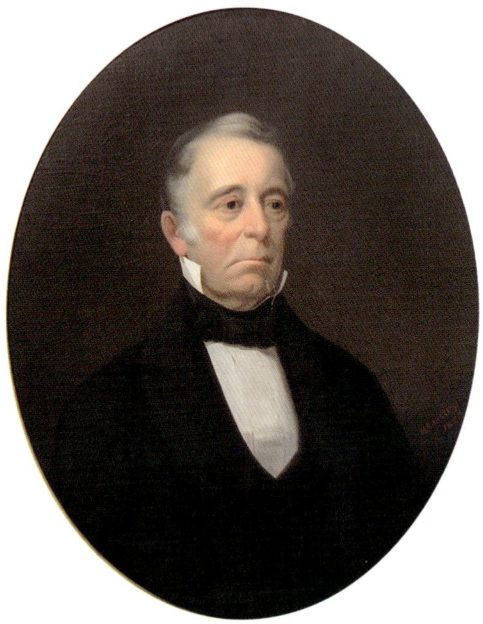

147

after Millard Fillmore became president. Johnson served during complex times, when the territories from the Mexican War were being assessed against the backdrop of national expansionist aspirations and the divisive slavery question as it related to the West. Over the brief period that Taylor was president, the administration would gradually veer toward northern sympathies. In 1861, long after Johnson had departed the attorney general's office, and as the Civil War rapidly approached, he participated in a last-ditch, futile Peace Congress in Washington.

148

Benjamin Franklin Butler, c. 1856

Oil on canvas, 34¾ × 27⅞ in. (88.3 × 70.8 cm) (sight measurements)

INSCRIBED CENTER RIGHT: Stanley / after C. B. King

PRESENT COLLECTION: U.S. Department of Justice, Washington, D.C.

PROVENANCE: The artist; present owner

Benjamin Franklin Butler was appointed attorney general of the United States in 1833 by President Andrew Jackson, and he remained in that position through part of the Martin Van Buren administration. In 1837 Van Buren asked him to serve as secretary of war. Sometime in the mid-1830s, Butler had his portrait painted by Charles Bird King, who was living in Washington, D.C., at the time.

King and Stanley were close friends and compatriots in the production of Indian portraits.[1] When their galleries of Indian portraits were first presented together at the Smithsonian in 1858, the museum's secretary, Joseph Henry, remarked that the combined exhibit comprised "the most valuable collection in existence of illustrations of the features, customs, and habits of the aborigines of this country."[2] When asked by the Franklin Pierce administration to paint portraits of notable attorneys general in 1856, it was probably a welcome task for Stanley to copy the King portrait of Butler. Butler was, at that date, living in New York, and King's likeness captured the noted barrister at the time of his service as U.S. attorney general.

1. See Andrew F. Cosentino, *The Paintings of Charles Bird King (1785–1862)* (Washington, D.C.: Smithsonian Institution Press, 1977), 49.

2. *Annual Report of the Board of Regents of the Smithsonian Institution . . . 1858* (Washington, D.C., Smithsonian Institutin, 1859), 41–42.

149

John Jordan Crittenden, 1856

Oil on canvas, 32¼ × 25⅛ in. (81.9 × 63.8 cm) (sight measurements, oval)

INSCRIBED CENTER RIGHT: J. M. Stanley. / 1856

PRESENT COLLECTION: U.S. Department of Justice, Washington, D.C.

PROVENANCE: The artist; present owner, 1856

John Jordan Crittenden was an extremely talented, versatile, and popular member of the Washington political scene in the first half of the nineteenth century. He was first elevated to the national stage in 1817 as U.S. senator from Kentucky and served off and on

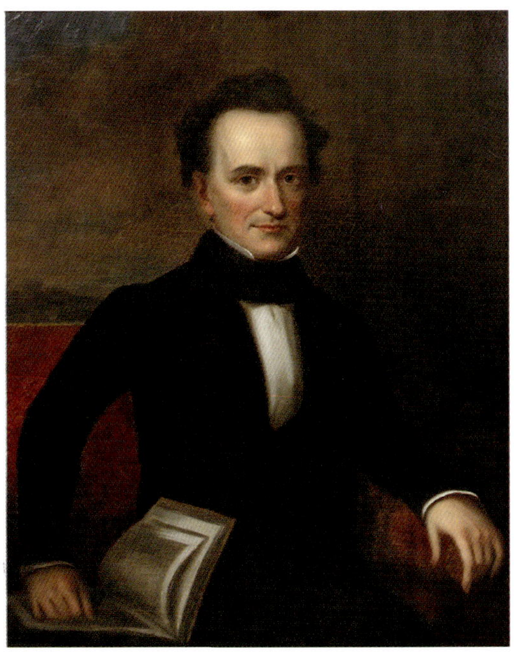

148

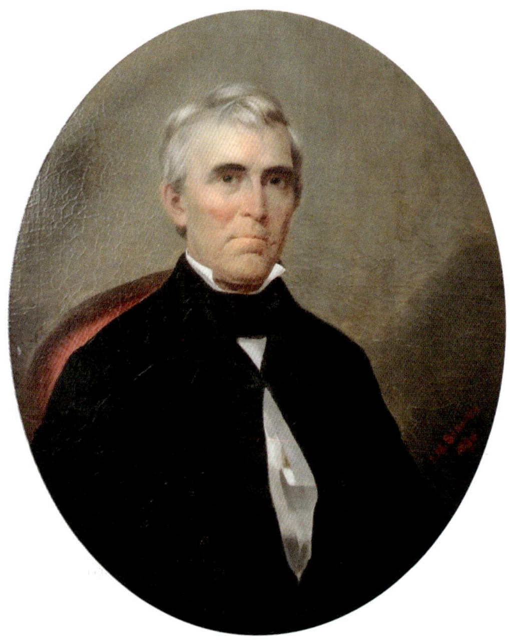

149

in that post for the next thirty years. A gifted lawyer, he also held the post of U.S. attorney once in 1827 for President John Quincy Adams and attorney general twice, in 1841 for Benjamin Harrison and in 1854 for Millard Fillmore.

Stanley, commissioned by the Franklin Pierce administration in 1856 to paint a series of eight portraits of U.S. attorneys general, completed this portrait that year. The two men shared few common interests regarding the West, as Crittenden had played a prominent role in opposing the Mexican War, subsequent Texas annexation, and the acquisition of Oregon from the British. But Crittenden, like Stanley, was a devout Unionist. He endeavored to sustain the Missouri Compromise as a strategy to preserve national stability in the years before the war broke out. Once the conflict was in progress, he successfully beseeched the Kentucky legislature to remain true to the Union.[1] Kentucky's decision was, as President Lincoln famously said, next to God's blessing, the most important contributor to the North's success.

1. See Crittenden's entry in Allen Johnson and Dumas Malone, eds., *Dictionary of American Biography*, vol. 2 (New York: Scribner, 1928), 546–49.

150

William Pinkney, 1856

Oil on canvas, 29¼ × 24½ in. (74.3 × 61.6 cm) (sight measurements)

PRESENT COLLECTION: U.S. Department of Justice, Washington, D.C.

PROVENANCE: The artist; present owner, 1856

William Pinkney served as U.S. Attorney General from 1811 to 1814 under President James Madison. He died in Washington, D.C., in 1822, some thirty-four years before Stanley came to paint this portrait. There was no photography in Pinkney's day, so there were no daguerreotypes for Stanley to copy. But there was a portrait in oils by the painter of America's revolutionary heroes, Charles Willson Peale, which was in the possession of Pinkney's grandson, William Pinkney Whyte of Baltimore. It provided a fine model for the later artist.

Pinkney was born in 1764. He studied law in Baltimore and, in 1788, was a member of the Constitutional Convention. At the turn of the century, he worked as part of the commission for Jay's Treaty and traveled to England with James Madison for negotiations with the British. Madison was impressed with Pinkney's skills and invited him to be part of his administration in 1811. This appointment was followed by many years of distinguished service to the Congress, both the House and the Senate, and in ambassadorial posts in Italy and Russia.

151

Edmund Jennings Randolph, 1856

Oil on canvas, 28 × 23¼ in. (71.1 × 59.1 cm) (sight measurements, oval)

INSCRIBED LOWER CENTER: STANLEY. / from Original

PRESENT COLLECTION: U.S. Department of Justice, Washington, D.C.

PROVENANCE: The artist; present owner, 1856

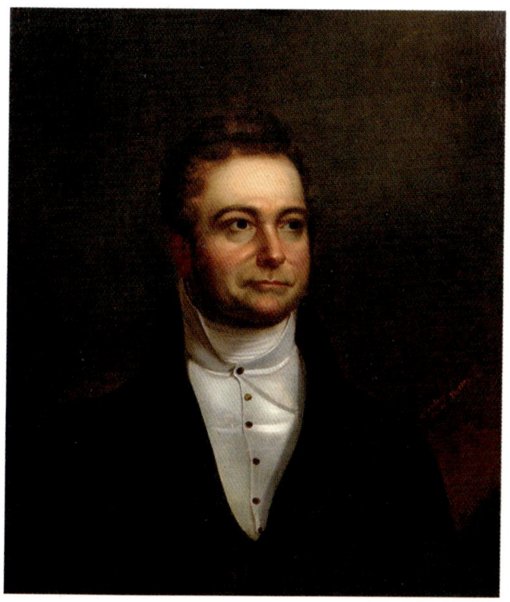

150

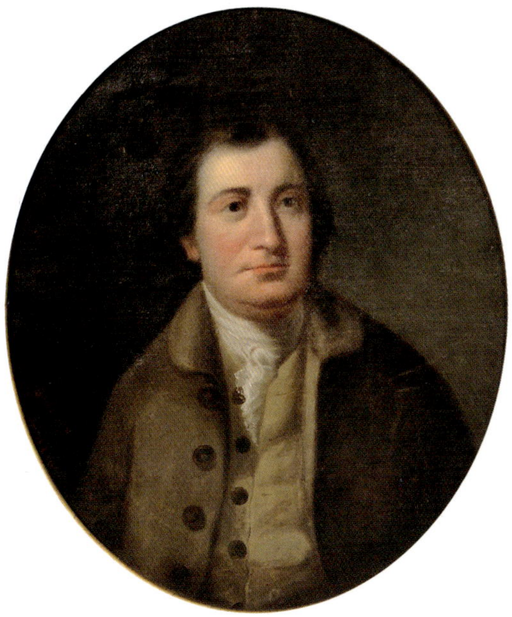

151

Edmund Randolph was a true son of Virginia. Born in Williamsburg and educated at William and Mary College, he was Virginia's attorney general in 1776 and her governor from 1786 to 1788. He was also the first attorney general of the United States, under George Washington, for whom he had previously provided personal legal counsel.

As a Virginia delegate to the Constitutional Convention in 1787, Randolph brought forward the Virginia Plan as a suggestion on how the new nation might govern itself. He was against the slave trade and in favor of a strong, republican central government. The final constitution adopted many of his plan's recommendations.

When Thomas Jefferson (Randolph's second cousin) gave up his seat in Washington's cabinet as the country's first secretary of state, Randolph was appointed to replace him. He labored on many complicated issues in that capacity, including finalizing Pinkney's Treaty and guiding the negotiations for the Treaty of San Lorenzo in 1795, which opened western navigation on the Mississippi River to Americans and fixed the boundaries between Spain and the United States.

152

Isaac Toucey, 1857

Oil on canvas, 31¾ × 24¾ in. (80.6 × 62.9 cm) (sight measurements)

INSCRIBED CENTER RIGHT: STANLEY / 1857[?]9

PRESENT COLLECTION: U.S. Department of Justice, Washington, D.C.

PROVENANCE: The artist; present owner

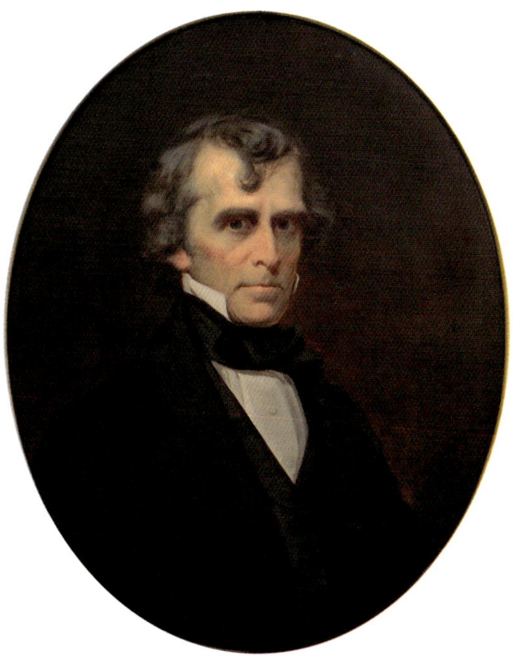

152

Stanley was very busy in the mid-1850s painting portraits of Washington, D.C., celebrities. The year 1857 was especially full in that regard, and his portrait of ex-governor and U.S. senator from Connecticut Isaac Toucey reveals the success of his prodigious output and the breadth of his political connections. Stanley was commissioned by the Department of Justice to paint a series of portraits documenting past and present attorneys general. Toucey had served as attorney general under President James K. Polk in 1848 and 1849, so this likeness showed his sitter over a decade older than when he held that office.

Toucey left the Senate in spring 1857 to take a position as secretary of the navy, a job he held until 1861. He was known as a southern sympathizer during those years and directed the U.S. Navy such that it favored the secessionist cause. So maligned was he during the war that the state of Connecticut opted to remove a portrait of him as governor that hung in the state house.[1]

1. Dumas Malone, ed., *Dictionary of American Biography*, vol. 19 (New York: Scribner, 1932), 601.

153

Caleb Cushing, 1857

Oil on canvas, 31⅞ × 25 in. (81.0 × 63.5 cm) (sight measurements, oval)

INSCRIBED CENTER RIGHT: J. M. Stanley. / From Carpenter [?] 1857

PRESENT COLLECTION: U.S. Department of Justice, Washington, D.C.

PROVENANCE: The artist; present owner

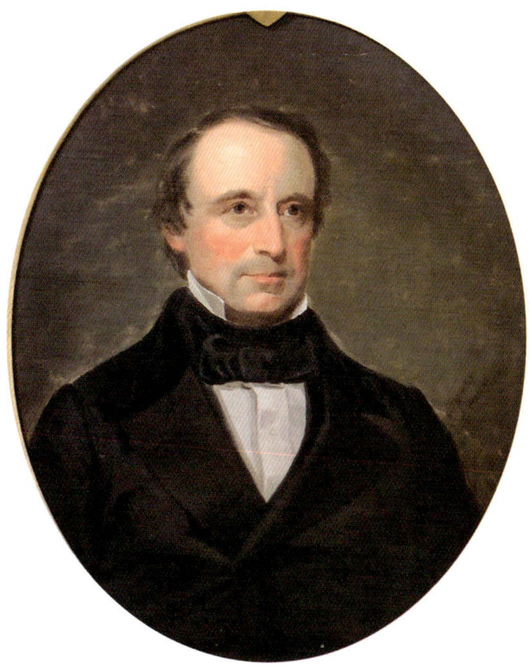

153

Through the late 1850s, Stanley used his political savvy to garner portrait commissions from various departments within the Franklin Pierce administration. Some were from life, but many were copied from existing portraits. The group of eight portraits done for the Department of Justice included an engaging likeness of Caleb Cushing, Pierce's attorney general spanning his full, albeit ill-fated, term from 1853 to 1857. It was copied from an existing portrait by an artist named Carpenter, whose full identity has not been confirmed but who is presumed to be the painter of several presidents, Francis Bicknell Carpenter of New York.

Cushing was from Massachusetts. Educated at Harvard, he came up through the ranks of his state legislature and the U.S. Congress (where he served 1834 to 1843). Cushing earned a reputation as a vigorous advocate for American expansion and in 1847 raised a regiment for and fought beside General Zachary Taylor in the Mexican War. He was serving as a Justice in the Massachusetts Supreme Court when Pierce recruited him.[1] Cushing was well equipped to provide legal counsel to and advocate for the infamous expansionist president.

Cushing is thought to have commissioned two other Stanley portraits of members of the Pierce administration in those years, the secretary of state, *William L. Marcy* (unlocated), and the secretary of the treasury, *James Guthrie* (cat. no. 146).[2]

1. Among the many biographical accounts of Cushing, perhaps the most usable is Lillian C. Buttre, *The American Portrait Gallery* (New York: J. C. Buttre, 1877), n.p.

2. This information comes from a fact sheet on the James Guthrie portrait supplied by the U.S. Treasury Department, Washington, D.C.

154

Captain John Smith and the Discovery of Washington, 1857

Captain John Smith and Party Landing at Jamestown; The Landing at Jamestown

Oil on canvas, 23⅝ × 35⅝ (60.0 × 90.5 cm)

PRESENT COLLECTION: Gilcrease Museum, Tulsa, Oklahoma (0126.1145)

PROVENANCE: The artist; John Carl Richberg, Knoxville, Tennessee; by descent to Donald R. Richberg, Charlottesville, Virginia, 1949; (Kennedy Galleries, New York, New York, 1956); Thomas Gilcrease, Tulsa, Oklahoma; present owner

LIFETIME EXHIBITIONS: J. C. McGuire and Co., Auctioneers, Washington Art Association Building (Auction Sale of Paintings), December, 20, 1858

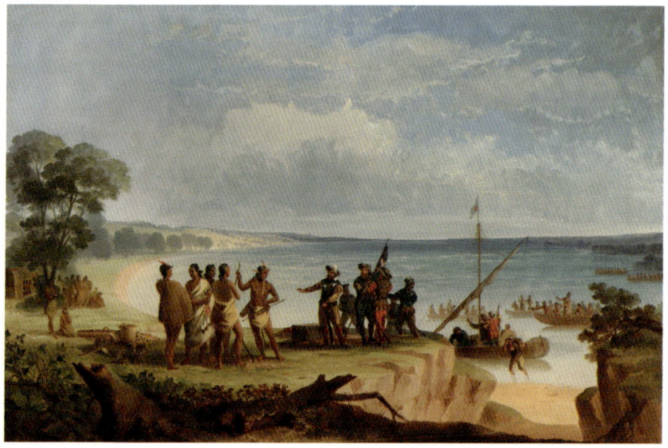

154

Since the 1940s, this painting has been known as *Captain John Smith and Party Landing at Jamestown.*[1] It was thought to have been painted in Washington, D.C., in 1857 while Stanley and his family were residents there. The latter assumption is correct; the title is not.

Under the header of "The Discovery of Washington City," the *National Intelligencer* announced on July 15, 1857, that one of its reporters had seen on Stanley's easel a painting that depicted the historic scene.[2] Two days later, in a write-up about local news, the *Washington Union* newspaper confirmed the sighting.[3]

Both papers noted Smith as the first white voyager to travel up the Potomac River. The *Washington Union* made much of the accurate portrayal of Stanley's Indians.[4] The other paper repeated the compliment but focused more on the setting, speaking of Greenleaf Point and its history as a place of considerable public interest at the confluence of the Potomac and Anacostia rivers. Stanley's oil was compared in thematic importance with paintings at the nation's capital, such as *Discovery of the Mississippi by de Soto*, by William Powell, and related closely to John Gadsby Chapman's often-reproduced 1841 painting of Smith's *Landing at Jamestown* (fig. 154.1).[5] Stanley's Indian figures may have been inspired by Theodore De Bry scenes painted in 1590 for John White in Virginia, and Smith's gesture in the Stanley painting is reminiscent of William Penn's outreached arms in Benjamin West's famous epic canvas *Penn's Treaty with the Indians* (Pennsylvania Academy of the Fine Arts, Philadelphia).

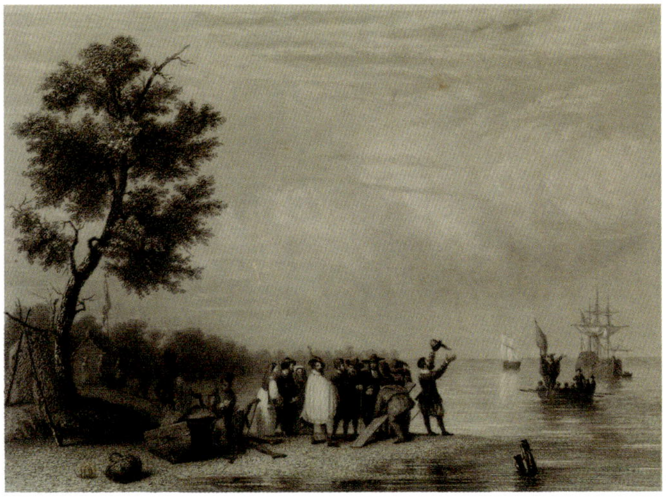

FIG. 154.1.
Moseley Isaac Danforth after John Gadsby Chapman, *Landing at Jamestown*, 1841. Etching and engraving on paper; 5 13/16 × 7 15/16 in. (14.8 × 20.2 cm). Courtesy Pennsylvania Academy of the Fine Arts (1928.18.9)

1. Donald R. Richberg to Stanley's granddaughter Alice Acheson, November 13, 1949, Stanley Papers.

2. "Local Intelligence," *National Intelligencer*, July 15, 1857.

3. "Local News," *Washington Union*, July 17, 1857.

4. Ibid.

5. See *New-York Mirror*, May 8, 1841, engraving by M. I. Danforth, for example.

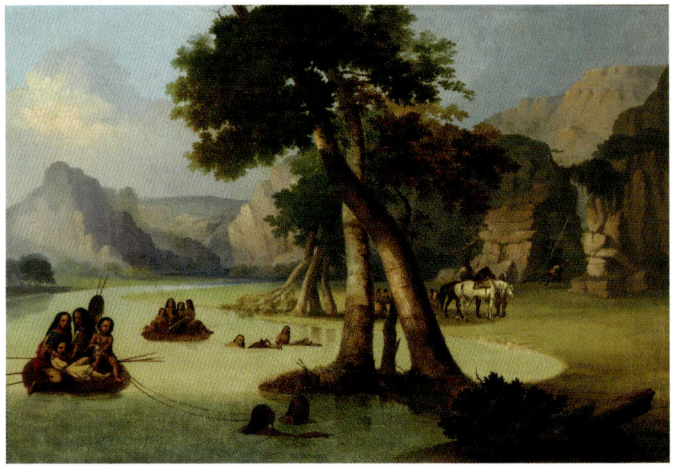

155

155
View on Milk River, 1857

View on Milk River—Minnesota Territory, Blackfoot Indian Crossing

Oil on canvas, 27 3/8 × 39 3/8 in. (69.5 × 100.0 cm)

INSCRIBED VERSO: View on Milk River / Min[nesota] Territory / Blackfoot Indian / crossing- Stanley / 1857

PRESENT COLLECTION: Gilcrease Museum, Tulsa, Oklahoma (0126.1138)

PROVENANCE: A. G. Seaman, New York, New York; Robert J. McKeon, Chappaqua, New York; (M. Knoedler and Co., New York, New York, 1952); Thomas Gilcrease, Tulsa, Oklahoma; present owner

The Stevens expedition crossed the lower Milk River several times during its trek west in 1853. Stanley produced a number of sketches along that course, two of which were worked into finished watercolors (cat. nos. 098 and 100) for the lithographers' illustrations in the final Stevens report of 1860. Stanley was given a special assignment to treat with the Piegan Indians farther up the river, and en route to a rendezvous with them, he crossed the Milk River some thirty miles beyond. It was here that he witnessed this scene, one that inspired him to paint at least two large canvases some years later.[1] The other is *Crossing the Milk River* (cat. no. 140), a slightly larger oil, which though not so colorful is more compelling as a composition. The grouping and poses of Indian women, children, and pets crossing the river are almost the same in both works.

Stanley was taken by the Piegan mode of river travel in buffalo hide bull boats. He incorporated these exotic vessels in several other finished paintings, including *Fort Benton Indians* (cat. no. 166).

1. Stevens, *Narrative and Final Report*, 116.

156
Peter Force, 1857

Oil on canvas, 34 × 27 in. (86.4 × 68.8 cm)

INSCRIBED LOWER RIGHT: J M Stanley / 1857

PRESENT COLLECTION: Rare Book and Special Collections Division, Library of Congress, Washington, D.C.

PROVENANCE: The artist; Peter Force; by descent to Charles Hunter, New Orleans, Louisiana; present owner, by gift, 1961

Peter Force, age sixty-seven when Stanley painted this portrait, was recognized for multiple careers as a publisher, a military officer (he had risen to the rank of major general), and a politician (he served as mayor of Washington, D.C., 1836–1840). But his true

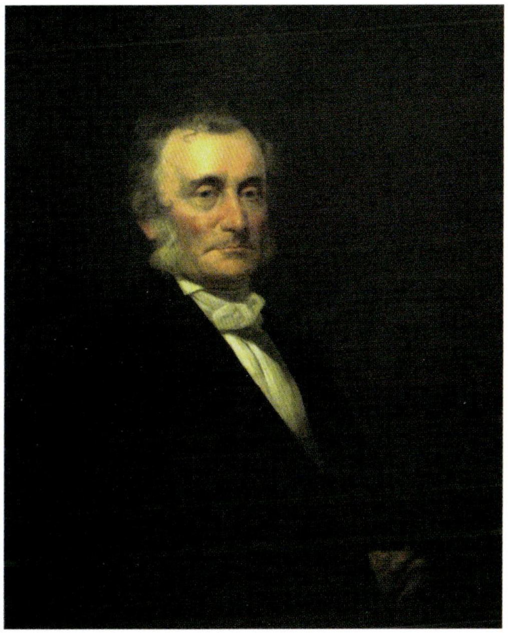

156

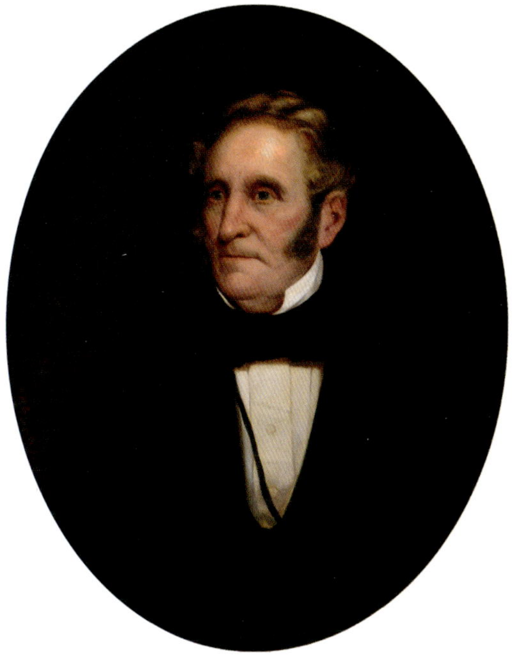

157

passion was history and books. In 1833, by an act of Congress, he was authorized to research and publish a mammoth multivolume history and bibliography of colonial America up to 1787 and the ratification of the U.S. Constitution. Known as the *American Archives: A Documentary History of the English Colonies of North America*, it comprised six series of six or more volumes each. He completed most of this work over the next twenty years, when the project was brought to a close.[1]

Over the course of Force's research, he amassed a vast personal library on the subject. In 1867, a year before Force died, Congress authorized $100,000 to purchase it for the Library of Congress. Consisting of about sixty thousand volumes and pamphlets, Force's library was regarded historically as one of the Library of Congress's largest and most formative collections.[2]

1. James Grant Wilson and John Fiske, *Appleton's Cyclopedia of American Biography* (New York: D. Appleton, 1898), 499.

2. Frederic R. Goff, "The Oldest Library in Washington: The Rare Book Division of the Library of Congress," *Records of the Columbia Historical Society* 70 (1969): 332–37.

157

Senator Thomas Hart Benton, 1857

Oil on canvas, 34 × 27 in. (86.4 × 68.8 cm) (oval)

INSCRIBED LOWER LEFT: J. M. Stanley 1857

PRESENT COLLECTION: Harry S. Truman Library and Museum, Independence, Missouri

PROVENANCE: The artist; R. J. Lackey by 1860; John Carl Richberg, Knoxville, Tennessee; Donald R. Richberg, Charlottesville, Virginia, 1949; by descent to his wife Florence W. Richberg, 1960; by gift to President Harry Truman, 1964; present owner

LIFETIME EXHIBITIONS: Fourth Annual Exhibition, Washington Art Association, Washington, D.C., 1860

When Stanley was working on his portraits of Washington dignitaries, like Zachary Taylor's appointee as the United States' first secretary of the interior, whose initial report in 1849 called for a transcontinental railroad, he made certain that he also included the true champion of Manifest Destiny, Senator Thomas Hart Benton of Missouri. This portrait was painted in Benton's last years, after he had fulfilled an ambitious career promoting the West and convincing the American people that it was their fate and calling to expand into the continent's farthest reaches.

Benton's son-in-law, John C. Fremont, was exploring the West at Benton's behest during the very years that Stanley was traveling the Santa Fe Trail and beyond in 1846 and across the Northwest to the Pacific Ocean in 1853. Much of Stanley's accomplishment as an artist was dependent on and motivated by Benton's nationalist vision, energy, and philosophy. Although Stanley, as a depicter of Indians rather than pioneers, painted relatively few works showing the Anglo expansion onto the frontier, one of his favorite outposts and subjects in the Far West was none other than the senator's namesake, Fort Benton.

When exhibited in the 1860 Fourth Annual Exhibition of the Washington Art Association, the portrait commanded favorable attention of the statesman's friends for its "faithfulness."[1]

1. "Washington Correspondence," *Frank Leslie's Illustrated Newspaper*, February 25, 1860, 200.

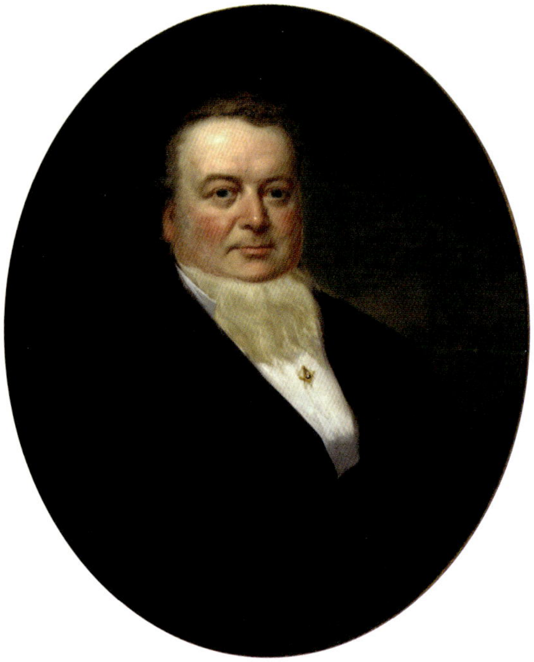

158

A Mason of Washington, D.C., 1857

Oil on canvas, 34 × 27 in. (86.4 × 68.6 cm) (oval)

INSCRIBED CENTER LEFT: J. M. Stanley / 1857

PRESENT COLLECTION: Private collection

PROVENANCE: Henry H. Glassie, Washington, D.C.; (Montrose Galleries, Bethesda, Maryland, 1979); present owner

The identity of this distinguished gentleman is unknown, as are the circumstances of the commission. Nonetheless, it is one of Stanley's most accomplished portraits. The likeness brings the sitter to life, the flourish in the flesh tones is sophisticated and vivacious, and the man's expression is commanding and engaging. Whoever the mason was, he got his money's worth from Stanley.

159

The Last of Their Race, 1857

The Doomed Race; The Last of the Race; The Last of His Race

Oil on canvas, 43 × 60 in. (109.2 × 152.4 cm)

INSCRIBED LOWER LEFT: J. M. Stanley / 1857

PRESENT COLLECTION: Buffalo Bill Center of the West, Cody, Wyoming (5.75)

PROVENANCE: The artist; (J. C. McGuire and Co., Washington, D.C.): Isaac I. Stevens; General Hazard Stevens; Major Richard Stevens Eskridge, Olympia, Washington; Helen Eskridge, Olympia, Washington, 1953; (J. N. Bartfield Galleries, New York, New York); present owner

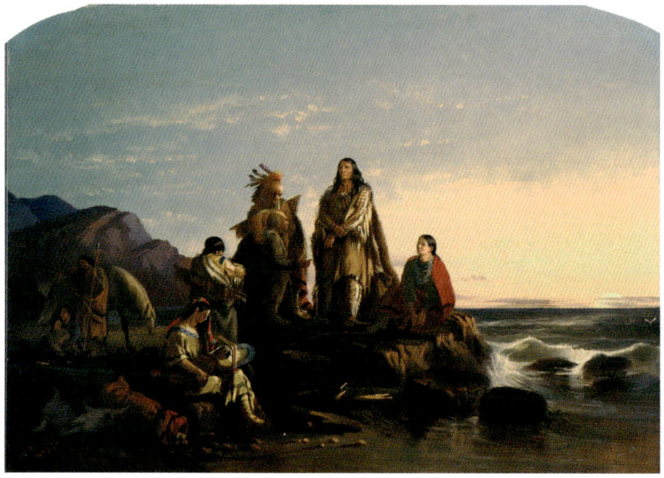

159

LIFETIME EXHIBITIONS: First Annual Exhibition, Washington Art Association (March 1857); Tenth Annual Exhibition of the Maryland Institute, Baltimore, Maryland (September 1857); J. C. McGuire and Co. Auctioneers, Washington Art Association Building (Auction Sale of Paintings), December 20, 1858; Michigan State Fair, Detroit, 1867; *A Great Sale of Paintings*, Dean, Brown and Co. and Mr. J. M. Stanley, St. Andrews Hall, Detroit, Michigan, 1867

Stanley's whole mission over more than a decade between 1842 and 1853 was to document the Native people of the West before their "passing."[1] He did his work with an expressed sense of urgency, hoping to paint them in their unspoiled state, prior to Anglo influence and acculturation taking sway. The resolve that he brought to the task was in good measure self-imposed and part of a marketing strategy, because the paintings could be more easily sold if the patrons felt these might be the last images obtainable before the Indians slipped into extinction and oblivion.

This oil, the first of two known versions of *The Last of Their Race* (see cat. no. 165), was completed in 1857. It was shown that March at the Washington Art Association and prompted a local poet, L. A. Christie, to reprint a prophetic poem he had written in 1854, which included these two lines: "Great Spirit, unto Thee / Thy children turn their face in their last agony."[2] The painting pictures a group of mostly Piegan Indians with their chief Seen From Afar and his sister, Natawista, on the far right, closest to the imposing sea toward which they are being pushed. The sun sets in the west, just as Stanley intended to propose to his patrons it was setting on Indian people.

1. Stanley implies this in the preface to his catalogue *Portraits of North American Indians*.

2. L. A. Christie, "Lines Suggested on Seeing Stanley's Painting of 'The Doomed Race' Now on Exhibition by the Washington A. Association," *National Intelligencer*, March 18, 1857.

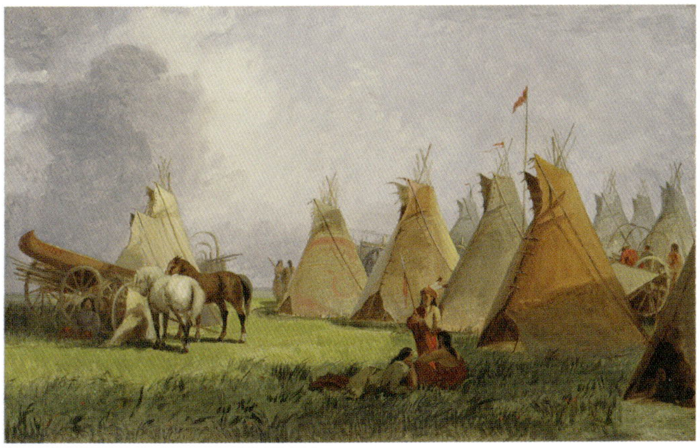

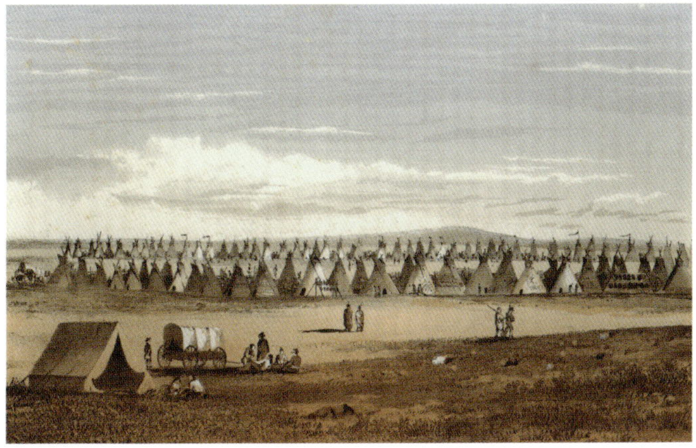

160

Camp of the Red River Hunters, 1857

Oil on canvas, 13¾ × 21⅛ in. (34.9 × 53.6 cm)

INSCRIBED LOWER RIGHT: Stanley / 1857

PRESENT COLLECTION: Amon Carter Museum of American Art, Fort Worth, Texas (1966.52)

PROVENANCE: The artist; probably Alexander Hamilton Redfield, Detroit, Michigan, 1857; [?]; (Kennedy Galleries, New York, New York, 1966); present owner, 1966

Stanley and Stevens had been particularly attracted to one of the Red River hunters' camps during their journey across the northern plains in 1853. The troop of Canadian hunters that the expedition encountered comprised 824 carts, 1,200 horses, and 1,300 people, "the whole," according to Stevens, "presenting a very fine appearance."[1] By summer 1854, about eight months after he had returned from his travels with Stevens, Stanley had painted a large panel for his frontier panorama *Scenes and Incidents of Stanley's Western Wilds* that pictured, among other things, his recollections of the Red River hunters. Stanley found the setting an especially joyful scene. According to the program for the panorama, "These lodges, and the smooth prairie round them, seem to contain many happy people." In all, it was "a picture of a happy time."[2] That same ebullience fills this later small oil, *Camp of the Red River Hunters*. The impressively scaled teepees shelter a group of men who have found a moment of relaxation beneath the long afternoon shadows. He subsequently painted a more panoramic watercolor of the camp that was lithographed and included in the official Stevens report (fig. 160.1).

This painting is thought to have been owned by Alexander Hamilton Redfield, perhaps acquired when Redfield sat for his portrait (cat. no. 161) with Stanley in 1858. As official agent for the Indians of the upper Missouri River in 1857, Redfield would have encountered the Red River hunters, who traveled south onto the plains each summer and autumn in pursuit of bison.

FIG. 160.1.
Sarony, Major, and Knapp after John Mix Stanley, *Camp of the Red River Hunters*, 1853–1855. Toned lithograph; 5¾ × 9 in. (14.6 × 22.9 cm). From Stevens, *Narrative and Final Report*, opp. p. 65. Courtesy McCracken Research Library, Buffalo Bill Center of the West, Cody, Wyoming

1. A more expansive view of this scene appears in Stevens, *Narrative and Final Report*, 65.

2. Donoho, *Scenes and Incidents*, 9.

161

Alexander Hamilton Redfield, 1858

Oil on canvas, 34½ × 27 in. (87.6 × 68.6 cm) (oval)

PRESENT COLLECTION: Amon Carter Museum of American Art, Fort Worth, Texas (1971.51)

PROVENANCE: The artist; Alexander Hamilton Redfield, Detroit, Michigan, 1858; by descent to Alexander H. Redfield, Jr.; Susan Novell, Washington, D.C.; Frank D. Gardner; Susan N. Gardner, Aledo, Texas, 1971; present owner, 1971

Alexander Hamilton Redfield was a noted Michigan attorney, a state senator, and a regent of the University of Michigan. A prominent member of the Democratic Party, he was awarded by President James Buchanan the position of agent for the Indians of the upper Missouri in 1857, following Alexander Culbertson's (cat. no. 080) retirement. Redfield hung his hat at Fort Union but traveled widely up and down the river, especially among the Sioux to the south.

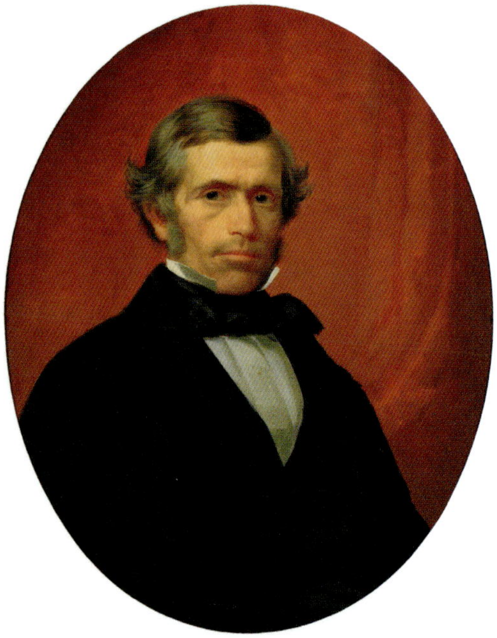

161

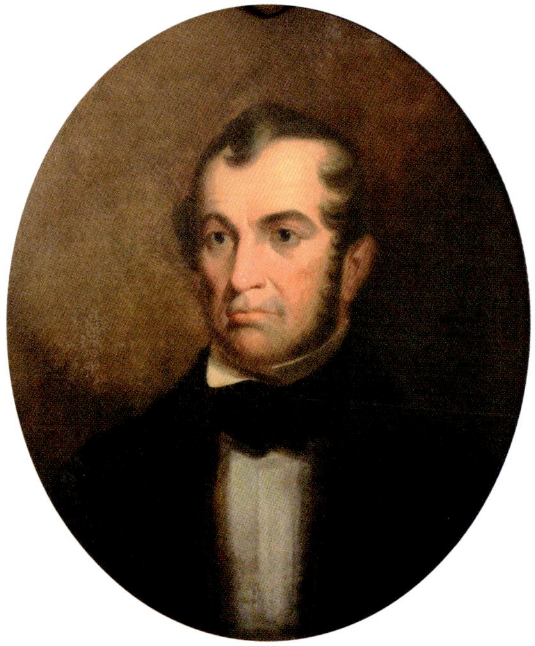

162

In 1858 Redfield helped arrange a treaty between the Yankton Sioux and the U.S. government, known as the Treaty of Washington. For this treaty, he brought a group of Sioux to the nation's capital. The treaty was signed on April 19, and Redfield, evincing a rather smug self-satisfaction, sat for his portrait with Stanley on the 25th of that month. The treaty ceded some 430,000 acres of prime land in Minnesota for the government's promise of $1.6 million over five years. From 1859 until 1861, when he was replaced by Republican President Abraham Lincoln, Redfield served as agent to the Yankton Sioux.

Redfield later became the comptroller of the City of Detroit and a state senator for that district.[1]

1. Biographical information on Redfield is provided in *Michigan Biographies*, vol. 2 (Lansing: University of Michigan Press, 1924), 223; and in Patience Nauta, of the Detroit Historical Department, to Julie Schimmel, March 9, 1982, and Susan N. Gardner to Willis Woods, of the Detroit Institute of Arts, May 21, 1970, Schimmel Papers.

162

Hugh Swinton Legaré, 1858

Oil on canvas, 25⅝ × 20¾ in. (65.1 × 52.7 cm) (sight measurements, oval)

INSCRIBED LOWER LEFT: J. M. Stanley. / from E. D. Marchant

PRESENT COLLECTION: U.S. Department of Justice, Washington, D.C.

PROVENANCE: The artist; present owner, 1858

Hugh Swinton Legaré was born in Charleston, South Carolina, in 1797. He studied law there and in Europe. When he returned from Europe in 1820, he promptly and successfully sought office within the state legislature. In the early 1840s, while serving North Carolina in the U.S. Congress, he attracted the attention of President John Tyler. Tyler invited Legaré to be his attorney general, a post that he filled for the next couple of years, until his death in 1843.

When Stanley was asked to paint portraits of noted U.S. attorneys general, Legaré was deceased, and the artist had to rely on the work of a previous likeness. Legaré's surviving sister, Mary Swinton Legaré Bullen, owned a portrait painted in around 1841 by the portraitist Edward Dalton Marchant. A visitor to Stanley's studio in 1858 saw his copy and deemed it "an excellent likeness and highly credible to the skill and taste of Mr. Stanley."[1] Marchant was known to have painted American presidents, including John Adams and George Washington in the early 1840s, but like Stanley's portrait of Legaré, these too were posthumous.[2]

1. From an untitled article, *Charleston Courier*, October 1, 1858, Stanley scrapbook.

2. These portraits are in the collection of the Smithsonian American Art Museum.

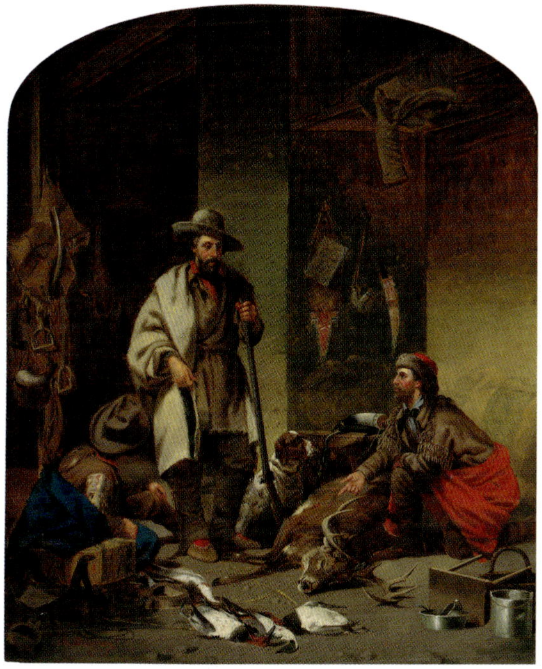

163

The Trapper's Cabin, 1858

The Huntsman's Cabin; The Disputed Shot; The Trappers

Oil on canvas, 36 × 29 in. (91.5 × 73.5 cm)

INSCRIBED LOWER LEFT: J. M. Stanley. / 1858

PRESENT COLLECTION: National Gallery of Art, Washington, D.C., Corcoran Collection, gift of William Wilson Corcoran (69.5)

PROVENANCE: The artist; William Wilson Corcoran, 1859; by gift to Corcoran Gallery of Art, 1869, by transfer to present owner, 2014

LIFETIME EXHIBITIONS: Philp's Gallery, Washington, D.C., 1858; J. C. McGuire and Co. Auctioneers, Washington Art Association Building (Auction Sale of Paintings), December 20, 1858; Third Annual Exhibition, Washington Art Association, Washington, D.C., 1858–1859; Eleventh Annual Exhibition of the Maryland Institute, Baltimore, Maryland, September, 1858

Stanley exhibited this painting as *The Trapper's Cabin* in Washington, D.C., in 1858 at the Philp's Gallery, where it was referred to as "the best thing so far coming off his easel."[1] A bit later that year, it was offered at auction at the Washington Art Association's annual exhibition under the title of *The Trappers*.[2] It was loaned by William Wilson Corcoran and hung in the same galleries as Arthur Fitzwilliam Tait's *Hunting Scene* and two George Caleb Bingham engravings of frontier democracy in action, *Stump Speaking* and *County Election, Mo.*[3] The Stanley painting shares the spirit of those other three works. It is all about both sportsmanship and politics.

The painting came to the Corcoran Gallery of Art as a gift in 1869 carrying the title *The Disputed Shot*, thus circumventing the observation that these are not really trappers at all, at least not in the normal western sense, even though they wear moccasins and buckskin jackets.[4] They are really hunters, posed in an unlikely interior filled with saddles and Indian accessories, discussing the fatal wound on a buck whitetail deer. As a genre piece, it is mildly engaging. As a history painting, it is vastly more interesting. Allegorically it provides a statement on the times, with the North and South debating the future of the West and the nation. The painting's completion in 1858, shortly after the Dred Scott decision of 1857 and the concomitant nullification of the 1820 Missouri Compromise, establishes a corollary to the contentiously divisive sectional debate over slavery. Like the painting of Stanley's contemporary William T. Ranney, *The Pipe of Friendship* (fig. 163.1), which shows frontiersmen having civil dialogue about the future of the West, Stanley's work is a testament to reasoned and peaceable interaction.[5]

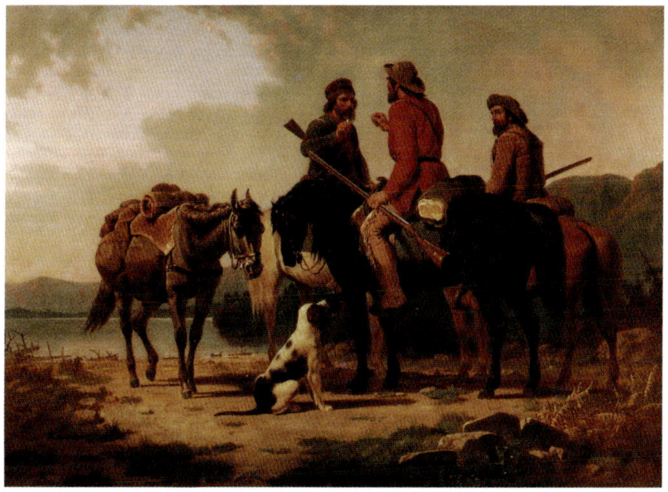

FIG. 163.1.
William Tylee Ranney,
The Pipe of Friendship, c. 1855.
Oil on canvas; 29½ × 40¼ in. (74.9 × 102.2 cm).
Private collection

1. The Philp's Gallery showing is mentioned in "Washington News and Gossip," *Washington Evening Star*, August 21, 1858. This is thought to be the painting's first exhibition.

2. "By J. C. McGuire & Co., Auctioneers," *Washington Evening Star*, December 13, 1858. See also *Catalogue of the Third Annual Exhibition of the Washington Art Association* (Washington: William H. Moore, Printer, 1859), no. 1. Stanley also exhibited a portrait of Commodore John Rodgers of the U.S. Navy as no. 156 (location unknown).

3. *Catalogue of the Third Annual Exhibition*, nos. 136, 189, 190.

4. Stanley was known to have painted two paintings of an actual trapper, Joseph Meek, in 1851. Titled *Flight of a Mountain Trapper* and *The Trapper's Escape*, they were shown in a section on the Blackfeet in Stanley's Indian Gallery. *The Trapper's Escape* and possibly *Flight of a Mountain Trapper* are thought to have survived the Smithsonian fire, although their present whereabouts are unknown.

5. For a full discussion of this reading of the painting, see Lisa Strong, "The Trappers," in *Corcoran Gallery of Art: American Paintings to 1945*, ed. Sarah Cash (Washington, D.C.: Corcoran Gallery of Art, 2006), 121; and for an analogous discussion of the Ranney paintings, see Linda Bantel and Peter H. Hassrick, *Forging an American Identity: The Art of William Ranney, With a Catalogue of His Works* (Cody, Wyo.: Buffalo Bill Historical Center, 2006), 148–50.

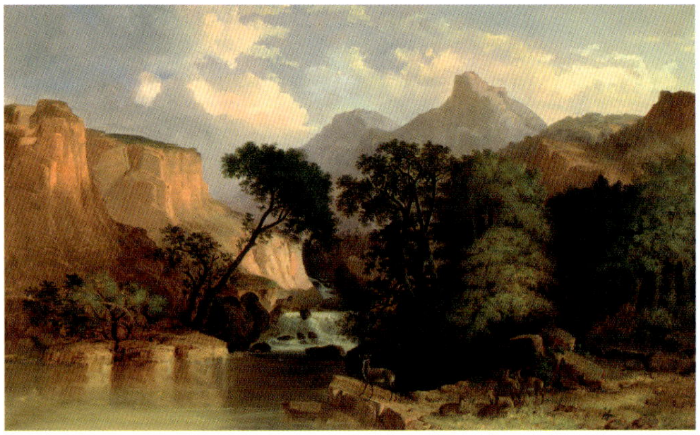

164

Landscape with Deer, c. 1858

Oil on canvas, 26⅛ × 40 in. (66.4 × 101.6 cm)

PRESENT COLLECTION: Private collection

PROVENANCE: The artist; Major General Isaac I. Stevens, Washington, D.C., 1858; by descent to Major Richard Stevens Eskridge, Olympia, Washington; by descent to Mary Eskridge, Washington, D.C.; by descent to Charles McKinley Saltzman; by descent to Charles E. Saltzman, New York; by descent to Cynthia Myrick Saltzman, c. 1971; by descent in the family; (Berry-Hill Galleries, New York, New York, 2003); present owner

In the mid-1850s, Stanley produced several bucolic landscapes. This enchanting view of cascades and deer in a mountain setting was painted for Isaac I. Stevens, who had hired Stanley in 1853 as official artist on his survey of a possible northern route for a transcontinental railroad. The scene is probably set somewhere in present-day Montana, perhaps along either the Marias River or the Teton River, both of which Stanley sketched as the survey party crossed them moving west (cat. nos. 104 and 105).

From Stanley's own oeuvre, this painting closely resembles his famous southwestern landscape *Chain of Spires along the Gila* (cat. no. 130). Both feature a majestic stag profiled against nature's spectacular backdrop. The geomorphology and foliage are dramatically different, but the message of an idealized Eden-like wilderness in the West is shared by both works. *Landscape with Deer* is also compositionally and spiritually resonant with views produced by another western artist of the time, George Caleb Bingham, in his version of *Deer in Landscape*, c. 1850 (fig. 164.1). While Bingham conveyed hints of the sublimity seen in earlier Hudson River School works, such as Thomas Cole's *Landscape with Tree Trunks* (1828, Museum of Art, Rhode Island School of Design), Stanley's scene appears less emotive, equally inviting, and more natural. The monochromatic unity of Bingham's and Stanley's works and their use of suffused atmosphere give them a poetic, transcendental character, one that art historian Barbara Novak has termed a "luminist classicism."[1]

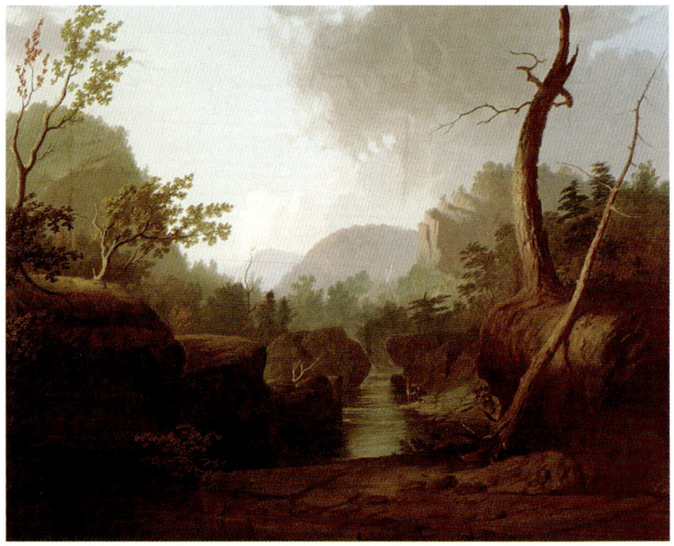

FIG. 164.1.
George Caleb Bingham,
Deer in Landscape, c. 1855.
Oil on canvas; 25 × 30 in. (63.5 × 76.2 cm).
Hunter Museum of American Art, Chattanooga, Tennessee; photograph by Piaget, courtesy Missouri Historical Society

1. Novak, *American Painting*, 105.

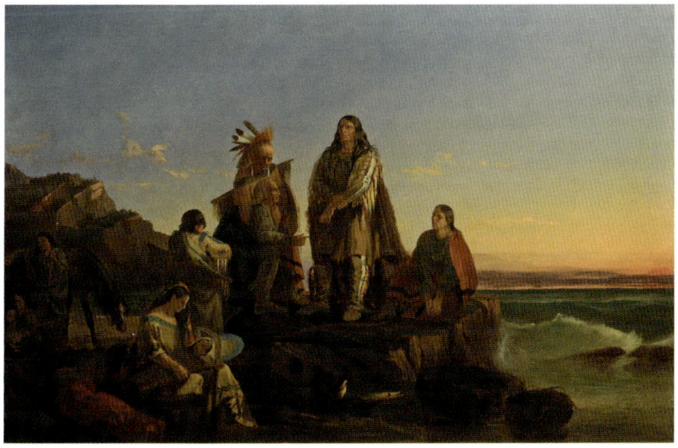

165

The Last of Their Race, c. 1859

Oil on canvas, 35 × 52 in. (88.9 × 132.1 cm)

INSCRIPTION: [Unsigned (in cut-down version)]

PRESENT COLLECTION: Nelda C. and H. J. Lutcher Stark Foundation, Stark Museum of Art, Orange, Texas (31.23.10)

PROVENANCE: The artist; Major Alexander Culbertson, Peoria, Illinois, c. 1850; William Herron, Peoria, Illinois; John W. Herron, Peoria, Illinois; Mrs. John W. Herron, Akron, Ohio; (Edward Eberstadt and Sons, New York, New York, 1958); H. J. Lutcher Stark, Orange, Texas, 1965; present owner

LIFETIME EXHIBITION: Peoria County Fair, Peoria, Illinois, 1859; Seventh Annual Fair of the Illinois State Agricultural Society, Freeport, Illinois, September 5–9, 1859

This work, a second version of his 1857 painting of the same title (cat. no. 159), was purchased by Stanley's friend and fellow lover of Indians, especially the Blackfeet, Alexander Culbertson (cat. no. 080). Culbertson had assisted Isaac Stevens in negotiations with the Indians at Fort Union and Fort Benton. He was married to the sister of the Blackfeet chief Seen From Afar, Natawista, both of whom are pictured prominently in the painting. Shortly after Culbertson's service to Stevens, he retired a wealthy man and moved to a large home in Peoria, Illinois. There he had room for several Stanley works, including this one, generally considered one of the artist's masterpieces. It was shipped to Culbertson in fall 1859 and was promptly placed on exhibition at the Peoria County Fair.[1]

This painting is somewhat smaller than the 1857 version, having been cut down to its present size from dimensions of 42½ × 60 inches. This trimming was done after 1942, when it was published in one of the early Stanley biographies, W. Vernon Kinietz's *John Mix Stanley and His Indian Paintings* (fig. 165.1).[2] Why this took place is unknown, but as a result, the signature and date were lost, as was one of the buffalo skulls in the foreground. It has several differences from the first version—the color of the horse, the articulation of the cliffs, and the hue of the setting sun—but the overall presentation is the same.

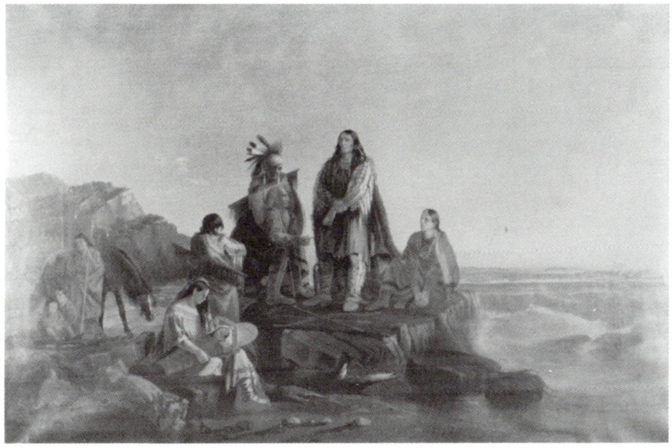

FIG. 165.1.
John Mix Stanley, *The Last of Their Race*, c. 1859.
Oil on canvas; 42½ × 60 in. (108.0 × 152.4 cm).
From Kinietz, *John Mix Stanley*.

1. See Wischmann, *Frontier Diplomats*, 276.

2. Kinietz, *John Mix Stanley*, 35.

166

Fort Benton Indians, 1859

Fort Benton Indians, Fort Benton, Montana; Friendly Indians Fleeing to Ft. Benton

Oil on canvas, 26½ × 38⅜ in. (67.3 × 97.4 cm)

INSCRIBED LOWER LEFT: Stanley 1859

PRESENT COLLECTION: American Museum of Western Art—The Anschutz Collection, Denver, Colorado

PROVENANCE: The artist; William A. Herron, Illinois, c. 1860; by descent to Mrs. William A. Herron, New York, New York; by descent in Herron family; (Hirschl and Adler Galleries, New York, New York, 1968); (James Graham Gallery, New York, New York, 1969); Dietrich Fine Arts Collection, Philadelphia, Pennsylvania, 1969; present owner, 1987

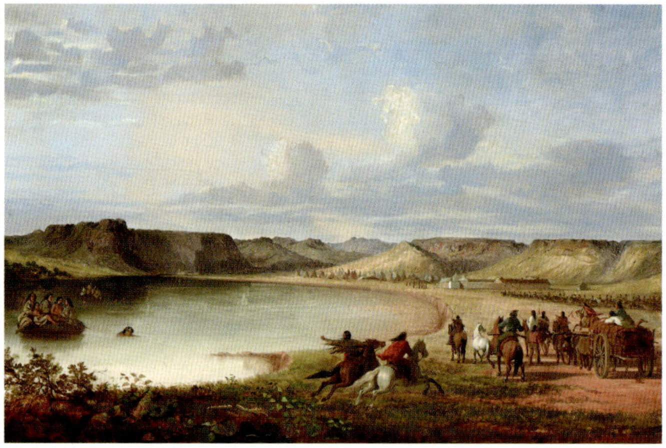

166

This painting is thought to portray Stanley (in the blue shirt) leading and encouraging a troop of thirty Piegan chiefs and their families to a grand council at Fort Benton on the upper Missouri River in 1853. He had been sent as a special envoy among the Piegans by Isaac Stevens and Alexander Culbertson (cat. no. 080) and had returned triumphantly with his prize. Stanley was considered invaluable as a diplomat among the Indians, and in this situation he proved himself a supreme emissary.[1]

Fort Benton was an extraordinary place for Stanley. His friend Alexander Culbertson had established the fort several years before Stanley arrived. He made many sketches of it, including a watercolor study (cat. no. 102) for the lithograph that appeared in the Stevens report.[2] Those images were criticized because the teepees beside the fort were drawn in too large a scale. That was corrected in this later oil and perhaps in the panel he devoted to it in his panorama *Scenes and Incidents of Stanley's Western Wilds*. While Stanley was painting that panel in 1854, Culbertson surprised him with a visit. "Why Culbertson," the artist exclaimed after a cordial greeting, "Do you remember that?" "Remember," replied his friend, "why, it's my own home—The Fort I built myself—the broad plain, the river, the hills; I know every one of them!" Stanley had even included what Culbertson remembered as "those Blackfeet crossing the river, with their buffalo skin canoes, just as I've seen them a thousand times."[3] Stanley had proven himself as a certified chronicler of the West as well as a kindred spirit with remarkable artistic skill.

1. For a description of the importance of council with the Piegans, see John C. Ewers, *The Blackfeet: Raiders of the Northwestern Plains* (Norman: University of Oklahoma Press, 1958), 208–11.

2. Stevens, *Narrative and Final Report*, 101.

3. Donoho, *Scenes and Incidents*, 14.

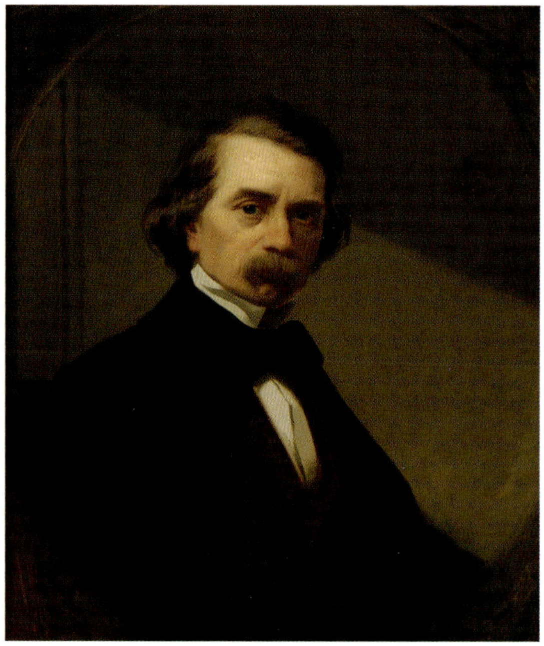

167

Self-Portrait, c. 1860

Oil on canvas, 29 × 24¼ in. (73.7 × 61.6 cm)

PRESENT COLLECTION: Gilcrease Museum, Tulsa, Oklahoma (0126.1139)

PROVENANCE: The artist; by descent to Mrs. Edith Stanley Bayles, Oak Park, Illinois; (M. Knoedler and Co., New York, New York); Thomas Gilcrease, Tulsa, Oklahoma, 1950; present owner

Over the years, several portraits were made of Stanley by other artists. In the mid-1840s, as Stanley's exhibiting career began to take shape with the emergence of his first Indian Gallery, he arranged to be painted by the New York portraitist Edmund L. Mooney (see fig 6.1). In 1851, his friend and colleague, the noted Troy portraitist Abel Moore, painted his likeness for display with Stanley's Indian Gallery. That replaced the Mooney version but did not survive the 1865 fire. Late in the artist's life, another worthy portraitist, Lewis T. Ives of Detroit, painted Stanley in oils, the whereabouts of which is unknown today.[1] A review of that painting appeared in a Detroit newspaper after Stanley's death in 1872. It was praised for its fidelity, and for those who knew Stanley personally, it was said to have elicited "deep emotional reminiscences."[2]

Stanley attempted several self-portraits during his career. One in the early 1840s was a dual portrait of the artist with one of his Indian subjects, an Iowa chief, Wo-Hum-Pa. The chief insisted that Stanley be portrayed shaking hands with him so that "when the Great Father [the President of the U.S.] saw it, he might know that he was a friend of the white man."[3]

The purpose of this *Self-Portrait* is unknown. It was probably painted for the family's enjoyment. It resembles a pencil drawing done by Henry Kirke Brown in Washington a few years earlier in 1858 (fig. 167.1). Brown, a distinguished sculptor and portraitist, had known Stanley since the early 1840s, when they were both in Troy, New York.

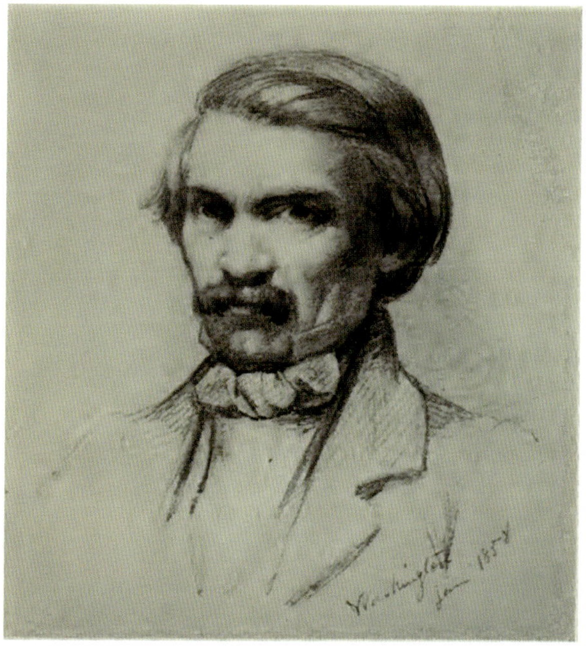

FIG. 167.1.
Henry Kirke Brown, *Portrait of John Mix Stanley*, 1858. Pencil on paper; dimensions unknown. Photograph courtesy Manuscript Division, Library of Congress, Washington, D.C.

1. This portrait, which was owned by Stanley's descendants, was illustrated as a frontispiece in Kinietz, John Mix Stanley. It was sold by the family to M. Knoedler and Co., New York, in 1971 and later was sold through the Kennedy Galleries, New York, in 1976.

2. "A Work of Art," unidentified Detroit newspaper clipping from the Schimmel Papers, presumed to date to 1872.

3. *Portraits of North American Indians*, 46.

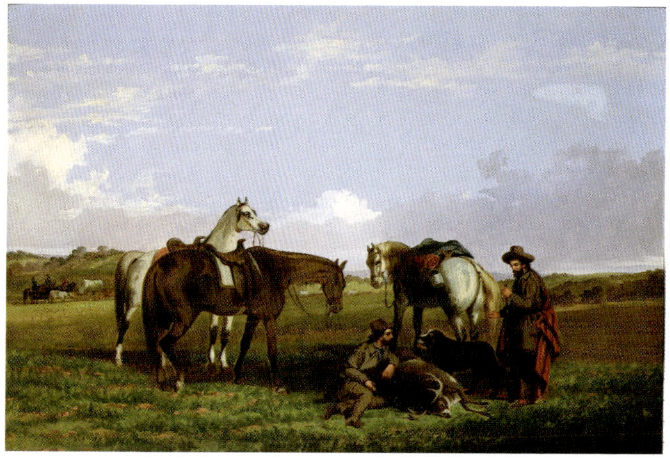

168

After the Hunt, c. 1860

Oil on canvas, 24 × 34⅛ in. (61.0 × 86.7 cm)

INSCRIBED LOWER LEFT: Stanley

PRESENT COLLECTION: The Rees-Jones Collection, Dallas, Texas

PROVENANCE: Major Richard Stevens Eskridge, Olympia, Washington; private collection, California; (Gerald Peters Gallery, Santa Fe, New Mexico); present owner

Only rarely in his later years did Stanley draw on his formative experiences from the Santa Fe Trail, when he was preparing large canvases. This is one of two known exceptions, the other being *Wagon Train: Break in the Journey* (cat. no. 134). But, around 1860, some dozen years after his trip across the Southwest with Kearny and Emory, the artist was inspired to recount one of his memories of life along the Arkansas River, somewhere between Independence, Missouri, and Bent's Fort.

Stanley was known as a skillful hunter and may have remembered this scene from some of his own exploits on the trek. Here two riflemen pose beside their prize, a rather corpulent buck deer that has been harvested for the larder of the wagon train that passes behind them. The hunters' staged pose with cradled rifles, a trusty dog, the adornment of a Hudson's Bay blanket, and the collective focus on the recent kill resembles that of several such compositions Stanley made of interior scenes, such as *The Trapper's Cabin* (cat. no. 163) and *Hunters and Traders* (cat. no. 172). Stanley was a master at directing focus to the salient subject in his paintings. Here it is the slain buck, and even the horses have trained their attention on the day's trophy. Without buffering trees to center the composition, three horses accomplish the artist's purpose.

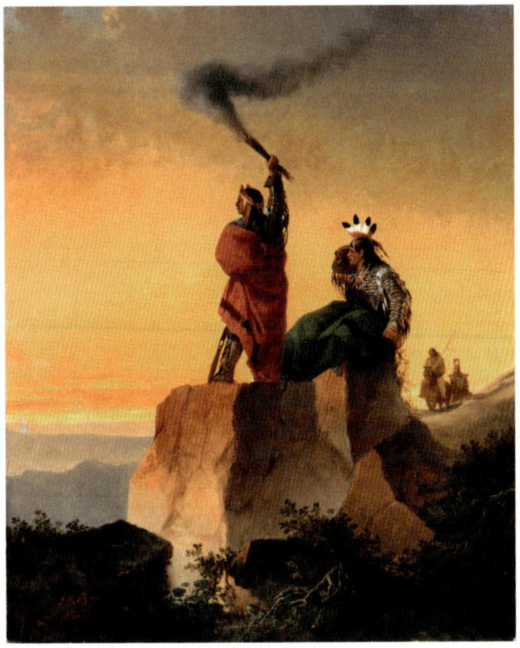

169

Indian Telegraph, 1860

Oil on canvas, 20 × 15½ in. (50.8 × 39.4 cm)

INSCRIPTION LOWER LEFT: J. M. Stanley / 1860

PRESENT COLLECTION: Detroit Institute of Arts, purchase, Popular Subscription Fund, 1901 (01.2); photograph courtesy Bridgeman Images

PROVENANCE: The artist; the artist's student Mrs. M. Noble Brainard, 1868; acquired by present owner, 1901

This was the first in a series of four known paintings Stanley titled *Indian Telegraph*. Painted in 1860, it was sold by Stanley to one of his Detroit pupils, Mrs. M. Noble Brainard, in 1868. It received national attention in 1893 when it was exhibited in the Michigan Pavilion at the World's Columbian Exposition in Chicago, and was purchased in 1901 by public subscription for the Detroit Institute of Arts. Though smaller in scale than the other versions of this title, this oil is remarkable for its brilliance and strength.

When promoted for sale by Mrs. Brainard in 1901, it was referred to as a picture "laid in the midst of the rugged Gila River country" and representing Apache Indians that Stanley had seen in 1846 while traveling with Lieutenant William Emory.[1] The reference is distinctly misguided, even though in a later version (cat. no. 208), the local press got it wrong again, claiming that too was a Gila River scene.[2] One of the first Stanley scholars, W. Vernon Kinietz, elaborated on the mythic tale, saying that Stanley and the expedition's guide, Kit Carson, had been held "hostages" during part of this scene.[3] The Indians are in fact Blackfeet warriors, Stanley's favorite tribe of the Northwest, with whom he spent considerable time in 1853 while on the railroad survey through present-day Montana. The man shading his eyes and looking at a responding puff of smoke in the distance is wearing a shirt similar to several that Stanley collected during his western trip and that are now in the Museum of the American Indian, Smithsonian Institution, Washington, D.C.

1. From label titled "indian telegraph," affixed to the back of the painting.

2. "Stanley's Chromos," *Detroit Free Press*, September 19, 1869.

3. Kinietz, *John Mix Stanley*, commentary for plate XIII.

170

Caleb Blood Smith, 1861

Oil on canvas, 50 × 40 in. (127.0 × 101.6 cm)

INSCRIBED LOWER LEFT: J. M. Stanley / 1861

PRESENT COLLECTION: U.S. Department of the Interior Museum, Washington, D.C. (INTR 01610)

PROVENANCE: The artist; present owner

171

Thomas Ewing, 1861

Oil on canvas, 50½ × 40¼ in. (128.3 × 102.2 cm)

INSCRIBED LOWER LEFT: J. M. Stanley / 1861

PRESENT COLLECTION: U.S. Department of the Interior Museum, Washington, D.C. (INTR 01605)

PROVENANCE: The artist; present owner

Stanley's portrait of Caleb Blood Smith was conceived as a companion work to his likeness of Thomas Ewing. Ewing had been the first secretary of the interior, serving under Presidents Zachary Taylor and Millard Fillmore in 1849 and 1850.[1] In 1861, when Smith and Ewing sat for Stanley, Smith was the current secretary. The two portraits are the same size and face one another as brackets in time.

Ewing had come to Washington in 1861 hoping to help avert civil war by attending a peace conference. Smith had been appointed Secretary as a political favor from President Lincoln for the efficacious support he had lent to Lincoln's nomination for the presidency. Smith was relatively ineffective in the job of secretary, mostly because of indifference to the job and the onset of poor health. He departed the position in 1862 to become a U.S.

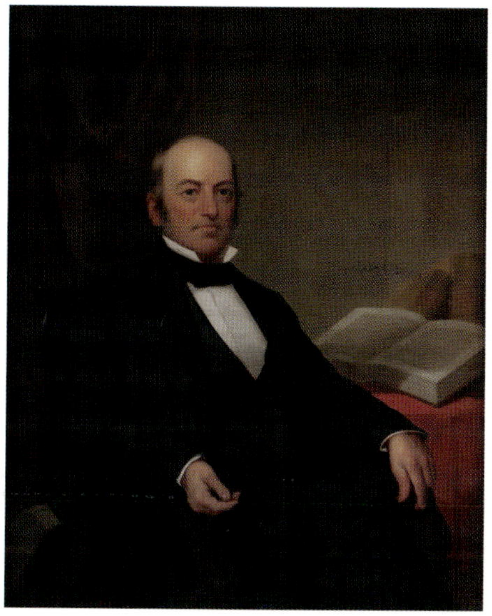

170

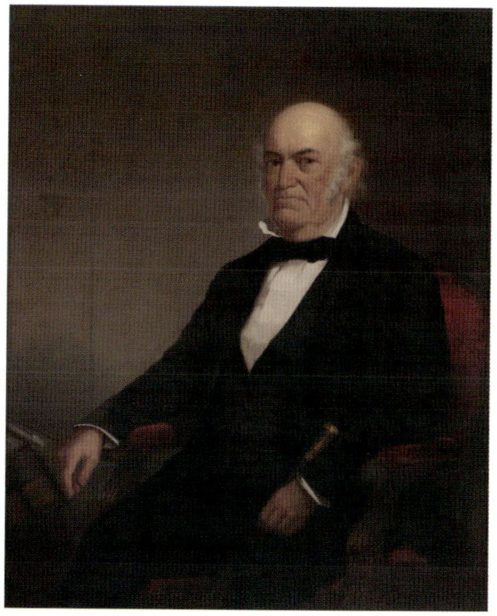

171

circuit judge in his home state of Indiana and died of his maladies in early 1864.[2]

Stanley painted Ewing near the close of a very distinguished political career. Ewing had been progressive in some respects, as when he brought the Bureau of Indian Affairs from the War Department into the Interior Department. He also initiated the formal inception of a transcontinental railroad with its mention in his first departmental report. Yet he was much less enlightened as an employer. He was known for rampant cronyism, which won him the nefarious sobriquet of "Butcher Ewing" from those he summarily dismissed in preference of political allies.

1. Wilson and Fiske, *Appleton's Cyclopedia*, 393.

2. Ibid., 558.

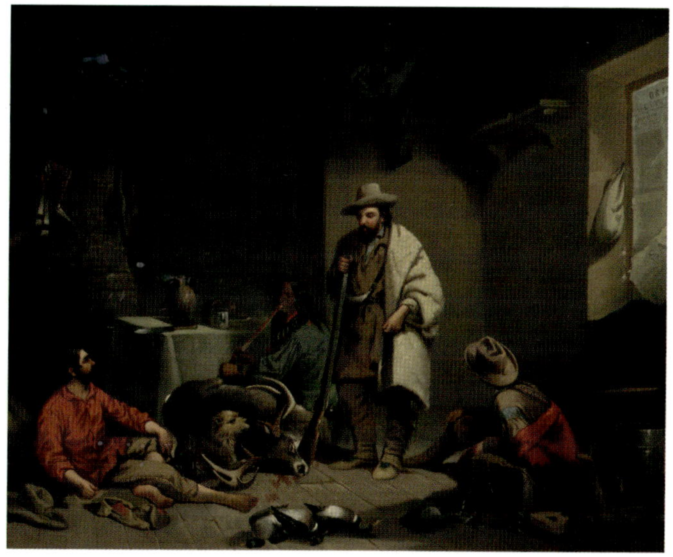

172

Hunters and Traders, 1862

Oil on canvas, 25¼ × 30¼ in. (64.1 × 76.8 cm)

INSCRIBED LOWER RIGHT: J. M. Stanley. 1862

PRESENT COLLECTION: Tim and Elaine Peterson

PROVENANCE: General William Burt Hickey, New York, New York to 1974; (Sotheby Parke Bernet, Inc. New York, New York, 1974); private collection; (unknown art dealer, Albany, New York); (Zaplin Lambert Gallery, Santa Fe, New Mexico); present owner

This canvas is as much a still-life painting as a genre scene. It is festooned with assorted objects from Stanley's western travels and experiences. There is a hint that the artist intended to locate the scene on the frontier, as he has painted an Oregon newspaper tacked over the window on the right side of the composition. Three Anglos and an Indian share the picture's stage with a group of dead ducks and a large buck deer. A trap, rifles, an Indian saddle and war club, and other accoutrements of the trapper suggest that these four men are fresh from the field of the hunt and are either engaging in tales of their enterprise or bargaining for distribution of their trophies.

Stanley was known for his own abilities as a hunter and was praised for his skills by both Emory and Stevens in their reports.[1] He painted two known canvases of mountain men (unlocated), but seemed more comfortable portraying Indian and western Anglo hunters in set pieces like this, in which they display their hunting exploits. The standing male figure at the center of this work may have been the same model he used in another hunting painting of the period, *After the Hunt* (cat. no. 168).

1. See, for example, Emory, *Notes*, 90; and Stevens, *Narrative and Final Report*, 103.

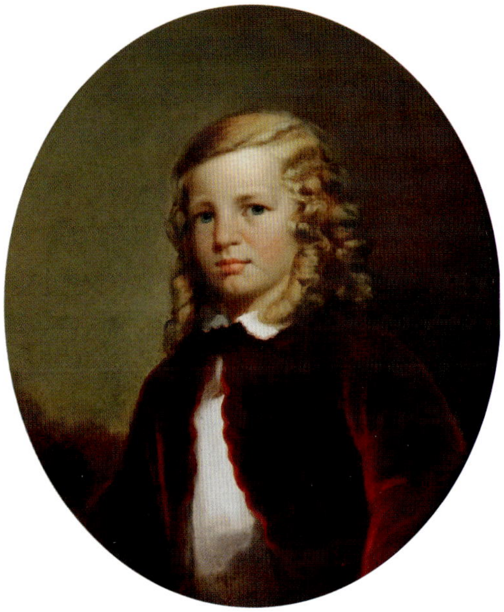

173

Louis Crandall Stanley, 1861

Oil on canvas, 27 × 22 in. (71.1 × 55.9 cm) (oval)

INSCRIBED LOWER LEFT: 1861

PRESENT COLLECTION: Collection of Eric and Sarah Daniels, great-great-granddaughter of the artist

PROVENANCE: The artist; Louis C. Stanley, Detroit, Michigan; by descent to his daughter Sarah L'Estrange Stanley Frantz, Saginaw, Michigan; Mrs. Fred R. (Joan) Meyer, Scottsville, New York; by descent to present owner

This portrait of the Stanleys' eldest child, Louis, is thought to have been painted in 1863, when he was about seven or eight years old.[1] The family was about to move to Detroit, where Louis would grow to maturity and prosper as an adult. He is painted in the fashion of formal European portraits of the eighteenth century, with his velvet jacket, long traces of blonde hair, and an air of nobility. Such was Stanley's estimation of his one and only male heir.

Louis received a public school education and went on to the University of Michigan and law school. He was admitted to the bar in 1877 and practiced as a corporate lawyer in Detroit for many years. His primary employer was the Grand Trunk Railway System, which he served for forty years. Louis and his wife, Jane Mahon Stanley, were married in 1889 and had four children.[2] Their first daughter, Sarah, inherited this portrait. Her younger sister, Alice, dedicated much of her life to researching her grandfather's art and perpetuating his legacy.

1. See Schimmel, "John Mix Stanley and Imagery," 385.

2. Clarence M. Burton, ed., *The City of Detroit, Michigan, 1701–1922*, vol. 3 (Ann Arbor: University of Michigan Library, 2005), 627–28.

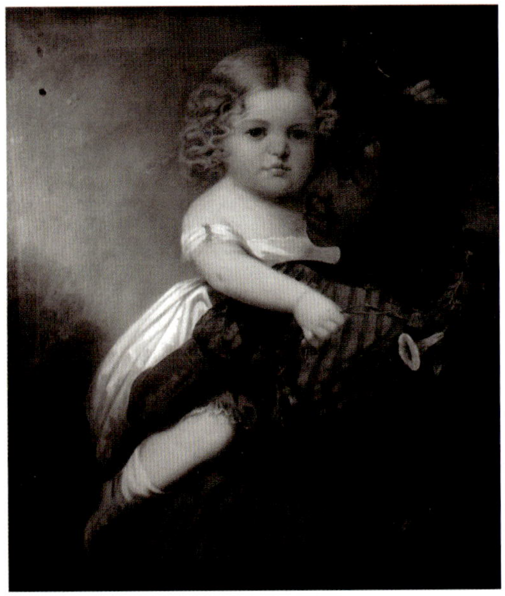

174

Clara and Sally, c. 1863

Clara Stanley and Slave Girl

Oil on canvas, 29¼ × 24½ in. (74.3 × 62.2 cm)

PRESENT COLLECTION: Last known, Mrs. Edith Stanley Bayles, Oak Park, Illinois

PROVENANCE: The artist; by descent to Mrs. Edith Stanley Bayles, Oak Park, Illinois

Clara was the Stanleys' second child. She was born in 1857, probably in Washington, D.C. The portrait pictures her, perhaps age three, looking out at the viewer with a hint of petulance in her expression. She holds a morning glory in her right hand, a symbol at the time of love and affection, which she appears to be enjoying from her nanny. The morning glory, which generally blooms for only a brief time, ironically also signified mortality. In this case, the latter meaning proved true. Clara died in 1873 in Detroit at age fifteen, just one year after her father.

Sally may not have been just a nanny. One of the alternate titles for the painting is *Clara Stanley and Slave Girl*. It is not known how many slaves the Stanley family had, if indeed any, but the portrait was apparently referred to by this title in the family. The painting was owned well into the 1950s by Clara's younger sister, Edith Stanley Bayles.

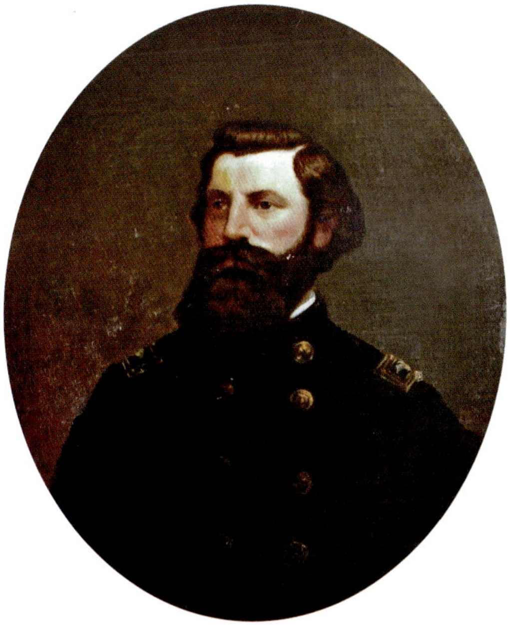

175

Colonel Charles M. Lum, 1863

Oil on canvas, 30¼ × 25½ in. (87.0 × 64.8 cm)

INSCRIBED: August, 1863

PRESENT COLLECTION: Detroit Historical Society, Michigan (1928.002)

PROVENANCE: The artist; Colonel Charles Lum, Detroit, Michigan; Detroit Light Guard, Michigan; present owner, 1928

Stanley is thought to have traveled to Detroit in spring 1863 with his second panorama, an epic extravaganza on the Civil War from the Union perspective. Titled *Polemorama* (a combination of the words "polemania," meaning the rage of war, and "panorama"), it was rather hyperbolically referred to as "one of the most truthful and magnificent of any subject ever presented to the American public."[1] Stanley resettled later that year from Washington, D.C., to Detroit. One of his first commissions must have been painting a portrait of a retired soldier who had seen distinguished service in the war, Colonel Charles Lum. The portrait is dated August 1863.

Lum was born in Stanley's hometown of Canandaigua, New York, in 1830. Like Stanley, he was also an artist by profession, being much celebrated in Detroit, where he settled as a painter of animals and scenic and religious pieces.[2] At the onset of the Civil War, Lum was a captain with the Detroit Light Guard, a local militia unit and popular men's social organization. As the war progressed, he received a commission of colonel for an infantry troop, the Tenth Michigan. He was wounded at the Battle of Bull Run in 1861 and returned to Detroit to recuperate and live out his life as an artist. Stanley depicted the veteran in his military uniform.[3]

1. From a clipping in an unidentified Detroit newspaper, February 19, 1863, Stanley scrapbook. For a description of the Civil War panorama, see Schimmel, "John Mix Stanley and Imagery," 130.

2. Arthur Hopkin Gibson, comp., *Artists of Early Michigan* (Detroit: Wayne State University Press, 1975), 163.

3. This biographical information is provided on the information sheet supplied by the painting's owner, the Detroit Historical Society.

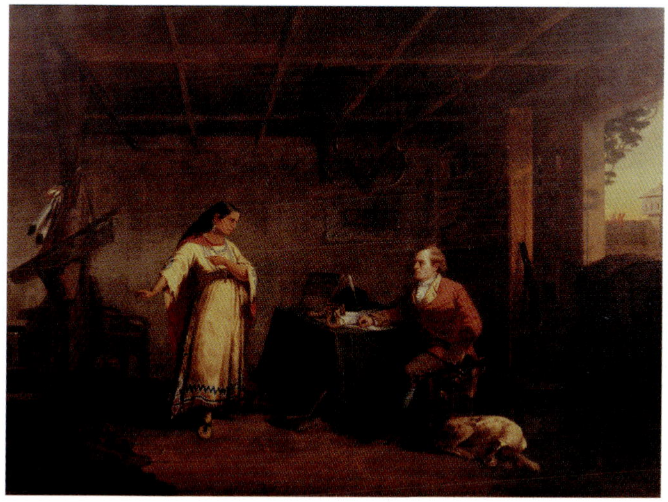

176

The Unveiling of the Conspiracy, 1863

Oil on canvas, 36 × 48 in. (91.4 × 121.9 cm)

INSCRIBED LOWER RIGHT: J. M. Stanley / 1863

PRESENT COLLECTION: Courtesy of the Burton Historical Collection, Detroit Public Library, Michigan

PROVENANCE: Vincent Field; by gift to present owner, c. 1926

LIFETIME EXHIBITIONS: Godfrey, Dean and Co., Detroit, Michigan, 1863; *Paintings and Sculpture on Exhibition at the Gallery of the Buffalo Fine Arts Academy*, Buffalo, New York, 1863; *Fine Arts Among the People*, Godfrey, Brown, Dean and Co., Detroit, Michigan, 1864

Stanley is generally considered a champion of Indian people. When it came to patronage, however, he knew that Anglos, not Indians, bought his paintings, and he readily threw in with the forces of conquest and civilization. Thus is the case with his portrayal of the famous Pontiac Conspiracy, and the Native defense of Ohio and Michigan lands after the French and Indian War, depicted in this painting.

The Ottawa chief Pontiac, whom many historians have claimed was a "man of great dignity," conspired with the assistance of the French and a host of northeastern tribes to push the English out of the region.[1] Pontiac hoped to surprise the English major Henry Gladwyn, who had charge of Fort Detroit in 1763, and take control of its strategic location. His plot was foiled and the enterprise eventually abandoned.

One hundred years after Pontiac's futile attempts to capture Fort Detroit, Stanley began making plans to move back to Detroit, the city of his youth, to re-establish a studio there. His début involved the presentation of this painting, inspired by Francis Parkman's book *The Conspiracy of Pontiac*.[2] Here an Ojibwe woman, Catherine, approaches Gladwyn with a pair of elk skin moccasins that the commander had ordered. She uses this delivery as a pretense to alert Gladwyn to Pontiac's impending attack. His state of unawareness is symbolized by the sleeping dog at his feet. Yet, once warned, Gladwyn is able to avert an attack. Pontiac is outsmarted, Catherine is allowed by Gladwyn to be beaten for her misstep, and Stanley celebrates the British victory, leaving his Indians out in the cold. The painting, said to "be of peculiar interest to" the citizens of Detroit, was seen as a valued historical document. It became the object of a city-wide subscription, though unsuccessful, to purchase for the Historical Society of Michigan.[3]

1. See for example, Bruce Catton, *Michigan: A Bicentennial History* (New York: Norton, 1976), 43.

2. Francis Parkman, *The Conspiracy of Pontiac and the Indian War After the Conquest of Canada* (Boston: Little, Brown, 1851). Stanley's use of this book is mentioned in "Unveiling the Conspiracy," *Detroit Free Press*, September 3, 1863.

3. See "The Historical Painting," *Detroit Free Press*, September 7, 1863; and "The Historical Painting, 'Unveiling the Conspiracy,'" *Detroit Free Press*, September 15, 1863.

177

Indian Telegraph, 1863

Oil on canvas, 20¼ × 30¼ in. (51.4 × 76.2 cm)

PRESENT COLLECTION: Tuscaloosa Museum of Art: Home of the Westervelt Collection, Tuscaloosa, Alabama

INSCRIBED LOWER RIGHT: J M Stanley 1863

PROVENANCE: Richard Manoogian, Detroit, Michigan; (Gerald Peters Gallery, Santa Fe, New Mexico, 1982); Gulf States Paper Corp., Tuscaloosa, Alabama; present owner

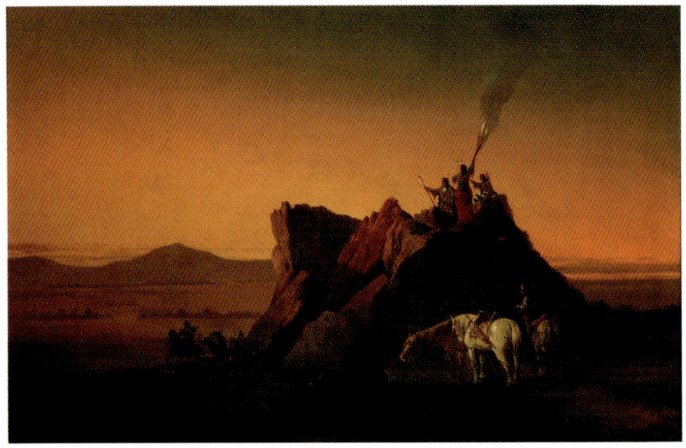

177

In the early 1860s, Stanley embarked on a series of works depicting Northern Plains Indians in the act of sending smoke signals (see for example cat. no. 169). Two of these, with the identical titles of *Indian Telegraph*, were thought to have been painted in 1863 (see cat. no. 178 for the other version). They are both the same size, 20 × 30 inches, have horizontal formats, and picture a group of three men on the crest of a pyramidal rocky prominence, one of whom extends his right arm and holds a flaming, smoking bundle of grasses. Another of the figures points into the distance, where it is assumed he has located a responding diaphanous message. In both pictures, the base of the outcropping is animated by the presence of other Indian warriors and horses.

Stanley favored this composition in these years. The people he placed on the rock crests, be they Anglo explorers as in *Scouts along the Teton River* (cat. no. 131) or Blackfeet men as here, assumed larger than life prominence in his vision of the West. There was no more ascendant place for his heroes of the western wilds than atop one of nature's pedestals, spanning with their gaze the nearly infinite horizon of that special landscape.

Stanley must have witnessed such a sight during his travels with Isaac Stevens, as the figures are undoubtedly Blackfeet men. The *Detroit Free Press* noted that Stanley had exhibited one of the two versions in a sales exhibition in fall 1863.[1] Perhaps it was this piece.

1. *Detroit Free Press*, November 9, 1863.

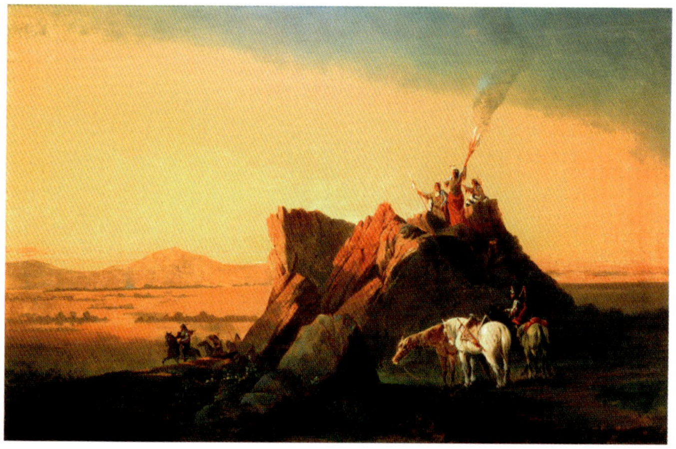

178

Indian Telegraph, c. 1863

Oil on canvas, 21 × 31 in. (53.3 × 78.7 cm)

INSCRIBED VERSO: signed

PRESENT COLLECTION: Private collection; photograph courtesy Gerald Peters Gallery, Santa Fe, New Mexico

PROVENANCE: (Gerald Peters Gallery, Santa Fe, New Mexico); present owner, 1997

This painting is similar to another oil of the same title (cat. no. 177) that Stanley painted in 1863. It differs from that work only slightly, particularly in the middle ground, where a body of water, presumably the Missouri River, flows instead of an expansive prairie. It points to the appeal of such scenes at this time, as patrons must have encouraged him to repeat the subject.

Revisionist art historians have addressed the public attraction to such works as epitomizing Anglo, bourgeois, racist attitudes toward the Indian. One scholar has stated that behind such "images is a hint of snide humor," a powerful hidden signifier that asserts "cultural superiority of industrial technology, that of the telegraph." Such contributors "to this smug sense of cultural superiority," as this and similar paintings are said to be, satisfied "the dominant white culture to whom" it "is addressed, and which will ultimately consume it."[1] Such cynical readings as this may be valid, but they require a broad, unsubstantiated view of history that denies the exotic charm that nurtured the popularity of Stanley's late work.

This version of *Indian Telegraph* is signed on the reverse and carries a label asserting that the subject derived from one of Stanley's experiences in the Southwest. This is a common faulty claim about these works, as the subject is distinctly one recorded on the northern plains.

1. J. Gray Sweeney, "Racism, Nationalism, and Nostalgia," in *Race-ing Art History: Critical Readings in Race and Art History*, ed. Kimberly N. Pinder (New York: Routledge, 2002), 159–60. Julie Schimmel, "John Mix Stanley (1814–1872)," in *Artists of Michigan from the Nineteenth Century*, ed. J. Gray Sweeney (Muskegon, Mich.: Muskegon Museum of Art, 1988), 52, presages Sweeney's assessment when she concludes about *Indian Telegraph* (cat. no. 169) that cultural "differences in habit were viewed as differences in basic worth."

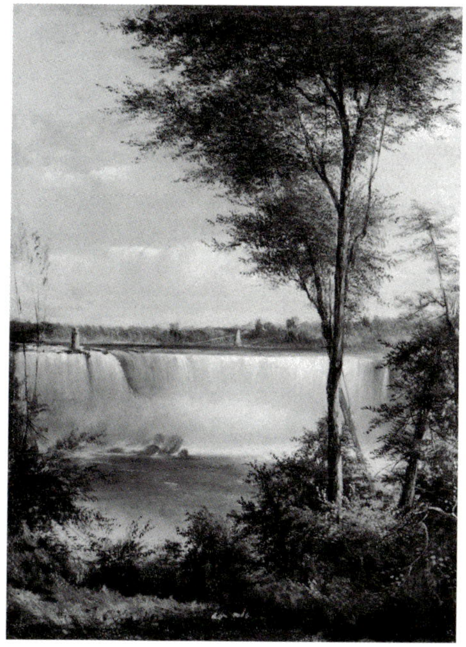

179

Peep at Niagara Falls, 1864

Oil on canvas, 14½ × 10½ in. (36.8 × 26.7 cm)

INSCRIBED VERSO: Peep at Niagara Falls 1864

PRESENT COLLECTION: Unlocated

PROVENANCE: Edith Stanley Bayles, Oak Park, Illinois; by descent to Dorothy E. Bayles; (M. Knoedler and Co., New York, New York, 1969); present owner

Family records suggest that Stanley and his family left Washington, D.C., in 1863 and settled for some months in Buffalo, New York.[1] His son Louis described the city as "a very pleasant" place, and he and his father frequented the docks to "see the shipping." Louis also described a summer visit in 1864 to see Niagara Falls, and it was perhaps on that occasion that the artist made this small cabinet painting of the view from the American side.[2]

Stanley had been drawn to waterfalls since his early years in Troy, when in 1842 he captured the power of *Cohoes Falls* (cat. no. 006). In the West he painted the Great Falls of the Missouri, the Peluse (Palouse) Falls near the Snake River, and the Cascades on the Columbia. In most of these views, he avoided presenting nature's spectacular features in grand scale. They are, by contrast, rather intimate observations, thus the title of this painting, a *Peep at Niagara Falls*.

1. From a typescript biography prepared by G. B. Catlin from information provided by Stanley's son Louis C. Stanley in 1924 in the Burton Historical Collection, Detroit Public Library.

2. Louis C. Stanley, "Buffalo," September 5, 1864, a handwritten account of the city and environs from an unidentified source in the Schimmel Papers.

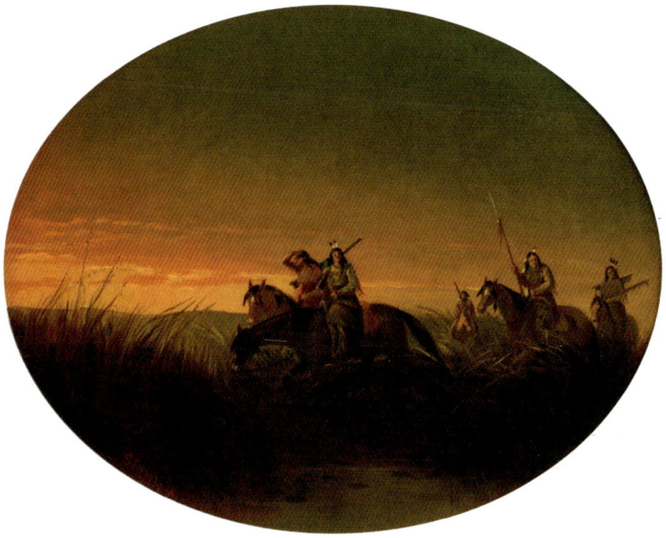

180

Scouting Party, 1864

Oil on canvas, 8 × 10¼ in. (20.3 × 26.0 cm) (oval)

INSCRIBED LOWER RIGHT MARGIN: 1864 / J. M. Stanley.

PRESENT COLLECTION: Tuscaloosa Museum of Art: Home of the Westervelt Collection, Tuscaloosa, Alabama

PROVENANCE: (Sotheby Parke Bernet, New York, New York, 1972); present owner

In 1864 Stanley moved to Detroit permanently. He was weary of life in Washington, D.C., and disappointed in the lack of congressional movement to acquire his Indian Gallery. Michigan provided a welcome change, and it was time for him to begin searching for alternate means of making a living beyond his portraiture and his failing hope of selling his Indian Gallery. This cabinet painting may have been an experiment in that direction, an effort to produce affordable paintings of his favorite Indian scenes for sale to patrons in the Midwest. It was the start of a series that he would continue through the next year, over a half dozen of which, including this oil, survive today.

Comparatively, when George Catlin had fallen on hard times in London in 1852, he tried a variety of approaches in an effort to salvage his vision. These included the production of drawing and watercolor portfolios, copies of his portraits and scenes of Indian life, and beginning in 1857, even a set of several hundred smaller oils painted in oval surrounds known as his "Cartoon Collection." These were substantially reduced in detail and presence. Although Stanley did not know of Catlin's series of small oils, his *Scouting Party* represented Stanley's similar attempt at seeking relief from hard times.

181

Sunset in the Desert, 1864

Oil on canvas, 18 × 30 in. (45.7 × 76.2 cm)

INSCRIBED LOWER LEFT: J. M. Stanley / 1864

LAST KNOWN COLLECTION: Belvedere Ranch Holdings, New Ulm, Texas; photograph courtesy Gerald Peters Gallery, Santa Fe, New Mexico

PROVENANCE: (Gerald Peters Gallery, Santa Fe, New Mexico); Belvedere Ranch Holdings, New Ulm, Texas

This gorgeous landscape of a sunset along the Gila River was painted as a remembrance of the artist's time with the Emory expedition that had traversed the Southwest eighteen years earlier in 1846. It resembles to some degree the scene he painted in the mid-1850s, *Chain of Spires along the Gila* (cat. no. 130), but instead of concentrating on the flora and fauna of the valley, Stanley now focused on the powerful effects of desert atmosphere and light. A golden red sky dominates the picture, revealing the psychological draw of the Far West as a space that approaches the divine. The West stands apart, beyond the immediate physical reach of the observer, but glows with a radiance that symbolizes the aspirations and national potential of the country as a whole. Americans were searching for motifs of national unity during and after the Civil War, and this 1864 masterpiece would have served as a mighty national emblem as the battles raged on.

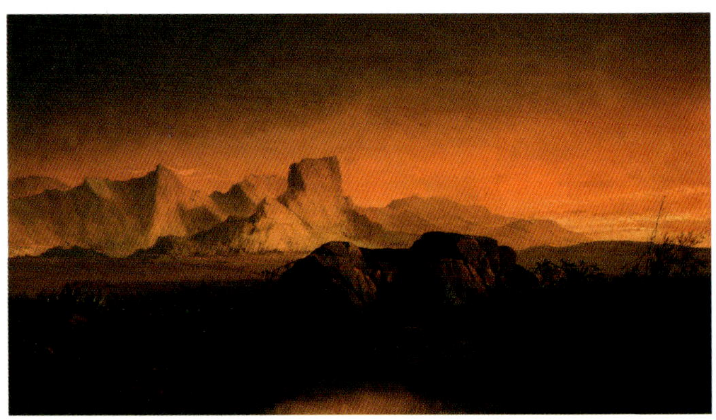

181

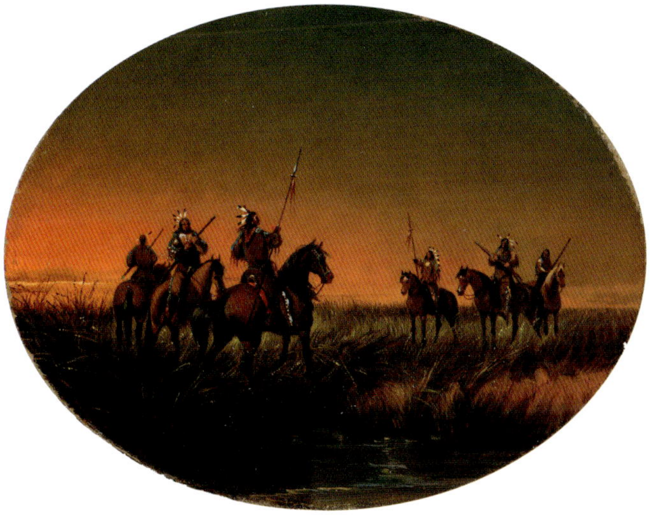

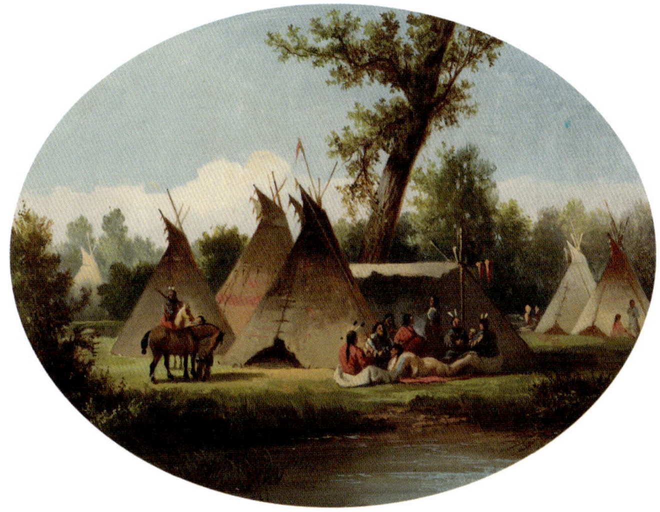

182

The Challenge, 1865

Oil on canvas, $7\frac{7}{8} \times 9\frac{7}{8}$ in. (20.0 × 25.1 cm) (oval)

INSCRIBED LOWER LEFT: J. M. Stanley

PRESENT COLLECTION: Detroit Institute of Arts, Michigan, gift of Mrs. Blanche Ferry Hooker, 1941 (41.65); photograph courtesy Bridgeman Images

PROVENANCE: The artist; Dexter Mason Ferry, Detroit, Michigan; by descent to Blanche Ferry Hooker, Detroit, Michigan; present owner by gift, 1941

LIFETIME EXHIBITIONS: J. M. Stanley's Studio, 159 Jefferson Avenue, Detroit, Michigan, 1867.

This small gem of a painting, sparkling with highlights on the mounted warriors and grass, is set against a rosy, opalescent backdrop of sky. It has a painterly tension accentuated by the posture of the horses and their riders. Stanley is not known to have portrayed scenes of intertribal warfare as did his contemporaries like George Catlin and Karl Bodmer, so this is an exception.

There is no way to know how the scene in *The Challenge* turns out, but confrontation seems real and the mood of the scene reveals that Stanley was at least wont to romanticize the potential for violent conflict. As with some of Bodmer's scenes, Stanley's painting pictures Blackfeet and Assiniboin warriors. Stanley's are preparing "for a fray," as one observer noted when seeing the work in the artist's studio. "Without greatly straining our imagination," wrote the critic, "the loud whoop, the desperate charge, the changing fortune of the fight, until . . . only one remains to carry the news of victory and the scalps of the slain to the tents of his tribe."[1] Such was the imagined outcome of this confrontation, at least in one viewer's mind.

1. "The Fine-Arts: A Visit to Stanley's Studio," *Detroit Free Press*, May 21, 1865.

183

Assiniboin Encampment on the Upper Missouri, 1865

Assiniboin Encampment

Oil on canvas, $7\frac{7}{8} \times 10\frac{7}{8}$ in. (20.0 × 27.6 cm) (oval)

INSCRIBED LOWER LEFT: J. M. Stanley

PRESENT COLLECTION: Detroit Institute of Arts, Michigan, gift of Mrs. William Fitzhugh Edwards, 1901 (01.6); photograph courtesy Bridgeman Images

PROVENANCE: The artist; Mrs. William Fitzhugh Edwards, Detroit, Michigan, 1901; present owner by gift, 1901

LIFETIME EXHIBITIONS: *Cabinet Pictures*, Stanley's Studio, Madison Avenue, Detroit, Michigan, 1865; J. M. Stanley's Studio, 159 Jefferson Avenue, Detroit, Michigan, 1867.

184

Assiniboin Camp, c. 1865

Oil on canvas, $8 \times 10\frac{1}{4}$ in. (20.3 × 25.9 cm) (oval)

PRESENT COLLECTION: Private collection; photograph courtesy Christie's, New York, and Bridgeman Images, New York

PROVENANCE: (Christie's, New York, New York, 1998); (Sotheby's, New York, New York, May, 2007); present owner

In May 1865, just four months after losing his Indian Gallery to the Smithsonian conflagration, Stanley opened his Detroit studio to a reporter from the *Detroit Free Press*. The reporter was thrilled to be among such a treasure house of art and artifacts as festooned Stanley's creative space. Despite the fact that Stanley had not been west for over ten years, the artist was like a deity to the writer, one whose familiarity with the West's "untrodden wildness" and the "untainted air of nature's wide domain" impressed him deeply.[1]

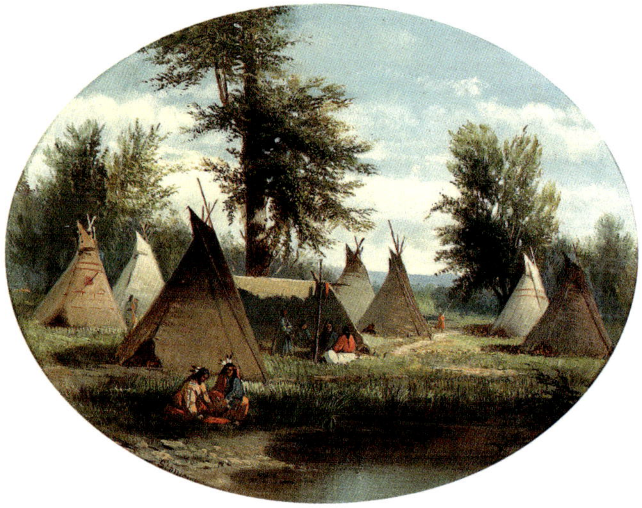

184

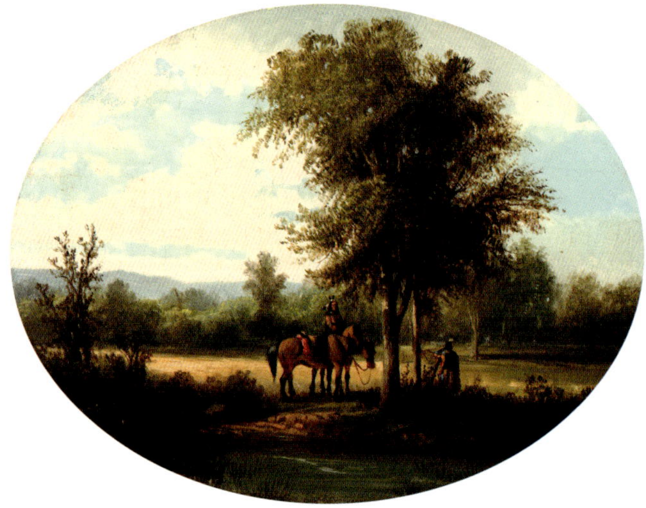

185

Of the things the reporter saw, he was especially struck by six or more cabinet pictures just then "receiving their finishing touches," and he described them at length.[2]

Assiniboin Encampment on the Upper Missouri was the first to take his notice, particularly because of its morning light and the limpid water of the river in the foreground. He mentioned also the card players in one of the figural groupings and the impressive hide lodges that punctuate the meadow.

Scholars have suggested that this, along with four other cabinet paintings in the series (cat. nos. 180, 182, 185, and 186), were part of an Indian Portfolio that Stanley ambitiously proposed to publish in the late 1860s. This oil was thought to have been included under the title *Prairie Indian Encampment*, but that is a slightly larger work that was painted about five years later (cat. no. 219). This and the other small-format cabinet paintings in the series were simply intended for sale.[3]

Stanley did at least one other oval cabinet painting of the same subject, this one simply titled *Assiniboin Camp* (cat. no. 184). Elements of the picture are adjusted slightly, but the feeling is refreshingly similar.

1. "The Fine-Arts: A Visit to Stanley's Studio," *Detroit Free Press*, May 21, 1865.

2. Ibid.

3. Kinietz, *John Mix Stanley*, 19–27; and Schimmel, "John Mix Stanley and Imagery," 147–48.

185
A Morning in Milk River Valley, c. 1865

Oil on canvas, 7⅞ × 10 in. (20.0 × 25.4 cm) (oval)

INSCRIBED LOWER LEFT: J. M. Stanley

PRESENT COLLECTION: Detroit Institute of Arts, Michigan, gift of Mrs. Blanche Ferry Hooker (41.66); photograph courtesy Bridgeman Images

PROVENANCE: Mrs. Blanche Ferry Hooker, Detroit Michigan; present owner by gift, 1941

LIFETIME EXHIBITIONS: *Cabinet Pictures*, Stanley's Studio, Madison Avenue, Detroit, Michigan, 1865; J. M. Stanley's Studio, 159 Jefferson Avenue, Detroit, Michigan, 1867

Although this could be just about any creek or river on the upper Missouri, Stanley chose to ascribe it to one of his favorite locations in the area, the Milk River valley. Beyond the landscape, it pictures only two men and their horses resting beneath a couple of cottonwood trees, one man in the shade and the other sunlit, patiently holding the horses. This is indeed a pastoral idyll. The Indians are the pure exemplars of natural man and their home, America's arcadia.

A man who saw this and the series of cabinet pictures that Stanley had produced in the mid-1860s spoke of the artist's extraordinary success with these works: "Considering the size of these paintings, their elaborate completeness, fidelity of detail, and natural truthfulness are really surprising. The figures of men and horses, though so minute, carry all, nevertheless, a distinct individuality about them that fully expresses the design of the artist. The landscapes and distant vistas are perfect gems in their way, and the skies are so perfectly draped, so mellow in tone, that they would delight the poet."[1] Calling on the poets to regard a painter's genius and proclaim nature's spectacle provided solace and respite from the agonies of the Civil War that raged near his old hometown of Washington, D.C.

1. "The Fine-Arts: A Visit to Stanley's Studio," *Detroit Free Press*, May 21, 1865.

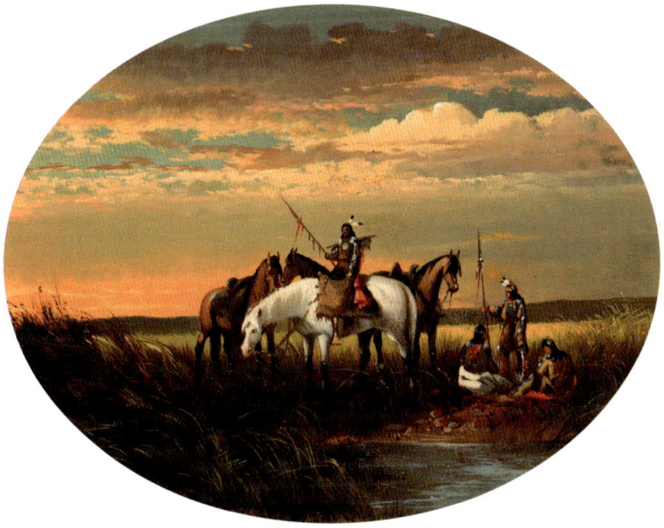

186

A Halt on the Prairie for a Smoke, 1865

Oil on canvas, 8⅞ × 11¼ in. (22.5 × 28.6 cm) (oval)

INSCRIBED LOWER LEFT: J. M. Stanley

PRESENT COLLECTION: Detroit Institute of Arts, Michigan, gift of Mrs. William Fitzhugh Edwards, 1901 (01.7); photograph courtesy Bridgeman Images

PROVENANCE: The artist; [?]; Mrs. William Fitzhugh Edwards, by 1901; present owner by gift 1901

LIFETIME EXHIBITIONS: *Cabinet Pictures*, Stanley's Studio, Madison Avenue, Detroit, Michigan, 1865

Indians halted on the prairie for a smoke was a fairly common theme for Stanley; thus it was a logical choice for one in a set of cabinet paintings that he worked on during the spring of 1865. These Plains warriors, in their moment of respite, attracted the attention of a visitor to Stanley's studio, a reporter from the *Detroit Free Press*. He was particularly smitten with the artist's achievement in rendering atmosphere, what he called "a gorgeous crimson-hued sky [that] shows the witching hour when the sun sinks to rest, and his parting beams rose-tint the luxuriant grass which fringes the edge of the lake or river."[1]

As with all the cabinet series, this oil is quite loosely painted. The figures are dashed off with miniature highlights suggesting feathers and beadwork. The intent must have been to execute these small canvases rapidly, perhaps in order to capture a scene as expeditiously as possible and thus make something of a manufacture of the works. Since they were intended for sale, he needed only to capture the essence of the narrative and scenery to achieve his purpose. These cabinet pictures may have been intended to be sold in sets of two or three. The Edwards family, who is thought to have purchased this piece, also acquired a companion work, *Assiniboin Encampment on the Upper Missouri* (cat. no. 183).

1. "The Fine-Arts: A Visit to Stanley's Studio," *Detroit Free Press*, May 21, 1865.

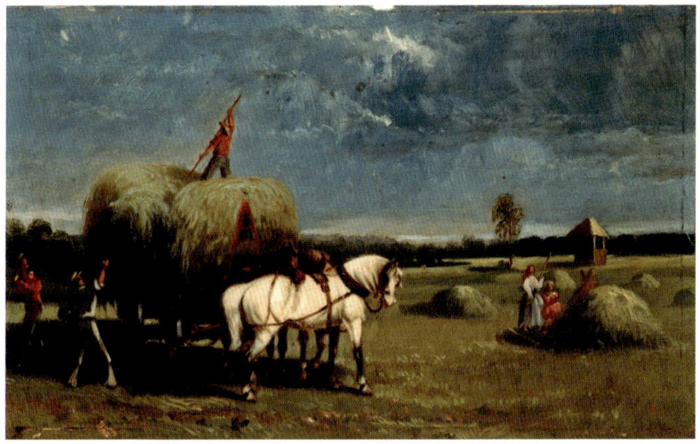

187

Haying, c. 1865

Oil on canvas, 8⅞ × 14¼ in. (22.5 × 36.2 cm)

PRESENT COLLECTION: Private collection

PROVENANCE: Mrs. Edith Stanley Bayles, Oak Park, Illinois; (M. Knoedler and Co., New York, New York); Gene Stapleton, Gross Point, Michigan; (Kennedy Galleries, New York, New York, 1980); (Sotheby's, New York, New York, 1982); present owner

Haying is a study for a larger, more finished work that Stanley completed in 1865, *The Last Load of Hay* (cat. no. 188). The free handling of the figures and the energetic treatment of the landscape details and sky suggest that this might be an on-the-spot work inspired by a summer's day farm visit. No doubt painted after the tragic news of the Smithsonian fire of the previous winter, which had burned just under 200 of his treasured Indian paintings, it suggests that the artist was emerging from the doldrums and searching successfully for themes and subjects for his art that were potentially marketable and not tied to his experiences in the West.

The pose of the horses and the inclusion of the woman and two children hinted at how important family was to Stanley. His wife, Alice, and the two of their three children born by this date, Louis and Clara, were surviving, so a painting that mixed the joy of the harvest with the harmony of spouses and children provided solace for a man anguished by life's inequities.

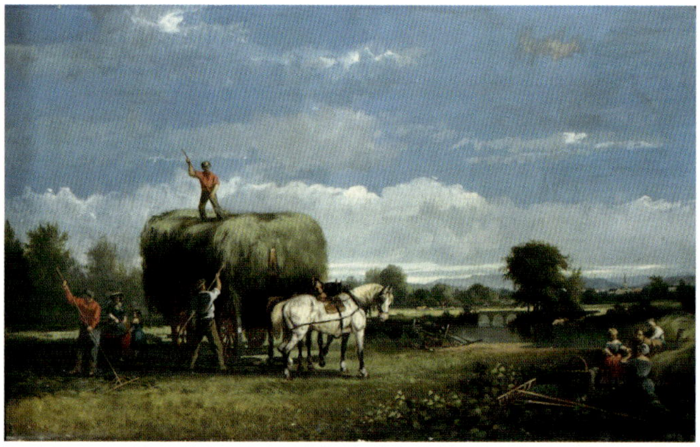

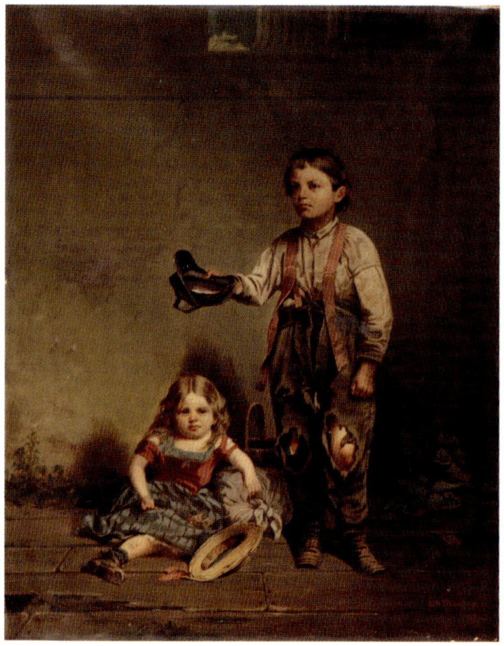

188

The Last Load of Hay, 1865

Oil on canvas, 18½ × 30½ in. (47.0 × 77.5 cm)

INSCRIBED LOWER LEFT: Stanley 1865

PRESENT COLLECTION: Detroit Institute of Arts, Michigan, gift of Mrs. Wilfred C. Leland (66.25); photograph courtesy Bridgeman Images

PROVENANCE: The artist; [?]; Mrs. Dean (Alice Stanley) Acheson, Washington, D.C.; by descent to Mr. and Mrs. Wilfred C. Leland; present owner by gift, 1966

LIFETIME EXHIBITIONS: M. S. Smith and Co. (jewelry store), Detroit, Michigan, 1866; St. Andrew's Hall, Detroit, Michigan, 1867

In the mid-1860s, when Stanley painted this oil, the theme of haying was popular in American art. Fanny F. Palmer, who worked for Currier and Ives in its prime, produced two paintings, *Haying Time—The First Load* and *Haying Time—The Second Load*, in 1868, reflecting the widespread appeal of such harvest scenes. Stanley dated this work 1865, and it appeared in the window of a Detroit jewelry store, M. S. Smith and Co., early the next year. The *Detroit Free Press* referred to it as a "fine new landscape" by the artist, "one taken from actual life."[1] This would imply that it was painted in Michigan, where Stanley was then residing. The same newspaper later mentioned the painting under its title "The Last Load of Hay."[2] Like Palmer's version, this painting generated public enthusiasm with its engaging charm. Another paper noted that it immediately engendered "universal interest and praise." Even a herd of cattle that passed the shop window was tempted by the harvest scene's offer of "repast."[3]

1. "A Favorite Criticism," *Detroit Free Press*, January 16, 1866.

2. "The Great Sale of Paintings at St. Andrews Hall," *Detroit Free Press*, December 19, 1867.

3. *Congressional Globe*, January 24, 1866.

189

Beggar Boy, 1865

Oil on canvas, 28⅝ × 22⅛ in. (72.7 × 56.2 cm)

INSCRIBED LOWER LEFT: Stanley 1865

PRESENT COLLECTION: The Fine Arts Museums of San Francisco, gift of George Mahon Stanley (1989.38)

PROVENANCE: The artist; Louis Crandall Stanley, Detroit, Michigan; by descent to George M. Stanley, Fresno, California; by gift to present owner, 1989

LIFETIME EXHIBITIONS: Ladies' Michigan State Fair, Detroit, 1865

In February 1865 Stanley exhibited four paintings at the Ladies' Michigan State Fair in Detroit. They were shown in a special fine art gallery that was said to have been the "most attractive feature of the Fair."[1] Stanley's display was intended to provide support for the fair's primary cause, to help with war relief efforts. Two of Stanley's submissions were his stock in trade, small Indian scenes (cat. nos. 191 and 192). The other two, somewhat less common examples of his work, were genre subjects related to the life of young boys in the city. One of these was the *Beggar Boy*, and the other was a painting titled *Market Boy* (unlocated). These followed a popular fashion in American art of painting impoverished city street urchins, a trend that would survive well into the twentieth century.

There is no way to corroborate this notion, but it might be assumed that the two genre pictures were considered by the artist as a companion set.[2] In the pattern of much nineteenth-century genre work, these two were probably produced as a morality statement. Though they sold separately, it might be expected that

Beggar Boy showed youths in distress, having to solicit handouts for survival, while the *Market Boy* very possibly featured the antithesis, an industrious lad who through hard work was rewarded with a productive, happy life.

1. "The Fine Art Gallery," *Broken Fetter*, February 28, 1865.

2. This might be assumed since the two paintings were exhibited together later at an exhibition of the Detroit Art Association. See *Catalogue: Detroit Art Association. First Exhibition* (Detroit: Detroit Art Association, 1876), nos. 123 and 124.

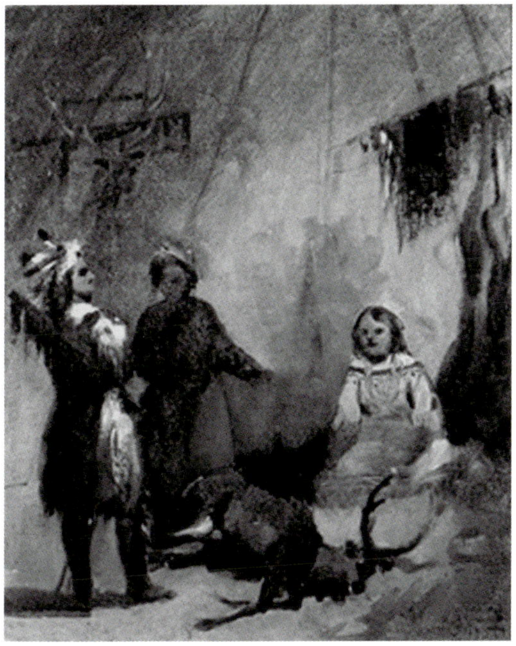

190

Hiawatha, a Study, c. 1865

Oil on paperboard, 12 × 9¾ in. (30.5 × 24.8 cm)

PRESENT COLLECTION: Private collection

PROVENANCE: (Kennedy Galleries, New York, New York); present owner

This sketch, related in tone and composition to the two small oils titled *Interior of Wigwam* (cat. nos. 191 and 192), may have been a preliminary study for a large painting that Stanley conceived after his return to Detroit. Its setting in the interior of a Plains Indian lodge, featuring three human figures, a dead deer, and hanging artifacts, would suggest that it is probably by Stanley's hand. The finished studio work is not known to exist either in the inventory of his known works or in the available Stanley literature. Given the generalized treatment of the figures, the narrative may also have nothing to do with Hiawatha, but rather be simply another variation on men bargaining for a buck, this time in front of a woman.

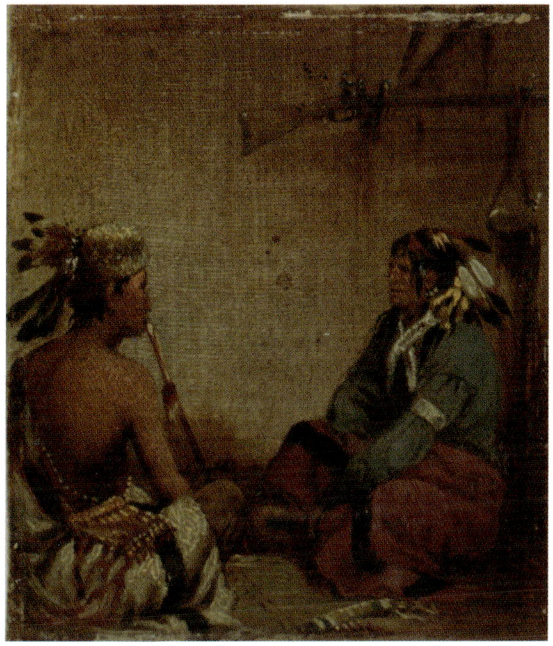

191

Interior of Wigwam, c. 1865

Oil on canvas, 4½ × 4 in. (11.4 × 10.2 cm)

INSCRIBED: [Signed with artist's initial] S; INSCRIBED VERSO: By Mr. Stanley / painter of the / celebrated Indian portraits at / Washington in the Smithsonian / Institute Lent to Mrs. Spicer conference / by Mr. I Stewart Jr. / 1865 Detroit

PRESENT COLLECTION: Private collection

PROVENANCE: (Bonhams, London, England, 2005); (Sotheby's, New York, New York, 2005); present owner

LIFETIME EXHIBITIONS: Ladies' Michigan State Fair, Detroit, 1865

192

Interior of Wigwam, c. 1865

Oil on canvas laid down on board, 4½ × 4 in. (11.4 × 10.2 cm)

INSCRIBED: [Unsigned]

PRESENT COLLECTION: Private collection

PROVENANCE: (Bonhams, London, England, 2005); (Sotheby's, New York, New York, 2005); present owner

LIFETIME EXHIBITIONS: Ladies' Michigan State Fair, Detroit, 1865

When Stanley resettled in Detroit in the early 1860s, he was determined to participate fully in the civic life of the community. Michigan was a major backer of the Union effort in the Civil War. Though he was too old to join the army, he could contribute in other ways.

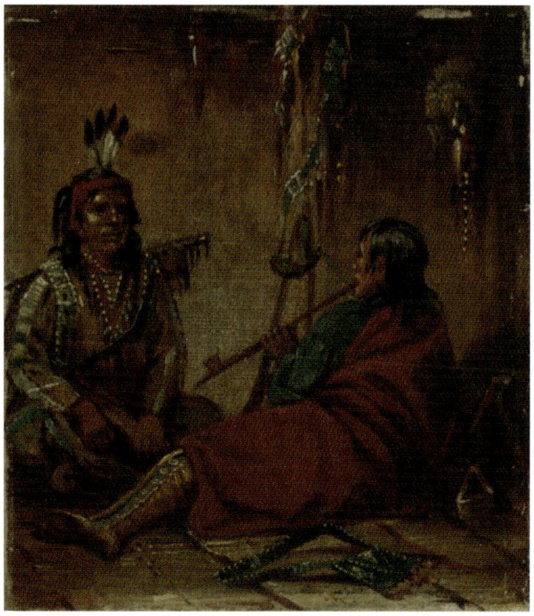

192

As an example, just a few weeks after he learned the sad news of the devastating fire at the Smithsonian, Stanley, though severely shaken, was participating in an anti-slavery event at the Ladies' Michigan State Fair organized by the Ladies Freedom Relief and Education Society of Detroit. Stanley contributed not one but five works to support the effort, four by his own hand and one, a still life, by his contemporary DeWitt Clinton Boutelle.[1] This duo is thought to have been part of Stanley's submission, along with another pair of oils, *Beggar Boy* (cat. no. 189) and *Market Boy* (unlocated).

If they were painted at the time, which is quite likely given their small size, sketchy execution, and dour palette, they would represent his gloomy mood and his desperate need to use his time effectively in order to begin recouping his losses with important salable works.

1. "Our Fair," *Broken Fetter*, February 28, 1865.

193
Western Landscape, c. 1865

Oil on canvas mounted on Masonite, 18½ × 30 in. (47.0 × 76.2 cm)

INSCRIBED LOWER LEFT: J. M. Stanley

PRESENT COLLECTION: Detroit Institute of Arts, Michigan, gift of Dexter M. Ferry, Jr. (15.14); photograph courtesy Bridgeman Images

PROVENANCE: The artist; Dexter Mason Ferry, Detroit, Michigan; by descent to Dexter M. Ferry, Jr., Detroit, Michigan; present owner, 1915

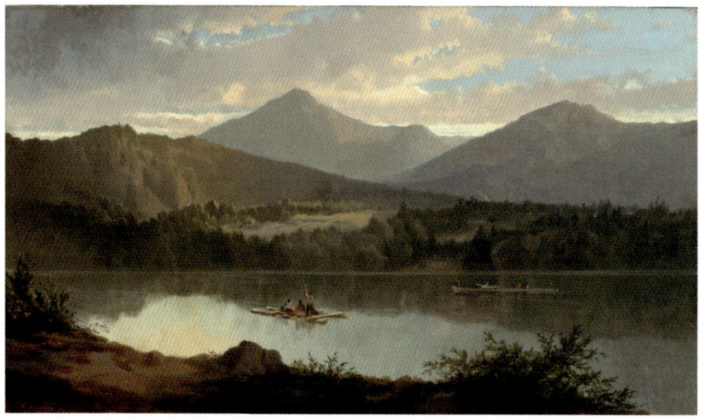

193

This painting has come down through history with the vague title *Western Landscape*. It carried that title when it was acquired by the Detroit Institute of Arts in 1915, a gift from the son of Stanley's patron, Michigan's premier seed merchant, Dexter M. Ferry. What stories Stanley and Ferry shared about the work are not known, but in the years since their association, much conjecture has prevailed in its description and dating.

In one of the painting's earliest twentieth-century showings, the Saint Louis Art Museum's seminal 1954 exhibition *Westward the Way*, it was referenced as a representation of the Sweetwater River in Wyoming and dated 1853.[1] More recent discussions of the painting suggest correctly that it portrays a scene on the Columbia River but incorrectly that it dates from the late 1840s, following the artist's first rather than second trip into the Northwest.[2]

The painting pictures a view of the Columbia River reminiscent of his 1852 *Scene on the Columbia River* (cat. no. 065). A similar group of Indians passes along the river in both works. The treatment of light and atmosphere, however, are quite different, the first being relatively crisp and lucid while this, the latter, evinces a more luminist, velvety ether as seen in such oils as *Landscape with Deer* (cat. no. 164) of about 1858 or *On the Snake River* (cat. no. 144) of about 1856. The fact that *Western Landscape* was purchased by Dexter Ferry might suggest that it was painted in Detroit, sometime after Stanley moved there in 1863.

1. Perry T. Rathbone, ed., *Westward the Way: The Character and Development of the Louisiana Territory as Seen by Artists and Writers of the Nineteenth Century* (Saint Louis: City Art Museum of St. Louis; Minneapolis: Walker Art Center, c. 1954), 50.

2. J. Gray Sweeney, "Western Landscape," in *American Paintings in the Detroit Institute of Arts*, vol. 1, *Works by Artists Born Before 1816*, ed. Nancy Rivard Shaw and Mary C. Black (New York: Hudson Hills Press, 1991), 184.

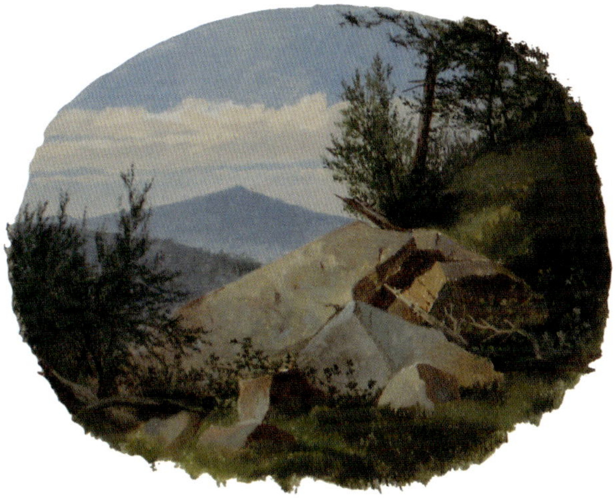

194

Rocks and Terrain, 1865

Oil on canvas, 9 × 12 in. (22.9 × 30.5 cm) (oval)

PRESENT COLLECTION: Private collection

PROVENANCE: The artist; Edith Stanley Bayles; by descent to Mrs. Dorothy E. Bayles, Oak Park, Illinois; (Kennedy Galleries, New York, New York); (M. Knoedler and Co., New York, New York); (Sotheby Parke Bernet, New York, New York, 1982); (Thompson Gallery, Woodstock, Connecticut, 1984); present owner

This handsome study of rocks, trees, and distant mountain is thought to have been painted in 1865 during the Stanley family's visit to the White Mountains of New Hampshire. Although it is unsigned and bears no inscriptions, it may have been conceived as a finished work. Many artists brought their plein-air paintings like this home and later signed and sold them in the marketplace.[1] This work's oval format suggests that it could be properly matted and promoted as a cabinet picture, a type of art that Stanley frequently produced in this period of his life.

In size and basic composition, *Rocks and Terrain* resembles his 1847 oil *View of Mount Graham* (cat. no. 039), from his Arizona trip with Lieutenant William Emory. Yet this later work is more complex in its balance of natural elements. The mountain is placed off center; its pyramidal peak is counterpoised with a huge, multifaceted boulder, whose geometries energize the scene and provide a barrier to physical incursion. Viewers must project their spirit into the scene because the corporeal world is closed to further intrusion. In the Arizona landscape, where Stanley wished to purvey the sense of accommodation for the sake of conquest, the mountain is centered in the composition and, psychologically at least, available for human assault.

1. See Eleanor Jones Harvey, *The Painted Sketch: American Impressions from Nature, 1830–1880* (Dallas: Dallas Museum of Art, 1998), 83–98.

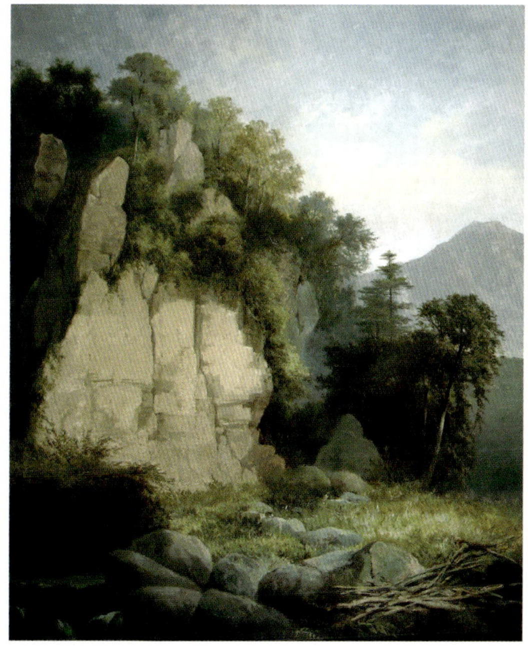

195

Eastern Landscape, c. 1865

Western Landscape

Oil on canvas, 29¾ × 24¾ in. (75.6 × 62.9 cm)

INSCRIBED LOWER RIGHT: Stanley

PRESENT COLLECTION: Private collection; photo courtesy of Kennedy Galleries

PROVENANCE: (Kennedy Galleries, New York, New York); private collection; (Scottsdale Art Auction, Scottsdale, Arizona, 2005); present owner

Given its scale, nearly 30 × 25 inches, this painting is probably a studio piece completed after Stanley returned to Detroit following his summer visit to the White Mountains in 1865. Although the painting bears no title, it is signed, which also connotes that it is a finished work. Yet, because of its intimate quality and freshness of execution, it has all the appearances of an in situ sketch from nature. It is reminiscent of rock studies by the first-generation Hudson River School artist Asher B. Durand.

Stanley evokes an inviting response. The brightly lit façade of the rock face reflects warmth on the glade in the foreground. A bundle of broken sticks in the lower right corner suggests that this might be a perfect spot to camp. It is almost certain that Stanley, who was traveling with his family, stayed in a hotel while touring the White Mountains. But the plein-air feeling of this canvas hints at his genuine bond with the outdoors and his fond remembrances of life in the field as an explorer-artist of the West.

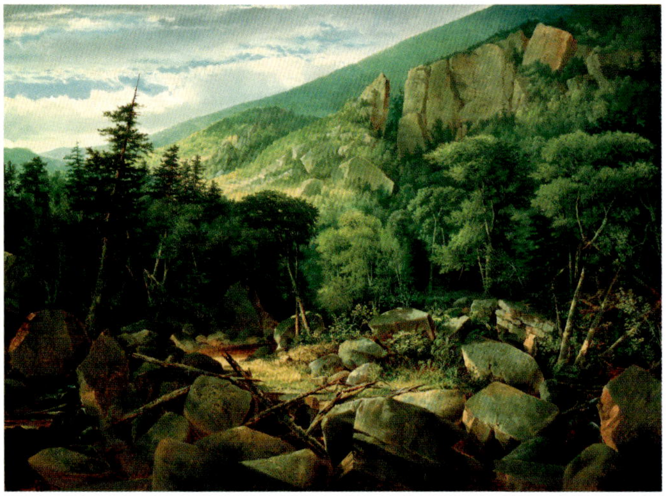

196

Under the Ledge, 1866

Under the Ledge, Mount Hayes near Gorham, New Hampshire

Oil on canvas, 36⅛ × 48½ in. (91.8 × 123.2 cm)

INSCRIBED LOWER RIGHT: J. M. Stanley 1866; INSCRIBED VERSO: Under the Ledge, Mount Hayes near Gorham, N. H. / J. M. Stanley

PRESENT COLLECTION: Private collection, Winchester, Virginia

PROVENANCE: The artist; Thomas L. McGraw; by descent to Dr. David Preston, 1883; descent through the family; (Macbeth Gallery, New York, New York, 1981); (Christie's, New York, New York, 1981); (Altman Fine Arts, New York, New York, 1987); (Gerald Peters Gallery, Santa Fe, New Mexico); (Sotheby's, New York, New York, 1991); (Sotheby's, New York, New York, 1993); (May and Associates, Scottsdale, Arizona, 1994); (Gerald Peters Gallery, New York, New York); present owner

LIFETIME EXHIBITIONS: M. S. Smith and Co. Detroit, Michigan, 1866

In August 1865 Stanley packed up his family and headed east from Detroit to New Hampshire. They went presumably on a vacation, though the artist was also provided a chance to paint the acclaimed White Mountains of northern New England.

This painting was one of the first of his landscape studies from that trip to be transferred to a large-scale canvas. It pictures a vista of the Leadmine Ledge at the base of Mount Hayes near the village of Gorham.[1] When it was completed in 1866, in Stanley's Detroit studio, a reporter from the local paper was summoned. He was impressed, lavishing praise on the painter's effort and summarizing that the work "combines all the distinguishing features of the beautiful scenery of the region." Stanley had long been recognized for his skills at rendering nature's greenery. The reporter noted this as well. "The trees, whose grouping and rich foliage constitute some of the most effective and charming points of the picture, [are] executed with a skill that could not be excelled."[2]

Hundreds of painters visited the White Mountains in these years. Stanley, fresh from the tragic loss of his Indian Gallery, was searching for a new direction for his talents. He painted several other landscapes as a result of the 1865 trip. This one is the most crisply colored and clearly delineated of the group. It may have a psychological implication as well. The rocky cliffs and jagged boulders in the scene may be symbolic of the obstacles he faced with his Indian Gallery lost to posterity.

1. I am grateful to Roger E. Belson of Henniker, New Hampshire, for this description of the scene.

2. "Art," *Detroit Free Press* (1866), incompletely cited clipping, Stanley scrapbook.

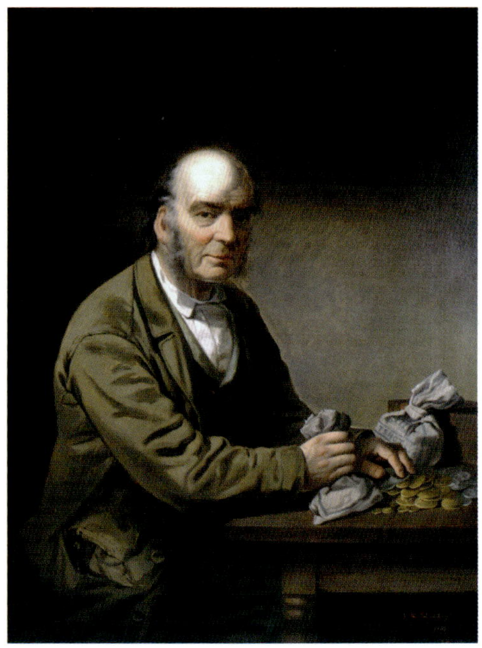

197

The Money Changer, 1866

Oil on canvas, 41½ × 35½ in. (105.4 × 90.2 cm)

INSCRIBED LOWER RIGHT: J. M. Stanley. / 1866. / Detroit. Mich

PRESENT COLLECTION: Private collection

PROVENANCE: The artist; Edith Stanley Bayles, Oak Park, Illinois; Dorothy E. Bayles, by descent; (Kennedy Galleries, New York, New York); (M. Knoedler and Co., New York, New York); (Frank H. Boos Gallery, Bloomfield Hills, Michigan, 2001); Graham Arader,

New York; (Sotheby's, New York, New York, 2009); (Arader Galleries, New York, New York, 2012); (Bonhams, New York, New York, 2013); present owner

T*he Money Changer* was painted in Detroit in 1866. It is a decidedly unaffectionate portrait of a man whose expression and gestures speak of parsimony and greed. It would seem that, from Stanley's viewpoint, money changers were the root of his and perhaps all society's problems. Money changers were, in Stanley's day, money brokers or lenders. Their fees and approachability may have been unreasonable, as this portrayal would imply, and Stanley obviously saw them as sinister figures in his world.

Stanley was notoriously bad with money, and he had a perpetually difficult time supporting his family with his art. In 1866, the year he painted this work, he was making every effort to finish his large historical painting *The Trial of Red Jacket* (cat. no. 212). He wrote his friend Isaac Strohm in Washington, D.C., early that year. "I hope soon to complete my Red Jacket," he scribed with shaky optimism, but continued, "I have been so occupied in fighting the wolf from the door that I have not been able to spend the time & money necessary to complete the painting."[1] Stanley was still trying to find a way to be compensated for his loss at the Smithsonian. Lawyers and congressmen were joined in his appeal. Yet, if the mood of this painting had anything to do with that endeavor, his hopes must not have been high. And, of course, in the end, they should not have been. Stanley received nothing for his loss. The U.S. government held onto its money.

1. Stanley to Isaac Strohm, January 16, 1866, Strohm Papers.

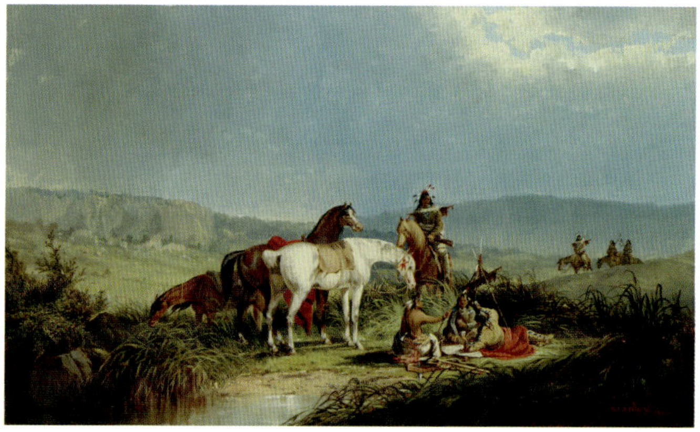

198

198

Indians Playing Cards, 1866

Oil on canvas, 16¼ × 26 in. (41.3 × 66.0 cm)

INSCRIPTION LOWER RIGHT: Stanley 1866

PRESENT COLLECTION: Detroit Institute of Arts, Michigan (43.60); photograph courtesy Bridgeman Images

PROVENANCE: Mr. and Mrs. Frederick K. Stearns, Detroit, Michigan; by gift to present owner

Stanley started to explore the theme of Indians playing cards in the mid-1850s (see cat. no. 136). Never particularly interested in showing the bellicose side of Plains Indian life, he chose genre subjects of peaceful repose and social intercourse rather than battle scenes favored by such contemporaries as Carl Wimar and Arthur Fitzwilliam Tait. Stanley pictured Indians thus engaged in two basic ways, as set pieces in the interior of lodges (*Gambling for the Buck*, cat. no. 206) or as part of broad western landscapes, as in *Indians Playing Cards*. In either case, the total focus of the compositions is on the game. The rider who has just arrived in the middle ground is attentive to the action (one of the players waves his card as if ready to slap it down in victory). Even the horses seem alert to the pastime.

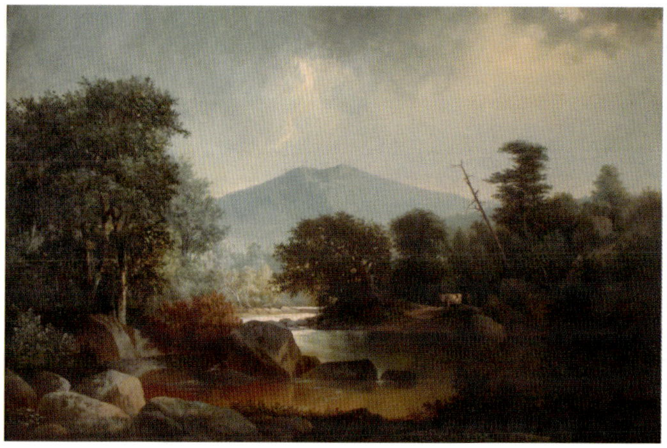

199

The River Bend, c. 1866

Mount Hood

Oil on canvas, 28 × 42 in. (71.1 × 106.7 cm)

INSCRIBED LOWER LEFT: Stanley

PRESENT COLLECTION: Private collection; photograph courtesy Christie's, New York, and Bridgeman Images, New York

PROVENANCE: Thomas L. McGraw; by descent to Sarah L. McGraw, Detroit Michigan, 1892; by descent to Ada Loop Harrison, Port Sanilac, Michigan, 1916; by descent to Stanley G. Harrison, 1925; Sanilac County Historical Society, by gift, 1964; (Frank H. Boos Gallery, Bloomfield Hills, Michigan, 1996); (Christie's, New York, New York, 1996); (Christie's East, New York, New York, 1997); present owner

In 1866, the *Detroit Free Press* announced that Stanley had produced what they termed the first in a series of sizable landscapes inspired by his 1865 late summer trip to the White Mountains in New Hampshire.[1] It was titled *Under the Ledge* and pictured Mount Hayes (cat. no. 196). About a year later, in spring 1867, the *Detroit Advertiser and Tribune* reported that he had just completed the third landscape in the White Mountain series, *Mount Carter and the Imp* (cat. no. 200).[2] Though incorrectly referred to over the years as a view of Mount Hood in Oregon, *The River Bend* is thought to be the second in his New England landscape series. The view pictures Mount Washington from the Peabody River south of Gorham.[3]

The River Bend was bought originally by Thomas and Sarah McGraw of Detroit. They were friends of the Stanley family, and Thomas was a partner with Hiram Walker in the tobacco business before Walker became involved in the sale and production of liquor.[4] That the painting was part of a White Mountain series may be borne out by the fact that its frame and size were identical to the painting that McGraw's partner, Walker, purchased in 1867, *Mount Carter and the Imp* (cat. no. 200).

1. "Art," *Detroit Free Press* (1866), incompletely cited news clipping, Stanley scrapbook.

2. "Mr. Stanley's Studio," *Detroit Advertiser and Tribune*, April 9, 1867.

3. For this description of the scene, I am grateful to Roger E. Belson, Henniker, New Hampshire.

4. For a discussion of this, see a typescript report by George p. Lawson, director, Sanilac Historical Museums, October 26, 1977, Schimmel Papers.

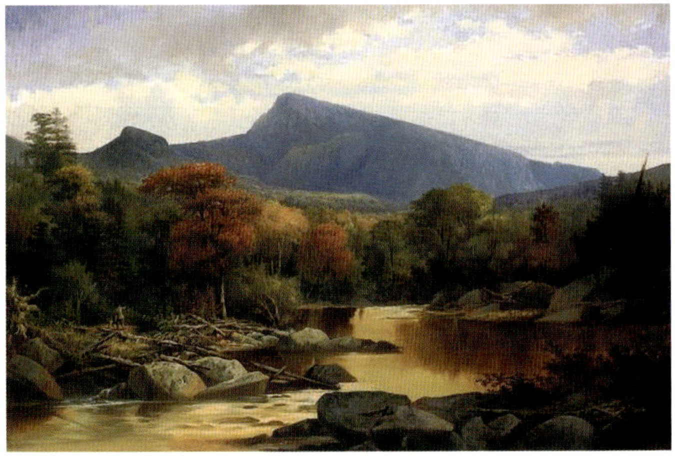

200

200

Mount Carter and the Imp, 1867

Hunter and Landscape; Autumn in the White Mountains

Oil on canvas, 28 × 40 in. (71.1 × 101.6 cm)

INSCRIBED LOWER RIGHT: Stanley

PRESENT COLLECTION: Owner and location unknown

PROVENANCE: Hiram Walker, Detroit, Michigan; by descent to private collection; (Frank H. Boos Gallery, Bloomfield Hills, Michigan 1987); (Sotheby's, New York, New York, March 1999); present owner

Stanley produced landscape paintings inspired by his visit to the White Mountains for a couple of years after his summer visit there in 1865. This view of North Carter Mountain and Imp Mountain from the Peabody River was painted in spring 1867 and was described by a newspaper reporter while it was in process.[1] "He has now upon his easel the third of his series of White Mountain landscapes, the subject in this case being a view of Mt. Carter and the Imp." Though incomplete at the time of the report, the painting foreshadowed "a work of great beauty and the most marked artistic merit."[2]

The painting combines landscape grandeur with an element of genre. In the middle distance is a male figure carrying a shotgun and a dead rabbit. The hunter is said to be Stanley's young son, Louis.

1. For the identification of the scene, I am grateful to Roger E. Belson, Henniker, New Hampshire.

2. "Mr. Stanley's Studio," *Detroit Advertiser and Tribune*, April 9, 1867.

201

Moonlight Adventure, 1867

Moonlight Adventure on the St. Clair River; Going for Strawberries; Spirit Lake, Minnesota by Moonlight

Oil on canvas, 11½ × 19½ in. (29.2 × 49.5 cm)

PRESENT COLLECTION: William L. Clements Library, University of Michigan, Ann Arbor

PROVENANCE: The artist; Emily Ward, Detroit, Michigan; William Van Dyke; by gift to present owner, 1944

Stanley produced only a handful of genre paintings, and most of those were created during his late years in Detroit. This moonlight river scene depicts a childhood recollection of Emily Ward, a doyenne of Detroit society in the 1860s. Emily was the sister of shipping and iron magnate Eber B. Ward, whose monumental portrait Stanley painted a few years later (cat. no. 224).

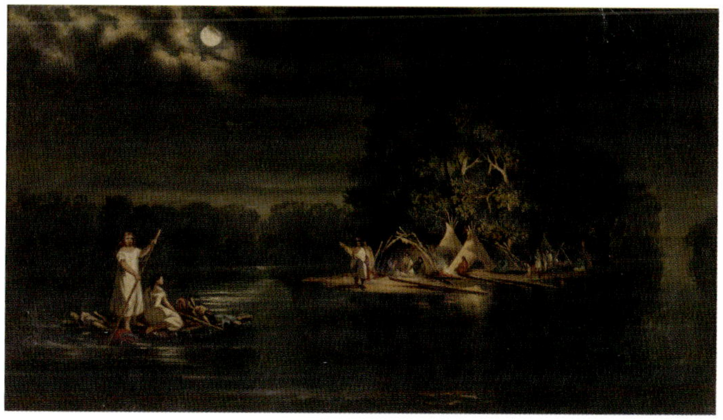

201

According to an account in the *Detroit Evening Journal* in 1887, the painting *Moonlight Adventure* depicts the tale of sixteen-year-old Emily afloat and adrift with her cousin on the St. Claire River near present-day Marine City, Michigan. They had crossed earlier in the day to the Canadian side to pick strawberries. Their boat drifted away while they were occupied, and they were forced to build a makeshift raft, which was carried downstream until it came to rest on an island. There a group of Indians rescued the young ladies, fed them, and transported them safely back home in their canoes.[1] Emily told Stanley the story while they were together on a river cruise one day. Stanley subsequently painted the small canvas and gave it to her as a present on her fiftieth birthday. It reflected a mellowed interpretation of Indians and their relation to Anglo women compared to his earlier abduction scenes and his large, racially distraught *An Osage Scalp Dance* of 1845 (cat. no. 025).

1. *Detroit Evening News*, March 26, 1887. I am grateful to Clayton Lewis, curator of graphic material, William L. Clements Library, Ann Arbor, for this information.

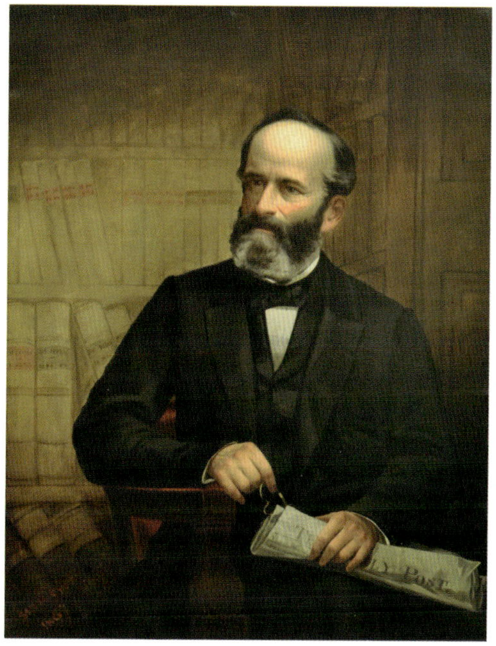

202

202
Frederick Morley, 1867

Oil on canvas, 39½ × 30⅜ in. (100.3 × 77.2 cm)

INSCRIBED LOWER LEFT: Stanley 1867

PRESENT COLLECTION: Detroit Historical Society, Michigan

PROVENANCE: The artist; Frederick Morley, Detroit, Michigan; [?]; Dr. S. S. Wittenberg, Detroit, Michigan; present owner, 1959

In spring 1867 Stanley moved into large quarters over a bank on Jefferson Avenue in Detroit. According to the *Detroit Advertiser and Tribune*, the accommodations consisted of at least two rooms, one said to have secured for him "the advantages of a commodious exhibition room for his paintings," and the other, a "suitable and admirably-lighted studio."[1] It was to this studio that he advertised for students to come and learn to draw and paint, so the space must have been large enough to provide for pupils as well.[2]

Stanley worked the Detroit newspapers as best he could to promote his art and his talents as a teacher. He befriended the media powerbrokers of the day and through them received direct support, such as the patronage of newsmen like Frederick Morley, who was the editor of the *Detroit Advertiser and Tribune* in the early 1860s. From 1867, the date of this portrait, until 1875, Morley was editor of the *Detroit Daily Post*. He is posed in this portrait with a copy of the *Post* in his hand and volumes of the archived newspaper behind him. His tight-lipped, sagacious expression reflects his self-estimation as a visionary journalist. He was also active in the Republican Party.

1. "Mr. Stanley's Studio," *Detroit Advertiser and Tribune*, April 9, 1867.

2. Schimmel, "John Mix Stanley and Imagery," 377.

203
Prairie Life, 1867
Indians Hunting; Scene from Indian Life

Oil on composition board, 10⁷⁄₁₆ × 8½ in. (26.5 × 21.6 cm)

INSCRIBED LOWER LEFT: Stanley / 1867

PRESENT COLLECTION: Cincinnati Art Museum, Centennial Gift of the Cincinnati Institute of Fine Arts from the Collection of Bishop Spence Burton (1981.131)

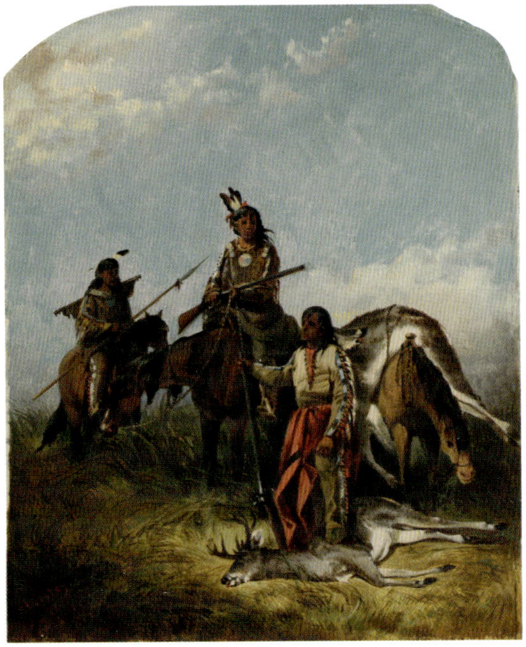

203

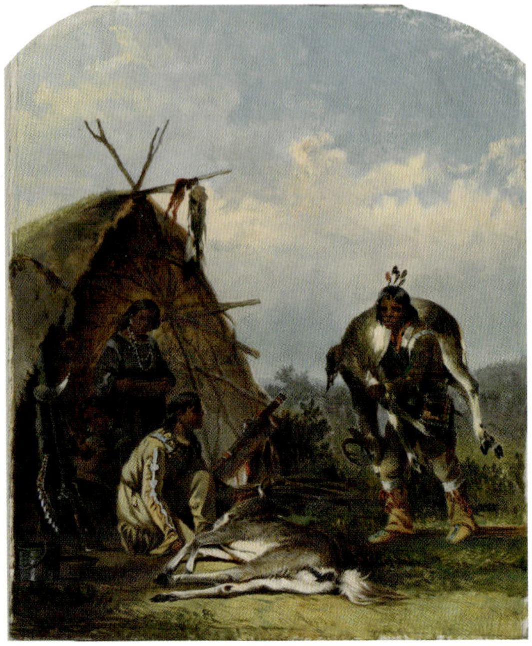

204

PROVENANCE: The artist; [?]; Steven H. and Martha Burton, Cincinnati, Ohio, 1878; Casper H. Burton, Cincinnati, Ohio, 1899; Bishop Spence Burton, Cincinnati, Ohio, 1931; Cincinnati Institute of Fine Arts, 1966; present owner, 1981

204

Camp Life, 1867

Indians with Deer; Scene from Indian Life

Oil on composition board, 10 7/16 × 8 1/2 in. (26.5 × 21.6 cm)

INSCRIBED LOWER LEFT: Stanley

PRESENT COLLECTION: Cincinnati Art Museum, Centennial Gift of the Cincinnati Institute of Fine Arts from the Collection of Bishop Spence Burton (1981.129)

PROVENANCE: The artist; [?]; Steven H. and Martha Burton, Cincinnati, Ohio, 1878; Casper H. Burton, Cincinnati, Ohio, 1899; Bishop Spence Burton, Cincinnati, Ohio, 1931; Cincinnati Institute of Fine Arts, 1966; present owner, 1981

These two cabinet pictures were created as a matched pair and were intended to be reproduced and marketed as chromolithographs. Stanley transported them to Berlin in spring 1868 along with four larger oil paintings.[1] He had titled them *Prairie Life* and *Camp Life*, and they were described at the time as "a very pretty pair of pictures, the former representing a group of hunters collected around the body of a newly killed deer, while the latter represents the hunters returning from the chase at sunset."[2]

It is likely that they were never, despite their coupled charm as Indian genre works, reproduced as lithographs. The Detroit newspapers welcomed the Berlin chromolithographs openly and enthusiastically when they were shipped back from Europe in 1869 and 1870. One paper wrote in 1869 that "Mr. Stanley is having his pictures chromed in Germany, by which means these valuable works are multiplied many times and supplied to the public at rates which bring them within the reach of all. The chromos are now coming back from Europe and are being put into the market as fast as they arrive."[3] There is no mention of prints made from these two works ever arriving, however, and no example chromolithographs survive today either. In all likelihood, Stanley for one reason or another probably brought the paintings back home with him. Perhaps the idea of a pair of small prints did not receive encouragement from Storch and Kramer, his German lithographers.

1. See "Art Matters," *Detroit Daily Post*, April 28, 1868.

2. "Our Home Artist," from an unidentified Detroit newspaper of 1868, Stanley Papers.

3. "Stanley's Chromos," *Detroit Free Press*, September 19, 1869.

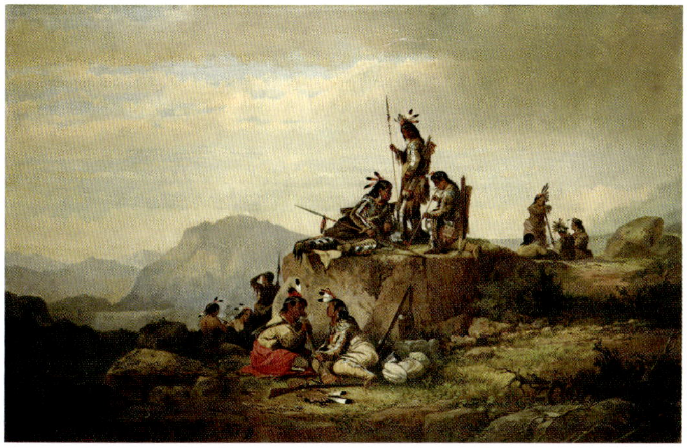

205

Group of Piegan Indians, 1867

Piegan-Blackfoot Group

Oil on canvas, 27 × 41 in. (64 × 103 cm) (sight)

INSCRIBED LOWER LEFT: J. M. Stanley / 1867—

PRESENT COLLECTION: Western History and Genealogy Department, Denver Public Library, Colorado, on loan to Denver Art Museum (C34–15)

PROVENANCE: Charles Hanah, Council Bluffs, Iowa; (Rosenstock Books, Denver, Colorado, 1939); present owner

Smoking among Plains Indians was a common practice, during ceremonies and for pleasure. In this Stanley painting, it was used as a genre motif, a cultural curiosity that would attract the interest of viewers. In the same way that Stanley has dressed all the men in this scene in their finest apparel, he has presented the act of leisure smoking as a special activity that afforded men a universal bond. These figures appear to be warriors who are perhaps resting after a military foray, so the action is one of relaxation, maybe even accomplishment.

Stanley has made a special effort to render a mountainous atmosphere and setting, both of which respond to experiences he had enjoyed during his trip west with Isaac Stevens in 1853. His job during that sojourn was equally to document the scenes they passed and to enhance their splendor in order to reinforce the attractiveness of a northern course for a transcontinental railroad. By the time this painting was produced, however, the railroad was already being built far to the south of Stevens's preferred route. Stanley was left then with creating a quintessentially gorgeous painting that, as art historian David Parks Curry has observed, is invested "with a still beauty that outlives mere reportage."[1]

1. David Parks Curry, *The Western Spirit: Exploring New Territory in American Art* (Denver: Denver Art Museum, 1989), 30.

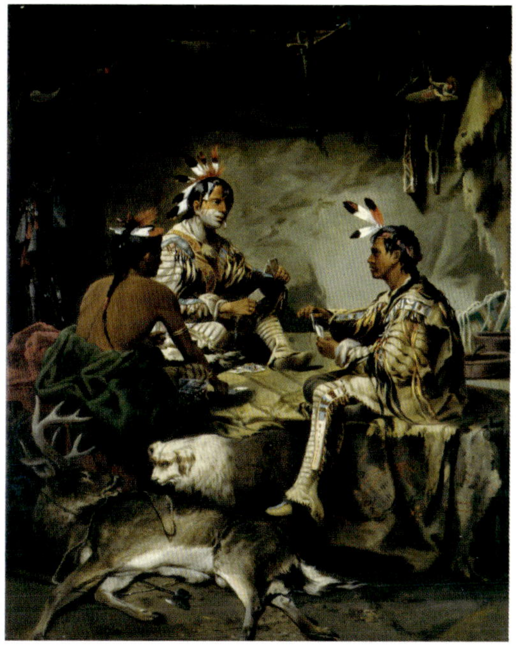

206

Gambling for the Buck, 1867

Oil on canvas, 20 × 15⅞ in. (50.8 × 40.3 cm)

INSCRIBED LOWER LEFT: J. M. Stanley / 1867

PRESENT COLLECTION: Nelda C. and H. J. Lutcher Stark Foundation, Stark Museum of Art, Orange, Texas (31.23.11)

PROVENANCE: George Stanley, Ann Arbor, Michigan, 1942; John Meddaugh Stanley, Washington, D.C., 1952; Mrs. Dean (Alice Stanley) Acheson, Washington, D.C.; H. J. Lutcher Stark, Orange, Texas, 1965; present owner

LIFETIME EXHIBITIONS: Fifth Annual Exhibition, Chicago Academy of Design, 1871

This is one of the first, if not the first, painting that Stanley produced with the expressed intention of having it reproduced as a chromolithograph. A Detroit newspaper referred to it as such, and its date would support that contention.[1] Stanley selected the theme from his long list of paintings that featured Indians at cards, dating back to the mid-1850s. He chose to place the figures in an interior setting, perhaps to put focus on the game and its suspense rather than on surrounding landscape distractions. The writer in the Detroit newspaper was fascinated with the physiognomies of the players, relishing the discovery that the artist had been able to distinguish "the individuality of every face."[2]

Others have viewed this painting as a pivotal work. Stanley scholar Julie Schimmel, for example, considers this a representation of a new vision of Indian people for the painter. Before this,

Stanley portrayed Indians as heroic figures, masters at survival with their prowess as hunters and warriors. Now he views them as noble, the scene having taken place following rather than during the hunt. By virtue of its monumental presence as a work of art and its portentous narrative, she has argued, it transcends the sphere of a simple genre painting to assume the proportions and stature of a history painting.[3] Remembering that his famous 1858 interior scene with hunters, *The Trapper's Cabin* (cat. no. 163), is regarded as a history painting more than a simple genre scene, such an analysis of this work has merit. In any event, *Gambling for the Buck* was certainly worthy of being preserved as a print for wide public distribution.

1. "Our Home Artists," unidentified Detroit newspaper clipping, Stanley Papers.

2. Ibid.

3. Schimmel, "John Mix Stanley and Imagery," 188–89.

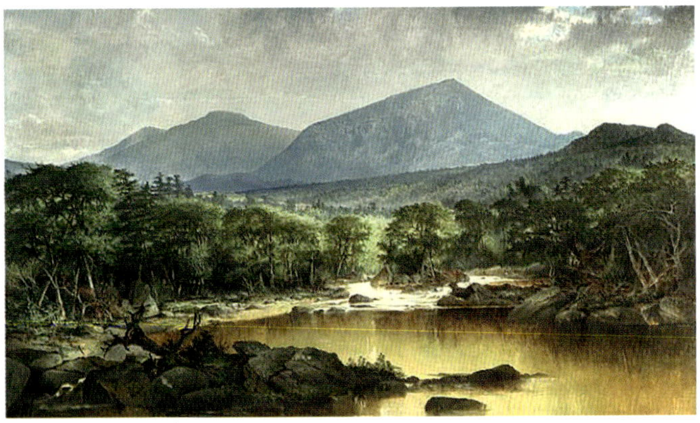

207

Mounts Washington and Madison, c. 1867

Oil on canvas, 48 × 60 in. (121.9 × 152.4 cm)

PRESENT COLLECTION: Unlocated

PROVENANCE: Unknown

LIFETIME EXHIBITIONS: M. S. Smith and Co., Detroit, Michigan, 1867

The whereabouts of this painting is unknown. It may be the second in the series of three White Mountain scenes that Stanley painted, as mentioned in a Detroit newspaper in April 1867.[1] The view is of Mount Washington (on the left; actually the taller of the two peaks) and Mount Madison (on the right) as seen from the conjunction of the Peabody and Androscoggin rivers. Although it is considered a rather unusual view, it is taken from Gorham, New Hampshire, where the Stanley family stayed during their White Mountain visit in 1865.[2] The painting was written up in the *Detroit Free Press* just as it was being finished. The reporter, who was spellbound before its spectacle, wrote, "Looking over the long stretch of intervening forest the eye is arrested with the grandeur of the mountain scenery."[3] The Stanley family made an ascent of Mount Washington during their stay in New Hampshire that is documented in a photograph of them near the weather station on the mountain's summit (fig. 207.1).

This ambitious oil exposes the duality of Stanley's landscape vision with the reverential yet openly mimetic perspective that he brought to nature's splendors. It is intentionally composed to lead the viewer's gaze toward the most formidable of the peaks in the distance. The water in the foreground provides a moment of calm, interrupted in the middle ground by the rushing of rapids and then overpowered by the mountain mass behind. His gentle temperament and spiritual embrace of nature are in evidence. In concert with the passing age of enlightenment, his vantage is an ordered, ideal world, one quite distant from the disastrous ordeals of the recent Civil War or his personal losses in 1865, which had preceded his recuperative journey to the New England highlands.

1. "Mr. Stanley's Studio," *Detroit Advertiser and Tribune*, April 9, 1867.

2. I am grateful to Roger E. Belson of Henniker, New Hampshire, for information about the scene.

3. "Magnificent Paintings," *Detroit Free Press*, March 14, 1867.

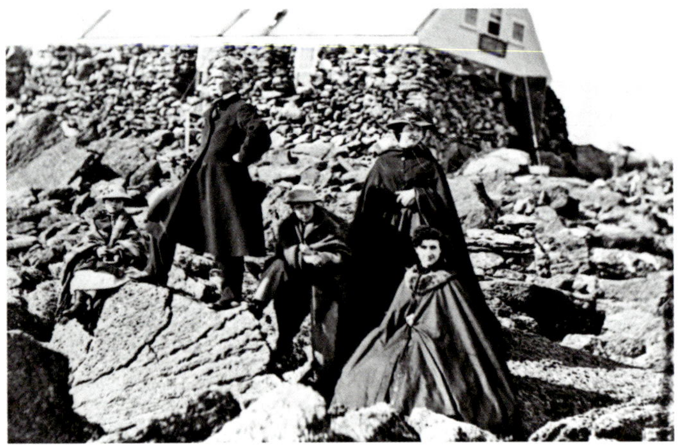

FIG. 207.1.
Unknown photographer,
Stanley Family at Summit of Mount Washington, 1865.
Photograph courtesy Julie Schimmel Papers

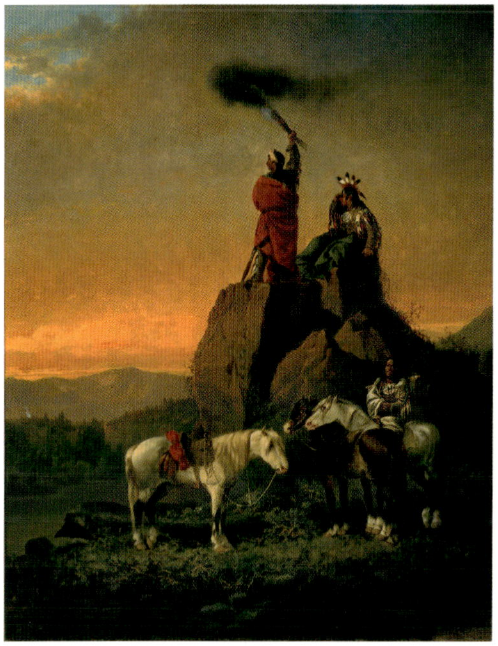

208

Indian Telegraph, 1868

The Smoke Signal

Oil on canvas, 30¼ × 23¼ in. (76.8 × 59.1 cm)

INSCRIBED LOWER LEFT: J. M. Stanley / 1868.

PRESENT COLLECTION: Rockwell Museum, Corning, New York

PROVENANCE: The artist; Diven Family, Elmira, New York, 1872; by descent to Lucy Diven French, Elmira, New York; Robert Rockwell, Corning, New York, 1963; present owner by gift, 1978

LIFETIME EXHIBITIONS: Dean, Brown and Co., Detroit, Michigan, 1868

The last of the paintings Stanley titled *Indian Telegraph* was intended to be reproduced as a chromolithograph. The theme had been quite popular for the artist, and it was thus selected along with six other subjects for broad public distribution. Just before Stanley left for Germany in spring 1868 to have the pieces reproduced, he invited the press to see his latest endeavor. A *Detroit Daily Post* reporter wrote that this was a particularly bright move on the artist's part.[1]

Despite the chromatic intensity in this painting being somewhat diminished from that of the earlier, smaller version of the vertical format (cat. no. 169), the *Detroit Daily Post* gave it a stunning appraisal. "The setting sun has gilded the western sky," they wrote in exaltation, "and far up toward the zenith a soft mellow light gives an exquisite tone to the whole, while in the form of the scout standing out in bold relief against the evening sky there is something indescribably striking, approaching even to grandeur."[2] Stanley's chromolithography enterprise was off to a lofty beginning.[3]

1. "Art Matters," *Detroit Daily Post*, April 28, 1868.

2. "Indian Telegraph," *Detroit Daily Post*, April 28, 1868.

3. For a description of the chromolithograph, see "Stanley's Chromos," *Detroit Free Press*, September 19, 1869. This source provides an incorrect description of the scene as being set in the "territory of the Apaches" in 1846 as opposed to the real source, the Stevens expedition on the northern plains in 1853. Whether Stanley related this misinterpretation to the reporter or not is unknown, but probable.

209

The Deer-Slayers, 1868

Hunters; The Hunters

Oil on canvas, 24 × 20 in. (61.0 × 50.8 cm)

INSCRIBED LOWER LEFT: J. M. Stanley / 1868

PRESENT COLLECTION: Private collection, Wyoming

PROVENANCE: The artist; J. P. Lieberman, Detroit, Michigan, by gift; by descent to private collection; (Sotheby's, New York, New York, 2004); present owner

As with several of the paintings Stanley created late in his career in order to make marketable prints, there are two versions of this work. The other (unlocated) is slightly smaller and probably a bit earlier, under the supposition that it stirred enough attention when painted to encourage the artist to replicate it for a chromolithographer to copy. This is the version that is thought to have been taken

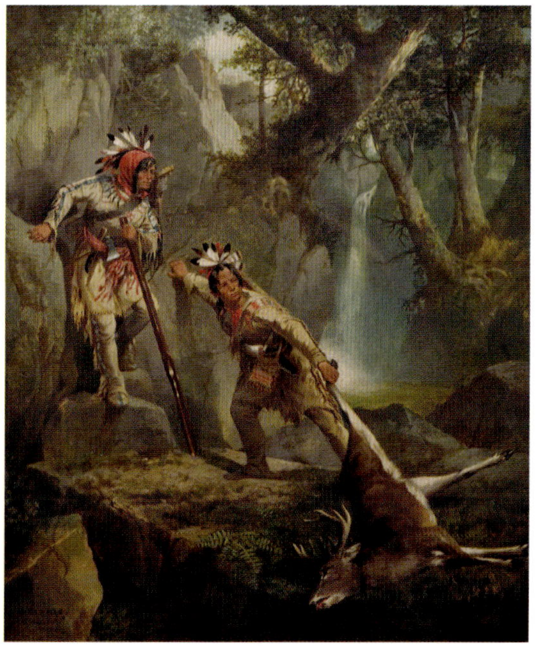

209

to Berlin for that purpose in 1868.[1] It is probably the painting that the *Detroit Daily Post* called "Hunters" when they reviewed the six paintings he was slated to carry to Germany that spring.[2]

About a year later, the prints began to arrive in Detroit. The chromolithographers, Storch and Kramer of Berlin, published a brochure promoting the first four completed prints and boasting that these were "the finest specimens of Chromo-Lithography yet presented to the public." The prints were exceedingly popular, as in fact the brochure guaranteed, and were made especially so because they followed Stanley's common refrain that they could not fail to excite the public "as souvenirs of a race that is fast dying out and will soon only survive in tradition." The publisher's description of the depicted scene was purely documentary, avoiding any assessment of the work's aesthetic merit. "This Chromo represents a couple of Indian Hunters who have just killed a deer in the Rocky Mountains. The animal having tumbled into a ravine, they are in the act of dragging the carcass up to the hights [*sic*] above." [3] The composition is actually quite complex, angles are counter posed, and linear tensions vivify the sense of exertion for the lead hunter, confirming the perils of the hunt.

1. This is implied in the essay accompanying the painting as it appeared in *Sotheby's: American Paintings, Drawings and Sculpture* (New York: Sotheby's, 2004), 234.

2. "Art Matters," *Detroit Daily Post*, April 28, 1868. Another Detroit newspaper referred to the work as "The Hunters" and applauded the print's fidelity to the original; see "Mr. Stanley's Chromos," *Detroit Free Press*, April 19, 1869.

3. *Just Published: Stanley Chromos, Four of the Series of Five Splendid Chromo-Lithographs Now Being Issued* (Berlin: Storch and Kramer, 1869).

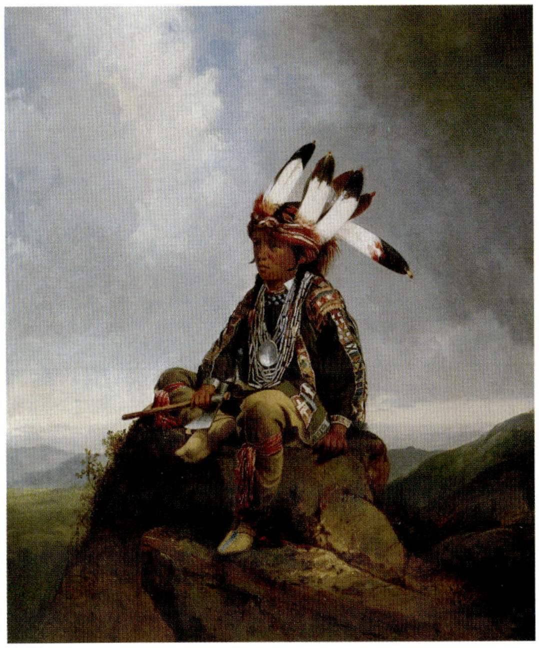

210

210

Young Chief Uncas, c. 1868

The Young Chief, Uncas

Oil on canvas, 24 × 20 in. (61.0 × 50.8 cm)

INSCRIBED LOWER RIGHT: J. M. Stanley

PRESENT COLLECTION: Autry National Center, Los Angeles, California (88.108.10)

PROVENANCE: The artist; Edith Stanley Bayles, Frances Q. Bayles, and Dorothy E. Bayles, Oak Park Illinois; (M. Knoedler and Co., New York, New York); Northern Natural Gas Company, Omaha, Nebraska, on loan to Joslyn Art Museum, Omaha, Nebraska, 1968; Enron Corporation, Houston, Texas, 1988; present owner

This is thought to be the first of two versions by Stanley of a young Indian seated atop a rocky prominence, peering out over an expansive, mountainous landscape (see cat. no. 211). The subject is dressed in the regalia of a mature warrior and holds a pipe tomahawk in his right hand. The pose is taken directly from an 1862 daguerreotype by Saint Paul photographer Joel Emmons Whitney, whom Stanley may have met at the beginning of his trip west with Isaac Stevens in 1853. The Whitney image is of a young Santee Sioux boy probably posed, in full adult attire including a peace medal, at Fort Snelling (fig. 5.12), and the photograph seems to have had wide circulation in the 1860s.[1]

Uncas, an ally of the British in the Northeast over several decades in the mid-seventeenth century, had been immortalized by James Fenimore Cooper in his historical novel *The Last of the Mohicans* of 1826. Uncas became the exemplar of Cooper's primary theme, the so-called doomed and disappearing Indian and, as such, inspired multiple painters to portray solitary Indians perched on precipices, staring into the distance, as magisterial symbols pondering their fate and that of their people.[2] Charles Deas' 1847 variation on the theme, *A Solitary Indian* (Autry National Center, Los Angeles), was known as *The Last Indian* when displayed in 1864.[3] Some artists produced such scenes by the handful, such as Stanley's contemporary, the Hudson River School painter Jesse Talbot, whose oil *Indian on a Cliff* (fig. 210.1) portrays an apprehensive, solitary figure whose vulnerable perch suggests a particularly uncertain future.

1. Whitney had set up business in Saint Paul in 1852. The photographer and subject were originally identified by Norman Feder, curator of American Indian Art at the Denver Art Museum, in a letter to Eugene Kingman at the Joslyn Art Museum in Omaha, March 3, 1969, in the archives of the Joslyn Art Museum. Other prints of the daguerreotype are found at the Minnesota Historical Society, St. Paul, and the Birmingham Reference Library, Birmingham, England.

2. See Schimmel, "John Mix Stanley (1814–1872)," 52.

3. See Clark et al., *Charles Deas*, 209.

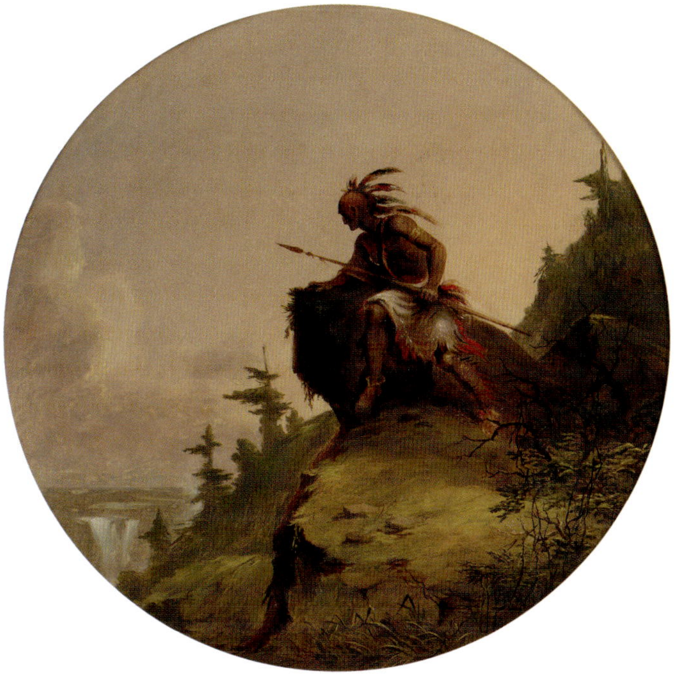

FIG. 210.1.
Jesse Talbot, *Indian on a Cliff*, c. 1841–1876.
Oil on canvas; 21 × 20 in. (53.3 × 50.8 cm).
Courtesy Robert L. Stuart Collection, New York Historical Society, on permanent loan from the New York Public Library

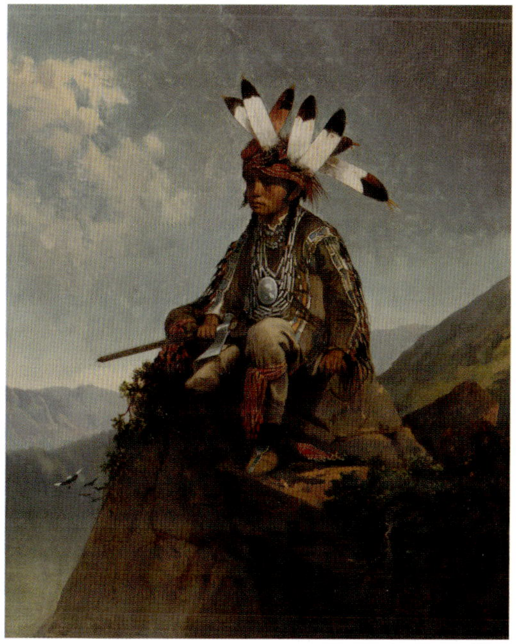

211

211

Young Chief, 1868

Uncas, the Young Chief; The Sentinel; Young Chief Uncas

Oil on canvas, 20 × 16 in. (50.8 × 40.6 cm)

INSCRIBED LOWER RIGHT: J. M. Stanley.

PRESENT COLLECTION: Haub Family Collection, Tacoma Art Museum, promised gift of Erivan and Helga Haub, 2014

PROVENANCE: Mrs. May Diven Liscum; A. W. Booth, 1949; M. Van Cleef Booth, Ithaca, New York, 1953; (Marathon Auction Company, Marathon, New York); (Wunderlich and Company, New York, New York); (Gerald Peters Gallery, Santa Fe, New Mexico); Haub Family, Wiesbaden, Germany; by gift to present owner

This is considered a second version of *Young Chief Uncas* (cat. no. 210). It was produced expressly as a model for a chromolithograph that was published in 1869 by the German firm Storch and Kramer. Stanley accompanied this painting and five others to Berlin in May 1868, where he contracted to have them reproduced as chromolithographs. When the painting was first mentioned, in the *Detroit Daily Post*, April 28, 1868, it was referred to simply as *Young Chief* with no allusion to Uncas. The article discussed Stanley's rationale for this, his latest commercial venture. The move was justified, they said, by the tragic loss of his collection to fire in 1865 made "irreparable, since no copies of these paintings exist. . . . To satisfy the demand for these pictures, as well as to secure their preservation, he has determined to cause chromo-lithographic copies to be made by the best European artists."[1] He was not about to have what remained of his legacy go up in smoke. By spring 1869, the first of the lithographs began to appear for sale in Detroit.[2]

Though closely patterned after the painting *Young Chief Uncas* (cat. no. 210) and the Joel Emmons Whitney daguerreotype of a Santee Sioux boy, *Ma-Za-Oo-Nie (Little Bird Hunter)* (fig. 5.12), this later version is more finished in the foreground, has a different and more dramatic arrangement of feathers in the boy's headdress, and enjoys a more clearly articulated sense of atmosphere. It is one of the true gems of Stanley's late career.[3]

1. "Art Matters," *Detroit Daily Post*, April 28, 1868. Although the newspaper referred to the work simply as *Young Chief*, a promotional brochure that was printed to accompany the chromolithographs titled it *Uncas, The Young Chief.*

2. *Detroit Advertiser and Tribune*, May 14, 1869. See Schimmel, "John Mix Stanley and Imagery," 153–56, for discussion of his lithographic endeavors.

3. The painting's association with these two portraits was first pointed out in a letter from Norman Feder, curator of American Indian Art at the Denver Art Museum, to Eugene Kingman at the Joslyn Art Museum, March 3, 1969, Schimmel Papers.

212

The Trial of Red Jacket, 1868

Oil on canvas, 66 × 108 in. (167.6 × 274.3 cm)

PRESENT COLLECTION: Buffalo and Erie Historical Society, Buffalo, New York

PROVENANCE: The artist; by descent to Louis C. Stanley and his sister Mrs. Edith Bayles; present owner, 1948

LIFETIME EXHIBITIONS: Exhibited in the cities of Detroit, Buffalo, New York, and Chicago (in the Fifth Annual Exhibition of the Chicago Academy of Design), 1868–1869

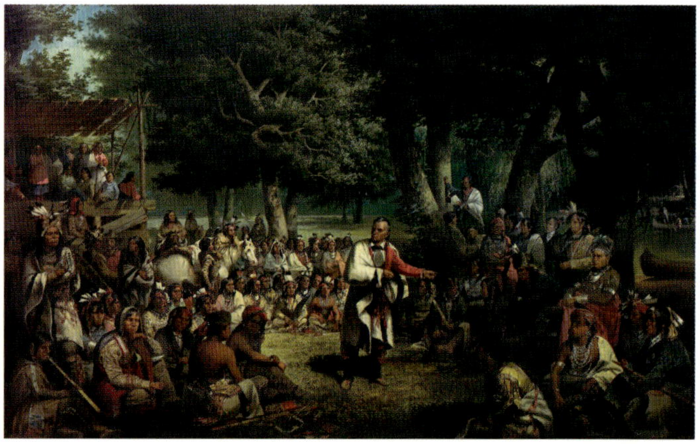

212

213

The Trial of Red Jacket, 1869

Oil on canvas, 23½ × 36⅛ in. (59.7 × 91.7 cm)

INSCRIBED LOWER CENTER, IN BROWN PAINT: J. M. Stanley / 1869

PRESENT COLLECTION: Smithsonian American Art Museum, Washington, D.C., gift of George M. Stanley (grandson of the artist) and family and museum purchase (1990.34)

PROVENANCE: The artist; by descent to George M. Stanley, Fresno, California; present owner, 1990

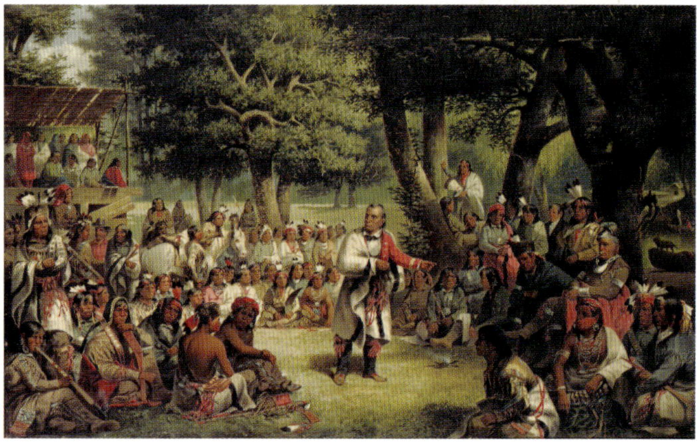

213

These paintings depict the renowned Seneca chief Red Jacket successfully defending himself against a wrongful accusation of witchcraft during his trial in 1802.[1] It is appropriate that Stanley depicts him speaking, since it was his eloquence as an orator that gained the chief fame. Other artists had painted Red Jacket's portrait, but Stanley was the first to do so as a history painting.[2] The larger work is a monumental canvas (6 × 9 feet) containing approximately seventy-two figures, including several portraits, and took Stanley five years to complete.[3]

The Seneca's territory was in upstate New York, in the environs of Buffalo. Stanley grew up in Buffalo, during the years 1816 to 1828, at the same time Red Jacket was living in the vicinity, and he knew the chief's story. Red Jacket, originally called Otetiani as a boy and renamed Sagoyewatha (Keeper Away) after 1780 because of his skills as a speaker, earned the sobriquet "Red Jacket" because of the red coat the British gave him in thanks for his help during the American Revolution. It was the Seneca's allegiance to Britain against the Americans, however, that lost them much of their land after the war and forced many of them to move to Canada. Red Jacket, however, stayed in the area until his death in 1830.

Stanley settled briefly in Buffalo in 1863, and it was then that he began the painting that he finished in Detroit in 1868.[4] Depicting Red Jacket with an outstretched arm and weight shifted to one foot as though he were about to take a step, Stanley captured the leader in a pose that dates back to classical times and Roman sculpture of their own great orators. Around his neck, Red Jacket wears the peace medal given to him by George Washington when he visited Washington, D.C., in 1792. The artwork was a success both to the critics and to the public: people paid a record $8,000 in admission fees to see the painting.[5] To take advantage of its popularity, Stanley had it lithographed in 1869. To this end, he painted a smaller version (cat. no. 213), almost identical to the larger work, that was sent to Berlin as a model for the chromolithographs.[6] M. S.

1. Red Jacket was accused of witchcraft by rival Seneca chief Cornplanter, who for personal gain wanted to negotiate with the newly established U.S. government over the tribe's lands and rights. He hoped to silence the eloquent Red Jacket, who was against ceding any of their land and would be an influential voice against Cornplanter's plans. Cornplanter's shaman, Handsome Lake, accused Red Jacket of witchcraft. Although Red Jacket won his case, he lost in the long run and spent his last years around Buffalo, dissolute and poor.

2. Charles Bird King and R. W. Weir both did more traditional half-length or bust portraits.

3. Schimmel, "John Mix Stanley and Imagery," 159.

4. According to Schimmel, ibid., 135, Stanley visited his sister, Mary Cornelius Stambach, and was looking for a city to relocate with his family. He eventually settled on Detroit.

5. Ibid., 159.

6. *The Trial of Red Jacket* was one of six paintings Stanley had chromolithographed in Berlin by the printing company Storch and Kramer.

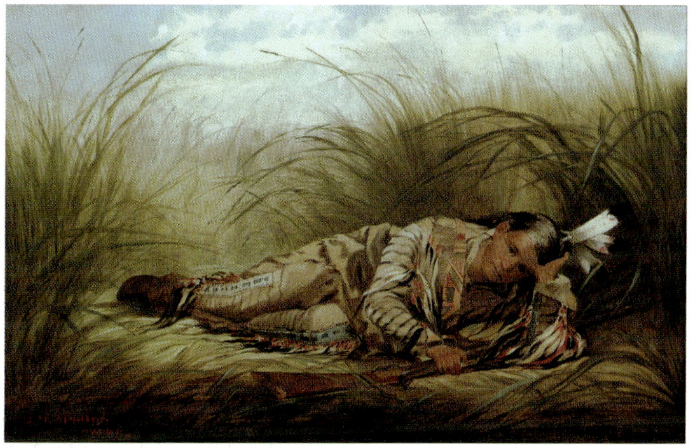

214

Snake in the Grass , 1868

Oil on canvas, 11¾ × 18 in. (29.8 × 45.7 cm)

INSCRIBED LOWER LEFT: J. M. Stanley / 1868

PRESENT COLLECTION: Autry National Center, Los Angeles, California (88.108.4)

PROVENANCE: The artist; [?]; Edith Stanley Bayles, Frances Q. Bayles, and Dorothy E. Bayles, Oak Park, Illinois; (M. Knoedler and Co., New York, New York); Northern Natural Gas Co., Omaha, Nebraska; Enron Corporation, Houston, Texas; present owner

Snake in the Grass provides a mix of conflicting sentiments and is therefore difficult to understand. On one account, it is a mournful work, suggesting not so much an Indian at rest as one who reclines to ponder his destiny. By the melancholy expression on the man's face, that fate appears to be rather unpromising. His pose suggests the theme of the 1856 sculpture *Dying Tecumseh*, by Ferdinand Pettrich (Smithsonian American Art Museum, Washington, D.C.), which was in the Smithsonian's collection in the 1860s, or another work that was a centerpiece in the Indian Gallery during the 1850s, a plaster cast of the Hellenistic sculpture *Dying Gaul*.

It has also been suggested that this work was intended to invite viewers into a reverie about the infinite breadth of the western prairies. Metaphorically, the introspective nature of the man's countenance ponders the question of life's meaning and humanity's place in its complex and expansive reach.[1]

Then again, Stanley may have painted it to contrast with the many artistic interpretations of Indian warriors lying in wait that appeared in the 1850s. George Caleb Bingham painted one memorable version, *The Concealed Enemy*, early in the decade (Stark Museum of Art, Orange, Texas), and Stanley's Baltimore colleague, Alfred Jacob Miller, used the theme frequently, as in *Pawnee Indians Watching the Caravan* (fig. 214.1), a watercolor painted for his Baltimore patron William T. Walters around 1858. If Stanley's *Snake in the Grass* does picture a warrior anticipating an attack, as the title suggests, it carries none of the menacing feeling of his contemporaries' versions.

In any event, Stanley considered it sufficiently meritorious to have it made into a chromolithograph in 1858. A few of these survive, but very few. The vast majority of the six chromolithographs published that year were, as the artist's son reported, "destroyed in a ware house fire with all our household goods in 1927."[2]

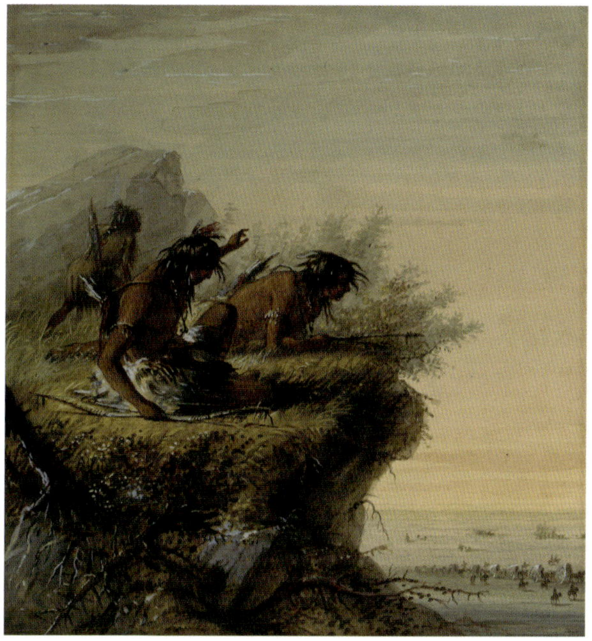

FIG. 214.1.
Alfred Jacob Miller, *Pawnee Indians Watching the Caravan*, 1858–1860.
Watercolor heightened with white on paper; 10⁷⁄₁₆ × 9⁷⁄₁₆ in. (26.5 × 24.0 cm).
Courtesy The Walters Art Museum, Baltimore, Maryland (37.1940.44)

1. See Brian W. Dippie, *West-Fever* (Los Angeles: Gene Autry Museum of Western Heritage; Seattle: University of Washington Press, 1998).

2. Undated letter from Louis Stanley to Ruth Gains in the Heye Foundation Archives, Huntington Free Library, New York.

215

Colonel Frank Graves, 1869

Oil on canvas, 43 × 31½ in. (109.2 × 80.0 cm)

INSCRIBED LOWER RIGHT: J. M. STANLEY / 1869

PRESENT COLLECTION: University of Arizona Museum of Art, Tucson (62.11.1)

PROVENANCE: The artist; Frank Graves family, Niles, Michigan; Mrs. Frances G. Emmons, Green Valley, Arizona, by descent; by gift to present owner

Stanley had known the Graves family at least since 1866, when he signed a page in a Graves family autograph album. It may have been at that time that the artist was asked if he might make a memorial portrait of a recently departed worthy in the Graves clan, Civil War hero Colonel Frank Graves.

Frank Graves was born in the southern Michigan town of Niles and was buried there twenty-eight years later, after suffering fatal wounds that spring in the Battle at the Wilderness in Virginia. Graves had mustered into the army as part of the Eighth Infantry, a Michigan volunteer unit. Because of the unit's widely varied engagements, they were referred to as "The Wandering Regiment." Before his death, Graves had led his company into the battles of Antietam in Maryland (September 1862), Vicksburg in Mississippi (June 1863), and Gettysburg in Pennsylvania (July 1863). His final engagement happened in Virginia, as General Ulysses Grant began his campaign to take Richmond.

Stanley's portrait of Graves was made from a daguerreotype, a practice that was not unfamiliar for artists after the war. He posed the colonel against a smoke-filled diagonal patch of foliated landscape. The greenish gold hue in the sky foretells of a potentially ominous situation on the horizon.

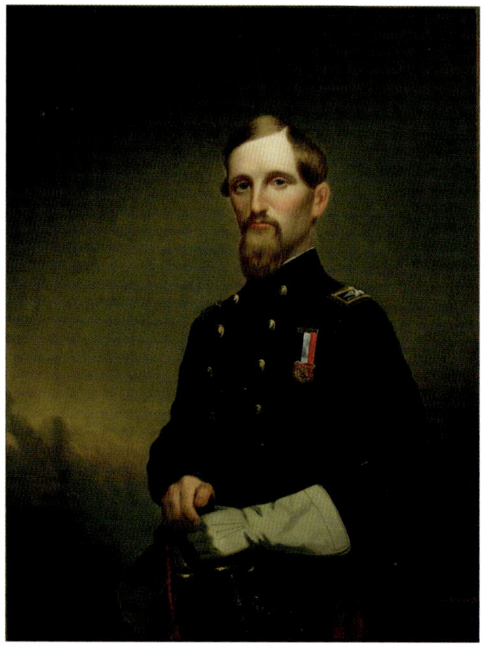

215

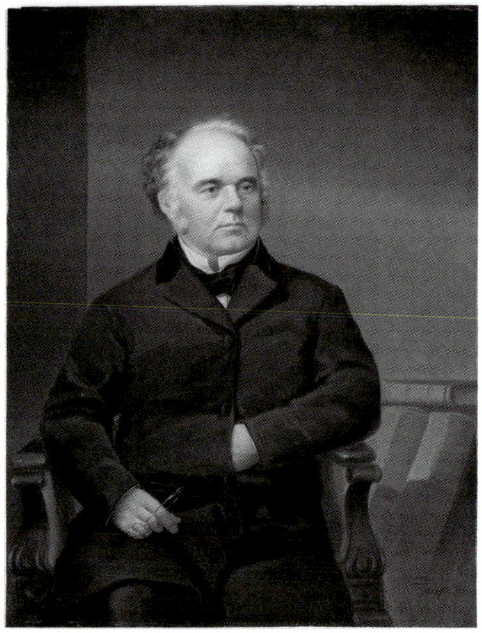

216

216

Samuel Mountfort Pitts, 1869

Oil on canvas, 48⅛ × 36 in. (122.2 × 91.4 cm)

INSCRIBED LOWER RIGHT: Stanley. 1869

PRESENT COLLECTION: Detroit Institute of Arts, Michigan, Founders Society Purchase, Gibbs-Williams Fund (58.364); photograph courtesy Bridgeman Images

PROVENANCE: The artist; Mrs. Samuel Pitts, Detroit, Michigan; Thomas Pitts, Detroit, Michigan; Lendall Pitts, Detroit, Michigan; Mrs. Lendall Pitts, Detroit, Michigan; present owner, 1958

This portrait of lumber baron Samuel Mountfort Pitts was painted for his widow, Sarah Merrill Pitts, in 1869. Samuel had died the previous year, so Stanley probably painted it from a photograph supplied by the family.[1] Stanley was accustomed to working from photographic imagery and thus was able to give Pitts a revivified countenance in this portrait. The fact that it was painted in almost total black and white would suggest a sense of mourning and posthumous remembrance.

Pitts was born in Maine and moved to Michigan after completing legal studies at Harvard University in 1830. He practiced law in Detroit for many years, but it was his investments in salt and lumber properties that brought him great wealth.

Stanley, perhaps at the behest of the Pitts family, painted Samuel in a similar pose as a painting by Joseph Badger of one of his most famous ancestors, John Pitts (Detroit Institute of Arts). John Pitts was the first of his family to immigrate to the United States from England. He made a fortune here and established a dynasty to which Samuel was partial heir.[2] Samuel, many generations later, ventured farther west, this time from Maine to Michigan, along the newly established Erie Canal. It was a voyage that must have felt equally daring and was one that proved just as rewarding as that of his ancestor.

1. See J. Gray Sweeney, "Samuel Mountfort Pitts, 1869," in Shaw and Black, *American Paintings*, 190.

2. For a description of this and other Pitts family portraits that came down through the family and were given to the Detroit Institute of Arts in the late 1950s, see Elizabeth H. Payne, "Pitts Family Portraits of the Eighteenth Century," *Antiques* 77 (January 1960): 87–89.

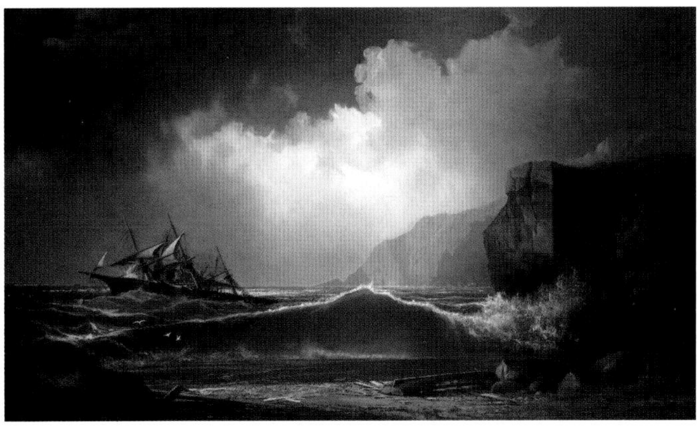

217

After the Storm on the Lee Shore, 1869

After the Storm

Oil on canvas, 37 × 60 in. (95.8 × 152.4 cm)

INSCRIPTION: [Unsigned]

PRESENT COLLECTION: D. Wigmore Fine Art, New York, New York

PROVENANCE: The artist; Mrs. L. D. Sanndors, Detroit, Michigan, 1883; Charlotte Public Library, Charlotte, Michigan, 1928; (Spanierman Gallery, New York, New York, 1994); (Sloan's, Washington, D.C., 2002); present owner

LIFETIME EXHIBITIONS: M. S. Smith and Co., Detroit, Michigan, 1869

This rather anomalous, unsigned work appeared in the display window of a Detroit jewelry store, M. S. Smith and Co., in fall 1869. There it caught the attention of a reporter from the *Detroit Daily Post*, a newspaper that was especially solicitous of Stanley's talents. The reporter commented that this was Stanley's "first attempt at a marine view," and that despite the artist's clumsy endeavor to picture "the fury of the storm-stirred waves of the ocean," the overall impression was a decided success. "The picture is a spirited one," he concluded, and "we think it will strike any beholder that the general treatment of the subject is admirable."[1]

A few details that a later reporter remembered seeing, such as a lighthouse on the shore and a lifeboat leaving the wreck, were evidently eliminated in the artist's final years. Since there was no signature, its attribution came into question a decade later, after Stanley died.[2] But at that time, one of Stanley's artist peers, Robert Hopkin, came forward to say he had not only seen it exhibited in the M. S. Smith and Co. window but also in Stanley's studio before it was finished.[3] Hopkin would have especially remembered this painting since marine pictures were a large part of his oeuvre. For Stanley, it represented a novel and intriguing theme, one of several different subjects he explored in his later years.

1. *Detroit Daily Post*, September 29, 1869.

2. These details are mentioned in a clipping, "Interesting Paintings Completed," from an unidentified Detroit newspaper of 1871, Stanley Papers.

3. R. Hopkin to the painting's first owner, Mrs. L. D. Sanndors of Detroit, November 7, 1883, Schimmel Papers.

218

Blackfeet Card Players, 1869

Blackfoot Card Players; Indians Playing Cards

Oil on canvas, 27¾ × 41¾ in. (70.5 × 106.0 cm)

INSCRIBED LOWER LEFT: J. M. Stanley. / 1869

PRESENT COLLECTION: American Museum of Western Art—The Anschutz Collection, Denver, Colorado

PROVENANCE: The artist; Major General Stewart Van Vliet, Washington, D.C.; by descent to Robert C. Van Vliet, son; by descent to Sarita Van Vliet, daughter; by descent to Marguerite Van Vliet, sister; Stuart Spraggins, Asheville, North Carolina, 1982; David S. Ramus, 1984; (Rosenstock Arts, Denver, Colorado, 1984); John F. Eulich Collection, Dallas, Texas, 1984; (Sotheby's, New York, New York, 1998); present owner

This is one of Stanley's most accomplished late paintings. It must have been one of his favorites, too, as it was chromolithographed. Unfortunately, even though the chromolithograph was one of the largest prints he ever produced (24 × 36 in.), few are known to have survived.[1] The painting resembles *Group of Piegan Indians*, 1867 (cat. no. 205), in composition, but it is bolder in its figural

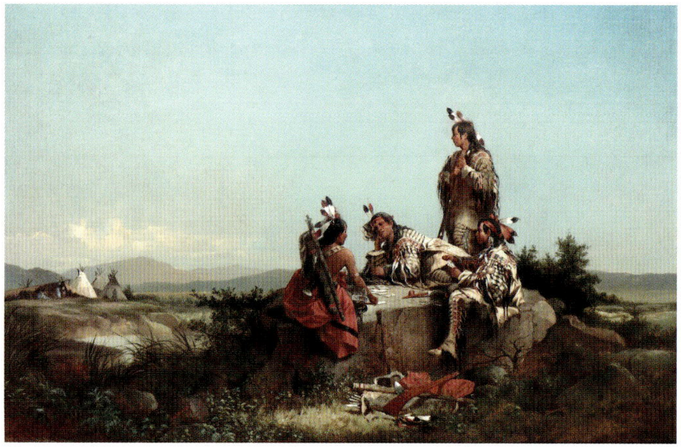

218

presentation and more skillfully drawn. Stanley's penchant for employing Indian gambling as a subject in his art was certainly gratified by this work.

Blackfeet Card Players was sent to Berlin in 1869, just as Stanley was receiving his first set of chromolithographs in Detroit. The local press described it as "unquestionably one of the finest works of his skillful brush in the field of art in which he stands without rival. The bold relief of the figures against the sky, their expressions, costumes and ethnic peculiarities, and the attractive landscape—all give to the picture a very striking effect."[2]

Stanley used Anglo models that he hired locally in the Detroit area and artifact props that he had collected during the Stevens expedition in 1853. A substantial number of Stanley's Northern Plains Indian studio objects were acquired by the Detroit sculptor Julius Theodore Melchers from the artist's widow. They were passed down to Melchers's son, the painter Gari Melchers, in 1903, and given by him to what is now the National Museum of the American Indian, Smithsonian Institution, in 1929. Among the surviving artifacts are a Teton Sioux gun-stock-shaped war club and a Blackfeet/Piegan man's shirt (fig. 4.3) that resemble accoutrements in the painting. Stanley sold the painting to Major General Stewart Van Vliet of Washington, D.C., who had served in the West at Fort Laramie during the mid-1850s.

1. Kinietz, *John Mix Stanley*, 28, 30.

2. "Mr. Stanley's Chromos," *Detroit Free Press*, April 19, 1869.

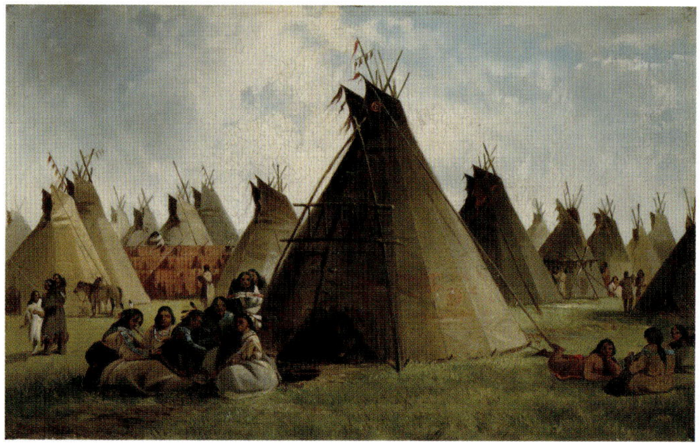

219

Prairie Indian Encampment, 1869

Oil on canvas, 9⅛ × 14⅛ in. (23.2 × 35.9 cm)

INSCRIBED LOWER LEFT: J. M. Stanley

PRESENT COLLECTION: Detroit Institute of Arts, Michigan, gift of Mrs. Blanche Ferry Hooker (41.63); photograph courtesy Bridgeman Images

PROVENANCE: The artist; Dexter M. Ferry, Detroit, Michigan; Mrs. Blanche Ferry Hooker, Detroit, Michigan; present owner by gift, 1941

Two paintings survive from Stanley's ill-fated last major project, his venture to produce a printed album containing fifty to one hundred color illustrations depicting various phases of Indian life in America. The images were to be drawn from his travels in the West over a dozen years, 1842 to 1854. This one was inspired by his time among the Assiniboins and Gros Ventres at Fort Union on the upper Missouri River. Though for purposes of the portfolio, Stanley elected to present this scene as a generic Plains Indian camp, he was specific in recounting his Fort Union memory of 1853 when he and Isaac Stevens were entertained in the tipi off a Gros Ventres chief. "This lodge" he recalled, "had been constructed with a truly remarkable elegance and attention to comfort." A travois, "the manner in which the lodge poles are used in transportation," leans against the façade of the hide structure. The camp as a whole, he concluded, presented "a no less novel than interesting spectacle."[1]

At least two original works survive from that moment back in 1853, a watercolor titled *Fort Union, and Distribution of Good to the Assiniboins* (cat. no. 096) and an untitled pencil drawing of a Gros Ventres tipi (cat. no. 074).

1. Quoted in Kinietz, *John Mix Stanley*, 26.

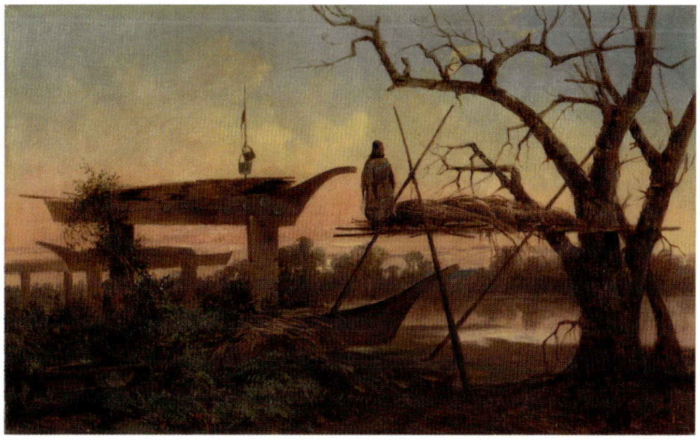

a far more complex work than the one Stanley produced for his portfolio and was beautifully engraved under the title *Chinook Burial* (fig. 133.1).[4]

1. "A National Loss," *Grand Rapids Eagle*, April 12, 1872.

2. These belong to the Museum of the American Indian, Smithsonian Institution, and were discussed in an article by Frederick Webb Hodge, "A Proposed Indian Portfolio by John Mix Stanley," *Indian Notes* 6, no. 4 (October 1929): 359–67. The whereabouts of the third painting, *Buffalo Hunt*, is not known.

3. Quoted in Kinietz, *John Mix Stanley*, 24; the complete essay on the painting appears on pages 21–24.

4. See Schoolcraft, *History of the Indian Tribes*, vol. 6. The whereabouts of the original painting is not known.

220

Chinook Burial Grounds, 1869

Chinook Burial

Oil on canvas, 9⅛ × 14⅛ in. (23.2 × 35.9 cm)

INSCRIBED LOWER LEFT: J. M. Stanley

PRESENT COLLECTION: Detroit Institute of Arts, Michigan, gift of Mrs. Blanche Ferry Hooker, 1941 (41.64)

PROVENANCE: The artist; Dexter Mason Ferry, Detroit, Michigan; by descent to Blanche Ferry Hooker, Detroit, Michigan; present owner by gift, 1941

In 1869 Stanley embarked on a project that he hoped would recoup his losses at the Smithsonian and permanently crown him the leading delineator of American Indian life. His idea was to provide a "pictorial history of Indian customs, manners, occupations, and religious rites" in what he called his "Indian Portfolio."[1] Three paintings are known to have been completed toward this endeavor, and two (this painting and cat. no. 219) are extant today. Press proofs for a printed preface and essays on the three paintings have also survived.[2] Sadly, Stanley died before the project could develop beyond this point.

The portfolio press-proof essay informed the viewer that the various scaffolds on the shore of the Columbia River bearing the Indian corpses indicated the relative stature of the deceased. The one on which the woman stands was for a poor man, one who could not afford a canoe to serve as his coffin or ornaments to decorate the site. Stanley noted that the painting carried a powerful symbolic message about the Chinooks and Indians as a whole. He said, though it was not true, that "the Chinooks are extinct."[3]

Stanley had been amongst the Chinook Indians both in 1847–1848 and 1853. He painted their fishing camps and other elements of their life. In 1857 Henry Rowe Schoolcraft invited him to submit a painting about their funerary practices for his monumental six-volume *History of the Indian Tribes of the United States*. It was

221

Mountain Landscape with Indians, c. 1870

Oil on canvas, 18 × 30¼ in. (45.7 × 76.8 cm)

PRESENT COLLECTION: Detroit Institute of Arts, Michigan, gift of the Wayne County Medical Society (59.312); photograph courtesy Bridgeman Images

PROVENANCE: David Whitney, Detroit, Michigan; Wayne County Medical Society, Detroit, Michigan; by gift to present owner, 1959

In 1865, when Stanley learned that his Indian Gallery had been destroyed by fire at the Smithsonian, he was living in Detroit. Through his efforts he had interested the Michigan State Legislature in buying the collection, but the fire preempted such a felicitous outcome. In this sad moment, he must have grasped at alternative courses for his career, and landscape painting provided one option. Among the paintings that the fire consumed were three views of Mount Hood in Oregon, and two similar views had adorned his now-defunct *Scenes and Incidents of Stanley's Western Wilds* panorama.[1] He had passed this vista most recently in 1853 on his way down the Columbia River with Isaac Stevens. Its

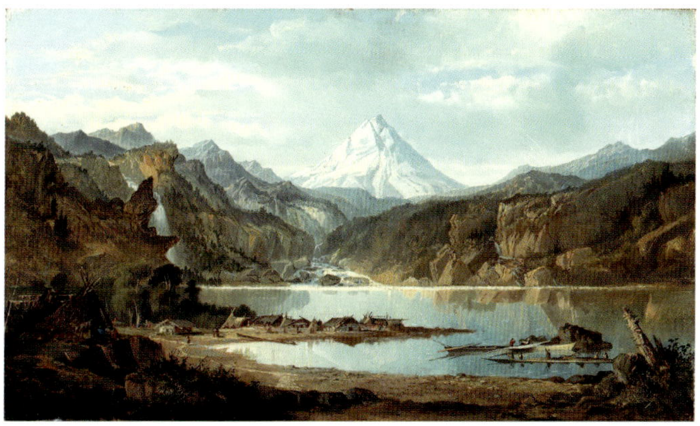

221

splendor was indelibly etched in his mind, and perhaps he had even taken photographs of the peak.

At this same time, the legendary western landscape painter Albert Bierstadt had unveiled his second monumental western landscape extravaganza. Bierstadt's chosen subject was also Mount Hood, which he had sketched in the fall and winter of 1864. His resulting 1865 magnum opus, *Mount Hood in Oregon* (fig. 223.1), created a national sensation. Most likely Stanley saw some of the rave reviews and began to conceive ideas for his own large-scale *Mount Hood from the Dalles* (cat. no. 223), for which this is a supremely detailed and beautiful study.

1. *Portraits of North American Indians*, 66, 68; and Donoho, *Scenes and Incidents*, 18–19.

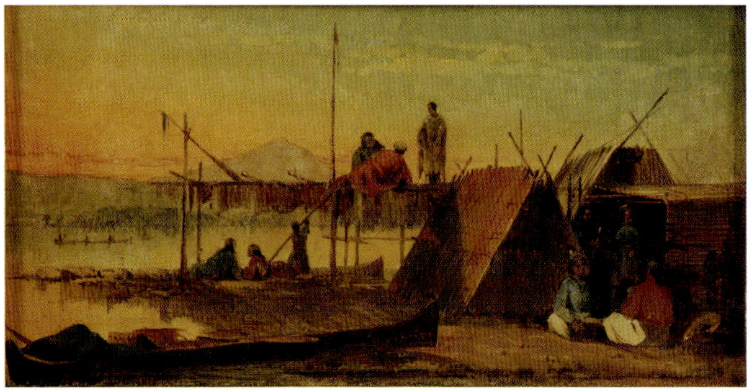

222

Indian Village Dalles, c. 1870

Mount Hood from the Dalles

Oil on canvas, 5 × 9 in. (12.7 × 22.9 cm)

INSCRIBED LOWER RIGHT: S—

PRESENT COLLECTION: Tuscaloosa Museum of Art: Home of the Westervelt Collection, Tuscaloosa, Alabama

PROVENANCE: (Detroit antique shop); Peter Coffey, Hartland, Michigan, 1981; (Stalker and Boos, Birmingham, Michigan, 1982); (Gerald Peters Gallery, Santa Fe, New Mexico); present owner, 1982

As Stanley prepared his landscape magnum opus, *Mount Hood from the Dalles* (cat. no. 223), in the late 1860s, he made studies of the Chinook Indians in order to animate the foreground. He had painted among the Chinooks in 1847–1848, and two of the portraits in his Indian Gallery were of a Chinook chief and an adult woman. He described the Chinooks at that time as being "few in number" and a tribe that once was a "powerful nation" but whose reduced population sustain themselves through fishing on the Columbia River.[1] He visited the area again in early November 1853 with Isaac Stevens, as they concluded their survey of the Northwest. One of Stanley's views of *Mount Hood and the Chinooks, Dalles*, appeared as plate 43 in the published report. The preliminary watercolor for that plate is found in this volume (cat. no. 115).

This oil study pictures Chinook Indians encamped along the Columbia, their proximity to the water and the racks of drying salmon evidencing their reliance on the river and the naturalness of their union with its rich resource. Mount Hood can be seen in the distance to the southwest, as the scene is set just below the Dalles, the first of the major set of rapids on the river. Despite the close view of the encampment and its inhabitants, the figures are adjunct decoration rather than ethnographic representations, with only generic regard for their costumes and no attention paid to their custom of flattening their heads.

1. See *Portraits of North American Indians*, 60, for entries on Stomaquea and Tel-Al-Lek, nos. 108 and 109.

223

Mount Hood from the Dalles, 1871

Oil on canvas, 57 × 92⅛ in. (144.8 × 234.0 cm)

INSCRIBED LOWER LEFT: J. M. Stanley / 1871

PRESENT COLLECTION: University of Michigan Museum of Art, gift of Mrs. Edith Stanley Bayles and the late Mrs. Jane C. Stanley (1940.426)

PROVENANCE: The artist; by descent to Louis C. Stanley, Detroit, Michigan; by descent to Jane C. Stanley (Louis C. Stanley's wife) and Edith Stanley Bayles (Louis's sister); by gift to present owner

With this grand rendition of Mount Hood, Stanley joined those members of the second-generation nineteenth-century American landscape painters, like Thomas Worthington Whittredge, who were drawn to the West. The precision and lucidity of Stanley's vision match Whittredge's clear American style of the same date and may respond as well to the Ruskinian specificity of Thomas Moran's western views of the early 1870s. It differs though from the luminous gradations of landscape splendor lavished on western scenes like *Mount Hood* (fig. 223.1) by the German aesthetic of Albert Bierstadt. Stanley's *Mount Hood from the Dalles* is controlled, meticulous, exalted, and fastidious. Its exactitude is so extraordinary that one scholar has suggested that this, and the related study (cat. no. 221), could be influenced by daguerreotypes that he took while on the Stevens expedition in that it "presents a sharply delineated work frozen in time and space by the precision of technique."[1]

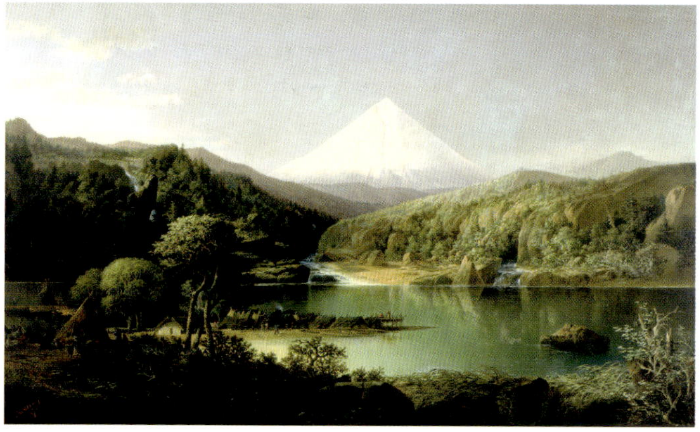

223

There is some indication that a similar painting may have been completed as early as 1866. Its description in a Detroit newspaper that year fits this work in all but size, it being 48 × 72 inches.[2] This 1871 version of the painting remained in the artist's possession through his lifetime and then was passed down through the family until the early 1940s.

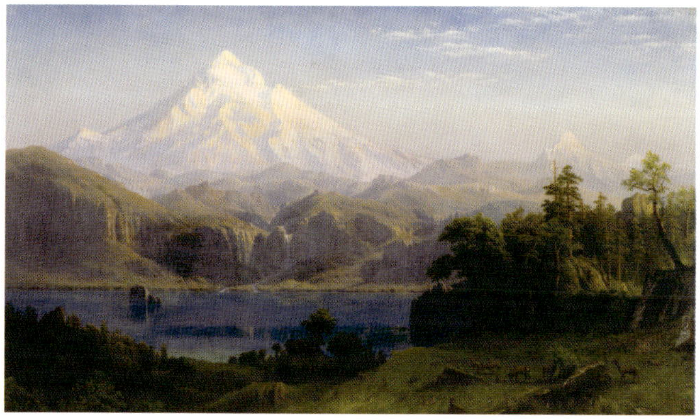

FIG. 223.1.
Albert Bierstadt, *Mount Hood*, 1869.
Oil on canvas; 51 × 60¼ in. (129.5 × 153.0 cm).
Courtesy Portland Art Museum,
gift of Henry Failing Cabell (53.21)

1. Delores Ann Kilgo, "The Sharp-Focus Vision: The Daguerreotype and the American Painter" (Ph.D. diss., University of Illinois at Urbana-Champaign, 1982).

2. "Art Matters," clipping in unidentified newspaper noted simply as "Detroit 1866," Stanley Papers. This earlier version may be the work that was offered for sale through lottery and noted in another clipping from the *Detroit Advertiser*, "A Picture of Mount Hood," Stanley Papers.

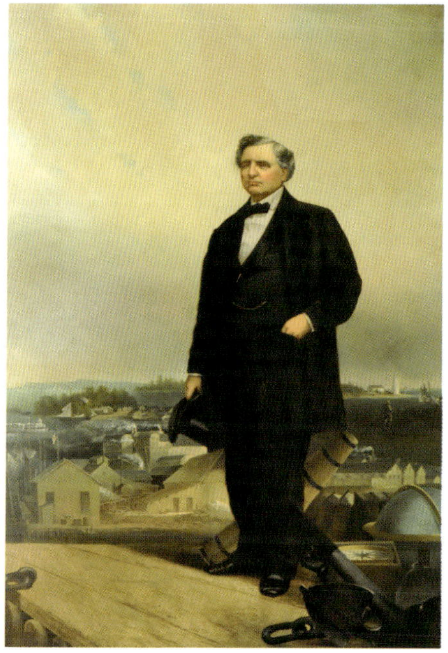

224

Eber Brock Ward, 1871

Oil on canvas, 144 × 60½ in. (365.8 × 153.7 cm)

INSCRIBED LOWER LEFT: J. M. Stanley 1871

PRESENT COLLECTION: Detroit Historical Society, Michigan (1959.200)

PROVENANCE: Michigan Historical Commission; present owner, 1959

Eber Brock Ward is generally recognized as Michigan's first true captain of industry. Ward was born in Canada, the son of a Great Lakes ship captain. He initially worked as a sailor but soon saved up enough money to acquire a part interest in a small schooner. From there he began to build a veritable navy of transport ships, both passenger and freight vessels. The first steamboat ever sailed on Lake Superior was built for him and operated by his company.[1]

In addition to his shipping empire, Ward was heavily invested in the iron and steel business. He explored multiple interests in the business, but it was his 1854 acquisition of the Eureka Iron and Steel Works in Wyandotte, Michigan, that propelled him into the top ranks of American enterprise. In 1864 he employed the first use of the Bessemer steel process in the United States. His iron and steel trade faltered in 1873, and he died two years later.[2]

This painting, though it emphasizes his experience in the shipping industry, celebrates Ward in his heyday. Commensurate with the exalted stature of its subject, this was perhaps the largest canvas Stanley ever painted.

1. I am grateful to Adam Lovell, curator of collections at the Detroit Historical Museum, for this information about Ward's career.

2. See Kenneth N. Metcalf, "Detroit . . . Steelmaker to the Nation," *Detroit Historical Society Bulletin* 18 (Summer 1962): 4–10.

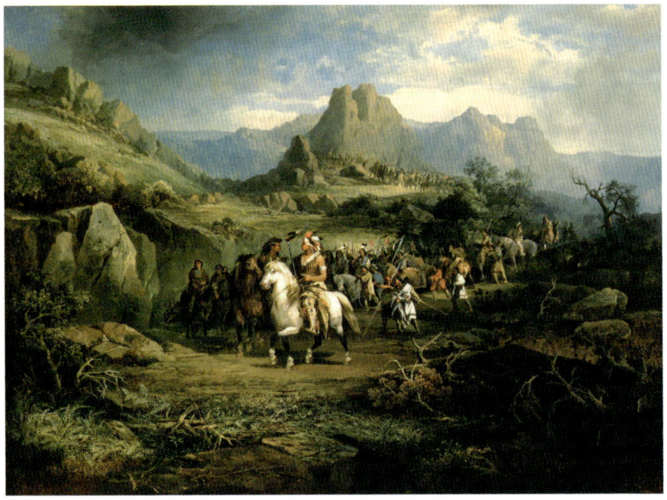

225

On the War Path, 1871

Oil on canvas, 36 × 48 in. (91.4 × 121.9 cm)

INSCRIBED LOWER LEFT: Stanley / [1]871

PRESENT COLLECTION: Private collection; image courtesy of Gerald Peters Gallery

PROVENANCE: Mr. James McMillan, Detroit, Michigan, c. 1872; Dr. and Mrs. Thornton I. Boileau, Birmingham, Michigan; (Gerald Peters Gallery, Santa Fe, New Mexico, 1997); (Thomas Nygard Gallery, Bozeman, Montana); present owner

LIFETIME EXHIBITIONS: M. S. Smith and Co., Detroit, Michigan, May 8, 1871

When Stanley first presented *On the War Path* to the public in 1871, a journalist from the *Detroit Free Press* wrote, "The story briefly told is this: The entire northern tribes are on the war-path. Hence we see representatives of all the various nations. Mr. Stanley, years ago, beheld a grand council of them, held at some days' journey from the very spot he represents."[1]

Throughout Stanley's later life, the Indian Wars in the West had raged. He had witnessed conflicts when traveling in the West, he saw Indians being displaced from their lands, and he attended councils where Natives listened as U.S. government officials dictated their future. It was in 1853 that Stanley accompanied a large procession of Piegan Indians to the council mentioned in the above quotation. Isaac Stevens, Stanley's good friend and governor to the newly created Washington Territory, had called the meeting and had asked Stanley to be his emissary.[2]

In *On the War Path*, however, Stanley does not depict a group of Indians who want to negotiate. Instead he paints a pan-Indian form of general resistance. Mounted and on foot, the warriors wear red war paint and carry spears, tomahawks, guns, and shields; scalps flap from several spears like ominous pennants. Based on his experiences in the West and inspired by events he witnessed, Stanley made *On the War Path* allegorical rather than historically factual. He lends some credibility to the scene by situating it in an actual place he had journeyed through and sketched, *Hell Gate—Entrance to Cadotts Pass from the West* (cat. no. 122).

Perhaps Stanley's last large painting, *On the War Path* was a tremendous success, and soon after its completion, Calvert Lithographing, Engraving and Map Publishing Company of Detroit began the year-long task to reproduce it as a chromolithograph. Sadly, Stanley died before it was completed but not before he saw and approved fifteen of the twenty stones that composed the scene.[3] M. S.

1. "On the War Path," *Detroit Free Press*, May 6, 1871.

2. Stevens was also the director of Indian affairs for the region.

3. James Bartlett, "On the War Path, by John Mix Stanley," *Antiques* 110, no. 3 (September 1976): 520. Fire, just as it had wiped out his Indian Gallery, destroyed the stones in 1872, ending the print run.

Chronology

Compiled by Emily C. Wilson

This chronology was adapted and expanded from the chronology by Julie Schimmel, "John Mix Stanley and Imagery of the West in Nineteenth-Century American Art" (Ph.D. diss., New York University, 1983). Italic entries denote events of general historical and sociocultural significance.

1814

JANUARY 17. John Mix Stanley is born in Canandaigua, New York, to Seth Stanley, Jr., a landowner and tavern keeper, and Sally McKinney Stanley. He will be the oldest of two, with younger sister, Mary Cornelia (b. 1816).

1816

By **JULY 9**, the family moves to Buffalo, New York. Seth Stanley, Jr., takes a job as a tavern keeper and tanner.

During this period, Buffalo was beginning to rebuild itself; the city was burned down by the British in the winter of 1813, during the War of 1812.

1818

The 49th parallel becomes the official border between Canada and the United States, with joint occupation of Oregon Territory.

1819

DECEMBER 28. Sally McKinney Stanley dies.

1820

The Missouri Compromise attempts to preserve the balance of power between free and slave states, and opens slavery to the west (repealed by the Kansas-Nebraska Act in 1854).

1825

The completed Erie Canal creates a waterway from the Atlantic to the Great Lakes, providing westward settlers access to Michigan and midwestern products transport east. The first annual rendezvous is held in Wyoming, bringing fur trappers and their suppliers together in one location for easier trade.

1826

James Fenimore Cooper publishes The Last of the Mohicans.

1828

At age fourteen, John Mix Stanley moves to Naples, New York, and becomes apprenticed to a wagon maker (until 1832).

1830

MAY 28. *President Andrew Jackson signs into law the Indian Removal Act, which grants tribes unsettled lands west of the Mississippi in exchange for Indian lands within existing southern states. Many tribes resist the new relocation policy.*

1832

Moves back to Buffalo, New York, probably working as a house and sign painter (until 1834).

Artist George Catlin begins his first series of trips up the Missouri and Mississippi rivers to document and paint American Indians (through 1836).

JULY 13. *Henry R. Schoolcraft locates the sources of the Mississippi River.*

1833

Swiss artist Karl Bodmer accompanies Prince Maximilian on an expedition up the Missouri River, retracing the route of Lewis and Clark (through 1834). Bodmer's eighty-one paintings illustrating the expedition will be published as lithographs in Travels in the Interior of America *(1843).*

1834

JULY 3. Seth Stanley, Jr., dies. John Mix Stanley moves to Detroit, Michigan, where his career shifts to portraiture under the influence of itinerant portrait painter James Bowman.

1835

Lewis Cass, a former governor of Michigan Territory, publishes the first illustrated portfolio of American Indian portraits. Washington Irving publishes his book on westward expansion, A Tour on the Prairies, *which discusses his travels from Independence, Missouri, to Fort Gibson, Oklahoma, in 1832 with U.S. commissioner of Indian tribes Henry Leavitt Ellsworth.*

1836

Travels throughout the Old Northwest (Michigan, Wisconsin, and Illinois) as an itinerant portrait painter, including Galena, Illinois, from at least February 24, 1838, to September 30, 1839, where he sets up a studio.

MARCH 2. *The Republic of Texas gains independence from Mexico and exists as a sovereign nation through 1846. Thomas L. McKenney, with James Hall, publishes the second illustrated portfolio of Indian American portraits (through 1844), based largely on works by Charles Bird King.*

1837

Michigan becomes the twenty-sixth state to join the union. Artist Alfred Jacob Miller is invited by Captain William Drummond Stewart of Scotland to sketch and paint his expedition to the Rocky Mountains and the annual rendezvous of fur trappers and traders. Catlin widely exhibits his Indian Gallery in Washington, D.C.; Baltimore; Philadelphia; New York City; Troy, New York; and Boston (through 1838).

1838

Lieutenant Charles Wilkes, U.S. Navy, commands the first U.S. exploring expedition of the Pacific Ocean, including mapping the coasts of Oregon, California, and Hawaii (through 1842). The U.S. Army Corps of Topographical Engineers is founded (and will merge with the Corps of Engineers during the Civil War).

1839

Travels to Fort Snelling, Minnesota, to paint American Indians.

Louis-Jacques-Mandé Daguerre invents the daguerreotype, the first photographic process. Over the next few years, the daguerreotype makes its way into the United States and becomes a popular medium for portraits.

1840

Travels to New York City, Philadelphia, Baltimore, and Troy, New York, as an itinerant painter.

Influenced by Catlin, artist Charles Deas travels through Minnesota, Wisconsin, Iowa, Nebraska, and Missouri to paint western life. Deas attempts to assemble an Indian gallery but is unsuccessful.

1841

MARCH. Settles in Troy, New York, as a portrait painter and forms a business partnership with Caleb Sumner Dickerman to create a gallery of Indian life.

Catlin publishes a book on his encounters with American Indians titled, Letters and Notes on the Manners, Customs, and Condition of the North American Indians.

Paints a family group, *The Williamson Family*, c. 1842 (cat. no. 007), in New York.

1842

SPRING. *John C. Fremont makes the first of his five expeditions across the plains (through 1853); his report on the expedition becomes the model for all later topographical surveys.*

SUMMER AND FALL. Travels to Fort Gibson, Oklahoma (then Arkansas Territory), with Dickerman; arrives in December. Paints American Indian portraits and scenes along the way.

1843

MARCH. Accompanies Col. Pierce M. Butler, U.S. commissioner, to Tehuacana Creek in the Republic of Texas to attend the first of three Indian peace councils. These peace councils provide Stanley the opportunity to paint prominent American Indians who represent their tribes at the talks, including a portrait of a Caddo Indian titled *Bin-tah, The Wounded Man* (cat. no. 015).

APRIL. Travels briefly with Butler to Shreveport, Louisiana.

JUNE. Attends a council at Tahlequah in Oklahoma Territory, where he paints *International Indian Council* (cat. no. 014). Stanley employs a daguerreotype camera to help him capture likenesses, including that of General Zachary Taylor, who attended the council and is present in Stanley's painting.

JULY. Travels with Dickerman to the western Arkansas River in Oklahoma to visit the Creek Indians.

AUGUST. Returns to Fort Gibson and paints portraits of Seminole Indians.

NOVEMBER–DECEMBER. Attends a council at Cache Creek, Oklahoma, and makes propaganda paintings promoting peace and other pageant ephemera.

1844

Lives in Fort Gibson, Oklahoma, and vicinity (until spring 1845). Here he paints portraits of several families, including the Ross family: John Golden, a Scots trader (cat. no. 018); his wife, Elizabeth, sister of Cherokee chief John Ross (cat. no. 019); and their three children, Eleanora (cat. no. 021), Lewis (cat. no. 022), and William (cat. no. 020).

1845

Translates his field sketches into finished paintings.

MAY. Travels with Dickerman from Arkansas Territory to St. Louis, Missouri. They are unsuccessful in making arrangements with the American Fur Company that would have allowed them to visit tribes around the upper Missouri and Platte rivers. Stanley leaves for Fort Leavenworth, Kansas, to make arrangements to travel with Col. Stephen Watts Kearny's expedition out west. Recent portraits are shipped back to Cincinnati with Dickerman.

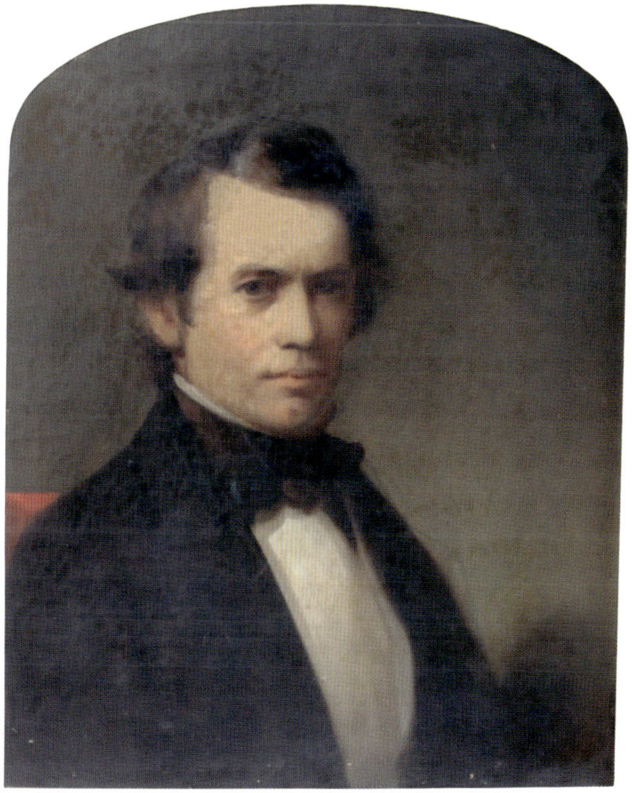

FIG. 6.1.
Edward Ludlow Mooney,
Portrait of John Mix Stanley, c. 1845.
Oil on Canvas. Private collection;
courtesy Julie Schimmel Papers

1846

JANUARY. Stanley's first exhibition, *Stanley's American Indians*, opens at Washington Hall, Cincinnati, Ohio. January 19–February 14, 1846. Travels to Apollo Rooms, Third Street, Louisville, Kentucky, March 3–11, 1846. Both exhibitions receive excellent reviews but suffer poor attendance.

APRIL. Travels to St. Louis and meets up with Josiah Gregg, a well-known trader on the Santa Fe Trail.

MAY 13. *Congress declares war on Mexico.*

MAY. Travels by caravan on the Santa Fe Trail from Westport Landing, Missouri, to Santa Fe, New Mexico (through August 31).

JUNE. *The United States signs a treaty with Great Britain establishing the border of Oregon Country at the 49th parallel.*

AUGUST 10. *Smithsonian Institution is founded.*

SEPTEMBER 25. Hired as a topographical draughtsman and embarks on a military expedition to occupy the northern provinces of Mexico with Stephen Watts Kearny, now a general, and surveyor William H. Emory, traveling from Santa Fe to San Diego. Paints American Indians from the Pima, Maricopa, and the Apache tribes, from which the portrait *Black Knife*, 1850 (cat. no. 064) was completed. Kit Carson serves as a guide for much of the expedition.

DECEMBER 6. Reaches San Diego and sees fighting against the Mexican Army.

DECEMBER 28. Travels by ship to San Francisco.

1847

APRIL. Completes sketches for Emory's *Notes of a Military Reconnoissance* (1848) while in San Francisco.

JULY. Travels through the Northwest and arrives in Oregon City. Paints American Indians such as the Chinooks, Calapooyas, Klamath, and Umpquas.

AUGUST. Travels farther north into present-day Washington state. Reaches and stays at the Wailetpu Mission.

OCTOBER 24. Reaches the Tshimakain (Chemakane) Mission near present-day Spokane. Paints the Walla Walla, Cayuse, and Nez Perce tribes.

NOVEMBER 22. Leaves Tshimakain (Chemakane) and heads south, just missing the November 29 Cayuse massacre at Wailetpu Mission.

DECEMBER 2. Travels to safety at Fort Walla Walla.

1848

JANUARY 8. Escorted to Fort Vancouver with survivors of massacre.

JANUARY 24. *Gold is found at Sutter's Mill in California, igniting the gold rush and large migrations west.*

LATE JANUARY. Returns to Oregon City; stays until the end of summer, painting portraits and scenes from the massacre.

FEBRUARY 2. *The Mexican-American war ends. The Treaty of Guadalupe Hidalgo cedes the territories of California and New Mexico to the United States.*

AUGUST 14. *Oregon becomes a U.S. Territory.*

AUGUST 16. Travels to and arrives in Honolulu, Hawaii.

NOVEMBER. King Kamehameha III of Hawaii asks Stanley to paint portraits of himself and Queen Kalama (cat. nos. 60 and 61). Twenty-three of Stanley's drawings are published as lithographs in Emory's *Notes of a Military Reconnoissance.*

1849

NOVEMBER 19. Departs from Honolulu.

William H. Emory begins his survey of the 1,800-mile border between Mexico and the United States (completed in 1855).

1850

SEPTEMBER 2. Travels to Troy, New York, where an exhibition of his works opens.

SEPTEMBER 9. *California becomes the thirty-first state in the union.*

OCTOBER 7. Travels to Albany, New York, for a month. His collection titled *Stanley's Indian Gallery* is exhibited at the Gallery of Fine Arts, Albany, New York, October 7–November 9, 1850, and at the Alhambra Building, New York, New York, October 7, 1850–March 7, 1851.

EARLY NOVEMBER. Travels to New York City and stays into the new year. Paints *Black Knife* (cat. no. 064).

1851

MARCH 23. Travels to New Haven, Connecticut, where works from his Indian Gallery are exhibited at the Adelphi Building. The exhibition opens March 23, 1851.

APRIL–MAY. Travels to nearby Hartford, where his Indian Gallery is exhibited at City Hall, April 22–May 5, 1851, then Springfield, Massachusetts, May–June 1851. Travels to Worchester and Lowell, Massachusetts.

JUNE. Partnership with Sumner Dickerman dissolves, making Stanley the sole owner of the North American Indian Portrait Gallery.

SEPTEMBER 17. *The Treaty of Fort Laramie guarantees safe passage for settlers migrating along the Oregon Trail and allows for the building of military outposts.*

1852

FEBRUARY. Three of Stanley's works are placed on exhibit at the first major art exhibition held in Detroit, at the Firemen's Hall.

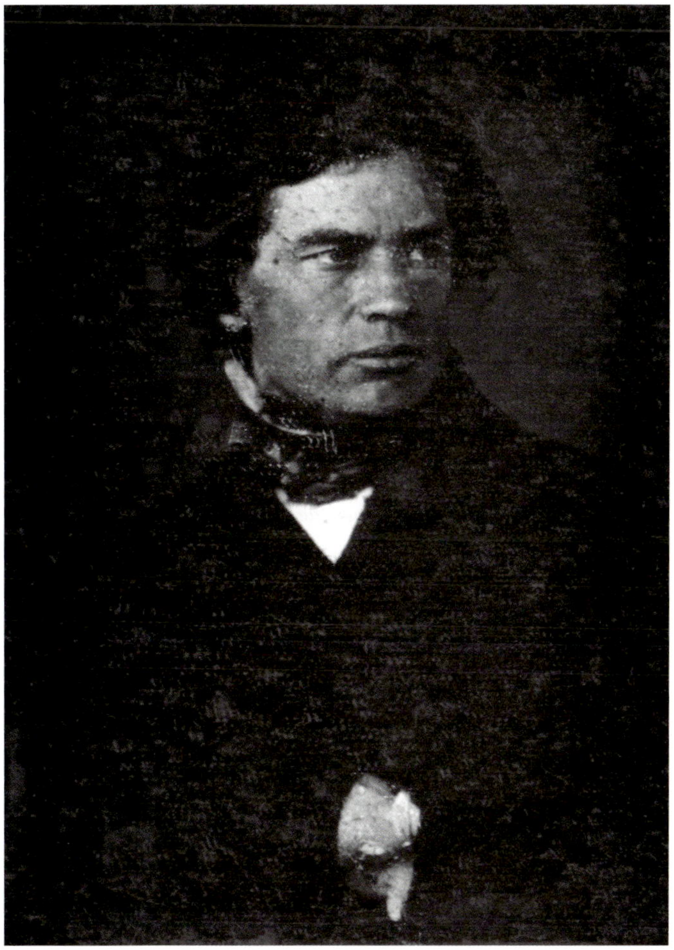

FIG. 6.2.
Unknown photographer, *Portrait of John Mix Stanley*, c. 1853. Daguerreotype; 2⅝ × 2⅛ in. (6.7 × 5.4 cm). Courtesy Julie Schimmel Papers

MARCH. Stanley deposits his Indian Gallery at the Smithsonian Institution. Exhibits *Portrait of General Scott* (unlocated) in his studio at 278½ Pennsylvania Ave between 11th and 12th streets, Washington, D.C. Exhibits *Flight of a Mountain Trapper*, 1851 (unlocated), and *The Trapper's Escape*, 1851 (unlocated), in the window of Taylor and Maury's bookstore, across the street from his studio.

DECEMBER. Smithsonian publishes a catalogue of Stanley's Indian Gallery, *Portraits of North American Indians*, to accompany the 152-item collection on view at the Smithsonian Institution Library. Stanley submits his first petition to Congress to purchase his gallery of Indian paintings.

1853

FEBRUARY 7. Several of Stanley's works are exhibited at the Gallery of Fine Arts, Firemen's Hall, Detroit, Michigan. Awarded First Diploma for *A Pueblo Chief on His Favorite Buffalo Horse*, 1853 (cat. no. 068), on exhibit at the First Annual Exhibition of the Metropolitan Mechanics Institute, east wing of the patent office, Washington D.C., along with *Black Knife, Version II* (cat. no. 072) and three private portraits, February 24–March 17, 1853.

MARCH 2. *Congress authorizes the Corps of Topographical Engineers to conduct eight separate surveys to find a preferred route for the transcontinental railroad. Washington Territory is established.*

EARLY MAY. Hired as an artist on the survey to determine a northern route for the Pacific railway from Saint Paul, Minnesota, to Puget Sound, by Isaac I. Stevens, survey leader and Washington Territory's new governor. Leaves Washington, D.C., and heads to St. Louis, Missouri.

MAY 27. Stays in Saint Paul and vicinity with Stevens, making final preparations. Stanley brings a daguerreotype apparatus with him to capture portraits.

JUNE 6. The survey officially begins.

OCTOBER 25. The survey reaches Puget Sound.

NOVEMBER. Leaves Oregon Territory for San Francisco.

DECEMBER 16. Leaves San Francisco by ship for New York City (arrives January 9, 1854). Returns to Washington, D.C., shortly after and stays in the area for the next nine years.

1854

Begins illustrating the texts for volumes 2 and 12 of the forthcoming twelve-volume publication of the pacific railroad surveys (1855–1860).

MAY 2. Marries Alice Caroline English, a young schoolteacher.

JUNE 8. *The Gadsden Purchase is approved, adding southern Arizona and southwestern New Mexico to the United States.*

Designs a travelogue panorama titled *Scenes and Incidents of Stanley's Western Wilds*. The forty-two scene panorama follows Stanley's expedition with Stevens. Exhibits panorama at the National Theater, Washington, D.C., September 7–13, 1854. Travels it to the Maryland State Fair, Baltimore, opening September 18, 1854; Philadelphia, Pennsylvania, fall 1854; U.S. Capitol rotunda, Washington, D.C., fall 1854; Odd-Fellows' Hall, Washington, D.C., opening December 6, 1854, and again April 1855; and Metropolitan Hall, Richmond, Virginia, May 1855.

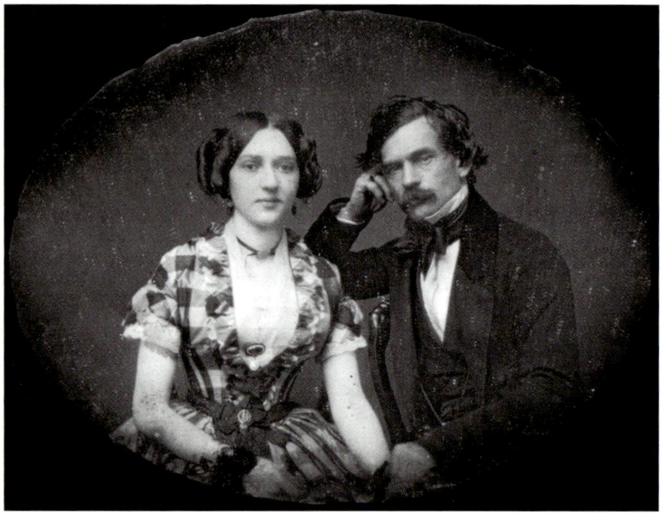

FIG. 6.3.
Unknown photographer, *Alice Caroline English and John Mix Stanley*, c. 1854. Daguerreotype; 2 11/16 × 3½ in. (6.8 × 8.9 cm). Courtesy Julie Schimmel Papers

SEPTEMBER. Stanley's Indian Gallery wins a silver medal at the First Annual Exhibition of the Virginia Mechanics Institute, 1000 East Marshall Street, Richmond, Virginia, September–October 1854, and a gold medal at the Seventh Annual Exhibition of the Maryland Institute for the Promotion of the Mechanical Arts, Maryland Institute, Baltimore, opening September 18, 1854.

1855

Provides several illustrations for the book *The U.S. Naval Astronomical Expedition . . .*

FEBRUARY 8. *Halting to Smoke*, 1855 (cat. no. 128), wins a silver medal at the Second Annual Exhibition of the Metropolitan Mechanics Institute, Smithsonian Institution Building, Washington, D.C., February 8—March 14, 1855.

MARCH 16. Exhibits *Halting to Smoke* (cat. no. 128) and *Seeking A Home*, 1855 (cat. no. 129), in the windows of Messrs. Galt and Brother Jewelry Store, Washington, D.C.

NOVEMBER 5. Stanley's son, Louis Crandall, is born (dies 1935). Paints *Chain of Spires along the Gila* (cat. no. 130), *Scouts along the Teton River*, c. 1855 (cat. no. 131), and *Wagon Train: Break in the Journey*, c. 1855 (cat. no. 134).

Henry Wadsworth Longfellow publishes The Song of Hiawatha.

1856

Active in the Washington Art Association (through 1860). Acting trustee of the National Gallery and School of Arts, which sought to put on exhibitions and hold professional art classes in the Washington, D.C., area, and treasurer, for a time, of the National Art Association, which endeavored to employ artists in the decoration of public buildings. Alexander Culbertson and his wife, Natawista, visit Stanley in Washington, D.C. Stanley Paints *A Family Group* (cat. no. 145).

1857

MARCH 2. Exhibits at the Third Annual Exhibition of the Metropolitan Mechanics Institute, Smithsonian Institution Building, Washington, D.C., March 2–30, 1857.

MARCH 6. *In the Dred Scott decision, the Supreme Court declares slavery legal in all the territories and denies citizenship to black Americans.*

MARCH 7. Exhibits *The Last of Their Race,* 1857 (cat. no. 159) at the First Annual Exhibition of the Washington Art Association, Corcoran Building, Washington, D.C., March 7–May 16, 1857. Submits a second unsuccessful petition to Congress to purchase the gallery of Indian paintings. Submits another petition to the Board of Regents of the Smithsonian to purchase the gallery at a reduced price, which is denied. Provides two illustrations for Henry R. Schoolcraft's, *History of the Indian Tribes of the United States* (1857).

APRIL 3. Exhibits *A Halt on the Prairie* (unlocated) in the windows of Galt and Brothers Jewelry Store, Washington, D.C.

SEPTEMBER 29. *The Last of Their Race* (cat. no. 159) wins a silver medal at the Tenth Annual Exhibition of the Maryland Institute, Baltimore.

1858

Daughter Clara is born (dies March 26, 1873).

JUNE. *The Pike's Peak Gold Rush creates a boom in prospecting and mining in present-day Colorado.*

AUGUST. Exhibits *The Trapper's Cabin*, 1858 (cat. no. 163), at Philp's Gallery, Pennsylvania Avenue, Washington D.C.

SEPTEMBER. Exhibits *The Trapper's Cabin* (cat. no. 163) at the Eleventh Annual Exhibition of the Maryland Institute.

DECEMBER 20. Exhibits *The Trapper's Cabin* (cat. no. 163), *The Last of Their Race*, 1857 (cat. no. 159), and *Mount Hood, Oregon* (unlocated), among other works at J. C. McGuire and Co., Washington Art Association Building, Washington, D.C., in an *Auction and Sale of Paintings*. During the year, exhibits at the Pennsylvania Academy of Fine Arts, Philadelphia.

1859

Serves as treasurer of the Washington Art Association for two years.

JANUARY 3. Exhibits at the Third Exhibition of the Washington Art Association, Washington, D.C., January–February 1859.

FEBRUARY 14. *Oregon enters the union as the thirty-third state.*

MAY 5. *Frederick W. Lander embarks on a government-sponsored road-building expedition from the South Pass in Wyoming to Fort Hall, Idaho. This expedition helps establish the reputation of painter Albert Bierstadt.*

SEPTEMBER 5. Alexander Culbertson exhibits the second version of *The Last of Their Race*, c. 1859 (cat. no. 165), at the Seventh Annual Fair of the Illinois State Agricultural Society in Freeport, Illinois, September 5–9, 1859.

DECEMBER 22. Exhibits a portrait, *Senator Thomas Hart Benton*, 1857 (cat. no. 157), among other works, at the Fourth Annual Exhibition of the Washington Art Association, Washington, D.C., December 22, 1859–February 9, 1860.

1860

APRIL 3. *The Pony Express launches its first mail route from St. Joseph, Missouri, to Sacramento, California, in a need to create faster communication with the West. The service lasts until 1861, when it becomes obsolete with the completion of the Pacific telegraph line linking New York with San Francisco.*

SEPTEMBER 1. Opens a School for Instruction in Drawing Landscape and Portrait Painting in the rooms of the former Washington Art Association.

1861

FEBRUARY 28. *Colorado becomes a territory.*

MARCH 4. *Abraham Lincoln takes office as the sixteenth president of the United States.*

APRIL 12. *The Civil War begins.*

Daughter Alice is born (dies in 1863).

1862

Stanley, along with several other artists, creates a seventy-seven scene panorama based on the Civil War titled *Polemorama*, which exhibits in Odd-Fellows' Hall, Washington, D.C., June 7–July 7, 1862, and travels to Tremont Hall, Boston, Massachusetts, August 11–late October 1862; Association Hall, Albany, New York, opening November 10, 1862; New Opera House, Buffalo, New York, February 3, 1863; Firemen's Hall, Detroit, Michigan, opening early March, 1863; and Anthony Hall, Schenectady, New York, February 2–6, 1864.

MAY 20. *The Homestead Act is signed into law, allowing settlers to buy up to 160 acres of land, which they could own after five years of residency and improvements to the land.*

JULY 1. *The Pacific Railway Act passes Congress, designating the 32nd parallel as the transcontinental route. The Union Pacific and the Central Pacific railroad companies begin construction.*

1863

JANUARY 1. *Lincoln signs the Emancipation Proclamation.*

Submits a third petition to Congress to purchase the gallery of Indian paintings.

SUMMER. Moves to Buffalo and later to Detroit; Stanley's family joins him in Detroit the next year.

SEPTEMBER. Paints *The Unveiling of the Conspiracy* (cat. no. 176) basing his subject on the book *Conspiracy of Pontiac and the Indian War* (1851), by Francis Parkman. Exhibits *The Unveiling of the Conspiracy* (cat. no. 176) at the Buffalo Fine Arts Academy, Buffalo, New York, in *Paintings and Sculpture on Exhibition at the Gallery of the Buffalo Fine Arts Academy*.

1864

During the year, *The Unveiling of the Conspiracy*, 1863 (cat. no. 176), is exhibited at Godfrey, Brown, Dean and Co., Detroit, Michigan, in *Fine Arts Among the People*. Begins painting more genre and landscape scenes.

NOVEMBER 29. *The Sand Creek Massacre occurs: U.S. Army Volunteers attack a camp of Cheyenne and Arapaho Indians, murdering two hundred people.*

1865

JANUARY. Michigan State Legislature is petitioned to purchase Stanley's Indian Gallery.

JANUARY 14. Stanley's Indian Gallery is destroyed in a fire at the Smithsonian Institution; only seven paintings survive.

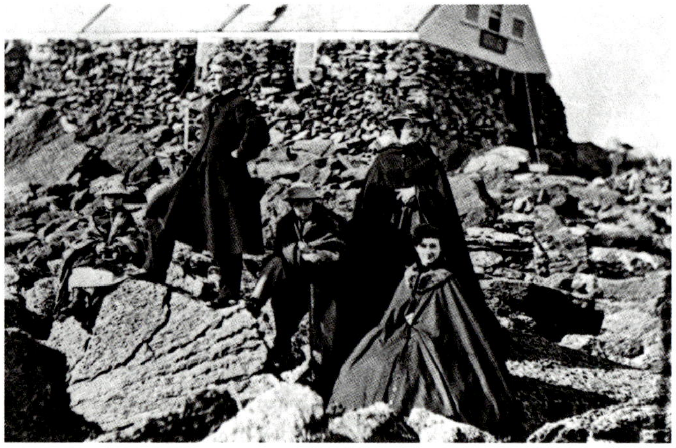

FIG. 6.4.
Unknown, *Stanley Family at Summit of Mount Washington*, c. 1865. Photograph courtesy Julie Schimmel Papers

FEBRUARY 28. Exhibits at the Ladies' Michigan State Fair, Merrill Hall, Adrian, Michigan.

MAY 9. *The Civil War ends.*

JULY. A selection of Stanley's American Indian paintings in P. T. Barnum's American Museum, New York City, burn to the ground with the museum.

AUGUST. Visits the White Mountains in New Hampshire with his family; paints and sketches the landscape. Exhibits *Assiniboin Encampment on the Upper Missouri*, 1865 (cat. no. 183), *Halting to Smoke* (cat. no. 128), *The Challenge*, 1865 (cat. no. 182), and *A Morning in Milk River Valley*, c. 1865 (cat. no. 185), at his studio on Madison Avenue, Detroit, Michigan.

1866

Produces numerous landscapes featuring the White Mountains of New Hampshire.

1867

MARCH. Advertises in the *Detroit Free Press* to attract pupils for painting and drawing instruction. Selected to join the newly formed Prismatic Club, whose purpose is to encourage the discussion of social culture (through 1872).

SEPTEMBER. *The Last of Their Race*, 1857 (cat. no. 159), is awarded a First Premium at the Michigan State Fair.

OCTOBER. *The Medicine Lodge Treaty is signed with Plains tribes, providing them peace and protection in exchange for their relocation to reservations in present-day Oklahoma.*

DECEMBER 20. Exhibits *The Last of Their Race*, 1857 (cat. no. 159), and other works at Messrs. Dean, Brown and Co., and Mr. J. M. Stanley, St. Andrews Hall, Detroit, in *A Great Sale of Paintings*. Stanley also has an exhibition at his studio on 159 Jefferson Avenue. Attempts to make albums of prints of his Indian Gallery but cannot find a publisher. Paints *Group of Piegan Indians* (cat. no. 205).

1868

Completes *The Trial of Red Jacket*, 1868 (cat. no. 212), which tours in Detroit, Buffalo, New York City, and Chicago.

MAY. Travels to Germany to get estimates from Storch and Kramer on chromolithography. Over the next three years, seven paintings are made into chromolithographs: *Young Chief* (cat. no. 211), *The Deer-Slayers* (cat. no. 209), *Indian Telegraph* (cat. no. 208), *Gambling for the Buck* (cat. no. 206), *The Trial of Red Jacket* (cat. no. 213), *Snake in the Grass* (cat. no. 214), and *Blackfeet Card Players* (cat. no. 218). During the year, Stanley exhibits *Indian Telegraph* (cat. no. 208) at Dean, Brown and Co., Detroit, Michigan, and in his studio on Woodward Avenue.

WINTER. Begins work on an illustrated Indian Portfolio (through 1869), depicting Indian life in America and based on his destroyed Indian Gallery, but is unable to find a publisher.

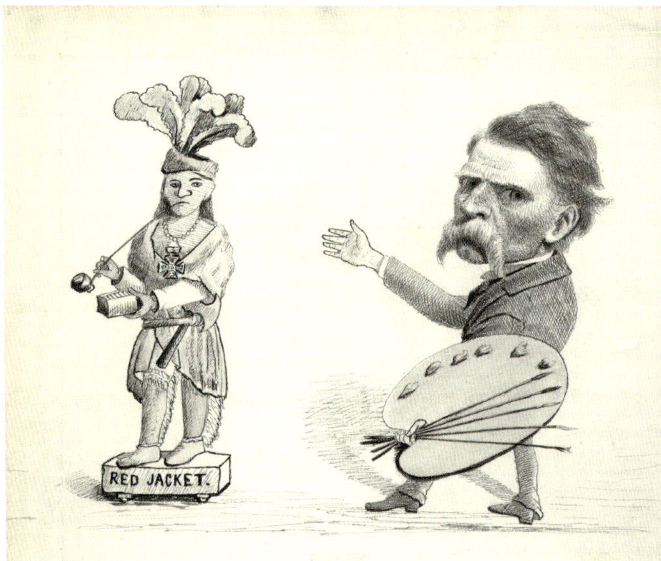

FIG. 6.5.
Lewis T. Ives, sketch of Stanley and Red Jacket, c. 1867. Ink and wash on paper; 6 × 7½ in. (15.2 × 19.1 cm) Prismatic Club of Detroit Collection; Walter P. Reuther Library, Wayne State University, Detroit, Michigan

1869

Paints *Prairie Indian Encampment* (cat. no. 219) and *Chinook Burial Grounds* (cat. no. 220), both of which were executed for Stanley's unpublished Indian Portfolio.

FEBRUARY 2. Exhibits at Wood's Art Gallery in New York. Daughter Edith is born. Sends a small version of *The Trial of Red Jacket* (cat. no. 213) to Berlin to be lithographed. Sometime in the year, he exhibits at J. R. Blodgett's Music Store, Main Street, Buffalo, New York.

MAY 10. *The first transcontinental railroad is completed, stretching from Sacramento to Omaha.*

1870

Helps found the Detroit Western Art Association and Gallery.

JUNE 27. Congress compensates Stanley's loss of his Indian Gallery by allowing him to bring twenty-one thousand prints into the country duty free.

1871

Daughter Ruth is born (dies July 26, 1872). Paints *Mount Hood from the Dalles* (cat. no. 223).

MARCH 3. *The Indian Appropriations Act no longer recognizes tribes as sovereign nations; individuals become wards of the federal government.*

APRIL 12. Stanley exhibits *The Trial of Red Jacket* (cat. no. 212), *Gambling for the Buck* (cat. no. 206), and other works at the Chicago Academy of Design Fifth Annual Exhibition.

JUNE–OCTOBER. *First federally funded U.S. Geological Survey explores the Yellowstone region in northwest Wyoming, led by Ferdinand V. Hayden and accompanied by Thomas Moran, painter, and William Henry Jackson, photographer. Survey results in Yellowstone becoming a national park in 1872.*

1872

APRIL 10. John Mix Stanley suffers a heart attack after an illness of several months and dies at the age of fifty-eight. His wife survives him, until her death in 1891.

DECEMBER. *William "Buffalo Bill" Cody makes his stage debut in the Wild West show,* Scouts of the Prairie.

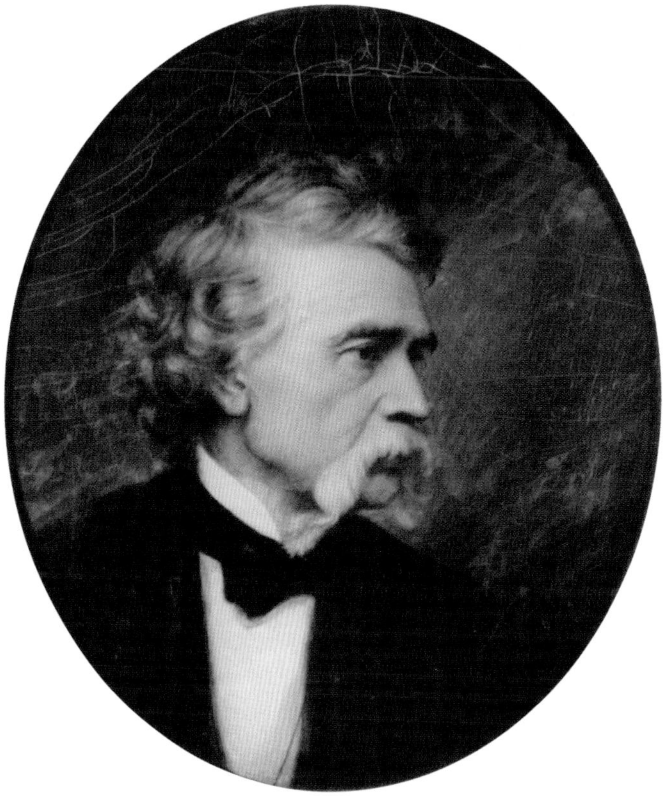

FIG. 6.6.
Lewis T. Ives, *John Mix Stanley*, 1872. Photograph; dimensions unknown. From Kinietz, *John Mix Stanley*, frontispiece.

Selected Bibliography

Compiled by Emily C. Wilson

Archival Resources

Bush-Brown, Henry Kirke. Papers. Manuscript Division, Library of Congress, Washington, D.C.

Catalogue of American Portraits. National Portrait Gallery, Smithsonian Institution, Washington, D.C.

Corcoran Gallery of Art. Curatorial Files. Corcoran Gallery of Art Archives, Washington, D.C.

Corcoran, William Wilson. Papers. Manuscript Division, Library of Congress, Washington, D.C.

Corcoran, William Wilson. Scrapbook. Corcoran Gallery of Art Archives, Washington, D.C.

Heye Foundation Archives. Huntington Free Library, New York.

Schimmel, Julie. Research Papers. Gerald Peters Gallery, Santa Fe, New Mexico.

Stanley, John Mix. Papers, 1830–1973. Archives of American Art, Smithsonian Institution, Washington, D.C.

Stanley, John Mix. Scrapbook, 1843–1868. Archives of American Art, Smithsonian Institution, Washington, D.C.

Stanley, John Mix. Vertical file. Smithsonian American Art Museum and National Portrait Gallery Library, Washington, D.C.

Stevens, Isaac. Letterbook. Office of Explorations and Surveys, Records of the Office of the Secretary of the Interior, National Archives, Washington, D.C.

Strohm, Isaac. Papers. Archives of the Cincinnati Museum Center, Ohio.

Washington Art Association. Constitution and bylaws. Corcoran Gallery of Art Archives, Washington, D.C.

Washington Art Association. Letterbook, 1856–1857. Archives and Manuscripts Collection, Historical Society of Washington, D.C.

Books, Catalogues, Pamphlets, and Articles

Abert, J. W. *Report of Lieut. J. W. Abert of His Examination of New Mexico*. Washington, D.C.: Wendell and Van Benthuysen, 1848.

Ames, Eric. "From the Exotic to the Everyday: The Ethnographic Exhibition in Germany." In *The Nineteenth-Century Visual Culture Reader*, edited by Vanessa R. Schwartz and Jeannene M. Przyblyski, 313–27. New York: Routledge, 2004.

Anderson, H. Allen. "The Delaware and Shawnee Indians and the Republic of Texas, 1820–1845." *Southwestern Historical Quarterly* 94 (October 1990): 231–60.

Anderson, Nancy K. "'Curious Historical Artistic Data': Art History and Western American Art." In *Discovered Lands, Invented Pasts: Transforming Visions of the American West*, by Jules David Prown et al., 1–36. New Haven, Conn.: Yale University Press, 1992.

Annual Report of the Board of Regents of the Smithsonian Institution . . . 1858. Washington, D.C.: Smithsonian Institution, 1859.

Arkelian, Marjorie. *Tropical: Tropical Scenes by the 19th Century Painters of California*. Oakland, Calif.: Oakland Museum, 1971.

Armstrong, Thomas. *An American Odyssey: The Warner Collection of Fine and Decorative Arts*. New York: Monacelli Press, 2002.

Ballinger, James. "John Mix Stanley, A 'Hudson River' Painter in Arizona." *Phoebus: A Journal of Art History* 3 (1981): 64–72.

Bantel, Linda, and Peter H. Hassrick. *Forging an American Identity: The Art of William Ranney, With a Catalogue of His Works*. Cody, Wyo.: Buffalo Bill Historical Center, 2006.

Bartlett, James. "On the Warpath, by John Mix Stanley." *Antiques* 110, no. 3 (September 1976): 520–21.

Bennett, Swannee, and William B. Worthen. *Arkansas Made: A Survey of the Decorative, Mechanical and Fine Art Production in Arkansas, 1819–1970*. Vol. 2. Fayetteville: University of Arkansas Press, 1990.

Berger, John. *Ways of Seeing*. New York: Viking, 1972.

Berkhofer, Robert F., Jr. *The White Man's Indian: Images of the American Indian from Columbus to the Present*. New York: Knopf, 1978.

Boehme, Sarah E. "Frontier America: The Artists' Environment." In *Frontier America: Art and Treasures of the Old West from the Buffalo Bill Historical Center*, by Paul Fees and Sarah Boehme, 27–28. New York: Abrams, 1988.

———. "Frozen in Time: Euro-American Portrayals of Indians." In *Powerful Images: Portrayals of Native America*, edited by Sarah E. Boehme, 35–62. Seattle: Museums West and University of Washington Press, 1998.

Boehme, Sarah E., ed. *Powerful Images: Portrayals of Native America*. Seattle: Museums West and University of Washington Press, 1998.

Boehme, Sarah E., Christian F. Feest, and Patricia Condon Johnston. *Seth Eastman: A Portfolio of North American Indians*. Afton, Ohio: Afton Historical Society Press, 1996.

Boime, Albert. *The Magisterial Gaze: Manifest Destiny and American Landscape Painting c. 1830–1865*. Washington, D.C.: Smithsonian Institution Press, 1991.

The Book of the Exhibition: Eleventh Annual Exhibition of the Maryland Institute for the Promotion of the Mechanic Arts. Baltimore: Samuel S. Mills Steam Press, 1858.

The Book of the Exhibition: Seventh and Eighth Exhibition of the Maryland Institute for the Promotion of the Mechanic Arts. Baltimore: Mills and Cox, 1854.

Bryant, Edwin. *What I Saw in California: Being the Journal of a Tour by the Emigrant Route and South Pass of the Rocky Mountains, across the Continent of North America, the Great Desert Basin, and through California, in the Years 1846, 1847*. Edited by Richard H. Dillon. Palo Alto, Calif.: Lewis Osborne, 1967.

Bryant, William Cullen. *The Poems of William Cullen Bryant*. Edited by Louis Untermeyer. New York: Heritage Press, 1947.

Burroughs, Clyde H. "Painting and Sculpture in Michigan." *Michigan History Magazine* 20 (Spring and Summer 1936): 393–409.

Burton, Clarence M., ed. *The City of Detroit Michigan, 1701–1922*. Vol. 3. Ann Arbor: University of Michigan Library, 2005.

Bushnell, David I., Jr. "John Mix Stanley, Artist-Explorer." In *Annual Report of the Smithsonian Institution for the Year Ending June 30, 1924*. Washington, D.C.: Government Printing Office, 1925.

Buttre, Lillian C. *The American Portrait Gallery*. New York: J. C. Buttre, 1877.

Cadbury, Warder H. *Arthur Fitzwilliam Tait, Artist in the Adirondacks: An Account of His Career and a Checklist of His Work*. Newark: University of Delaware Press, 1986.

Calvin, Ross, ed. *Lieutenant Emory Reports: A Reprint of Lieutenant W. H. Emory's Notes of a Military Reconnoissance*. Albuquerque: University of New Mexico Press, 1951.

Cash, Sarah. *Corcoran Gallery of Art: American Paintings to 1945*. Manchester, Vt.: Hudson Hills Press, 2011.

Catalogue: Detroit Art Association. First Exhibition. Detroit: Detroit Art Association, 1876.

Catalogue of the Fourth Annual Exhibition of the Washington Art Association. Washington, D.C.: Henry Polkinhorn, 1860.

Catalogue of the Third Annual Exhibition of the Washington Art Association. Washington, D.C.: William H. Moore, 1859.

Catlin, George. *Letters and Notes on the Manners, Customs, and Condition of the North American Indians*. 2 vols. London: David Bogue, 1844.

Catton, Bruce. *Michigan: A Bicentennial History*. New York: Norton, 1976.

Chalmers, Claudine. *Chronicling the West for Harper's: Coast to Coast with Frenzeny and Tavernier in 1873–1874*. Norman: University of Oklahoma Press, 2013.

Chinen, Jon J. *The Great Mahele: Hawaii's Land Division of 1848*. Honolulu: University of Hawaii Press, 1958.

Clapper, Michael. "'I Was Once a Barefoot Boy!': Cultural Tensions in a Popular Chromo." *American Art* 16, no. 2 (2002): 16–39.

Clark, Carol. "Charles Deas." In *American Frontier Life: Early Western Paintings and Prints*, edited by Alan Axelrod, 51–78. New York: Cross River Press, 1987.

Clark, Carol, Joan Carpenter Troccoli, Frederick E. Hoxie, and Guy Jordan. *Charles Deas and 1840s America*. Norman: University of Oklahoma Press, 2009.

Clarke, Dwight L., ed. *The Original Journals of Henry Smith Turner with Stephen Watts Kearny to New Mexico and California, 1846–1847*. Norman: University of Oklahoma Press, 1966.

———. "Soldiers Under Stephen Watts Kearny." *California Historical Society Quarterly* 45 (June 1966): 132–48.

Cobb, Josephine. "The Washington Art Association: An Exhibition Record." In *Records of the Columbia Historical Society of Washington, D.C., 1963–1965*, edited by Francis Coleman Rosenberger, 122–90. Washington, D.C.: Columbia Historical Society, 1966.

Coen, Rena. "David's *Sabine Women* in the Wild West." *Great Plains Quarterly* 2, no. 2 (Spring 1982): 67–76.

———. "The Indian as the Noble Savage in Nineteenth Century American Art." Ph.D. diss., University of Minnesota, 1969.

———. *Painting and Sculpture in Minnesota, 1820–1914*. Minneapolis: University of Minnesota Press, 1976.

Comment, Bernard. *The Painted Panorama*. New York: Abrams, 1999.

Cook, James W., ed. *The Colossal P. T. Barnum Reader: Nothing Else Like It in the Universe*. Urbana: University of Illinois Press, 2005.

Cooper, Helen A., ed. *Life, Liberty, and the Pursuit of Happiness: American Art from the Yale University Art Gallery*. New Haven, Conn.: Yale University Press, 2008.

Cooper, James Fenimore. *The Last of the Mohicans: A Narrative of 1757*. Reprint ed. Franklin Center, Pa.: Franklin Library, 1982.

Cosentino, Andrew J. *The Paintings of Charles Bird King (1785–1862)*. Washington, D.C.: Smithsonian Institution Press, 1977.

Cosentino, Andrew J., and Henry H. Glassie. *The Capital Image: Painters in Washington, 1800–1915*. Washington, D.C.: Smithsonian Institution Press, 1983.

Cronon, William. "Telling Tales on Canvas: Landscapes of Frontier Change." In *Discovered Lands, Invented Pasts: Transforming Visions of the American West*, by Jules David Prown et al., 37–88. New Haven, Conn.: Yale University Press, 1992.

Curry, David Parks. *The Western Spirit: Exploring New Territory in American Art*. Denver: Denver Art Museum, 1989.

Dippie, Brian W. *Catlin and His Contemporaries: The Politics of Patronage*. Lincoln: University of Nebraska Press, 1990.

———. "The Moving Finger Writes: Western Art and the Dynamics of Change." In *Discovered Lands, Invented Pasts: Transforming Visions of the American West*, by Jules David Prown et al., 89–116. New Haven, Conn.: Yale University Press, 1992.

———. *The Vanishing American: White Attitudes and U.S. Indian Policy*. Middletown, Conn.: Wesleyan University Press, 1991.

———. "The Visual West." In *Oxford History of the American West*, ed. Clyde A. Milner II, 674–705. New York: Oxford University Press, 1994.

———. *West-Fever*. Los Angeles: Gene Autry Western Heritage Museum; Seattle: University of Washington Press, 1998.

Donoho, Thomas S. *Scenes and Incidents of Stanley's Western Wilds*. Washington D.C., 1854.

Drake, Samuel G. *Indian Captivities; or, Life in the Wigwam*. Auburn, N.Y.: Derby and Miller, 1853.

Draper, Benjamin P. "John Mix Stanley, Pioneer Painter." *Antiques* 61 (March 1942): 180–82.

Drumm, Stella M., ed. *Down the Santa Fe Trail and into Mexico: The Diary of Susan Shelby Magoffin, 1846–1847*. Lincoln: University of Nebraska Press, 1982.

Drury, Clifford Merrill. *Elkanah and Mary Walker, Pioneers among the Spokanes*. Caldwell, Idaho: Caxton Press, 1940.

———. *First White Women Over the Rockies: Diaries, Letters, and Biographical Sketches of the Six Women of the Oregon Mission Who Made the Overland Journey in 1836 and 1838*. Glendale, Calif.: Arthur H. Clark, 1966.

Emory, William H. *Notes of a Military Reconnoissance, from Fort Leavenworth, in Missouri, to San Diego, in California, including part of the Arkansas, Del Norte, and Gila Rivers*. Washington, D.C.: Wendell and Van Benthuysen, 1848.

Evanson, Jeffrey W., comp. *Art of the Lewis and Clark Trail*. Bismarck, N.Dak.: Whisper'n Waters, 2003.

Ewers, John C. "Artists' Choices." *American Indian Art Magazine* 7, no. 2 (Spring 1982): 45.

———. *Artists of the Old West*. Garden City, New York: Doubleday, 1973.

———. "Barter for a Bride." *American West* 5 (November 1968): inside cover.

———. *The Blackfeet: Raiders of the Northwestern Plains*. Norman: University of Oklahoma Press, 1958.

———. "The Emergence of the Plains Indian as the Symbol of the North American Indian." In *Annual Report of the Smithsonian Institution for 1964*, 530–44. Washington, D.C.: Government Printing Office, 1965.

———. *Gustavus Sohon's Portraits of Flathead and Pend d'Oreille Indians, 1854*. Smithsonian Miscellaneous Collections 110, no. 7. Washington, D.C.: Smithsonian Institution Press, November 26, 1948.

Fees, Paul, and Sarah Boehme. *Frontier America: Art and Treasures of the Old West from the Buffalo Bill Historical Center*. New York: Abrams, 1988.

Fitzpatrick, Gary L. *The Early Mapping of Hawai'i*. Honolulu: Editions Limited, 1986.

Forbes, David W. *Encounters with Paradise: Views of Hawaii and Its People, 1778–1941*. Honolulu: Honolulu Academy of Arts, 1992.

Foreman, Grant. *Advancing the Frontier: 1830–1860*. Norman: University of Oklahoma Press, 1933.

———. *Indian Removal: The Emigration of the Five Civilized Tribes of Indians*. Norman: University of Oklahoma Press, 1972.

Frank, Robin Jaffee. "John Mix Stanley and the Isaac I. Stevens Railroad Survey Expedition of 1853." In *Life, Liberty, and the Pursuit of Happiness: American Art from the Yale University Art Gallery*, edited by Helen A. Cooper, 292–93. New Haven, Conn.: Yale University Press, 2008.

Fryd, Vivien Green. *Art and Empire: The Politics of Ethnicity in the United States Capitol, 1815–1860*. New Haven, Conn.: Yale University Press, 1992.

Fulton, Maurice Garland., ed. *Diary and Letters of Josiah Gregg: Southwestern Enterprises, 1840–1847*. Norman: University of Oklahoma Press, 1941.

Galvin, John, ed. *Western America in 1846–1847: The Original Travel Diary of Lieutenant J. W. Abert, Who Mapped New Mexico for the United States Army*. San Francisco: John Howell, 1966.

Gene Autry Western Heritage Museum. *The West Explored: The Gerald Peters Collection of Western American Art*. Santa Fe: Gerald Peters Gallery, 1988.

Gibson, Arthur Hopkin, comp. *Artists of Early Michigan*. Detroit: Wayne State University Press, 1975.

Glanz, Dawn. *How the West Was Drawn: American Art and the Settling of the Frontier*. Ann Arbor, Mich.: UMI Research Press, 1992.

———. "The Iconography of Western Expansion in American Art, 1820–1870." Ph.D. diss., University of North Carolina, 1978.

Goetzmann, William H. *Army Exploration in the American West, 1803–1863*. New Haven, Conn.: Yale University Press, 1959.

———. *Exploration and Empire: The Explorer and the Scientist in the Winning of the American West*. New York: Knopf, 1966.

———. "The Grand Reconnaissance." *American Heritage* 23 (October 1972): 44–59, 92–95.

Goetzmann, William H., and William N. Goetzmann. *The West of the Imagination*. 2nd ed. Norman: University of Oklahoma Press, 2009.

Goff, Frederic R. "The Oldest Library in Washington: The Rare Book Division of the Library of Congress." *Records of the Columbia Historical Society* 70 (1969): 332–37.

Goode, William H. *Outposts of Zion with Limnings of Mission Life*. Cincinnati: Poe and Hitchcock, 1863.

Green, Constance McLaughlin. *Washington Village and Capital, 1800–1878*. Princeton, N.J.: Princeton University Press, 1962.

Gurney, George, and Therese Thau Heyman, eds. *George Catlin and His Indian Gallery*. New York: Norton, 2002.

Hackler, Rhonda E. A. *Royal Portraits of Hawai'i in 'Iolani Palace*. Honolulu: 'Iolani Palace, 1982.

Haltman, Kenneth. *Looking Close and Seeing Far: Samuel Seymour, Titian Ramsay Peale, and the Art of the Long Expedition, 1818–1823*. University Park: Pennsylvania State University Press, 2008.

Hansen, Emma I. *Memory and Vision: Arts, Cultures, and Lives of Plains Indian People*. Seattle: University of Washington Press, 2007.

Harris, Neil. *Humbug: The Art of P. T. Barnum*. Boston: Little, Brown, 1973.

Harthorn, Sandy, and Kathleen Bettis. *One Hundred Years of Idaho Art, 1850–1950*. Boise, Idaho: Boise Art Museum, 1990.

Harvey, Eleanor Jones. *The Painted Sketch: American Impressions from Nature, 1830–1880*. Dallas: Dallas Museum of Art, 1998.

Hassrick, Peter H. *The American West: Out of Myth, Into Reality*. Washington, D.C.: Trust for Museum Exhibitions, 2000.

———. "Artists Employed on United States Government Expeditions to the Trans-Mississippi West before 1850." Master's thesis, University of Denver, 1969.

———. *Drawn to Yellowstone: Artists in America's First National Park*. Seattle: University of Washington Press, 2002.

———. *Treasures of the Old West: Paintings and Sculpture from the Thomas Gilcrease Institute of American History and Art*. New York: Abrams, 1984.

———. *The Way West: Art of Frontier America*. New York: Abrams, 1978.

Heilbron, Bertha. "Frontier Artists: Before the Camera Brought Back an Authentic Picture of Pioneer Minnesota." *American Heritage* 1, no. 2 (Winter 1950): 13.

Heydt, Stephanie Mayer, Mindy N. Besaw, and Emma L. Hansen. *Art of the American Frontier from the Buffalo Bill Center of the West*. Atlanta: High Museum of Art, 2013.

Hight, Kathryn S. "Doomed to Perish: George Catlin's Depictions of the Mandan." In *Reading American Art*, edited by Marianne Doezema and Elizabeth Milroy, 150–62. New Haven, Conn.: Yale University Press, 1998.

———. "The Frontier Indian in White Art, 1830–1876: The Development of a Myth." Ph.D. diss., University of California, Los Angeles, 1987.

Hills, Patricia. "The American Art-Union as Patron for Expansionist Ideology in the 1840s." In *Art in Bourgeois Society, 1790–1850*, edited by Andrew Hemingway and William Vaughan, 314–39. Cambridge and New York: Cambridge University Press, 1998.

———. *The Painters' America: Rural and Urban Life, 1810–1910*. New York: Praeger, 1974.

———. "Picturing Progress in the Era of Westward Expansion." In *The West as America: Reinterpreting Images of the Frontier, 1820–1920*, edited by William H. Truettner, 97–147. Washington, D.C.: National Museum of American Art and Smithsonian Institution Press, 1991.

Hobbs, Richard Gear. *Glamorous Galena and Jo Daviess County: The Little Switzerland of Illinois*. Galena, Ill.: Gazette Print, 1939.

Hodge, Frederick Webb. "A Proposed Indian Portfolio by John Mix Stanley." *Indian Notes* 6, no. 4 (October 1929): 359–67.

Holt, Roy D. *Heap Many Texas Chiefs*. San Antonio: Naylor Press, 1966.

Honour, Hugh. *The European Vision of America*. Cleveland: Cleveland Museum of Art, 1976.

Horan, James D. *The McKenney-Hall Portrait Gallery of American Indians*. Devon, UK: Bramhall House, 1986.

Huhndorf, Shari. *Going Native: Indians in the American Cultural Imagination*. Ithaca, N.Y.: Cornell University Press, 2003.

Huhtamo, Erkki. *Illusions in Motion: Media Archaeology of the Moving Panorama and Related Spectacles*. Cambridge, Mass.: MIT Press, 2013.

Hunt, David C. "John Mix Stanley: Survey Artist and Indian Painter." *American Scene* 12, no. 4 (1971): 1–20.

———. *John Mix Stanley: Survey Artist and Indian Painter*. Tulsa, Okla.: Thomas Gilcrease Institute of American History and Art, 1971.

Hunter, Albert, ed. *The Washington and Georgetown Directory, Strangers' Guide-Book For Washington and Congressional and Clerks' Register*. Washington, D.C.: Kirkwood and McGill, 1853.

Hussey, John A. *The History of Fort Vancouver*. Tacoma: Washington State Historical Society, 1957.

James, Edwin. *An Account of an Expedition, from Pittsburgh to the Rocky Mountains*. Philadelphia: H. C. Carey and I. Lea, 1822.

James, Juliet Helena Lumbard. *Sculpture of the Exposition Palaces and Courts; Descriptive Notes on the Art of the Statuary at the Panama-Pacific International Exposition, San Francisco*. San Francisco: H. S. Crocker, 1915.

Janson, Anthony F. *Worthington Whittredge*. Cambridge: Cambridge University Press, 1990.

Johns, Elizabeth. *American Genre Painting: The Politics of Everyday Life*. New Haven, Conn.: Yale University Press, 1991.

———. "Settlement and Development: Claiming the West." In *The West as America: Reinterpreting Images of the Frontier, 1820–1920*, edited by William H. Truettner, 191–235. Washington, D.C.: National Museum of American Art and Smithsonian Institution Press, 1991.

Johnson, Allen, and Dumas Malone, eds. *Dictionary of American Biography*. Vol. 2. New York: Scribner, 1928.

Josephy, Alvin M., Jr. *The Artist Was a Young Man*. Fort Worth, Tex.: Amon Carter Museum, 1970.

Joslyn Art Museum. *Artists of the Western Frontier: Selections from the Northern Natural Gas Company Collection*. Omaha, Neb.: Joslyn Art Museum, 1978.

Just Published: Stanley Chromos, Four of the Series of Five Splendid Chromo-Lithographs Now Being Issued. Berlin: Storch and Kramer, 1869.

Kamakawiwo'ole Osorio, Jonathan Kay. *Dismembering Lāhui: A History of the Hawaiian Nation to 1887*. Honolulu: University of Hawaii Press, 2002.

Kane, Paul. *Paul Kane's Frontier: Including Wanderings of an Artist zmong the Indians of North America, by Paul Kane*. Edited by J. Russell Harper. Austin: University of Texas Press, 1971.

Karpenstein, Katherine. "Illustrations of the West in Congressional Documents 1843–1863." Master's thesis, University of Rochester, 1953.

Kett, H. F. *The History of Jo Daviess County, Illinois*. Chicago: H. F. Kett, 1878.

Kilgo, Delores Ann. "The Sharp-Focus Vision: The Daguerreotype and the American Painter." Ph.D. diss., University of Illinois at Urbana-Champaign, 1982.

Kinietz, W. Vernon. *John Mix Stanley and His Indian Paintings*. Ann Arbor: University of Michigan Press, 1942.

Kinsey, Joni L. "John Mix Stanley," In *The West as America: Reinterpreting Images of the Frontier, 1820–1920*, ed. William H. Truettner, 368. Washington, D.C.: National Museum of American Art and Smithsonian Institution Press, 1991.

———. *Plain Pictures: Images of the American Prairie*. Washington, D.C.: Smithsonian Institution Press, 1996.

———. *Thomas Moran's West: Chromolithography, High Art, and Popular Taste*. Lawrence: University Press of Kansas, 2006.

Kloss, William. *Art in the White House: A Nation's Pride*. Washington D.C.: White House Historical Association, 1992.

Kort, Pamela, and Max Hollein, eds. *I Like America: Fictions of the Wild West*. Munich: Prestel, 2006.

Lanman, Charles. *Catalogue of W. W. Corcoran's Gallery*. Washington, D.C., 1857.

Leja, Michael. *Looking Askance: Skepticism and American Art from Eakins to Duchamp*. Berkeley: University of California Press, 2004.

Lett, Amanda, Patricia Hills, Peter John Brownlee, and Randy Ramer. *Perfectly American: The Art-Union and Its Artists*. Tulsa, Okla.: Gilcrease Museum, 2011.

Levine, Lawrence. *Highbrow, Lowbrow: The Emergence of Cultural Hierarchy in America*. Cambridge, Mass., and London: Harvard University Press, 1988.

Lister, Kenneth R. *Paul Kane, the Artist: Wilderness to Studio*. Toronto: Royal Ontario Museum Press, 2010.

Lockley, Fred. *History of the Columbia River Valley*. Chicago: S. J. Clarke, 1928.

Longfellow, Henry Wadsworth. *The Song of Hiawatha and Other Poems*. Reader's Digest ed. Pleasantville, N.Y.: Reader's Digest Association, 1989.

Malone, Dumas, ed. *Dictionary of American Biography*. Vol. 4. New York: Scribner, 1930.

———, ed. *Dictionary of American Biography*. Vol. 11. New York: Scribner, 1933.

———, ed. *Dictionary of American Biography*. Vol. 19. New York: Scribner, 1939.

Maps and Illustrations of the American Board of Commissioners for Foreign Missions, September 1846. Boston: Board of Commissioners for Foreign Missions, 1846.

Marzio, Peter C. *The Democratic Art: An Exhibition on the History of Chromolithography in America, 1840–1900*. Fort Worth, Tex.: Amon Carter Museum of Western Art, 1979.

McDermott, Francis. *Seth Eastman, Pictorial Historian of the Indian*. Norman: University of Oklahoma Press, 1961.

McKenney, Thomas Loraine. *The Indian Tribes of North America: With Biographical Sketches and Anecdotes of the Principal Chiefs*. 3 vols. Edinburgh: J. Grant, 1933.

McKenney, Thomas L., and James Hall. *History of the Indian Tribes of North America*. Vol. 2. Philadelphia: Frederick W. Greenough, 1838.

McLaughlin, Castle. *Arts of Diplomacy: Lewis and Clark's Indian Collection*. Cambridge, Mass.: Peabody Museum of Archaeology and Ethnology, Harvard University, 2003.

McMahan, Virgil E. *The Artists of Washington, D.C., 1796–1996*. Vol. 1, *A Directory of Painters, Sculptors, and Engravers Born Before 1900*. Washington, D.C.: Artists of Washington, D.C., 1995.

Meserve, John Bartlett. "Chief William Potter Ross." *Chronicles of Oklahoma* 5 (March 1937): 21–29.

Metcalf, Kenneth N. "Detroit . . . Steelmaker to the Nation." *Detroit Historical Society Bulletin* 18 (Summer 1962): 4–10.

Michigan Biographies. Vol. 2. Lansing: University of Michigan Press, 1924.

Mitchell, Lee Clark. *Witnesses to a Vanishing America: The Nineteenth-Century Response*. Princeton, N.J.: Princeton University Press, 1981.

Montana Historical Society. *An Art Perspective of the Historic Pacific Northwest: From the Collection of Dr. and Mrs. Franz R. Stenzel, Portland, Oregon*. Helena: Montana Historical Society, 1963.

Moore, Robert J., Jr. *Native Americans: A Portrait: The Art and Travels of Charles Bird King, George Catlin, and Karl Bodmer*. Edison, N.J.: Chartwell Books, 2002.

Moulton, Gary E. *John Ross, Cherokee Chief*. Athens: University of Georgia Press, 2004.

———, ed. *The Journals of the Lewis and Clark Expedition*. Vol. 5. Lincoln: University of Nebraska Press, 1988.

Mullan, John. *Report on the Construction of a Military Road from Fort Walla-Walla to Fort Benton*. Washington, D.C.: Government Printing Office, 1863.

National Convention of Artists. *Proceedings of the National Convention of Artists: Held March 20, 22, and 23, 1858 at the Smithsonian Institute, Washington, D.C., Together with the Proceedings of the 2d and 3d Conventions*. Washington, D.C.: William H. Moore, 1860.

Newcomb, William W., Jr. *German Artist on the Texas Frontier: Friedrich Richard Petri*. Austin: University of Texas Press, 1978.

Nicandri, David L. "Isaac I. Stevens and the Expeditionary Artists of the Northern West." In *Encounters with a Distant Land: Exploration and the Great Northwest*, edited by Carlos A. Schwantes, 133–48. Moscow: University of Idaho Press, 1994.

———. "John Mix Stanley: Paintings and Sketches of the Oregon Country and Its Inhabitants." *Oregon Historical Quarterly* 88, no. 2 (Summer 1987): 149–73.

———. *Northwest Chiefs: Gustav Sohon's Views of the 1855 Stevens Treaty Councils*. Tacoma: Washington State Historical Society, 1986.

Novak, Barbara. *American Painting of the Nineteenth Century*. New York: Praeger Publishers, 1976.

———. *Nature and Culture: American Landscape, 1825–1865*. New York: Oxford University Press, 1980.

Oettermann, Stephan. *The Panorama: History of a Mass Medium*. New York: Zone Books, 1997.

Oliver, Christopher. "Civic Visions: The Panorama and Popular Amusement in American Art and Society, 1845–1870." Ph.D. diss., University of Virginia, forthcoming.

Palmquist, Peter E. *Pioneer Photographers from the Mississippi to the Continental Divide: A Biographical Dictionary, 1839–1865*. Stanford, Calif.: Stanford University Press, 2005.

Parkman, Francis. *The Conspiracy of Pontiac and the Indian War After the Conquest of Canada*. Boston: Little, Brown, 1851.

Payne, Elizabeth H. "Pitts Family Portraits of the Eighteenth Century." *Antiques* 77 (January 1960): 87–89.

Pennington, Estill Curtis. *Passage and Progress in the Works of William Tylee Ranney*. Augusta, Ga.: Morris Museum of Art, 1993.

Penny, H. Glenn. *Kindred by Choice: Germans and American Indians since 1800*. Chapel Hill: University of North Carolina Press, 2013.

Perry, Claire. *Young America: Childhood in 19th-Century Art and Culture*. New Haven, Conn.: Yale University Press, 2006.

Pipes, Nellie B. "John Mix Stanley, Indian Painter." *Oregon Historical Quarterly* 33, no. 3 (September 1932): 250–58.

Portraits of North American Indians, with Sketches of Scenery, Etc., Painted by J. M. Stanley. Washington, D.C.: Smithsonian Institution, 1852.

Proceedings of Annual Conventions of the National Art Association Held at Washington City, from 1858 to 1860, Inclusive. Washington, D.C.: William H. Moore, 1860.

Prown, Jules David, Nancy K. Anderson, William Cronon, Brian W. Dippie, Martha A. Sandweiss, Susan P. Schoelwer, and Howard R. Lamar. *Discovered Lands, Invented Pasts: Transforming Visions of the American West*. New Haven, Conn.: Yale University Press, 1992.

Rasmussen, William M. S. "Art of the Nineteenth-Century Government Explorations in the West: Changing Concepts of the Western Landscape." Master's thesis, University of Delaware, 1975.

Ratcliffe, Sam DeShong. *Painting Texas History to 1900*. Austin: University of Texas Press, 1992.

Rathbone, Perry T., ed. *Westward the Way: The Character and Development of the Louisiana Territory as Seen by Artists and Writers of the Nineteenth Century*. St. Louis: City Art Museum of St. Louis; Minneapolis: Walker Art Center, c. 1954.

A Record of the First Exhibition of the Metropolitan Mechanics Institute, Held in the East Wing of the Patent Office, February–March, 1853. Washington, D.C.: Henry Polkinhorn, 1853.

A Record of the Second Exhibition of the Metropolitan Mechanics Institute. Washington, D.C.: Henry Polkinhorn, 1855.

Reis, Peter. *From Long Grass to Short Grass Prairie: A Vision of the American West, 1850–1920*. Bozeman, Mont.: Thomas Nygard Gallery, 1998.

Rhees, William J. *An Account of the Smithsonian Institution*, 27. Washington, D.C.: Thomas McGill, 1858.

Ridgely, James L., and Paschal Donaldson, eds. *The Odd-Fellows' Offering for 1848*. New York: Edward Walker, 1848.

Roberts, Jennifer. *Transporting Visions: The Movement of Images in Early America*. Berkeley: University of California Press, 2014.

Rosaldo, Renato. *Culture and Truth: The Remaking of Social Analysis*. Boston: Beacon Press, 1993.

Ross, Marvin C., ed. *The West of Alfred Jacob Miller*. Norman: University of Oklahoma Press, 1968.

Rossi, Paul A., and David C. Hunt. *The Art of the Old West: From the Collection of the Gilcrease Institute*. New York: BBS, 1995.

Rothenberg, Marc, ed. *The Papers of Joseph Henry*. Vol. 8, *January 1850–December 1853: The Smithsonian Years*. Washington, D.C.: Smithsonian Institution, 1972.

Samuels, Peggy. *Samuels' Encyclopedia of Artists of the American West*. Secaucus, N.J.: Castle, c. 1985.

Sandweiss, Martha A. *Print the Legend: Photography and the American West*. New Haven, Conn., and London: Yale University Press, 2002.

———. "The Public Life of Western Art." In *Discovered Lands, Invented Pasts: Transforming Visions of the American West*, by Jules David Prown et al., 117–34 . New Haven, Conn.: Yale University Press, 1992.

Sawyer, Charles H. *John Mix Stanley: A Traveller in the West*. Ann Arbor: University of Michigan Museum of Art, 1969.

Sayre, Gordon M. *The Indian Chief as Tragic Hero: Native Resistance and the Literatures of America, from Moctezuma to Tecumseh*. Chapel Hill: University of North Carolina Press, 2009.

Schimmel, Julie. "Images of the Dispossessed." In *Henry Farny Paints the Far West*. Cincinnati, Ohio: Cincinnati Art Museum, 2007.

———. "Inventing 'the Indian.'" In *The West as America: Reinterpreting Images of the Frontier, 1820–1920*, edited by William H. Truettner, 149–89. Washington, D.C.: National Museum of American Art and Smithsonian Institution Press, 1991.

———. "John Mix Stanley (1814–1872)." In *Artists of Michigan from the Nineteenth Century*, edited by J. Gray Sweeney, 39–40, 49–54. Muskegon, Mich.: Muskegon Museum of Art, 1987.

———. "John Mix Stanley and Imagery of the West in Nineteenth-Century American Art." Ph.D. diss., New York University, 1983.

———. *Stark Museum of Art: The Western Collection, 1978*. Orange, Tex.: Stark Museum of Art, 1978.

Schoolcraft, Henry Rowe. *Historical and Statistical Information Respecting the History, Condition and Prospects of the Indian Tribes of the United States*. 6 vols. Philadelphia: J. B. Lippincott, 1851–1857.

———. *History of the Indian Tribes of the United States: Their Present Condition and Prospects, and a Sketch of their Ancient Status*. Philadelphia: J. B. Lippincott, 1857.

Second Annual Exhibition of the Washington Art Association. Washington, D.C.: Henry Polkinhorn, 1857.

Sides, Hampton. *Blood and Thunder: The Epic Story of Kit Carson and the Conquest of the American West*. New York: Doubleday, 2006.

Skolnick, Arnold. *Paintings of the Southwest*. Albuquerque: University of New Mexico, 2002.

Slotkin, Richard. *The Fatal Environment: The Myth of the Frontier in the Age of Industrialization, 1800–1890*. Middleton, Conn.: Wesleyan University Press, 1985.

Sotheby's: American Paintings, Drawings and Sculpture. New York: Sotheby's, 2004.

Stafford, Barbara. *Voyage into Substance: Art, Science, Nature and the Illustrated Travel Account*. Cambridge, Mass.: MIT Press, 1984.

Stanley, John Mix. *Portraits of North American Indians with Sketches of Scenery, Etc.* Washington, D.C.: Smithsonian Institution, 1852.

Stevens, Isaac I. *Narrative and Final Report of Explorations for a Route for a Pacific Railroad, near the Forty-seventh and Forty-ninth Parallels of North Latitude from Saint Paul to Puget Sound*. Vol. 12, book 1 of *Reports of Explorations and Surveys, to Ascertain the Most Practicable and Economical Route for a Railroad from the Mississippi River to the Pacific Ocean*. Washington, D.C.: Thomas H. Ford, 1860.

Stokes, I. N. Phelps, and Daniel C. Haskell. *American Historical Prints*. New York: New York Public Library, 1933.

Stone, Horatio. *Addresses before the Washington Art Association, Feb. 24, 1857 and Feb. 10, 1858*. Washington, D.C.: Cornelius Wendell, 1858.

———. *National Art: An Address Delivered before the Washington Art Association, February 10, 1858*. Washington, D.C.: Cornelius Wendell, 1858.

Stott, Annette. "Prairie Madonnas and Pioneer Women: Images of Emigrant Women in the Art of the Old West." *Prospects: An Annual of American Cultural Studies* 21 (October 1996): 299–325.

Strong, Lisa. *Sentimental Journey: The Art of Alfred Jacob Miller*. Fort Worth, Tex.: Amon Carter Museum, 2009.

———. "The Trappers." In *Corcoran Gallery of Art: American Paintings to 1945*, edited by Sarah Cash, 120–21. Washington, D.C.: Corcoran Gallery of Art, 2006.

Swanson, John R. *Source Material on the History and Ethnology of the Caddo Indians*. Washington, D.C.: Smithsonian Institution, Bureau of American Ethnology, 1942.

Sweeney, J. Gray. *Masterpieces of Western American Art*. New York: Gramercy, 1996.

———. "Racism, Nationalism, and Nostalgia." In *Race-ing Art History: Critical Readings in Race and Art History*, edited by Kimberly N. Pinder, 155–68. New York: Routledge, 2002.

———. "Western Landscape." In *American Paintings in the Detroit Institute of Arts*, vol. 1, *Works by Artists Born Before 1816*, ed. Nancy Rivard Shaw and Mary C. Black, 184. New York: Hudson Hills Press, 1991.

Taft, Robert. *Artists and Illustrators of the Old West, 1850–1900*. New York: Scribner, 1953.

———. "The Pictorial Record of the Old West. XV. John M. Stanley and the Pacific Railroad Reports." *Kansas Historical Quarterly* 20, no. 1 (February 1952): 1–23.

Taragin, Davira. *Corcoran*. Washington, D.C.: Corcoran Gallery of Art, 1976.

Trenton, Patricia, and Peter H. Hassrick. *The Rocky Mountains: A Vision for Artists in the Nineteenth Century*. Norman: University of Oklahoma Press, 1982.

Troccoli, Joan Carpenter. *First Artist of the West: George Catlin Paintings and Watercolors from the Collection of Gilcrease Museum*. Tulsa, Okla.: Gilcrease Museum, 1993.

———. *Painters and the American West: The Anschutz Collection*. New Haven, Conn.: Yale University Press, 2000.

———. *Painters and the American West: The Anschutz Collection*. Vol. 2. Denver: American Museum of Western Art, 2013.

———, ed. *West Point: Points West*. Denver: Institute of Western American Art, Denver Art Museum, 2002.

Truettner, William H. *The Natural Man Observed: A Study of Catlin's Indian Gallery*. Washington, D.C.: Smithsonian Institution Press, 1979.

———. *Painting Indians and Building Empires in North America, 1710–1840*. Berkeley: University of California Press, 2010.

———, ed.. *The West as America: Reinterpreting Images of the Frontier, 1820–1920*. Washington, D.C.: National Museum of American Art and Smithsonian Institution Press, 1991.

Tuckerman, Henry T. *Book of the Artists: American Artist Life, Comprising Biographical and Critical Sketches of American Artists: Preceded by an Historical Account of the Rise and Progress of Art in America*. New York: Putnam, 1867.

Tuttle, Charles Richard. *General History of the State of Michigan*. Detroit: R. D. S. Tyler, 1873.

Tyler, Ron, ed. *Alfred Jacob Miller: Artist on the Oregon Trail*. With a catalogue by Karen Dewees Reynolds and William R. Johnston. Fort Worth, Tex.: Amon Carter Museum, 1982.

———, ed. *American Frontier Life: Early Western Painting and Prints*. New York: Abbeville Press, 1987.

———, ed. *Prints of the American West*. Fort Worth, Tex.: Amon Carter Museum, 1983.

U.S. War Department. *Reports of Explorations and Surveys to Ascertain the Most Practicable and Economical Route from the Mississippi River to the Pacific Ocean*. 12 volumes. Washington, D.C.: A. O. P. Nicholson and Thomas H. Ford, 1855–1860.

Victor, Frances Fuller. *River of the West*. 1870. Reprint, Oakland, Calif.: Brooks-Sterling, 1974.

Viola, Herman J. *Exploring the West*. New York: Abrams, 1988.

———. *The Indian Legacy of Charles Bird King*. Washington, D.C.: Smithsonian Institution Press and Doubleday, 1976.

———. *Indians of North America: Paintings by Henry Inman from the D. Harold Byrd, Jr. Collection*. Cody, Wyo.: Buffalo Bill Historical Center, 1983.

Viola, Herman J., with H. B. Crothers and Maureen Hannan. "The American Indian Genre Paintings of Catlin, Stanley, Wimar, Eastman and Miller." In *American Frontier Life: Early Western Painting and Prints*, edited by Ron Tyler et al., 131–66. Fort Worth, Tex.: Amon Carter Museum, 1987.

Wallace, Edward S. *The Great Reconnaissance: Soldiers, Artists, and Scientists on the Frontier, 1848–1861*. New York: Little, Brown, 1955.

Webber, Charles Wilkins. *The Hunter Naturalist*. New York: Putnam, 1854.

———. *Wild Scenes and Song-Birds*. New York: Riker Thorne, 1855.

Weber, David J. *Richard H. Kern: Expeditionary Artist in the Far Southwest, 1848–1853*. Albuquerque: University of New Mexico Press, 1985.

Wilson, C. P. "Early Western Paintings." *Beaver* 280 (June 1949): 12–13.

Wilson, James Grant, and John Fiske. *Appleton's Cyclopedia of American Biography*. New York: D. Appleton, 1898.

Wischmann, Lesley. *Frontier Diplomats: Alexander Culbertson and Natoyist-Siksina'*. Spokane, Wash.: Arthur H. Clark, 2000.

———. *Frontier Diplomats: Alexander Culbertson and Natoyist-Siksina' among the Blackfeet*. Norman: University of Oklahoma Press, 2004.

Withington, Mary C. *A Catalogue of Manuscripts in the Collection of Western Americana Founded by William Robertson Coe*. New Haven, Conn.: Yale University Press, 1952.

Exhibition Checklist

BUFFALO BILL CENTER OF THE WEST, CODY, WYOMING:
JUNE 6–AUGUST 29, 2015

GILCREASE MUSEUM, TULSA, OKLAHOMA:
OCTOBER 3, 2015–JANUARY 4, 2016

TACOMA ART MUSEUM, TACOMA, WASHINGTON:
FEBRUARY 1–APRIL 29, 2016

Le Grand Morehouse, 1838
Muscatine Art Center, Muscatine, Iowa (cat. no. 001)

The Williamson Family, c. 1842
The Metropolitan Museum of Art, New York, New York (cat. no. 007)

Bin-Tah, The Wounded Man, 1843
Yale University Art Gallery, New Haven, Connecticut (cat. no. 015)

Eleanora C. Ross, 1844
Gilcrease Museum, Tulsa, Oklahoma (cat. no. 021)

John Golden Ross, 1844
Gilcrease Museum, Tulsa, Oklahoma (cat. no. 018)

Ko-rak-koo-kiss, a Towoccono Warrior, 1844
Smithsonian American Art Museum, Washington, D.C. (cat. no. 017)

Lewis Anderson Ross, 1844
Gilcrease Museum, Tulsa, Oklahoma (cat. no. 022)

Boy with Birds, c. 1846
Private collection, Salt Lake City, Utah (cat. no. 027)

The Ruins of Casa Grande, 1846
Peabody Museum of Archaeology and Ethnology, Harvard University, Cambridge, Massachusetts (Buffalo Bill Center of the West venue only) (cat. no. 028)

Valley of the Mimbres, 1846
Private collection, Washington, D.C. (cat. no. 029)

Butte on the Del Norte, 1847
Eiteljorg Museum of American Indians and Western Art, Indianapolis, Indiana (cat. no. 032)

Fort Vancouver, c. 1847
Beinecke Rare Book and Manuscript Library, Yale University, New Haven, Connecticut (cat. no. 048)

The Ruins of the Casa Grande, 1847
Buffalo Bill Center of the West, Cody, Wyoming (cat. no. 041)

San Felippe, New Mexico, 1847
Stark Museum of Art, Orange, Texas (cat. no. 030)

View in the Sierra Mimbres, 1847
Stark Museum of Art, Orange, Texas (cat. no. 033)

Asa Lawrence Lovejoy, 1848
Oregon Historical Society, Portland, Oregon (cat. no. 056)

Black Knife, Version I, 1850
Smithsonian American Art Museum, Washington, D.C. (cat. no. 064)

Oregon City on the Willamette River, c. 1852
Amon Carter Museum of American Art, Fort Worth, Texas (cat. no. 066)

Scene on the Columbia River, 1852
Tacoma Art Museum, Tacoma, Washington (cat. no. 065)

"Ah Dolle" Red Feathers, 1853
National Anthropological Archives, Smithsonian Institution, Washington, D.C. (Tacoma Art Museum venue only) (cat. no. 076)

Untitled (Fort Union), 1853
Private collection (cat. no. 075)

Untitled (teepees, dog and Fort Union), 1853
Private collection (cat. no. 074)

Buffalo Hunt, 1854
Gilcrease Museum, Tulsa, Oklahoma (cat. no. 082)

Major Alexander Culbertson, 1854–1855
Fort Benton Museums, Fort Benton, Montana (cat. no. 080)

Dalles of the Columbia [River] Looking Westward, 1854–1855
Yale University Art Gallery, New Haven, Connecticut (Gilcrease Museum venue only) (cat. no. 115)

Fort Benton, 1854–1855
Yale University Art Gallery, New Haven, Connecticut (Buffalo Bill Center of the West venue only) (cat. no. 102)

Maple River, 1854–1855
Yale University Art Gallery, New Haven, Connecticut (Buffalo Bill Center of the West venue only) (cat. no. 091)

Mt. Baker and Cascade Range, from Whitby's Island, 1854–1855
Yale University Art Gallery, New Haven, Connecticut (Tacoma Art Museum venue only) (cat. no. 127)

Nez Perces Indians, 1854–1855
Yale University Art Gallery, New Haven, Connecticut (Tacoma Art Museum venue only) (cat. no. 109)

Puget Sound and Mt. Rainier from Whitby's Island, 1854–1855
Yale University Art Gallery, New Haven, Connecticut (Gilcrease Museum venue only) (cat. no. 125)

Sheyenne River, 1854–1855
Yale University Art Gallery, New Haven, Connecticut (Tacoma Art Museum venue only) (cat. no. 092)

Teton Valley, 1854–1855
Yale University Art Gallery, New Haven, Connecticut (Buffalo Bill Center of the West venue only) (cat. no. 105)

Tshimikaine Mission, 1854–1855
Yale University Art Gallery, New Haven, Connecticut (Gilcrease Museum venue only) (cat. no. 113)

Chain of Spires along the Gila, 1855
Phoenix Art Museum, Phoenix, Arizona (cat. no. 130)

Crossing the Milk River, c. 1855
Autry National Center, Los Angeles, California (cat. no. 140)

Scouts along the Teton River, c. 1855
Gilcrease Museum, Tulsa, Oklahoma (cat. no. 131)

Untitled, Teton Valley Scene, c. 1855
Buffalo Bill Center of the West, Cody, Wyoming (cat. no. 132)

Wagon Train: Break in the Journey, c. 1855
American Museum of Western Art—The Anschutz Collection, Denver, Colorado (cat. no. 134)

A Family Group, c. 1856
Diplomatic Reception Rooms, Department of State, Washington, D.C. (cat. no. 145)

On the Snake River, c. 1856
Collection of Larry A. Sheakley (cat. no. 144)

Camp of the Red River Hunters, 1857
Amon Carter Museum of American Art, Fort Worth, Texas (cat. no. 160)

The Last of Their Race, 1857
Buffalo Bill Center of the West, Cody, Wyoming (cat. no. 159)

The Trapper's Cabin, 1858
National Gallery of Art, Washington, D.C. (cat. no. 163)

After the Hunt, c. 1860
The Rees-Jones Collection, Dallas, Texas (cat. no. 168)

Self-Portrait, c. 1860
Gilcrease Museum, Tulsa, Oklahoma (cat. no. 167)

Hunters and Traders, 1862
Tim and Elaine Peterson (cat. no. 172)

Indian Telegraph, 1863
Tuscaloosa Museum of Art: Home of the Westervelt Collection, Tuscaloosa, Alabama (cat. no. 177)

The Unveiling of the Conspiracy, 1863
Detroit Public Library, Detroit, Michigan (cat. no. 176)

A Halt on the Prairie for a Smoke, 1865
Detroit Institute of Arts, Detroit, Michigan (cat. no. 186)

Assiniboin Encampment on the Upper Missouri, 1865
Detroit Institute of Arts, Detroit, Michigan (cat. no. 183)

Gambling for the Buck, 1867
Stark Museum of Art, Orange, Texas (cat. no. 206)

Group of Piegan Indians, 1867
Denver Public Library, Denver, Colorado (cat. no. 205)

The Deer-Slayers, 1868
Private collection, Wyoming (Buffalo Bill Center of the West venue only) (cat. no. 209)

Indian Telegraph, 1868
The Rockwell Museum, Corning, New York (cat. no. 208)

The Trial of Red Jacket, 1868
Buffalo History Museum, Buffalo, New York (cat. no. 212)

Young Chief, 1868
Tacoma Art Museum, Tacoma, Washington (cat. no. 211)

Chinook Burial Grounds, 1869
Detroit Institute of Arts, Detroit, Michigan (cat. no. 220)

Prairie Indian Encampment, 1869
Detroit Institute of Arts, Detroit, Michigan (cat. no. 219)

Uncas, the Young Chief, 1869
Amon Carter Museum of American Art, Fort Worth, Texas (fig. 1.5)

Mountain Landscape with Indians, c. 1870
Detroit Institute of Arts, Detroit, Michigan (cat. no. 221)

Index

Page numbers in italic type refer to illustrations.